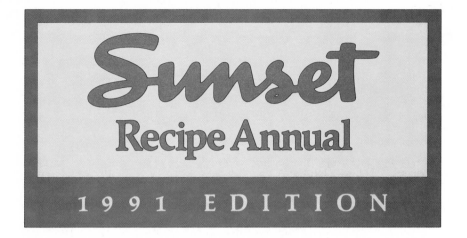

Sunset
Recipe Annual
1991 EDITION

Every *Sunset Magazine* recipe and
food article from 1990

By the *Sunset* Editors

Salmon and Walla Wallas (page 188)

Sunset Publishing Corporation ■ **Menlo Park, California**

Another Great Year at *Sunset*

Grab an apron and some hungry guests. Another annual feast from *Sunset Magazine* is about to begin.

As in previous editions of the *Sunset Recipe Annual*, this collection serves forth every food article published in the past year's 12 monthly issues of *Sunset Magazine*.

What's new from 1990? This year you'll notice a special emphasis on using everyday cuts of meat in reduced-fat ways, plus our regular attention to the fresh foods of each season. We also enjoy fresh ideas, and continue to supply some surprises, such as April's "smashing dessert," that will take your breath away. And such long-appreciated monthly features as *Chefs of the West*, *Kitchen Cabinet*, and *Menus* also appear on cue.

If you are new to the adventure of cooking and entertaining with *Sunset's Recipe Annuals*, you'll soon understand why other cooks have been collecting each year's edition since the series began in 1987. If you are one of these collectors yourself, you've probably already set the table in anticipation of this year's recipes.

Either way, we invite you to sample all that piques your palate in the pages ahead. An elegant wine-tasting dinner? A slice of our readers' favorite fruit pie? Some squeaky cheese from Finland? Or a 15-minute family meal featuring tortillas with spinach and mozzarella cheese? These and a year's worth of other tempting choices appear in this banquet from 1990's *Sunset Magazine*.

All material in this book originally appeared in the 1990 issues of *Sunset Magazine* and was created by the following editors, illustrators, and photographers:

Food and Entertaining Editor
Sunset Magazine
Jerry Anne Di Vecchio

Food Staff
Sunset Magazine
Linda Anusasananan, Senior Editor
Sandra Bakko Cameron
Paula Smith Freschet
Bernadette Hart
Karyn Lipman
Annabel Post
Betsy Ann Reynolds
Christine B. Weber

Illustrations
David Broad (*Chefs of the West*)
Alice Harth (*Sunset's Kitchen Cabinet*)

Photography
Glenn Christiansen
Peter Christiansen
Norman A. Plate
Darrow M. Watt
(See page 368 for individual credits)

Recipe Annual was produced by *Sunset Books.*

Contributing Editors
Cornelia Fogle
Helen Sweetland
Susan Warton

Design
Williams & Ziller Design

Front cover: Vegetable Focaccia Milano (recipes start on page 52) featuring, clockwise from top, toppings of eggplant, olives, and tomato. Photography by Kevin Sanchez. Design by Susan Bryant. Photo styling by Susan Massey-Weil. Food styling by Sue Brownlee.

Back cover: Hazelnut & Mint Zabaglione (recipe on page 95). Photography by Peter Christiansen.

Sunset Magazine
   Editor: William R. Marken
Sunset Books
   Editor: Elizabeth L. Hogan

First printing March 1991

Fresh Fruit Creations (page 204)

Contents

A Letter from Sunset

DEAR READER,

Except for employing more ovens, pans, and editors, *Sunset's* food and entertaining department is probably a lot like your own kitchen at home—a place where dishes clatter, bread bakes, a baby squalls, the phone rings. Our staff members lead complex lives, just as you do. Our families include toddlers to teenagers, and some of us have reached the empty-nest stage.

Our firsthand experience combining family life with careers qualifies us to produce stories that address the realities you face when shopping, cooking, and entertaining. These are some of our favorite memories of 1990:

Shortcuts to a quick, great meal are welcome at any time of year, but especially in **January,** when everyone wants to unwind after the holidays. We suggest a choice of filled pastas—purchased ready-to-cook from a supermarket or delicatessen—to use in an appetizer, soup, salad, or main course. Also this month, look for an intriguing background report on tapioca.

In **February,** we wake up winter menus with Singapore pancakes, which look like coconut cobwebs, to serve with an accompanying chicken curry. You can also delve into the real issues concerning oysters, one of the world's most celebrated celebration foods.

March is the month for meat-and-potato lovers. Learn how to lower fat even in well-marbled cuts, then feast on lamb shoulder or pork baby back ribs. Teaming these moist and tender meats with potatoes, grains, or pastas, it's easy to reach the weight and health goal of consuming no more than 30 percent of your calories in fats.

Changing to a Latin rhythm for an **April** party, we feature a Brazilian seafood stew known as *moqueca.* Equally dramatic this month is the shimmering dessert "bowl" that you smash with a spoon before sprinkling its caramelized sugar shards over servings of "floating island."

For **May,** we bake an airy Italian bread called *bomba.* Then we showcase cheeses of the Pacific Northwest, luring you to take a trip or send for a taste by mail (addresses are included).

Sunset food editors—like many Sunset readers—juggle office and family responsibilities in their busy lives. Clockwise from left, you see Lisa (Linda's younger daughter); student intern Diana Fair; Betsy Reynolds; Linda Anusasananan; Chalida (Linda's older daughter); retester Allene Russell; Annabel Post; Danielle and mother Paula Freschet; Jerry Di Vecchio (empty-nester); Karyn Lipman; Christine Weber; and Sandra Bakko Cameron with sons Gregory and Matthew.

June brings a summer spectrum of delectable fresh-fruit pies—strawberry pink to huckleberry blue.

In **July,** we offer a bonus section on the "Good Foods of Summer," packed with exciting yet easy-going recipes for picnics, barbecues, and other outdoor meals. We also devise a way to make old-fashioned pickles on a 1990 timetable—overnight.

To cool off in **August,** sip gazpacho made with the season's dazzling crop of orange, yellow, white, and green as well as traditional red tomatoes. Or serve a cross-cultural lemonade made with aromatic lemon grass, an herb borrowed from Southeast Asian cooks.

In **September,** we report on the continuing poultry revolution. New cuts and new ways to cook make the difference between a 375-calorie, 3½-hour chicken dinner (from a 1930s *Sunset* story) and today's 156-calorie, 15-minute herb-fragrant update.

October reviews the new market apples, such as the Fuji. We try baking with soy flour for a protein boost. When little goblins show up for Halloween, we ladle them soup from a pumpkin shell.

Thanksgiving steals the show in **November,** but we take a new slant each year. Our 1990 menu can dress up, with such glamorous ingredients as prosciutto and foie gras. Or, if you'd prefer a more informal dinner, just substitute the simpler foods also suggested.

For **December,** we wrap up the year in a festive mood, reporting grand family parties shared with us by our readers. But when you need something simple and hearty during this hectic month, you can turn to the *Menus'* section for a work-night supper of Costa Rican Beef Soup.

Whether you're hosting dozens of party guests or two for tea, you'll find a wealth of choices throughout this *Recipe Annual.* And because we understand, firsthand, your basic concerns, we've made sure that our recipes are not only delicious, but also realistic to prepare.

Enjoy them!

Jerry Di Vecchio

Jerry Anne Di Vecchio
Food and Entertaining Editor
Sunset Magazine

Dessert again? Paula Freschet prepares for one of several pie tastings as daughter Danielle—in the office to model for a different story—observes.

Retesters check each recipe after copy is written. From left, they include Bernadette Hart, Test Kitchen Director; Sally Baumgartner; Dorothy Decker; Jean Strain; Jerry Di Vecchio, Food and Entertaining Editor; Joyce Chowla; Allene Russell.

An Annual Tradition

1987
1988
1989
1990

Starting with The Best of Sunset in 1987, each Recipe Annual that followed has been a keepsake edition of the previous year's food articles and recipes from Sunset Magazine.

TO USE OUR NUTRITION INFORMATION

Sunset recipes contain nutrition information based on the most current data available from the USDA for calorie count; grams of protein, total fat, and carbohydrate; and milligrams of sodium and cholesterol.

This analysis is usually given for a single serving, based on the largest number of servings listed for the recipe. Or it's for a specific amount, such as per tablespoon (for sauces), or by a unit, as per cooky.

The nutrition analysis does not include optional ingredients or those for which no specific amount is stated (salt added to taste, for example). If an ingredient is listed with an alternative —such as unflavored yogurt or sour cream—the figures are calculated using the first choice. Likewise, if a range is given for the amount of an ingredient (such as ½ to l cup butter), values are figured on the first, lower amount.

Recipes using regular-strength chicken broth are based on the sodium content of salt-free homemade or canned broth. If you used canned salted chicken broth, the sodium content will be higher.

Filled Pasta with Vegetable Confetti (page 10)

Salute the new year with a
festive supper inspired by flavors of the Southwest, featuring
a New Mexican version of the hearty pork stew called pozole.
Or experiment with ready-to-cook filled pasta, now widely
available with various interiors and wrappers. Other ideas to
brighten January days include savory scones to complement a
hearty soup or salad, four time-saving entrées cooked in the
microwave oven, bold appetizers from Thailand, a pair
of unusual vegetable salads, and slow-cooked
stews for satisfying winter suppers.

Santa Fe Stew

EW YEAR'S EVE *in Bruce Johnson's Santa Fe home calls for pozole (spelled posole locally). This hearty stew of pork, chilies, and dry corn is popular throughout New Mexico; it's based on a feast-day dish of local Indians. Santa Fe pozole is festive on its own, and less complex than its Mexican counterpart.*

SANTA FE
DESERT SUPPER

New Year Pozole
Flour Tortillas   Green Salad
Bizcochitos
Hibiscus-flower Punch   Beer

You can make the pozole, cookies, and punch at least a day in advance.

Look for dried hibiscus flowers, chilies, and pozole (dry corn—canned hominy is the easy alternative) in supermarkets or Mexican groceries. If pozole is moist-packed, it will be refrigerated or frozen.

NEW YEAR POZOLE

3 cups dry pozole or 4½ cups moist-pack pozole (also called nixtamal; thaw if frozen), rinsed well; or 2 cans (1 lb. 13 oz. *each*) hominy, drained
   About 3 quarts regular-strength chicken broth
2½ pounds boned pork shoulder or butt (fat trimmed), cut into 1½-inch chunks
1 medium-size onion, chopped
8 cloves garlic, minced or pressed
2 tablespoons ground dry New Mexico or California chilies, or chili powder
½ teaspoon *each* dry oregano leaves and pepper
   Roasted chilies (directions follow) or 1 can (7 oz.) diced green chilies
   Salt
   Sour cream and green onions (optional)

Pozole brings together chunks of pork, fresh and dry chilies, onions, garlic, and hominy or dry corn (also called pozole).

If using pozole (or nixtamal), fill a 5- to 6-quart pan about ⅔ full with water. Add pozole and bring to a boil over high heat. Boil 5 minutes, then drain.

Add 8 cups broth to pozole. Bring to a boil, cover, and simmer until kernels are just tender to bite, about 2 hours. As needed, add water to keep kernels covered by ½ inch. (Omit these steps if you're using hominy.)

In another 5- to 6-quart pan, combine pork, onion, garlic, ground chilies, oregano, pepper, and 1 cup broth. Bring to a boil, cover, and simmer rapidly on medium heat for 30 minutes. Uncover pan; stir often on medium-high heat until broth evaporates, meat is streaked

with brown, and drippings are richly browned. Add 1 cup broth and stir drippings free. Add pozole and liquid (or hominy and 8 cups broth) and roasted chilies.

Bring mixture to a boil, cover, and simmer gently until pork is very tender when pierced, about 1½ hours. Measure pozole and add enough more broth to make a total of about 14 cups. If made ahead, cool, then cover and chill up to 3 days. Reheat until simmering. Ladle pozole into bowls. Add salt, sour cream, and green onions to taste. Makes about 3½ quarts, 6 to 8 servings. —*Bruce Johnson, Santa Fe.*

PER SERVING: 485 calories, 24 g protein, 33 g carbohydrates, 28 g fat, 79 mg cholesterol, 740 mg sodium

Roasted chilies. Place 1 pound **fresh poblano** (also called pasilla) or Anaheim (California) **chilies** in a rimmed 10- by 15-inch pan. Broil 2 to 3 inches below heat until skins are charred, about 7 minutes. Turn chilies; broil until charred, about 4 minutes longer. Drape with foil and let cool. Pull off and discard skins, stems, and seeds; rinse chilies and chop.

BIZCOCHITOS

2 tablespoons brandy or water
1½ teaspoons anise seed
1 cup (½ lb.) butter or margarine; or use half lard or solid shortening
¾ cup sugar
1 large egg
1 teaspoon baking powder
   About 3 cups all-purpose flour
¼ cup sugar mixed with 1 teaspoon ground cinnamon

In a small bowl, mix brandy with anise. Cover and let stand at least 20 minutes.

In a large bowl, beat butter and sugar with a mixer until fluffy, then beat in egg and brandy mixture. Mix in baking powder and 3 cups flour. Cover and chill dough until firm, at least 2 hours or up to 2 days.

Ladle dense, hearty pozole into wide soup bowls and top with dollops of sour cream and sliced green onions. Serve this Southwestern stew with green salad and flour tortillas, then finish with anise-flavored cookies.

On a floured board, roll half the dough at a time to ⅛ inch thick (keep balance chilled; dough is hard to handle as it warms and softens). Cut shapes with floured cooky cutters. Place cookies about 1 inch apart on greased 12- by 15-inch baking sheets. Sprinkle with sugar-cinnamon mixture. Bake 2 pans at a time in a 350° oven until golden, 12 to 15 minutes; switch pan positions halfway through baking. Transfer cookies to racks to cool.

Serve cookies, or package airtight and hold up to 2 days; freeze to store longer. Makes about 7½ dozen, 1½-inch size. — *Karen Aubrey, Santa Fe.*

PER COOKY: 43 calories, 0.5 g protein, 5.4 g carbohydrates, 2.1 g fat, 7.9 mg cholesterol, 26 mg sodium

HIBISCUS-FLOWER PUNCH

    3 ounces (2¼ cups) dried hibiscus
       (jamaica) flowers
    3¼ quarts water
    1¼ cups sugar

In a 4- to 5-quart noncorrodible pan (stainless steel, porcelain-clad) over high heat, bring hibiscus, water, and sugar to a boil; stir often. Boil 2 minutes. Cover and chill 6 to 8 hours. Pour through a fine strainer into a pitcher; discard flowers. If made ahead, cover and chill up to 2 days. Pour into ice-filled glasses. Makes about 3 quarts, 6 to 8 servings.

PER CUP: 126 calories, 0.3 g protein, 32 g carbohydrates, 0.3 g fat, 0 mg cholesterol, 0.6 mg sodium

Pasta Short-Cutters

W HAT COMES IN SQUARES, *circles, twists, half-moons, and triangles?* One answer is filled pasta—including agnolotti, anolini, ravioli, ravolini, tortelloni, and tortellini.

Once considered only a restaurant entrée or a time-consuming home project, filled pasta can now be called fast food. Today it's widely available—fresh, frozen, dry, or vacuum-packed—in supermarkets as well as in pasta shops and delicatessens.

Start with ready-to-cook pasta as a short-cut to a quick meal. Here we use this versatile ingredient in an entrée, salad, appetizer, and soup. The pasta comes with different fillings and wrappers; all are interchangeable in these recipes.

Colorful confetti of finely diced green zucchini and red bell pepper sautéed in thyme butter goes over round anolini.

FILLED PASTA WITH VEGETABLE CONFETTI

About ½ pound refrigerated, frozen, or vacuum-packed filled fresh pasta, or about ¼ pound filled dry pasta

¼ cup (⅛ lb.) butter or olive oil

1 medium-size zucchini, ends trimmed, cut into ¼-inch cubes

1 small red bell pepper, stemmed, seeded, and finely diced

1 clove garlic, pressed or minced

6 sprigs (*each* 4 in.) fresh thyme, or ½ teaspoon dry thyme leaves

2 tablespoons pine nuts or slivered almonds

Salt and pepper

Grated parmesan cheese

In a 3- to 4-quart pan, bring about 2 quarts water to a boil. Add pasta and boil gently, uncovered, until barely tender to bite, 4 to 6 minutes for refrigerated or frozen pasta, 10 to 12 minutes for vacuum-packed, 20 to 25 minutes for dry. Drain well.

Meanwhile, in a 10- to 12-inch frying pan, melt butter over medium heat. Add zucchini, red pepper, garlic, and thyme. Stir often for 3 minutes. Add nuts and continue stirring until zucchini and nuts begin to brown, 3 to 5 minutes longer. Add hot pasta and mix lightly. Add salt, pepper, and cheese to taste. Makes 2 servings.

PER SERVING: 609 calories, 22 g protein, 51 g carbohydrates, 37 g fat, 62 mg cholesterol, 633 mg sodium

BASIL PASTA SALAD

About 1 pound refrigerated, frozen, or vacuum-packed filled fresh pasta, or about ½ pound filled dry pasta

½ cup olive oil

¼ cup white wine vinegar

½ cup chopped fresh basil leaves, or ¼ cup dry basil leaves

½ teaspoon pepper

2 cups (14 oz. *total*) cherry tomatoes, stemmed and cut in half

1 small cucumber, quartered lengthwise, seeded, and thinly sliced
Salt

Romaine lettuce leaves, rinsed and crisped

Greek-style or black ripe olives (optional)

Fresh basil sprigs (optional)

In a 5- to 6-quart pan, bring about 3 quarts water to a boil. Add pasta and boil gently, uncovered, until just barely tender to bite, 4 to 6 minutes for refrigerated or frozen pasta, 10 to 12 minutes for vacuum-packed, 20 to 25 minutes for dry. Drain pasta; rinse with cold water and drain.

In a large bowl, mix oil, vinegar, chopped basil, and pepper. Lightly mix in pasta, tomatoes, and cucumber. Add salt to taste. Spoon onto lettuce-lined plates. Garnish with olives and basil sprigs. Serves 6 to 8.—*April Linton, Seattle.*

PER SERVING: 307 calories, 10 g protein, 27 g carbohydrates, 18 g fat, 0 mg cholesterol, 203 mg sodium

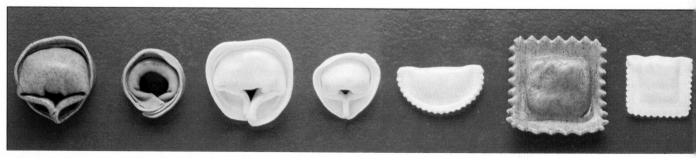

Ready-made, filled pasta comes in various shapes and sizes; choices include twisted spinach or egg tortelloni or smaller tortellini, semicircular agnolotti, square ravioli or smaller ravolini, and round anolini.

Spinach tortelloni float in chicken broth thick with shredded escarole and other vegetables—green peas, chopped onion, and chunky carrots. Nutmeg and lemon enhance soup's flavors.

Dip crisp-fried tortellini dusted with parmesan cheese and basil into cocktail sauce for party appetizers.

FRIED PASTA CRISPS

About ½ pound refrigerated or thawed frozen small (about ¾ in.) filled fresh pasta
Salad oil
⅓ cup grated parmesan cheese
1 teaspoon dry basil leaves
⅛ to ¼ teaspoon cayenne
Garlic salt
Cocktail sauce (optional)

If the pasta does not feel moist and supple, cover with boiling water and let stand until softened, about 5 minutes. Drain well. Spread soaked pasta on a 10- by 15-inch baking pan lined with paper

towels. Blot pasta gently with paper towels and let dry about 5 minutes. (If pasta feels moist, omit soaking and drying step.)

Meanwhile, pour about ½ inch oil into a 10-inch frying pan or 5-quart pan. Heat oil until it reaches 350° on a thermometer. Place about ⅓ of the pasta in pan. Cook, turning occasionally, until golden and crisp, 2 to 3 minutes. Remove with a slotted spoon and drain on 10- by 15-inch pan lined with paper towels. Serve pasta, or keep warm in a 200° oven up to 30 minutes while frying remaining pasta.

In a bag, mix cheese, basil, cayenne, and garlic salt to taste. Add warm pasta; shake to coat. Pour into bowl. Offer pasta with cocktail sauce for dipping. Makes 60 to 80 appetizers, 10 to 12 servings.

PER SERVING: 97 calories, 4 g protein, 7.7 g carbohydrates, 5.6 g fat, 1.7 mg cholesterol, 107 mg sodium

FILLED PASTA WITH ESCAROLE IN BROTH

2 tablespoons olive oil
1 large onion, chopped
2 large carrots, peeled and chopped
1 strip (4 in.) pared lemon peel (yellow part only)

10 cups regular-strength chicken broth
About 1 pound refrigerated, frozen, or vacuum-packed filled fresh pasta, or about ½ pound filled dry pasta
1 package (10 oz.) frozen petite peas, thawed
6 cups (8 oz.) shredded escarole
Freshly grated or ground nutmeg
Lemon wedges
Salt

In a 5- to 6-quart pan, stir oil, onion, carrots, and lemon peel over medium-high heat until onion is soft, 5 to 8 minutes.

Add broth (if using dry pasta, also add 1 cup water) and bring to a boil. Add filled pasta and boil gently, uncovered, just until barely tender to bite, 4 to 6 minutes for refrigerated or frozen pasta, 10 to 12 minutes for vacuum-packed, 20 to 25 minutes for dry. Stir in peas and escarole; cook just until escarole wilts, 1 to 2 minutes.

Ladle soup into bowls. Dust generously with nutmeg. Offer lemon wedges and salt to taste. Makes 6 to 8 servings.

PER SERVING: 282 calories, 15 g protein, 34 g carbohydrates, 10 g fat, 0 mg cholesterol, 327 mg sodium

Savory Scones

UNLIKE MOST SCONES, *these biscuit wedges offer robust and savory flavors instead of sweetness. Packed with herbs, chilies and cheese, or with oats and seeds, they make excellent companions to soups, salads, and hearty entrées.*

They're easy to make. Simply mix together dry ingredients; add butter, eggs, and milk; knead dough lightly, and shape. A food processor is even quicker—but take care to avoid overmixing.

To store scones: When cool, wrap the rounds airtight and hold at room temperature up to 1 day, or freeze to store longer. To reheat, unwrap scones (thaw wrapped, if frozen) and place on a 12- by 15-inch bak-ing sheet. Bake in a 350° oven until warm, 8 to 10 minutes.

CHILI CHEESE SCONES

- 2 cups all-purpose flour
- ½ cup yellow cornmeal
- 1 tablespoon baking powder
- 1 to 2 teaspoons crushed dried hot red chilies
- ½ teaspoon ground cumin
- ¼ cup (⅛ lb.) butter or margarine, cut into ½-inch pieces
- ¼ pound cheddar cheese
- 2 large eggs
- ½ cup milk

In a food processor or large bowl, whirl or mix flour, cornmeal, baking powder, chilies, and cumin until combined. Add butter; whirl or rub with your fingers until coarse crumbs form. If using a food processor, cut cheese into 1-inch chunks and whirl until shredded; otherwise, shred cheese and stir into flour mixture.

Beat eggs and milk to blend; set aside 2 tablespoons of the mixture. Add remainder to flour mixture and whirl or stir just until evenly moistened.

Scrape dough onto a floured board and knead about 6 turns or until dough holds together. Divide dough in half. Pat each half into a ¾-inch-thick round 5 to 6 inches in diameter. Set rounds well apart on an oiled 12- by 15-inch baking sheet. With a knife, cut each round not quite through to form 6 equal wedges. Brush rounds with the reserved egg mixture.

Bake in a 400° oven until golden brown, about 18 minutes. Serve hot or warm, breaking along scores. Makes 12 wedges.

PER WEDGE: 189 calories, 6.4 g protein, 21 g carbohydrates, 8.4 g fat, 57 mg cholesterol, 220 mg sodium

OAT & SEED SCONES

Follow steps for **chili cheese scones,** but for ingredients use 2 cups **all-purpose flour**; 1 cup **regular rolled oats**; 1 tablespoon **baking powder**; 2 teaspoons **caraway seed**; 1 teaspoon **fennel seed**; ½ teaspoon **celery seed**; ½ cup (¼ lb.) **butter** or margarine, cut into ½-inch pieces; 2 **large eggs;** and ½ cup **milk.**

PER WEDGE: 191 calories, 4.8 g protein, 21 g carbohydrates, 9.5 g fat, 58 mg cholesterol, 201 mg sodium

WHEAT & HERB SCONES

Follow steps for **chili cheese scones,** but for ingredients use 1½ cups *each* **all-purpose flour** and **whole-wheat flour;** 1 tablespoon **baking powder;** 1 teaspoon **dry basil leaves;** ½ teaspoon *each* **dry oregano leaves** and **dry thyme leaves;** ½ cup (¼ lb.) **butter** or margarine, cut into ½-inch pieces; 2 **large eggs;** and ½ cup **milk.**

PER WEDGE: 195 calories, 5.1 g protein, 23 g carbohydrates, 9.2 g fat, 58 mg cholesterol, 201 mg sodium

Season cornmeal dough with dried hot chilies and cumin. Then form into rounds.

Score rounds deeply to make wedges, cutting almost but not quite through.

Serve warm herb-seasoned scones, packed with chilies and cheese, with a hearty soup for a satisfying winter supper. To eat, break scone rounds into wedges where scored. Wrap any extra scones airtight for later use; scones freeze well.

Microwave Meals

NO TIME TO COOK? *With the help of your microwave oven, you can prepare and cook dinner for two in about 30 minutes. These four full-meal dishes use fresh, lean foods from the supermarket.*

Recipes are designed for medium- and full-size microwave ovens (0.7 to 1.5 cubic feet inside, 600 to 700 watts). Since cooking times are affected by variations in power as well as exact weight and starting temperature of foods, check for doneness at minimum times given, then add cooking time in 30-second intervals.

When you cover foods with plastic wrap for microwave cooking, be sure the wrap is made for this purpose.

MICROWAVE SALMON & VEGETABLES WITH FENNEL & ORANGE

- 4 small (*each* about 2-in. diameter) thin-skinned potatoes
- 2 small (*each* about ¾ in. thick and ⅓ to ½ lb.) salmon steaks or fillets
- ¼ teaspoon fennel seed
- ½ pound asparagus, tough ends trimmed
- Orange or lemon wedges

Peel a thin strip from center of each potato, then evenly arrange potatoes around perimeter of a rimmed nonmetal platter. Cover platter loosely with plastic wrap and cook at full power (100 percent) in a microwave oven for 5 minutes.

Arrange fish pieces opposite each other on platter, with thickest part of fish on outside of dish. If using steaks, tuck tips in (see picture below); for fillets, fold any thin edges under. Sprinkle fish with fennel. Cover and cook at full power for 2 minutes.

Place asparagus in a single layer in center of platter, with stems to outside. Cover and cook at full power until fish is just opaque in center (cut to test) and asparagus is tender-crisp to bite, 3 to 5 minutes. Offer with orange wedges to squeeze over fish and vegetables. Serves 2.

PER SERVING: 342 calories, 35 g protein, 28 g carbohydrates, 10 g fat, 84 mg cholesterol, 77 mg sodium

MICROWAVE CHICKEN COUSCOUS

- ¾ cup water
- 2 tablespoons raisins
- ¼ teaspoon ground cinnamon
- ⅓ cup couscous
- 4 chicken thighs (about 1¼ lb. *total*), skinned
- 1 medium-size zucchini (ends trimmed), diagonally sliced
- 1 cup regular-strength chicken broth
- 2 tablespoons tomato paste or catsup
- 1 teaspoon ground cumin
- ⅛ teaspoon cayenne
- 1 clove garlic, minced or pressed
- 1 small can (8¾ oz.) garbanzos, drained
- 1 medium-size bell pepper, cored, seeded, and cut into 1½-inch chunks

Place water, raisins, and cinnamon in a 1- to 1½-quart nonmetal bowl. Cover with a lid or plastic wrap and cook in a microwave oven at full power (100 percent) until water boils, about 2 minutes. Remove from oven, stir in couscous, cover tightly, and let stand.

Meanwhile, evenly arrange chicken, bone up, around perimeter of shallow 2- to 2½-quart nonmetal baking dish; place zucchini in center.

In a bowl, mix chicken broth, tomato paste, cumin, cayenne, garlic, and garbanzos. Pour mixture over chicken and zucchini. Cover with a lid or plastic wrap and cook the mixture at full power for 5 minutes.

Turn chicken over and arrange bell pepper chunks evenly in dish. Cover and cook at full power until meat is no longer pink at bone (cut to test), 7 to 8 minutes. Stir couscous and offer with meat, vegetables, and sauce. Serves 2.

PER SERVING: 503 calories, 44 g protein, 62 g carbohydrates, 9.2 g fat, 138 mg cholesterol, 676 mg sodium

MICROWAVE CURRIED TURKEY & BROCCOLI

Buy the kind of ramen noodles that have seasoning in a separate packet; save the packet for other uses.

- 1 tablespoon salad oil
- 1 medium-size onion, cut into thin slivers
- 1 teaspoon curry powder
- ½ teaspoon ground ginger
- ¼ teaspoon ground cinnamon
- 3 cups broccoli flowerets

Salmon and vegetables cook right on their serving platter. For best heat distribution, place asparagus stems and thickest part of fish toward outside of dish, where energy is most intense.

Slender strands of curried turkey and onion cook in the microwave with broccoli flowerets and ramen noodles. When you use plastic wrap to cover food during cooking, be sure the wrap is made for this purpose.

¾ cup regular-strength beef broth mixed with 2 teaspoons cornstarch and 1 tablespoon minced fresh cilantro (coriander)

½ pound thinly sliced cooked turkey or cooked ham, cut into very thin strips about 3 inches long

1¼ cups water

1 package (3 oz.) dry ramen noodles, broken up slightly

In a shallow 1- to 1½-quart nonmetal baking dish, stir oil, onion, curry, ginger, and cinnamon to mix. Cover with a lid or plastic wrap and cook at full power (100 percent) in a microwave oven until onion is limp, 4 to 5 minutes.

Stir in broccoli and broth mixture. Cover and cook at full power until sauce bubbles, 4 to 5 minutes. Stir in turkey. Cover and let stand.

Place water in a shallow 1- to 1½-quart nonmetal container. Cover with a lid or plastic wrap and cook in a microwave oven on full power until water boils, 2 to 4 minutes. Stir in noodles, cover tightly, and let stand for 2 minutes. Drain, then drift broccoli mixture to spoon on noodles. Serves 2.

PER SERVING: 493 calories, 46 g protein, 48 g carbohydrates, 14 g fat, 87 mg cholesterol, 135 mg sodium

EGGS & BACON VEGETABLE SOUP

4 slices bacon

1 small onion, chopped

1 medium-size carrot, peeled if desired, thinly sliced diagonally

1 small turnip, peeled and diced

1 small (about ¼ lb.) russet potato, peeled and diced

1 teaspoon dry basil leaves

1¾ cups regular-strength chicken broth

1 can (14½ oz.) low-sodium stewed tomatoes

2 cups cleaned, lightly packed spinach leaves, cut in slivers

4 large eggs (to sterilize shells just before using eggs, dip eggs in and out of boiling water to cover)

Place bacon in a single layer on 6 layers of paper towels. Cover with 2 paper towels. Cook at full power (100 percent) in a microwave oven until bacon is brown and crisp, 3 to 4 minutes. Crumble bacon and set aside.

In a deep 2- to 2½-quart nonmetal container, stir onion, carrot, turnip, potato, basil, and broth. Cover with lid or plastic wrap and cook at full power until carrot is barely tender to bite, 7 to 9 minutes. Stir in tomatoes and spinach. Gently crack eggs into soup, spacing them evenly. Carefully prick each yolk with the tines of a fork.

Cover and cook at full power until yolks are done to your liking, about 5 minutes for soft-cooked. Top portions with bacon. Makes 2 servings.

PER SERVING: 417 calories, 24 g protein, 40 g carbohydrates, 19 g fat, 559 mg cholesterol, 501 mg sodium

Full-meal soup combines carrots, tomatoes, spinach, and other vegetables with poached egg; prick yolk carefully with a fork before cooking. Offer microwaved bacon as a topping. Breadsticks make a crisp accompaniment.

Bold Thai Appetizers

A PROVOCATIVE MIX *of flavors teases your palate in these appetizers from Thailand.*

Marinate thin slices of pork in coconut milk, fish sauce, and garlic, then skewer meat and grill; dip in hot, tart sauce to eat. Or make a chili and garlic paste; cook with pork and shrimp for a mildly hot relish to eat with raw vegetables.

The combination of ingredients emphasizes Southeast Asian flavors. Make the recipes either with the ethnic ingredients found in some supermarkets and Asian grocery stores, or use the readily available alternatives for similar results.

Thai chef Vatcharin Bhumichitr, of London's Chiang Mai restaurant, created the pork skewers. Vorachoon Yuchinda and Narin Chotipanang, of Bangkok's Lemongrass Restaurant, created the red relish to eat with vegetables.

SKEWERED MARINATED PORK
(Moo Ping)

- 2 cloves garlic, pressed or minced
- ¼ teaspoon ground coriander
- 2 tablespoons fish sauce (*nuoc nam* or *nam pla*) or soy sauce
- 1 tablespoon light soy sauce
- ½ cup coconut milk (or whipping cream with ¼ teaspoon coconut extract)
- 1 tablespoon sugar
- ½ teaspoon ground white pepper
- 1 pound lean boneless pork such as leg or loin
- Fresh cilantro (coriander) sprigs
- Sauce (recipe follows)

Mix garlic, ground coriander, fish sauce, light soy, coconut milk, sugar, and pepper.

Cut pork into ⅛-inch-thick strips about 3 inches long and 1½ inches wide. Coat pork with coconut mixture. Cover and chill at least 30 minutes or up to 4 hours. Meanwhile, soak thin bamboo skewers in water for about 20 minutes.

Weave skewers through meat strips so meat lies flat. Place on a grill 4 to 6 inches above a solid bed of hot coals (you can hold your hand at grill level only 2 to 3 seconds). Cook, turning once, until browned on both sides, 5 to 7 minutes total. Transfer to platter; garnish with cilantro. Offer sauce in a bowl to spoon onto each serving. Makes 18 to 22 skewers, 8 appetizer servings.

PER SERVING (NO SAUCE): 123 calories, 13 g protein, 3.2 g carbohydrates, 6.5 g fat, 39 mg cholesterol, 162 mg sodium

Sauce. Mix 2 tablespoons **lemon juice**, 1 tablespoon **fish sauce** (*nuoc nam* or *nam pla*) or soy sauce, 2 tablespoons **light soy sauce**, 1 teaspoon **cayenne**, 1 tablespoon **sugar**, and 1 tablespoon chopped **fresh cilantro** (coriander). Makes ⅓ cup.

PER TEASPOON: 7.3 calories, 0.3 g protein, 1.3 g carbohydrates, 0.1 g fat, 0 mg cholesterol, 130 mg sodium

SPICY VEGETABLE DIP
(Nam Prik Ong)

Serve mild chili relish warm with crisp lettuce leaves, cucumber slices, cabbage wedges, or tender green beans.

- 6 dry California (Anaheim) or New Mexico chilies
- 1 small dried hot red chili
- ¼ teaspoon ground coriander
- 1 teaspoon shrimp paste (*gapi*) or anchovy paste
- 4 shallots
- 10 cloves garlic
- 1 teaspoon salad oil
- ⅛ pound (¼ cup) ground lean pork
- ⅓ pound medium (43 to 50 per lb.) shrimp, shelled, deveined, and minced
- 2 tablespoons lime juice
- 1 teaspoon sugar
- Fish sauce (*nuoc nam* or *nam pla*), soy sauce, or salt
- 5 cherry tomatoes, stemmed and cut in half

Remove and discard stems and seeds from California and hot chilies. Crumble chilies into a bowl, and soak in hot water to cover until soft, 20 to 30 minutes; drain chilies.

In a food processor or blender, combine the chilies, coriander, shrimp paste, shallots, and garlic (chop shallots and garlic first if using a blender); whirl until mixture forms a smooth paste, scraping bowl often, 5 to 15 minutes.

Pour oil into an 8- to 10-inch frying pan and place over medium heat. Add chili mixture. Stir often until chili paste is fragrant and turns darker in color, about 5 minutes. Add pork; stir until meat is crumbly, about 3 minutes. Add shrimp and stir, cooking until they turn pink, about 2 minutes. Add lime juice, sugar, and fish sauce to taste. Stir in tomatoes. Serve warm or at room temperature. Makes 1¾ cups, 8 to 10 appetizer servings.

PER SERVING: 45 calories, 4.4 g protein, 4.1 g carbohydrates, 1.3 g fat, 23 mg cholesterol, 47 mg sodium

Bold, spicy appetizers—chili paste with vegetables, or grilled pork skewers with soy-based sauce—go with chilled dry Chenin Blanc or dry Gewürztraminer.

Surprising Salads

To a westerner, *salads are many things served many ways. They frequently harbor unexpected and refreshing combinations of ingredients. Here, we present two such surprising recipes.*

The first takes a new look at potato salad. Instead of boiling, you slice the potatoes, oven-fry them to a golden brown color, then serve them warm or at room temperature with a light dressing of balsamic vinegar, parsley, and green onion.

The second salad is a colorful mix of two tender squash: green zucchini and yellow crookneck. You cook them whole to get a pleasantly firm texture, scoop out the seedy centers, and slice to create decorative half-moon shapes.

Serve the salads together, perhaps with cheese and bread for a simple meal; or offer them separately, when your menu calls for potatoes or squash. Both salads use an unusually small amount of oil.

Oven-fried Potato Salad

1½ pounds small (about 1½-in. diameter) red thin-skinned potatoes

   About 2 tablespoons olive oil or salad oil

2 tablespoons balsamic vinegar

½ cup thinly sliced green onion

3 tablespoons minced parsley

¼ teaspoon pepper

   Salt

Scrub potatoes and cut into ⅛-inch-thick slices (to brown evenly, slices must be uniformly thick); discard the ends of the potatoes.

Brush 2 baking pans, each 10 by 15 inches, with oil. Arrange slices in a single layer; lightly brush tops of potatoes with more oil. Bake in a 450° oven until both sides are deep, golden brown, about 25 minutes. Check frequently after 10 minutes for even browning; turn over slices that are not cooking evenly, or move to a cooler or hotter area of pan, as needed.

As slices are browned, transfer with a wide spatula to a serving bowl. (If made ahead, let stand, uncovered, up to 3 hours.) To potatoes, add vinegar, onion, parsley, and pepper; mix gently. Add salt to taste. Makes 6 to 8 servings.

PER SERVING: 94 calories, 1.6 g protein, 14 g carbohydrates, 3.5 g fat, 0 mg cholesterol, 6.7 mg sodium

Oven-browned potato slices and half-rings of zucchini and crookneck squash form the bases for two unusual salads. Serve together or separately.

Green & Yellow Squash Salad

1½ pounds *each* zucchini (about 1½-in. diameter) and yellow crookneck squash (about 2-in. diameter in thickest part), rinsed

½ cup minced red onion

¼ cup lemon juice

2 tablespoons minced fresh or 2 teaspoons dry basil leaves

1 tablespoon minced fresh or 1 teaspoon dry oregano leaves

1 tablespoon extra-virgin olive oil or salad oil

In a 6- to 8-quart pan, bring 3 quarts water to a boil over high heat. Add zucchini and crookneck; simmer, uncovered, until just tender when pierced, about 8 minutes. Drain; immerse squash in ice water just until cold; drain. If made ahead, cover and chill up until next day.

Trim off squash ends; discard. Cut squash in half lengthwise. Using a spoon, scrape out and discard seeds. Cut squash halves crosswise into ⅜-inch-thick slices.

In a bowl, combine onion, lemon juice, basil, oregano, and oil. Add squash and mix gently. Makes 6 to 8 servings.

PER SERVING: 46 calories, 1.8 g protein, 6.6 g carbohydrates, 2 g fat, 0 mg cholesterol, 4.7 mg sodium

Simmered Suppers

S LOW SIMMERING *transforms fibrous meat and vegetables into succulent stews for satisfying winter suppers.*

Our first stew, which pairs veal with escarole, cooks on top the range. In the other, a panful of vegetables is seasoned with a little pork; they bake together.

BRAISED VEAL WITH ESCAROLE

- 3 to 4 tablespoons olive oil
- 3 pounds boneless veal shoulder, cut into 1-inch cubes
- 2 ounces thinly sliced prosciutto, cut into thin shreds
- 1 large onion, finely chopped
- 1 large carrot, finely chopped
- 1½ cups water
- 1 cup dry white wine
- 2 quarts (about 1½ lb.) lightly packed shredded escarole

- 4 teaspoons cornstarch
  Salt and pepper
  Lemon wedges (optional)

Pour 1½ tablespoons oil into a deep 12-inch frying pan or 6-quart pan over high heat. Add half of the veal. Cook, stirring often, until meat is browned, 5 to 8 minutes. Remove browned pieces from pan and set aside. Repeat to cook remaining meat.

To pan, add 1 tablespoon oil (if needed), prosciutto, onion, and carrot. Stir over high heat until onion is limp, about 5 minutes. Return veal to pan. Add 1 cup water and the wine. Cover and simmer, stirring occasionally, until meat is tender to bite, about 1 hour. Add escarole, a portion at a time if it doesn't all fit at once; cook, stirring, until it wilts, 2 to 3 minutes. Mix cornstarch and remaining water; stir into meat. Stir until boiling. Add salt and pepper to taste. Spoon into a warm dish. Offer lemon

wedges to squeeze onto stew to season to taste. Makes 6 to 8 servings.

PER SERVING: 319 calories, 35 g protein, 5.6 g carbohydrates, 17 g fat, 152 mg cholesterol, 304 mg sodium

RATATOUILLE WITH PORK

- 2 pounds pork shoulder or butt, trimmed of fat and cut into 1-inch cubes
- 2 tablespoons olive oil
- 1 large onion, chopped
- 2 cloves garlic, pressed or minced
- 1 large (about 1⅓ lb.) eggplant, stem trimmed off, cut into 1-inch cubes
- 3 large (about 1⅓ lb. *total*) red thin-skinned potatoes, scrubbed and cut into 1-inch cubes
- 3 large (about ½ lb. *total*) carrots, peeled and sliced diagonally ¼ inch thick
- 2 pounds (about 2 heads) fresh fennel, stems and root ends trimmed, cut into 1-inch pieces
- 2 large (about 1 lb. *total*) red bell peppers, stemmed, seeded, and cut into 1-inch squares
- 1 can (28 oz.) pear-shaped tomatoes
- ½ teaspoon crushed dried hot red chilies
- ½ teaspoon fennel seed
  Salt and pepper

Place pork and oil in a 12- by 17-inch roasting pan; spread meat in a single layer. Bake in a 450° oven until meat is browned, 25 to 30 minutes.

Remove pan from oven and reduce heat to 400°. To pan, add onion, garlic, eggplant, potatoes, carrots, fresh fennel, bell peppers, tomatoes (including juices: break tomatoes up with a spoon), chilies, and fennel seed; stir to mix. Cover pan and return to oven; bake until eggplant is almost soft when pressed, 1¼ to 1½ hours. Uncover and continue baking, stirring occasionally, until meat is very tender when pierced and pan juices reduce slightly, about 45 minutes longer. Add salt and pepper to taste. Ladle into bowls. Makes about 8 servings.

PER SERVING: 291 calories, 23 g protein, 31 g carbohydrates, 9 g fat, 60 mg cholesterol, 321 mg sodium

Chunks of veal shoulder—simmered with prosciutto, carrot, and onion, then streaked with shreds of escarole—are presented on noodles with lemon wedge.

Putting Tapioca's Magic to Work

CONJURING CHILDHOOD MEMORIES, tapioca recalls visions of warm pudding swarming with tender, clear beads that resembled fish eggs. Ever wonder what those gelatinous pearls really were?

They are a starch from the root of the tropical cassava or manioc plant. To reach an edible form, the toxic root is washed, peeled, and leached of its toxins, then finely ground. Repeated washing and draining follow. As the starch washes out, it is collected, dried, then pulverized to make a fine flour.

Pearl tapioca, large or small, is made from the flour mixed with water. The resulting dough is shaped into pellets and toasted on a griddle to create a hard shell. Pellets are then dried thoroughly. These hard beads need to be soaked several hours to soften before cooking.

Quick-cooking tapioca is a mixture of tapioca flour and water that is cooked, dried, and then ground again to make small, even pieces. The precooking and the granular size make your preparation time considerably shorter.

One of tapioca's great attributes is its ability to hold moisture. When heated in liquid, particles swell and become transparent. Use the flour and quick-cooking and small-pearl tapiocas as you would cornstarch—as thickeners. Stir only until your mixture boils; stirring after boiling may make tapioca mixtures stringy.

Tapioca flour renders a smooth, clear sauce. Quick-cooking and small-pearl tapiocas swell and become clear but retain their shape. All three forms perform well in juicy fruit pies—even those with high acid, such as the fresh pineapple pie that follows. Wheat flour and cornstarch may break down (liquefy) in acid mixtures.

Because of its size, the large-pearl tapioca is less effective for thickening and is best used when you want to add a chewy, bouncy texture—perhaps to a pudding.

Quick-cooking tapioca is widely available. Look for the tapioca flour and pearl tapiocas in Asian markets. Pearl tapiocas are also available in some supermarkets.

FRESH PINEAPPLE PIE

- ¼ cup small-pearl (⅛-in.) tapioca, quick-cooking tapioca, or tapioca flour
- ¾ cup sugar
- 5 cups ½-inch chunks peeled, cored fresh pineapple (about 2 lb., trimmed)
- ½ teaspoon grated lime peel
- 1 tablespoon lime juice
  Pastry for a 2-crust 9-inch pie, rolled to fit pan

Mix small-pearl tapioca with 1 cup water; let stand until soft, at least 3 hours or up to overnight; drain. (Omit this step with quick-cooking tapioca or tapioca flour.)

Mix sugar with tapioca until blended. Add pineapple, lime peel, and lime juice; mix gently. Let stand at least 15 minutes.

Line a 9-inch pie pan with 1 round of pastry. Fill pan with fruit mixture. Cover with remaining pastry. Trim pastry to within ½ inch of pan rim; fold edges under, flush to rim. Flute edges to seal. Slash top in several places. Set in a foil-lined 10- by 15-inch baking pan. Bake on the bottom rack of a 400° oven until juices bubble through slashes in center, 50 to 60 minutes. Cool completely. Cut into wedges. Makes 6 servings.

PER SERVING: 370 calories, 3.2 g protein, 57 g carbohydrates, 16 g fat, 0 mg cholesterol, 277 mg sodium

To thicken plentiful juices of fresh pineapple pie, add beads of quick-cooking tapioca.

CREAMY PEARL TAPIOCA PUDDING

- ¾ cup small- (⅛-in.) or large- (¼-in.) pearl tapioca
- 1½ cups water
- 2 cups milk
- ½ cup sugar
- 2 large egg yolks
- 1 teaspoon vanilla

Soak tapioca in water until most of the water is absorbed, 3 hours for small-pearl, 8 to 12 hours for large-pearl. Drain.

In the top of a double boiler, combine soaked tapioca, milk, and sugar. Cook over simmering water, stirring occasionally, until tapioca is tender to bite and translucent, 25 to 30 minutes for small-pearl, 1½ hours for large-pearl.

In a small bowl, beat egg yolks and vanilla to blend. Stir about ½ cup of the hot tapioca into yolks, then stir mixture back into pan. Serve warm or cool; cover and chill up until next day. Makes 4 servings.

PER SERVING: 306 calories, 5.6 g protein, 56 g carbohydrates, 6.9 g fat, 153 mg cholesterol, 65 mg sodium

Four forms of tapioca are flour, quick-cooking, small-pearl, and large-pearl. When heated in liquid, particles swell and become transparent. Use first three kinds as thickeners; pearl varieties add chewy, bouncy texture to tapioca pudding.

Pistachio Biscotti

PALE GREEN PISTACHIOS *dot these slices of biscotti, the classic twice-baked Italian cooky. First, you bake cooky dough in flat loaves, then slice the loaves and bake the pieces until firm and golden. Add lemon icing for a sweet-tart accent.*

LEMON-TIPPED PISTACHIO BISCOTTI

> 5 tablespoons butter or margarine, at room temperature
> ½ cup sugar
> 1½ teaspoons grated lemon peel
> 2 large eggs
> 1 teaspoon vanilla
> 2 cups all-purpose flour
> 2 teaspoons baking powder
> 1 cup shelled, salted, roasted pistachios, coarsely chopped
>   Lemon icing (recipe follows)

In a large bowl, beat butter, sugar, and lemon peel until well blended. Add eggs, 1 at a time, beating well after each addition. Stir in vanilla. Mix flour and baking powder; add dry ingredients to butter mixture and stir to blend thoroughly. Mix in nuts.

Divide dough in half. On a lightly floured board, shape each portion into a long roll, about 1½ inches in diameter. Place rolls on a greased 12- by 15-inch baking sheet, spacing them 3 inches apart. Flatten rolls to make ½-inch-thick loaves. Bake in a 350° oven for 15 minutes.

Remove from oven and cut loaves crosswise into about ½-inch-thick slices. Lay slices, cut side down, on the baking sheet (at this point you need another sheet to bake cookies all at once). Return to oven and bake until biscotti look dry and are lightly browned, about 10 min-

Offer nut-studded, lemon-iced biscotti with hot cider or tea; try dunking the firm cookies (un-iced end) into your steaming drink.

utes (change pan positions halfway through baking). Transfer biscotti to racks to cool.

Spread icing on about 1 inch of one end of each biscotti. When icing firms, serve cookies. Or store biscotti airtight up to 1 week, or freeze up to 1 month. Makes 4½ dozen.

PER COOKY: 57 calories, 12 g protein, 7.9 g carbohydrates, 2.4 g fat, 11 mg cholesterol, 29 mg sodium

Lemon icing. In a small bowl, combine 1 cup sifted **powdered sugar,** ½ teaspoon grated **lemon peel,** and 1 to 1½ tablespoons **lemon juice.** Mix enough to make icing easy to spread.

A Flaming Spanish Favorite, Simplified

LECHE FRITA, *or fried milk, is a Spanish twist on custard. But here the method gets modernized. Instead of pan-frying, this simplified version uses the oven. The process is easier and much less harried.*

Traditionally, fried milk starts with a nicely flavored egg and milk pudding made sturdy by cornstarch. The pudding is chilled, cut into squares, coated with crumbs, and fried. Inside the fragile crust, the pudding becomes delectably tender.

To make oven-fried milk, you start the same way. Coat chilled rectangles of pudding with butter, then with crisp almond macaroon crumbs, and bake at high heat. For a dramatic and flavorful option, you can flame the oven-fried custards with a liqueur. Offer whipped cream for a subtle texture contrast.

If you want, you can serve part of the dessert one day and part another.

OVEN-FRIED ALMOND MILK

- ½ **cup cornstarch**
- ¾ **cup sugar**
- 4 **cups milk**
- 1 **teaspoon grated lemon peel**
- 4 **large egg yolks**
- ¼ **teaspoon almond extract**
  About 6 tablespoons melted butter or margarine
  About 1 cup crushed crisp almond macaroons (such as Italian-style amaretti; about 20 cookies, 2 in. wide)
- ¼ **cup sliced almonds**
  Strawberries (optional)
- ½ **cup almond-flavored liqueur such as amaretto (optional)**
- 1 **cup whipping cream, softly whipped**

In a 3- to 4-quart pan, mix cornstarch with sugar. Smoothly stir in the milk and add lemon peel. Stirring, cook on high heat until mixture is boiling. Remove from heat; whisk some of the hot sauce into egg yolks. Stir yolks into pan and return to low heat; stir for 5 minutes. Stir in almond extract, then pour hot cornstarch-custard mixture into an oiled 9-inch-square pan and smooth the surface. Let cool, then cover custard with plastic wrap and refrigerate until firm, at least 4 hours or as long as 3 days.

Run a knife along pan edge to release custard, then invert pan onto a sheet of foil or waxed paper. Tap pan to release the custard. Cut custard into 9 equal squares.

Pour melted butter into a shallow pan, and put cooky crumbs in another.

Gently lift a custard square from foil, turn in butter to coat all surfaces, then turn in crumbs, patting them lightly onto all sides. Lay squares about 1 inch apart in a 10- by 15-inch baking pan. Repeat to coat as many pieces of custard as desired. (If you save some of the custard to serve another day, keep uncoated portions covered and chilled; cover crumbs airtight; remelt left-over butter to continue.)

Sprinkle tops of coated custard squares with almonds; if desired, cover and chill up to 4 hours.

Bake coated squares, uncovered, in a 450° oven until sizzling and lightly browned, about 10 minutes; let cool about 5 minutes (if you move custards while too hot, they're apt to break).

As custards cool, warm dessert plates. For easy presentation, put plates on a large tray. With a wide spatula, transfer a piece of custard to each plate; garnish with strawberries. Pour the liqueur into a 1- to 2-cup pan and place on medium-high heat until hot to touch. Present the dessert at the table; light the liqueur in the pan and ladle it, flaming, onto each dessert. Offer whipped cream from a small bowl to add to taste. Makes 9 servings.

PER SERVING: 405 calories, 6.7 g protein, 39 g carbohydrates, 25 g fat, 191 mg cholesterol, 177 mg sodium

Almond milk pudding is chilled, cut into squares, coated with butter and crisp macaroon crumbs, and oven-browned at high heat. Flame with liqueur to finish crisp-creamy dessert.

Cook leeks, potatoes, clams, and bacon for chowder.

CLAM & LEEK CHOWDER

2½   **pounds (about 4 large) leeks**
3   **large (about 1½ lb. *total*) red thin-skinned potatoes, scrubbed**
4   **slices bacon, cut into thin slivers**
¼   **cup all-purpose flour**
3   **cups regular-strength chicken broth**
1   **teaspoon dry thyme leaves**
½   **teaspoon pepper**
3   **cups milk**
3   **cans (6½ oz. *each*) chopped clams**

Remove and discard green tops and root ends from leeks; split in half lengthwise and rinse well. Thinly slice leeks; cut potatoes into ½-inch cubes.

In a 5- to 6-quart pan, stir bacon over medium-high heat until crisp, about 5 minutes. Drain and discard all but 2 tablespoons fat. Add leeks; stir often until limp, about 5 minutes. Sprinkle flour over leeks and stir until flour coats leeks. Stir in broth, thyme, pepper, and potatoes; bring to a boil. Cover and simmer until potatoes are tender when pierced, about 15 minutes. Add milk and clams (including juices). Stir often over low heat until hot, about 5 minutes. Makes 6 to 8 servings. —*Susan Sproat, Redding, Calif.*

PER SERVING: 266 calories, 13 g protein, 34 g carbohydrates, 9 g fat, 40 mg cholesterol, 545 mg sodium

---

Chop fresh cilantro to sprinkle over baked rice laced with green chilies and corn.

GREEN CHILI RICE

1   **tablespoon salad oil**
1   **large onion, chopped**
2   **large eggs**
2   **cups unflavored yogurt**
¼   **teaspoon salt (optional)**
⅛   **teaspoon pepper**
3   **cups cooked rice**
3   **cans (4 oz. *each*) diced green chilies**
1   **package (10 oz.) frozen corn kernels**
1   **cup (4 oz.) shredded cheddar cheese**
¼   **teaspoon chili powder**
½   **cup chopped fresh cilantro (coriander)**

In an 8- to 10-inch frying pan, combine oil and onion. Stir often over medium-high heat until onion is faintly browned, about 12 minutes; set aside.

In a large bowl, beat eggs to blend with yogurt, salt, and pepper. Add onion, rice, chilies, and corn; mix together. Pour mixture into an oiled shallow 3-quart baking dish. Sprinkle with cheese and chili powder. Bake in a 375° oven just until hot in center, about 25 minutes. Sprinkle with cilantro. Scoop out portions and serve hot. Makes 10 to 12 servings. —*Carolyn McClure, Scottsdale, Ariz.*

PER SERVING: 173 calories, 7.5 g protein, 23 g carbohydrates, 6 g fat, 48 mg cholesterol, 270 mg sodium

---

Onion, capers, and raisins form sauce for braised chicken.

SPICED CHICKEN WITH CAPERS

2   **tablespoons salad oil**
4   **boned, skinned chicken breast halves (about 1 lb. *total*)**
1   **large onion, thinly sliced**
2   **cloves garlic, pressed or minced**
¼   **teaspoon ground cinnamon**
¼   **teaspoon ground cloves**
½   **cup orange juice**
2   **tablespoons raisins**
1   **tablespoon drained capers**
    Parsley sprigs (optional)
    Salt and pepper

Pour oil into a 10- to 12-inch frying pan over high heat. When oil is hot, add chicken breasts and cook until both sides are lightly browned, turning once, 4 to 6 minutes total. Lift out chicken; set aside.

Reduce heat to medium-high. Add onion and garlic to pan; stir often until onion is faintly browned, about 6 minutes. Stir in cinnamon, cloves, orange juice, raisins, and capers. Return chicken to pan. Cover and simmer over low heat until chicken is white in thickest part (cut to test), about 5 minutes.

Transfer chicken and juices to a serving dish; garnish with parsley. Add salt and pepper to taste. Makes 4 servings. —*Carmela Meely, Walnut Creek, Calif.*

PER SERVING: 229 calories, 27 g protein, 11 g carbohydrates, 8.4 g fat, 66 mg cholesterol, 131 mg sodium

HALIBUT WITH TOMATOES & DILL

- ½ **cup thinly sliced green onion**
- 2 **cloves garlic, pressed or minced**
- 2 **tablespoons chopped fresh dill weed or ½ teaspoon dry dill weed**
- 2 **tablespoons olive oil**
- 1 **pound cherry tomatoes, cut in half**
- 4 **halibut steaks (6 to 8 oz.** *each)*
- 2 **tablespoons lemon juice**
  Fresh dill sprigs (optional)
  Salt and pepper

Mix the onion, garlic, dill weed, and oil. Place tomatoes, cut side up, in a 9- by 13-inch baking pan or dish. Distribute onion mixture evenly over tomatoes.

Bake, uncovered, on top rack in a 425° oven for 25 minutes.

Meanwhile, rinse fish, pat dry, and place in a 9- by 13-inch baking pan. Drizzle lemon juice over fish and cover. After tomatoes have baked 25 minutes, place fish on bottom rack. Bake until tomatoes are browned and fish looks just barely translucent in thickest part (cut to test), 10 to 12 minutes.

Transfer fish to a platter. Stir fish juices into tomatoes; spoon mixture over fish. Garnish with dill sprigs. Add salt and pepper to taste. Serves 4. — *Heide Gohlert, Cheney, Wash.*

PER SERVING: 276 calories, 37 g protein, 6.7 g carbohydrates, 11 g fat, 54 mg cholesterol, 104 mg sodium

Cherry tomatoes baked with garlic and fresh dill top oven-steamed halibut steaks.

WINTER RED SLAW

- ½ **cup thinly sliced red onion**
- 2 **tablespoons chopped almonds or salted roasted almonds**
- 2 **cups (about 5 oz.) finely shredded red cabbage**
- 1 **large Red Delicious apple, cored and coarsely chopped**
- ¼ **cup unflavored yogurt**
- ½ **teaspoon grated lemon peel**
- 2 **tablespoons lemon juice**
- 2 **tablespoons boysenberry (or other berry) preserves**
- ¾ **teaspoon ground coriander**
  Salt and pepper

Soak red onion in ice water to cover until crisp, about 15 minutes. Drain.

Meanwhile, in a 6- to 8-inch frying pan, stir unroasted nuts over medium-low heat until golden, about 5 minutes. Set aside. (Omit this step if using purchased roasted nuts.)

In a large bowl, combine shredded cabbage, apple, and onion. Mix together the yogurt, lemon peel, lemon juice, boysenberry preserves, and coriander. Pour yogurt dressing over cabbage mixture and mix until blended. Pour into serving bowl. Sprinkle with almonds. Add salt and pepper to taste. Makes 4 servings. — *Brandy Johnstone, La Luz, N.M.*

PER SERVING: 104 calories, 2.4 g protein, 20 g carbohydrates, 2.6 g fat, 0.8 mg cholesterol, 18 mg sodium

Mix red cabbage, lemon, apple, onion, and almonds for winter salad.

ORANGE PUDDING CAKE

- 3 **large eggs, separated**
- 1 **cup sugar**
- 1½ **cups milk**
- ½ **teaspoon grated orange peel**
- ⅓ **cup orange juice**
- ⅓ **cup all-purpose flour**
- 1 **teaspoon vanilla**
  Lightly sweetened whipped cream (optional)
  Fine shreds of orange peel (optional)

In a large bowl, beat egg whites until foamy. With beater on high speed, gradually beat in ¼ cup sugar until stiff, moist peaks form; set aside.

In a small bowl, beat egg yolks until thick. Stir in milk, grated orange peel, and orange juice. Add remaining ¾ cup sugar, flour, and vanilla; beat just until smooth. Add yolk mixture to beaten whites; fold gently just until blended. Pour into a 9-inch quiche dish (1½ in. deep) or 10-inch pie dish.

Set dish in a slightly larger baking pan in a 350° oven. Pour about 1 inch boiling water into outer pan. Bake until center of pudding appears set when gently shaken, about 35 minutes. Serve warm or cool. Garnish with cream and shreds of orange peel. Makes 6 to 8 servings. — *Lois Dowling, Tacoma.*

PER SERVING: 178 calories, 4.4 g protein, 33 g carbohydrates, 3.4 g fat, 86 mg cholesterol, 47 mg sodium

Cake is on top, pudding underneath in this orange dessert.

DERIVED FROM A SHE-CRAB SOUP conceived in Maryland's Chesapeake Bay, and brought to us from Hawaii, Matt Cabot's crab soup might truly be called nationwide. Instead of blue crab, this version uses Dungeness; instead of crab roe, hard-cooked eggs serve for added enrichment; instead of cream, as a sop to the calorie-conscious, Cabot uses milk. Marylanders newly arrived in the West brag about the flavor of blue crab, but they're eager enough to eat our Western crabs (which are bigger anyway) and will even concede that ours have more meat and less shell than the blues.

CRAB SOUP

    2   tablespoons butter or margarine
    1   medium-size onion, chopped
    3   tablespoons cornstarch
    2   quarts low-fat or whole milk
    1   bottle (8 oz.) clam juice
    ½   cup dry sherry
    1   teaspoon Worcestershire
    1   pound shelled cooked crab
    1   hard-cooked egg or 3 hard-cooked
        egg yolks, rubbed through a fine
        strainer
        Salt and pepper

Melt butter in a 4- to 5-quart pan over medium heat. Add onion and stir often until golden, 10 to 15 minutes. Smoothly mix cornstarch with about ¼ cup of the milk, then add mixture along with remaining milk to pan. Stir often until boiling; turn heat to medium-low and add clam juice, sherry, Worcestershire, and crab. Stir gently until hot. Ladle into bowls. Sprinkle egg onto portions, and add salt and pepper to taste. Makes about 3 quarts, 8 or 9 servings.

PER SERVING: 211 calories, 18 g protein, 15 g carbohydrates, 8.2 g fat, 98 mg cholesterol, 347 mg sodium

Matt Cabot

Kailua, Hawaii

R.D. HORWITZ'S MARRIAGE of Mexican enchiladas and Jewish blintzes was made not in heaven but in San Diego—but it is still a happy match. Nevertheless, he is accurate in naming his creation "Culture Shock Blintzes."

Mr. Horwitz got the idea when, having decided to make chicken enchiladas for brunch, he found himself without tortillas.

The logical thing was to substitute crêpes. These eggy pancakes look somewhat like tortillas and can, like them, be used for packaging other food. In a traditional blintz, the crêpe is folded like an envelope around a cheese filling, lightly fried, and served with fruit or jam. But it can contain other foods as well.

The crêpe, though more tender than the tortilla, holds together well enough to make an attractive package, and portions left uncovered by sauce are not likely to turn into leather, as tortillas (especially those made of corn) too often do.

CULTURE SHOCK BLINTZES

    1   tablespoon salad oil
    1   medium-size onion, chopped
    1   small green bell pepper, stemmed,
         seeded, and diced
    1   large can (15 oz.) tomato sauce
    2½   tablespoons chili powder
    1   cup diced cooked chicken
         Crêpes (recipe follows)
    1   cup (4 oz.) shredded jack cheese
    1   medium-size firm-ripe avocado,
         peeled, pitted, and sliced
         About ¾ cup sour cream or small-
         curd cottage cheese
         Purchased salsa and sliced ripe
         olives (optional)

Pour oil into a 10- to 12-inch frying pan over medium heat; add onion and green

"Derived from a soup conceived in Chesapeake Bay, and brought to us from Hawaii, this crab soup might truly be called nationwide."

pepper, and stir often until onion is limp and slightly browned, about 10 minutes. Stir in ½ of the tomato sauce and 1 tablespoon of the chili powder. Simmer, stirring occasionally, about 10 minutes. Add chicken and simmer until mixture is reduced to about 1¾ cups, about 10 minutes. Remove from heat and let cool.

In a 1- to 1½-quart pan, combine remaining tomato sauce and remaining 1½ tablespoons chili powder. Place over medium heat and cook to blend flavors, 3 to 5 minutes. If made ahead, cover and chill chicken and tomato mixtures up until next day.

Spoon an equal amount of the chicken mixture down the center of each crêpe, leaving a 1¼- to 1½-inch margin of crêpe at each end of the chicken. Fold ends over filling, then roll each crêpe to enclose the filling. Place blintzes, seams down, in an oiled 8- by 12- or 9- by 13-inch baking dish or pan. Spoon tomato sauce evenly over blintzes, then evenly sprinkle with cheese. Bake, uncovered, in a 350° oven until cheese is melted and blintzes are hot throughout, 20 to 25 minutes.

Serve blintzes garnished with avocado slices. Offer sour cream, salsa, and ripe olives to add to taste. Makes 4 to 6 servings.

PER SERVING: 409 calories, 20 g protein, 26 g carbohydrates, 26 g fat, 193 mg cholesterol, 656 mg sodium

Crêpes. With an electric mixer, or in a blender, mix until smooth 3 **large eggs** and ¾ cup **all-purpose flour.** Mix in 1 cup **milk** and ⅛ teaspooon **salt** (optional).

Place a 6- to 7-inch crêpe pan (or frying pan with a nonstick finish) over medium-high heat. When hot, add 1 teaspoon **salad oil;** rotate pan to coat evenly with oil, then pour out excess and reserve (you will need about 1 tablespoon total).

Add to pan about 2 tablespoons of the batter; quickly tilt pan to spread mixture evenly. Cook until the crêpe is dry to touch. Turn crêpe over with a wide spatula and cook for 15 seconds longer. Turn

out of pan onto a plate. Repeat to cook remaining crêpes, stacking as cooked, and adding oil to pan as needed. Makes 12 to 16 crêpes.

If made ahead, wrap crêpes airtight and chill up to 4 days; let come to room temperature before separating to serve.

R D Hormuz

San Diego

E GGPLANT IS THE BELLE *of the* Solanaceae *family, an extended clan that includes the above-reproach potato and tomato, scoundrels like tobacco, and out-and-out thugs like deadly nightshade. Its glossy, deep purple hue is lovely, but, since the name eggplant will never take prizes for euphony, decorators and designers refer to the color (and the French refer to the whole vegetable) as aubergine.*

While some eggplant varieties actually do resemble eggs in both shape and coloring, and others come in browns, creams, greens, and reds, the most familiar shade is purple. For generations, melon-size deep purple fruits were the only ones in the market, but the slender Japanese (also called Oriental—and even French) varieties are coming on strong, and Dean Terlinden uses these in his Simply Perfect Eggplant recipe. Notice that tomato, a frequent companion of eggplant, is present here in dried form. This variation makes for a rich tomato flavor without the accompanying soupiness.

SIMPLY PERFECT EGGPLANT

- 3 to 4 tablespoons salad oil
- 6 Oriental eggplants (about 1 lb. *total*), stemmed and cut crosswise into ½-inch-thick slices
- ¼ cup dried tomatoes
- 1 small onion, finely chopped
- ½ pound mushrooms, minced
- 1 small red bell pepper, stemmed, seeded, and chopped
- 1 teaspoon *each* finely chopped parsley, fresh oregano leaves, and fresh marjoram leaves; or use parsley and ½ teaspoon *each* dry leaves of oregano and marjoram
- Salt and pepper

"Eggplant is the belle of the Solanaceae family."

Coat a 10- by 15-inch pan with some of the oil. Lay eggplant slices side-by-side in pan; brush tops with oil (you'll need 1 to 2 tablespoons). Bake in a 425° oven until browned and very soft when pressed, about 25 minutes.

Meanwhile, put tomatoes in a small bowl and barely cover with boiling water; let stand at least 5 minutes. Drain tomatoes and finely chop.

Pour 2 tablespoons oil into a 10- to 12-inch frying pan over medium heat. When oil is hot, add tomatoes, onion, mushrooms, bell pepper, parsley, oregano, and marjoram; stir often until mushrooms are slightly browned, 10 to 15 minutes. Keep mixture warm.

Arrange eggplant slices on a platter and top with onion mixture. Season vegetables to taste with salt and pepper. Makes 4 to 6 servings.

PER SERVING: 117 calories, 2.8 g protein, 13 g carbohydrates, 7 g fat, 0 mg cholesterol, 15 mg sodium

Dean W. Terlinden

Long Beach, Calif.

January Menus

Chase away the chill of winter with these warming family meals. For a cozy evening at home with a movie, serve pan-browned bratwurst and spaetzle, with spicy gingerbread à la mode for dessert.

Pumpkin pancakes laced with cinnamon and nutmeg welcome the family to a weekend breakfast.

Serve creamy risotto dotted with buds of broccoli and cauliflower with sliced cooked ham and a green salad for a winter supper.

MOVIE NIGHT SUPPER

**Pan-browned Bratwurst
Red Onion Marmalade
Swiss Chard with Garlic
Buttered Spaetzle
Gingerbread   Cinnamon Ice Cream
Apple Cider   Dark Beer**

For a snug evening at home, rent your favorite movie and prepare this hearty, quick, portable meal to serve buffet-style and eat from trays.

Pale, fat bratwurst are cooked sausages that need only to be heated and browned. The sweet-sour onion marmalade can be made several days ahead. Stir-fry slivered Swiss chard or boil the leaves, then season with minced or pressed garlic and extra-virgin olive oil. Purchase prepared spaetzle and cook as package directs (or cook egg noodles). For dessert, use your favorite gingerbread recipe, or buy prepared gingerbread. Serve it warm with ice cream. To give the ice cream cinnamon flavor, stir 1 teaspoon ground cinnamon into 1 quart slightly softened vanilla ice cream; you can store it in the freezer up to a week.

Assemble the meal on trays to carry to the TV room. Put the gingerbread in to bake or reheat just before you eat, so it will be warm and waiting when you finish.

For an easy dessert, serve a wedge of warm, spicy gingerbread with a scoop of cinnamon ice cream.

PAN-BROWNED BRATWURST

Accompany with red onion marmalade.

- **6 bratwurst (about 1¾ lb. total)**
- **2 tablespoons butter or margarine**

In a 10- to 12-inch frying pan at least 2 inches deep, bring to boil enough water to cover sausages. When water is boiling, add sausages and remove from heat. Let stand 10 minutes; drain off water. With a fork, pierce each bratwurst in several places. Return pan to medium-high heat; add butter and cook sausages, turning as needed, until lightly browned. Makes 6 servings.

PER SERVING: 489 calories, 21 g protein, 3.1 g carbohydrates, 43 g fat, 101 mg cholesterol, 882 mg sodium

RED ONION MARMALADE

- **2 tablespoons butter or margarine**
- **2 pounds red onions, peeled and thinly sliced**
- **⅓ cup sugar**
- **½ teaspoon pepper**
- **1 cup white wine**
- **½ cup red wine vinegar**

In a 10- to 12-inch frying pan, melt the butter over medium-high heat. Mix in onions, sugar, and pepper. Cover and cook, stirring occasionally, until onion is very limp and its juices have evaporated, 10 to 12 minutes.

To onions, add wine and vinegar; stir occasionally until liquid evaporates, about 25 minutes. Serve warm. If made ahead, let cool, cover, and chill up to 3 days. Reheat to serve. Makes 2½ cups.

PER ¼ CUP: 76 calories, 1 g protein, 13 g carbohydrates, 2.5 g fat, 6.2 mg cholesterol, 26 mg sodium

PANCAKE BREAKFAST

**Pink & White Grapefruit Segments
Spiced Pumpkin Pancakes
Maple Syrup
Rosemary Bacon Twists
Café au Lait   Hot Cocoa**

Spicy pumpkin pancakes go with whimsical herbed bacon spirals.

Alternate segments of pink and white grapefruit on salad plates; place on the table for early arrivals. Put bacon in to bake while you mix pancake batter. If you have an electric griddle, set it on a cart by the table so the cook can have company as pancakes brown. Offer makings for café au lait—hot milk, hot coffee—so each cup can be blended to taste.

SPICED PUMPKIN PANCAKES

- **2 cups all-purpose flour**
- **2 tablespoons sugar**
- **2 teaspoons baking powder**
- **1 teaspoon baking soda**
- **1 teaspoon ground cinnamon**
- **½ teaspoon ground nutmeg**
- **¼ teaspoon salt**
- **1¾ cups nonfat milk**
- **1 cup canned pumpkin**
- **2 large eggs**
- **2 tablespoons salad oil**
  Butter or margarine
  Warm maple syrup

In a bowl, mix flour, sugar, baking powder, baking soda, cinnamon, nutmeg, and salt. In another bowl, beat to blend milk, pumpkin, eggs, and oil. Add flour mixture and stir until just moistened.

On a lightly oiled or nonstick griddle over medium heat, pour batter in ¼-cup

Movies at home share billing with this hearty, buffet-style supper of pan-browned bratwurst, sweet-sour onion marmalade, stir-fried Swiss chard, and hot buttered spaetzle.

portions at least 1 inch apart. Cook until bubbles form on tops and bottoms are browned, about 1 minute. Turn with a spatula and cook until brown on bottoms, about 1 minute longer. To serve, accompany with butter and syrup. Makes 6 servings.

PER SERVING: 274 calories, 9.3 g protein, 43 g carbohydrates, 43 g fat, 72 mg cholesterol, 431 mg sodium

ROSEMARY BACON TWISTS

12 slices bacon
2 teaspoons crumbled dry rosemary

Gently twist bacon strips to form spirals and lay side-by-side in a 10- by 15-inch pan. Sprinkle evenly with rosemary. Bake in a 350° oven for 10 minutes. With a wide spatula, transfer bacon to paper towels to drain; do not untwist spirals. Discard fat and wipe pan clean.

Return bacon to pan and put back in the oven; bake until bacon is crisp and browned, about 15 minutes longer. Drain spirals briefly on paper towels, then serve. Makes 6 servings.

PER SERVING: 74 calories, 3.9 g protein, 0.3 g carbohydrates, 6.3 g fat, 10 mg cholesterol, 203 mg sodium

(Continued on next page)

RISOTTO SUPPER

Sliced Cooked Ham
Winter Flower Bud Risotto
Salad Greens with Oil & Vinegar
Tangelos   Blood Oranges
Crisp Butter Cookies
Dry Sauvignon Blanc
Mineral Water

This creamy risotto is full of edible flower buds: broccoli and cauliflower.

If you have ham left from the holidays, serve it; if not, buy sliced cooked ham. Make the salad as the risotto cooks. Offer a choice of citrus with cookies.

WINTER FLOWER BUD RISOTTO

2 cups *each* cauliflower flowerets and broccoli flowerets
3 tablespoons butter or margarine
1 large onion, chopped
2 cloves garlic, minced or pressed
1 cup short-grain (pearl) rice
½ cup dry white wine
3 to 3¼ cups regular-strength chicken broth
1 cup (4 oz.) grated parmesan cheese
   Freshly ground pepper

In a 3- to 4-quart pan, bring 2 quarts water to a boil. Add cauliflower; cook 3 minutes. Add broccoli; cook until both vegetables are tender when pierced, about 2 minutes more; drain. Immerse vegetables immediately in ice water; when cold, drain.

In a 10- to 12-inch frying pan, melt butter over medium-high heat. Add onion and garlic; stir often until onion is faintly browned, 5 to 8 minutes. Add rice and stir until it is slightly translucent, 2 to 3 minutes. Mix in wine and 3 cups broth. Stir often until mixture boils. Reduce heat; simmer gently, uncovered, for 10 minutes. Stir in broccoli and cauliflower.

Cook mixture until rice is tender to bite and liquid is absorbed, about 10 minutes. Add remaining broth if rice starts to stick. Stir in ½ cup parmesan; pour risotto into a bowl. Offer remaining parmesan and pepper to add to taste. Serves 6.

PER SERVING: 306 calories, 14 g protein, 34 g carbohydrates, 13 g fat, 30 mg cholesterol, 455 mg sodium

FEBRUARY

Niçoise Sandwich (page 36)

Join us for an oyster-tasting party, as we sample and compare different kinds. You'll learn how to choose, store, and shuck oysters, and we also suggest party-planning tips and dipping sauces. A Singapore cook shares her recipe for cobweb pancakes, an unusual bread flavored with coconut milk and served with spicy chicken curry. For hearty February meals, we offer substantial sandwiches and oven-braised shanks. Cholesterol-conscious cooks will find recipes, as well. And for Valentine's Day, surprise someone special with an edible candy corsage.

Come for an Oyster Tasting

IF YOU EXULT *in the freshness of an ocean breeze, you know the flavor of oysters on the half-shell. Perhaps no other food captures the essence of the sea so well. And oyster lovers have reason to rejoice: the half-shell market is improving, with better quality, variety, and availability.*

But outside of restaurants, where oysters arrive magically chilled and shucked, this shellfish may seem more intimidating than enticing. For starters, why do oysters have so many different names? Which kinds taste best? How do you get an oyster open? Once they're open, how do you keep them cold and level so they hold their juices? If you use ice, how do you deal with the melt?

We offer a guide to selecting, storing, and serving one of the world's grand celebration foods. We'll show you how to shuck and serve oysters with ease, and suggest simple sauces to accent their flavor.

How Many Kinds? How Many Names?

A glance at an oyster bar's menu might make you think there are dozens of oysters. In fact, just four primary species are sold in this country: Pacific, Eastern, Olympia, and European flat. A fifth species, from Chile, has limited availability.

The proliferation of names arises because Pacifics and Easterns—the most widely grown oysters—are frequently labeled according to the area they're from, rather than by species. For example, Yaquina Bay (Oregon) and Quilcene (Washington) oysters are both Pacifics.

Geographic nomenclature has merit because oysters, being filter-feeders, pick up different flavors depending on the amount of salt and other nutrients in the water, and on the types of food the oysters eat. One area might give oysters a more vegetative flavor, while another might impart a brinier taste. These factors also affect flesh color. Seasonal changes (like rainfall) influence both flavor and texture.

Within the same species, some variations are consistent from one geographic area to another, but others aren't. If you want to experience distinct differences, include more than one species in your tasting.

Species not only taste different but look different, as you'll notice in the picture below. Following is a thumbnail guide to different species; they're listed in order of availability in the West.

Pacific oysters, the commonest species in the West, have a distinct, full, briny flavor. Their shells are deeply ridged and may be nearly black to purple, green, or oyster gray. Flesh is usually gray-white to tan, with a mantle (the ruffled-looking edge of the meat) that is beige-gray to black. Seed originally came to the U.S. from Japan, and this oyster is now grown from California to Alaska (as well as in New Zealand and Australia). Production has doubled in the last few years to 25 percent of the nation's total oysters.

Most Pacifics are farm-raised; small, plump, milder ones are chosen for half-

shell consumption. Some Pacifics grow to the astonishing length of 12 inches.

The Kumamoto, a Pacific variety, tastes similar to other Pacifics but is sweeter. A fairly small oyster with an especially deep-ridged cup, it is farm-raised in California, Oregon, and Washington.

Eastern oysters, native to the Atlantic and Gulf of Mexico coasts, have a mild flavor. Their tan-colored, flat shells may be oblong to rounded. Meat is usually gray to tan, with a light-colored mantle. Growing areas stretch from northern Canada to Texas, with Louisiana the greatest producer. (You may see the term "blue point" used generically for Eastern oysters; it originally applied to those from Blue Point, New York.)

Oysters from the Eastern U.S. are flown to the West and are available at many fish stores and supermarkets here. Some are farm-raised, others are from wild beds.

In recent years, problems with pollution, diseases, and overharvesting have somewhat limited supplies of Eastern oysters, especially from the Chesapeake Bay area. Various regulatory controls also restrict the number harvested. In 1988, though, the Gulf of Mexico region still produced 51 percent of this country's oysters.

Olympia oysters, the only ones native to the West coast, are prized for their sweet flavor, distinct metallic aftertaste,

Four primary species of oysters are sold in this country. The most widely grown kinds, Pacific and Eastern, are usually labeled for area in which they're grown. Differences in geography and climate affect flavors and color.

Grand tasting of oysters served on the half-shell makes an informal party. Have several different kinds from different areas to compare; serve oysters well chilled and level on crushed ice atop trays rigged to catch the melt. You can shuck your own oysters—just follow the steps on page 32—or hire a shucker. Simple accompaniments show off the oysters best.

Oh Shucks, How Do I Open This Oyster?

SHUCKING AN OYSTER is all in the wrist. It doesn't require much strength, though it does require the proper knife and a little practice.

First scrub oysters with a stiff brush under cold running water. Use an oyster knife (available in some fish stores, cookware shops, and restaurant supply stores)—never a regular kitchen knife, which is not stiff enough and can be dangerous. Long, narrow oyster knives can easily reach into larger shells; shorter knives are handy for smaller oysters (the shorter knife illustrated in steps 1 and 2 also has a slip guard).

You can shuck oysters up to 3 hours in advance. Keep them well chilled and level in a bed of crushed ice, with oyster meat and juices cupped in the shells.

1 *Wrap an oyster in a towel, letting hinge (look for a small opening) stick out. Keep shell flat, cup side down, and firmly hold it on a flat surface. With knife horizontal, firmly insert tip ¼ inch into hinge.*

2 *With a twist of the wrist, turn knife sideways so it will sever the hinge and pop the shell open.*

3 *Slide knife along inside of top shell to sever the muscle that connects meat and shell; discard top shell. Sever muscle along bottom shell. Wipe off any fragmentary bits of shell.*

---

and tiny greenish shells. Meat ranges from tan to copper-purple; the mantle can be beige to black. Originally found from Los Angeles to northern British Columbia, Olympia oysters nearly died out in the 1920s from pollution and overharvesting.

With greater interest in oysters, the little Olympia is enjoying a revival in the waters of southern Puget Sound and, on a very small basis, in northern California as well. Most of the harvest still comes from wild beds, though aquaculturists are working on farm production. Olympias are slow-growing—sometimes taking five years to reach the size of a quarter.

European flat oysters have a mild, slightly sweet, metallic flavor. Shells are round and flat and may be white or tan to greenish; flesh is usually tan with a tan mantle. This oyster is often incorrectly called Belon after an oyster-growing area in France. Most of the "European" oysters you'll find in America are actually raised in small quantities on the East and West coasts.

Chilean oysters, new to the West in 1989, look like large Olympia oysters and taste like a cross between Olympias and European flats. Shells are gray-green; flesh is pale. So far, only restaurants offer these South American imports.

HOW TO CHOOSE & STORE OYSTERS

Your selection may be based on availability as well as on your preference for milder, sweeter, or more full-flavored species. You should also observe the following precautions as you buy and store oysters (for more safety tips, see facing page).

Buy from approved sources. To be certified, shellfish growers and processors must meet state standards for cleanliness and safety. Every box of oysters that goes to a retailer should have a tag with a certification.

Buy oysters from a store you trust, where shellfish is kept clean and cold. Oysters should have tightly closed shells and feel heavy for their size. They should smell clean, not sulfurous. Ones that close when tapped are all right to eat, but they may be dry.

Oysters in their shells are alive; they need air, moisture, and a cool environment. If you buy them in a plastic bag, open it as soon as you get home. Store oysters cup side down, to retain juices, and topped with damp towels.

Keep oysters chilled (below 40°), and don't store more than a few days. Raw oysters contain some bacteria, which cool temperatures keep in check. If oysters are held above 40° for more than a few hours, the bacteria can quickly multiply to harmful levels. Even when stored at ideal temperatures, oysters deteriorate with time, so buy them close to when you plan to use them. Eat shucked oysters within a few hours.

When preparing oysters, keep hands, tools, and work surfaces clean to avoid contamination from any other sources.

PLANNING AN OYSTER-TASTING PARTY

Enjoying oysters at home needn't be a daunting prospect. The biggest job is getting them shucked. Your first few may go slowly, so practice a little ahead of time, following the drawings on the facing page. For a party, you may want to shuck all the oysters in advance, starting a few hours ahead, or just open a couple of dozen and do the rest after guests arrive.

Another option is to hire a professional shucker from a restaurant or a catering company that serves a lot of oysters. One shucker can open about 200 oysters an hour. Cost for this service varies from as low as $15 an hour for shucking only (you provide the oysters) to a $300 flat rate including set-up, oysters, and a minimum time period.

Crushed ice (not cubes) works best for keeping shucked oysters cold and steady. One method we like for capturing melting ice is to place small cans (of equal height) in a deep roasting pan, then top them with a piece of stiff, foil-covered cardboard that is slightly smaller in dimensions than the pan. Place crushed ice on top of the cardboard to make a solid oyster bed; the pan will gather drips. You can drape fabric around the pan to dress it up.

To steady oysters on plates, rest them on crushed ice or crumpled napkins.

Plan on about a dozen oysters per person. Depending on availability, consider offering at least two species, and perhaps Pacifics from a couple of areas, so you can compare flavors.

Simple accompaniments show off oysters best. Offer one or both of the following sauces, as well as lemons, buttered pumpernickel bread to clear the palate, and very dry champagne or wine such as a dry Sauvignon Blanc. You'll also need forks, napkins, small plates, and a container for empty shells.

PER ¼-OUNCE SHUCKED SMALL PACIFIC OYSTER: 5.8 calories, 0.7 g protein, 0.4 g carbohydrates, 0.2 g fat, 3.9 mg cholesterol (estimated), 7.8 mg sodium

Being on the Safe Side with Oysters

ENJOYING OYSTERS, as described on the preceding pages, also requires some cautions. Because oysters are filter-feeders, they pick up any contaminants in the water where they live. Manmade pollution occasionally threatens some oyster beds. Naturally occurring bacteria and viruses, though harmless to oysters, may prove unpleasant or even toxic to people.

The U.S. Food and Drug Administration says raw oysters are safe to eat if growers and consumers follow a few guidelines.

May through August, buy oysters from cold waters. Safe waters include the north Pacific and north Atlantic coasts of Canada and parts of the U.S. (reaching into northern California), and New Zealand and Australia. In other areas, harmful microorganisms may increase as water warms; conservative experts suggest caution April through November.

Oysters in waters that get warm in the summer spawn then; they're safe to eat, but spawning gives them a mushy texture that isn't very palatable. Now being introduced are tropical species such as the *Suminoe*, which spawn at even higher temperatures and have a longer harvest season. Also underway is work on genetically altered triploids—which spawn very little.

If you suspect an oyster is bad, don't eat it. If you have eaten a dubious one, watch for symptoms such as tingling or numbness of the face and mouth, muscular weakness, chills, fever, head-ache, nausea, diarrhea, and abdominal pain; if you experience any of these, see a doctor immediately.

Don't eat raw oysters if you have liver problems, an iron imbalance, or a weakened immune system. One bacterium, *Vibrio vulnificus*, sometimes present from April through November in oysters from the southeastern Atlantic coast and Gulf of Mexico, can cause fatal blood poisoning. It's also recommended that pregnant women not eat raw oysters.

If you're harvesting your own, obey posted warnings about polluted waters and paralytic shellfish poisoning (PSP, or red tide). PSP is caused when shellfish, then humans, ingest a toxin produced by a few species of dinoflagellates. These microscopic organisms occasionally multiply greatly, appearing as a red color when the water temperature rises.

To check the safety of oyster beds, here are numbers to call. *Alaska:* Environmental Conservation, (907) 465-2609; *California:* Health Services, (707) 576-2145; *Oregon:* Environmental Services, (503) 229-6313; *Washington:* Environmental Health, Shellfish, (206) 753-5992.

For more details, send for a free publication, *For Oyster And Clam Lovers, The Water Must Be Clean* (number 85-2200); write to Consumer Inquiries, FDA, 5600 Fishers Lane, Rockville, MD 20857. Many libraries have the article "Fewer Months Safe for Eating Raw Gulf Oysters" (*FDA Consumer,* June 1988).

MIGNONETTE SAUCE FOR OYSTERS

½ cup white wine vinegar
¼ cup water
1½ tablespoons minced shallot
¾ teaspoon coarse-ground pepper

In a bowl, mix vinegar, water, shallot, and pepper. If made ahead, cover and chill up to 3 hours. Makes about ¾ cup, enough for 72 oysters (½ teaspoon each).

PER ½ TEASPOON: 0 calories, 0 g protein, 0.1 g carbohydrates, 0 g fat, 0 mg cholesterol, 0 mg sodium

TART CHILI-CUCUMBER SALSA

½ cup peeled, seeded, and finely diced cucumber
2 tablespoons seasoned rice vinegar (or use 2 tablespoons white wine vinegar and ½ teaspoon sugar)
1 tablespoon minced fresh cilantro (coriander)
1 tablespoon minced red or green jalapeño chili

In a bowl, mix cucumber, vinegar, cilantro, and chili. If made ahead, cover and chill up to 3 hours. Makes ⅔ cup, enough for 64 oysters (½ teaspoon each).

PER ½ TEASPOON: 0.7 calories, 0 g protein, 0.2 g carbohydrates, 0 g fat, 0 mg cholesterol, 0.1 mg sodium

Singapore Pancakes—to Sop Up Curry

COCONUT COBWEBS *may sound like some kind of lacy filament billowing in a palm tree. But these webs are a special bread eaten with curry in Singapore.*

In our kitchens, Violet Oon, editor of the Food Paper in Singapore, demonstrated how to make the bread (roti jala). She pours a thin batter into a special cup with five funnels, then swirls the batter onto a hot griddle. She makes her pancakes rather soft, so they can sop up the flavorful sauce of the curry. If you prefer firmer pancakes, cook them longer or make them ahead and reheat in the oven until crisp.

Since roti jala funnels are not readily available here, you can easily fashion your own from a can, punctured with a nail.

The curry starts with a roasted blend of spices. For a short-cut, use a purchased Indian curry powder. (You can substitute rice or French bread for the pancakes.)

Begin the meal with a salad of sliced cucumbers, red onion, and pineapple, dressed with lime juice and chopped peanuts. End with icy canned litchis, served with sliced kiwi fruit.

COBWEB PANCAKES
(Roti Jala)

2 cups all-purpose flour
½ teaspoon salt
About 1½ tablespoons salad oil
2 large eggs
1 cup canned coconut milk mixed with 2 cups water; or 3 cups cow's milk mixed with 1 teaspoon coconut extract
Roti jala cup (directions follow)

In a blender, whirl until smooth flour, salt, 1 tablespoon oil, eggs, and the milk mixture.

Place a griddle or 10- to 12-inch frying pan over medium heat. Brush pan with oil. Over the hot pan, quickly fill the roti jala cup with at least ½ cup batter. At once, move the cup to drizzle a series of continuous overlapping circles of the batter from the center to the edge of the pan, making a large, round lacy pancake about 8 inches in diameter. (If batter spatters so much when it hits the pan that the line breaks, lower heat slightly.) Pancake should be thin and lacy; don't use excessive batter, and empty any extra back into the bowl.

Cook until pancake is lightly browned on bottom, about 1 minute; turn over with a wide spatula and lightly brown other side, about 1 minute. Remove from pan. Repeat process to cook all remaining batter.

If made ahead, stack pancakes, separated by paper towels. Cool, cover, and chill up until next day. Reheat in a single layer on 12- by 15-inch baking sheets in a 350° oven until warm, about 3 minutes; if you like them crisp, bake 2 to 3 minutes

longer. Fold in eighths, if desired. Serve warm or at room temperature. Makes 18 to 24 pancakes, 6 servings.

PER PANCAKE: 70 calories, 1.8 g protein, 8.2 g carbohydrates, 3.4 g fat, 18 mg cholesterol, 52 mg sodium

Roti jala cup. With a 4d finishing nail, make 5 holes about 1 inch apart in the bottom of a clean, empty 8-ounce food can (about 3½ in. tall and 2½ in. wide).

SINGAPORE CHICKEN CURRY

8 cloves garlic
1¾ cups (about 10 large) chopped shallots
10 slices (about the size of a quarter) fresh ginger
½ cup homemade curry powder (recipe follows), or purchased
1 broiler-fryer chicken (3½ lb.), cut up; or 3½ pounds chicken thighs
5 tablespoons salad oil
½ cup coconut milk; or ½ cup cow's milk and ¼ teaspoon coconut extract
2 pounds (about 4 medium size) russet potatoes, peeled and cut into 1- by 2-inch chunks
About 2 teaspoons sugar
Salt
Fresh cilantro (coriander) sprigs, optional

In a food processor or blender, combine garlic, shallots, and ginger; whirl, scraping container often, until finely ground. Mix ¼ cup of the curry powder with 3 tablespoons water. Mix the curry paste and half the ginger mixture (if made ahead, cover and chill remaining ginger mixture up until the next day).

If desired, remove and discard skin from chicken. Rinse chicken and pat dry. Rub the curry-ginger mixture all over chicken pieces. If made ahead, cover and chill up until the next day.

Place oil in a 5- to 6-quart pan over medium-high heat. When oil is hot, add remaining ginger mixture; cook for 3 minutes, stirring often. Mix remaining curry powder with 3 tablespoons water and add to the pan. Stir often for 2 to 3 minutes. Add the marinated chicken and cook, turning often, until yellow on both sides, about 7 minutes.

Add 1 cup water and the coconut milk; cover and simmer for 10 minutes. Add potatoes; cover and simmer until meat is no longer pink at thigh bone (cut to test)

Folded in eighths, cobwebs go with chicken-potato curry. Use pancakes to sop up fiery sauce.

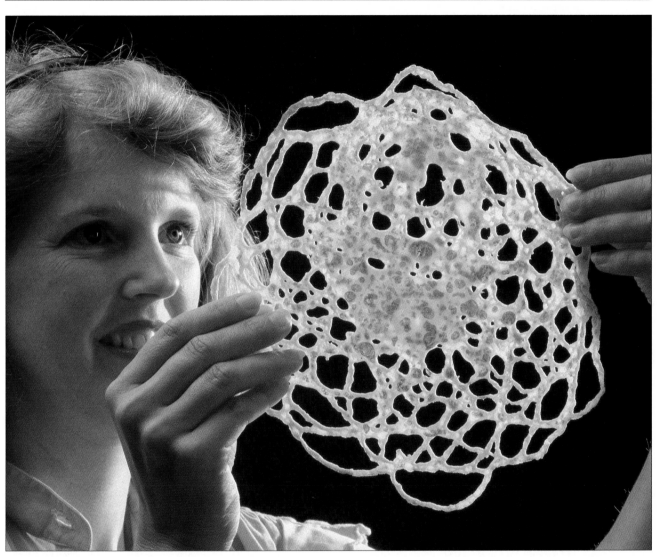

See-through web is actually a coconut-flavored pancake to eat with hotly spiced curry. Thin streams of batter are drizzled in a series of overlapping circles onto a hot griddle to cook briefly. If made ahead, stack pancakes, separated by paper towels; cool, cover, and refrigerate, then reheat to serve.

and potatoes are tender when pierced, 30 to 40 minutes.

Add sugar and salt to taste. If made ahead, cool, cover, and chill up until next day. Reheat, covered, over low heat until hot, 10 to 15 minutes; stir often. Skim and discard fat. Spoon into dish; garnish with cilantro. Serves 6.

PER SERVING: 717 calories, 39 g protein, 42 g carbohydrates, 45 g fat, 135 mg cholesterol, 153 mg sodium

Homemade curry powder. In a 10- to 12-inch frying pan, combine ⅓ cup **coriander seed,** ¼ teaspoon **white peppercorns,** and 2 **whole cloves;** stir often over medium-low heat for 3 minutes.

Add 2½ tablespoons **cumin seed,** 1 tablespoon **fennel seed,** 9 **small dried hot red chilies,** and 6 **whole cardamom pods,** hulled; stir just until chilies begin to brown, 3 to 4 minutes. Add 1 table-

spoon **ground turmeric,** ½ teaspoon **ground cinnamon,** and ¼ teaspoon **ground nutmeg;** continue stirring until spices become fragrant, about 2 minutes.

In a blender, whirl spices as fine as possible. If desired, sift mixture in fine strainer to remove coarse bits. Store airtight up to 1 month. Makes about ½ cup.

Prime-Time Sandwiches

JAZZED UP ENOUGH *to qualify as dinner, these hearty sandwiches make handsome entrées for relaxed, informal meals. And with make-ahead steps in each recipe, sandwich assembly is quick.*

The first features easy-to-cook roasted pork loin. Earthy Mediterranean vegetables dominate in the second sandwich; both come from David Page of San Francisco. The third sandwich, inspired by salad niçoise, makes use of fresh tuna.

PORK LOIN ON RYE WITH APPLE CHUTNEY

- 1 boned, rolled, and tied center-cut pork loin (2 to 2¼ lb., about 3 in. diameter)
  Marinade (recipe follows)
- 12 slices sandwich caraway-rye bread
  Coarse-grain mustard
  Apple chutney (recipe follows)
- 6 large butter lettuce leaves, washed and crisped

Place pork in a heavy plastic bag (1-gal. size); add marinade, seal bag, and rotate to mix ingredients. Chill at least 2 hours or until next day; turn occasionally.

Lift meat from marinade; discard marinade. Place meat, fat up, in a 9- by 13-inch pan. Roast at 375° until a thermometer inserted in center registers 155°, 50 to 60 minutes. Set on a carving board. Tilt pan; skim and discard fat. Save drippings. Cut meat into ¼-inch-thick rounds.

Coat 6 slices of bread generously with mustard, and set each on a plate. Top each slice with equal amounts of meat and drippings. Add chutney, lettuce, and remaining bread to complete each sandwich. Makes 6 entrée servings.

PER SERVING WITHOUT CHUTNEY: 498 calories, 32 g protein, 28 g carbohydrates, 29 g fat, 98 mg cholesterol, 348 mg sodium

Marinade. Combine 1 tablespoon *each* **honey** and minced **fresh** (or 1 teaspoon dry) **sage leaves,** 1 clove minced **garlic,** 1 teaspoon crushed **juniper berries,** and ¼ teaspoon **coarse-ground pepper.**

Apple chutney. Peel, core, and chop 2 large (about 1 lb. *total*) **Newtown Pippin apples;** chop ½ small **onion;** seed and finely chop ½ **lemon;** stem, seed, and chop ½ small **red bell pepper;** mince enough **fresh ginger** to make 2 table-spoons; and mince or press 1 clove **garlic.** Mix together.

In a 2- to 3-quart pan over high heat, combine ⅓ cup **apple cider** or white wine vinegar and ⅔ cup firmly packed **light brown sugar;** stir until sugar dissolves. Add apple mixture, ⅛ teaspoon **cayenne,** and ½ teaspoon **salt.** Bring to a boil, reduce heat, and simmer, uncovered, stirring often, until mixture is reduced to about 2 cups. Let cool. Use, or cover and chill up to 3 weeks. Makes about 2 cups.

PER TABLESPOON: 44 calories, 0.1 g protein, 11 g carbohydrates, 0.1 g fat, 0 mg cholesterol, 37 mg sodium

GRILLED VEGETABLES ON CORNBREAD

Bake cornbread in an 8-inch-square pan; use your favorite recipe or mix.

- 4 small (about 1¼ lb. *total*) leeks
- 1 small (about ¾ lb.) eggplant
- 1 tablespoon olive oil
  Cornbread (see above)
  Dried tomato relish (recipe follows)
- ½ pound fontina cheese, shredded

Trim and discard root and tough stems of leeks; cut in half lengthwise, rinse well, and drain. Cut off eggplant stem, then cut eggplant lengthwise in 8 wedges.

Brush vegetables with oil and place on a grill 4 to 6 inches above a bed of medium coals (you should be able to hold your hand at grill level 4 to 5 seconds). Turn often until vegetables brown and eggplant is very soft when pressed, 8 to 10 minutes for leeks, 15 to 20 minutes for eggplant. If made ahead, let stand up to 6 hours.

Cut cornbread into 4 equal triangles and split horizontally. Lay bread, cut side up, on a 12- by 15-inch baking sheet. Arrange leeks and eggplant equally on bread; top equally with tomato relish and cheese. Broil 6 inches from heat until cheese melts, 3 to 4 minutes. With a wide spatula, place 2 triangles on each of 4 dinner plates. Makes 4 entrée servings.

PER SERVING: 898 calories, 27 g protein, 76 g carbohydrates, 55 g fat, 183 mg cholesterol, 849 mg sodium

Dried tomato relish. Combine 2 table-spoons **balsamic** or red wine **vinegar;** 3 tablespoons **olive oil;** 2 tablespoons *each* drained, minced **dried tomatoes packed in oil** and **Greek-style olives;** 1 table-spoon minced **fresh** (or 1 teaspoon dry) **rosemary leaves;** and 1 clove minced **garlic.**

NIÇOISE SANDWICH

- About 1 pound tuna, cut into 4 1-inch-thick pieces, rinsed and patted dry
- 1 tablespoon olive or salad oil
- ½ baguette (1-lb. size, 3 in. diameter)
  Caper aïoli (recipe follows)
- 1 medium-size firm-ripe tomato, cored and sliced
- 8 canned anchovies, drained
  Vegetables (directions follow)
- ½ cup niçoise olives (optional)
- 4 large butter lettuce leaves, washed and crisped

Brush fish with oil and lay on a grill 4 to 6 inches above a solid bed of hot coals (you can hold your hand at grill level only 2 to 3 seconds). Cook, turning once, until outside is firm and opaque, inside is moist and pink (cut to test), about 5 minutes.

Cut baguette into 4 equal pieces, then split almost in half horizontally. Spread the inside of each piece with 1 table-spoon aïoli sauce. Add tomato slices and tuna, crossing 2 anchovies over each piece of fish. Place sandwiches on dinner plates; accompany with vegetables and olives on lettuce leaves. Add the remaining aïoli to taste. Makes 4 entrée servings.

PER SERVING WITHOUT AÏOLI SAUCE: 606 calories, 38 g protein, 59 g carbohydrates, 24 g fat, 85 mg cholesterol, 698 mg sodium

Caper aïoli. In blender or food processor, whirl 1 tablespoon *each* **lemon juice** and **water,** 2 large **egg yolks,** 2 cloves **garlic,** and 1 tablespoon drained **capers.** In thin, steady stream, add 5 tablespoons *each* **olive oil** and **salad oil.** Use; or cover and chill up to 5 days. Makes about ¾ cup.

PER TABLESPOON: 110 calories, 0.5 g protein, 0.3 g carbohydrates, 12 g fat, 35 mg cholesterol, 20 mg sodium

Niçoise vegetables. You need 2 cups *each* **red** and/or **yellow bell pepper** strips, cold cooked **green beans,** and cold boiled tiny **red thin-skinned potatoes.**

Crossed with anchovies, grilled tuna sits atop tomato slice on split baguette section. Inspired by salade niçoise, this hearty sandwich is accompanied by strips of red and yellow bell pepper, cold cooked green beans, and boiled tiny red potatoes. Spoon a lively caper aïoli sauce over fish and vegetables.

Lean, Oven-Braised Shanks

I**N THE SEARCH** *for lean cuts of meat, some extremely flavorful choices get overlooked because their rich taste is assumed to come from fat. Shanks are a perfect example of meats that fit this neglected slot. When shanks of beef, veal, or lamb are oven-braised to tenderness, then skimmed of fat, calories coming from fat are below 30 percent.*

Because shanks are muscular and designed to work hard, they are full of connective tissue composed of the protein collagen. Cooked in moist heat, this connective tissue softens and dissolves to give meat a luxurious, melting taste.

Here we oven-braise beef, veal, and lamb shanks, browning them first in the dry heat of the oven to bring out their intense natural flavors. Then seasonings and liquid go into the pan, and the meat is tightly covered. Even though the shanks cook at 400°, they simmer gently, taking a bit of time to cook but needing no attention. And if you want to cook them ahead, they reheat quickly for an easy-to-prepare supper on the following day.

A bonus with these recipes is the richly browned, fat-free juices that make a lean gravy. For thicker juices, blend cornstarch with water, then stir a little at a time into boiling juices to desired consistency. Serve the meat with baked potatoes, which can cook along with the meat. Or serve with rice or an interesting grain, such as hot cooked wheat berries, millet, or quinoa.

BRAISED BEEF SHANKS

6 **beef shanks,** *each* **about 1¾ inches thick (about 6 lb.** *total***)**
4 **cups regular-strength beef broth**
1 **lemon, unpeeled, chopped (discard seeds)**
1 **teaspoon dry marjoram leaves**
1 **dry bay leaf**
½ **teaspoon black peppercorns**
¼ **teaspoon coriander seed**
1 **tablespoon cornstarch**
2 **tablespoons balsamic or red wine vinegar**
   Salt

Lay shanks in a single layer in a close-fitting pan about 9 by 13 inches. Bake, uncovered, in a 400° oven until browned, about 35 minutes. Remove from oven and turn shanks over. Add broth, lemon, marjoram, bay leaf, peppercorns, and coriander. Cover pan tightly with foil. Return to oven and bake until meat is tender enough to pull apart easily, 2 to 2½ hours.

With a slotted spoon, lift shanks gently from pan and set in a single layer on a platter; keep warm.

Pour broth through a fine strainer into a 1-quart measure; press any liquid from residue into cup; discard residue.

If made ahead, cover and chill broth and meat up until next day. If shanks are chilled, reheat in foil-covered pan in a 400° oven until warm, 15 to 20 minutes. Put on platter; keep warm.

In a small bowl, combine cornstarch with 2 tablespoons water; set aside.

With a spoon, skim fat from broth and discard (if chilled, lift off hard fat). In a 10- to 12-inch frying pan, bring broth and vinegar to boiling on high heat; boil, uncovered, until reduced to 1½ to 2 cups, 8 to 12 minutes. Stir in cornstarch mixture and stir until boiling.

Pour into a small pitcher; add to meat to taste, along with salt. Makes 6 servings.

PER SERVING: 324 calories, 51 g protein, 3.8 g carbohydrates, 10 g fat, 118 mg cholesterol, 100 mg sodium

BRAISED VEAL SHANKS

Follow directions for **braised beef shanks** (preceding), but instead of beef use 6 **veal shanks,** *each* about 6 inches long (about 6 lb. *total*). Bake until the meat is very tender and pulls easily from the bones, about 1½ hours.

ESTIMATED PER SERVING BASED ON VEAL SHOULDER (USDA data not available for shanks; the shoulder is a slightly fattier cut): 393 calories, 67 g protein, 3.8 g carbohydrates, 10 g fat, 287 mg cholesterol, 170 mg sodium

BRAISED LAMB SHANKS

Follow directions for **braised beef shanks** (preceding), but instead of beef use 6 **lamb shanks** (about 5½ lb. *total*). Bake until meat is very tender and pulls easily from the bones, about 2 hours.

PER SERVING: 280 calories, 44 g protein, 3.8 g carbohydrates, 8.8 g fat, 145 mg cholesterol, 106 mg sodium

Oven-browned and braised to tender succulence, beef shanks retain subtle flavors of well-seasoned cooking liquid. Meat pulls easily from bone. Skimmed of fat, rich juices make a lean gravy to spoon over shanks.

Low-Cholesterol, Low-Fat Recipes

FAT IS JUST ONE PART *of the cholesterol issue, and cholesterol confuses because you can't see it and you can't taste it. So how do you control your intake, and how do you determine how much is too much?*

The American Heart Association and National Institute of Health evaluate on the basis of total fat, kind of fat, and percentage of calories contributed by fat. If a recipe, such as the green chili with white beans and the carrot cake that follow, is well balanced in fats, protein, and carbohydrates, it can usually meet the goal of 30 percent or fewer calories coming from fat. Even though the chili is made with a well trimmed cut of pork usually considered fatty, calories contributed by fat are only 28 percent, with 4 grams saturated fat and 76 milligrams cholesterol per serving.

Because the cake is made with vegetable oil instead of solid fats, there is no cholesterol, and the saturated fat is less than 1 gram a serving.

Lean pork, green bell peppers, chilies, and canned or home-cooked white beans make a savory chili for those watching their intake of cholesterol and fat. For a thin chili, cook covered; for a thicker chili, cook uncovered to desired consistency.

GREEN CHILI WITH WHITE BEANS

- 3 tablespoons salad oil
- 2 large green bell peppers, stemmed, seeded, and thinly sliced crosswise
- 2 cups sliced green onions (including tops)
- 8 cloves garlic, minced or pressed
- 4 teaspoons ground cumin
- 6 cans (13 oz. *each*) tomatillos
- 4 large cans (7 oz. *each*) diced green chilies
- 6 cans (15 oz. *each*) white kidney beans (cannellini), drained; or 9 cups drained cooked small white beans
- 3 pounds lean boneless pork shoulder or butt, trimmed of fat and cut into ½-inch cubes
- 4 teaspoons dry oregano leaves
- ½ teaspoon cayenne
- ½ cup lightly packed fresh cilantro (coriander) leaves

In a 10- to 12-quart pan over medium-high heat, combine oil, bell peppers, green onions, garlic, and cumin. Stir often until onions are limp, about 5 minutes. Mix in tomatillos (break up with a spoon) and liquid, chilies, beans, pork, oregano, and cayenne.

Bring to a boil; reduce heat and simmer, stirring occasionally, until pork is tender when pierced, about 1¾ hours. For a thin chili, cook covered; for thicker chili, cook uncovered to desired consistency. Reserve a few cilantro leaves; chop remaining leaves. Stir chopped cilantro into chili; garnish with reserved leaves. Serves 12.

PER SERVING: 441 calories (28% fat, 40% carbohydrates, 32% protein), 14 g total fat, 4 g saturated fat, 76 mg cholesterol, 44 g carbohydrates, 36 g protein, 1,231 mg sodium

CARROT CAKE

- 1 cup *each* all-purpose flour and whole-wheat flour
- 1½ tablespoons ground cinnamon
- 1 teaspoon ground nutmeg
- 2 teaspoons *each* baking soda and baking powder
- ½ teaspoon salt
- 1 cup firmly packed brown sugar
- ½ cup granulated sugar
- 1 can (about 8 oz.) crushed pineapple packed in pineapple juice
- ¾ cup salad oil
- 6 large egg whites
- 1 teaspoon vanilla
- 3 cups finely shredded carrots
- 1½ cups golden raisins
  Pineapple glaze (recipe follows)

In a large bowl, stir together all-purpose flour, whole-wheat flour, cinnamon, nutmeg, soda, baking powder, salt, brown sugar, and granulated sugar. Set aside.

Drain pineapple, reserving the juice. Place pineapple, oil, egg whites, vanilla, and carrots in large bowl of an electric mixer; beat until well combined. Add pineapple mixture and raisins to flour mix; stir until evenly moistened. Spoon into a well-greased, flour-dusted 9- by 13-inch baking pan.

Bake in a 350° oven until a toothpick inserted in center of cake comes out clean, about 45 minutes. Let cool in pan on a rack. Pour the pineapple glaze over the cake. Cut into 2- by 2¼-inch pieces. Makes 24 servings.

PER SERVING: 216 calories (28% fat, 67% carbohydrates, 5% protein), 7 g total fat, 0.9 g saturated fat, 0 mg cholesterol, 37 g carbohydrates, 3 g protein, 173 mg sodium

Pineapple glaze. Stir 1½ cups sifted **powdered sugar** with about ¼ cup **reserved pineapple juice** until mixture is smooth and has a good pouring consistency.

Buttery Cookies Made with Cornmeal

A PLEASING GRITTINESS *characterizes these buttery cookies. Cornmeal is responsible, giving them a tantalizing texture.*

Choose from slice-and-bake refrigerator wafers, tender spritz made with a cooky press, or twice-baked fennel biscotti.

All the cookies keep well stored airtight at room temperature, but freeze them to keep longer than the recommended time. For even browning if you bake two pans in one oven, switch pan positions when cookies are about halfway done.

CORNMEAL WAFERS

> ½ cup (¼ lb.) butter or margarine, at room temperature
> ⅔ cup sugar
> 1 large egg
> 1 teaspoon vanilla
> 1 cup all-purpose flour
> 1 cup yellow cornmeal
> 1 teaspoon baking powder

With an electric mixer, beat butter and sugar until creamy. Beat in egg and vanilla until blended. In another bowl, mix together the flour, cornmeal, and baking powder. Gradually add to butter mixture, stirring, until completely blended.

Directly on plastic wrap or waxed paper, shape dough into 2 rolls about 2 inches in diameter; wrap and chill (freeze if using margarine) until firm, at least 2 hours or up to 3 days.

Unwrap dough. Using a sharp knife, cut into ⅛-inch-thick slices. Place slices about 2 inches apart on greased 12- by 15-inch baking sheets. Bake in a 325° oven until pale gold, 15 to 18 minutes. Transfer cookies to racks to cool. Serve, or store airtight up to 2 weeks. Makes about 4 dozen.

PER COOKY: 50 calories, 0.6 g protein, 7 g carbohydrates, 2.1 g fat, 11 mg cholesterol, 30 mg sodium

CORNMEAL SPRITZ

> 1 cup (½ lb.) butter or margarine, at room temperature
> About ½ cup sugar
> 2 large egg yolks
> 1 teaspoon vanilla
> ½ teaspoon almond extract
> 1½ cups all-purpose flour
> 1 cup yellow cornmeal
> ½ teaspoon baking powder

Cookies with crunch: cornmeal adds texture to twice-baked biscotti, spritz hearts and flowers made with a cookie press, and slice-and-bake refrigerator wafers.

In large bowl with electric mixer, beat butter and ½ cup sugar until creamy. Add egg yolks, vanilla, and almond extract; beat until smooth. In another bowl, mix flour, cornmeal, and baking powder; gradually add to butter mixture, blending well.

Place dough in a cooky press fitted with a design plate, packing dough firmly and evenly. Force out onto greased 12- by 15-inch baking sheets, spacing cookies about 1 inch apart. (If you don't have a press, roll dough into ¾-inch balls and press to about ¼ inch thick with the flat bottom of a glass dipped in sugar.)

Bake in a 350° oven until edges are lightly browned, 12 to 14 minutes. At once transfer cookies to racks to cool. Serve, or store airtight up to 2 weeks. Makes 7½ to 10 dozen cookies, each about 1½ inches wide.

PER COOKY: 28 calories, 0.3 g protein, 2.2 g carbohydrates, 1.6 g fat, 8.7 mg cholesterol, 18 mg sodium

CORNMEAL BISCOTTI

> ¾ cup sugar
> ½ cup (¼ lb.) butter or margarine, melted
> 2 tablespoons fennel seed
> 1 tablespoon rum or water

> 1 teaspoon vanilla
> 3 large eggs
> 1¾ cups all-purpose flour
> 1 cup yellow cornmeal
> 1½ teaspoons baking powder
> 1 cup pine nuts or coarsely chopped almonds

In a bowl, mix sugar with butter, fennel, rum, and vanilla. Beat in eggs. Mix flour, cornmeal, and baking powder; stir into sugar mixture. Mix in nuts. Cover and chill until firm, 2 to 3 hours.

Directly on greased 12- by 15-inch baking sheets, shape dough with your hands into flat loaves about ½ inch thick and 2 inches wide down length of pan; keep loaves 1 inch from pan ends and 2 inches apart.

Bake in a 375° oven until lightly browned, about 20 minutes. Remove from oven and let loaves stand until cool enough to touch. Cut crosswise on pans into ½- to ¾-inch-thick slices. Place slices close together, cut sides down, on pans.

Bake in a 350° oven until lightly toasted, 15 to 18 minutes. Transfer to racks to cool. Serve, or store airtight up to 3 weeks. Makes 5 to 7 dozen.

PER COOKY: 44 calories, 1 g protein, 5.4 g carbohydrates, 2.2 g fat, 13 mg cholesterol, 22 mg sodium

Candy Corsage

H ELP CUPID *spread the frivolity of Valentine's Day by surprising someone special with an arrangement of edible flowers and leaves.*

Almond-based marzipan, found in most supermarkets, is as moldable as clay and makes this project child's play. Leaves for the roses are of painted chocolate.

Marzipan dries on standing, so flowers taste best if made only a few hours ahead. The leaves keep much longer.

MARZIPAN ROSES WITH CHOCOLATE LEAVES

    7 ounces (⅔ cup) marzipan
       Food coloring (optional)
       Salad oil
       Chocolate leaves (directions
       follow)

To tint marzipan, knead in food coloring by the drop until it's the shade desired; to have several colors, divide marzipan into 2 or 3 equal portions and tint separately.

Shape marzipan, or each colored portion, into an oval roll about 1 inch in diameter; enclose roll or rolls in plastic wrap and chill for about 1 hour.

To make each rose, use a sharp knife to cut 6 or 7 slices, each about ¹⁄₁₆ inch thick, from a marzipan roll. Lightly coat your fingers and a smooth, flat surface with oil to prevent sticking. With fingertips, flatten slices to even thickness; pinch any tears to patch and smooth.

Curl 1 slice marzipan lengthwise into a cylinder that flares out slightly at one end. Wrap another slice around center petal, slightly overlapping second slice's sides; flare out new petal at top and pinch gently at base to hold together. Repeat steps as you add remaining petals; delicately flare 1 end of each petal away from the center. Press narrow (stem) end to flatten so rose sits upright; cover with plastic wrap to prevent drying. Repeat to make remaining roses.

If made ahead, place roses in a single layer in a rimmed pan, cover tightly with plastic wrap, and store up to 6 hours at room temperature.

To present, arrange 1 or several roses with chocolate leaves in a decorative box. Serve as a confection or use to decorate desserts. Makes about 8 roses.

PER ROSE: 100 calories, 1.3 g protein, 22 g carbohydrates, 1 g fat, 0 mg cholesterol, 2.7 mg sodium

For Valentine's Day, surprise someone special with this pretty and edible gift— fancifully packaged chocolate leaves and multicolored marzipan roses.

Chocolate leaves. Rinse and pat dry 12 to 16 small, sturdy, **nontoxic leaves** such as citrus or camellia. In 1- to 1½-quart pan, stir 4 ounces chopped **semisweet chocolate** over lowest heat just until melted. With a small brush, thickly paint backs of leaves (not over edges) with chocolate.

Set leaves, chocolate up, on a flat pan; chill until chocolate is firm, then carefully peel leaves away. If made ahead, wrap airtight and chill up to 3 days.

PER LEAF: 36 calories, 0.3 g protein, 4 g carbohydrates, 2.5 g fat, 0 mg cholesterol, 0.1 mg sodium

More February Recipes

OTHER FEBRUARY ARTICLES *offered several unusual new appetizers, a spicy wild rice salad that travels well, and a satisfying asparagus entrée.*

SWEET POTATOES WITH CAVIAR

An intriguing variation on tiny baked potatoes with caviar and sour cream, these appetizers change only one ingredient: oven-browned slices of sweet potato form the base. The potatoes' creamy-crisp sweetness combines with sour cream's cool smoothness and caviar's salty tang.

For even more subtle flavor, try satsuma-imo, a sweet potato found in Japanese markets in winter months. It's lighter-colored inside, and still quite sweet. You can also use yams, but watch carefully, as they brown faster.

2 **pounds sweet potatoes (about 2-in. diameter), scrubbed and ends trimmed**
About 3 tablespoons salad oil
About ¼ cup inexpensive caviar such as flying fish roe (*tobiko*), crab roe (*masago*), or lumpfish, whitefish, or salmon caviar
About ½ cup sour cream

Cut the sweet potatoes into ¼-inch-thick rounds. Oil 2 rimmed pans, each 10 by 15 inches, then distribute the slices in a single layer.

Brush tops of slices with oil. Bake in a 400° oven until slices are golden brown on bottom; turn slices over and continue baking until both sides are browned, about 25 minutes total (potatoes at rim of pan tend to darken faster; move to center of pan as you turn slices). After 10 minutes, alternate pan positions.

Meanwhile, put caviar in a fine strainer. Rinse under cool running water; drain well and keep cold.

With a wide spatula, transfer potato slices to a platter in a single layer. Dot each slice equally with sour cream, then fish roe. Pick up to eat while warm, or serve at room temperature. Makes about 60 pieces, 12 to 15 servings.

PER PIECE: 29 calories, 0.6 g protein, 3.8 g carbohydrates, 1.3 g fat, 7.1 mg cholesterol, 19 mg sodium

PETITE TOMATO & BASIL GOUDA FONDUE

Baby goudas, those compact cheese rounds available in most supermarkets, are ideally shaped for this made-in-the-microwave fondue appetizer. Fresh vegetables and herbs add color and flavor.

1 **small whole (7-oz.-size) gouda cheese**
2 **small (about 4 oz. *total*) Roma-type tomatoes, cored and diced**
1 **tablespoon finely chopped fresh basil leaves**
1 **small (8 oz.) sliced and toasted baguette**

Remove coating from gouda; carefully scoop out center of cheese, leaving a ¼-inch-thick shell. Set shell aside. Coarsely chop scooped-out cheese into small pieces and place in a microwave-safe bowl; mix in tomatoes and basil.

Cook, uncovered, in a microwave oven at half-power (50 percent) for 1 minute. Stir, then continue cooking at half-power, stirring every 20 seconds, until cheese is bubbling, 1½ to 2 minutes longer.

Set cheese shell on a plate; surround with baguette slices. Pour cheese mixture into shell, pushing into corners to fill shell and accommodate fondue.

Hollowed-out gouda holds melted fondue quickly made in the microwave with cheese from the center. Spread on toasted baguette slices to eat.

Serve hot to scoop onto toast; cut up warmed shell to eat. Makes 4 or 5 appetizer servings.

PER SERVING: 279 calories, 14 g protein, 27 g carbohydrates, 12 g fat, 46 mg cholesterol, 590 mg sodium

PETITE CHILI & ONION GOUDA FONDUE

Follow directions for **petite tomato and basil gouda fondue,** omitting tomatoes and basil. With chopped cheese, mix 1 tablespoon **canned chopped green chilies,** 1 chopped **green onion** (including top), and ¼ teaspoon **ground cumin.**

PER SERVING: 274 calories, 14 g protein, 26 g carbohydrates, 12 g fat, 46 mg cholesterol, 599 mg sodium

FRUIT & SPICE WILD RICE SALAD

Nonwilting and durable, this wild rice salad is a good traveler for potlucks and winter picnics. It also appeals because it is low in fat. The toasted flavor of the rice is highlighted by spices that simmer with it; the savory broth becomes the dressing.

- 1 cup wild rice, rinsed and drained
- 4 cups regular-strength chicken broth
- 1 tablespoon mustard seed
- 1 tablespoon coriander seed
- 1 teaspoon dry thyme leaves
- ½ teaspoon ground allspice
- ½ cup chopped dates
- ½ cup (4 oz.) dried peaches, cut into small pieces
- ¼ cup pecans, chopped
- ¼ cup chopped green onions
- ½ cup chopped parsley
- ¼ cup lemon juice
   Green-leaf or butter lettuce, rinsed and crisped (optional)
   Salt and freshly ground pepper

In a 2- to 3-quart pan, combine rice, broth, mustard, coriander, thyme, and allspice. Bring to a boil on high heat; cover and simmer until rice is tender to bite, 45 to 55 minutes. Drain rice in a fine strainer, reserving about ½ cup of the broth for salad (and the balance for other uses). Let rice stand until lukewarm.

In a large bowl, combine rice with dates, peaches, pecans, green onions, parsley, lemon juice, and ½ cup broth; mix well. If made ahead, cover and chill up until next day; serve cool or at room

For a satisfying vegetarian entrée, spoon rich-tasting tofu-mushroom sauce over tender-crisp spears of asparagus.

temperature. For a moister salad, add more of the broth. Garnish salad with lettuce leaves; add salt and pepper to taste. Makes 6 to 8 servings. —*Gladys Kent, Port Angeles, Wash.*

PER SERVING: 186 calories, 5.2 g protein, 35 g carbohydrates, 3.7 g fat, 0 mg cholesterol, 33 mg sodium

ASPARAGUS WITH TOFU-MUSHROOM SAUCE

Tender-crisp asparagus topped with a rich-tasting sauce of minced mushrooms and creamy tofu makes a satisfying entrée.

- ¾ pound mushrooms, rinsed and minced
- 2 tablespoons salad oil
- ¼ teaspoon Oriental sesame oil
- 2 teaspoons grated fresh ginger
- 1 tablespoon soy sauce
- 2 tablespoons oyster sauce (or 1 more tablespoon soy sauce)
- ¼ cup regular-strength chicken broth
- 1 carton (14 to 16 oz.) firm tofu, drained and cut into ½-inch cubes
- 1 pound asparagus, tough ends trimmed
- 4 green onions, ends trimmed and thinly sliced

In a 10- to 12-inch frying pan, combine mushrooms, salad oil, sesame oil, and ginger. Cook, uncovered, over medium-high heat until all liquid from mushrooms evaporates, about 15 minutes; stir often.

Add soy, oyster sauce, and broth; stir until simmering. Gently mix tofu (cubes break easily) with sauce until tofu is warm, 3 to 5 minutes; keep warm.

Meanwhile, bring about 1 inch water to boiling in a 10- to 12-inch frying pan over high heat. Add asparagus and boil, uncovered, until just tender when pierced, about 4 minutes. Drain and arrange spears equally on 4 dinner plates. Spoon sauce equally across asparagus; sprinkle with onions. Makes 4 servings. —*Pin Pin Liu, Orinda, Calif.*

PER SERVING: 280 calories, 23 g protein, 14 g carbohydrates, 17 g fat, 0 mg cholesterol, 639 mg sodium

Wholesome tea bread gets pleasing moistness from buttermilk and sweet prunes.

PRUNE BREAD

- 1 cup (8 oz.) pitted prunes, chopped
- ¼ cup (⅛ lb.) butter or margarine
- 1 cup sugar
- 1 large egg
- 2 teaspoons vanilla
- 1 cup whole-wheat flour
- 1½ cups all-purpose flour
- 1½ teaspoons baking powder
- 1 teaspoon baking soda
- 1 cup buttermilk

In a 1- to 1½-quart pan, put prunes in 1 cup water. Bring to a boil over high heat; simmer until prunes are plumped, about 1 minute. Drain well, reserving ½ cup liquid; set aside.

In a bowl, cream butter with sugar, then beat in egg and vanilla. Mix whole-wheat and all-purpose flours, baking powder, and soda. Add alternately dry ingredients, prune liquid, and buttermilk, stirring until evenly moistened. Stir in prunes. Pour into 2 greased 4- by 8-inch loaf pans. Bake in 350° oven until golden brown, 50 to 55 minutes. Cool 15 minutes, then invert loaves from pans. If made ahead, let cool, then wrap airtight up until next day; freeze to store longer. Makes 2 loaves, each 1¼ pounds.—*LaFawn P. James, Citrus Heights, Calif.*

PER OUNCE: 75.6 calories, 1.4 g protein, 14 g carbohydrates, 1.5 g fat, 8.7 mg cholesterol, 57 mg sodium

---

Color and crunch characterize this lean vegetable salad with Asian overtones.

ORIENTAL WINTER SALAD

- 1 tablespoon sesame seed
- 1 pound carrots, peeled and cut into thin diagonal slices
- 4 cups broccoli flowerets
- 1½ cups thin diagonal slices celery
- 1 medium-size onion, cut into thin wedges
- ¼ cup rice vinegar or white wine vinegar
- 2 tablespoons soy sauce
- 1 teaspoon honey
- 1 teaspoon Oriental sesame oil
  About 12 large butter lettuce leaves, washed and crisped

In a 6- to 8-inch frying pan, stir sesame seed over medium-high heat until golden brown, 3 to 4 minutes. Pour from pan and let cool.

In a wok or 5- to 6-quart pan, place carrots, broccoli, celery, and onion on a rack over 1 inch boiling water. Cover and steam on high heat until barely tender when pierced, about 5 minutes. Immerse vegetables in ice water; when cold, drain.

In a large bowl, mix together vinegar, soy sauce, honey, sesame oil, and vegetables. Arrange lettuce on 6 salad plates, then spoon vegetables and dressing onto lettuce; sprinkle with sesame seed. Serves 6.—*Lyn Avila, Sebastopol, Calif.*

PER SERVING: 90.5 calories, 4.7 g protein, 16 g carbohydrates, 1.9 g fat, 0 mg cholesterol, 416 mg sodium

---

POCKET BREAD CALZONES

- 2 tablespoons butter or margarine
- 1 clove garlic, minced or pressed
- 1 small onion, chopped
- ¼ pound mushrooms, thinly sliced
- 1 carton (15-oz. size, or 2 cups) ricotta cheese
- 6 ounces mozzarella cheese, grated
- 2 cups finely diced cooked ham
- ¼ cup minced parsley
- 1 teaspoon dried oregano leaves
- 6 pocket breads (6 in. diameter)

In an 8- to 10-inch frying pan, melt 1 tablespoon butter over medium-high heat. Add garlic, onion, and mushrooms. Cover and cook until mushrooms give off juice, about 2 minutes. Uncover and stir often until mushrooms are browned, 5 to 7 minutes more. In a bowl, mix together cooked vegetables, ricotta and mozzarella cheeses, ham, parsley, and oregano.

Carefully slit each bread along edge and open about a third. Gently spoon equal amounts of filling into each pocket. Place on a pair of 12- by 15-inch baking sheets. Melt remaining butter and brush it evenly on bread tops. Bake in 400° oven until toasted, 12 to 15 minutes. Serves 6.—*Carmela M. Meely, Walnut Creek, Calif.*

PER SERVING: 480 calories, 30 g protein, 42 g carbohydrates, 20 g fat, 82 mg cholesterol, 1,318 mg sodium

Quick-fix calzones start with purchased pocket bread rounds.

MEDITERRANEAN SPINACH

2 teaspoons olive oil
1 clove garlic, minced or pressed
½ cup chopped green onion
½ teaspoon dry dill weed
⅓ pound Roma-type tomatoes, cored and chopped
1¼ pounds spinach, washed and drained, stems and wilted leaves removed
¼ cup crumbled feta cheese
½ cup calamata or black ripe olives, pitted if desired
Salt and freshly ground pepper

In a 5- to 6-quart pan over medium-high heat, combine oil, garlic, green onion, and dill weed. Stir often until onion is limp, about 3 minutes. With a slotted spoon, transfer mixture to a bowl; add tomatoes.

Add spinach to the pan and stir over medium heat until just wilted, about 2 minutes. With a slotted spoon, transfer to a serving platter; spread out slightly. Top with onion-tomato mixture. Sprinkle with feta cheese and olives. Add salt and pepper to taste. Makes 4 servings. —*Barbara Jacque, Van Nuys, Calif.*

PER SERVING: 106 calories, 4.9 g protein, 6.9 g carbohydrates, 7.8 g fat, 7.5 mg cholesterol, 305 mg sodium

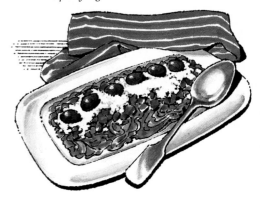

Bright green spinach, red tomatoes, and white feta make a pretty vegetable dish.

HOT & SWEET CHICKEN

1 tablespoon grated orange peel
1 cup orange juice
3 tablespoons lemon juice
2 tablespoons Worcestershire
1 tablespoon Dijon mustard
½ teaspoon liquid hot pepper seasoning
½ cup currant jelly
1 broiler-fryer chicken (3 to 3½ lb.), cut into pieces
3 cups hot cooked rice
1 tablespoon cornstarch mixed with 2 tablespoons water

In a 1- to 1½-quart pan, stir peel, orange and lemon juices, Worcestershire, mustard, liquid pepper, and jelly over medium heat until jelly melts.

Rinse chicken and pat dry. Arrange all but breast in 12- by 15-inch metal pan; brush with sauce. Bake in 400° oven 20 minutes; baste with sauce halfway through. Add breast; bake, basting often, until meat at thigh is no longer pink (cut to test), about 25 minutes.

Put chicken and rice on a platter; keep warm. Skim and discard fat from juices. Add remaining sauce to pan. With heat on high, add cornstarch mixture and stir until boiling. Offer with chicken. Makes 4 or 5 servings. —*Laura Getschmann, Bremerton, Wash.*

PER SERVING: 543 calories, 35 g protein, 60 g carbohydrates, 16 g fat, 105 mg cholesterol, 288 mg sodium

Shiny amber glaze for chicken is sweet-tart from currant jelly, spicy from hot sauce.

POTATO CAKE

1 small (about 6 oz.) baked russet potato, peeled and cooled
½ cup (¼ lb.) butter or margarine, at room temperature
1 cup sugar
2 large eggs
1¼ cups all-purpose flour
1 teaspoon baking powder
½ cup water
4 ounces semisweet chocolate, finely chopped
¼ cup finely chopped almonds
Sliced almonds (optional)

Smoothly mash potato. In a large bowl, cream together butter and sugar. Add potato and eggs, and beat to blend well. Mix together flour and baking powder. Alternately add dry ingredients and water to creamed mixture, moistening evenly. Stir in chocolate and chopped almonds. Pour batter into a greased and flour-dusted 9-inch round or heart-shaped cake pan.

Bake in a 350° oven until browned, 40 to 45 minutes. Let cool 20 minutes in pan, then invert onto a plate. Serve warm or cool; garnish with sliced almonds. If made ahead, let cool, wrap airtight, and store at room temperature up to 2 days. Makes 6 to 8 servings. —*M. Cederblade, Fowler, Colo.*

PER SERVING: 399 calories, 5.4 g protein, 52 g carbohydrates, 20 g fat, 84 mg cholesterol, 189 mg sodium

For Valentine's Day, bake this tender, chocolate-flecked cake in a heart-shaped pan.

DID NOT THE ARIZONA CLAM *ages ago fall from endangered-species status to that of fossil? How, then, to explain Gary Kiefer's recipe? It transpires that the clams were roused from beds on some bay, beach, or estuary far from the arid Sonoran sands—and made the journey into less hospitable climes in that well-traveled but rather inglorious vessel, the can. Dr. Kiefer explains that it's not the bivalve but the chowder that is Arizonan.*

The soup gets its character from the presence of mild green chilies. These have long lent excitement to much Southwestern cooking, and without them this dish would be merely Manhattan chowder—a somewhat anemic minestrone with clams.

ARIZONA CLAM CHOWDER

- 2 slices bacon, cut into ¼-inch pieces
- 1 medium-size onion, chopped
- 1 large fresh mild green chili such as Anaheim (or California) or poblano (or pasilla), stemmed, seeded, and chopped
- 1 stalk celery, chopped
- 1 large (about 8 oz.) thin-skinned potato, peeled and diced
- ¼ teaspoon dry thyme leaves
- 1 can (10 oz.) whole baby clams
- 2 bottles (8 oz. each) clam juice
- 1 can (14½ oz.) tomatoes
  Salt and pepper
  Warm flour tortillas

In a 3- to 4-quart pan, cook bacon over medium heat until lightly browned, about 5 minutes; stir often. Add onion, chili, and celery, and cook, stirring often, until vegetables are slightly browned, 10 to 14 minutes. Stir in potato, thyme, clams and their liquid, clam juice, and tomatoes and their liquid (break up tomatoes with a spoon). Bring to a boil, cover, reduce heat, and simmer until potato is tender to bite, 15 to 20 minutes.

Ladle into individual bowls. Season to taste with salt and pepper; accompany with tortillas. Makes 4 or 5 servings.

PER SERVING: 135 calories, 7.5 g protein, 14 g carbohydrates, 5.9 g fat, 24 mg cholesterol, 736 mg sodium

Sy Kiefer

Scottsdale, Ariz.

ANYONE WHO CAN RECALL *his youth can recall a malt's deeply satisfying flavor. Joe Kretlow blends malted milk powder with ice cream and chopped malted milk balls into a voluptuous dessert worthy of a Big Occasion.*

CHOCOLATE MALTED ICE CREAM TORTE

- 1 gallon vanilla or marble fudge ice cream
- 1 cup malted milk powder
  Graham cracker crust (recipe follows)
  About 4 ounces chocolate-covered malted milk balls, coarsely chopped

Transfer ice cream to a large bowl and place in refrigerator until soft enough to stir but not melted, about 45 minutes. Add malted milk powder and beat until well blended. Quickly spread ice cream mixture evenly in crumb crust, then sprinkle with chopped candy, patting it lightly into ice cream.

Cover and freeze until firm, at least 4 hours; seal airtight to store up to 2 weeks. Dip a knife in hot water; run between torte and pan rim; remove pan

"The soup gets its character from the presence of mild green chilies."

rim. Put torte on a plate; cut dessert into wedges. Makes 10 to 12 servings.

PER SERVING: 569 calories, 10 g protein, 74 g carbohydrates, 27 g fat, 91 mg cholesterol, 398 mg sodium

Graham cracker crust. In a small bowl, stir together 1 cup finely crushed **graham cracker crumbs**, 3 tablespoons **sugar**, 1 teaspoon **ground cinnamon**, 3 tablespoons cool melted **butter** or margarine, and 2 tablespoons finely grated **semisweet chocolate**. Press crumb mixture over bottom of a pan (9 or 10 in. across and at least 3 in. deep) with removable rim.

Orinda, Calif.

THE STROGANOFF (*or Stroganov*) *family first came to prominence as merchants and pioneer developers of Siberia. Originally a rough, tough crew, by the 19th century they had become noblemen and diplomats. It is quite conceivable that during this time they engaged a French chef who one day presented a new and wonderful creation christened in the family's honor.*

Stroganoff, in one of its simplest forms, consists of beef or veal thinly sliced and lightly browned in butter, then finished with seasonings and that old Russian favorite, sour cream. Another form finishes the lightly browned meat in a sauce of stock and tomato concentrate thickened with flour and butter. Alan Kunz' Chicken Stroganoff takes the best of both basic styles and adds further subtle touches. Most notable is the use of chopped dried tomatoes instead of the more usual tomato paste concentrate.

CHICKEN STROGANOFF

- ½ cup dried tomatoes
- ¼ cup all-purpose flour
- ¼ teaspoon pepper
- 2 whole chicken breasts (about 2 lb. *total*), boned, skinned, and cut into ¾-inch cubes
- 3 tablespoons *each* butter or margarine and salad oil
- 1 medium-size onion, chopped
- ½ pound mushrooms, sliced
- 2 cloves garlic, minced or pressed

- 1 teaspoon cornstarch blended with 2 teaspoons water
- 1 cup sour cream
- ½ cup regular-strength chicken broth
- 1 cup dry white wine
- ½ teaspoon *each* grated fresh ginger and dry thyme leaves
- 2 tablespoons dry sherry
  Hot cooked rice
  Chopped parsley

Put tomatoes in a small bowl and just barely cover with boiling water; let stand to soften.

In a plastic or paper bag, combine flour and pepper; add chicken cubes and shake until evenly coated. Lift chicken from flour and shake off excess.

In a 10- to 12-inch frying pan, melt half of the butter in half of the oil over medium-high heat. Add chicken, about half at a time, without crowding; brown well and cook just until white in the center (cut to test), about 5 minutes for each portion. Turn pieces with a spatula as needed. As browned, lift chicken from pan with a slotted spoon and set aside.

To pan, add remaining butter and oil, onion, mushrooms, and garlic; stir often and cook until mushrooms are lightly browned, about 15 minutes. Meanwhile, drain and coarsely chop the tomatoes. Also stir the cornstarch mixture into the sour cream.

Stir broth, wine, ginger, thyme, and sherry into pan. Stir until boiling, then add tomatoes, chicken with any juices, and sour cream mixture. Stir until boiling. Accompany with rice; sprinkle parsley over stroganoff and rice. Serves 4.

PER SERVING: 542 calories, 40 g protein, 21 g carbohydrates, 36 g fat, 134 mg cholesterol, 239 mg sodium

Walnut Creek, Calif.

JUST WHAT IS A BRISKET? *Try to recall the look of a prize steer at the county fair. Washed, curried, and marcelled, it stands in bedding so deep that its legs are hidden and its massive trunk seems to float like a ship on a sea of straw. The prow of that ship is the brisket—the portion over the breastbone and between the forelegs.*

Generally considered tough and coarse of grain, brisket is not, generally speaking, a highly esteemed cut (although it is a top

choice for corned beef). But it has a fine flavor—and long, slow, moist cooking can make it tender. Marinating before cooking also helps make the meat more succulent. Wally Lauterbach anoints the brisket with a mixture of seasonings, lets it absorb flavor overnight, then bakes it for several hours. The meat slices beautifully, is fork-tender, and is nicely complemented by its spicy sauce.

BAKED BRISKET OF BEEF

- 2 tablespoons chili powder
- 1½ teaspoons pepper
- 1 teaspoon crushed dry bay leaves
- ¾ teaspoon salt or garlic salt
- 1 piece center-cut beef brisket (4 to 5 lb.), trimmed of surface fat
- 4 teaspoons liquid smoke
  Hot and spicy sauce (recipe follows)

Mix chili powder, pepper, bay leaves, and salt. Rub mixture all over meat. Place meat in a 2-inch-deep pan about 10 by 14 inches. Cover and chill at least 6 hours or up until next day.

Rub meat on both sides with liquid smoke; cover tightly with foil. Bake in a 325° oven until meat is very tender when pierced, about 4½ hours. Transfer beef to a board and cut into thin slices. Skim fat from pan juices and stir juices into the hot and spicy sauce. Add sauce to meat to taste. Makes 10 to 12 servings.

PER SERVING: 214 calories, 28 g protein, 0.9 g carbohydrates, 10 g fat, 83 mg cholesterol, 256 mg sodium

Hot and spicy sauce. In a 2- to 3-quart pan, combine 1 bottle (14 oz., 1⅓ cups) **catsup**, ½ cup **water**, 1 teaspoon **liquid smoke**, 2 teaspoons **celery seed**, 3 tablespoons firmly packed **brown sugar**, 3 tablespoons **Worcestershire**, 3 tablespoons **dry mustard**, ⅓ cup **butter** or margarine, and ¼ teaspoon **cayenne**. Bring to a boil, stirring, over medium-high heat. If made ahead, cover and chill up until next day; reheat to serve. Makes 2 cups.

PER TABLESPOON: 39 calories, 0.5 g protein, 4.8 g carbohydrates, 2.1 g fat, 5.1 mg cholesterol, 165 mg sodium

Brewster, Wash.

February Menus

IT MAY BE THE SHORTEST MONTH *of the year, but February is long on special occasions. In joint celebration of Valentine's Day and the presidents' birthdays, we suggest a simple, make-ahead breakfast combining heart-shaped shortbread and cherries.*

Two other meals offer soothing suppers to warm you on cold winter nights. One is a light, quick-cooking dinner based on a seafood soup. The second features a more substantial, slow-simmering beef and olive stew, served with couscous.

And don't overlook one more reason to celebrate this month: the brief burst of glorious summer fruit from below the equator. Take advantage of it to brighten any of these menus.

VALENTINE BREAKFAST

Oat Shortbread Hearts
Gouda or Sharp Cheddar Cheese
Fresh Cherries or Dried Cherries
Cherry Preserves   Tangerines
Earl Grey Tea

Romance your sweetheart with heart-shaped shortbread to eat with cheese and cherry preserves. As an added treat, serve a bowlful of imported fresh cherries. If you can't find fresh fruit, consider sweet or sour dried cherries (available in some supermarkets or gourmet markets).

Bake the shortbread in small heart-shaped cooky molds or an 8- to 9-inch heart-shaped or round cake pan. The shortbread can be made up to several days ahead. Set cheese out in a wedge, letting guests cut off pieces to eat on the whole-grain cookies with fruit or preserves.

OAT SHORTBREAD HEARTS

½ cup (¼ lb.) butter or margarine
¼ cup sugar
1 cup whole-wheat flour
½ cup regular rolled oats

In a large bowl, beat butter and sugar with a mixer until creamy. Add flour and oats; mix until incorporated. (Or in a food processor, whirl butter—cut into chunks—sugar, and flour just until butter is cut into tiny bits, then add oats and whirl until dough holds together.)

Firmly pat dough into 8 to 10 greased heart-shaped cooky molds (each heart about 2½ in. at widest point), or use a greased 8- to 9-inch heart-shaped or round cake pan. Bake in a 325° oven until shortbread is a deeper gold color, 40 to 45 minutes. If you use a large heart-shaped or round pan, cut shortbread in wedges while hot, or, with a knife or cooky cutter, cut hearts in shortbread in pan, leaving shapes in place.

Let shortbread cool in pan on rack about 15 minutes. Loosen cooky edges in small molds with knife tip, then invert cookies onto rack. For shortbread baked in a single pan, lift pieces out of pan and arrange on a serving plate. Serve warm or cool. If made ahead, cool and store airtight up to 3 days. Makes 8 to 10 cookies, 4 or 5 servings.

PER COOKY: 156 calories, 2.3 g protein, 16 g carbohydrates, 9.7 g fat, 25 mg cholesterol, 94 mg sodium

For an easy and romantic breakfast, offer oat and whole-wheat shortbread hearts to eat with gouda cheese and cherry preserves.

SEAFOOD SOUP SUPPER

Dressed Greens
Fish & Pea Soup
Parsley Toast
Brownies à la Mode
or Lemon Sorbet & Kiwi Fruit
Dry Sauvignon Blanc
Sparkling Water

This tarragon-scented fish soup makes a relatively light and lean complete meal. Splurge on a sinful dessert of homemade or purchased brownies topped with vanilla ice cream, or—for a more virtuous ending— try scoops of lemon sorbet with sliced kiwi fruit.

Rinse and crisp the salad greens and bake the parsley toast. Then make the quick-cooking soup. As it simmers, dress the greens with a homemade or purchased dressing.

FISH & PEA SOUP

- 3 large (about 1¾ lb. *total*) leeks
- 2 tablespoons salad oil
- 1 clove garlic, pressed or minced
- 1 large carrot, peeled and chopped
- 1 cup dry white wine or regular-strength chicken broth
- 6 cups regular-strength chicken broth
- 1 dry bay leaf
- 1 teaspoon dry tarragon leaves
- 1½ to 2 pounds boned and skinned lean white-flesh fish (such as rockfish or grouper), cut into 1-inch chunks
- 1 package (10 oz.) frozen petite peas, broken apart
  Salt and pepper

Trim and discard root ends and dark green tops from leeks. Split leeks in half lengthwise; rinse thoroughly. Thinly slice leeks crosswise.

In a 5- to 6-quart pan, combine oil, leeks, garlic, and carrot. Stir occasionally over medium heat until leeks are limp, 6 to 8 minutes. Add wine, broth, bay leaf, and tarragon. Bring to a boil; simmer, uncovered, for 5 minutes. Add fish chunks and peas; cook, covered, over low heat until fish is just barely translucent in thickest part (cut to test), 5 to 7

Ladle chunks of fish and lean broth into wide bowls. Serve fish soup with a green salad, and offer slices of parsley toast to dip into flavorful broth.

minutes. Ladle soup into a large tureen or 6 wide soup bowls. Add salt and pepper to taste. Makes 6 servings.

PER SERVING: 290 calories, 34 g protein, 18 g carbohydrates, 8.9 g fat, 53 mg cholesterol, 228 mg sodium

PARSLEY TOAST

- About 6 ounces slender baguette, cut diagonally into ½-inch-thick slices
- 3 tablespoons extra-virgin olive oil
- 3 tablespoons chopped parsley

Lay bread in a single layer on wire racks on 2 baking sheets, 12- by 15-inch size. Mix oil and parsley. Brush bread tops with all the oil mixture.

Bake in a 350° oven until bread is crisp and golden, about 15 minutes. Serve warm or cool. Makes 6 servings.

PER SERVING: 143 calories, 2.6 g protein, 16 g carbohydrates, 7.8 g fat, 0.8 mg cholesterol, 165 mg sodium

MEDITERRANEAN SUPPER

Beef & Olive Stew
Hot Couscous
Wilted Curly Endive
Sliced Peaches or Pineapple
with Orange-flavor Liqueur
Cabernet Sauvignon   Milk

On a lazy rainy day, you can start this slow-simmering stew in the afternoon. Once started, it needs little attention. Brighten the meal with south-of-the-equator fresh peaches or tropical pineapple drizzled with liqueur.

Start the stew about 3 hours before you plan to serve. Or make it ahead and reheat. Shortly before it is ready, bring about 2 cups regular-strength chicken or beef broth to a boil and stir in 1½ cups couscous. Cover and let stand until liquid is absorbed, about 5 minutes.

Also rinse 1 to 1½ pounds curly endive; cut it into 3-inch lengths. Place a 10- to 12-inch frying pan with about 1 tablespoon olive oil on high heat. When hot, add endive and cook just until lightly wilted, 1 to 2 minutes; serve hot.

(Continued on next page)

BEEF & OLIVE STEW

3 pounds boneless beef chuck, fat trimmed, cut into 1-inch cubes
1 tablespoon soy sauce
1 large onion, chopped
1 clove garlic, pressed or minced
2 tablespoons minced fresh ginger
1 cup dry red wine
1 can (15 oz.) tomato purée
1½ cups water
1 teaspoon dry rubbed sage leaves
1 cup green olives (ripe or Spanish-style), pitted if desired
Salt and pepper

In a 5- to 6-quart pan, combine beef and soy sauce. Cover pan tightly and bring to a boil over medium heat. Let meat simmer in its juices for 30 minutes.

Uncover and cook over high heat until pan juices evaporate, about 15 minutes. Stir often until meat is richly browned, about 5 minutes more. Add onion, garlic, and ginger; stir until onion is limp, about 5 minutes. Add wine, tomato purée, water, and sage. Cover and simmer, stirring occasionally, until meat is almost tender when pierced, about 1½ hours. Stir in olives. Cover and simmer until meat is very tender when pierced, about 30 minutes longer. Skim and discard fat. Pour into a serving bowl. Add salt and pepper to taste. Serves 6 to 8.

PER SERVING: 271 calories, 26 g protein, 8.1 g carbohydrates, 15 g fat, 84 mg cholesterol, 850 mg sodium

MARCH

Oaxacan Black Bean & Oxtail Soup (page 58)

Steaming, satisfying soups
from Mexico, accented with chilies and spices, brighten
the final days of winter. To salute spring, we suggest
lunch outdoors (if weather permits) with dishes featuring
the season's asparagus and fresh fruits, accompanied by
compatible wines. Focaccia, an Italian flat bread from Milan,
appears in a variety of tasty versions this month. For
company meals, consider one of our beef tenderloin entrées or
a feast celebrating the Persian New Year. For lighter meals, try
our imaginative fish dishes and pasta-and-vegetable entrées.

Focaccia

Varying from city to city and baker to baker, Italian flat bread boasts a seemingly endless array of names, shapes, textures, and toppings.

In Milan, it is known as focaccia. Thicker and softer than pizza, the bread features baked vegetables atop a springy mattress of olive oil–anointed dough. A plain version is also very typical; the only seasoning is fruity olive oil and salt. Regardless of the topping, focaccia is a satisfying snack served with a glass of wine, a distinctive companion for salad or soup, or even the base of a light meal with cheese or meat and a green salad.

Either make your own yeast dough (recipe at right) or—for a very acceptable short-cut—use several loaves of purchased frozen bread dough. If you want to get a head start, make the dough and let it rise slowly overnight in the refrigerator; you can also thaw frozen bread dough in the refrigerator overnight.

While the dough rises the second time, bake the raw vegetable you have selected: eggplant, potatoes, tomatoes, zucchini, or onion. If your topping choice is cured olives, simply drain them.

With your fingers, make impressions all over the puffy, oiled dough; neatly arrange the toppings on the dough and bake.

These savory flat breads taste best warm from the oven; however, you can also eat them at room temperature or reheated.

VEGETABLE FOCACCIA MILANO

2 tablespoons olive oil
Focaccia dough (recipe follows); or 2 loaves (1 lb. *each*) frozen white bread dough, thawed and kneaded together
Vegetable topping (choices follow)
Salt and pepper

Coat bottom of a 10- by 15-inch baking pan with 1 tablespoon of the oil. Place dough in pan. Press and stretch dough to fill pan evenly. (If dough is too elastic, let rest a few minutes and stretch again; repeat as needed.) Cover pan lightly with plastic wrap and let dough rise in a warm place until about doubled, 45 to 60 minutes.

Drizzle 1 tablespoon oil over dough. With your fingers, gently press dough down all over, forming dimples in the surface. Also gently push dough to fit into pan corners. Evenly cover dough with topping. Sprinkle lightly with salt and pepper.

Bake in a 400° oven until dough is well browned on edges and bottom, 35 to 45 minutes (if topping is brown before bread is done, lightly cover with foil for last 10 to 15 minutes). Cut while hot, warm, or cool. If made ahead, cover and hold up to 8 hours at room temperature. To reheat, bake, lightly covered, in a 350° oven until warm to touch, 10 to 15 minutes. Makes 12 servings.

Focaccia dough. In a large bowl, sprinkle 1 package **active dry yeast** over 1½ cups **warm water** (110°) and let stand for 5 minutes to soften.

Stir in ½ teaspoon **salt** and 2 tablespoons **olive oil.** Add 2½ cups **all-purpose flour;** stir to blend. Beat with an electric mixer until dough is elastic and stretchy, 3 to 5 minutes. Stir in 1⅓ cups more **flour.**

To knead with a dough hook, beat until dough is stretchy and cleans sides of bowl, 5 to 7 minutes; if dough is sticky, add more flour, 1 tablespoon at a time.

To knead by hand, scrape dough onto a floured board and knead until smooth and springy, 5 to 10 minutes. Place in an oiled bowl; turn dough over to oil top.

Cover bowl (either method) with plastic wrap. Let dough rise until doubled, about 45 minutes in a warm place, or in the refrigerator until the next day. Knead on a lightly floured board to expel air.

Vegetable toppings

Choose one of the following focaccia toppings:

Eggplant. Remove stem and seeds from 1 large **red bell pepper.** Coarsely chop pepper. Remove stems from 2 medium-size (about 2 lb. *total*) **eggplant.** Cut eggplant into ¾-inch cubes. In a 10- by 15-inch baking pan, mix eggplant, pepper, and 3 tablespoons **olive oil.** Bake in a

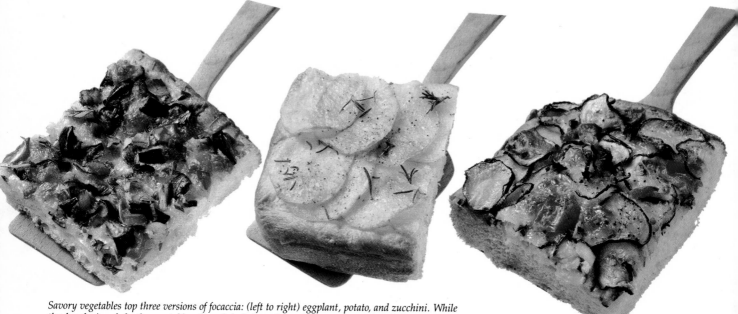

Savory vegetables top three versions of focaccia: (left to right) eggplant, potato, and zucchini. While the dough rises, bake the vegetables. Once baked, focaccia can be cut and served while hot, warm, or cool. Enjoy it as a hearty snack or with salad or soup for a light meal.

450° oven, stirring once, until eggplant begins to soften and lightly brown, 20 to 25 minutes. Evenly sprinkle 2 cups (8 oz.) shredded **mozzarella cheese** over dimpled dough. Scatter eggplant mixture over cheese. After baking, sprinkle with 2 tablespoons chopped **parsley**.

PER SERVING: 288 calories, 8.8 g protein, 35 g carbohydrates, 12 g fat, 15 mg cholesterol, 166 mg sodium

Potato. Peel 3 large (about 2 lb. *total*) **russet potatoes.** Cut the potatoes crosswise into ⅛-inch-thick slices. In a 10- by 15-inch baking pan, mix potatoes with ¼ cup **olive oil,** 1 tablespoon **fresh** or dry **rosemary leaves,** and ¼ teaspoon **pepper.** Spread potatoes in an even layer. Bake in a 400° oven until potatoes begin to turn translucent and light gold, 15 to 20 minutes. Cool about 5 minutes, then gently loosen potatoes from pan with a wide spatula and carefully separate slices. Arrange evenly over dimpled dough.

PER SERVING: 282 calories, 5.7 g protein, 43 g carbohydrates, 9.6 g fat, 0 mg cholesterol, 97 mg sodium

Tomato. Coat a 10- by 15-inch baking pan with 1 tablespoon **olive oil.** Core and cut 2 pounds (about 9 large) **Roma-type tomatoes** lengthwise into ½-inch-thick slices. Lay tomato slices in pan in a single layer, overlapping slightly if needed. Drizzle 2 tablespoons **olive oil** over tomatoes. Bake in a 450° oven until tomatoes look dry and pan juices evaporate, 20 to 30 minutes. Gently loosen tomato slices from pan with a wide spatula. Evenly space slices over dimpled dough. Sprinkle with 1 teaspoon *each* **dry basil leaves** and **dry oregano leaves.**

PER SERVING: 230 calories, 5 g protein, 34 g carbohydrates, 8.4 g fat, 0 mg cholesterol, 98 mg sodium

Zucchini. Trim ends from 5 medium-size (about 1⅓ lb. *total*) **zucchini.** Cut zucchini crosswise into ⅛-inch-thick slices. Core ⅓ pound (about 3 medium-size) **Roma-type tomatoes.** Cut tomatoes into ½-inch cubes. In a 10- by 15-inch baking pan, mix tomatoes, zucchini, 1 teaspoon **dry marjoram leaves,** and 3 tablespoons **olive oil.** Bake in a 450° oven, stirring once, until zucchini begins to turn translucent and all pan juices evaporate, 20 to 25 minutes.

Sprinkle 2 cups (8 oz.) shredded **mozzarella cheese** evenly over dimpled dough. Distribute zucchini mixture over cheese.

PER SERVING: 279 calories, 8.7 g protein, 33 g carbohydrates, 12 g fat, 15 mg cholesterol, 165 mg sodium

(Continued on next page)

Warm or cool, focaccia is enjoyable as an accompaniment to salad, soup, or cheese, or as a savory snack. Press fingertips into risen dough to create dimples for olive oil and spread dough evenly in pan. Top with cooked vegetables and herbs, and bake until dough is well browned.

Onion. Slice 3 medium-size (about 1½ lb. *total*) **onions** in half lengthwise, then cut into ¼-inch-thick slices. In a 10- by 15-inch pan, mix onions and 2 tablespoons **olive oil.** Bake in a 450° oven, stirring occasionally, until onions are limp but not brown, about 20 minutes. Stir in ¼ cup **golden raisins** and 1 tablespoon chopped, drained **canned anchovies.** Scatter mixture evenly over dimpled dough.

PER SERVING: 238 calories, 5.6 g protein, 37 g carbohydrates, 7.4 g fat, 0.8 mg cholesterol, 149 mg sodium

Olive. Cut 20 to 25 **pitted Spanish-style olives** (at least 1 in. long) in half lengthwise.

After pressing dough with fingers to dimple the surface, press olive halves, cut side down, into dough, spacing about 1 inch apart. Evenly sprinkle 1 teaspoon **dry thyme leaves** over dough.

PER SERVING: 195 calories, 4.5 g protein, 31 g carbohydrates, 5.7 g fat, 0 mg cholesterol, 248 mg sodium

FOCACCIA WITH OLIVE OIL & SALT

   3 **to 4 tablespoons extra-virgin olive oil**
      Focaccia dough (recipe on page 52)
      Coarse salt

Drizzle 1 tablespoon oil over bottom of a 10- by 15-inch baking pan. Place dough in pan. Press and stretch dough to evenly fill pan; if dough is too elastic, let it rest a few minutes and stretch again; repeat as needed. Cover pan lightly with plastic wrap and let dough rise in a warm place until doubled, about 45 to 60 minutes.

Drizzle 2 tablespoons oil over dough. With your fingers, gently press dough down all over, forming dimples in surface. Also gently push dough to fit into pan corners. Lightly sprinkle with salt.

Bake in a 400° oven until dough is well browned, 30 to 35 minutes. (If made ahead, cool, wrap airtight, and hold at room temperature up to 8 hours. To reheat, bake, lightly covered, in a 350° oven until warm, 12 to 15 minutes.) If desired, brush with remaining oil and serve hot or at room temperature. Serves 12.

PER SERVING: 207 calories, 4.4 g protein, 31 g carbohydrates, 7.3 g fat, 0 mg cholesterol, 92 mg sodium

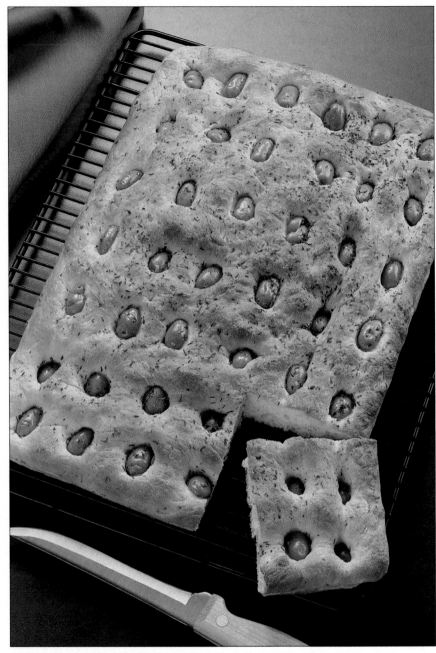

Spanish-style olives, cut into halves and embedded in the bread, add another dimension to basic focaccia. Thyme leaves speckle the surface.

A Salute to Spring

A SPRINGTIME SALUTE *suitably describes this meal to enjoy indoors or out, depending upon the whim of the weather. Asparagus, coming into bountiful supply, leads off as an appetizer salad, served with a prosciutto dressing. Cheese-speckled braided bread goes with both the first course and the main dish salad.*

Grilled chicken, made aromatic by fruit wood smoldering on the coals, is served warm or cool, accompanied by a fresh mango sauce with Oriental influence; this tropical fruit has just returned to the market after its winter hiatus.

Western strawberries top the perfume-rich but calorie-conservative cool dessert mousse of canned litchis and fruity Gewürztraminer wine.

Although these dishes are robust in flavor, they are surprisingly compatible with white wines—dry or with a touch of sweetness—that have distinctive fruit character. Tina and Walt Dreyer of Grand Cru Vineyards, seeking dishes to show off their own dry Sauvignon Blanc, dry Chenin Blanc, and Gewürztraminer, created this menu.

Asparagus & Prosciutto Salad
Gruyère Braids
Dry Sauvignon Blanc
Smoked Chicken Salad with
Mango-Sesame Dressing
Dry Chenin Blanc
Litchi-Gewürztraminer Mousse
Gewürztraminer, Dry or Late Harvest

Convenient make-ahead steps are built into each recipe.

ASPARAGUS & PROSCIUTTO SALAD

2 **pounds asparagus**
   Prosciutto dressing (recipe on page 56)
1 **lemon, cut into 8 wedges**

Snap off and discard tough ends of asparagus; peel stalks, if desired. In a 10- to 12-inch frying pan, bring 1 inch water to boiling on high heat. Add asparagus and cook, uncovered, until tender when pierced, about 4 minutes; drain. At once, immerse asparagus in ice water;

Fruity white wines accompany each part of lunch. Dry Chenin Blanc complements smoked chicken salad with mango-sesame dressing and cheese-speckled braided bread.

Appetizer of asparagus features lemon and prosciutto dressing; serve with dry Sauvignon Blanc.

Chicken breasts for smoked chicken salad are grilled, covered, over smoldering fruit wood chips.

when cool, drain. If made ahead, cover and chill up until next day.

Evenly divide asparagus among 8 salad plates; spoon dressing over asparagus and accompany with lemon wedges to squeeze on to taste. Makes 8 servings.

PER SERVING: 105 calories, 4.5 g protein, 4.8 g carbohydrates, 8.6 g fat, 8.1 mg cholesterol, 325 mg sodium

Prosciutto dressing. Cut ¼ pound thinly sliced **prosciutto** into fine slivers. Combine in a 10- to 12-inch frying pan with 1 tablespoon **olive oil** and 2 cloves **garlic,** minced or pressed.

Cook over medium heat, stirring often, until prosciutto and garlic are golden, 8 to 10 minutes. Remove from heat and stir in 3 tablespoons *each* **extra-virgin olive oil** and **lemon juice** and 2 teaspoons **Dijon mustard.** If made ahead, pour into a small jar, cover, and let stand up until next day. Stir before using.

GRUYÈRE BRAIDS

- 1 **package active dry yeast**
- ¼ **cup warm water (110°)**
- ¾ **cup dry white wine, such as dry Chenin Blanc (or water)**
- 1 **tablespoon sugar**
  About 3½ cups all-purpose flour
- ¾ **cup (⅜ lb.) butter or margarine, at room temperature, cut into chunks**
- 5 **large eggs**
- ½ **pound gruyère cheese, cut into ¼-inch cubes**

In a large bowl, mix yeast and water; let stand until yeast is softened, about 5 minutes. Stir in wine, sugar, and 1 cup flour. Using a heavy spoon or an electric mixer, beat the butter into the dough. Add 4 eggs, 1 at a time, beating well after each addition. Stir in 2½ more cups of flour.

To knead with a dough hook, beat at high speed until dough is smooth, satiny, and not sticky when lightly touched, about 10 minutes. Stir in the cheese.

To knead by hand, vigorously pull dough in large handfuls from bowl, then toss back repeatedly until dough pulls

from hands and bowl and is satiny and smooth looking, about 20 minutes (because extra flour is not worked in, dough is quite soft). Press cheese into dough.

Cover dough, kneaded by either method, with plastic wrap. Let rise in a warm place until doubled, about 1 hour. If made ahead, chill up until next day.

On a floured board, dust dough lightly with flour, then knead to expel air. Divide dough in 6 equal portions. With floured hands, shape 3 portions into ropes, each 15 inches; use as little flour as possible on the board to prevent sticking. Lay ropes 1 inch apart on an oiled 12- by 15-inch baking sheet; pinch ropes together at 1 end. Braid, then pinch ends to seal. Repeat to shape remaining braid on another pan. Lightly cover with plastic wrap; let rise until puffy, about 30 minutes.

Uncover braids; beat remaining egg to blend and brush over dough, taking care not to let egg drip onto pan. Bake in a 400° oven until a rich golden brown, 25 to 30 minutes. (If using 1 oven, switch pan positions after 15 minutes.) Serve warm or cool. If made ahead, wrap airtight and freeze; thaw unwrapped. To reheat, set loaves on baking sheets and place in a 350° oven until warm, about 20 minutes. Makes 2 loaves, about 1¼ pounds *each*.

PER 1-OUNCE SLICE: 103 calories, 3.6 g protein, 8.4 g carbohydrates, 6 g fat, 42 mg cholesterol, 63 mg sodium

SMOKED CHICKEN SALAD WITH MANGO-SESAME DRESSING

> 1 tablespoon *each* chopped fresh ginger and grated orange peel
>
> ⅓ cup *each* soy sauce, orange juice, and oyster sauce (or 1 more tablespoon soy sauce and 1 tablespoon brown sugar)
>
> 8 boned chicken breast halves (about 3 lb. *total*)
>
> About 1 cup fruit wood chips, such as cherry or apple
>
> 4 quarts assorted tender lettuces or mesclun, rinsed and crisped
>
> 1 *each* medium-size red and yellow bell pepper, stemmed, seeded, and thinly sliced
>
> Chive blossoms (optional)
>
> Mango dressing (recipe follows)

In a bowl, combine ginger, peel, soy, orange juice, and oyster sauce. Skin chicken, if desired. Add chicken to bowl, mix, cover, and chill 4 hours or until next day; mix several times.

To cook on a gas barbecue, preheat as directed, about 15 minutes. When hot, adjust for indirect cooking on high heat. Pour wood chips into disposable pan; set on heat distributor directly above flame and cover barbecue. When chips smoke, turn heat to medium-low. Place drained breasts onto indirect heat area of grill; quickly cover.

To cook in a charcoal barbecue, ignite 40 charcoal briquets on firegrate; when lightly covered with gray ash, about 30 minutes, push coals into a ring along edge of grate. Evenly space 4 to 6 more briquets on coals. Set grill 4 to 6 inches above coals; lay drained breasts on center of grill (not over coals). Drop wood chips onto coals, cover barbecue, and open dampers.

Cook chicken until no longer pink in thickest sections (cut to test), 15 to 20 minutes. Serve meat hot or cool; cut across the grain into ½-inch strips.

Divide lettuce equally among 8 dinner plates. On each plate, arrange equal portions of chicken and peppers over lettuce; garnish with chive blossoms. Offer

Strawberry fan tops light litchi mousse that's made and served with aromatic Gewürztraminer. Dessert can be made up to a day ahead.

dressing from a small bowl or pitcher to add to taste. Makes 8 servings.

PER SERVING WITHOUT DRESSING: 342 calories, 39 g protein, 9.2 g carbohydrates, 16 g fat, 109 mg cholesterol, 1,268 mg sodium

Mango dressing. Peel 2 ripe **mangoes** (about 1½ lb. *total*). Slice fruit from pits; discard pits. In a food processor or blender, purée mango with 2 tablespoons *each* **Oriental sesame oil** and **balsamic vinegar** and ⅓ cup **orange juice.**

PER TABLESPOON: 16 calories, 0.1 g protein, 2.5 g carbohydrates, 0.8 g fat, 0 mg cholesterol, 0.3 mg sodium

LITCHI-GEWÜRZTRAMINER MOUSSE

To sterilize egg shells, dip whole eggs in and out of boiling water to cover; crack shell and separate eggs to use at once.

> 2 cans (20 oz. *each*) litchis
>
> 2 packages (2 teaspoons *each*) unflavored gelatin
>
> 1¾ cups fruity Gewürztraminer
>
> 2 large egg whites
>
> ½ cup sugar
>
> ¾ cup whipping cream
>
> 8 medium-size strawberries, rinsed and drained

Drain litchis and reserve 1 cup syrup (save balance for other uses, if desired). Smoothly purée litchis in a blender or food processor, then rub purée through a fine strainer into a 2- to 3-quart pan; discard pulp. Add the 1 cup syrup, gelatin, and wine; let stand about 5 minutes to soften gelatin.

Stir often over medium-high heat until gelatin is melted. Chill mixture, covered, until the consistency of egg whites, about 3 hours (if mixture thickens too much, reheat and repeat this step).

When gelatin mixture is about ready to use, whip egg whites until foamy. Beating at high speed, gradually add sugar, 1 tablespoon at a time, and whip until whites hold soft, shiny peaks. With unwashed beaters, whip cream in another bowl until it holds soft peaks.

Gently whisk the whites, cream, and litchi mixture until blended. Pour mixture equally into 8 (1-cup-size) dessert bowls. Cover and chill until set, at least 4 hours or up until next day. Garnish each with a sliced berry. Makes 8 servings.

PER SERVING: 261 calories, 3.2 g protein, 41 g carbohydrates, 7.2 g fat, 25 mg cholesterol, 74 mg sodium

Mexican Soups

STEAMING SOUPS *comfort with warmth and homespun flavor. Accented with chilies and spice, these versions have a Oaxaca, Mexico, heritage. Choose from a south-of-the-border bouillabaisse, a thick black bean soup with sherry, or a chunky vegetable chowder.*

MEXICAN SHELLFISH CHOWDER

Fish broth (recipe follows), or 2½ quarts regular-strength chicken broth
½ cup dry white wine
1 dry bay leaf
2 cloves garlic, pressed or minced
⅛ teaspoon powdered saffron
4 to 6 fresh jalapeño chilies, stemmed, seeded, and minced
3 large (about 1½ lb. *total*) firm-ripe tomatoes, cored and cut up
18 small clams in shell, suitable for steaming, scrubbed
2 pounds boned, skinned fish such as rockfish, halibut, grouper, lingcod; use 1 or several kinds
½ pound sea scallops, rinsed and sliced crosswise ½ inch thick
½ pound medium-large (36 to 42 per lb.) shrimp, shelled and deveined
¼ cup chopped fresh cilantro (coriander)
Salt and pepper
Lime wedges

In a 6- to 8-quart pan, combine broth, wine, bay leaf, garlic, saffron, and chilies. Cover and bring to a boil, then simmer, covered, 20 to 30 minutes.

Meanwhile, in a food processor or blender, whirl tomatoes to coarsely purée. Add to pan; cover and bring to a boil. Add clams, cover, and simmer 5 minutes. Cut fish into ½-inch cubes. Add fish, scallops, and shrimp to pan; cover and simmer until clams pop open and remaining shellfish is barely translucent in thickest part (cut to test), 3 to 5 minutes. Sprinkle with cilantro. Ladle seafood and broth into bowls. Add salt, pepper, and lime to taste. Makes 9 or 10 servings.

PER SERVING: 157 calories, 25 g protein, 6.2 g carbohydrates, 3.1 g fat, 61 mg cholesterol, 158 mg sodium

Fish broth. In a 6- to 8-quart pan, combine 2½ quarts **regular-strength chicken broth,** 3 pounds **fish heads** and **carcasses,** and 1 large **onion,** sliced. Simmer, covered, for 30 minutes. Pour through a strainer set over a bowl. Discard fish parts and onion. Makes 2½ quarts.

OAXACAN BLACK BEAN & OXTAIL SOUP

1 tablespoon salad oil
2 pounds beef oxtails
2 large onions, chopped
4 cloves garlic, pressed or minced
5 quarts regular-strength beef broth
1½ cups dry sherry
2 teaspoons ground cumin
1 teaspoon cayenne
½ teaspoon ground allspice
4 cups (about 2 lb.) dry black beans
Salt and pepper
Tortilla strips (recipe on page 60)
¾ cup thinly sliced green onion
About 1½ cups (6 oz.) shredded jack cheese (optional)
1 large ripe tomato, cored and diced

Pour oil into an 8- to 10-quart pan on high heat. Add oxtails and cook, turning often, until well browned, 8 to 10 minutes. Remove meat from pan. Add chopped onion and garlic; stir often until limp, about 6 minutes. Return meat to pan and add broth, sherry, cumin, cayenne, and allspice. Cover and simmer for 1 hour.

(Continued on page 60)

Bouillabaisse, Mexican-style, features clams, shrimp, and fish in a saffron and tomato broth base; chilies add a bit of fire.

Thick soup of black beans and oxtails comes from Oaxaca, Mexico. Just before serving, add a decorative topping of crisp tortilla strips, diced tomatoes, sliced green onion, and shredded jack cheese to richly spiced potage.

Sort beans; remove and discard debris. Rinse beans and drain. Add to broth. Bring to a boil, then cover and simmer until meat is very tender when pierced and beans are soft to bite, 1½ to 2 hours.

Lift out oxtails; let cool. Whirl about half of the beans and soup in a blender or food processor, a portion at a time, until puréed. Return purée to pan. Pull off meat and tear into bite-size shreds; return meat to soup; discard bones and fat. (If made ahead, cool, cover, and chill up to 3 days.) Simmer, covered, until meat is hot. Add salt and pepper to taste. Ladle into bowls. Add tortilla strips, green onion, cheese, and tomato. Serves 10 or 11.

PER SERVING: 528 calories, 29 g protein, 71 g carbohydrates, 15 g fat, 0 mg cholesterol, 158 mg sodium

Tortilla strips. Cut 3 **corn tortillas** (6-in. size) into ¼-inch strips. Pour about ½ inch **salad oil** into an 8- to 10-inch frying pan over medium-high heat. When oil is 350° on a thermometer, add about ¼ of the strips; stir often until crisp, 1 to 2 minutes. Remove with a slotted spoon; drain on paper towels. Repeat to cook remainder. Sprinkle with **salt** to taste. If made ahead, store airtight up to 1 day.

MEXICAN VEGETABLE SOUP

- 2 **tablespoons salad oil**
- 1 **clove garlic, pressed or minced**
- 3 **to 5 fresh jalapeño chilies, stemmed, seeded, and chopped**
- 1 **large onion, chopped**
- 1 **teaspoon cumin seed**
- 2 **quarts regular-strength chicken broth**
- 1 **pound (about 2 medium-size) chayotes**
- 4 **small (about 10 oz.** *total***) carrots, peeled and thinly sliced**
- 2 **stalks (about 5 oz.** *total***) celery, thinly sliced**
- 3 **medium-size (about ¾ lb.** *total***) zucchini, ends trimmed and cut into ½-inch cubes**
- 2 **large (about 1 lb.** *total***) firm-ripe tomatoes, cored and cut into ½-inch cubes**
- 1 **package (10 oz.) frozen petite peas**
  Salt and pepper

Colorful confetti of vegetables laces chili- and cumin-speckled broth. Serve this satisfying soup with crusty rolls for lunch or supper.

In a 6- to 8-quart pan, combine oil, garlic, chilies, onion, and cumin. Stir often over medium-high heat until onion is limp, about 5 minutes. Add broth, cover, and bring to a boil.

Meanwhile, peel chayotes only if skin is tough, then cut into ½-inch cubes (slice through edible seed). Add chayotes, carrots, and celery to broth. Cover and simmer 5 minutes. Add zucchini; cover and simmer until carrots are tender when pierced, 10 to 15 minutes. Add tomatoes and peas; cook just until hot, about 1 minute. Ladle into bowls. Add salt and pepper to taste. Makes 8 servings.

PER SERVING: 141 calories, 6.3 g protein, 18 g carbohydrates, 5.6 g fat, 0 mg cholesterol, 137 mg sodium

Getting the Most Out of Tenderloin

A PREMIUM CUT, *beef tenderloin makes a grand roast. But to get maximum value from this ultratender meat, you need to trim and compactly tie it so it will cook equally throughout. For an evenly shaped roast, select the center cut of the tenderloin (the whole tenderloin is tapered at one end). Next, remove the silvery membrane, if present; left in place, the membrane shrinks as the meat cooks, making the roast fatter on one end.*

Tenderloin's smooth flavor takes well to sprightly but simple seasonings. Brush the first roast with a sharp-salty-pungent blend of hoisin sauce, oyster sauce, fresh ginger, and sherry. The second roast features coriander seed and peppers with wine and butter.

ROAST TENDERLOIN ORIENTAL

- 1 **center-cut beef tenderloin with some surface fat, about 5 pounds**
  Oriental sauce (recipe follows)
- 1 **large onion, diced**
- ½ **cup** *each* **regular-strength beef broth and dry sherry**

Rinse tenderloin and pat dry. Neatly trim surface fat (and any easy-to-reach, large intramuscular chunks) from meat. If a tough silver-colored membrane is present, slide a thin, sharp knife under it at one end of the tenderloin to separate it from the meat. Hold this section of the membrane taut and cut against it to remove. Discard fat and membrane. For a compact, even shape, tie roast snugly with cotton string at about 2-inch intervals.

Set roast in a 10- by 15-inch baking pan and generously brush meat with Oriental sauce; pat onion in a thin layer around meat.

Bake in a 450° oven until a thermometer inserted in center of thickest part of meat registers 125° for rare, about 25 minutes; 135° for medium, about 35 minutes; or 145° for well done, about 45 minutes. Brush meat twice with sauce during cooking; push onion close to meat if onion begins to scorch. Transfer tenderloin to a platter and let stand in a warm place for 15 minutes so juices settle. Snip strings free and remove.

Meanwhile, add remaining sauce, beef broth, and sherry to pan with onion; stir to scrape browned bits free. Bring to a boil over high heat; pour into a small bowl.

Cut roast into thick or thin slices and accompany with sauce. Makes 10 to 12 servings. —*George Tate, Portland.*

PER SERVING: 250 calories, 32 g protein, 4.9 g carbohydrates, 10 g fat, 94 mg cholesterol, 372 mg sodium

Oriental sauce. Mix together ¼ cup **hoisin sauce;** 2 tablespoons *each* **oyster sauce** and **dry sherry;** 2 tablespoons minced **fresh ginger;** and 2 cloves **garlic,** minced or pressed.

PEPPERED TENDERLOIN WITH GREEN ONION–CORIANDER SAUCE

- 1 **center-cut beef tenderloin with some surface fat, about 5 pounds**
- 2 **tablespoons coarsely crushed black peppercorns**
- 1½ **cups dry white wine**
- ¼ **cup (⅛ lb.) butter or margarine**
- 2 **tablespoons coriander seed**
- 1 **tablespoon** *each* **soy sauce and Dijon mustard**
- 1 **cup diagonally sliced green onions (including tops)**

Rinse tenderloin and pat dry. Neatly trim surface fat (and any easy-to-reach intramuscular chunks) from meat. If a tough silver-colored membrane is present, slide a thin, sharp knife under it at one end of tenderloin to separate from the meat. Hold this section of the membrane taut and cut against it to remove. Discard fat and membrane. For a compact, even shape, tie roast snugly with cotton string at about 2-inch intervals.

Set roast in a 10- by 15-inch baking pan and firmly pat pepper all over it.

In a 1- to 1½-quart pan, combine wine, butter, coriander, soy, and mustard. Over medium-low heat, bring mixture to a simmer; remove from heat. Lightly brush some of the sauce on roast.

Bake roast in a 450° oven until a thermometer inserted in center of the thickest part registers 125° for rare, about 25 minutes; 135° for medium, about 35 minutes; or 145° for well done, about 45 minutes. Brush meat twice with sauce during cooking. Transfer roast to a platter and let stand in a warm place for 15 minutes for juices to settle, then snip strings free and remove.

Bring sauce to a boil on high heat; stir in onion and pour into a bowl. Cut roast into thin or thick slices. Accompany with sauce. Makes 10 to 12 servings.

PER SERVING: 271 calories, 32 g protein, 2.1 g carbohydrates, 14 g fat, 104 mg cholesterol, 246 mg sodium

Pepper-coated tenderloin, cut into thick or thin slices, makes an elegant entrée. Snugly tied into a compact roll, the roast cooks evenly and quickly.

Feasting for Persian New Year

THE VERNAL EQUINOX *marks the beginning of Persian New Year, Norooz— a time when Persians celebrate the rebirth of nature and its blessings for mankind. Following 3,000-year-old traditions, they prepare their homes for the holiday by cleaning, decorating, and creating ceremonial displays that symbolize the four elements of life—fire, air, water, and earth —and seven "gifts from nature." These sometimes include candles, a bowl of water with goldfish, a potted hyacinth, vinegar, sprouted wheat or lentils, apples, jujube fruit, and garlic.*

In Palo Alto, California, Niloufar and Hamid Farzaneh celebrate the new year in time-honored style, gathering family and friends to share good wishes, presents, and the lavish but surprisingly easy-to-achieve feast described here.

Rice, fragrant with herbs and tinged golden with saffron, is the base of the meal. Smoked fish—authentically, a very salty shad—is served with it. Generous quantities of fresh herbs, feta cheese, and cool yogurt also go alongside. Pickled vegetables and an egg custard redolent with more herbs are optional additions. For dessert, it's rice again—but now as a delicate rosewater and saffron-scented sweet pudding.

Look for long-grain basmati rice and saffron at well-stocked supermarkets, specialty food stores, or Middle Eastern or Indian stores. In place of the traditional shad, you may prefer to use more available (and less salty) smoked trout, whitefish, or mackerel. Pickled garlic, vegetables in brine, rose water, and Persian flat breads (taftoon and barbari) can be purchased at Middle Eastern markets. Rose water is also sold at liquor stores and some supermarkets.

Hostess Niloufar Farzaneh presents platter of saffron and herbed rice with smoked fish, centerpiece of Persian feast. Accompaniments include sesame flat bread, rice crust, pickled garlic, and yogurt (plain or with cucumber and raisins).

PERSIAN NEW YEAR DINNER

Saffron & Herb Rice with Smoked Fish

Fresh Herb Platter

Yogurt with Cucumber or Unflavored Yogurt

Herb Custard

Pickled Garlic   Vegetables in Brine

Taftoon   Barbari

Saffron Rice Pudding   Dates

Ice Water   Hot Tea

Accompany the aromatic rice with fresh herbs and tangy crumbs of feta cheese, or wrap the cheese and herbs in bread to eat. Pocket bread, sesame-crusted chewy bread, and sweet French bread are suitable alternatives for taftoon and barbari.

To simplify the meal, you can omit the custard and the purchased pickled and brined vegetables. Make the yogurt mixture or, if you're in a hurry, use plain yogurt.

The herb platter, yogurt sauce, savory custard, and sweet pudding can be prepared in advance. Cook the herb rice shortly before serving.

SAFFRON & HERB RICE WITH SMOKED FISH
(Sabzi Polo Ba Mahi)

  6 cups white basmati rice or long-grain white rice

  2 teaspoons salt (optional)

  ½ cup salad oil

1½ cups chopped fresh cilantro (coriander)

1½ cups chopped fresh dill or ½ cup dry dill weed

1 cup chopped parsley

½ cup thinly sliced green onions

3 garlic chives, ends trimmed (or 3 unpeeled cloves garlic and 3 green onions, ends trimmed)

½ teaspoon saffron threads, crushed (or ¼ teaspoon powdered saffron), dissolved in ¼ cup hot water
About 3 tablespoons olive oil

1½ to 2 pounds smoked trout, mackerel, or whitefish (at room temperature), cut crosswise into about 3-inch lengths

3 or 4 limes, cut in half

Pour rice into a heavy 8- to 10-quart pan, add water to cover, and stir vigorously. Drain and repeat until water remains clear; drain. Add about 4 quarts of water and salt. Bring to a boil, uncovered, over high heat. Boil until rice is slightly translucent on surface but still firm to bite, 6 to 8 minutes. Drain rice in a colander; rinse with cool water and drain well.

Rinse and dry pan. Pour ¼ cup of the salad oil into pan. Gently mix rice (avoid breaking grains) with cilantro, dill, parsley, and onions. Add about ½ of the rice to the pan. Add ¼ cup water.

Pile remaining rice on rice in pan, pushing to center of pan to form a cone, with rice touching pan sides at bottom only 1 to 2 inches high. Lay garlic chives on rice. Pour ¾ of the saffron mixture and remaining salad oil evenly over rice.

Cover pan with a double layer of paper towels and tightly cover with lid. Cook over high heat just until steam begins to escape from pan, 8 to 10 minutes. Reduce heat to very low and cook until rice is tender to bite, 15 to 20 minutes.

Lift off garlic chives and reserve. Scoop out loose rice and mound on a large platter. Drizzle with the remaining saffron mixture and olive oil to taste. Set the reserved garlic chives on top of rice. Place fish pieces around rice. Garnish with lime halves. With a spatula, scrape the pan to remove chunks of rice crust and place them on another platter. Makes 10 to 12 servings.

PER SERVING: 508 calories, 20 g protein, 78 g carbohydrates, 15 g fat, 13 mg cholesterol, 398 mg sodium

FRESH HERB PLATTER
(Sabzi-Khordan)

2 cups (1 oz.) lightly packed fresh basil leaves, rinsed and crisped

2 cups (1 oz.) lightly packed fresh mint leaves, rinsed and crisped

2 cups (1 oz.) lightly packed cilantro (coriander) sprigs, rinsed and crisped

2 cups rinsed, trimmed radishes

¾ pound feta cheese, cut into about ½-inch-thick slices

10 to 12 green onions, ends trimmed

Arrange basil, mint, cilantro, radishes, feta cheese, and onions on a platter. (If made ahead, cover and chill up to 6 hours.) Makes 10 to 12 servings.

PER SERVING: 86 calories, 4.6 g protein, 3.6 g carbohydrates, 6.3 g fat, 25 mg cholesterol, 323 mg sodium

YOGURT WITH CUCUMBER
(Mast-o Khiar)

1 quart unflavored yogurt

1 small (14 oz.) thin-skinned European cucumber, ends trimmed off, chopped

⅓ cup thinly sliced green onions

½ cup golden raisins

3 tablespoons chopped fresh mint

3 tablespoons chopped fresh dill or 1½ tablespoons dry dill weed

2 cloves garlic, pressed or minced

¼ cup chopped walnuts

¼ teaspoon pepper
Salt
Fresh rose petals (optional), pesticide-free and rinsed
Fresh dill sprigs or dry dill weed

Mix yogurt with cucumber, onions, raisins, mint, chopped dill, garlic, walnuts, pepper, and salt to taste. Garnish with rose petals and dill sprigs. Serve, or cover and chill up to 4 hours. Makes 6 cups, 10 to 12 servings.

PER TABLESPOON: 11 calories, 0.6 g protein, 1.5 g carbohydrates, 0.3 g fat, 0.6 mg cholesterol, 6.9 mg sodium

HERB CUSTARD
(Kookoo-ye Sabzi)

8 large eggs

1 teaspoon all-purpose flour

½ teaspoon salt, or to taste

¼ teaspoon pepper

¼ cup salad oil, or melted butter or margarine

1 cup chopped parsley

1 cup chopped lettuce

¾ cup chopped chives or green onions

½ cup chopped fresh dill

¼ cup chopped fresh cilantro (coriander)

⅓ cup coarsely chopped walnuts
Walnut halves or chunks (optional)

Beat eggs to blend. Add flour, salt, pepper, and 3 tablespoons oil. Beat well. Add parsley, lettuce, chives, dill, cilantro, and chopped walnuts; mix well. Brush remaining 1 tablespoon oil over sides and bottom of a 7- by 11-inch baking dish or pan. Pour egg mixture into the baking dish.

Bake in a 350° oven until custard jiggles only slightly in center when gently shaken, 18 to 20 minutes. Serve hot or at room temperature. (If made ahead, cool, cover, and chill up until next day.) Cut into pieces. Garnish with nuts. Makes 10 to 12 servings.

PER SERVING: 121 calories, 5 g protein, 2.4 g carbohydrates, 10 g fat, 183 mg cholesterol, 142 mg sodium

SAFFRON RICE PUDDING
(Shole-Zard)

1½ cups medium-grain white rice
About 6 cups water

½ teaspoon ground cardamom

¼ teaspoon powdered saffron

1 cup sugar

¼ cup (⅛ lb.) butter or margarine

1 tablespoon slivered almonds

2 tablespoons rose water
Ground cinnamon

In a 3- to 4-quart pan, combine rice and 6 cups water. Bring to a boil over high heat; reduce heat and simmer, uncovered, until rice is tender to bite, about 20 minutes.

Mix cardamom and saffron in 2 tablespoons hot water. Add saffron mixture, sugar, butter, slivered almonds, and rose water to rice; stir to blend. Simmer, uncovered and stirring occasionally, until creamy and slightly thicker, 8 to 10 minutes. Spoon into a bowl; serve warm or cool. (If made ahead, cover and chill.)

Spoon or dust ground cinnamon decoratively over pudding. Makes 10 to 12 servings.

PER SERVING: 201 calories, 2.1 g protein, 37 g carbohydrates, 4.9 g fat, 10 mg cholesterol, 41 mg sodium

Salads with Fresh Fruit & a Little Heat

A LITTLE HEAT *intensifies the flavor of the fruit in these cool-weather salads.*

WARM PEAR SALAD WITH FENNEL CONSERVE

About ¾ pound fennel, stems and base trimmed off, feathery green tops reserved

1 small onion, minced
2 tablespoons butter or margarine
¼ cup regular-strength chicken broth
3 tablespoons rice vinegar
1 teaspoon sugar
½ teaspoon anise seed
2 medium-size (about 1⅓ lb. *total*) firm-ripe pears
2 tablespoons lemon juice
Watercress sprigs, rinsed and crisped
4 wedges *each* orange and lemon

Chop feathery fennel tops; reserve. Finely chop remaining fennel. In a 10- to 12-inch frying pan, cook fennel and onion in 1 tablespoon butter over medium-high heat, stirring often, until onion is lightly browned, about 8 minutes. Add broth, vinegar, sugar, and anise. Cover and simmer 10 minutes. Uncover and stir on high heat until liquid evaporates, 7 to 8 minutes. Pour into a bowl; set aside.

Cut pears in half and remove cores. Rub cut sides with some of the lemon juice. Lay pears cut side down. Starting about ½ inch from stem end, make ¼-inch-thick slices lengthwise down each pear. Rub top of fruit with lemon juice.

In the frying pan, melt remaining butter over medium-high heat. With a wide spatula, carefully transfer 2 pear halves, one at a time and skin side up, to pan. Gently press down on each pear half to fan out slices. Cover pan and cook until pears are lightly brown on bottom, about 3 to 4 minutes. Gently transfer pears to a platter; keep warm. Repeat to heat remaining pears.

Place 1 pear half on each of 4 salad plates. Spoon ¼ of the fennel mixture beside fruit; sprinkle pears and fennel with chopped fennel tops. Garnish with watercress; accompany with orange and lemon wedges to squeeze onto salads. Makes 4 servings.

PER SERVING: 128 calories, 1.8 g protein, 17 g carbohydrates, 6.3 g fat, 15 mg cholesterol, 152 mg sodium

Handsome salad teams sautéed pear fan and cooked fennel conserve. Garnish with watercress and squeeze wedges of lemon and orange over salad.

WILTED SPINACH SALAD WITH ORANGE

1 large (about 10 oz.) onion, thinly sliced
¼ cup balsamic or red wine vinegar
1 tablespoon salad oil
1 teaspoon dry tarragon leaves
1 teaspoon grated orange peel
2 medium-size oranges (cut off peel and white membrane; segment fruit)
About ⅓ pound (about 8 cups, lightly packed) rinsed and crisped spinach leaves

In a 10- to 12-inch frying pan, combine onion, vinegar, oil, tarragon, and peel. Cover and simmer until onions are tender-crisp when pierced, 8 to 10 minutes. Uncover and gently stir in orange segments. Put spinach into a salad bowl; pour the orange mixture onto leaves. Mix and serve at once. Makes 4 servings.

PER SERVING: 100 calories, 2.5 g protein, 16 g carbohydrates, 3.8 g fat, 0 mg cholesterol, 31 mg sodium

BROILED PINEAPPLE SALAD WITH BASIL

¼ cup honey
2 tablespoons cider vinegar
1 tablespoon minced candied ginger
1 teaspoon crumbled dry basil leaves
1 medium-size (about 3 lb.) pineapple, peeled and cored
Fresh basil sprigs

In a 1- to 1½-quart pan, stir honey, vinegar, ginger, and dry basil over low heat until warm and well mixed; set aside.

Cut pineapple into ½-inch rounds or wedges. Place in a single layer in a 10- by 15-inch rimmed pan. Evenly spoon honey mixture onto fruit. Broil fruit 4 inches from heat until warm and glazed, 3 to 4 minutes. With a wide spatula, transfer pineapple to 4 salad plates; spoon pan juices onto fruit. Garnish with basil sprigs. Makes 4 servings.

PER SERVING: 111 calories, 0.5 g protein, 29 g carbohydrates, 0.5 g fat, 0 mg cholesterol, 3.6 mg sodium

Pasta with Cheese & Vegetables

ATISFYING, QUICK & ATTRACTIVE, *these two pasta-and-vegetable entrées, both suggested by readers, are also rich in complex carbohydrates.*

In the first dish, a sauce of gorgonzola cheese blended with broth lightly coats linguine. The pasta contrasts delicately in flavor and texture with smooth avocado slices and crunchy sunflower seeds, both served on top.

The second dish teams curly twists of pasta with a robust and colorful mix of vegetables.

AVOCADO LINGUINE

- 1 **large (about 10 oz.) firm-ripe avocado**
- 2 **tablespoons lemon juice**
- 1 **pound dry linguine**
- 1 **cup (4 oz.) crumbled gorgonzola or cambozola cheese**
- ⅓ **cup regular-strength chicken broth**
- 2 **tablespoons minced parsley**
- ⅓ **cup toasted shelled sunflower seeds**

Peel, pit, and slice avocado into ½-inch-thick wedges. Place wedges on a plate and coat with lemon juice; set aside.

In a 5- to 6-quart pan, bring 3 quarts water to a boil on high heat. Add linguine and cook, uncovered, until pasta is just tender to bite, about 10 minutes. Drain well; return pasta to pan and set on low heat.

Add gorgonzola and broth to pan; mix, lifting with 2 forks, until cheese melts and most of the liquid is absorbed. Pour onto a warm platter and arrange avocado on pasta; sprinkle with parsley and sunflower seeds. Serves 4 to 6.—*Thea L. Pyle, Grays River, Wash.*

PER SERVING: 475 calories, 17 g protein, 62 g carbohydrates, 18 g fat, 16 mg cholesterol, 324 mg sodium

WINTER GARDEN PASTA

- ¾ **pound Swiss chard**
- 3 **tablespoons extra-virgin olive oil or salad oil**
- 1 **pound mushrooms, sliced**
- 1 **medium-size onion, chopped**
- 3 **cloves garlic, minced or pressed**
- 1 **pound dry pasta twists**
- ½ **cup regular-strength chicken broth**
- ½ **cup freshly grated parmesan cheese**
- 1½ **pounds Roma-style tomatoes, cored and chopped**

Long strands of linguine, coated with light gorgonzola sauce, are topped with crisp sunflower seeds and mellow avocado. Serve with a crusty loaf of bread.

Rinse and drain chard. Trim off and discard discolored ends of stems; cut stems from leaves. Separately, finely chop leaves and stems.

Pour oil into a 10- to 12-inch frying pan over medium-high heat. Stir in the chard stems, mushrooms, onion, and garlic. Cover pan and simmer until mushrooms exude juice and onions are limp, about 6 minutes.

Meanwhile, bring 3 quarts water to a boil in a 5- to 6-quart pan over high heat.

Add pasta and cook until tender to bite, about 10 minutes.

As pasta cooks, uncover frying pan and stir vegetables until liquid evaporates and mushrooms are brown. Add broth and chard leaves; stir on high heat until chard is just wilted, about 1 minute. Remove from heat and keep warm.

Drain pasta well and pour into a bowl. Pour chard-mushroom mixture onto pasta, sprinkle with ¼ cup of the cheese, then top with tomatoes. Mix to serve. Offer remaining cheese to add to taste. Makes 4 to 6 servings.—*Sheryl G. Lee, Garden Valley, Calif.*

PER SERVING: 434 calories, 17 g protein, 69 g carbohydrates, 11 g fat, 6.4 mg cholesterol, 280 mg sodium

Brussels Sprouts Come to the Party

Sprinkle parmesan over hot slaw of shredded Brussels sprouts and prosciutto; border of raw sprout leaves garnishes platter.

TINY CABBAGE LOOK-ALIKES *with a more pronounced flavor, Brussels sprouts appear here three ways. By the leaf, they form showy appetizers. Served whole, they are tartly glazed and offered as a vegetable dish. Shredded, they make a bold slaw.*

CAVIAR CUPS

48 **large, perfect Brussels sprouts leaves**
About 2 tablespoons black, red, or golden caviar
About ¼ cup sour cream
About 1 tablespoon minced shallots or red onion

Put leaves in a colander in the sink, then evenly pour about 1 quart boiling water over them. Immediately immerse leaves in ice water. When cold, drain.

Put caviar in a fine sieve and hold under cold running water to rinse well. Tap sieve to remove as much moisture as possible.

Nest 1 leaf in another; repeat for all leaves. Set leaf cups on a platter. To each cup add about ½ teaspoon sour cream; top with about ¼ teaspoon caviar and ⅛ teaspoon onion. If made ahead, cover and chill up to 2 hours. Makes 24; allow 3 or 4 per serving.

PER PIECE: 11 calories, 0.6 g protein, 0.7 g carbohydrates, 0.7 g fat, 8.9 mg cholesterol, 22 mg sodium

Like a little cup, blanched sprout leaves cradle sour cream, onion, and caviar.

BRUSSELS SPROUTS WITH MUSTARD GLAZE

¼ **cup slivered almonds**
4 **cups Brussels sprouts**
2 **tablespoons cider vinegar**
3 **tablespoons firmly packed brown sugar**
1 **tablespoon Dijon mustard**
1 **tablespoon butter or margarine**
Salt

In a 6- to 8-inch frying pan, stir nuts over medium-high heat until golden, about 2 minutes. Pour from pan; set aside.

Discard sprouts' coarse outer leaves; rinse sprouts and drain. In a wok or 4- to 5-quart pan, place sprouts on a rack over 1 inch boiling water. Cover and steam on high heat until tender when pierced, about 15 to 20 minutes.

Meanwhile, in a 10- to 12-inch frying pan, stir vinegar, sugar, mustard, and butter over medium-high heat until bubbling vigorously. Add sprouts and almonds; stir to mix well. Pour into a bowl; add salt to taste. Makes 4 servings.

PER SERVING: 157 calories, 4.7 g protein, 20 g carbohydrates, 7.7 g fat, 7.7 mg cholesterol, 168 mg sodium

HOT BRUSSELS SPROUTS SLAW

1 **pound Brussels sprouts**
2 **tablespoons butter or margarine**
2 **cloves garlic, minced or pressed**
3 **ounces thinly sliced prosciutto, cut in slivers**
¾ **cup regular-strength chicken broth**
2 **tablespoons shredded parmesan cheese**

Discard coarse outer leaves of sprouts. Rinse sprouts and break off about 1 cup large leaves; set aside. With a knife or food processor, finely shred sprouts.

In a 10- to 12-inch frying pan over medium-high heat, stir butter, garlic, and prosciutto until meat is browned, 5 to 7 minutes. Add sprouts and broth; stir on high heat until sprouts are tender to bite, about 6 minutes. Mound on a platter and surround with reserved leaves. Sprinkle with parmesan. Makes 4 to 6 servings.

PER SERVING: 101 calories, 5.8 g protein, 7.1 g carbohydrates, 6.2 g fat, 19 mg cholesterol, 378 mg sodium

Fat-Lowering Strategies with High-Fat Meats

DOES WATCHING FAT *in your diet mean you can't enjoy some of your favorite cuts of meat? Not if you watch portion size and balance the meat—and its fat—with complex carbohydrates. Fat should amount to 30 percent or less of the calories you consume; these satisfying, nutritious recipes achieve that with pasta and potatoes.*

Also, you can trim off surface fat and cook meats in ways that render out a lot of the intramuscular fat. These recipes are also examples of this technique.

The first starts with lamb shoulder, lavishly streaked with fat. By cooking it with moist heat, skimming fat from pan juices, then browning the meat, you eliminate many calories. Then mix the lean juices with noodles and broccoli.

Pork baby back ribs (from the loin section) are much leaner than pork spareribs. Nutritional analysis is available only for pork loin; we arrived at our data by weighing the trimmed edible portion of loin from the cooked ribs.

OVEN-BRAISED LAMB SHOULDER WITH GARLIC, NOODLES & BROCCOLI

- 2 **heads (about ¼ lb.** *total***) garlic**
- 1 **lamb shoulder (4 to 5 lb.), surface fat trimmed off**
  About 2 cups regular-strength beef broth
- 1 **pound broccoli**
- 10 **ounces dry wide egg noodles**
  Salt and pepper (optional)

Peel 1 head garlic and cut each clove in half (cut largest cloves in thirds). Cut 1-inch-deep gashes all over lamb shoulder and poke a garlic piece into each cut. Set shoulder, curved bones down, in a 9-by 13-inch pan. Cut remaining garlic head in half horizontally and put, cut side down, beside lamb in pan. Add 2 cups broth and seal pan tightly with foil.

Bake in a 400° oven for 1½ hours; uncover (avoid hot steam), turn shoulder over, re-cover, and bake until meat pulls easily from bone, about 1½ hours longer.

Lift garlic pieces from pan with a slotted spoon and set aside. Using 2 large spoons, carefully transfer shoulder to a platter. Pour pan juices into a 2-cup measure and return shoulder to pan. If made ahead, let meat, garlic, and juices cool, then cover and chill up to 2 days.

Skim fat (or lift off if chilled) and discard. Squeeze garlic from peel, mash thoroughly, and add to pan juices. You should have 1 cup juices; if not, add broth to make this amount. Brush meat with about 2 tablespoons of the juices. Reduce oven heat to 350° and bake meat, uncovered, until browned, about 10 minutes—45 minutes if chilled. Heat juices and keep warm.

Meanwhile, trim off and discard tough ends of broccoli; thinly slice broccoli. In a 4- to 5-quart pan on high heat, bring about 3 quarts water to a boil. Add noodles and broccoli. Cook, uncovered and stirring occasionally, until noodles and broccoli are tender to bite, about 7 minutes. Drain and return to pan. Add remaining meat juices to pan and mix, lifting with 2 forks; keep warm.

When shoulder is browned, set on a warm platter; pile noodles and broccoli beside it. Because of the bone structure, shoulder is awkward to carve; pull meat off with forks; offer bones for gnawing. Add salt and pepper to taste. Makes 6 to 8 servings.

PER SERVING: 457 calories, 44 g protein, 36 g carbohydrates, 15 g fat, 156 mg cholesterol, 147 mg sodium

OVEN-BAKED PORK BABY BACK RIBS WITH SMALL POTATOES & MUSTARD GREENS

- 3 **pounds pork baby back ribs**
- 3 **cups regular-strength chicken broth**
- 3 **pounds small (about 1½-in.-diameter) thin-skinned potatoes, scrubbed**
- ⅓ **cup hoisin sauce (Chinese bean sauce) or purchased barbecue sauce**
- 1 **pound mustard greens, tough stems trimmed off, rinsed and thinly shredded**

Well-trimmed lamb shoulder, baked with moist heat, becomes succulent as internal fat melts and flows into pan juices. Skimmed of fat, lean juices season broccoli and noodles.

In 2 metal baking pans, each 10 by 15 inches, evenly divide ribs, setting curved side up. Pour 1½ cups broth over ribs in each pan; tightly cover pans with foil. Bake in a 400° oven for 1 hour.

Lift foil (avoid steam), turn ribs over, and tuck potatoes around them. Seal pans and bake until potatoes are tender when pierced, about 1 hour. Uncover pan, transfer potatoes to a platter, and keep warm. Drain juices into a bowl; skim off and discard fat.

Lay all the ribs in 1 pan. Brush equally with ¼ cup hoisin sauce. Broil 8 inches from heat until ribs are browned, about 5 minutes.

Meanwhile, return meat juices to the other pan; add remaining hoisin sauce and mustard greens. Stir over high heat until greens are wilted, about 4 minutes. Spoon greens onto platter; add ribs. Cut ribs apart to serve. Makes 6 to 8 servings.

ESTIMATED PER SERVING: 315 calories, 20 g protein, 27 g carbohydrates, 10 g fat, 53 mg cholesterol, 419 mg sodium

A Light Coat for Fish

AROMATIC JACKETS *of flavor baked on fish add distinctive seasonings and an attractive finish. To venture beyond the typical coats of flour or crumbs, we suggest using pink peppercorns or dry mushrooms for a lighter, livelier touch.*

Pink peppercorns poached to softness and baked on swordfish or halibut add a delicate spice and attractive color. (Some individuals are allergic to pink peppercorns—as others are to shellfish. If the peppercorns are new to you, and if you have food sensitivities, first taste a very small amount, then wait about 2 hours to see if you have any adverse reaction.)

Dry porcini mushrooms whirled to a powder make a surprisingly intense complement to salmon fillets.

PINK PEPPERCORN SWORDFISH

⅓ cup pink peppercorns

4 swordfish or halibut steaks, *each* 1 inch thick and 5 to 6 ounces (1¼ to 1½ lb. *total*)

4 teaspoons honey

1 can (15 oz.) pickled sliced beets, drained

4 large butter lettuce leaves, rinsed and crisped
Salt

Combine peppercorns and about 2 cups water in a 1- to 1½-quart pan. Bring to a boil on high heat and simmer to soften slightly, about 4 minutes. Drain well.

Rinse fish, pat dry, and lay well apart in a lightly oiled 10- by 15-inch baking pan. Brush each steak with 1 teaspoon of honey, then spoon peppercorns equally atop fish, spreading in a single layer.

Bake in a 400° oven until the fish is no longer translucent but still looks moist in the thickest part (cut to test), about 10 minutes.

With a wide spatula, transfer fish to warm dinner plates; accompany with beets presented on the lettuce leaves. Season to taste with salt. Makes 4 servings.

PER SERVING: 319 calories, 36 g protein, 29 g carbohydrates, 7.1 g fat, 66 mg cholesterol, 438 mg sodium

Pink peppercorns top baked swordfish steaks; their flavor penetrates as the fish cooks. Pickled beets make refreshing companion.

PORCINI-CRUSTED SALMON WITH ASPARAGUS IN BROTH

¼ ounce (about ⅓ cup) dry porcini mushrooms (also called cèpes)

2 tablespoons fine dry bread crumbs

4 boned and skinned salmon fillets, *each* about 1 inch in thickest section and 4 to 5 ounces (1 to 1¼ lb. *total*)
About 2 tablespoons melted butter or margarine

3 cups regular-strength chicken broth

2 cups thin diagonal asparagus slices
Toasted and buttered baguette slices (optional)
Salt and pepper

In a blender or food processor, whirl mushrooms until a coarse powder; add crumbs and whirl to mix, then pour into a wide pan or onto a sheet of waxed paper.

Rinse salmon and pat dry. Turn fish in mushroom mixture, pressing to coat well all over. Lay fish, flattest side down and well apart, in a lightly oiled 10- by 15-inch baking pan; pat remaining crumbs on fish. Drizzle fish evenly with butter.

Bake in a 400° oven until salmon is opaque but still looks moist in thickest part (cut fish to test), about 10 minutes.

Meanwhile, bring broth to boil in a 3- to 4-quart pan on high heat. Add asparagus and simmer, uncovered, until just tender when pierced, about 4 minutes. Ladle equal amounts of broth and asparagus into 4 wide, shallow soup bowls. With a wide spatula, set a salmon fillet in each bowl. Accompany with baguette toast; add salt and pepper to taste. Makes 4 servings.

PER SERVING: 284 calories, 27 g protein, 11 g carbohydrates, 15 g fat, 78 mg cholesterol, 197 mg sodium

More March Recipes

OTHER MARCH ARTICLES *suggest tiny bite-size biscuits, with sweet and savory versions for teatime treats or party appetizers, and a chocolate dessert that is lower in fat than it appears.*

CINNAMON-SUGAR BISCUIT BITES

Miniature biscuits, whether savory or sweet, make tender-crunchy nibbles at teatime or as party appetizers. Whole-wheat flour gives them hearty color and flavor, while yeast, used unconventionally (no rising), makes them light and tender.

    3   tablespoons sugar
    ¾   teaspoon ground cinnamon
    1   package active dry yeast
    2   tablespoons warm water (110°)
    ¾   cup whole-wheat flour
    ½   cup all-purpose flour
    1½ teaspoons baking powder
    ¼   teaspoon baking soda
    2   tablespoons cold butter or
        margarine, cut into small pieces
    ½   cup buttermilk

In a small bowl, mix half the sugar with half the cinnamon; set aside.

In another small bowl, mix together the yeast and water; let stand about 5 minutes to soften.

In a large bowl, mix whole-wheat and all-purpose flours, remaining sugar and cinnamon, baking powder, and baking soda. Cut in butter with a pastry blender, or rub mixture between your fingers until it is the texture of coarse meal. Add yeast and buttermilk; stir to moisten dough evenly. With your hands, pat dough to incorporate all the crumbs.

Drop dough in about 2-teaspoon-size mounds about ½ inch apart on 1 or 2 lightly oiled 12- by 15-inch baking sheets. Sprinkle dough evenly with reserved cinnamon-sugar mixture. Bake in a 350° oven until lightly browned, about 15 minutes; if using 2 pans, alternate pan positions halfway through baking. Serve warm; if made ahead, let cool on pan and cover airtight up to next day. Uncover, and return to 350° oven until warm, about 5 minutes. Makes about 3 dozen.

PER BISCUIT: 30 calories, 0.8 g protein, 5 g carbohydrates, 0.8 g fat, 2 mg cholesterol, 38 mg sodium

ALMOND-PARMESAN BISCUIT BITES

Follow directions for **cinnamon-sugar biscuit bites** (preceding), omitting sugar and cinnamon. Decrease **whole-wheat flour** to ½ cup and add 3 tablespoons **grated parmesan cheese** and ¼ cup **chopped toasted almonds** to the dry ingredients.

PER BISCUIT: 30 calories, 1 g protein, 3.4 g carbohydrates, 1.4 g fat, 2.4 mg cholesterol, 46 mg sodium

COCOA MERINGUE MOUNTAINS WITH HEARTS OF CHOCOLATE MOUSSE

Appearances can be deceiving. This cocoa dessert looks decadent, but it's actually lower in fat than you'd suspect.

Each meringue mountain is made with egg whites and cocoa; additional cocoa gives a deep chocolate flavor to the light mousse inside. The meringues can be baked well in advance and then filled with mousse several days ahead. It's easier to form the meringues with a pastry bag, but you can also use a spoon.

    5   large egg whites
    ½   teaspoon cream of tartar
    1¼ cups sugar
        About ⅓ cup unsweetened cocoa
        Chocolate mousse (recipe follows)

From cooking parchment (with paper supplies in supermarkets, or in cookware stores), cut 2 sheets, *each* 11 by 15 inches; on each, trace 8 circles, *each* about 2½ inches in diameter and 1 inch apart. Place on 2 baking sheets, 12- by 15-inch size.

In a large mixing bowl, beat egg whites and cream of tartar with a mixer at high speed until frothy. Gradually add sugar, 1 tablespoon at a time, beating at high speed and scraping bowl occasionally, until whites hold stiff, moist peaks and sugar is dissolved (taste to test). Gradually add 4 tablespoons cocoa, beating at high speed until mixed; scrape bowl often.

Spoon meringue into a pastry bag fitted with a star tip about ½ inch wide. Twist top of bag to enclose meringue tightly. (Or use the back of a spoon to shape cups and tops, using about ⅓ cup meringue for each cup and top.)

To make the cups, pipe meringue onto paper, starting in the middle of 1 circle and spiraling out to fill area evenly within the drawn line. Then pipe another layer of meringue on top of the first, forming a rim that makes a cup about 1½ inches tall. Repeat to make 7 more cups.

To make the tops, pipe meringue around circle's perimeter and spiral in, filling area evenly. Next, pipe a smaller circle on top of the first, continuing the spiral until you have a cone-shaped mound that is about 1½ inches tall.

Bake tops and cups in a 250° oven until meringues are firm to touch, about 1 hour; switch pan positions halfway through baking. Turn off heat and let meringues dry in closed oven for 2 hours. Let cool. (If made ahead, immediately package in an airtight moistureproof container; meringues keep well up to 1 week.)

Place meringue cups on a platter. Spoon about ¼ cup chocolate mousse into each cup, then set a meringue cone on top of each. Cover meringues lightly, but airtight, with plastic wrap and chill at least 1 hour or up to 2 days. Sift remaining cocoa over meringues. Makes 8 servings.

PER SERVING: 320 calories, 4.7 g protein, 52 g carbohydrates, 13 g fat, 17 mg cholesterol, 50 mg sodium

Chocolate mousse. In a 1- to 1½-quart pan, combine ½ cup **whipping cream** and 1 package (6 oz. or 1 cup) **semisweet chocolate baking chips.** Stir often over medium-low heat just until chocolate is smoothly melted and blended with cream. Cover and chill until cold, at least 1 hour or up until next day.

In a small bowl, beat 2 **large egg whites** with a mixer at high speed until frothy. Gradually add 4 tablespoons **sugar,** 1 tablespoon at a time, and continue to beat until whites hold soft, distinct peaks.

Whip chocolate mixture at high speed until it holds soft peaks. Gently fold with whites and ½ teaspoon **vanilla** until smoothly blended. Use or cover and chill up to 2 hours.

Serve date squares with milk for breakfast or a snack.

DATE NUT CHEDDAR SQUARES

- 1½ cups (8 oz.) chopped dates
- ¾ cup water
- ½ cup sugar
- 2 tablespoons butter or margarine
- 2 cups all-purpose flour
- 1 cup chopped walnuts or almonds
- 1½ teaspoons ground cinnamon
- 1 teaspoon baking soda
- 1½ cups (6 oz.) shredded cheddar cheese
- 1 large egg

In a 2- to 3-quart pan, combine dates, water, sugar, and butter. Over high heat, bring mixture to a boil. Let cool at least 30 minutes.

In a large bowl, stir together flour, walnuts, cinnamon, baking soda, and cheese. Beat egg to mix well with date mixture; pour into flour mixture. Stir until batter is evenly moistened.

Spread batter in a buttered 9- by 13-inch baking pan. Bake in a 325° oven until golden brown around edges and firm when lightly touched in center, about 25 minutes. Cool slightly and cut into about 2-inch squares. Serve hot to cool, or, to store, cool and wrap airtight for up to 3 days; freeze for longer storage. Makes 24 pieces. — *Joan Cunningham, Moscow, Idaho.*

PER PIECE: 153 calories, 4 g protein, 20 g carbohydrates, 6.7 g fat, 19 mg cholesterol, 92 mg sodium

---

Couscous pasta is flavored with ginger, nuts, fruit, vegetables.

GOLDEN CURRIED COUSCOUS

- 1½ cups regular-strength chicken broth
- ½ cup golden raisins
- ¼ cup lemon juice
- 2 tablespoons minced crystallized ginger
- 2 tablespoons butter or margarine
- ½ teaspoon curry powder
- 1 cup couscous
- ⅓ cup thinly sliced celery
- ¼ cup thinly sliced green onion
- 2 tablespoons chopped fresh cilantro (coriander)
- ⅓ cup coarsely chopped roasted and salted pistachios
- Cilantro sprigs (optional)

In a 2- to 3-quart pan over high heat, bring broth to a boil. Stir in raisins, lemon juice, ginger, butter, curry powder, and couscous.

Cover pan and remove from heat; let stand at least 5 minutes, or up to 3 hours. Stir with a fork. If made ahead, cover and chill up until next day.

Mix in celery, green onion, and chopped cilantro. Mound couscous onto a platter; sprinkle pistachios on top of the couscous and garnish with cilantro sprigs. Serve warm or at room temperature. Makes 4 servings. — *Sally Vog, Springfield, Ore.*

PER SERVING: 332 calories, 7.9 g protein, 52 g carbohydrates, 12 g fat, 16 mg cholesterol, 104 mg sodium

---

Golden cheese melts over savory turkey and green chili casserole.

WESTERN TURKEY CASSEROLE

- 1 pound boned and skinned turkey breast
- 2 tablespoons salad oil
- 1 small onion, chopped
- 1 cup prepared taco sauce
- 2 cups (½ lb.) shredded jack cheese
- ¼ cup all-purpose flour
- 4 large eggs
- ¾ cup milk
- 2 cans (7 oz. *each*) whole green chilies

Cut turkey into ¼-inch-thick slices. To a 10- to 12-inch frying pan over medium heat, add oil, turkey, and onion. Stir often until turkey is white outside and slightly pink in center (cut to test), about 5 minutes. Add taco sauce.

Mix cheese and flour, then beat in eggs and milk. Slice chilies open and remove any seeds.

Cover bottom of a greased 8- to 9- by 10- to 11-inch shallow casserole with half the chilies. Top with half the turkey and half the milk and cheese mixture. Repeat steps to use remaining ingredients. Bake, uncovered, in a 350° oven until the top is golden brown, about 40 minutes. Let stand at least 5 minutes, then spoon from casserole. Makes 6 servings. — *Jean Slaughter, Las Vegas.*

PER SERVING: 390 calories, 33 g protein, 15 g carbohydrates, 22 g fat, 226 mg cholesterol, 1,008 mg sodium

SWEET SPICE SPAGHETTI SAUCE

- 4 slices bacon, chopped
- 1 pound ground lean beef
- 4 medium-size onions, chopped
- 1 cup finely chopped celery
- 2 cloves garlic, minced or pressed
- 2 tablespoons minced parsley
  Spice blend (recipe follows)
- 3 cans (15 oz. *each*) tomato sauce
- 1 can (6 oz.) tomato paste
- 2 tablespoons red wine vinegar

In a 5- to 6-quart pan over medium-high heat, stir bacon and beef frequently until well browned, about 15 minutes. Discard fat. Add onions, celery, garlic, parsley, and spice blend. Stir often until onions

are limp, about 20 minutes. Add tomato sauce, tomato paste, and vinegar. Simmer, uncovered, until reduced to 2 quarts, about 1 hour. If made ahead, cover and chill up to 5 days; reheat to use. Makes 2 quarts. —*Marla Melton, Bend, Ore.*

PER CUP: 223 calories, 14 g protein, 21 g carbohydrates, 9.9 g fat, 37 mg cholesterol, 1,230 mg sodium

Spice blend. Combine 1 tablespoon firmly packed **brown sugar;** ½ teaspoon *each* **ground cinnamon, dry oregano leaves, pepper, rubbed sage,** and **dry thyme leaves;** ¼ teaspoon *each* **ground cloves** and **ground nutmeg.**

Sweet and spicy overtones give spaghetti sauce subtle, complex flavor.

ORIENTAL FISH PATTIES

- 1 pound boned and skinned firm white-flesh fish (lingcod, rockfish, sole), finely chopped
- 3 medium-size (about 1½ lb.) boiled thin-skinned potatoes, peeled and shredded
- ¼ cup minced parsley
- 1 large egg
- ⅔ cup fine dry bread crumbs
- 2 tablespoons *each* soy sauce and Worcestershire
- 1 tablespoon black or regular (white) sesame seed
  About ¼ cup salad oil
  Lemon wedges

In a large bowl, mix together fish, potatoes, parsley, egg, ⅓ cup bread crumbs, soy sauce, Worcestershire, and sesame seed. Shape each ⅓ cup of the mixture into a 3-inch-wide patty; as shaped, coat lightly with remaining bread crumbs.

Put 2 tablespoons oil in a 10- to 12-inch frying pan over medium heat (to speed cooking, use 2 frying pans). When hot, add patties without crowding. Cook, turning once, until golden brown on both sides, about 8 minutes *total*. Keep warm while remaining patties cook; add oil as needed. Serve with lemon. Makes 16 to 18 patties. —*Arlene Stangel, Palo Alto, Calif.*

PER PATTY: 107 calories, 6.2 g protein, 10 g carbohydrates, 4.6 g fat, 34 mg cholesterol, 179 mg sodium

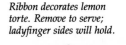

Fish, cooked potatoes, and Asian seasoning become fish patties.

LEMON TORTE WITH LADYFINGERS

- 2 boxes (3 oz. *each*) cooked lemon pudding mix, or 6 cups of your favorite lemon pie filling
- 1 cup whipping cream
- 1 large package (8 oz.) cream cheese
- ¾ cup powdered sugar
- 1 cup (1 jar, 10 oz.) apricot jam
- 1 teaspoon vanilla
- 1 baked (10 oz.) pound cake
- 1 package (3 oz.) ladyfingers

Make pudding as directed on package; let cool. Whip cream until it holds soft peaks; fold into cool pudding.

Beat cream cheese with sugar, jam, and vanilla until smooth.

Cut cake into ⅜-inch slices. Stand ladyfingers vertically, flat side to center, against inside of a 10-inch cheesecake pan with removable rim. Cover bottom with ⅓ of cake slices, cut to fit. Gently spread ⅓ of the cheese mixture over cake. Spread ⅓ of the pudding over cheese mixture, then cover with ⅓ of cake slices, cut to fit. Repeat, making 2 more layers of filling, and finishing with pudding on top. Cover and chill at least 6 hours or up until next day. Remove rim. Makes 16 servings. —*Maryalice Tilman, San Jose, Calif.*

PER SERVING: 382 calories, 5.6 g protein, 49 g carbohydrates, 19 g fat, 139 mg cholesterol, 158 mg sodium

Ribbon decorates lemon torte. Remove to serve; ladyfinger sides will hold.

IN YET ANOTHER TRIUMPH *of cross-cultural cuisine, Emmett Duncan's Stir-fried Calabacitas brings a Chinese technique to a Mexican squash mélange. This being no simple undertaking, it's no wonder that the story of this dish spans many years and two hemispheres.*

In what was then known as Peking, Sister Francetta and Sister Regia were interned during the Japanese occupation of China and later detained by the subsequent communist regime. After their release through a joint effort of the American, British, and Chinese Red Cross organizations, the sisters chose to remain in the Far East, and eventually they taught Chinese cooking classes in Tokyo. It was there that Mr. Duncan learned the stir-fry technique, which he later adapted to other cuisines.

STIR-FRIED CALABACITAS

- 1 **pound lean boneless pork**
- 2 **tablespoons dry white wine**
- 1½ **teaspoons dry oregano leaves**
- ¾ **teaspoon ground cumin**
- 1 **clove garlic, minced or pressed**
- 1 **medium-size onion**
- 3 **tablespoons olive oil**
- 1 **pound zucchini, ends trimmed and cut into ¼-inch-thick slices**
- 1 **small red bell pepper, stemmed, seeded, and diced**
- 1 **cup corn kernels, frozen or fresh**
- 1 **can (4 oz.) diced green chilies**
- 3 **tablespoons water**
- 1 **medium-size firm-ripe tomato, peeled and cut into small wedges**
   Salt and pepper

Trim and discard excess fat from pork, then cut meat into thin slices. In a bowl, mix meat with wine, oregano, cumin, and garlic; set aside.

Cut onion in half horizontally, then vertically, then cut into ½-inch-thick wedges. Pour 1 tablespoon oil into a wok or 12-inch frying pan over high heat. When oil is hot, add onion; stir-fry for 1 minute, then add zucchini, bell pepper, corn, chilies, and water. Stir-fry until squash is tender-crisp to bite, 5 to 7 minutes. Pour from pan and set aside.

Add remaining 2 tablespoons oil to pan; when oil is hot, add half the meat and stir-fry until no longer pink, about 2 minutes. Lift from pan with a slotted spoon and add to vegetables. Repeat to cook remaining meat, then return vegetable mixture to pan and stir until hot. Mix in the tomato, and season to taste with salt and pepper. Makes 5 or 6 servings.

PER SERVING: 201 calories, 15 g protein, 12 g carbohydrates, 11 g fat, 39 mg cholesterol, 160 mg sodium

Emmett Duncan

Albuquerque

"The sisters taught Chinese cooking classes in Tokyo."

HETEROSIS SOUNDS LIKE *something you treat with mouthwash; in fact, it is the technical term for hybrid vigor, a quality often displayed by the offspring of widely differing parents. Hybrid vegetable varieties, for instance, are often heralded as improvements over their parent stock.*

Chefs of the West are old hands at creating culinary heterosis by hybridizing the foods of different ethnic groups. A recent example is Randall Richardson's Sichuan Guacamole, a felicitous cross between Southwestern avocado dip and southwestern Chinese seasonings.

SICHUAN GUACAMOLE

- 1 **teaspoon sesame seed**
- 1 **large (about 10 oz.) ripe avocado**
- ½ **teaspoon minced fresh ginger**
- ¼ **teaspoon Chinese five spice**
- 1 **clove garlic, minced or pressed**
- ¼ **to ½ teaspoon Sichuan hot bean sauce or other hot chili paste**
- ½ **teaspoon *each* Oriental sesame oil and soy sauce**
- 1 **teaspoon lemon juice**
- 2 **tablespoons chopped fresh cilantro (coriander)**
   Salt
- 2 **tablespoons *each* diced tomato or red bell pepper and finely chopped red onion**
   Shrimp chips

Stir sesame seed in a 6- to 8-inch frying pan over medium heat until golden; pour out of pan and set aside.

Pit and peel avocado. Put on a large rimmed plate with ginger, five spice, garlic, bean sauce, sesame oil, soy sauce, lemon juice, and cilantro. Coarsely mash avocado with a fork or potato masher, mixing in seasonings. Add salt to taste. Scrape into a serving bowl and sprinkle guacamole with sesame seed, tomato, and onion. Scoop guacamole onto shrimp chips to eat. Makes about 1 cup.

PER TABLESPOON: 25 calories, 0.3 g protein, 1.3 g carbohydrates, 2.2 g fat, 0 mg cholesterol, 13 mg sodium

Camarillo, Calif.

I T'S DIFFICULT TO CONCEIVE *of a location in the contiguous 48 states that is as far as 60 miles from a pizzeria. But Chaco Canyon, in New Mexico, is just such a place. It is, in fact, 60 miles from the nearest store—a situation that can readily lead to acute oligopizzia, or pizza deficiency. (Don't bother to look it up; this is the term's first, and possibly last, use.)*

Although the Piersons now live in Moab, Utah, and have the nearby services of four pizza parlors (at a recent count), they once were stationed in Chaco Canyon. To supply their pizza cravings between trips to town, Lloyd Pierson had to improvise, using staples from pantry shelf, refrigerator, or freezer. This is the result.

PIERSON PIZZA

- ¾ pound ground lean beef
- 1 small onion, finely chopped
- ½ teaspoon *each* dry basil leaves, dry oregano leaves, and dry rosemary leaves
- ¼ teaspoon pepper
- 1 small clove garlic, minced or pressed
- 2 cups baking mix (biscuit mix)
- ½ cup milk
- ⅓ cup hamburger pickle relish, drained
- ½ cup tomato-based chili sauce
- 1½ cups (6 oz.) shredded mozzarella cheese

"To supply their pizza cravings between trips to town, Lloyd Pierson had to improvise."

In a bowl, mix together the beef, onion, basil, oregano, rosemary, pepper, and garlic; set aside.

In another bowl, stir together baking mix and milk. With greased hands, pat and stretch dough over bottom and sides of a greased 12-inch pizza pan.

Bake crust in a 375° oven for 10 minutes. Remove from oven and evenly spread relish over dough, then crumble meat mixture evenly over relish. Dot top of pizza with chili sauce, spreading as much as possible with a spatula.

Bake on lowest rack in a 450° oven for 15 minutes, then sprinkle with cheese. Continue to bake until cheese is bubbly and crust is golden brown, 8 to 10 minutes more. Let stand 5 minutes, then cut into wedges. Makes 4 to 6 servings.

PER SERVING: 469 calories, 20 g protein, 42 g carbohydrates, 24 g fat, 68 mg cholesterol, 1,110 mg sodium

Moab, Utah

T HE PENNSYLVANIA DUTCH *(actually Pennsylvania Germans) enjoy a salad familiarly known as wilted lettuce. Its dressing, poured hot over the greens, is based on bacon fat and vinegar. It doesn't sound appealing, but (as the Pennsylvania Dutchman would say) it eats good. An effete modern-day version is the spinach salad prepared at your table by a waiter with moves like those of a professional* magician or an orchestra conductor. Larry Parker's Wilted Romaine is a more robust descendant of the Pennsylvania greens.

Parker makes a cooked dressing with bacon fat, vinegar, sugar, milk, and egg, then adds it to a mix of romaine, onion, olives, and (surprise!) diced kohlrabi—which confers crunchiness and a note of mystery. An optional addition of thinly sliced salami converts the mixture to a full-meal salad.

WILTED ROMAINE

- 1 large head (about 1 lb.) romaine, rinsed and crisped
- 1 large (about 1¼ lb.) kohlrabi
- 1 medium-size mild onion
- ¼ pound thinly sliced dry salami (optional)
- 1 can (2¼ oz.) sliced ripe olives, drained
- 4 slices bacon, cut into ½-inch pieces
- ⅓ cup red wine vinegar
- 3 tablespoons sugar
- 1 large egg
- 2 tablespoons milk
  Salt and pepper

In a large salad bowl, tear romaine into bite-size pieces. Peel and finely dice kohlrabi. Cut onion in half lengthwise, then thinly slice through the layers to form crescent-shaped pieces. Cut salami into thin strips. Add kohlrabi, onion, salami, and olives to romaine.

In an 8- to 10-inch frying pan, cook bacon over medium heat until crisp; stir often. Meanwhile, in a small bowl, stir together vinegar, sugar, egg, and milk.

Discard all but 1 tablespoon bacon drippings, then add vinegar mixture to pan. Stir over low heat until dressing is thick enough to lightly coat a metal spoon. Pour hot dressing over romaine mixture and mix well, seasoning to taste with salt and pepper. Makes 8 servings.

PER SERVING: 91 calories, 3.1 g protein, 8.2 g carbohydrates, 5.3 g fat, 31 mg cholesterol, 135 mg sodium

Bremerton, Wash.

March Menus

L IGHT, FRESH FLAVORS *sparkle through these three menus, reflecting the delights of the new season that's just around the corner.*

For a change from more usual breakfast fare, begin the day with the taste and texture contrasts of this ham stir-fry.

You can bake the crisp wafers ahead. Stir-fry the slivered ham and pea pods while warming the papaya halves and cooking the rice; this is a good time to try the new quick-cooking brown rice—consider it as your cereal.

HAM & PEA POD STIR-FRY WITH PAPAYA

- 2 medium-size (about 1 lb. *each*) ripe papayas
- 2 tablespoons melted butter or margarine
- 1 package (6 oz.) sliced cooked ham, finely slivered
- ¼ pound edible-pod peas, ends and strings removed
  Sauce (recipe follows)

Cut papayas lengthwise in half (do not peel); remove seeds. Set, cut side up, in a 9- by 13-inch baking pan; brush with half the butter. Bake in a 375° oven until very warm, about 15 minutes.

Meanwhile, place a 10- to 12-inch frying pan over medium-high heat. When hot, add remaining butter and ham; stir-fry until meat is slightly tinged with brown, about 5 minutes. Add peas and stir-fry for about 3 minutes. Stir sauce, then add to pan; stir until sauce boils. Spoon stir-fry equally into papayas. Makes 4 servings.

PER SERVING: 221 calories, 11 g protein, 23 g carbohydrates, 9.9 g fat, 41 mg cholesterol, 703 mg sodium

Sauce. Combine ¼ cup **water**, 1 tablespoon *each* **honey** and **lemon juice**, ½ teaspoon **ground ginger**, ½ teaspoon **Chinese five-spice** (or ⅛ teaspoon *each* anise seed, ground allspice, ground cinnamon, and ground cloves), and 2 teaspoons **cornstarch.**

Not your ordinary breakfast: this colorful stir-fry of cooked ham and tender pea pods is served in warm papaya halves with crisp, golden won ton wafers and rice.

WON TON WAFERS

Separate 1 package (7 oz., or half of a 14-oz. size) **won ton wrappers** and lay out flat; if desired, cut in rounds with a 3-inch-diameter cutter and discard the outside edges.

Melt 1½ tablespoons **butter** or margarine. Lightly brush 2 rimmed 10- by 15-inch baking pans with butter. Lay wrappers close together in a single layer in pans; brush tops lightly with remaining butter.

Bake in a 375° oven until golden, about 6 minutes; switch pan positions halfway through baking. Serve; or if made ahead, let cool, then package airtight and store up to 2 days. Makes about 30.

PER PIECE: 23 calories, 0.8 g protein, 3.6 g carbohydrates, 0.6 g fat, 1.6 mg cholesterol, 7.7 mg sodium

The oven and the barbecue share duties in this menu. It's easy for a family supper, but interesting enough for guests.

Right after the squash goes into the oven, start the charcoal (or gas barbecue). When the squash has cooked about 15 minutes, put the grits in the oven, too. Then assemble the meat for grilling.

For dessert, buy a poundcake or make your own. Serve thin slices topped with sliced peeled kiwi fruit.

GRILLED SKIRT STEAK WITH ROSEMARY & SWEET PEPPERS

- **2 pounds skirt steak, trimmed of excess fat, cut crosswise into 6 equal pieces**
- **1 *each* small green, red, and yellow bell pepper (or all 1 color), stemmed, seeded, and cut into sixths**
  Marinade (recipe follows)
  About 12 sprigs fresh rosemary, *each* 3 inches long
  Salt and pepper

Place meat and peppers in a heavy plastic bag (1-gallon size); add marinade, seal bag, and rotate to coat food. Chill 30 minutes or until next day; turn occasionally.

On each of 6 metal skewers (12- to 15-in. size), weave 1 piece of meat and 3 bell pepper pieces (one of each color), rippling slightly. Tuck sprigs of rosemary between meat and skewer.

Place on a grill 4 to 6 inches above a solid bed of hot coals (you should be able to hold your hand at grill level only 2 to 3 seconds). Cook steaks until done to your liking, 3 to 5 minutes a side for rare; turn often and brush with marinade. Season to taste with salt and pepper. Makes 6 to 8 servings.

PER SERVING: 215 calories, 21 g protein, 13 g carbohydrates, 13 g fat, 58 mg cholesterol, 70 mg sodium

Marinade. Combine thoroughly 1 tablespoon *each* **lemon juice** and **olive oil** and ⅓ cup **dry red wine**.

BAKED BANANA SQUASH

Lay a 2-pound piece of **banana squash**, cut side down, in a 9-inch-square pan; cover tightly. Bake in a 350° oven until flesh is tender when pierced, about 1 hour. Cut squash through shell into serving pieces, or scoop from shell; add **salt** and **pepper** to taste. Serves 6.

PER SERVING: 57 calories, 1.3 g protein, 15 g carbohydrates, 0.1 g fat, 0 mg cholesterol, 5.1 mg sodium

GARLIC & WHITE CHEDDAR GRITS

- **4 cups regular-strength chicken broth**
- **1 clove garlic, minced or pressed**
- **1 cup quick-cooking hominy grits**
- **2½ cups (10 oz.) shredded white cheddar cheese**
- **2 large eggs**
- **½ cup milk**

In a 3- to 4-quart pan, bring broth and garlic to a boil over high heat. Stirring, slowly add the grits. Reduce heat and simmer, uncovered, for 5 minutes; stir frequently.

Remove from heat and stir in 1½ cups cheese until melted. Add eggs and milk; beat until thoroughly blended. Pour into a buttered, shallow 2-quart baking dish; sprinkle evenly with remaining cheese.

Bake, uncovered, in a 350° oven until top is golden brown, 45 to 50 minutes. Makes 6 to 8 servings.

PER SERVING: 240 calories, 13 g protein, 17 g carbohydrates, 13 g fat, 89 mg cholesterol, 248 mg sodium

(Continued on next page)

Skirt steak is grilled with bell peppers and rosemary for an easy entrée. Accompany with baked banana squash and garlic-cheese grits.

SPRING SOUP & SANDWICH

Asparagus, Shrimp & Watercress Soup
Grilled Port Salut Cheese Sandwiches
Fresh Fennel & Cucumber Sticks
Raspberry Sorbet
Pinot Grigio Milk

Springtime colors brighten this lean, quickly prepared soup. Serve with sandwiches for lunch or supper.

Cut vegetables into sticks or chunks and immerse in ice water to crisp; then start the soup. While soup heats, toast cheese sandwiches (without using any fat) in a toaster-grill or a covered frying pan on medium heat. For a refreshingly light wine with fruity character, choose a Pinot Grigio or dry Sauvignon Blanc.

ASPARAGUS, SHRIMP & WATERCRESS SOUP

¾ pound asparagus
7 cups (or 4 cans, 14½ oz. *each*) regular-strength chicken broth
1 teaspoon *each* grated lemon peel and dry tarragon leaves
⅛ teaspoon white pepper
1 ounce dry capellini or dry coil vermicelli
¾ pound medium-size shrimp (40 to 45 per lb.), shelled and deveined
2 cups watercress sprigs, rinsed and drained
3 tablespoons lemon juice

Snap off and discard tough ends of asparagus, then cut spears into ½-inch-thick diagonal slices.

In a 4- to 5-quart pan, bring broth, lemon peel, tarragon, and pepper to a boil on high heat; add capellini. Return to boiling; simmer 4 minutes. Add asparagus and shrimp; simmer, uncovered, until shrimp are opaque in center (cut to test), about 3 minutes. Stir in watercress, then lemon juice. Serve promptly (on standing, the heat and lemon juice make the green vegetables lose their bright color). Makes 10 cups, 4 to 6 servings.

PER SERVING: 113 calories, 14 g protein, 7.7 g carbohydrates, 2.7 g fat, 70 mg cholesterol, 138 mg sodium

Floating Islands in a Caramelized Sugar Crystal Bowl (page 78)

APRIL

Surprise your guests
this month with a "smashing" dessert—meringue islands
floating atop custard sauce, presented in an edible bowl of
caramelized sugar; serve into dishes, then shatter the
container into shards for topping. For an international accent
to spring entertaining, we suggest a Brazilian menu
featuring seafood stew or a homey Russian dinner from
Finland with traditional meat-filled cabbage rolls. Australian
cooks also share lamb recipes with our readers. To complement
April meals, we offer a variety of breads and vegetable dishes.

A Smashing Dessert

Startle and delight *guests when you break the shimmery-looking bowl pictured on the facing page. It may appear to be Venetian glass, but in reality it's edible caramelized sugar.*

Use it as a container to present the classic dessert, floating islands. The bowl holds soft oven-poached meringues (the islands). You "float" the meringues in individual dishes with custard sauce, then shatter the caramelized bowl into small shards for a crackly sweet topping to sprinkle over the white puffs.

The caramelized sugar bowl is surprisingly easy to make. You heat sugar until it melts and turns a rich amber, then pour the resulting syrup into a foil-lined pizza pan. As it begins to firm, invert the warm round over a bowl to mold it. Once cool, the bowl holds its shape for several days, if it is kept airtight. The meringues and custard can be made a day ahead.

In a large bowl, combine reserved egg whites and cream of tartar. Beat with a mixer at high speed until foamy. Gradually add remaining ⅓ cup sugar, beating until whites hold soft, shiny peaks.

Fill a 12- by 17-inch roasting pan with about ¾ inch boiling water. From a large spoon, drop egg-white mixture into water in 8 to 10 equal-size scoops; do not overlap. Carefully transfer pan to a 350° oven; bake, uncovered, until golden brown, 12 to 15 minutes. With a slotted spoon, transfer cooked meringues to a wire rack to drain and cool. Lift rack and use a paper towel to blot remaining moisture from meringue bottoms. If made ahead, cover and chill up until next day.

To present, mound meringues in sugar bowl and top with berries. At the table, spoon meringues and berries into individual bowls, adding custard sauce. Using a large spoon, crack sugar bowl into small pieces; sprinkle a few fragments over each meringue. Makes 8 to 10 servings.

Per Serving with 1 Tablespoon Sugar Bowl: 233 calories, 6.5 g protein, 33 g carbohydrates, 8.1 g fat, 145 mg cholesterol, 102 mg sodium

Caramelized sugar bowl. Have at hand 2 tablespoons melted **butter** or margarine. Smoothly line a 14-inch pizza pan with foil; brush foil with half the butter. Set pan in a 200° oven to keep warm. Also invert a 4- to 8-inch-tall bowl with a flat bottom that measures 2 to 4 inches across onto a foil-covered, 14-inch pizza pan or a 10- by 15-inch baking pan. Brush outside of bowl with remaining butter; put in oven.

Floating Islands in a Caramelized Sugar Crystal Bowl

- 6 **large eggs, separated**
- ⅔ **cup sugar**
- 1½ **teaspoons vanilla**
- 3⅓ **cups milk**
- 3 **tablespoons orange-flavor liqueur**
- ¼ **teaspoon cream of tartar**
    Caramelized sugar bowl (recipe follows)
- 1 **cup sliced strawberries**

In a small bowl, whisk yolks to blend with ⅓ cup sugar and vanilla. In the top of a double boiler over medium-high heat, bring milk to scalding. Whisk about ½ cup milk into egg mixture, then return mixture to milk in pan. Place pan over barely simmering water and stir often until custard coats a metal spoon in a smooth, opaque layer, 15 to 20 minutes.

At once, set pan with custard into ice water; stir until cool. Stir in liqueur. Pour custard into a pitcher. Cover and chill until cold, about 1 hour or up until next day.

1 *Cook sugar, shaking pan often, until it melts and forms an amber-colored syrup.*

2 *Pour hot caramelized syrup into a warm well-buttered, foil-lined pizza pan.*

3 *Tilt pan to spread hot syrup. As it begins to set but is still hot, thin out with spatula.*

4 *Loosely mold warm caramel over warm buttered bowl to shape glassy container.*

5 *Serve oven-poached meringues with strawberries in bowl of caramelized sugar.*

Pour 1½ cups **sugar** into a 10- to 12-inch nonstick frying pan and set over medium-high heat. Cook, shaking pan often, until most of the sugar liquefies. Reduce heat to medium to medium-low; shake pan often until all sugar melts and turns amber-colored, 30 to 45 minutes total.

At once, pour and scrape caramelized syrup into warm, foil-lined pizza pan; quickly tilt to spread syrup as thinly as possible. As syrup begins to set, use a buttered spatula to pull it gently and evenly out from edges to make it thinner (no need, though, to fill pan or have round edges). Let syrup stand until it's firm when pan is tilted but still pliable and warm, 3 to 4 minutes. (If caramel gets rigid before you are able to mold it, place in oven until pliable, 5 to 10 minutes.)

Lift foil from pan and invert caramel over bottom of warm bowl. With potholder-protected hands, immediately press sides of caramel *loosely* around bowl (if you press after caramel is cool, it will crack). When cool enough to touch but still slightly pliable, 2 to 4 minutes, peel off foil and gently loosen sugar bowl from sides of mold. Let cool on mold until firm, about 5 minutes. Gently remove sugar bowl from mold. Use, or wrap airtight up to 3 days. Makes 1 bowl.

6 *Duck for cover as brittle bowl of caramelized sugar gets cracked. Meringue puffs, custard, and fruit have been spooned into individual dishes to await a final garnish.*

7 *Shards of glassy sugar "bowl" top baked meringues floating on custard.*

Samba Stew

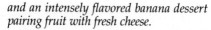

LIKE A SAMBA, *the Brazilian seafood stew called* moqueca *(moh-keh-ka) has a tropical beat. Delicate, fresh seafood and smooth coconut milk—with hints of musky* dendê *palm oil and fiery chili— mingle to form a festive syncopation in this popular dish.*

Hilza da Silva, raised in Brazil, now cooks moqueca for friends and for catering clients in the Los Angeles area. She serves this version for eight with fried white rice, as well as a savory topping called farofa

and an intensely flavored banana dessert pairing fruit with fresh cheese.

The meal reflects Africa's and Europe's culinary impact on Bahia, a state on Brazil's Atlantic coast. Bahian dishes are distinguished by a strong African influence on their combination of European and native ingredients—chilies, coconut, palm oil, manioc root (in farofa).

You start moqueca by cooking elements separately to make a flavorful broth. Then put the stew together with an assortment of

seafood and a touch of brightly colored palm oil, and simmer briefly.

The Brazilian recipes that accompany the moqueca go well with other meals, as well. Try the crunchy farofa on scrambled eggs or with curries. The dessert makes a sweet conclusion to any dinner.

Spice shops and stores catering to Latinos sell ingredients for the authentic version of this meal: coconut milk, dendê palm oil, Brazilian hot chilies (called pimienta *or* malagueta*) in oil, fresh Mexican cheese, and manioc (also called* farina, *cassava, or* gari*). Or use alternatives suggested. Many supermarkets have coconut milk and Oriental chili oil.*

Dendê palm oil ranges in color from orange to deep red and may be liquid to solid (cold firms it up). Since the oil has no flavor substitute, omit it if you can't find it; the stew and farofa will be different but still good.

One mail-order source for coconut milk, palm oil, and manioc is Ratto's International Grocers, 821 Washington St., Oakland, CA 94607. To order by telephone, call (800) 228-3515 in California, (800) 325-3483 elsewhere.

Brazilians ordinarily use only the oil from the preserved chilies because the chilies themselves are so incendiary. But sensation seekers can add chili bits to their portions of moqueca.

FLAVORS OF BAHIA

Moqueca
Fried Rice   **Green Salad**
Farofa with Dendê Palm Oil
Banana Sweet with
Fresh Cheese & Fruit
Mineral Water or Beer

Though salad isn't typically Brazilian, you may want to add it to the menu.

Cook rice while moqueca simmers. Farofa goes together quickly at the last minute. The banana paste dessert takes about an hour; you can make it up to a week ahead.

Brilliant colors of seafood, peppers, and palm oil accent coconut-rich broth of moqueca, a Brazilian seafood stew. Accompaniments include fried rice and crunchy farofa.

MOQUECA

⅓ cup minced garlic
1 medium-size yellow or white onion, cut into slivers
1 cup sliced green onions
¼ cup olive oil
1 pound medium-size (43 to 50 per lb.) shrimp, shelled (reserve shells) and deveined
1 can (8 oz.) tomato sauce
2¼ cups regular-strength chicken broth
1 can (14 oz.) canned or thawed frozen coconut milk
¾ cup lemon juice
2 dry bay leaves
1 *each* medium-size green and red bell peppers, stemmed, seeded, and chopped
¼ cup dendê palm oil (optional)
2 teaspoons oil from preserved Brazilian chilies, or 4 teaspoons Oriental chili oil
1½ pounds boned and skinned swordfish, cut into 8 equal pieces
1 pound small clams in shells (suitable for steaming), scrubbed
1 pound New Zealand green mussels or domestic blue mussels in shells, scrubbed, with beards pulled off
½ pound (at least 8) large sea scallops, rinsed
½ pound bay scallops (or sea scallops), rinsed

In a 5- to 6-quart pan over medium heat, cook garlic and yellow and green onions in 2 tablespoons olive oil until very limp, stirring often, 12 to 15 minutes. Scrape out of pan and set aside.

To pan, add remaining olive oil and shrimp shells (set meat aside). Stir often until shells turn opaque, 2 to 3 minutes. Add tomato sauce and chicken broth; bring to a simmer on medium-high heat, then simmer, stirring often, for 10 minutes longer.

Pour broth mixture through a fine strainer into a bowl, pressing shells to extract liquid; discard shells. Return liquid to pan with onion mixture, coconut milk, lemon juice, bay leaves, and bell peppers. Bring to a boil over medium-high heat; simmer, stirring often, until bell peppers are tender to bite, about 10 minutes. (At this point, you can cover and chill broth and seafood separately for up to 1 day.)

Add palm and chili oils and bring to a boil. Gently stir in shelled shrimp, swordfish, clams, and mussels. Return to a simmer and cook for 2 minutes. Gently stir in sea and bay scallops; simmer until shells open, 3 to 4 minutes longer. Serves 8. — *Hilza da Silva, Sherman Oaks, Calif.*

PER SERVING WITHOUT PALM OIL: 433 calories, 42 g protein, 13 g carbohydrates, 24 g fat, 129 mg cholesterol, 488 mg sodium

PER SERVING WITH PALM OIL: 493 calories, 42 g protein, 13 g carbohydrates, 31 g fat, 129 mg cholesterol, 488 mg sodium

FRIED RICE

¼ cup salad oil
1 tablespoon minced garlic
½ cup coarsely chopped onion
3 cups long-grain white rice
5 cups water
  Salt

In a 3- to 4-quart pan over medium-high heat, stir oil, garlic, and onion until garlic is golden, about 5 minutes. Add rice and stir until it's slightly opaque, about 5 minutes. Add water and bring to a boil, then cover and simmer until liquid is absorbed, about 15 minutes. Add salt to taste. Serves 8.

PER SERVING: 317 calories, 4.8 g protein, 57 g carbohydrates, 7.1 g fat, 0 mg cholesterol, 3.9 mg sodium

FAROFA WITH DENDÊ PALM OIL

¼ cup coarsely chopped onion
2 tablespoons coarsely chopped fresh cilantro (coriander)
¼ cup dendê palm oil or olive oil
1 cup broth from moqueca (recipe preceding) or regular-strength chicken broth
2¾ cups (1¼ lb.) manioc flour (also called *farina, cassava,* or *gari*), or farina for hot cereal

In a 10- to 12-inch frying pan over medium-high heat, stir onion and cilantro in oil until cilantro is very limp, about 3 minutes. Add broth and manioc flour; stir often until liquid is absorbed and manioc is slightly toasted, about 3 minutes. If made ahead, cover and let stand up to 30 minutes. Makes 8 servings.

PER SERVING: 289 calories, 6.7 g protein, 48 g carbohydrates, 7.3 g fat, 0 mg cholesterol, 8.6 mg sodium

Fresh fruit and cheese accompany spoonful of sweet brown banana paste dessert.

BANANA SWEET WITH FRESH CHEESE & FRUIT

1½ pounds (about 4 medium-size) ripe (skins with brown spots) bananas, peeled
¾ cup sugar
½ cup water
½ pound fresh Mexican cheese (such as *panela* or *queso fresco*) or jack cheese, sliced
1 large (about 1¼ lb.) ripe papaya or mango, peeled and sliced
1 pint strawberries, rinsed and drained
  Fresh mint sprigs and lime wedges

In a 10- to 12-inch nonstick frying pan over medium heat, bring bananas, sugar, and water to a boil. Mash bananas and stir often until mixture turns a caramel color and holds together in a soft mass, about 45 minutes; to avoid scorching, stir more often as mixture thickens.

Use warm or cool; if made ahead, cover and chill up to 1 week. Spoon banana sweet onto plates with cheese, papaya, and berries; garnish with mint and lime. Makes about 1 cup banana sweet, enough for 8 servings.

PER SERVING: 284 calories, 8.1 g protein, 45 g carbohydrates, 9.2 g fat, 25 mg cholesterol, 154 mg sodium

A Russian Dinner from Finland

THE HEARTY, TRADITIONAL *cuisine of Russia offers many recipes that work surprisingly well for Western cooks. Tourists may not encounter these home-style kinds of foods at the source—yet. But from Alexander Nevski's, a Russian restaurant in neighboring Finland, comes this handsome menu featuring plenty of make-ahead steps. It serves six.*

You may need to order fish trimmings for the broth several days in advance. Broth, cabbage rolls, and spiced syrup can be made a day ahead. Add a green salad if you like.

Serve the broth plain or with bite-size pieces of puff pastry. To make your own, use 1 sheet frozen puff pastry (half of a 17¼ oz. package), thawed. Cut with a floured, decorative 1-inch-wide cutter and place pieces slightly apart on 2 ungreased 12- by 15-inch baking sheets. Brush pastries with milk and sprinkle lightly with minced fresh dill. Bake in a 350° oven until golden, 10 to 12 minutes; switch pan positions halfway through baking.

A mellow dry red wine, such as a Merlot, goes well with the meal.

RICH FISH BROTH

2½ quarts water
 1 cup dry white wine
 4 pounds bones, trimmings, and heads (gills removed) of lean, white-flesh fish (such as rockfish, lingcod, or perch), rinsed well
 2 large onions, sliced
 2 large carrots, peeled and sliced
 ½ cup chopped parsley
 1 dry bay leaf
 1 teaspoon *each* whole cloves and black peppercorns
    About 2 tablespoons lemon juice
 1 tablespoon minced fresh dill
    Salt

In a 6- to 8-quart pan on high heat, bring to boiling the water, wine, fish scraps, onions, carrots, parsley, bay leaf, cloves, and peppercorns. Cook, uncovered, until liquid is reduced by half, 1¼ to 1½

A delicately spiced fish broth, its flavor enriched by simmering with fish trimmings and bones, is served with puff pastry bites.

hours. With a slotted spoon, remove carrots; set aside.

Pour broth into a bowl. Rinse pan; place a colander in pan. Line colander with damp cheesecloth. Pour broth mixture into colander. When cool to touch, gather cloth edges and twist tightly to squeeze out as much liquid as possible; remove colander and discard residue. (If made ahead, cover and chill up until next day.) Return broth to boiling. Add carrots and 2 tablespoons lemon juice. Ladle into six bowls; garnish with dill, and add lemon juice and salt to taste. Serves 6.

PER SERVING: 61 calories, 5.1 g protein, 9.5 g carbohydrates, 0.4 g fat, 18 mg cholesterol, 217 mg sodium

RUSSIAN CABBAGE ROLLS

 ½ cup pearl barley
 1 large (2½ to 3 lb.) head cabbage
 1 pound boned veal round or boned and skinned turkey thigh
    All-purpose flour
    About 1 tablespoon *each* butter or margarine and olive oil
 1 small red bell pepper, stemmed, seeded, and slivered
    At least ¼ cup sour cream
 ⅔ cup *each* regular-strength chicken or beef broth and slivered kosher-style dill pickles

    Salt and pepper
    Smetana sauce (recipe follows)
 1 loaf (1 lb.) frozen whole-wheat bread dough, thawed
 1 large egg yolk, beaten with 1 tablespoon water

Rinse barley and combine in a 1- to 1½-quart pan with 2 cups water. Bring to a boil, cover, and simmer until barley is tender to bite, about 30 minutes. Drain; set aside.

Meanwhile, in a 6- to 8-quart pan, bring 4 to 5 quarts water to a boil over high heat. Core cabbage and, with a spoon, submerge head in water for 20 seconds. Lift out cabbage; when cool to touch, gently pull off (don't tear) softened outer leaves. Repeat until you have 12 to 14 large leaves (save extra cabbage for other uses).

Return leaves, about 4 at a time, to boiling water and cook until pliable, 2 to 4 minutes; drain well. Cut thick section of stem from back of each leaf.

Cut meat across grain into ¼-inch-wide strips. Coat strips with flour; shake off excess. Put 1 tablespoon *each* butter and oil in a 10- to 12-inch frying pan over medium-high heat. When hot, add half of the meat at a time and cook, stirring often, until lightly browned, 5 to 7

Fold blanched cabbage leaf over meat-and-barley filling; roll to seal. Snugly fit rolls into casserole, drizzle with sauce, top with dough, and bake.

minutes; transfer with a slotted spoon to a bowl. Add more butter and oil if needed.

In pan, cook bell pepper until limp, about 5 minutes, stirring often. Remove from heat and mix in ¼ cup sour cream, broth, pickles, barley, meat and juices, and salt and pepper to taste. Divide in portions to match the number of leaves (smaller for small leaves). Mound 1 portion in center of each leaf cup. Fold sides over filling, then roll to enclose. Place rolls, seam down, in a shallow 3½- to 4-quart (10- by 14-in. oval) casserole. If made ahead, cover and chill up until next day.

Pour hot smetana sauce evenly over rolls. On a lightly floured board, roll dough slightly larger than casserole top. Lay dough over rolls; fold excess dough under and press against inside rim of casserole. Cover lightly with plastic wrap and let rise in a warm place until puffy, 15 to 25 minutes. Brush egg mixture over dough. Bake in a 350° oven until top is richly browned, 40 to 45 minutes. To serve, break through bread with a spoon; scoop out rolls and sauce to serve with bread. Offer sour cream to add to taste. Serves 6.

PER SERVING: 591 calories, 28 g protein, 63 g carbohydrates, 26 g fat, 119 mg cholesterol, 815 mg sodium

Smetana sauce. In a 1- to 2-quart pan over medium-high heat, stir 2 tablespoons **butter** or margarine with 2 tablespoons **all-purpose flour** until mixture is smooth and bubbling. Whisk in 1½ cups **regular-strength chicken** or beef **broth** and 1 tablespoon **tomato paste;** stir until sauce boils. Remove from heat; stir in 6 tablespoons **sour cream.** Add **pepper** to taste. Use hot.

Oranges with Spiced Rum Syrup

In a 1½- to 2-quart pan, bring to boiling ½ cup **sugar,** 1½ cups **water,** and 2 teaspoons **whole cloves;** boil until reduced to ¾ cup. Remove from heat and stir in 2 tablespoons **rum.** Let stand until cool or, if made ahead, cover and chill up to 5 days.

With a sharp knife, cut peel and membrane from 4 large **oranges.** Slice fruit into dessert bowls; add syrup. Serves 6.

PER SERVING: 139 calories, 1 g protein, 32 g carbohydrates, 0.4 g fat, 0 mg cholesterol, 2 mg sodium

Succulent cabbage rolls bake under topping of whole-wheat dough. To serve, cut through golden crust and scoop out rolls and sauce.

Australian Ways with Lamb

AUSTRALIAN COOKS *bring a practiced skill to cooking lamb. It's as familiar on dinner tables there as beef and chicken are here. So it's only natural that cooks have discovered innumerable ways to vary presentations. Lamb-loving Westerners will also appreciate these new flavors.*

Dining out in Australia's largest city reveals some new trends in cooking lamb. Sydney's Macleay Street Bistro combines tradition and invention, braising lamb shanks in red wine to serve with lentils. To brighten the dish, chefs add a garnish of chopped fresh tomato, chive stems, and a bouquet of mâche or tiny lettuce leaves.

Franca Corino, a native of Italy's Piedmont region, settled in the Australian Gold Rush town of Mudgee—about a 3-hour drive northwest of Sydney. (Mudgee, an Aboriginal word, means "nest in the hills.") For many years, she ran the Craigmoor Winery restaurant and featured, at the noon buffet, a leg of lamb seasoned with olive oil, garlic, and one of her favorite wines, a dry Semillon produced by her husband, Carlo. Beneath the roasting lamb, she tucked small halved potatoes to absorb the savory juices.

The result resembles the traditional Australian Sunday dinner of roast lamb with potatoes and two or more vegetables, but with an update: Mrs. Corino cooks the lamb only to medium-rare, a practice that is gradually replacing the Aussie preference for well-done meat.

Some butchers in larger Australian cities display a wide variety of ready-to-cook lamb cuts conveniently seasoned, marinated, stuffed, or skewered. These meats are ready to pop into the oven, into the frying pan, or onto the "barbie." Worth duplicating at home is one favorite from Sydney's Double Bay section, a shoulder roast stuffed with spinach and pine nuts.

Another Mudgee cook, Louise Wilson, takes an easy, informal approach to lamb. Cubed lamb shoulder needs no browning before it goes into a deep casserole to make an oven stew. Tart apple, white wine, and tangy malt vinegar counter the meat's naturally sweet flavor.

Lamb shanks oven-braised in red wine are served with savory lentils and a colorful garnish. Recipe comes from a bistro "down under."

MACLEAY STREET LAMB SHANKS WITH SAVORY LENTILS

- 2 tablespoons salad oil
- 6 large lamb shanks, 5½ to 6 pounds total, bones cracked
- 1 large onion, thinly sliced
- 2 medium-size carrots, thinly sliced
- 2 stalks celery, thinly sliced
- 3 cloves garlic, minced or pressed
- 6 sprigs fresh thyme (each about 4 in. long), coarsely chopped; or ½ teaspoon dry thyme leaves
- 1 cup dry red wine
- 1¾ cups or 1 can (14½ oz.) regular-strength chicken broth
  Savory lentils (recipe follows)
- 1 small, firm-ripe tomato, cored and finely chopped
  Whole or chopped chives
  Salt and pepper

Pour oil into a 5- to 6-quart pan that can go into the oven. Place on medium-high heat. When oil is hot, add lamb shanks, 2 or 3 at a time (do not crowd), and brown well on all sides. Remove from pan as browned, and brown remaining shanks. Spoon out pan drippings; return 1 tablespoon to pan and save the remainder for lentils (recipe follows). Return shanks to pan along with the onion, carrots, celery, garlic, thyme, wine, and broth. Cover and bake in a 400° oven until lamb is very tender when pierced, 2 to 2½ hours.

Spoon lentils into wide, deep bowls or rimmed dinner plates; top equally with cooked vegetables, lamb shanks, and meat juices. Sprinkle with chopped tomato and chives; season to taste with salt and pepper. Makes 6 servings.

PER SERVING: 668 calories, 49 g protein, 53 g carbohydrates, 29 g fat, 98 mg cholesterol, 165 mg sodium

Savory lentils. Pour **reserved drippings** from lamb shanks into a 2- to 3-quart pan. Finely chop 1 large **onion** and add to pan; stir often over medium heat until onion is limp but not brown, 6 to 8 minutes.

Sort through 2 cups (1 lb.) **lentils**, removing debris. Rinse and drain lentils, then add to onion along with 3½ cups **regular-strength chicken broth.** Bring to a boil on high heat. Cover, reduce heat, and boil gently until lentils are tender to bite, about 35 minutes. Add **salt** and **pepper** to taste.

FRANCA'S ROAST LAMB

    1   leg of lamb, 6 to 6½ pounds
    4   cloves garlic
    2   cups dry white wine such as
        Australian or domestic dry
        Semillon
    3   tablespoons fresh or 1 tablespoon
        dry rosemary leaves
    2   tablespoons olive oil
   16   to 20 small (1½- to 2-in.-diameter)
        thin-skinned red potatoes
    2   teaspoons *each* butter or
        margarine and all-purpose flour
        Salt and pepper

Trim and discard surface fat from lamb. Thinly slice 2 cloves of the garlic; make small, shallow cuts in surface of lamb and insert a garlic slice into each.

In a large plastic bag set in a pan, combine wine, rosemary, oil, and remaining

garlic, minced or pressed; add lamb, turning to coat. Seal bag and chill at least 4 hours or up until next day; turn bag over several times.

Cut potatoes in half and place, cut sides down, in a 12- by 15-inch roasting pan. Place a V-rack in pan. Remove lamb from marinade; reserve marinade. Place lamb on the rack. Insert a meat thermometer in thickest part of meat, touching the bone. Roast, uncovered, in a 350° oven, until thermometer registers 135° for medium-rare (145° in the center of the largest muscle), about 2 hours.

Transfer lamb and potatoes to a platter and keep warm. Skim and discard fat from pan, if necessary. Add butter to pan and melt on medium heat. Blend in flour, then smoothly mix in the reserved marinade; stir to scrape free browned bits. Stirring, bring to a boil on high heat. Pour into a bowl. Slice meat and serve with potatoes and sauce; add salt and pepper to taste. Makes 8 to 10 servings.

PER SERVING: 345 calories, 40 g protein, 15 g carbohydrates, 13 g fat, 138 mg cholesterol, 109 mg sodium

LAMB SHOULDER ROAST WITH SPINACH & PINE NUTS

        About ¾ pound spinach
    2   tablespoons olive oil
    ¼   cup pine nuts
    1   small onion, finely chopped
    1   clove garlic, minced or pressed
    ½   teaspoon dry oregano leaves
        Coarsely ground pepper
    ½   cup soft bread crumbs
    1   lamb shoulder, 4 to 4½ pounds,
        boned
        Salt

Discard roots, coarse stems, and yellowed leaves of spinach. Wash leaves well. Stack leaves, then cut crosswise into about ½-inch-wide slivers. Set aside.

In a 5- to 6-quart pan over medium heat, combine oil and nuts; stir often until nuts are golden, about 6 minutes. Remove from pan with a slotted spoon; set aside. Add onion to pan; cook, stirring often, until limp but not browned, 4 to 6 minutes. Add garlic, oregano, ⅛ teaspoon pepper, and spinach. Stir just until spinach is limp, about 2 minutes. Remove from heat and mix in crumbs and nuts.

Trim and discard most of the surface fat from lamb. Lay meat flat, boned side up, and cover with plastic wrap. With a

flat mallet, pound meat gently and firmly to flatten evenly. Spread spinach mixture over the meat, leaving about a 1½-inch margin on all sides. Starting from the most irregular long side, roll meat up snugly. Use string to tie snugly at about 1½-inch intervals.

Place meat, fat side up, on a rack in a 12- by 15-inch roasting pan. Sprinkle generously with pepper. Insert a meat thermometer in center. Roast, uncovered, in a 350° oven until thermometer registers 145° for medium-rare, about 1 hour and 15 minutes. Slice roast ½ inch thick. Add salt to taste. Serves 6 to 8.

PER SERVING: 308 calories, 30 g protein, 4.9 g carbohydrates, 19 g fat, 102 mg cholesterol, 146 mg sodium

LOUISE WILSON'S OVEN LAMB STEW

    2   to 2½ pounds boneless lamb
        shoulder, fat trimmed, cut into
        1-inch cubes
    ¾   teaspoon dry rosemary leaves
    ¼   teaspoon pepper
    2   cloves garlic, minced or pressed
    2   medium-size tart apples, peeled,
        cored, and sliced ¼ inch thick
    4   to 6 medium-size carrots, thinly
        sliced
    1   can (14½ oz.) pear-shaped
        tomatoes
    ½   cup dry white wine
    2   tablespoons malt vinegar
    1   tablespoon Worcestershire
    1   tablespoon all-purpose flour
        mixed smoothly with 2
        tablespoons water
        Salt

Mix lamb with rosemary, pepper, and garlic. Place about a third of the meat in a deep 3- to 3½-quart casserole; cover with apple slices. Add another third of the lamb and cover with carrots, then add remaining lamb.

Whirl tomatoes in food processor or blender until puréed. Mix with wine, vinegar, and Worcestershire; pour over lamb. Cover casserole tightly. Bake in a 375° oven until lamb is very tender when pierced, 2½ to 3 hours; stir once or twice after 1 hour.

Skim and discard fat from stew, if necessary. Stir flour mixture into stew. Cover and return to oven until liquid bubbles, about 5 minutes. Add salt to taste. Makes 6 servings.

PER SERVING: 220 calories, 20 g protein, 17 g carbohydrates, 8.2 g fat, 71 mg cholesterol, 223 mg sodium

Fila Stands in for Puff Pastry

A QUICK, LIGHTWEIGHT SUBSTITUTE *for puff pastry, fila dough comes in paper-thin sheets. Buttered sparingly and stacked, they create a layered pastry that's easy to work with and much less rich than the classic puff pastry alternative.*

Simply cut the fila stacks into one of a variety of shapes and fill them to make a main dish, a napoleon look-alike, or a savory appetizer.

Sold refrigerated or frozen, fila dough is fragile and needs attentive handling. To thaw, leave airtight in refrigerator for about 8 hours; this method minimizes accumulation of moisture, which can make sheets gummy. When using, keep it airtight except when actually working with it; air dries fila quickly and makes it brittle. You can refreeze what you don't use, or keep it in the refrigerator 3 or 4 days (although it's inclined to mold).

FILA CALZONE

  16 sheets fila dough (about ¾ lb.), thawed if frozen
      About ½ cup (¼ lb.) melted butter or margarine
      Chicken-vegetable filling (recipe follows)

Keep fila covered with plastic wrap, except when using, to prevent drying and breaking. Lay 1 sheet of fila on a flat surface and brush lightly with melted butter. Lay another sheet on top of the first and brush lightly with butter. Repeat for 2 more layers, but do not butter the top layer. Repeat process to make 3 more 4-layer stacks.

With an 8-inch plate or pan as a guide, use a very sharp knife to cut 2 rounds from each fila stack; reserve scraps, if desired. Put 1 round on a 12- by 15-inch baking sheet; put ⅛ of the filling on half the round, leaving about a ¾-inch rim. Fold plain half over filling. Working quickly, lightly brush entire edge with water; roll rim over a few times, to meet the filling. Press rolled rim firmly to seal. Push filled calzone to the end of the pan; repeat process to fill and shape 3 more calzones. Using another 12- by 15-inch baking sheet, repeat to fill remaining fila for 4 more calzones.

Brush tops of calzones lightly with melted butter, then carefully cut a 1-inch slit in the center of the top of each. If desired, arrange fila stack trimmings in a single layer around calzones; brush lightly with butter. Bake calzones in a 350° oven until fila is golden brown, about 25 minutes. With a wide spatula, carefully slide calzones onto plates and serve at once. Offer scraps as an accompaniment. Makes 8.

PER CALZONE: 392 calories, 18 g protein, 35 g carbohydrates, 20 g fat, 70 mg cholesterol, 341 mg sodium

Chicken-vegetable filling. Coarsely chop 2 large **red bell peppers;** 2 **zucchini** (about 1 lb. total), ends trimmed; and 1 small **onion.** In a 10- to 12-inch frying pan over medium-high heat, stir-fry vegetables in 3 tablespoons **olive oil** until barely tender when pierced, about 5 minutes. Transfer vegetables to a bowl.

To frying pan add ½ cup **dry white wine;** 2 tablespoons *each* chopped **fresh thyme leaves** and **fresh basil leaves** (or 1½ teaspoons *each* of dry herbs); and 1 large firm-ripe **tomato,** cored, seeded, and finely diced.

Bring to a boil and cook until reduced to about ½ cup, 7 to 10 minutes; remove from heat. Mix 1½ tablespoons **cornstarch** with 1 tablespoon **water;** add to tomato mixture along with vegetables and 2½ cups **cooked chicken** cut into ½-inch cubes. Season to taste with **salt, pepper,** and 2 to 3 tablespoons **lemon juice.** If made ahead, cover and chill up until next day.

FILA NAPOLEONS

   4 sheets fila dough (about 3 oz.), thawed if frozen
   2 tablespoons melted butter or margarine
   ¼ cup granulated sugar
      Berry cream filling (recipe follows)
      Powdered sugar

Lay 1 sheet of fila on a flat surface. Brush lightly with butter and sprinkle with 1 tablespoon sugar. Lay another sheet on top of first; brush lightly with butter and sprinkle with 1 tablespoon sugar. Repeat with remaining fila, butter, and sugar to make a 4-layer stack.

Cut the fila stack into 24 equal rectangles, each about 2 by 4 inches. Place rectangles slightly apart on 2 lightly buttered 12- by 15-inch baking sheets.

Golden, flaky fila calzone holds a moist filling of cooked chicken cubes, coarsely chopped fresh vegetables, and herbs.

Neat rectangles of sugared and buttered fila stacks bake to golden brown. Assemble in tiers with berry cream filling to make fast, spectacular napoleons.

down into cup, fitting smoothly against bottom and sides, with edges poking up. Spoon filling equally into cups.

Bake in a 350° oven until filling feels set when lightly touched and fila is golden brown and crisp, about 20 minutes. Let cool about 5 minutes. With the tip of a blunt knife, gently ease pastries from pan and serve warm. If made ahead, let cool, then package airtight and chill up until next day. To reheat, set pastries in a 10- by 15-inch pan and place in a 400° oven until hot, 10 to 15 minutes. Makes 24.

PER PIECE: 100 calories, 3.2 g protein, 6.5 g carbohydrates, 6.9 g fat, 30 mg cholesterol, 132 mg sodium

Artichoke filling. Dice 1 package (9 oz.) thawed **frozen artichoke hearts.** In an 8- to 10-inch frying pan over medium-high heat, cook the artichokes with 2 tablespoons **butter** or margarine until slightly browned, 5 to 6 minutes.

In a bowl, beat 1 large **egg** with ½ cup **half-and-half** (light cream) until blended. Add 1 cup (8 oz.) **ricotta cheese,** ½ cup grated **parmesan cheese,** and 2 tablespoons finely chopped **fresh basil leaves** or 1½ teaspoons dry basil leaves. Add the warm artichoke mixture and **salt** and **pepper** to taste; mix well.

Bake in a 350° oven until rectangles are golden brown and crisp, about 20 minutes. With a wide spatula, carefully transfer fila rectangles to racks to cool. If made ahead, store airtight up to 3 days.

To assemble, use half the berry cream filling to top 8 of the fila rectangles equally. Spread cream to make level on pastries, then align another fila rectangle on top of each of the first 8. Top with remaining filling.

Level cream, then set remaining fila, sugared side up, on each pastry. Dust liberally with powdered sugar. Serve; or chill, lightly covered, no longer than 1 hour. Makes 8 servings.

PER SERVING: 212 calories, 2.3 g protein, 24 g carbohydrates, 12 g fat, 41 mg cholesterol, 100 mg sodium

Berry cream filling. Beat 1 cup **whipping cream** until it will hold soft peaks, then mix in ¼ cup **powdered sugar** and ½ teaspoon **vanilla.** Gently fold in 1 cup rinsed and drained **raspberries.** Use at once.

FILA FLOWER APPETIZERS

  16 **sheets fila dough (about ¾ lb.), thawed if frozen**
  5 **or 6 tablespoons melted butter or margarine**
    Artichoke filling (recipe follows)

Keep fila covered with plastic wrap, except when using, to prevent drying and breaking. Lay 1 sheet of fila on a flat surface and brush lightly with melted butter. Lay another sheet on top of the first; brush lightly with butter. Repeat for 2 more layers; do not butter the top layer. Repeat to make 3 more 4-layer stacks.

Cut each stack into 12 equal squares. To make each cup, center 1 square on buttered muffin cup (2 in. wide); set another square on top, rotating so there are 8 corners. Gently press center of fila

Flower-like appetizers are baked in muffin cups with artichoke and ricotta cheese filling.

Matzo Bagels

BY TRADITION, *many Jews do not eat leavened breads during Passover. One result of this proscription is a bagel made without flour and yeast, but with matzo meal and egg; a spicy variation contains currants and cinnamon. Another is a biscuit made with crushed matzos and egg.*

These unleavened breads are dense in texture. They're best eaten the day of baking.

BOILED & BAKED MATZO MEAL BAGELS

⅓ **cup salad oil**
⅔ **cup water**
   About 1 cup matzo meal
 2 **large eggs, separated**
¼ **teaspoon cream of tartar**
 2 **tablespoons sugar**
 1 **large egg yolk beaten with
    1 tablespoon water**

In a 2- to 3- quart pan, combine oil and water. Bring to boiling on high heat. All at once, dump 1 cup matzo meal into pan; stir vigorously until evenly moistened. Remove from heat and let stand until cool enough to touch. Add 2 egg yolks, 1 at a time, beating well.

In a bowl, whip whites and cream of tartar on high speed until frothy. Gradually add 1 tablespoon sugar, beating on high speed until whites hold stiff peaks. Beat half the whites into matzo mixture, then fold in remaining whites until mixed.

Meanwhile, in a 4- to 5-quart pan over high heat, bring 3 quarts water and remaining 1 tablespoon sugar to a boil; adjust heat to keep at a gentle boil. Also, oil a 12- by 15-inch baking sheet and sprinkle lightly with matzo meal.

Divide dough into 6 equal portions. Coat hands with matzo meal and firmly shape each portion into a 2½-inch-diameter round. Dip thumb in matzo meal, then make a hole with thumb through the center of each round. Transfer bagels on a wide spatula, 1 at a time, into simmering water; cook 5 minutes. With a slotted spoon, lift each bagel from water and set on prepared baking sheet.

Brush bagels with yolk mixture. Bake in a 375° oven until golden brown, 40 to 50 minutes. Serve hot or cool. Makes 6 bagels, 1 or 2 for a serving.

PER BAGEL: 239 calories, 4.7 g protein, 22 g carbohydrates, 15 g fat, 106 mg cholesterol, 23 mg sodium

BAKED MATZO MEAL BAGELS WITH CURRANTS & SPICE

⅓ **cup salad oil**
⅔ **cup water**
 1 **cup matzo meal**
 1 **tablespoon sugar**
¼ **cup dried currants or raisins**
½ **teaspoon ground cinnamon**
 3 **large eggs**

In a 1½- to 2-quart pan, combine oil and water. Bring to boiling on high heat. All at once, dump 1 cup matzo meal into pan; stir vigorously until moistened. Let stand until cool enough to touch. Add sugar, currants, cinnamon, and eggs, 1 at a time, beating well after each.

Divide dough into 6 equal portions. Moisten hands with water and shape each portion firmly into a ball. Space balls well apart on a nonstick or oiled 12- by 15-inch baking sheet. Dip thumb in water; press to make a hole in the center of each round.

Bake in a 375° oven until golden brown and crisp, 40 to 45 minutes. Serve hot or cool. Makes 6 bagels, 1 or 2 for a serving.

PER BAGEL: 255 calories, 5.6 g protein, 25 g carbohydrates, 15 g fat, 106 mg cholesterol, 33 mg sodium

MATZO BISCUITS

⅓ **cup salad oil**
⅔ **cup water**
 2 **cups coarsely crushed matzo
    (about 6 pieces, about 6-in.
    square), plain or egg and onion
    flavor**
 3 **large eggs**

In a 1½- to 2-quart pan, combine oil and water. Bring to boiling on high heat. All at once, dump crushed matzo into pan; stir vigorously until evenly moistened. Let matzo mixture stand until cool enough to touch. Add eggs, 1 at a time, beating well after each.

Lightly oil a 12- by 15-inch baking sheet. Drop mixture in about ¼-cup mounds about 2½ inches apart on pan; flatten with back of spoon to make about 1 inch thick. Bake in a 375° oven until golden brown, 35 to 40 minutes. Serve hot, at room temperature, or cool. Makes 10 biscuits; allow 1 or 2 for a serving.

PER BISCUIT: 157 calories, 3.7 g protein, 15 g carbohydrates, 8.9 g fat, 64 mg cholesterol, 19.3 mg sodium

Bagel look-alikes and biscuits are made with matzo meal; egg glaze gives shine. Dense in texture, they are best eaten the day of baking.

Graham Flour in Breads & Muffins

BACK IN THE 1800s, *Sylvester Graham—a strong advocate of healthful living—introduced a radically new flour made using the entire wheat kernel.*

Originally, graham flour was less finely milled (ground) and coarser in texture than regular whole-wheat flour. But as interest in the flavor and nutritional value of whole-grain flours has increased, the precise distinction between graham flour and whole-wheat flour has blurred.

You may find that your market carries graham flour, whole-wheat flour that's also labeled graham, or just whole-wheat flour. The first two will usually be coarser in texture than the last, but all three can be used interchangeably.

We take advantage of the distinctive toasted flavor of graham or whole-wheat flour in three breads.

The sturdy muffins, made with graham flour only, are dotted with tart bites of dried apricot. The loaf, studded with bits of chocolate, is more tender because it contains part all-purpose flour. Both these breads are good with butter or cream cheese for breakfast; or offer them as a mid- or late-day snack with tea or coffee. The yeast bread is a hearty mix of graham flour, cornmeal, and all-purpose flour; slices are particularly good toasted.

APRICOT GRAHAM MUFFINS

1½   **cups graham or whole-wheat flour**
½   **cup toasted wheat germ**
3   **tablespoons granulated sugar**
2   **teaspoons baking powder**
1   **teaspoon baking soda**
½   **cup chopped dried apricots**
½   **cup chopped pecans or walnuts**
5   **tablespoons butter or margarine, melted and cooled**
2   **large eggs**
1   **cup unflavored yogurt**
  About 3 tablespoons firmly packed brown sugar

In a bowl, mix graham flour, wheat germ, granulated sugar, baking powder, soda, apricots, and nuts. In another bowl, beat to blend butter, eggs, and yogurt; add to dry mixture and stir just until moistened.

Spoon batter into well-greased 2½-inch muffin-pan cups, filling to the rim. Sprinkle brown sugar evenly over each muffin.

Bake in a 375° oven until edges are golden brown and center is firm to touch, about 20 minutes. Let cool slightly, then tip muffins out of pan. Serve warm, or cool on racks. If made ahead, store cool muffins airtight and hold at room temperature until next day; freeze to keep longer (thaw wrapped).

To reheat, wrap a single layer of muffins in foil and place in a 325° oven until hot, about 10 minutes. Makes about 12. —*Ayako Hill, Sacramento.*

PER MUFFIN: 206 calories, 5.9 g protein, 25 g carbohydrates, 10 g fat, 60 mg cholesterol, 218 mg sodium

GRAHAM & CHOCOLATE LOAF

2   **cups graham or whole-wheat flour**
1   **cup all-purpose flour**
1   **cup (6-oz. package) semisweet chocolate baking chips or raisins**
½   **cup chopped almonds or walnuts**
½   **cup firmly packed brown sugar**
1½   **teaspoons baking soda**
½   **teaspoon salt**
2   **large eggs**
1½   **cups buttermilk**

In a large bowl, mix graham flour, all-purpose flour, chocolate, nuts, sugar, soda, and salt. In a small bowl, beat eggs and buttermilk to blend; add to dry ingredients, stirring until moistened. Pour batter into a buttered 5- by 9-inch loaf pan.

Bake in a 350° oven until edges begin to pull from pan sides and toothpick inserted in center of loaf comes out clean, about 1 hour. Let cool in pan 10 minutes. Tip bread out of pan and let cool on a rack. Slice to serve; if made ahead, store loaf airtight at room temperature up to 3 days; freeze to store longer (thaw wrapped). Makes 1 loaf, about 2½ pounds.

PER OUNCE: 80 calories, 2.2 g protein, 13 g carbohydrates, 2.8 g fat, 14 mg cholesterol, 73 mg sodium

GRAHAM & CORNMEAL YEAST BREAD

2   **packages active dry yeast**
1½   **cups warm water (110°)**
1   **cup evaporated milk**
2   **tablespoons honey**
1   **tablespoon salad oil**
1   **teaspoon salt**
  About 3 cups all-purpose flour
2   **cups graham or whole-wheat flour**
1½   **cups yellow cornmeal**
1   **large egg, beaten to blend**

Graham or whole-wheat flour imparts toasty flavor and hearty texture to yeast bread with cornmeal, muffins with apricots, and a loaf with chocolate.

In a large bowl, sprinkle yeast over the water; let stand until yeast is softened, about 5 minutes. Add milk, honey, oil, salt, and 2½ cups all-purpose flour.

Beat mixture with a heavy spoon until the dough is well mixed and slightly stretchy. Add graham flour and cornmeal; mix with spoon until ingredients are moistened. Cover bowl with plastic wrap and let stand in a warm place until dough doubles in volume, about 1½ hours.

To knead with a dough hook, beat on high speed until dough no longer sticks to bowl, about 10 minutes; add remaining all-purpose flour as required.

To knead by hand, scrape dough onto a board coated with remaining all-purpose flour. Knead until dough is elastic and no longer sticky, about 10 minutes.

Divide kneaded dough in half. Shape each piece into a 6-inch round and place each on an oiled 12- by 15-inch baking sheet. Cover lightly with plastic wrap and let rise in a warm place until puffy, about 30 minutes. Remove plastic and brush loaves with egg.

Bake loaves in a 350° oven until richly browned, 45 to 50 minutes. (If using 1 oven, switch pan positions after 25 minutes.) Cool loaves on racks; serve warm or cool. If made ahead, wrap cool loaves airtight and hold at room temperature up until next day; freeze to store longer (thaw wrapped). Makes 2 loaves, each about 1½ pounds.

PER OUNCE: 73 calories, 2.3 g protein, 14 g carbohydrates, 1 g fat, 72 mg cholesterol, 53 mg sodium

Flour Tortillas—Soft or Crisp

SOFT AND PLIABLE *like a Mexican tortilla, or dry and brittle like Scandinavian crisp bread, this dough works either way. Cornmeal and ready-to-eat cereal add flecks of flavor to the wheat-flour base. Roll dough thin and bake to serve like a tortilla or soft taco; cook it twice to use as crisp bread.*

If you don't find the cereal mix in the supermarket, try a health-food store (or use bran cereal or puffed wheat).

FLOUR TORTILLAS PLUS

- 1 **cup ready-to-eat 9-grain cereal**
- 1 **cup yellow or white cornmeal**
- 2 **tablespoons salad oil**
- 1 **cup water**
  About 2¾ cups all-purpose flour
- 2 **teaspoons baking powder**

In a food processor, whirl cereal until half is finely ground. Add cornmeal, oil, and water; whirl to mix. (Or whirl cereal in a blender, then mix in a bowl with remaining ingredients.)

Mix 2¼ cups flour with baking powder. Whirl into cereal mixture until dough forms ball, about 30 seconds. If required, add more flour, 2 tablespoons at a time. (Or stir ingredients together and knead on a floured board until smooth and elastic, about 5 minutes.) Cover dough with plastic wrap and let stand until relaxed and elastic, at least 10 minutes.

Divide dough into 12 equal pieces; keep covered with plastic wrap or waxed paper to prevent drying. Shape 1 piece at a time into a ball; press each to make a round about 3 inches wide. Roll out on a floured board to make an 8-inch-wide round; flip often, adding flour to prevent sticking. Repeat for all balls; stack with plastic wrap or waxed paper between each layer.

In an ungreased 10- to 12-inch nonstick frying pan or on a nonstick griddle over medium-high heat, cook each tortilla, turning often, until dry and flecked with brown but still soft and flexible, about 4 minutes. Brush off excess flour and stack, as cooked, in an envelope made of foil. Serve warm. If made ahead, let cool. Keep airtight up to 2 days. Makes 12 tortillas. —*T.R. Mafit, Roseburg, Ore.*

PER TORTILLA: 135 calories, 3 g protein, 24 g carbohydrates, 2.6 g fat, 0 mg cholesterol, 72 mg sodium

Top warm tortilla with cheese, turkey, asparagus, and pimientos. When cheese starts to melt, fold tortilla to enclose filling.

Crisp tortillas. Follow recipe for **flour tortillas plus** (preceding). Quickly immerse each tortilla (warm or cool) in water; drain briefly. Lay rounds side-by-side on 12- by 15-inch baking sheets. Bake in a 500° oven for 4 minutes. Turn tortillas over with a wide spatula; bake until crisp, 1 to 2 minutes longer. If using 2 pans, switch positions halfway through baking.

TURKEY-ASPARAGUS SOFT TACOS

- 12 **medium-size (about ½ lb.) asparagus spears**
- 6 **flour tortillas plus (recipe precedes), warm and soft**
- 6 **ounces thinly sliced fontina cheese**
- ¾ **pound thinly sliced cooked turkey breast, cut into strips**
- 1 **jar (3 oz.) sliced pimientos**

Snap off and discard tough ends of asparagus. In a deep 10- to 12-inch nonstick frying pan over high heat, bring about 1 inch water to boiling. Add asparagus; cook, uncovered, until barely tender when pierced, 3 to 5 minutes. Drain and immerse in ice water. When cool, drain and set aside.

Dry pan and set on medium heat. Lay tortillas in pan, 1 at a time (use 2 pans to speed cooking), and quickly top each with ⅙ of the cheese, turkey, asparagus spears, and pimientos. Heat just until cheese begins to melt, about 1 minute; lift tortilla to fold in half over filling.

Hold tacos to eat, or serve on plates. Makes 6 servings.

PER TACO: 344 calories, 28 g protein, 27 g carbohydrates, 13 g fat, 72 mg cholesterol, 293 mg sodium

French Vinegar by Way of Boise

TURNING WINE *into vinegar is a natural transformation that's been understood for centuries. The basic chemistry is a two-step affair: yeast feeds on sugar in fruit juice, turning it into alcohol and creating wine. When the wine sours, the alcohol changes to vinegar.*

Romaine Galey Hon, of Boise, wanted to make vinegar the way she'd seen it made in French homes. In this process, adding a starter culture of bacteria and yeast cells—known as the "mother"—to small vats of wine slowly converts the wine to vinegar.

The problem for home vinegar makers is getting a mother to use as a starter. Ms. Hon attempted many methods, then worked with Dr. Russell Centanni, a microbiologist at Boise State University, who helped identify reliable procedures.

Unpasteurized vinegar, available in health- or natural-food stores, proved the best basis for producing a mother. When this vinegar is mixed with wine and water and stored in a warm place, a thin gelatinous film of bacteria and yeast cells grows over the surface. This film can convert alcohol to vinegar. Add more wine and water, and the mother converts them, in a month or so, to more vinegar.

You can continue to produce vinegar as long as you feed the mother proportionally correct amounts of wine and water and do not fill the container too full (the process needs oxygen). A good container to use is a large, clear, wide-mouth glass or plastic jar.

The mixture must stay in a consistently warm (70° to 85°) place. At higher or lower temperatures, the process may slow down or stop.

Because the jar is covered with porous fabric to provide ample air, contamination by molds and other bacteria can be a problem. Keep the developing vinegar in a clean place. If mold appears, or if peculiar non-vinegar odors develop, discard the mixture, sterilize the jar, and start again. While the wine is in the process of changing to vinegar, it has a strong acidic aroma. If you find this unpleasant, store the mixture away from your living quarters.

This homemade vinegar makes an excellent condiment. Use it to flavor foods as you would any wine vinegar; it's especially good on salads such as the one at right.

However, since you cannot determine its exact acid level, do not use it for canning or pickling, *procedures which require a certain percentage of acidity for food safety.*

HOMEMADE WINE VINEGAR

To create a mother. Rinse a 2- to 4-quart clear, wide-mouth glass or plastic jar with water. Pour ¾ cup dry red or white **wine** into the jar. Screw on lid and shake jar vigorously. Remove lid and let stand 5 to 10 minutes. Repeat shaking and airing wine 2 or 3 times; this helps eliminate any harmless gas that may have been added to wine to prevent the growth of vinegar bacteria. Add 1 cup **unpasteurized vinegar** and ¼ cup **water** (diluting the wine makes it easier for the vinegar bacteria to grow); shake to blend.

Rinse a double thickness of cheesecloth (about 3 in. larger than top of jar) and squeeze dry; place over the jar's rim and secure with a rubber band. Place jar in a warm place (70° to 85°), out of direct sunlight and away from house plants (so their microorganisms can't contaminate the vinegar). Let sit undisturbed until a whitish gelatinous film (about ⅛ in. thick) forms on the surface (this is the mother); it will probably take 2 to 4 weeks. Some liquid will evaporate.

To make vinegar. Aerate 3 cups **wine** (red or white, whichever you started with for the mother) by shaking it vigorously in a covered 2- to 4-quart jar; remove lid and let stand about 5 minutes. Repeat 2 or 3 more times. Add 1½ cups **water,** shake briefly to blend, and add to container with vinegar mother; do not fill jar more than ⅔ full.

The mother may dissipate when you add liquid, but it will form again. Rinse the cheesecloth until clean and replace on jar; secure with rubber band. Let stand at 70° to 85° until vinegar tastes as you like, 1 to 3 months (disturb as little as possible). During that time, the mother will grow thicker and eventually settle; then another will form on top. Extra mothers can be removed and transferred to other jars to start more vinegar: always add 2 parts aerated wine to 1 part water.

When the mixture tastes like vinegar, pour it through a fine strainer lined with 4 layers of damp muslin or fine-mesh cheesecloth. The vinegar is ready to use; return mother to vinegar-making jar.

To keep a mother from growing in the strained vinegar, you can chill the vinegar, covered.

Or pasteurize it to store at cool room temperature. Pour vinegar into a 3- to 4-quart pan. Cover and bring to boil over high heat, then boil for 3 minutes. Cool. Line the strainer with more clean, damp muslin or fine-mesh cheesecloth and pour vinegar through it, then into bottles. Cap bottles and keep in a cool place. If a mother starts to grow, repeat boiling process or refrigerate vinegar.

When you remove vinegar, feed the mother with aerated **wine** and **water** (2 parts wine to 1 part water, in any amount that does not fill the container more than ⅔ full), and repeat.

You can add more wine any time before the vinegar is ready, but it's best to collect leftover wines in the refrigerator, then add a large amount at one time. The mother works best undisturbed. And adding more wine before the current batch is ready dilutes the vinegar's acidity, delaying its progress. It's simpler to start a new batch. The first complete process makes about 1 quart.

GREENS WITH TARRAGON VINAIGRETTE

    8 cups (about 6 oz.) bite-size pieces
      butter lettuce, rinsed and crisped
    5 cups (about 3 oz.) bite-size pieces
      curly endive, rinsed and crisped
    1 cup cherry tomatoes, stemmed
      and cut in halves
    ¼ cup olive oil
    2 tablespoons homemade red or
      white wine vinegar (recipe
      precedes)
    1 clove garlic, pressed or minced
    1 tablespoon minced fresh or
      1 teaspoon dry tarragon leaves
      Salt and pepper

In a large salad bowl, combine the butter lettuce, curly endive, and tomatoes.

Mix together the olive oil, vinegar, garlic, and tarragon. Pour over greens and tomatoes and mix together. Add salt and pepper to taste. Makes 6 to 8 servings.

PER SERVING: 72 calories, 0.7 g protein, 2.5 g carbohydrates, 7.1 g fat, 0 mg cholesterol, 6.2 mg sodium

Three-Vegetable Soufflé

VERSATILE VEGETABLE SOUFFLÉS, *combined in layers or baked separately, lend a colorful note to party menus.*

In the first recipe, purées of spinach, carrot, and broccoli are stacked and baked to make a tricolor vegetable dish. Carrots or broccoli can also be the base of one-vegetable soufflés. Just make a triple batch of either purée. All these soufflés can be made ahead and served at room temperature or reheated. Egg and a little flour help these dense soufflés maintain their structure.

THREE-TIERED VEGETABLE SOUFFLÉ

Spinach purée (recipe follows)
Carrot purée (recipe follows)
Broccoli purée (recipe follows)
**Extra-virgin olive oil, lemon
  wedges, and pepper (optional)**

Oil a 9-inch-diameter cake pan (at least 2 in. deep) with removable rim. Spread spinach purée evenly over bottom of pan. Spread carrot purée over spinach, then top with the broccoli purée, spreading evenly. Bake in a 400° oven until top feels firm when gently pressed in center, about 45 minutes. Remove from oven and serve hot to room temperature.

If made ahead, let cool, then cover and chill up to 2 days. To reheat, cover with foil and bake in a 400° oven until warm in center (make a small cut to test), 40 to 45 minutes.

Slip a knife around pan sides, then carefully remove rim. Place soufflé on a plate; cut into wedges and offer oil, lemon, and pepper to add to taste. Makes 12 servings.

PER SERVING: 104 calories, 6.8 g protein, 14 g carbohydrates, 2.9 g fat, 106 mg cholesterol, 85 mg sodium

Spinach purée. Discard stems and yellow leaves from 1¾ pounds **spinach.** Wash leaves well and drain (you should have about 9 cups, lightly packed). Place leaves in a 5- to 6-quart pan; cook, covered, over medium heat, stirring several times, until leaves are wilted. Pour leaves into a colander set in a bowl; let drain. When cool to touch, squeeze excess liquid from spinach with your hands, reserving liquid.

In a food processor or blender, smoothly purée spinach with 3 tablespoons of the reserved liquid; 2 **large eggs;** ¼ cup **all-purpose flour;** 2 cloves

Multicolored wedge of vegetable soufflé boasts three savory layers: spinach, carrot, and broccoli. Soufflé can be made ahead and served at room temperature or reheated.

garlic, minced or mashed; and 1 teaspoon grated **lemon peel.** Add **salt** to taste.

Carrot purée. In a 2- to 3-quart pan, bring to a boil 1 cup **water** and 1 tablespoon chopped **fresh thyme leaves** or 1 teaspoon dry thyme leaves. Add 3 slender (½ lb. total) **carrots,** peeled and quartered, and 1 small **onion,** coarsely chopped. Cook, covered, over medium-high heat until carrots are very tender when pierced, about 20 minutes; drain well. In a food processor or blender, smoothly purée carrots, onion, 2 **large eggs,** and ¼ cup **all-purpose flour.** Add **salt** to taste.

Broccoli purée. Cut off and discard tough ends from ½ pound **broccoli;** peel stems. Chop enough flowerets and peeled stems to make 2 cups. In a 2- to 3-quart pan, bring 1½ cups **water** to a boil. Add broccoli and 1 small **onion,** coarsely chopped; cook, covered, over medium-high heat until broccoli is just tender when pierced, about 8 minutes. Drain thoroughly; spread out on paper towels and pat dry. In a food processor

or blender, smoothly purée broccoli mixture, 2 **large eggs,** and ¼ cup **all-purpose flour.** Add **salt** to taste.

SOLO VEGETABLE SOUFFLÉ

Follow the recipe for **three-tiered vegetable soufflé** (preceding), but make only 1 vegetable purée with either the carrots or broccoli (the spinach mixture is very dense when used on its own), tripling the ingredients.

Cook the mixture as directed for carrot or broccoli purée in a 5- to 6-quart pan. If using the blender, purée vegetables in 2 batches. Bake as directed. Accompany the broccoli or carrot soufflé with the extra-virgin olive oil, lemon wedges, and pepper to add to taste. Or top the carrot soufflé with shredded **fontina cheese** and minced **parsley.** Each soufflé makes 12 servings.

PER SERVING BROCCOLI SOUFFLÉ: 109 calories, 7.5 g protein, 15 g carbohydrates, 3 g fat, 106 mg cholesterol, 60 mg sodium

PER SERVING CARROT SOUFFLÉ WITHOUT CHEESE: 103 calories, 5 g protein, 15 g carbohydrates, 2.8 g fat, 106 mg cholesterol, 51 mg sodium

Turnips in a Whole New Light

FREQUENTLY OVERLOOKED *and often lacking for advocates, turnips tend to be relegated to use as a flavor backup in soups and stews. In fact, though, this root can more than hold its own and adapts readily to many cooking methods. When paired with appropriate seasonings, turnips' natural sweetness is enhanced.*

These two recipes present turnips in a flattering light. In the first, cooked turnips are mashed with potatoes and mixed with roasted garlic and onion. In the second, turnip wedges are basted with a mixture of lime juice, chili powder, cumin, and cilantro, then oven-roasted until golden and tender.

Either dish makes a fine accompaniment for grilled or roasted meats.

MASHED TURNIPS & POTATOES WITH ROASTED GARLIC & ONIONS

Try this as a robust alternative to plain mashed potatoes.

- 2 tablespoons olive or salad oil
- 1 large (about ½ lb.) onion, chopped
- 3 large heads garlic (about 9 oz. total), unpeeled
- 1¼ pounds (about 2 large) turnips, peeled
- 1½ pounds (about 2 large) russet potatoes, peeled
- 1½ cups regular-strength chicken broth
- ¼ cup low-fat or whole milk
  Salt and pepper

Pour oil into a 10- by 15-inch baking pan. Add onion and mix until evenly coated. Push onion to 1 side to make room for garlic. Cut garlic heads in half crosswise. Set garlic, cut sides down, in pan.

Roast garlic and onion in a 375° oven until garlic is very tender when pierced all the way to the center and onions are browned, about 45 minutes; stir onions (without disturbing garlic) occasionally during cooking. Set aside until cool enough to handle.

Meanwhile, quarter the turnips and potatoes. Place them in a 3- to 4-quart pan with chicken broth. Bring the broth to a boil over high heat, then cover and simmer until vegetables are very tender when pierced and cooking liquid is almost all gone, 25 to 35 minutes. Check frequently to avoid scorching.

While turnips and potatoes are cooking, squeeze garlic out of papery husks (discard husks) and place in a small bowl. With the back of a spoon, mash garlic to a smooth paste. Mix in roasted onions. Set mixture aside.

Transfer turnips and potatoes to a large bowl and, with an electric mixer or potato masher, beat hot vegetables until they are in small lumps. (If desired, run vegetables through a food mill to remove any tough turnip fibers.)

Add the milk and the garlic-onion mixture; beat until vegetables are smooth and creamy. Spoon into a shallow 1½- to 2-quart casserole.

Broil 4 inches from heat until top is dappled with golden brown spots, about 5 minutes. Serve hot; add salt and pepper to taste. Makes 6 servings.

PER SERVING: 192 calories, 5.2 g protein, 32 g carbohydrates, 5.5 g fat, 0.8 mg cholesterol, 81 mg sodium

OVEN-ROASTED TURNIPS WITH CILANTRO & LIME

- 3 pounds (about 4 large) turnips
- 1 cup lightly packed fresh cilantro (coriander) leaves, minced
- ¼ cup lime juice
- 2 tablespoons extra-virgin olive oil or salad oil
- 1 tablespoon honey
- 1 teaspoon chili powder
- ½ teaspoon ground cumin
  Salt and pepper

Peel turnips and cut into ½-inch wedges. Spread out in a 9- by 13-inch baking pan. Set aside.

Combine cilantro with lime juice, oil, honey, chili powder, and cumin; stir until well blended. Pour about half the mixture over the turnips and gently mix until all wedges are evenly coated.

Roast in a 450° oven until wedges are browned and very tender when pierced, about 50 minutes, basting every 10 minutes with remaining cilantro mixture until all is used. Transfer to a platter and serve warm. Add salt and pepper to taste. Makes 6 servings.

PER SERVING: 93 calories, 1.5 g protein, 13 g carbohydrates, 4.9 g fat, 0 mg cholesterol, 110 mg sodium

Smooth and creamy, mashed turnips and potatoes are flavored with sweet roasted garlic and onion. Serve with grilled or roasted meats.

Polenta: Savory or Sweet

SOFT OR FIRM, SAVORY OR SWEET, coarsely ground cornmeal—known as polenta—is a versatile, healthy, and tasty addition to a meal.

When cooked with lots of water, polenta swells up to a creamy consistency. Spoon a simple tomato and Italian sausage sauce over the hot mush for a satisfying family supper.

Cooked with less liquid (here we use orange juice) and sweetened, the firmer polenta goes into molds. Serve with fruit for breakfast or dessert.

Look for polenta in many supermarkets or Italian delicatessens. Or substitute finer-ground yellow cornmeal for the polenta.

SOFT POLENTA WITH SAUSAGE SAUCE

- 1 **pound mild or hot Italian sausages (or use a combination of both)**
- 1 **can (28 oz.) pear-shaped tomatoes**
- 1½ **cups polenta or yellow cornmeal**
  Salt
  Grated parmesan cheese (optional)

Squeeze sausages from casings into a 10- to 12-inch frying pan. Stir over high heat until browned and crumbly, about 5 minutes. Remove and discard all fat.

Pour tomatoes, including liquid, into pan. With a spoon, break tomatoes into small pieces. Boil gently, uncovered, stirring occasionally, until sauce is thick and most of the liquid evaporates, 15 to 20 minutes.

Meanwhile, in a 4- to 5-quart pan, bring 7 cups water to a boil. Gradually add polenta, stirring until blended. Reduce heat to low and stir often with a long-handled spoon until polenta is smooth and soft to bite (be careful: mixture is very hot and spatters) and thick enough to flow only slightly when mounded, 8 to 10 minutes. Add salt to taste. At once pour polenta into a bowl and top with sausage sauce. Add parmesan cheese to taste. Makes 6 servings.

PER SERVING: 331 calories, 15 g protein, 34 g carbohydrates, 15 g fat, 43 mg cholesterol, 726 mg sodium

ORANGE POLENTA CAKE

- ½ **teaspoon grated orange peel**
- 2½ **cups orange juice**
- ½ **teaspoon salt (optional)**
- 1 **cup polenta or yellow cornmeal**
- ¼ **cup honey**
- 2 **tablespoons butter or margarine**
- 2 **tablespoons sweetened, shredded dry coconut (optional)**
  About 2 cups peeled sliced fruit (such as kiwi fruit, oranges, bananas)
- 1 **cup unflavored yogurt, sweetened to taste with honey (optional)**

In a 2- to 2½-quart pan, bring orange peel, juice, and salt to a boil. Gradually add polenta, stirring until blended. Boil gently, uncovered, stirring with a long-handled spoon over medium heat, until thick, about 1 to 1½ minutes (be careful: hot mixture splatters). Reduce heat to low; stir until polenta stops flowing after spoon is drawn across pan bottom, 3 to 5 minutes. Stir in honey and butter.

Spoon equal portions of the hot mixture into 4 or 5 buttered custard cups or decorative molds (½- to ¾-cup size). Press polenta solidly into cups. Let cool at least 5 minutes, or up to 30 minutes. Run a knife around edge of each mold and invert onto plates. If made ahead, cover and hold at room temperature up to 2 hours.

Stir coconut in a 6- to 8-inch frying pan over medium heat until golden, about 5 minutes. If made ahead, cool and wrap coconut airtight up until the next day.

Serve polenta cakes hot, warm, or at room temperature. Sprinkle cakes with toasted coconut. Offer fruit and yogurt to add to each portion. Makes 4 or 5 servings.—*Lisa Sturgis, Temecula, Calif.*

PER SERVING: 353 calories, 4.5 g protein, 75 g carbohydrates, 5.6 g fat, 12 mg cholesterol, 52 mg sodium

Firm orange polenta cake, served with fruit and yogurt, is a nutritious breakfast. Individual portions are shaped in buttered custard cups or decorative molds.

More April Recipes

OTHER APRIL ARTICLES *suggest a refreshing watercress and pear salad and a selection of lively zabaglione desserts.*

WATERCRESS & PEAR SALAD WITH FIG & GINGER DRESSING

An exotic combination of textures and flavors—buttery pear, crisp watercress, dried fig and crystallized ginger dressing—distinguishes this lively-tasting salad. Sherry wine vinegar balances the sweetness of the figs.

- 3 tablespoons chopped crystallized ginger
- 6 dried figs (about 4 oz. total)
- ½ cup sherry wine vinegar or seasoned rice vinegar
  About ¾ cup water
- ⅓ cup extra-virgin olive oil or salad oil
- 2 medium-size (about 1¼ lb. total) firm-ripe Comice or Anjou pears
- 4 cups (12 oz.) lightly packed watercress sprigs, rinsed and crisped

Assertive purée of dried figs and ginger dresses fan of sliced ripe winter pear. Serve on bed of fresh watercress sprigs.

In a 1- to 1½-quart pan, combine ginger, figs, vinegar, and ½ cup water. Bring to a boil on high heat, then cover tightly and simmer until figs are very tender when pierced, about 40 minutes. Set covered pan aside to cool completely.

Drain cooking liquid into a glass measure; add water to make ⅔ cup liquid total. Choose 3 nicely shaped figs; cover and set aside up until next day. Place remaining figs, cooking liquid, and oil in a blender; whirl until smooth. If made ahead, cover and chill up until next day.

Core pears; cut lengthwise into ¼-inch-thick slices. Divide watercress and place sprigs equally on each of 6 salad plates. Fan equal portions of the pear slices on each plate. Cut reserved figs in half and set 1 half-fig at base of each fan. Spoon dressing over pears. Serves 6.

PER SERVING: 201 calories, 1 g protein, 24 g carbohydrates, 13 g fat, 0 mg cholesterol, 17 mg sodium

SPIRITED ZABAGLIONE

Tiny bubbles, whipped into heating egg yolks, wine, and sugar, create the classic Italian dessert zabaglione, best enjoyed warm. Because you can make it in minutes and vary its flavor with different liquids—dry or late-harvest wines, or liqueurs—it's perfect for emergencies.

- 4 large egg yolks
- 2 tablespoons sugar
- ¼ cup dry or late-harvest wine or liqueur (choices follow)
  Seasoning accents (choices follow)
  Garnish (optional, choices follow)

In a round-bottom zabaglione pan or top of a double boiler, beat together egg yolks, sugar, wine, and seasonings.

Place round-bottom pan over medium gas heat or high electric heat; set double-boiler top over simmering water. Whip mixture constantly with a wire whip or electric mixer until foam is just thick enough to briefly hold a peak when whip is withdrawn, 5 to 6 minutes. Volume should triple or quadruple. Immediately pour zabaglione into 4 dessert goblets. Garnish as desired. Makes 4 servings.

Late-harvest wine & thyme zabaglione. Follow recipe for **spirited zabaglione** (preceding); add 3 more tablespoons **sugar.** Use ¼ cup **late-harvest white wine,** such as Johannisberg Riesling or Sauvignon Blanc. Season with 1 teaspoon **lemon juice** and ¼ teaspoon minced **fresh thyme leaves** or ⅛ teaspoon dry thyme leaves. Garnish with **thyme sprigs.** Serves 4.

PER SERVING: 133 calories, 3 g protein, 16 g carbohydrates, 6 g fat, 272 mg cholesterol, 9 mg sodium

Anisette & lime zabaglione. Follow recipe for **spirited zabaglione** (preceding); use ¼ cup **anisette liqueur** and 2 tablespoons **water.** Season with ¾ teaspoon grated **lime peel** and ½ teaspoon **poppy seed.** Garnish with **lime wedges** to squeeze onto zabaglione. Serves 4.

PER SERVING: 130 calories, 3 g protein, 11 g carbohydrates, 6 g fat, 272 mg cholesterol, 8 mg sodium

Chocolate & chili zabaglione. Follow recipe for **spirited zabaglione** (preceding); use ¼ cup **chocolate-flavor liqueur** and 2 tablespoons **water.** Season with 1 teaspoon grated **orange peel,** ½ teaspoon **vanilla,** and ⅛ to ¼ teaspoon **crushed dried hot red chilies.** Garnish with **semisweet chocolate curls.** Serves 4.

PER SERVING: 131 calories, 3 g protein, 11 g carbohydrates, 6 g fat, 272 mg cholesterol, 8 mg sodium

Hazelnut & mint zabaglione. Place ⅓ cup **hazelnuts** in 9-inch pie or cake pan. Bake in 350° oven until golden under skin (crack 1 open to check), about 20 minutes. Follow recipe for **spirited zabaglione** (preceding); use ¼ cup **hazelnut-flavor liqueur** and 2 tablespoons **water.** Season with 2 teaspoons minced **fresh mint leaves.** Serve with hot nuts; garnish with **mint sprigs.** Makes 4 servings.

PER SERVING: 174 calories, 4 g protein, 12 g carbohydrates, 10 g fat, 272 mg cholesterol, 9 mg sodium

A little cream mixed with lemon helps dressing cling to crisp salad leaves.

JEAN'S DRESSING WITH MIXED GREENS

Jean's dressing (recipe follows)
6 cups (about ½ lb. total, untrimmed) lightly packed, rinsed, and crisped butter lettuce leaves
5 cups (about 6 oz. *total*) lightly packed, rinsed, and crisped watercress sprigs, Belgian endive, or radicchio (or a combination)
Salt and pepper

Makes 8 or 9 servings.—*Jean Rappaport, Los Angeles.*

PER SERVING: 70 calories, 0.8 g protein, 13 g carbohydrates, 7.1 g fat, 3.7 mg cholesterol, 11 mg sodium

Jean's dressing. In a large salad bowl, whisk together ¼ cup **salad oil** or extra-virgin olive oil, 3 tablespoons **lemon juice,** 2 tablespoons **whipping cream,** 1 tablespoon minced **onion,** and 1 clove **garlic,** minced or pressed. Use or, if made ahead, cover and chill up until next day. Makes about 1 cup.

Steamed dill dumplings top ground beef chili; serve with crunchy, sour dill pickles.

CHILI WITH DILL DUMPLINGS

1 pound ground lean beef
1 large (about 8 oz.) onion, chopped
1 large (about 8 oz.) green bell pepper, stemmed, seeded, and chopped
1 tablespoon salad oil
3 tablespoons chili powder
1 can (28 oz.) tomatoes
2 cans (15 oz. each) butter beans
Dumpling dough (recipe follows)
Dill pickles

In a 4- to 5-quart pan over high heat, combine beef, onion, bell pepper, and oil. Stir often until meat is crumbled and browned, about 25 minutes. Stir in chili powder, and tomatoes and beans with their liquids. Simmer, uncovered, to blend flavors, about 15 minutes.

Drop dough in about 2-tablespoon portions onto chili. Cover and cook until dumplings are dry in centers (cut to test), about 20 minutes. Accompany with pickles. Makes 4 to 6 servings.—*Mrs. Joseph Farah, Lake Oswego, Ore.*

PER SERVING: 497 calories, 26 g protein, 47 g carbohydrates, 24 g fat, 95 mg cholesterol, 878 mg sodium

Dumpling dough. In a bowl, combine 1 cup **all-purpose flour,** 1½ teaspoons **baking powder,** and ½ teaspoon **dry dill weed.** Blend 1 **large egg,** ½ cup **milk,** and 1 tablespoon **salad oil.** Add liquids to flour mixture; stir until moistened.

Simmer zucchini, onion, bacon, and basil in broth; whirl to a smooth soup.

ZUCCHINI SOUP

5 slices bacon
3 pounds zucchini, ends trimmed, chopped
1 large (about 8 oz.) onion, chopped
3 tablespoons chopped fresh basil leaves or 2½ teaspoons dry basil leaves
1 clove garlic
5 cups regular-strength chicken broth
Fresh basil leaves (optional)
Salt and pepper
Freshly grated parmesan cheese or finely shredded jarlsberg cheese (optional)

In a 6- to 8-quart pan over medium-high heat, stir bacon often until crisp, 5 to 8 minutes; discard drippings. To pan, add zucchini, onion, basil, garlic, and broth. Bring to a boil and simmer, uncovered, until zucchini is soft when mashed, about 15 minutes.

In a blender, whirl half the zucchini mixture at a time until smoothly puréed. If made ahead, cover and chill up to 3 days; to serve, return to pan over medium heat and stir until steaming.

Ladle hot soup into wide bowls; garnish with basil leaves. Add salt, pepper, and cheese to taste. Makes about 10 cups, 8 to 10 servings.—*Audree Swanson, Arcadia, Calif.*

PER SERVING: 58 calories, 3.9 g protein, 6 g carbohydrates, 2.5 g fat, 2.7 mg cholesterol, 82 mg sodium

ONION, PEA & PEANUT SALAD

- 1 large (about 8 oz.) red onion, thinly sliced
- 5 tablespoons rice vinegar
- 1 tablespoon soy sauce
- 2 tablespoons finely chopped mango chutney
- 2 packages (10 oz. each) frozen petite peas, thawed and well drained
- 16 large butter lettuce leaves, rinsed and crisped
- ½ cup salted peanuts

Put onion slices in a deep bowl and add water to cover. With your hands, squeeze slices until almost limp. Drain, rinse, and drain again. To onions in bowl, add ¼ cup vinegar and about 2 cups *each* ice cubes and water; let slices stand until crisp, 20 to 30 minutes; drain. Add remaining vinegar, soy sauce, and chutney to onions. If made ahead, cover and chill up until next day.

Stir peas with onion mixture. Lay 2 lettuce leaves, cup sides up, on each of 8 salad plates. Spoon salad equally onto lettuce leaves; sprinkle with nuts. Makes 8 servings. —*Pat Albertson, Palm Springs, Calif.*

PER SERVING: 120 calories, 6.2 g protein, 15 g carbohydrates, 4.8 g fat, 0 mg cholesterol, 315 mg sodium

Butter lettuce cradles salad of tiny peas, red onion, and salted peanuts.

APPLE COUNTRY CHICKEN

- 1 large (about 8 oz.) Golden Delicious apple, cored
- 1 large (about 8 oz.) onion
- 1 teaspoon curry powder
- 2 cups apple juice or cider
- 1 tablespoon lemon juice
- ¼ pound mushrooms, sliced
- 1 teaspoon chicken-flavor instant bouillon
- 3¼ to 3½ pounds chicken thighs, skinned
- 1 tablespoon all-purpose flour
- 2 tablespoons sliced green onion
- 1 cup unflavored yogurt (optional)

Chop apple and large onion; set aside.

In a 12-inch frying pan or 5- to 6-quart pan over medium heat, stir curry until slightly darker, about 4 minutes. Add apple, onion, 1½ cups apple juice, lemon juice, mushrooms, and bouillon; bring to a boil. Add chicken; cover and simmer until meat is no longer pink at bone (cut to test), about 30 minutes. With a slotted spoon, transfer chicken to a platter and keep warm.

Blend remaining juice and flour. Add to pan and stir often on high heat until reduced to 3 cups; pour over chicken. Garnish with green onions; add yogurt to taste. Makes 4 or 5 servings. —*Carolyn E. Gilbaugh, Wenatchee, Wash.*

PER SERVING: 300 calories, 34 g protein, 23 g carbohydrates, 7.2 g fat, 140 mg cholesterol, 373 mg sodium

Skinned chicken thighs simmer in sauce of apple juice, apple, curry, onion, and sliced mushrooms.

FRESH STRAWBERRY CREAM TORTE

- 1 package (8 oz.) cream cheese
- ½ cup sugar
- 1 cup whipping cream
  Nut crust (recipe follows)
- 3 cups strawberry halves

In a bowl, beat cheese and sugar at high speed until fluffy. Still beating, pour cream into cheese in a thin stream (if added too fast, mixture thins). Spread cream mixture evenly in crust. (If made ahead, cover and chill up until next day.) Mound strawberries on cream; remove pan rim. Makes 9 to 12 servings. — *Monica Barton, San Jose, Calif.*

PER SERVING: 364 calories, 4.2 g protein, 27 g carbohydrates, 28 g fat, 74 mg cholesterol, 181 mg sodium

Nut crust. In a blender or food processor, whirl ½ cup **pecans** or walnuts to a fine powder. To processor add 1½ cups **all-purpose flour,** 2 tablespoons **sugar,** and ¾ cup (⅜ lb.) chilled **butter** or margarine, in chunks. Whirl until mixture holds together. Or rub with fingers to make fine crumbs; pat into a ball. Press dough over bottom and 1 inch up the sides of a 9-inch-diameter cake pan with removable rim.

Bake in a 325° oven until a rich golden brown, 30 to 40 minutes. Cool in pan. If made ahead, wrap airtight and keep up until next day.

Bright strawberries rest on sweet cream cheese filling in cooky crust with ground nuts.

CHEFS OF THE WEST *are old hands at making salads, but they're often guarded when it comes to sharing their recipes for salad dressings. The thinking seems to be that anyone can chop, tear, tatter, and slice a variety of vegetables, but it takes a special talent to whip up a dressing that elevates the produce above mere rabbit food. We are grateful to Rodney Garside for declassifying the recipe for his Creamy French Dressing.*

The creaminess results from the thorough agitation a blender brings to the oil, vinegar, wine, and egg. Garlic and mustard add tang, and catsup or chili sauce confers a rosy hue, as well as a touch of sweetness.

CREAMY FRENCH DRESSING

⅓ cup salad oil
¼ cup catsup or tomato-based chili
  sauce
1 clove garlic, minced or pressed
  (optional)
3 tablespoons red wine vinegar
½ teaspoon dry mustard
1 large egg
3 tablespoons dry red wine

In a blender whirl oil, catsup, garlic, vinegar, mustard, egg, and wine for about 15 seconds. Serve, or pour into an airtight container and chill up to 1 week.

(If you are concerned about the safety of raw egg in dressing, chill mixture 48 hours before serving.) Makes about 1¼ cups; allow 1 to 2 tablespoons for a serving.

PER TABLESPOON: 40 calories, 0.4 g protein, 1 g carbohydrates, 3.7 g fat, 10 mg cholesterol, 37 mg sodium

Rodney Garside

Tuolumne, Calif.

WHY CREOLE *and not Cajun Shrimp Cakes? It probably makes little difference what you call them. Paul Prudhomme, a recognized authority, says that although Creole is an older and more citified cuisine than Cajun, the resemblances are greater than the differences. He prefers* to call them both simply Louisiana cooking. Gordon Nartker's shrimp cakes, if they were Cajun, would probably contain a half-dozen more herbs and spices.

Nartker's recipe calls for 3 tablespoons of liquid hot pepper seasoning; ever mindful of possible litigation, we have reduced this quantity. If you are a professional fire-eater, you may use the full amount.

CREOLE SHRIMP CAKES

1 to 2 tablespoons salad oil
1 cup chopped onion
¾ cup chopped green bell pepper
¾ cup diced celery
2 cans (8 oz. each) tomato sauce
1 cup regular-strength chicken broth
1 teaspoon dry oregano leaves
½ teaspoon ground cumin
½ to 1 teaspoon liquid hot pepper
  seasoning
2 large eggs
1½ cups cooked long-grain white rice
½ cup oat bran
¾ pound shelled cooked tiny shrimp
  Lime or lemon wedges

"Chefs of the West are often guarded when it comes to sharing their recipes for salad dressings."

Pour 1 tablespoon oil into a 3- to 4-quart pan over medium heat; add onion, bell pepper, and celery. Stir often until vegetables are soft, about 10 minutes; add a little more oil if vegetables stick. Mix in tomato sauce, broth, oregano, cumin, and hot pepper seasoning to taste. Bring to a boil, then reduce heat and simmer, uncovered, for 10 minutes; set aside.

In a bowl, beat eggs to blend with rice, oat bran, and about 1 cup of the tomato sauce mixture.

Divide rice mixture equally among 6 very well greased 2½-inch muffin cups. Bake in a 350° oven until rice cakes are dry to touch, about 25 minutes.

When cakes are ready, invert onto a platter and keep warm. Return sauce to high heat and stir until boiling; add shrimp to sauce and pour into a bowl. Garnish cakes with lime wedges.

On individual plates, ladle sauce onto cakes and squeeze on lime juice to taste. Makes 6 first-course or 3 entrée servings.

PER FIRST-COURSE SERVING: 340 calories, 20 g protein, 76 g carbohydrates, 5.8 g fat, 181 mg cholesterol, 642 mg sodium

Gordon E. Matthew

Littleton, Colo.

S AMUEL NASH'S "SALSA" *has affinities both with its Mexican namesake and with Spanish gazpacho; you could think of it as* gazpacho firma.

The Mexican product is loosely based on tomato, onion, garlic, green and red bell peppers, and vinegar, while Nash's Mediterranean version also includes cucumber and basil, with oil to smooth. Thoroughly Mediterranean feta cheese goes into the mixture at the very end. Then you eat it— either as an independent dish or mixed with leafy greens as a salad.

MEDITERRANEAN SALSA

    4   medium-size (about 2 lb. total) firm-ripe tomatoes, cored, seeded, and chopped
    4   green onions (ends trimmed), thinly sliced
    ½   cup seeded and diced cucumber
    ½   cup finely diced green or red bell pepper

"If you are a professional fire-eater, you may use the full amount."

    ¼   cup olive oil
    2   tablespoons white wine vinegar
    1   teaspoon pepper
    1   clove garlic, minced or pressed (optional)
    1   tablespoon dry basil leaves
    ½   teaspoon dry marjoram leaves
    6   ounces feta cheese, crumbled

In a large bowl, combine tomatoes, onions, cucumber, bell pepper, oil, vinegar, pepper, garlic, basil, and marjoram. If made ahead, cover and chill up until next day. Stir in feta cheese. Makes about 5 cups, 5 or 6 servings as a vegetable dish.

PER SERVING: 190 calories, 5.7 g protein, 9.2 g carbohydrates, 15 g fat, 25 mg cholesterol, 329 mg sodium

Samuel A. Nash

Merced, Calif.

I T'S HARD TO BEAT *a pork tenderloin: think of your favorite bites of a pork chop; then think of a piece of meat big enough to provide those bites from several chops; then imagine being freed from the work of getting the meat off the bone.*

Because it is very tender and has been trimmed of waste, the cut is somewhat expensive, but it's well worth the cost— especially when enhanced by a marinade and barbecued over hot coals.

Harold Merkow's marinade, Asian in inspiration, has an unusual ingredient— powdered instant orange-flavor drink mix; we included it for authenticity but offer it as an alternative to freshly grated orange peel.

There's enough marinade to season another tenderloin, if you want more.

BARBECUED PORK TENDERLOIN

    1   pork tenderloin (¾ to 1 lb.)
    1   clove garlic, minced or mashed
    ¾   teaspoon ground ginger
    ⅛   teaspoon crushed dried hot red chilies
    ½   teaspoon dry mustard
    2   tablespoons firmly packed brown sugar
    ½   teaspoon grated orange peel, or ½ teaspoon powdered instant orange-flavor drink mix
    1   tablespoon salad oil
    3   tablespoons rice vinegar
    1   tablespoon soy sauce
    1   teaspoon cornstarch

Trim and discard excess fat and membrane from pork. In a deep bowl, stir to mix garlic, ginger, chilies, mustard, brown sugar, orange peel, oil, vinegar, and soy. Roll pork in mixture, then cover and chill at least 30 minutes or up to 3 hours; turn meat over several times.

Lift meat from marinade, drain briefly, and place on a lightly greased grill, 4 to 6 inches above a solid bed of hot coals (you can hold your hand at grill level for only 2 to 3 seconds). Brush pork with marinade, cover grill, and open dampers. Cook meat, turning to brown evenly and basting occasionally with marinade, until a meat thermometer inserted into thickest portion registers 150° to 155°, about 20 minutes. Transfer to a platter and keep warm. Add water to remaining marinade to make ½ cup *total*. Add cornstarch and stir over high heat until boiling.

To serve, cut meat crosswise into thin slices and spoon sauce onto slices. Makes 3 servings.

PER SERVING: 215 calories, 24 g protein, 12 g carbohydrates, 7.5 g fat, 74 mg cholesterol, 404 mg sodium

Harold J Merkow

Phoenix

April Menus

CELEBRATE APRIL *with a picnic lunch in the park, a bunny-shaped cake for Easter brunch, and a hot-cold main-dish salad for supper.*

PORTABLE LUNCH

Warm-up Vegetable Soup
Mashed Avocado   Tortilla Chips
Dry Salami   Sandwich Rolls
Grapes   Chocolate Chip Cookies
Fruit Juice in Boxes

Stow this lunch in a basket or a backpack and head out to enjoy the springtime air.

Only the soup needs temperature control; carry it in a thermos. Mash several ripe avocados, then flavor to taste with lemon juice, Dijon mustard, and salt; bring along as a dip for chips and a spread for salami sandwiches (allow about ⅛ lb. cold meat for a serving). Buy or make cookies. Plan to refresh en route with grapes and some of the individual cartons of juice.

WARM-UP VEGETABLE SOUP

1 tablespoon olive oil or salad oil
1 medium-size onion, chopped
½ pound mushrooms, sliced
1 teaspoon *each* dry oregano leaves, dry basil leaves, and dry marjoram leaves
6 cups (or 1 large can, 49½ oz.) regular-strength chicken broth
1 medium-size (about 6 oz.) thin-skinned potato, peeled and cut into ½-inch cubes
1 pound banana squash, peeled and cut into ½-inch cubes
¾ cup shell-shaped dry pasta
1 cup diced Roma-type tomatoes

To a 5- to 6-quart pan over medium heat, add oil, onion, and mushrooms; stir often until vegetables are tinged with brown, about 10 minutes. Stir in oregano, basil, marjoram, broth, potato, and squash. Bring mixture to a boil; cover and simmer until potatoes are tender to bite, about 15 minutes. Add pasta; simmer, covered, until tender to bite, about 8 minutes. Stir in tomato. If made ahead, let cool, cover, and chill up until next day; reheat to boiling to serve.

A stop in the woods: after a brisk walk, refresh with mugs of hot vegetable soup, salami sandwiches with avocado spread, and fruit and cookies for dessert.

To transport, pour soup into a vacuum bottle (at least 3-qt. size); serve within 3 hours. Makes 6 servings.

PER SERVING: 185 calories, 7.3 g protein, 30 g carbohydrates, 4.4 g fat, 0 mg cholesterol, 62 mg sodium

This carrot cake, shaped like a rabbit, is easy to assemble; children can help. It's perfect for Easter, of course, but appropriate for any April weekend.

After the egg hunt, present eggs to enjoy with fruit and the moist carrot cake. Bake the cake and frost it the night before, or save the decorating step to be part of the morning's fun.

BUNNY CARROT MUFFIN CAKE

Cut ears from stiff pink or white paper and stick behind head of frosted bunny. Use jelly beans or raisins for eyes.

- ½ cup (¼ lb.) butter or margarine
- 1 cup sugar
- 1 teaspoon grated orange peel
- 2 large eggs
- 2 cups shredded carrots
- 1⅓ cups all-purpose flour
- 1½ teaspoons baking powder
- 1 teaspoon ground cinnamon
- ¼ teaspoon ground nutmeg
- ½ cup chopped almonds or walnuts
  Cheese frosting (recipe follows)
  About 1 cup sweetened shredded dry coconut

Beat butter, sugar, and peel until fluffy. Beat in eggs, 1 at a time. Stir in carrots. Mix flour with baking powder, cinnamon, nutmeg, and nuts; stir into butter mixture. Pour into a buttered, floured 9-inch cake pan. Bake in a 350° oven until cake is firm in center when lightly pressed, about 25 minutes. Set on rack 15 minutes, then invert cake onto rack to cool. If made ahead, cover and chill up until next day.

Cut cake in half crosswise. Spread ¼ cup frosting on 1 piece; align second piece on top. Follow illustration above to

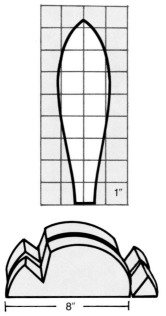

Cut wedge from cake halves for bunny's tail; make ears from stiff pink or white paper. Each square on ear equals 1 inch.

cut wedge for tail; from the round side of the cake, about 3 inches along perimeter from cut edge, cut a wedge about 2 inches wide at the outer edge and 2 inches deep (the notch is the dip behind the bunny's head). Tilt cake upright on cut side on a plate. Set wedge at end opposite V cut. Frost cake and pat with coconut. Add ears and eyes. Serve or, if made ahead, cover and chill up until next day. Makes 8 servings.

PER SERVING: 509 calories, 8.4 g protein, 57 g carbohydrates, 29 g fat, 116 mg cholesterol, 325 mg sodium

Cheese frosting. Beat together 1 large package (8 oz.) **cream cheese,** ½ cup **powdered sugar,** ¼ cup **unflavored yogurt,** and ½ teaspoon **vanilla.**

Stir-fried ground lamb in a savory sauce tops rice in lettuce leaves.

Coconut fur turns carrot muffin cake into Easter bunny with jelly bean eyes. If you like, garnish with carrots and watercress.

The day before, you can make the grapefruit relish and crisp the greens for the salad. About 30 minutes before serving, start the rice, then cook the lamb mixture and assemble the salad.

LAMB TUMBLE SALAD

- 1 tablespoon salad oil
- 1 pound ground lean lamb
- ¼ cup minced shallots or onions
- 1 garlic clove, minced or pressed
- ¾ cup minced fresh or ⅓ cup dry mint leaves
  Cooking sauce (recipe follows)
- 16 to 20 large leaves of butter lettuce, red-leaf lettuce, or radicchio, rinsed and crisped
  About 3 cups hot cooked white rice

Pour oil into a 10- to 12-inch frying pan over medium-high heat. When oil is hot, add lamb, shallots, and garlic. Stir and crumble meat frequently until it is well browned, 12 to 15 minutes. Add ⅔ cup of the mint and the cooking sauce and stir until boiling; remove from heat. Arrange lettuce leaves equally, cupped side up, among 4 dinner plates. Mound rice equally onto leaves, then spoon lamb mixture over rice; sprinkle with remaining mint. Serve at once. Makes 4 servings.

PER SERVING: 494 calories, 24 g protein, 44 g carbohydrates, 24 g fat, 76 mg cholesterol, 586 mg sodium

Cooking sauce. Mix together 2 teaspoons **cornstarch,** 1¼ teaspoons **hot chili oil** (or ¼ teaspoon crushed dried hot red chilies), 1 tablespoon **Oriental** sesame oil, 2 tablespoons **soy sauce,** and ¼ cup *each* **dry sherry** and **regular-strength chicken broth.**

FRESH GRAPEFRUIT RELISH

Select 3 medium-size (about 3 lb. total) **pink grapefruit.** With a vegetable peeler, pare yellow layer from peel of 2 grapefruit. Cut peel into long, thin shreds. In a 1½- to 2-quart pan, cover peel with 3 cups **water.** Bring to a boil; drain. Add ½ cup water, ¼ cup **sugar,** and ¼ cup chopped **crystallized ginger** to peel in pan. Boil on high heat, uncovered, until most of the liquid has evaporated, about 8 minutes; do not scorch. Remove from heat.

Cut peel from all grapefruit and cut segments free, catching juice in a bowl. Add 2 tablespoons juice to peel. If made ahead, cover and chill up until next day. Spoon fruit, juice, and peel into bowls. Serves 4.

PER SERVING: 170 calories, 1.3 g protein, 43 g carbohydrates, 0.2 g fat, 0 mg cholesterol, 10 mg sodium

Bomb Bread (page 104)

Informal meals for friends and family take the May spotlight. We begin with an intriguing bread, shaped like a bomb and full of hot air, that puffs and browns into a hollow balloon as it bakes. For casual outdoor entertaining, assemble a spaghetti-bar supper — guests top pasta with their choice of raw and cooked garnishes. Each of our nine easy family entrées can be ready to serve in about 15 minutes. Other articles include an introduction to Northwest cheeses and recipes for light salads, a stacked deli sandwich, and ice cream cones.

Italian Bomba Bread

FULL OF HOT AIR *and shaped like a bomb, this intriguing bread is aptly named in Italian:* bomba. *And at the table it's a stunning knockout—another translation for "bomba."*

Inspired by a bread he encountered in Italy, Franco Galli, of Il Fornaio America, developed this chewy-crisp, shapely cousin to pocket bread. In his restaurants, fast-cooking disks of dough go into a very hot brick pizza oven. As heat hits the thin dough rounds, they puff and brown to form ballooned hollows.

At home, you can get just as spectacular results by baking in a conventional oven. Make the yeast dough up to a day ahead or within an hour of baking.

The bread is at its best freshly baked. And because it takes only minutes to cook, you might invite guests to participate in making it. Roll dough into thin rounds, then bake one at a time for a showy appetizer. If they don't puff, check the oven temperature with a thermometer to make sure the oven's hot enough. Also handle the thin dough round carefully; beware of punctures. And even if they don't puff perfectly, bombas are delicious anyway.

Serve bread shiny with brushed-on extra-virgin olive oil. At the table, "explode" the bomb by cutting it open, then enjoy with prosciutto, olives, or cheese—and a mellow, smooth red wine such as a Chianti, Dolcetto, Merlot, or Rhône-style (French or domestic).

In minutes, wood-fired restaurant oven bakes bombas to golden brown; you can get the same results at home in a conventional oven.

BOMB BREAD
(Bomba)

- 1 **package active dry yeast**
- 2 **cups warm water (110°)**
  About ½ cup extra-virgin olive oil
- 1 **teaspoon salt**
  About 6 cups all-purpose flour

In a large bowl, soften yeast in warm water, about 5 minutes. Add ¼ cup olive oil and salt. Add 3½ cups flour; beat until dough is stretchy and elastic. Stir in 2¼ cups more flour.

To knead with a dough hook, beat the dough at high speed until it is stretchy and elastic, and comes away cleanly from sides of bowl, about 3 to 5 minutes; if dough is still sticky, add more flour, 1 tablespoon at a time.

To knead by hand, scrape dough onto a floured board and knead until smooth and elastic, about 10 minutes; add flour, as required, to prevent sticking. Place in a large bowl.

After kneading either way, cover dough with plastic wrap. Let rise in a warm place until doubled, about 1 hour; or let rise in refrigerator overnight. Punch dough down. On a well-floured board, divide dough into 5 equal pieces. Working with 1 portion of dough at a time, lightly knead to make a smooth ball (keep remaining dough covered with plastic wrap). With a floured rolling pin, roll ball evenly into a round ⅛ inch thick and 11 inches wide; occasionally lift round and dust with flour to prevent sticking. Carefully transfer round to a greased 12- by 15-inch baking sheet (take ·care to keep evenly thick and avoid puncturing).

Bake, 1 at a time, on the bottom rack of a 550° oven until golden all over and puffed, 4 to 6 minutes. (While 1 bread bakes, roll out another portion of dough.) Transfer hot breads to serving board, and brush with remaining olive oil. Serve hot or warm. To avoid flattening, use a sharp or serrated knife to cut into wedges. Makes 5 loaves, ½ pound each, enough for 8 servings.

PER OUNCE: 93 calories, 2 g protein, 14 g carbohydrates, 3 g fat, 0 mg cholesterol, 56 mg sodium

Thin round of yeast dough inflates with hot air as it bakes in hot oven; cooking takes only 4 to 6 minutes. Easy yeast dough can be made up to a day ahead, if you wish, or just before baking. Handle the thin dough round carefully to avoid punctures.

Glistening with extra-virgin olive oil, hollow bomba "explodes" when you cut it open at the table. For an eye-catching appetizer, serve the chewy-crisp bread warm with prosciutto and olives and a mellow red wine.

Step Up to the Spaghetti Bar

THE SPAGHETTI'S READY, *and you use it as the foundation on which to create your own pasta meal—lean to lavish, plain to fancy. As at a salad bar, at this garden party you pick and choose among a colorful collection of garnishes; some just need heating, some should cook a bit, some are enjoyed as is. Mix and warm them with cooked plain spaghetti. The barbecue is the obvious answer to your need for plenty of cooking space, but camp stoves and portable burners work well, too.*

This menu is designed for 8 to 10 hungry people as enthusiastic about the cooking as about the eating.

SPAGHETTI-BAR SUPPER

Spaghetti Ready on the Barbecue
Raw & Cooked Garnishes
Green Salad   Sourdough Bread
Strawberries   Grapes   Nectarines
Biscotti or Amaretti Cookies
Orvieto or Dry Sauvignon Blanc
Mineral Water

Have at least 1 frying pan (6- to 10-in. sizes are best) for every 3 guests. Have pot-holders and cooking spoons handy.

SPAGHETTI READY ON THE BARBECUE

Raw and cooked garnishes (choices follow)
About 1 cup extra-virgin or regular olive oil
Ready spaghetti (recipe follows)
About ½ pound freshly grated parmesan cheese

Have a barbecue with a solid bed of hot coals (you should be able to hold your hand at grill level for only 1 to 2 seconds). When charcoal briquets are almost covered with ash, scatter 10 to 15 more over coals to maintain steady heat, then add same amount every 30 minutes until you expect to cook no more than 30 minutes more. Or fire up several portable burners, such as camp stoves.

Add to a frying pan, without crowding, your choice of garnishes and a little oil to moisten. Place over heat and stir often until ingredients are cooked to suit your taste. Then add a portion of spaghetti and stir until it is warm, about 2 minutes. At this point you may want to add more garnishes (ones that don't need any cooking). Then pour the pasta onto a plate, top with cheese, and eat.

Wipe pan with paper towels and set aside until ready to try another combination. Makes 8 to 10 servings.

Ready spaghetti. In a 6- to 8-quart pan, bring 4 quarts water to a boil on high heat. Add 2 pounds **dry thin spaghetti** or vermicelli. Cook, uncovered, until tender to bite, about 12 minutes. Drain, pour into a large bowl, and mix well with 2 tablespoons **olive oil**. If made ahead, cover lightly and let stand up to 4 hours; mix again before serving. Makes about 15 servings, 1-cup size.

PER CUP: 239 calories, 7.5 g protein, 46 g carbohydrates, 2.5 g fat, 0 mg cholesterol, 1.2 mg sodium

RAW & COOKED GARNISHES

Browned Italian sausage nuggets. Remove casings from 1 pound *each* **mild and hot Italian sausage** (or use all 1 kind). Crumble meat into a 10- to 12-inch frying pan; cook over medium-high heat, stirring often, until well browned, 25 to 30 minutes; discard fat. If made ahead, cover and chill up to 2 days. Makes 3 cups.

PER ¼ CUP: 179 calories, 11 g protein, 0.8 g carbohydrates, 14 g fat, 43 mg cholesterol, 510 mg sodium

Tiny shrimp. Put 1 pound **shelled cooked tiny shrimp** in a small bowl.

PER ¼ CUP: 37 calories, 7.9 g protein, 0 g carbohydrates, 0.4 g fat, 74 mg cholesterol, 85 mg sodium

Golden onions. Peel and thinly slice 4 large (about 2 lb. total) **onions.** Put onions and 2 tablespoons **olive oil** in a 5- to 6-quart pan. Stir often on medium-high heat until onions are golden and sweet-tasting, 35 to 40 minutes. If made ahead, cover and chill up to 2 days. Makes 2 cups.

PER ¼ CUP: 65 calories, 1.2 g protein, 7.5 g carbohydrates, 3.6 g fat, 0 mg cholesterol, 2 mg sodium

Sautéed mushrooms. Rinse and drain 1 pound small (about 1-in. caps) **mushrooms.** In a 10- to 12-inch frying pan, combine mushrooms and 1 tablespoon **olive oil.** Cover and cook over medium heat until mushrooms are juicy, then uncover. Stir often on medium-high heat until liquid evaporates and mushrooms are lightly browned, 5 to 10 minutes longer. If made ahead, cover and chill up to 2 days. Makes about 1¾ cups.

PER ¼ CUP: 33 calories, 1.3 g protein, 3 g carbohydrates, 2.2 g fat, 0 mg cholesterol, 2.6 mg sodium

Red pimientos. Drain 2 small jars (4 oz. each) chopped **pimientos;** put pimientos into a small bowl. Makes 1 cup.

PER TABLESPOON: 1.9 calories, 0 g protein, 0.4 g carbohydrates, 0 g fat, 0 mg cholesterol, 1.7 mg sodium

Marinated artichokes. Pour 1 jar (6 oz.) **marinated artichoke hearts** and marinade into a small bowl. Makes about ¾ cup.

PER TABLESPOON DRAINED ARTICHOKES: 13 calories, 0.3 g protein, 1.1 g carbohydrates, 1.1 g fat, 0 mg cholesterol, 73 mg sodium

Green & gold vegetable confetti. Trim ends from 2 medium-size **zucchini.** Peel 2 medium-size **carrots.** Rinse and drain vegetables, then finely shred in a food processor or on a shredder. Mix to blend colors. If made ahead, cover and chill up to 4 hours. Makes about 4 cups.

PER ¼ CUP: 6.8 calories, 0.3 g protein, 1.5 g carbohydrates, 0 g fat, 0 mg cholesterol, 3.8 mg sodium

Cherry tomatoes. Stem, rinse, and halve 2 cups **cherry tomatoes.** Put in a small bowl; if done ahead, cover and let stand up to 4 hours. Makes 2 cups.

PER ¼ CUP: 9.4 calories, 0.4 g protein, 2.2 g carbohydrates, 0.1 g fat, 0 mg cholesterol, 3.9 mg sodium

Green onions. Trim ends from 8 **green onions,** then thinly slice onions and tops, and mound in a small bowl. If made ahead, cover and chill up to 4 hours. Makes 1¼ cups.

PER TABLESPOON: 1.5 calories, 0.1 g protein, 0.3 g carbohydrates, 0 g fat, 0 mg cholesterol, 0.2 mg sodium

Bell pepper slivers. Remove stems and seeds from 2 medium-size **yellow** or green **bell peppers** (or 1 of each color), then cut into thin slivers. Place in a small bowl. If made ahead, cover and chill up to 4 hours. Makes about 2 cups.

PER ¼ CUP: 4.6 calories, 0.2 g protein, 0.9 g carbohydrates, 0.1 g fat, 0 mg cholesterol, 0.5 mg sodium

Herb bouquet. Rinse and drain fresh herbs such as **basil, thyme, sage,** and **oregano;** put stems into a small vase with water. Or have jars of the dried herbs.

Garlic bowl. You need ½ cup minced **garlic;** buy prepared minced garlic, or mince or mash your own; spoon into a small bowl.

PER TABLESPOON: 15 calories, 0.6 g protein, 3.3 g carbohydrates, 0 g fat, 0 mg cholesterol, 1.7 mg sodium

Buffet spread offers the makings for pasta tailored to taste. Choices range from cooked tiny shrimp to raw zucchini and carrot. To frying pan of ingredients heated on the barbecue, guests add cooked spaghetti, then warm mixtures on the grill. Make small portions and try several combinations. With salad, bread, and fruit for dessert, it's a party!

Nine Quick Family Meals

ULTRASIMPLE AND FLEXIBLE, *these recipes provide quick meals for 2 to 4 people. Here we've taken three almost effortless dishes, each complete in about 15 minutes, and varied the short ingredient lists to make six more dishes.*

The advantage of these loosely structured recipes is that you can keep many of the ingredients on hand, in the cupboard, the refrigerator, and the freezer. Chances are, you'll find ways to improvise further.

One dish is based on filled flour tortillas that you bake crisp and hot. The second is fish cakes, featuring any seafood from fresh crab to canned tuna. The last dish takes its cue from risotto, with pasta instead of rice cooking in flavorful liquid to make a thick, soothing soup.

TORTILLA PACKETS WITH SPINACH & MOZZARELLA CHEESE

Use the microwave oven to thaw spinach quickly.

- 1 **package (10 oz.) frozen chopped spinach, thawed**
- 4 **flour tortillas (7-in. diameter)**
- 1 **tablespoon olive oil**
- ½ **pound mozzarella cheese, sliced**
- 4 **cloves garlic, minced**
- ½ **cup prepared spaghetti sauce**

This handy dinner takes 15 minutes to make. Hot tortilla packets, served with broccoli, nestle on top of warmed spaghetti sauce.

Toddler and mom fill warm tortilla with sliced mozzarella, garlic, and spinach.

Squeeze moisture from spinach; set spinach aside.

Lay tortillas in a single layer in 2 ungreased baking pans (10- by 15-in. size); brush tops with oil. Place in a 500° oven until tortillas are warm and more flexible, about 1 minute. Turn over tortillas.

Working quickly, place equal portions of cheese, garlic, and then spinach in center of each tortilla, mounding ingredients onto one another. Overlap opposite sides of each tortilla onto filling, then bring ends together to make closed packets. Turn packets flap side down to hold shut, and place well apart in one of the pans.

Bake in a 500° oven until tortillas are golden, about 6 minutes. Meanwhile, warm spaghetti sauce over direct heat or in a microwave oven. Spoon 2 tablespoons sauce per packet onto each of 2 to 4 dinner plates. Set tortilla packets into the sauce. Makes 2 to 4 servings.

PER SERVING: 315 calories, 16 g protein, 22 g carbohydrates, 19 g fat, 44 mg cholesterol, 559 mg sodium

Tortilla packets with pears & blue cheese. Follow directions for **tortilla packets with spinach and mozzarella cheese,** preceding, but omit spinach, garlic, and spaghetti sauce. Instead of oil, use melted **butter** or margarine. Instead of mozzarella use **blue cheese** such as cambozola or Bavarian blue, broken in chunks.

Peel, core, and thinly slice 1 large ripe **pear.** Rub slices lightly with **lemon juice** (about 1 tablespoon) to slow darkening. Fill each packet with cheese and ⅛ of the pear slices; bake. Serve with remaining fruit and **freshly ground pepper.**

PER SERVING: 326 calories, 14 g protein, 21 g carbohydrates, 21 g fat, 50 mg cholesterol, 961 mg sodium

Enchilada packets. Follow directions for **tortilla packets with spinach and mozzarella cheese,** preceding, but omit spinach. Instead of mozzarella, use ¾ pound sliced **jack cheese.** Instead of garlic, use 3 tablespoons minced **onion.** Use **prepared enchilada sauce** or salsa instead of spaghetti sauce.

PER SERVING: 436 calories, 23 g protein, 17 g carbohydrates, 31 g fat, 74 mg cholesterol, 869 mg sodium

CRAB CAKES

- 1 large egg
- 1 slice white bread, crust trimmed off and discarded, and bread crumbled
- ½ pound shelled cooked or drained canned crab
- 2 tablespoons minced bell pepper
- 2 tablespoons mayonnaise
- ⅛ teaspoon cayenne
- 1 tablespoon salad oil
  Seafood cocktail sauce

With a fork, beat egg with bread crumbs to moisten evenly. Add crab, bell pepper, mayonnaise, and cayenne; stir vigorously to break up crab into flaky pieces.

Pour oil into a 10- to 12-inch frying pan over medium heat. When oil is hot, spoon crab in 4 or 6 equal mounds into pan; flatten to make 1-inch-thick cakes. Cook until cake bottoms are lightly browned, about 5 minutes. Turn the crab cakes over with a wide spatula and cook until bottoms are lightly browned, about 4 minutes longer. Offer cocktail sauce. Makes 2 or 3 servings.—*Diane Rodgers, Burlingame, Calif.*

PER SERVING: 228 calories, 18 g protein, 3.9 g carbohydrates, 15 g fat, 173 mg cholesterol, 319 mg sodium

Salmon cakes. Follow directions for **crab cakes,** preceding, but omit cayenne and seafood sauce. Instead of crab, use 1 can (7½ oz.) **salmon,** drained, and add 1 teaspoon **curry powder.** Accompany with **Major Grey chutney** and **lemon wedges.**

PER SERVING: 236 calories, 15 g protein, 4.3 g carbohydrates, 17 g fat, 120 mg cholesterol, 395 mg sodium

Tuna cakes. Follow directions for **crab cakes,** preceding, but omit cayenne and seafood sauce. Instead of crab, use 1 can (6½ oz.) **tuna packed in water** or oil, drained. Add 2 tablespoons drained **capers** and ½ teaspoon **dry tarragon leaves** or dry thyme leaves. Serve with **seasoned rice vinegar** or white wine vinegar.

PER SERVING: 116 calories, 19 g protein, 3.6 g carbohydrates, 2.3 g fat, 115 mg cholesterol, 305 mg sodium

Canned salmon goes into crusty, curry-scented cakes seasoned with chutney and lemon. Warm peas in the same frying pan.

PASTA RISOTTO WITH ASPARAGUS

- 1 cup dry tiny pasta in rice, star, or letter shapes
- 3 cups regular-strength chicken broth
- 2 cups 1-inch-long asparagus pieces
  About ½ cup shredded parmesan cheese

In a 2- to 3-quart pan on high heat, bring pasta and broth to a boil. Reduce heat and boil gently, uncovered, 5 minutes. Add the asparagus pieces and simmer until pasta absorbs much of the liquid and the mixture is like thick soup, 7 to 10 minutes; stir often to prevent sticking.

Stir in ¼ cup cheese. Serve pasta risotto in wide bowls; offer additional parmesan to add to taste. Makes about 4 cups, 2 or 3 servings.

PER SERVING: 357 calories, 19 g protein, 55 g carbohydrates, 6.5 g fat, 11 mg cholesterol, 305 mg sodium

Spaghetti risotto with peas. Follow directions for **pasta risotto with asparagus,** preceding, but omit cheese. Use **spaghetti** broken into roughly ½-inch lengths instead of tiny pasta. After pasta has cooked 10 minutes, add 1 package (10 oz.) **frozen petite peas** instead of asparagus. When cooked, add 2 teaspoons **Oriental sesame oil.**

PER SERVING: 242 calories, 11 g protein, 37 g carbohydrates, 5.3 g fat, 0 mg cholesterol, 181 mg sodium

Tortellini risotto with green cabbage. Follow directions for **pasta risotto with asparagus,** preceding, but omit the parmesan cheese. Use 1 package (9 oz.) **fresh tortellini** (refrigerated or frozen) instead of the tiny pasta, **regular-strength beef broth** instead of the chicken broth, and 3 cups finely shredded **green cabbage** instead of the asparagus pieces. Accompany with **sour cream** to add to taste.

PER SERVING: 288 calories, 15 g protein, 40 g carbohydrates, 7.6 g fat, 0 mg cholesterol, 313 mg sodium

Northwest Cheeses

H OME TO THE COUNTRY'S *most contented cows (Washington is first among all 50 states in milk production per cow), the Northwest generates plenty of raw material for one of its fastest-growing cottage industries—cheesemaking. And the cuisine-conscious new producers don't stop at cows; they're using goats' and sheep's milk, too.*

A tasting party is a great reason to get together with friends and try some of the new, high-quality, limited-production Northwest cheeses (and maybe rediscover some old favorites). Some are sold in supermarkets. For the rest, look in specialty cheese shops, fancy food stores, and health-food stores throughout the West.

Or, to add some earthy authenticity to your cheese shopping, travel to a dairy farm. On page 112, we list farms and production facilities you can visit. Often you can taste and buy cheese on the premises; some also ship by mail. And many show you the cheesemaking process.

Fourth-generation cheesemaker Lora Lea Misterly shows off aging room at Quillisascut Cheese Company, northwest of Spokane.

THE NORTHWEST, A-CHEESING MORE TODAY THAN EVER IN ITS LONG PRODUCTION HISTORY

Commercial cheesemaking in the Northwest started at Tillamook, Oregon, in 1899 and focused for years on traditional cheddar, jack, colby, and Swiss. Today, selection is far more eclectic—and business is thriving. In May, Tillamook—perhaps the West's best-known producer—is set to open a $4-million viewing and manufacturing addition at its coastal plant.

Some Northwest cheesemaking reflects the ethnic heritage of the local community. A Dutch influence, for example, is evident in the gouda and edam production of Yakima Valley Cheese in Sunnyside, Washington. And in Salmon, Idaho, home of many Basques, Salmon Valley Cheese uses sausage flavors of linguisa and chorizo in its cheddar.

Well-supplied with milk from its dairy herds, Washington State University was inspired in 1943 to try making cheese; since then, its Cougar Gold has been a regional favorite. And WSU's short course in cheesemaking is more popular every year (see listing 12 on page 112).

Experiments by today's cheesemaking entrepreneurs have led to the availability of many cheeses that are either new to the area or just plain new. (Carla Koford of Portland, for example, makes fresh Guernsey milk mozzarella and plans to market one that's made, as in Italy, from water buffalo milk.)

KEY TO CHEESES SHOWN ON FACING PAGE

A Gouda
B Smoked baby Swiss
C Aged hard goat cheese
D Aged goat cheese with dried tomatoes and basil
E Aged goat cheese with mold
F Jack with linguisa seasoning
G Marbled cheddar and jack cheese
H Havarti cheese, made "light-style"
I Extra-sharp aged cheddar
J Edam
K Fresh goat cheese with herbs
L Natural Cougar Gold
M Camembert
N Sweetened fresh goat cheese and strawberry torta
O String cheese
P Jack with jalapeño chilies
Q Oregon blue-vein cheese
R Quark
S Sweetened goat cheese spread with pecans
T Aged goat cheese with lavender and fennel seed
U Jack

(Continued on page 112)

Star suppliers of raw material in Tillamook, Oregon, take well-deserved rest in dairy pasture along State Highway 6.

Northwest cheese-tasting party pairs cheeses with fruit and raw vegetables, crusty breads, and regional wines. Mix and match flavors to discover the cheeses' diverse character. Letters at left identify the cheeses shown here; the area produces many more.

THE CHEESY NORTHWEST: A FOUR-STATE DIRECTORY

Except for Appel, the producers listed below all have some sort of retail outlet. If you can't visit, you can mail-order from listings with an asterisk. Some places also have viewing windows or rooms; to see cheese being made, call ahead to check schedules.

WASHINGTON

1 *Appel Farm Quark,* c/o Langerfeld Imports, 580 E. Wiser Lake Rd., Lynden 98264; (206) 354-1125. Quark is a spreadable cheese that tastes like a mix of yogurt, cream cheese. Mail-order only.

2 *Pleasant Valley Dairy,* 6804 Kickerville Rd., Ferndale 98248; (206) 366-5398. Raw-milk classic Dutch gouda and farmstead cheese (firmer and more tart than gouda). Mail-order October to April 15. No store, but visitors can buy cheese in 2-pound wheels; call ahead.

3 *Washington Cheese Company,* 900 E. College Way, Mount Vernon 98273; (206) 424-3510. Tours, retail shop. Cheddar and cheddar varieties (such as smoked salmon cheddar), plain and flavored jack, mozzarella, low-fat cheeses. Open 9 to 5:30 Mondays through Saturdays.

4 *Sally Jackson Cheese,* Star Route 1, Box 106, Oroville 98844. Highlights of more than 24 cheeses are aged sheep's cheese wrapped in chestnut leaves, or rubbed with cocoa or wood ash; flavored soft chèvres; hard goat cheese flavored with dried Roma tomato, oregano, and basil; hard cow's milk cheese with herbs. Limited mail-order sales. Write to arrange a farm visit.

5 *Quillisascut Cheese Company,* 2409 Pleasant Valley Rd., Rice 99167; (509) 738-2011. Spanish-style goat's milk manchego is sold young (soft, sweet, nutty flavor) or aged (firm, piquant, good for grating). Also aged goat cheese with herbs. Maceres is a spread of aged and fresh goat cheese. Mail-order October through April. Visitors welcome to the rustic 26-acre farm; call ahead.

6 *Green River Cheese Co.,* 8260 S. 192 St., Kent 98032; (206) 872-7600. Office sells mozzarella in 1- and 5-pound loaves, 9 to 5 weekdays.

7 *Mazza Cheese Co.,* 1515 Puyallup St., Sumner 98390; (206) 863-3857. Mozzarella, provolone, feta. Call for a tour.

8 *Olympia Cheese Co.,* 3145 Hogum Bay Rd. N.E., Olympia 98506; (206) 491-5330. Cheddars and jacks, colby, string cheese, provolone, havarti, cream cheese, low-fat cheeses. Store, open 9 to 5 Mondays through Saturdays, offers samples. No viewing.

9 *Darigold Cheese Plant,* 67 S.W. Chehalis Ave., Chehalis 98532; (206) 748-8826. Cheddar, colby, jack made here, by Washington's largest cheese producer. No viewing. Store is open 8 to 5 weekdays.

10 *Mount Capra Cheese,* 279 S.W. 9th St., Chehalis 98532; (206) 748-4224. Makes feta-style Olympic, cheddar-type Alpine, herb goat cheese. Mail-orders locally year-round, out-of-state in winter. Store open 9 to 5 weekdays.

11 *Yakima Valley Cheese Company,* 100 Alexander Rd., Sunnyside 98944; (509) 837-6005. Known for gouda and edam. Store and viewing hours are 9:30 to 5 Mondays through Saturdays.

12 *Washington State University Creamery,* Troy Hall 101, Pullman 99164; 335-4014. No viewing. Store sells Cougar Gold, Viking (mild white cheese), cheddar. Cheeses come in cans but require refrigeration. Offers 3-day course in cheesemaking in March.

OREGON

13 *Tillamook County Creamery Association,* Box 313, Tillamook 97141; (503) 842-4481. Cheddar (some aged), colby, jack, and flavored versions of each. Large cheese and gift shop, with viewing, is open 8 to 6 daily. Restaurant features grilled cheese sandwiches.

14 *Blue Heron French Cheese Company,* 2001 Blue Heron Dr., Tillamook 97141; (503) 842-8281. Store in a picturesque barn sells camembert, brie, other cheeses; wine tasting. No viewing. Cheese now made out-of-state.

15 *Tall Talk Dairy,* 11961 S. Emerson Rd., Canby 97013; (503) 266-1644. Goat feta, jack, and spreadable flavored cheese. Tours of dairy by arrangement.

16 *Curly's Dairy,* 2310 Mission St. S.E., Salem 97302; (503) 362-2401. Cottage cheese and soft cream cheese. Store open 8 to 5 weekdays, 8 to 4 Saturdays. No viewing.

17 *Singing Winds Dairy,* 17225 Beck Rd., Dallas 97338; (503) 623-3021. Raw goat cheddar, pasteurized chèvres (herb and plain). Tour by appointment.

18 *Bandon Foods, Inc.,* Box 1668, Bandon 97411; (503) 347-2456. Best-known for cheddars, including a full cream cheddar and 12 flavored ones. Store sells cheese and gifts. Viewing windows, and a video on cheesemaking.

19 *Rogue Gold Dairy, Inc.,* 234 S.W. Fifth St., Grants Pass 97526; (503) 476-7786. Mild to sharp and raw-milk cheddars, flavored jacks. No viewing. Write or call for brochure.

20 *Rogue River Valley Creamery,* 311 N. Front St., Central Point 97502; (503) 664-2233. Oregon blue-vein (the only blue cheese produced in the West), cheddar, jack. Sales 9 to 5 weekdays; viewing.

21 *Klamath Falls Creamery,* 1310 Main St., Klamath Falls 97601; (503) 884-5101. Crater Lake cheddar and jack, and gift packs sold 8 to 5 weekdays.

IDAHO

22 *Rollingstone Chèvre,* 27349 Shelton Rd., Parma 83660; (208) 722-6460. At least 24 kinds of chèvre, including cheese layered with pesto and pistachio, dried tomato and basil, or Italian strawberry preserves; $10 to $16 a pound. Call to arrange a farm visit.

23 *Swiss Village,* Box 280, Nampa 83653; (208) 467-4424. Cheddar, longhorn cheddar, jack, marbled cheeses, flavored cheeses, low-fat cheeses. Retail hours are 8 to 6 Mondays through Saturdays, 10 to 5 Sundays. Restaurant and gift shop. Tours by arrangement.

24 *Salmon Valley Cheese,* Box B, Salmon 83467; (208) 756-3213. Baby Swiss, cheeses with linguisa or chorizo seasoning, and "dairy lite" havarti. Shop open 10 to 4 Mondays through Saturdays; tours by appointment.

MONTANA

25 *Glacier Mountain Cheese,* Box 268, Gallatin Gateway 59730; (406) 763-4433. Cheddar, colby, jack, and curds. Viewing from shop, which is open 9 to 5 weekdays, 10 to 6 Saturdays.

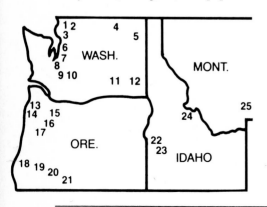

A Salad Newcomer: Mizuna

A NEWCOMER FOR SALADS *is showing up in many supermarkets: mizuna* (Brassica japonica). *Curiously, this mild-flavored and tender-firm member of the mustard family is not used in salads in its native land, Japan. There, where raw salads are unusual, mizuna is instead featured in soups and broth-based main dishes.*

Mizuna's jagged, feathery leaves are medium to light green, with a white vein running from the tip down. The full-bodied taste of mizuna is like that of arugula or frisée (baby curly chicory), but without the bite. You can sample mizuna in the dishes below.

Pieces of mizuna are often present in mixtures of tender leaves sold as mesclun. Mizuna is also sold in bunches; the stem end is sometimes a bit woody and should be trimmed off and discarded.

Mizuna is easy to grow (directions follow). Where summers aren't too hot and dry, plant batches in sequence, starting in May, so you have an ongoing crop. In hot-summer climates, wait until August or September to plant.

Mizuna seeds are fairly easy to find in Japanese nurseries and general merchandise or hardware stores. You can also get them through a number of specialty vegetable and Oriental vegetable catalogs. Here are two sources (price covers one pack of seeds and postage): Kitazawa Seed Co., 1748 Laine Ave., Santa Clara, Calif. 95051 ($2.50); Nichols Garden Nursery, 1190 N. Pacific Highway, Albany, Ore. 97321 ($1.85).

Feathery mizuna leaves (left) with mild, distinct flavor are tender-crisp in salads. Ladle dressing, tinted with puréed mizuna, over salad of mizuna and Belgian endive (right).

MIZUNA SALAD WITH MIZUNA DRESSING

- 4 **medium-size heads (about 1 lb. total) Belgian endive**
- ¾ **pound mizuna, bare stem ends trimmed off and yellow or bruised leaves discarded**
   Mizuna dressing (recipe follows)
   Salt and pepper

Rinse and drain endive and mizuna. Wrap loosely in towels and place in a plastic bag. Chill 30 minutes or up to 3 days.

Separate large leaves from endive and arrange 6 to 8, tips outward, on each of 8 salad plates. Sliver remaining endive finely and mound equally in the center of each salad. Reserve ¾ cup mizuna for dressing. Cut remaining mizuna into 2- to 3-inch pieces and top salads equally. Individually, add dressing and salt and pepper to taste. Serves 8.

PER SERVING WITHOUT DRESSING: 16 calories, 1.4 g protein, 3.1 g carbohydrates, 0.1 g fat, 0 mg cholesterol, 12 mg sodium

Mizuna dressing. In a food processor or blender, smoothly purée reserved **mizuna** (see above), ½ cup *each* **lowfat unflavored yogurt** and **mayonnaise,** 2 teaspoons *each* **lemon juice** and **soy sauce,** and 1 clove **garlic.** If made ahead, cover and chill up to 3 days. Makes about 1½ cups.

PER TABLESPOON: 37 calories, 0.3 g protein, 0.6 g carbohydrates, 3.7 g fat, 2.9 mg cholesterol, 58 mg sodium

SAUTÉED MIZUNA & ORECCHIETTE

- ¾ **pounds dry orecchiette (ear-shaped) pasta or pasta twists**
- ¼ **cup extra-virgin olive oil**
- 1 **pound mizuna, bare stem ends trimmed off and yellow or bruised leaves discarded, coarsely chopped**
- ¼ **teaspoon crushed dry hot red chilies**
   About ½ cup freshly grated parmesan cheese

In a 6- to 8-quart pan on high heat, bring about 4 quarts water to boiling. Add pasta and cook, uncovered, just until tender to bite, 6 to 10 minutes.

Meanwhile, place a 5- to 6-quart pan over high heat and add oil. When oil is hot, add mizuna. Stir until leaves are wilted, 2 to 4 minutes.

Drain pasta well and pour into a warm, wide bowl. Add mizuna and lift pasta with 2 forks to mix. Sprinkle with chilies and parmesan cheese; mix again. Makes 5 or 6 servings.

PER SERVING: 346 calories, 13 g protein, 46 g carbohydrates, 13 g fat, 6 mg cholesterol, 173 mg sodium

HOW TO GROW MIZUNA

Mizuna does best in full sun. Sow seeds directly in the ground, planting ¼ inch deep and a few inches apart; or start seeds in flats, then transplant later. With adequate moisture and good drainage, plants should thrive until the first hard frost. Mizuna will grow year-round indoors, or outdoors if weather is mild.

Seeds germinate in about 7 days. The sprouts are tasty, but for full-flavored leaves, harvest the light-colored greens in 3 to 7 weeks, when several thin stalks form a rosette of narrow leaves. As plants age, pick only tender leaves.

Classic Spinach Combinations

F EATURED IN *many classic combinations, particularly with cheese or chicken, spinach holds its color better than many green vegetables. But fresh spinach shrinks dramatically when cooked, so knowing how much to start with is a challenge. In these three main dishes, we give guidelines—and the option of using frozen spinach.*

SPINACH CASSEROLE

- 1 tablespoon butter
- 1 medium-size onion, chopped
- 4 large eggs
- 1 tablespoon red wine vinegar
- 1 cup chopped cooked spinach (directions follow)
- 1½ cups (¾ pt.) small-curd cottage cheese
- ¾ pound jack cheese with jalapeños, shredded
- ¼ cup freshly grated parmesan cheese

In an 8- to 10-inch frying pan, combine butter and onion; stir often over medium heat until onion is gold and tastes sweet, about 20 minutes. In a large bowl, beat to blend eggs, vinegar, spinach, cottage cheese, and jack cheese; stir in onion mixture.

Pour evenly into a buttered shallow 1½-quart casserole (at least 2 in. deep);

Baked pineapple and chicken breasts, seasoned with honey and mustard sauce, line up across a bed of hot cooked spinach.

sprinkle top with parmesan cheese. Bake in a 350° oven until center feels firm when lightly pressed, 35 to 40 minutes. Let cool about 10 minutes; spoon from casserole. Makes 6 to 8 servings.— *Metchtild Martin, Vashon, Wash.*

PER SERVING: 281 calories, 21 g protein, 5 g carbohydrates, 26 g fat, 164 mg cholesterol, 576 mg sodium

Cooked spinach. To make 1 cup of the cooked vegetable, you need 10 ounces fresh **spinach,** including leaves and stems. Purchase about 1 pound; trim off roots and discard bruised and yellow leaves.

Rinse leaves thoroughly, then drain. Place in a 5- to 6-quart pan on high heat. Stir frequently until leaves wilt, 2 to 4 minutes. Pour from pan into a colander. Press firmly with back of a spoon to remove excess moisture. Use hot or cool.

To use frozen spinach, thaw chopped or whole leaves in a microwave oven or at room temperature, then drain and press as directed for cooked spinach, preceding; 1 package (10 oz.) yields 1 cup.

MACADAMIA CHICKEN MELT

- 4 boned and skinned (about 1½ lb. total) chicken breast halves
- 1 piece, about 1 pound, peeled, cored pineapple (about 2 lb. unpeeled), cut into 4 equal slices
- ¼ cup Dijon mustard
- 3 tablespoons honey
- 1 tablespoon salad oil
- 1 tablespoon lime juice
- 2 cups cooked spinach (see spinach casserole, preceding)
- 2 tablespoons chopped salted macadamias
  Salt and pepper

Place chicken and pineapple side-by-side on rack in a 12- by 14-inch broiling pan. In a bowl, mix mustard, honey, oil, and lime juice; spoon ½ the mixture evenly over meat and fruit. Bake, uncovered, in a 450° oven, until meat is white in thickest part (cut to test), 12 to 15 minutes.

If spinach is cold, reheat and put on a platter (stir in an 8- to 10-inch frying pan over high heat or put on a microwave-safe platter in a microwave oven at full power, 100 percent, for about 1 minute).

Also warm extra sauce (in a microwave-safe bowl or 1- or 2-cup pan on high heat). Top spinach with meat and fruit; drizzle with sauce. Sprinkle with nuts; add salt and pepper to taste. Makes 4 servings.—*Bonnie Mandoe, Haiku, Hawaii.*

PER SERVING: 401 calories, 44 g protein, 35 g carbohydrates, 11 g fat, 98 mg cholesterol, 693 mg sodium

GREEN & RED LASAGNA

- 1 cup cooked spinach (see spinach casserole, preceding)
  About 2 cups (1 carton, 15-oz. size) part-skim or whole-milk ricotta cheese
- 2 large eggs
- ⅓ cup freshly grated parmesan cheese
- ¼ teaspoon pepper
- ⅛ teaspoon ground nutmeg
  Lasagna sauce (directions follow)
- ½ pound dry lasagna noodles
- ¾ pound mozzarella cheese, shredded

In a large bowl, mix well spinach, ricotta, eggs, parmesan, pepper, and nutmeg.

In a 9- by 13-inch casserole, evenly spread ¼ of the lasagna sauce. Arrange ⅓ uncooked noodles over sauce. Sprinkle with ⅓ of the spinach mixture. Repeat layers, ending with sauce. Sprinkle with mozzarella cheese. Cover tightly with foil; if made ahead, chill up until next day.

Bake, covered, in a 375° oven until hot in center, about 1 hour (1 hour and 30 minutes, if chilled). Let lasagna stand 10 minutes, then cut it into rectangles and lift out portions with a wide spatula. Makes 6 to 8 servings.—*Elizabeth DuBuisson, Coeur d'Alene, Idaho.*

PER SERVING: 422 calories, 25 g protein, 41 g carbohydrates, 19 g fat, 106 mg cholesterol, 987 mg sodium

Lasagna sauce. In a 10- to 12-inch frying pan over medium heat, combine 1 tablespoon **olive oil,** 3 cloves **garlic** (minced or pressed), 2 large **onions** (chopped), 1 large **red bell pepper** (stemmed, seeded, and chopped), and ½ pound sliced **mushrooms.** Stir often until liquid evaporates and onion is limp, 10 to 15 minutes. Add 1 can (15 oz.) **tomato sauce,** 1 can (6 oz.) **tomato paste,** 1 teaspoon **dry oregano leaves,** 2½ teaspoons **dry basil leaves,** 1 tablespoon **soy sauce,** and ½ cup **dry red wine.** Stirring, bring to a boil. Use hot or reheated.

Light Chinese Salads

UNLIKE MOST WESTERN SALADS, *these two Chinese versions use only minimal oil. Their refreshing flavor comes from a generous splash of lean and mellow rice vinegar—and a few zesty seasonings.*

Look for the Asian ingredients in Asian markets or some supermarkets.

CHINESE HOT & SOUR CHICKEN-NOODLE SALAD

- 1 whole chicken breast (about 1¼ lb.), split
- 8 ounces dry linguine
- 1 tablespoon Sichuan peppercorns or black peppercorns
- ¾ teaspoon crushed dried hot red chilies
- 3 tablespoons salad oil
- ⅓ cup rice vinegar or cider vinegar
- 2 tablespoons soy sauce
- ¼ cup chopped fresh cilantro (coriander)
- 1 small cucumber, thinly sliced

In a 5- to 6-quart pan, bring about 3 quarts water to a boil. Add chicken, cover, and bring to a boil. Remove from heat and let stand, covered, until meat is white in thickest part (cut to test), about 20 to 25 minutes. Lift out chicken, let cool, and reserve water. Remove and discard skin and bones; tear chicken into bite-size shreds. If made ahead, cover and chill chicken and water until the next day.

Bring water to a boil and add linguine. Boil, uncovered, until just tender to bite, 6 to 8 minutes. Drain; immerse in cold water until cool, then drain well again.

Remove any debris from Sichuan peppercorns. In a 6- to 8-inch frying pan, toast the peppercorns over medium-low heat until fragrant, about 2 to 3 minutes; shake pan often. Pour peppercorns into a blender and whirl until finely ground.

Add chilies and oil to pan; cook over low heat until chilies just begin to brown, about 3 minutes. Let cool and add ground Sichuan pepper, vinegar, soy sauce, and cilantro.

On a shallow dish, arrange a bed of noodles; cover with cucumber and chicken. Pour dressing evenly over salad and mix to blend. Makes 4 to 6 servings.

PER SERVING: 277 calories, 15 g protein, 31 g carbohydrates, 9.8 g fat, 30 mg cholesterol, 371 mg sodium

Mix egg noodles, shredded chicken, and cucumber with vinegar tantalizingly spiced with chilies and Sichuan peppercorns.

CELLOPHANE NOODLES WITH SESAME DRESSING

- 6 ounces dry bean threads (cellophane noodles)
- ½ ounce (½ cup) dried lily buds (optional; also called golden needles or tiger lily buds)
- 2 large (8 oz. total) carrots, shredded
- 4 green onions, ends trimmed, cut into thin shreds
- 2 tablespoons sesame seed
- 3 tablespoons salad oil
- ½ cup rice vinegar or cider vinegar
- 2 tablespoons soy sauce
- 2 tablespoons sugar
- 1 tablespoon minced fresh ginger
  Salt

In a 5- to 6-quart pan, bring about 3 quarts water to a boil. Add bean threads.

Remove from heat. Stir to separate noodles. Add lily buds and let stand until noodles are soft and pliable, 10 to 15 minutes. Lift out lily buds. Remove and discard hard tips from lily buds; cut into 3-inch lengths. Drain noodles well. If desired, cut noodles to shorter lengths.

In a large bowl, combine noodles, lily buds, carrots, and green onions. Cover and chill until cold, about 1 hour or until the next day. Drain again, if needed.

In a 6- to 8-inch frying pan over medium heat, combine sesame seed and oil. Shake pan often until seeds are golden, 3 to 5 minutes. Let cool. Add vinegar, soy sauce, sugar, and ginger. Pour over noodles and mix to blend. Add salt to taste. Makes 6 servings.

PER SERVING: 215 calories, 1.5 g protein, 34 g carbohydrates, 8.4 g fat, 0 mg cholesterol, 357 mg sodium

Deli Favorites Stacked

GREAT DELI FAVORITES—*matzo, pastrami, chopped liver—join forces in this stacked sandwich. It's a cool make-ahead main dish for a spring supper. The cut slices show off ribbons of each flavor, and go with a refreshing cabbage salad.*

The recipe looks long, but each simple segment can be made as much as a day ahead. You frost thin sheets of matzo (handle carefully—they crack easily) with the fillings, stack them, and mellow in the refrigerator until the matzo softens enough to cut neatly.

If observing Jewish dietary laws, broil livers on a rack and discard juices. You will need a little more chicken broth or schmaltz (rendered chicken fat) to make the chopped mixture spreadable.

MATZO SANDWICH TORTE

    Cabbage salad (recipe follows)
 4 matzos (each about 6 in. square),
    plain or flavored with egg and
    onion
¾ pound thinly sliced, fat-trimmed
    pastrami
    Chopped liver (recipe follows)
    About ½ cup chopped red onion

 2 medium-size (about ¼ lb. total)
    Roma-type tomatoes, peeled
    (optional), cored, and thinly sliced
    Dilled egg salad (recipe follows)
    Thinly sliced red onion rings
    Dill pickles

Spoon 1 cup lightly packed cabbage salad into a strainer; place over bowl of cabbage salad and press out as much salad dressing as possible. Lay 1 matzo on a flat platter and cover with pastrami in an even layer, flush with edges. Pat pressed salad over pastrami to make an even layer.

Lay another matzo on the counter; scoop chopped liver onto it, then spread in an even layer, flush with edges, using a long spatula. Set matzo on top of cabbage salad; press gently to settle it evenly and align matzo edges. Sprinkle liver with chopped onion.

Lay the third matzo on the counter and cover with tomato slices. Dot with the egg salad, then spread in an even layer, flush with edges. Set this matzo on top of the stack; press gently to settle evenly and align matzo edges. Cover with the last matzo, pressing gently to settle evenly and align edges. Loosely drape torte with plastic wrap, sealing

edges to keep moisture in. Chill at least 6 or up to 24 hours.

Unwrap torte and garnish with onion slices. Drain dressing from remaining cabbage salad, and spoon salad into a bowl. With a sharp, serrated knife, cut torte in half through the middle; then cut each half in 4 equal pieces. Accompany with cabbage salad and pickles. Makes 8 servings.

PER SERVING: 246 calories, 19 g protein, 18 g carbohydrates, 11 g fat, 279 mg cholesterol, 661 mg sodium

Cabbage salad. Rinse and drain 1 small (about 1½ lb.) **napa cabbage;** finely shred cabbage in a food processor or with a sharp knife.

In a large bowl, mix together ½ cup **rice vinegar,** 3 tablespoons chopped **fresh cilantro** (coriander), 1 tablespoon **Oriental sesame oil** or salad oil, and 2 teaspoons **sugar.** Add cabbage and mix. If made ahead, cover and chill up until next day. Makes 6 cups.

PER ½ CUP SERVING: 23 calories, 0.7 g protein, 2.9 g carbohydrates, 1.2 g fat, 0 mg cholesterol, 6.8 mg sodium

Chopped liver. In a 10- to 12-inch frying pan over medium heat, melt 1 tablespoon **schmaltz** (rendered chicken fat) or salad oil. Add 1 large **onion,** chopped; stir often until it is faintly browned and sweet tasting, about 20 minutes. Scrape the onion and drippings into a food processor or blender.

Rinse ½ pound **chicken livers,** pulling off any fat. Pat livers dry. Return frying pan to medium heat and add 1 more tablespoon **schmaltz** or salad oil. When hot, add livers. Turn livers frequently, cooking just until they are slightly pink in center (cut to test), about 5 minutes. Pour in with onion.

Chop 1 hard-cooked **large egg;** add to livers. Whirl until smoothly puréed. If needed to make mixture spreadable (about the consistency of soft peanut butter), add **regular-strength chicken broth,** 1 tablespoon at a time. Add **salt** to taste. If made ahead, cover and chill up until next day. Makes about 1 cup.— *Phyllis Hart, Petaluma, Calif.*

Dilled egg salad. Finely chop in a food processor or finely mash with a fork 2 tablespoons **mayonnaise,** 2 teaspoons **Dijon mustard,** ¼ teaspoon **Worcestershire,** ¼ teaspoon **dry dill weed,** and 4 hard-cooked **large eggs.** If made ahead, cover and chill up until next day. Makes about 1 cup.

Fat slice of sandwich torte shows off layers of pastrami, chopped liver, and egg salad. Sheets of matzo separates the flavors, and rings of red onions garnish top.

Cooking with Fresh Shiitakes & Chanterelles

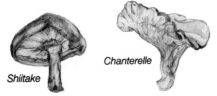

Shiitake

Chanterelle

Shiitake has gills in roundish cap. Chanterelle is irregular, gills run into stem.

AS DISTINCTIVE IN FLAVOR *as their better-known dried counterparts, though milder tasting, fresh shiitake and chanterelle mushrooms enrich these simple dishes. Both mushrooms are often available in well-stocked supermarkets, but since chanterelles are not cultivated, their supply is irregular.*

The first dish is grilled flank steak with Asian seasonings and a shiitake sauce. In the second, couscous is penetrated by the woodsy flavor and aroma of chanterelles.

FLANK STEAK WITH SHIITAKE SAUCE

- ¼ cup hoisin sauce or 3 tablespoons soy sauce
- ¼ cup red wine vinegar
- 1 tablespoon Oriental sesame oil
- 3 tablespoons minced fresh cilantro (coriander)
- 2 cloves garlic, minced or pressed
- 1 flank steak (1½ to 2 lb.), fat trimmed
  Fresh shiitake sauce (recipe follows)
- 2 to 3 thinly sliced green onions, including tops

In a deep bowl, mix together hoisin sauce, vinegar, sesame oil, cilantro, and garlic; add steak and turn to coat. Cover and chill at least 2 hours or up until next day. Turn meat over several times.

Lift meat from marinade. Set aside 2 tablespoons marinade; reserve remainder. Place steak on a grill 4 to 6 inches above a solid bed of hot coals (you should be able to hold your hand at grill level only 2 to 3 seconds). Cook meat, turning to brown evenly and basting often with reserved marinade, until it is done to your liking, 10 to 12 minutes for rare (cut to test).

Slice meat thinly across the grain. Pour any meat juices and the 2 tablespoons marinade into fresh shiitake sauce; stirring, bring sauce to a boil on high heat. Arrange meat slices on dinner plates. Spoon sauce equally onto or alongside meat. Sprinkle with onions. Makes 4 to 6 servings.

PER SERVING: 311 calories, 26 g protein, 9.7 g carbohydrates, 18 g fat, 57 mg cholesterol, 453 mg sodium

Fresh shiitake sauce. Cut off and discard tough stems from 1 pound **fresh shiitake mushrooms.** Rinse and drain caps, then cut into ¼-inch-wide slices.

In a 10- to 12-inch frying pan, combine mushrooms, 2 tablespoons **salad oil,** and 2 tablespoons minced **fresh ginger;** stir often on medium-high heat until mushrooms are lightly browned, about 10 minutes.

Pour 3 cups **regular-strength chicken** or beef **broth** into pan. Boil, stirring often, on high heat until sauce is reduced to 2 cups, 15 to 20 minutes. If made ahead, let cool, cover, and chill up until next day. Dissolve 1 tablespoon **cornstarch** with a little of the broth; stir into pan. Stir on high heat until boiling; keep warm as steak cooks.

COUSCOUS WITH CHANTERELLES & HERBS

- 4 to 5 ounces fresh chanterelles
- 2 tablespoons olive oil or salad oil
- ½ cup finely chopped onion
- 2 teaspoons minced fresh or 1 teaspoon crumbled dry rosemary leaves
- 1 teaspoon minced fresh or ½ teaspoon crumbled dry thyme leaves
- 1¾ cups regular-strength chicken broth
- 1 cup couscous
- ¼ cup grated parmesan cheese

If ends of chanterelles are tough or discolored, trim them off. Immerse mushrooms in water and swish vigorously to remove debris; at once lift from water and drain well. Finely chop mushrooms.

In a 10- to 12-inch frying pan over medium-high heat, combine chanterelles, oil, onion, rosemary, and thyme. Cover and cook until mushrooms get juicy, 3 to 5 minutes. Uncover and stir often until juices evaporate and mushrooms are lightly browned, about 10 minutes. Add broth and bring to a boil. Stir in couscous, then cover tightly and remove from heat. Let stand until liquid is absorbed, about 5 minutes. With a fork, fluff couscous, then stir in parmesan. Makes 6 servings.

PER SERVING: 154 calories, 5.3 g protein, 20 g carbohydrates, 6 g fat, 2.6 mg cholesterol, 82 mg sodium

Fresh shiitake mushrooms are base of sauce for grilled and thinly sliced flank steak. Look for the distinctively flavored mushrooms in well-stocked supermarkets.

French Bistro Dinner

A T ITS BEST, *French bistro cuisine is simple, unpretentious food well prepared and generously proportioned. This cooking also tends to highlight a region's local ingredients, as you'll find in this easy supper we enjoyed in Burgundy. You can easily manage this meal at home.*

A crisp oven-browned cake of sliced potatoes with herbs bakes while you prepare the Swiss chard and season the thick double-cut lamb ribs with an aromatic paste of juniper berries. As the chops brown, cook the chard. The tender leaves cook more quickly than the stems, so separate them and cook the stems first; add the leaves later, along with a tangy bit of Roquefort cheese. Or you can choose another vegetable, such as spinach or green beans, or offer a green salad.

The chop drippings become the base for a flavorful sauce to spoon on the meat.

A smooth red wine such as a light French Burgundy (a St. Morey Denis, for example) or California Pinot Noir complements the meal.

For dessert, offer a soft ripe cheese such as St. André to go with ripe pears.

Dining alfresco, French-style: double-thick lamb chops, pan-browned with juniper berries, are served with crisp herbed potato cake and Swiss chard in Roquefort cream.

LAMB RIB CHOPS WITH JUNIPER BERRIES

You may have to special-order rib lamb chops cut with 2 bones for each piece. Or buy rack of lamb and have it cut through at every other rib.

Juniper berry paste (recipe follows)
4 **to 6 double-rib lamb chops (2 to 2½ lb. total), excess fat trimmed**
2 **tablespoons butter or margarine**
½ **cup** *each* **regular-strength chicken or beef broth and dry red wine**
2 **tablespoons minced shallots**

Rub juniper berry paste evenly over each chop. Melt half the butter in a 10- to 12-inch frying pan over medium heat. Add chops and cook, turning as needed, until meat is well browned on both sides and still pink in center (cut to test), 18 to 20 minutes total. (The drippings will be blackened.) Transfer chops to a platter; keep warm.

To pan, add broth, wine, and shallots; bring to a boil on high heat, stirring to loosen browned bits. Boil until reduced to ⅓ cup. Remove from heat and add remaining butter, stirring until melted. Pour sauce over chops. Makes 4 servings.

PER SERVING: 227 calories, 20 g protein, 2.4 g carbohydrates, 15 g fat, 80 mg cholesterol, 132 mg sodium

Juniper berry paste. Combine 2 tablespoons crushed **dry juniper berries** with 1 teaspoon **coarse-ground pepper** and 1 large clove **garlic,** minced or pressed.

CRISP HERBED POTATO CAKE

4 **large (about 2¼ lb. total) russet potatoes**
⅓ **cup melted butter or margarine**
¾ **teaspoon** *each* **dry rosemary leaves and dry thyme leaves**
Salt

Peel potatoes and carefully cut into ⅛-inch-thick slices. Combine butter and herbs. Coat the inside of a 12-inch ovenproof frying pan or 14-inch pizza pan with some of the herb butter. Neatly arrange potato slices, overlapping, in concentric circles to form an even layer in pan. Drizzle remaining butter over potatoes.

Bake on the bottom rack in a 450° oven until potato cake is well browned and crisp on top and bottom (lift with a spatula to check), about 1 hour.

Invert a platter onto frying pan. Hold together (using hot pads) and invert potato cake onto platter. With a sharp knife, cut potatoes into wedges. Season to taste with salt. Makes 4 servings.

PER SERVING: 322 calories, 4.6 g protein, 42 g carbohydrates, 16 g fat, 41 mg cholesterol, 173 mg sodium

SWISS CHARD IN ROQUEFORT CREAM

2 **pounds Swiss chard, stem ends trimmed**
1 **tablespoon butter or margarine**
¼ **cup whipping cream**
1 **ounce (¼ cup) Roquefort cheese**
Freshly ground pepper

Wash Swiss chard well and drain. Cut stems out of leaves and slice stems crosswise into ¼-inch pieces. Slice leaves into 1- to 2-inch widths.

Melt butter in a 4- to 5-quart pan over medium-high heat. Add stems; stir often until limp, about 8 minutes. Add leaves and cream; cover and stir occasionally until leaves are wilted, about 3 minutes. Uncover, add cheese, and stir frequently on high heat until most of the liquid boils away, 3 to 4 minutes. Season to taste with pepper. Makes 4 servings.

PER SERVING: 144 calories, 6.4 g protein, 9.8 g carbohydrates, 10 g fat, 31 mg cholesterol, 590 mg sodium

Geoduck: Don't Let Its Name or Looks Intimidate You

CERTAINLY NO BEAUTY, *and decidedly firm (almost crisp) to chew, the giant geoduck (pronounced "gooey duck") clam wins diners with its delicate, sea-fresh taste. Harvested in the Pacific Northwest under regulations to preserve supply, clams average 2 to 3 pounds in their gaping shells. In the West, good Asian fish markets frequently sell them.*

A live clam's freshness is easily determined by smell, which should—as with any fresh clam—be as clean as an ocean breeze. Dying or dead geoducks deteriorate rapidly to stinking. Keep on ice until ready to clean; overnight from purchase is usually safe.

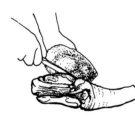

Although intimidating, geoducks are easy to clean. Rinse in shell with cool water, then slip a sharp knife between shell and flesh to release clam; discard shell.

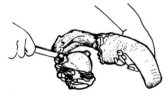

Cut and pull ovoid stomach free from siphon (neck) and mantle (breast). Portions of the stomach are sometimes edible, but we suggest you discard it.

After a quick dip in boiling water, pull thin skin from siphon and mantle and discard.

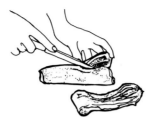

Slit siphon open lengthwise; rinse well to remove any sand. A 2- to 3-pound (in the shell) geoduck yields ½ to 1 pound meat. Because of its texture and flavor, the siphon is considered choice eating raw.

Both the siphon and the tenderer mantle are excellent when finely chopped and barely heated in chowder. Our recipe comes from Shuckers Restaurant in Seattle. The chowder is also tasty with canned clams.

SHUCKERS GEODUCK CHOWDER

- ⅓ **pound sliced bacon, chopped**
- ¼ **pound andouille sausage, chopped; or bulk pork sausage, crumbled**
- 1 **small onion, chopped**
- ½ **cup diced celery**
- 1 **small green bell pepper, stemmed, seeded, and diced**
- 2 **medium-size (about 1 lb. total) firm-ripe tomatoes, cored and diced**
- 2 **teaspoons** *each* **dry oregano leaves, dry basil leaves, and dry thyme leaves**
- 1 **teaspoon filé powder (optional) Chowder base (recipe follows)**
- 2 **cups (about ½ lb.) sliced fresh or frozen okra**
- ½ **to ¾ pound cleaned geoduck siphon and/or mantle (see preceding), finely chopped; or 3 cans (6¾-oz. size) chopped clams, drained and rinsed**

In a 5- to 6-quart pan over medium heat, combine bacon, sausage, and onion; stir often until well browned, 10 to 15 minutes. Spoon out and discard fat.

Add to pan the celery, bell pepper, tomato, oregano, basil, thyme, filé powder, and chowder base. Bring mixture to a boil (if made ahead, let cool, cover, and chill until next day; reheat to continue). Add okra and cook just until tender when pierced, about 4 minutes. Add geoduck, stir, and remove from heat immediately. Ladle chowder into bowls. Makes 6 to 8 servings. —*Ludger Szmania, Seattle.*

PER SERVING: 126 calories, 9 g protein, 11 g carbohydrates, 5.5 g fat, 20 mg cholesterol, 505 mg sodium

Chowder base. Mix together ¼ cup **tomato paste,** 1 bottle (8 oz.) **clam juice,** 1 can (12 oz.) **tomato juice,** and 1½ cups **regular-strength chicken broth.**

GEODUCK SASHIMI

> About ½ **pound cleaned geoduck siphon (see preceding)**
> 1 **tablespoon** *each* **soy sauce and seasoned rice vinegar**
> 1 **teaspoon minced fresh ginger (optional)**
> About 1 **tablespoon powdered wasabi mixed with 1 tablespoon water**
> About ¼ **cup pickled sliced ginger, drained**

Thinly slice geoduck across the siphon, keeping slices aligned. Slide a wide spatula under slices; holding in place, put on a platter. In a small bowl, mix together soy sauce, rice vinegar, and fresh ginger. Pinch wasabi to make a small cone. Place sauce, wasabi, and pickled ginger beside sliced clam. If made ahead, cover and chill up to 2 hours. Dip geoduck into sauce and eat with wasabi and ginger to taste; use chopsticks or forks. Makes 6 to 8 appetizer servings.

PER SERVING: 45 calories, 3.8 g protein, 6.7 g carbohydrates, 0.3 g fat, 9.6 mg cholesterol, 162 mg sodium

For sashimi, dip slices of geoduck into sauce of soy and rice vinegar. Offer with pickled ginger and wasabi (Japanese horseradish).

Ice Cream Irresistibles

ICE CREAM OR SORBET *in cones can be quickly dressed up to make a walk-about dessert treat.*

Coat a scoop of ice cream on a cone with a confection and freeze the cone upright. When ice cream is hard, dip the cone quickly into melted chocolate, then sprinkle with extras of the first coating. Cones will keep in the freezer for up to 2 weeks, ready to eat.

Here we give a choice of flavors; don't hesitate to mix and match.

DOUBLE MINT & CHOCOLATE CONES

Use the chocolate wafer candies with firm green (not soft white) mint centers.

1 **package (6 oz.) thin chocolate and mint wafer candy, coarsely chopped**

1 **quart mint flavor ice cream with chocolate bits**

8 **purchased ice cream sugar cones Cone stand (directions follow)**

1 **bag (12 oz., 2 cups) semisweet chocolate baking chips**

¼ **cup solid shortening**

Set aside ½ cup chopped candy. Put remaining candy on a large piece of waxed paper. Lightly press a round scoop (about ½ cup) of ice cream onto 1 cone. Holding cone, roll ice cream in candy to coat. At once, set cone upright in cone stand in freezer. Repeat for remaining cones and freeze, uncovered, until ice cream is very firm, at least 1 hour or up to 6 hours.

Combine chocolate chips and shortening in a 2-cup glass measure. Set container in about 1 inch of almost boiling water (take extreme care not to get water in chocolate) and let stand until chocolate is softened; stir until smooth.

Or, in a microwave oven, heat chips and shortening in a 2-cup glass measure, uncovered, for 1 minute at full power (100 percent); stir. Heat for another 30 seconds and stir; repeat, heating 5 seconds at a time, until chocolate is completely melted. Let cool for 5 minutes.

Working quickly, invert 1 cone and dip into chocolate to coat ice cream. Let excess chocolate drip back into container. At once, sprinkle coating with ⅛ of the reserved candy. Set cone upright

in stand in freezer. Repeat for remaining cones. (Save extra chocolate for other uses.) Freeze until ice cream is very firm, about 30 minutes. Serve, or wrap each cone airtight; freeze up to 2 weeks. Makes 8 servings.

PER CONE: 559 calories, 6.6 g protein, 62 g carbohydrates, 35 g fat, 34 mg cholesterol, 113 mg sodium

Cone stand. Buy a 3-inch-thick 10- by 12-inch piece of rigid plastic foam. With a sharp knife, carve 8 holes about 3½ inches apart, each 1 inch deep and ½ inch wide; put stand in freezer.

MILK CHOCOLATE & TOFFEE CONES

Stir ½ cup **slivered** or coarsely chopped **blanched almonds** in an 8- to 10-inch frying pan over medium heat until golden, 5 to 7 minutes. Let cool, then chop finely. Follow directions for **double mint and chocolate cones** (recipe precedes), using mixture of browned almonds and 1 package (6 oz.) **almond brittle chips** instead of mint candy.

Use **coffee ice cream** instead of mint flavor with chocolate bits, and **milk chocolate baking chips** instead of semisweet chips.

PER CONE: 542 calories, 9.5 g protein, 69 g carbohydrates, 28 g fat, 37 mg cholesterol, 130 mg sodium

WHITE CHOCOLATE & COCONUT CONES

Follow directions for **double mint and chocolate cones** (recipe precedes), using 1 cup (3½ oz.) lightly packed **dry sweetened shredded coconut** in place of the mint candy. Use **raspberry sorbet** instead of mint flavor ice cream with chocolate bits, and **white chocolate baking chips** instead of semisweet chips.

PER SERVING: 497 calories, 4 g protein, 70 g carbohydrates, 23 g fat, 7.2 mg cholesterol, 112 mg sodium

Candy-studded chocolate shell surrounds mint-chip ice cream. Made ahead, dipped cones are ready to please any age. Experiment with different flavors and toppings.

Horned Melon

IT LOOKS AS LETHAL *as a hand grenade, and its name sounds intimidating, but horned melon is just as innocuous as its more familiar cucumber, gherkin, and melon relatives.*

When ripe, the fruit turns an even, deep shade of orange-gold. Inside the firm, inedible shell, the interior resembles a seedy cucumber; each pale white, tender seed is surrounded by a sack of transparent, fluorescent green, jellylike pulp. The pulp tastes like a refreshing blend of cucumber, banana, and lime. Some call the fruit "jelly melon"; one grower has trademarked the name "kiwano" to identify his crop.

Horned melon, originally from Africa, is in supermarkets almost year-round because it's harvested in the fall in California and in (our) spring in New Zealand. The fruit keeps, under controlled conditions, up to 6 months.

If you can't find ripe fruit with orange-colored skin, make sure immature fruit's green skin is dappled with flecks of yellow and cream. It should have no punctures, bruises, mold, or soft spots (check ends and spine tips, especially). If damaged, fruit will rot before it ripens.

Keep immature fruit unwrapped in a dry location at room temperature (ideal is 70° to 72°); do not chill, or ripening will cease. It may take several weeks to months for the fruit to ripen.

To get acquainted with this fruit, we offer two simple serving suggestions. Both take advantage of the pulp's distinctive and decorative look.

How to use a horned melon. Cut a 4- to 5-inch-long melon (about ¾ lb.) in half and with a spoon scoop out pulp (protect hand from spiky "horns" with a potholder); discard shell. One fruit yields ½ to ⅔ cup pulp; allow 2 or 3 tablespoons for a serving.

Nutritional information not available.

Horned melon salad. Spoon **melon pulp** over sliced **oranges** splashed lightly with **balsamic vinegar.**

Horned melon sundaes. Spoon **melon pulp** over scoops of **lime sherbet** or vanilla ice cream.

Ripe horned melon is deep shade of orange gold. Inside the inedible shell, green jellylike pulp surrounds fruit's pale, tender seeds.

Spooned over sherbet, green pulp adds an intriguing texture and mild, exotic tang.

Cooky Cameos

PRETTY AS A PICTURE, *these flower-topped cookies make perfect treats for May Day or Mother's Day. With a little supervision, youngsters can shape the cooky frames, spread the syrup "glue," then anchor the edible flowers. An adult should do the baking and make the syrup.*

POSY COOKIES

> 3 pared strips of orange peel (orange part only), each 3 inches long
> 1 cup sugar
> ⅓ cup water
> Cooky frames (recipe follows)
> About 2 dozen edible flowers (choices follow), rinsed and drained dry, stem ends pinched off

In a 1- to 1½-quart pan, boil peel, sugar, and water on high heat (don't stir) until syrup reaches 238°; for accurate reading, tilt pan so syrup covers thermometer base. Discard peel; let syrup stand undisturbed until warm to touch, 30 to 40 minutes.

Into each cooky frame, spread 1 teaspoon syrup, then press in 1 or 2 flowers. Let stand until syrup is firm, about 4 hours; if held longer, wrap airtight (do not stack) up until next day. Makes 16.

PER COOKY: 199 calories, 2.1 g protein, 28 g carbohydrates, 9.1 g fat, 40 mg cholesterol, 93 mg sodium

Cooky frames. Rub with your fingers until fine crumbs 2 cups **all-purpose flour,** ¼ cup **sugar,** and ¾ cup (⅜ lb.) **butter** or margarine, cut into chunks. Stir in 1 **large egg** until dough sticks together. Pat 2-tablespoon-size balls of dough into 3-inch rounds, each at least 1 inch apart, on 1 or 2 baking sheets, each 12 by 15 inches. Pinch cooky edges to make rims; press rims lightly with tines of a fork.

Bake in a 300° oven until golden, about 30 minutes. If using 1 oven, switch pan positions after 15 minutes. Let cool on pan. If made ahead, store airtight up until next day; freeze to store longer.

Edible flowers. Select pesticide-free unbruised primroses (except Chinese primroses, *Primula obconica*), johnny-jump-ups, nasturtiums, roses (petals only), violas, or violets.

Gently press fresh flowers into tacky syrup. Syrup may turn opaque.

Edible posies held fast by sugar syrup in shortbread frames make charming sweets for mother or grandma on Mother's Day.

More May Recipes

OTHER MAY ARTICLES FEATURE *a curried vegetable stew that's quick to prepare and cook, and cocoa-dusted jalapeño truffles, an uncooked sweet with a tingling afterglow.*

GARBANZO CURRY

Potatoes and garbanzos absorb the flavors of this curried vegetable stew by soaking up the slightly hot juices while simmering with bits of onion, celery, and bell pepper. Served with rice, the dish is a meal in itself; the vegetables and grain balance to provide complete protein. It takes only minutes to assemble and simmers for about a half-hour.

    2 tablespoons olive oil or salad oil
    1 large (about ½ lb.) onion, chopped
    5 or 6 celery stalks, ends trimmed,
       chopped
    1 large red or green bell pepper,
       stemmed, seeded, and coarsely
       chopped
    4 cloves garlic, minced or pressed
    3½ cups regular-strength chicken
       broth
    1⅓ pounds (about 6 medium-size)
       thin-skinned red potatoes,
       scrubbed and cut into 1-inch
       chunks
    2 cans (15½ oz. each) garbanzos,
       drained and rinsed
    1 can (6 oz.) tomato paste
    1 tablespoon curry powder
    ¼ teaspoon cayenne
    3 cups hot cooked rice
       Chopped green onion

Tinted gold by curry, garbanzos and potatoes form base of this vegetable stew.

In a 5- to 6-quart pan over medium heat, combine the oil, onion, celery, bell pepper, and garlic. Stir occasionally until vegetables are tender to bite, about 7 minutes.

Stir in broth, potatoes, garbanzos, tomato paste, curry, and cayenne. Cover and simmer on medium heat until potatoes are tender when pierced, 30 to 40 minutes. Make a ring of the hot rice on a rimmed platter and mound curry mixture in the center. Or spoon rice onto plates and ladle curry over rice. Sprinkle with chopped green onion. Makes 6 or 7 servings. —*Joan Launier, Merced, Calif.*

PER SERVING: 427 calories, 13 g protein, 79 g carbohydrates, 6.9 g fat, 0 mg cholesterol, 629 mg sodium

JALAPEÑO TRUFFLES

Sweet heat is the surprise in these confection truffles. You make a syrup with jalapeño chilies, then add it to uncooked powdered-sugar fondant. Shaped into balls and dusted with cocoa, the effect is cool with a tingling afterglow.

    6 fresh jalapeño chilies (about 5 oz.
       total)
    ¼ cup white vinegar
    ½ cup granulated sugar
    ¼ cup (⅛ lb.) butter or margarine,
       at room temperature
    1 tablespoon grated orange peel
       About 3 cups powdered sugar
    ¼ cup unsweetened cocoa

Wearing rubber gloves, stem, seed, and mince jalapeños (do not touch eyes).

In a 1- to 2-quart pan, combine chilies, vinegar, and granulated sugar. Bring to a boil on high heat, stirring until sugar is dissolved. Continue to boil, without stirring, until thermometer reads 220° (you may need to tilt pan to pool syrup for an accurate reading), about 6 to 7 minutes. Let stand until cool, at least 15 minutes.

Cocoa-dusted truffles are cool white inside, but warmed by jalapeño chilies.

In a bowl, beat butter with an electric mixer until fluffy. Still beating, add jalapeño syrup and orange peel. Stir in 3 cups powdered sugar, then beat until mixture holds its shape when patted into a ball. If too soft and sticky, stir in a little more powdered sugar. Divide mixture into 1-tablespoon portions. Shape each into a ball to make a truffle.

Roll truffles in cocoa to coat completely. Place truffles on a plate, slightly apart. Cover and chill until firm, at least 30 minutes or up to 2 weeks. Makes 25.

PER PIECE: 92 calories, 0.3 g protein, 19 g carbohydrates, 2 g fat, 4.9 mg cholesterol, 19 mg sodium

Strawberry jam adds sweetness to fresh fruit shake.

FROZEN STRAWBERRY BREAKFAST SHAKE

3 cups strawberries, rinsed, drained, and hulled

2 large eggs

1½ cups nonfat milk

1 medium-size ripe banana, peeled and sliced

2 tablespoons strawberry jam

½ teaspoon vanilla

4 pretty strawberries, rinsed and drained

On a 10- by 15-inch baking pan, place hulled berries in a single layer without touching. Freeze until hard, about 1 hour. If done ahead, pack fruit airtight when firm, and freeze up to 2 weeks.

In a 1- to 1½-quart pan, bring 2 cups water to boiling over high heat. Immerse eggs in water and boil exactly 1 minute; lift out with a slotted spoon. Let cool 10 minutes.

Break eggs into a blender or food processor. Add milk, frozen strawberries, banana, jam, and vanilla; whirl until smoothly puréed. Pour into 4 tall glasses; garnish with pretty whole berries. Makes about 4½ cups, 4 servings. — *Beulah Fabris, San Mateo, Calif.*

PER SERVING: 160 calories, 7.4 g protein, 32 g carbohydrates, 3.2 g fat, 108 mg cholesterol, 68 mg sodium

FLORENTINE SPINACH SOUP

1 tablespoon olive oil

½ cup *each* thinly sliced celery and green onion

2 teaspoons anise seed

1 pound spinach, stems trimmed, leaves rinsed and drained; or 1 package (10 oz.) frozen spinach leaves

3 cups regular-strength chicken broth

¼ teaspoon freshly ground pepper

Lemon wedges

Freshly shredded parmesan cheese

Pour oil into a 3- to 4-quart pan over medium-high heat. When oil is hot, add celery, onion, and anise seed to pan; stir

Spinach gives this light, lean soup its flavor and bright green color.

occasionally until vegetables just begin to brown, 8 to 10 minutes. Add spinach, broth, and pepper; bring to a boil, then reduce heat and simmer 10 minutes.

Pour hot soup, a portion at a time, into a blender or a food processor, and whirl until smoothly puréed. Pour soup into bowls. Offer lemon wedges and cheese to add to taste to individual portions. Makes 4 servings. — *J. Hill, Sacramento.*

PER SERVING: 80 calories, 4.5 g protein, 5.9 g carbohydrates, 5 g fat, 0 mg cholesterol, 118 mg sodium

Stir-fry vegetables, then sprinkle with pine nuts.

BOK CHOY, MUSHROOM & TOMATO STIR-FRY

¼ cup pine nuts

1½ pounds bok choy

1 tablespoon salad oil

¼ pound mushrooms, sliced

¼ cup rice vinegar

¼ pound cherry tomatoes, stemmed and quartered

Place pine nuts in a wok or 12-inch frying pan. Stir frequently or shake pan often over medium-high heat until nuts are golden, about 3 to 4 minutes. Pour from pan and set aside.

Remove and discard wilted leaves from bok choy. Cut stalks from leaves.

Slice stalks diagonally into ½-inch-wide pieces. Cut leaves crosswise into ½-inch-wide strips. Separately, rinse stalks and leaves well; drain.

Place the pan over high heat; add oil. When oil is hot, add stem pieces, mushrooms, and vinegar. Stir-fry until most of the liquid evaporates and vegetables begin to brown, 8 to 10 minutes. Add leaves; stir-fry just until leaves are wilted, 1 to 2 minutes. Stir in tomatoes and sprinkle with nuts. Makes 4 servings. — *Michelle Elliot, Newport Beach, Calif.*

PER SERVING: 113 calories, 5.6 g protein, 8.1 g carbohydrates, 8.5 g fat, 0 mg cholesterol, 117 mg sodium

BAKED CHILI PUFF

- ½ pound jack cheese
- 2 large cans (7 oz. each) whole green chilies
  Egg batter (recipe follows)
- 1 cup (4 oz.) shredded cheddar cheese
- 1 cup homemade or purchased guacamole
- 1 small firm-ripe tomato, cored and diced

Cut jack cheese into enough equal-size sticks to match the number of chilies; insert a piece of the jack cheese into each chili. Arrange stuffed chilies in a single layer in a buttered 1½- to 2-quart casserole (about 2 in. deep).

Spread egg batter evenly over chilies. Sprinkle batter with cheddar cheese. Bake in a 350° oven until casserole is puffed and appears set when shaken, 18 to 20 minutes. Scoop out portions with a spoon and top each with guacamole and tomato. Makes 6 servings. —*Ruth Hagerman, Colorado Springs, Colo.*

Egg batter. Separate 3 **large eggs.** In a large bowl, whip whites at high speed until they hold moist, distinct peaks. In another bowl, use same beaters to whip yolks with 2 tablespoons **milk** and 3 tablespoons **all-purpose flour.** Gently fold yolks into whites; use at once.

PER SERVING: 379 calories, 20 g protein, 14 g carbohydrates, 28 g fat, 160 mg cholesterol, 1025 mg sodium

Fluffy egg batter buries cheese-stuffed chilies; sprinkle with more cheese, then bake.

BLACK CURRANT PORK CHOPS

- 6 center-cut pork chops (about 2½ lb. total), excess fat trimmed off
  Freshly ground pepper
- 1 tablespoon butter or margarine
- 3 tablespoons black currant preserves or currant jelly
- 1½ tablespoons Dijon mustard
- ¼ cup raspberry vinegar or white wine vinegar

Sprinkle chops generously with pepper. Melt butter in a 10- to 12-inch frying pan over medium-high heat. Add chops and cook, turning as needed, until well browned on both sides, 8 to 10 minutes total.

Combine preserves with mustard; spoon evenly over chops. Reduce heat to medium low; cover and cook until chops are still moist and look faintly pink to white in the center (cut to test), about 10 minutes total. With a slotted spoon, transfer chops to a serving platter; cover and keep warm.

Add raspberry vinegar to pan; bring to a boil over high heat, stirring to loosen browned bits. Boil sauce, uncovered, until reduced to about ¼ cup, 3 to 4 minutes. Spoon sauce over chops. Makes 4 to 6 servings. —*Carmela Meely, Walnut Creek, Calif.*

PER SERVING: 252 calories, 28 g protein, 7.8 g carbohydrates, 11 g fat, 85 mg cholesterol, 217 mg sodium

Pork chops are glazed with jam, mustard, and vinegar; serve with rice.

WHITE CHOCOLATE ANGEL PIE

- ¾ cup slivered almonds
- 4 large egg whites
- ½ teaspoon cream of tartar
- 1 teaspoon vanilla
- 1 cup sugar
- 1 cup whipping cream
- 6 ounces white chocolate, coarsely chopped

Place almonds in an 8- or 9-inch-wide pan. Bake, shaking occasionally, at 350° until toasted, 8 to 10 minutes.

In a blender or food processor, coarsely chop ½ cup almonds. Set aside.

In a large bowl, beat egg whites, cream of tartar, and vanilla at high speed

with an electric mixer until frothy. Gradually whip in sugar, beating until whites hold stiff, glossy peaks. With the back of a spoon, spread meringue in a well-greased 9-inch pie pan, pushing meringue high on pan sides to resemble a pie shell. Bake in 300° oven until meringue is firm and dry but not browned, about 30 minutes; cool.

Whip cream until it holds soft peaks; fold in chopped almonds and chocolate. Spoon into meringue shell. Cover and chill at least 2 hours or up to 8 hours. Sprinkle with slivered nuts; cut in wedges. Makes 8 servings. —*Lois Dowling, Tacoma.*

PER SERVING: 384 calories, 6 g protein, 42 g carbohydrates, 22 g fat, 37 mg cholesterol, 56 mg sodium

White chocolate, whipped cream, and toasted almonds fill crisp meringue shell.

THE CUISINE *of the Indian subcontinent is an ancient and varied one. But to most American diners it simply means curry—a notion that amuses Indians if it does not annoy them. As more Indian restaurants open, our appreciation of the complexity of the country's cuisine grows. One concept that has caught on is* tandoori cooking—*named for the* tandoor, *a very hot clay or brick oven that sears the surface of meat or fish, creating a crisp and richly colored crust.*

The crust and the meat take their flavor from a blend of herbs, spices, lime, vinegar, and yogurt used as a marinade and basting sauce. These spices are the soul of Indian cooking and are more important, in fact, than the tandoor itself. Tandoori dishes can be, and often are, barbecued over coals, baked in an oven, or cooked on a rotisserie.

After marinating chicken legs in a classic tandoori marinade, S. M. Estvanik grills them. For deeper flavor penetration, some cooks remove the skin, slash the meat in several places, and rub in marinade.

TANDOORI BARBECUED CHICKEN

- 2 tablespoons white wine vinegar
- ¼ cup lime juice
- ½ teaspoon crushed dried hot red chilies
- ½ teaspoon cumin seed
- 1 teaspoon ground turmeric
- 1½ teaspoons paprika
- ¼ cup chopped fresh cilantro (coriander)
- 3 cloves garlic
- 1 tablespoon minced fresh ginger
- ¼ cup chopped parsley
- 1 cup unflavored low-fat yogurt
- 6 to 8 chicken legs (drumsticks with thighs attached, about 2¾ to 3½ lb. *total*)

In a blender or food processor, whirl vinegar, lime juice, chilies, cumin, turmeric, paprika, cilantro, garlic, ginger, and parsley until smoothly puréed. Put in a large bowl, add yogurt, and mix well.

Rinse legs and pat dry. Make a cut through to thigh and drumstick bones along entire length of each leg. Add chicken to yogurt mixture; mix to coat thoroughly. Cover and chill at least 1 hour or up until next day.

In a barbecue with a lid, ignite 50 to 60 charcoal briquets on the fire grate. When coals are dotted with gray ash, push equal amounts to opposite sides of grate. Place grill 4 to 6 inches above height of coals. Drain legs briefly and lay them on grill, but not directly over coals. Cover barbecue, open drafts, and cook until chicken is no longer pink at bone in thickest part (cut to test), about 40 minutes. Baste frequently with remaining yogurt mixture. Makes 6 to 8 servings.

PER SERVING: 285 calories, 31 g protein, 3.8 g carbohydrates, 16 g fat, 105 mg cholesterol, 120 mg sodium

Seattle

WITH SHRIMP AT THE PRICE *they are, one should make every effort to enhance, and not conceal, their flavor. Jambalayas and gumbos are fine if you operate a shrimp boat, but the rest of us would prefer a more subtle approach, like Robert Gates' Shrimp de Jonghe. Gates enjoyed it*

"Spices are the soul of Indian cooking."

in a Chicago South Side restaurant years ago and has reconstructed a recipe for us.

Samuel Johnson once said that the keenest of human pleasures is to do a good deed by stealth and have it discovered by accident. Re-creating a favorite restaurant dish by memory and experiment (and getting it right) is a similar pleasure.

SHRIMP DE JONGHE

- 2 tablespoons butter or margarine
- 1 clove garlic, minced or pressed
- 1 tablespoon finely chopped parsley
- 1 tablespoon chopped chives
- ¼ teaspoon Worcestershire
- 3 tablespoons seasoned fine dry bread crumbs
- ⅛ teaspoon pepper
- 1 pound medium-large (36 to 42 per lb.) shrimp, shelled and deveined
- ¼ cup dry sherry
  Paprika

In a 10- to 12-inch frying pan over medium heat, stir together until hot the butter, garlic, parsley, chives, Worcestershire, 1 tablespoon of the crumbs, and pepper. Add shrimp and stir often just until they turn pink but are still translucent and moist-looking in center (cut to test), 3 to 4 minutes. Evenly arrange shrimp with butter mixture in 4 individual casseroles (each about ¾-cup size). Add sherry to pan, scraping browned bits free; spoon liquid equally over shrimp. Evenly sprinkle remaining crumbs over shrimp, then dust lightly with paprika.

Bake, uncovered, in a 400° oven until crumbs are lightly toasted, 5 to 8 minutes. Makes 4 servings.

PER SERVING: 178 calories, 20 g protein, 6.8 g carbohydrates, 7.5 g fat, 156 mg cholesterol, 349 mg sodium

San Francisco

THE BEAN IS THE DONKEY *of the vegetable world, bearing up under derision while it carries a big load of nutrition, especially in parts of the world where meat is a luxury. Since pre-Columbian times in Mexico, the bean has been a significant source of protein. More recently, the refried bean has become a staple on the Mexican-American restaurant combination plate.*

Modestly refried (when judged by Mexican standards for fat added), Carter Wilson's dish consists of beans that have been boiled, mashed, then cooked again with seasonings. More traditional refried beans start as a sort of thick porridge; then the mixture solidifies rapidly, forming a crust around the edges. Any left over for another meal quickly takes on the appearance of a lava field and the texture of fudge—but still tastes good.

Wilson's concoction passes the porridge stage quickly and goes right to the solid state with his Idaho Pinto Bean Cakes. A ham hock and chicken broth enrich the bean flavor in the boiling process. After the beans are mashed and seasoned, the mixture is shaped into round cakes and cooked yet again.

IDAHO PINTO BEAN CAKES WITH SALSA

- 1 cup dry pinto beans or 2 cans (15-oz. size) pinto beans
- 1 small (about 1½ lb.) smoked ham hock, cut in half and rinsed
- 3½ cups or 2 cans (14½ oz. each) regular-strength chicken broth
- 4 slices bacon, chopped
- ¼ cup *each* finely chopped onion and red bell pepper
- 2 large cloves garlic, minced or pressed
- 1 medium-size fresh jalapeño chili, stemmed, seeded, and finely chopped
- 2 tablespoons finely chopped fresh cilantro (coriander)
- ½ teaspoon ground cumin
- ¼ teaspoon pepper
- ⅓ cup yellow cornmeal
  About 4 tablespoons salad oil
  Homemade or purchased salsa

Sort dry beans, discarding any debris; rinse beans and place in bowl. Cover with cold water and let soak overnight.

Drain soaked beans and place in a 3- to 4-quart pan along with ham hock and broth. Bring to a boil over high heat, then cover, reduce heat, and simmer until beans are tender to bite, 1 to 1¼ hours. (Omit these steps if using canned beans.) Drain liquid from beans, cooked dry or canned, and place beans in a large bowl. Reserve cooking liquid and ham hock for other uses, such as soup. Mash the beans with a potato masher until mixture sticks together; set aside.

In a 10- to 12-inch frying pan over medium heat, cook bacon until crisp, stirring often. Add onion, bell pepper, garlic, and jalapeño. Stir often until onion is limp, about 10 minutes. Add onion mixture to mashed beans along with cilantro, cumin, and pepper; mix well. If warm, cover and chill until cool, at least 1 hour or up until next day.

Spread cornmeal on a sheet of waxed paper. Shape bean mixture, ⅛ at a time, into cakes about ½ inch thick and 2½ inches across; as formed, coat each cake all over with cornmeal and set slightly apart on another sheet of waxed paper.

Rinse and dry the frying pan, then add 2 tablespoons of the oil and set over medium-high heat. When oil is hot, add cakes without crowding; cook until golden brown on both sides. Lift out and keep warm until all are browned; add more oil as needed. Serve bean cakes with salsa to add to taste. Makes 8; allow 1 or 2 for each serving.

PER PIECE: 234 calories, 12 g protein, 18 g carbohydrates, 13 g fat, 19 mg cholesterol, 453 mg sodium

Hagerman, Idaho

May Menus

A SPECIAL LUNCH *for mother on her day leads off this month's menus; junior cooks will find it easy to manage. Chicken stir-fry is the base of a quick supper, and baked-ahead meat-filled buns can reheat in a microwave oven for a serve-yourself breakfast.*

MOTHER'S DAY LUNCH

Falafel Pie
Cucumber & Jicama Salad
Chocolate-dipped Strawberries
Iced Tea   Zinfandel

Falafel mix (seasoned garbanzo meal) combined with ground-turkey sausage makes a piquant meat pie; both ingredients are available at supermarkets.

Check the freezer case for turkey sausage. Thaw either in the refrigerator overnight or in the microwave oven according to manufacturer's directions. Look for falafel mix in the same section as rice and rice mixes, or with the fancy foods.

While the pie bakes, make a salad of 2 cups diced peeled jicama and 2 cups diced European cucumbers; season to taste with rice vinegar and salt. Serve on rinsed and crisped butter lettuce leaves.

Purchase chocolate-dipped strawberries, or serve berries with powdered sugar.

FALAFEL PIE

- 3 large eggs
- ¾ cup nonfat milk
- 1 package (8 oz.) falafel mix
- 1 pound ground-turkey sausage or ground turkey
- 1 small can (4 oz.) diced green chilies
- 1 cup low-fat unflavored yogurt
  Lime wedges

In a large bowl, beat eggs, milk, and falafel mix until evenly moistened. To another bowl, add ½ cup of the falafel mixture, turkey sausage, and green chilies; stir to mix well.

Smoothly spread turkey-falafel mixture in an 8- by 12-inch oval casserole at least 1¾ inches deep. Spread remaining falafel over meat mixture. Bake in a 350° oven until well browned, about 45 minutes. Spoon from casserole. Add yogurt

Offering easy-to-make falafel-turkey pie they baked themselves, youngsters treat on Mother's Day. Accompany with salad, and serve chocolate-dipped strawberries for dessert.

---

and squeezes of lime juice to taste to individual portions. Makes 4 or 5 servings.

PER SERVING: 348 calories, 28 g protein, 27 g carbohydrates, 14 g fat, 158 mg cholesterol, 824 mg sodium

CHICKEN PLATTER SUPPER

**Chicken & Mushrooms
with Couscous
Hot Asparagus
Poached Pears
Toasted Almond Ice Cream
Chardonnay
Fruit-flavor Mineral Water**

Fast and fresh, this simple meal uses couscous made creamy with milk.

First, pound and cut up boned chicken, then cook onion-mushroom mixture. When you heat milk for the couscous, also heat the water and cook asparagus. Drain the asparagus as soon as it is tender-crisp; keep vegetables warm.

CHICKEN & MUSHROOMS WITH COUSCOUS

- 1 **pound boned and skinned chicken thighs**
- 2 **tablespoons butter or margarine**
- 1 **large onion, chopped**
- ¾ **pound mushrooms, sliced**
- 1 **tablespoon cornstarch**
- 1 **cup regular-strength chicken broth**
- 3 **tablespoons dry sherry (or 3 more tablespoons regular-strength chicken broth)**
- 2 **tablespoons soy sauce**
- ⅛ **teaspoon cayenne**
- 2 **cups low-fat milk**
- 1½ **cups couscous**

Place chicken between sheets of plastic wrap and pound with a flat mallet until about ¼ inch thick. Discard plastic wrap and cut chicken into ½-inch-wide strips; set aside.

In a 10- to 12-inch frying pan, melt 1 tablespoon butter over medium-high heat; add onion and mushrooms. Stir often until liquid evaporates and onion is golden and sweet-tasting, about 15 minutes. Lift onion mixture from pan with a slotted spoon and set aside.

Meanwhile, in a small bowl, smoothly mix cornstarch with ¼ cup broth, the sherry, soy sauce, and cayenne; set aside.

In a 2- to 3-quart pan, bring remaining ¾ cup broth and the milk to boiling over high heat. Stir in couscous; cover, remove from heat, and let stand at least 7 or up to 10 minutes. Stir with a fork.

Add remaining butter to frying pan and melt over high heat. Add chicken and stir-fry until meat is tinged with brown and no longer pink in center (cut to test), 4 to 5 minutes. Return onion mixture to pan; add cornstarch mixture and stir until sauce bubbles, 1 to 2 minutes; remove from heat. Stir couscous with a fork and mound on a warm platter; pour chicken beside couscous. Makes 4 or 5 servings.

PER SERVING: 446 calories, 31 g protein, 56 g carbohydrates, 10 g fat, 92 mg cholesterol, 606 mg sodium

BOW FOR BREAKFAST

**Baked Breakfast Bow
Fresh Pineapple Slices
Chopped Crystallized Ginger
Orange Juice   Herbal Tea**

Chinese bow are buns—usually steamed, though sometimes baked—filled with meat and other ingredients. Here, we offer a Western version, stuffed with beef.

Depending on how you need to budget your time, you can serve bow immediately after baking or store them. If you make the buns a day ahead, chill overnight, then reheat buns in the morning, one at a time, in a microwave oven; bow can also be reheated together in a regular oven. Offer with thinly sliced pineapple strewn with finely chopped candied ginger.

(Continued on next page)

Pour hot stir-fry made with chicken thigh strips onto warm platter beside creamy, quick couscous and warm spears of asparagus.

BAKED BREAKFAST BOW

1 **loaf (1 lb.) frozen honey-wheat or whole-wheat bread dough, thawed**
Sage beef filling (recipe follows)

On a lightly floured board, divide dough into 16 equal pieces; shape each piece into a ball, then cover with plastic wrap to prevent drying. Working with 1 piece at a time, pat ball into about a 3-inch round, then roll into a 4½-inch-wide round, turning dough over and flouring board as required to prevent sticking.

Spoon about 2 tablespoons (1⁄16) of the filling in the center of the round; pull edges of dough over filling and pinch together to seal. Set filled bun, pinched side up, on a greased 12- by 15-inch bak-ing sheet (you will need 2 pans); keep covered with plastic wrap. As each bun is shaped, place about 2 inches from others on pan. Let rise in a warm place until puffy-looking, about 20 minutes.

Bake, uncovered, in a 350° oven until richly browned, about 25 minutes. Serve warm or, if made ahead, let cool, wrap airtight, and chill up to 2 days.

To reheat buns 1 at a time in a micro-wave oven, set between sheets of paper towels; cook on half-power (50 percent) until hot to touch, 1 to 2 minutes.

To reheat buns all at once, set slightly apart on a baking sheet and bake in a 350° oven until hot to touch, about 12 minutes. Makes 16; allow 2 per serving.

PER BUN: 169 calories, 7.6 g protein, 8.4 g carbohydrates, 15 g fat, 23 mg cholesterol, 169 mg sodium

Sage beef filling. In a 10- to 12-inch fry-ing pan over medium heat, combine 1 pound **ground lean beef;** 1 large **onion,** chopped; and 1 tablespoon **salad oil.** Stir often until meat is crumbled and well browned, about 25 minutes.

Meanwhile, in a small bowl, smoothly blend 1 tablespoon **cornstarch** with ¾ cup **regular-strength beef broth** and 2 tablespoons **cider vinegar;** set aside.

To browned meat add 2 tablespoons grated **parmesan cheese,** 2 teaspoons **dry rubbed sage,** 1 teaspoon **caraway seed,** and ¼ teaspoon **pepper;** mix well. Add cornstarch mixture and stir until bubbling. Season to taste with **salt.** Let cool; if made ahead, cover and chill up until next day. Makes about 2 cups.

Lattice-topped Apricot Pie (page 135) and Orange Blossom–Strawberry Pie (page 133)

JUNE

Sun-ripened fruit, served
fresh or enclosed in flaky pastry, is one of summer's pleasures.
This month readers share their favorite fruit pies—simple,
piled high with fruit, and visually appealing. Outdoor chefs
will find fresh ideas for cooking steak and sauce together on
the barbecue. For warm June days, we suggest main-dish
salads and several dishes seasoned with the cooling flavor of
fresh mint. Ready for something different? Try our Japanese
breakfast with a Western twist, experiment with exotic eggs,
or spend a leisurely day making Finnish-style cheese.

131

Summer Fruit Pies

S UN-RIPENED FRUIT, *served fresh or cooked in a flaky crust, is a classic summer dessert. Pioneers, cherishing the harvest of their newly planted orchards and gardens, considered fruit pies a joy of the season. They're just as popular today.*

Last year, we asked readers to share their favorite summer fruit pie recipes with us. Hundreds of letters poured in from all over the West, from points including big cities, remote ranches, and just about everywhere in between. From this cooperative outpouring, we taste-tested our way to the 11 grand pies offered in these pages.

Our tally showed berries collectively (strawberries, blueberries, and other bush berries like raspberries and blackberries) to be the most popular pie filling. But the individual fruit that came out on top was the peach. (We set aside candidates using spring rhubarb or late-summer or fall fruits; we'll look at them when those fruits are in season.)

To our surprise, many of your recipes were quite similar; we merely selected fine, representative examples.

Like the readers who wrote to us, our tasters preferred pies that were simple, ungimmicky, filled with fruit, and visually appealing because of the color and texture of the fruit. You might even call these pies

old-fashioned; sometimes, it would seem, no matter how innovative your spirit, the most forthright presentation can't be improved upon.

Choices of double-crust pies include confections laden with boysenberries or blackberries (page 134), cherries or apricots (page 135). The open-faced pies make showy displays of raw or cooked fruit. Pies of strawberries and blueberries (page 133) are topped with cooked glazes of the same berries. Cooked contrasting-fruit glazes top mangoes with orange juice (page 136), and nectarines with mulberries, blackberries, or ollalieberries (page 137). Melted jelly sparkles on the mixed berries and cream pie (page 135). And cream bakes with fruit in the open-faced pies of peaches (page 136), raspberries (page 132), and plums (page 135).

For the crust, whether double or open-faced, some readers prefer ready-to-use pastry dough or pie crust mix; others make their own pastry. We offer a good basic recipe below; it produces a crust that is both tender and flaky, fine for any of these pies.

A word of warning: these recipes weren't conceived with calorie-cutting in mind. Even the nutritionally virtuous seem to agree that a good summer pie warrants a splurge.

FRENCH RASPBERRY PIE

- 6 cups raspberries
- 1 cup sugar
- ¼ cup quick-cooking tapioca
- ½ teaspoon ground cinnamon
- ¼ teaspoon salt (optional)
- 1 cup sour cream
  Unbaked pastry for a single-crust 9-inch pie (see box, below)

Rinse berries and drain dry on absorbent towels. In a small bowl, mix sugar, tapioca, cinnamon, and salt. Stir in sour cream; let stand 15 minutes to soften tapioca.

Put 4½ cups raspberries into pastry shell; reserve remaining berries for garnish.

Pour sour cream mixture evenly over raspberries in pastry shell. Set pie in a foil-lined 10- by 15-inch pan. Bake in 400° oven on the lowest rack until filling is bubbly and surface is browned, 45 to 55 minutes. If rim begins to darken excessively, drape with strips of foil. Let cool, then pile remaining berries on top of pie. If made ahead, cover and chill up until next day. Cut into wedges. Serves 8 or 9. —*Pamela Parr, Richland, Wash.*

PER SERVING: 334 calories, 3.3 g protein, 50 g carbohydrates, 15 g fat, 11 mg cholesterol, 74 mg sodium

---

The Art of the Pie Crust

W HEN BAKING PIES, place them on the lowest rack of the oven so the bottom of the crust can brown well. Because the pastry rim is thin, it cooks faster; if you want to keep the pie crust an even color, you can tent any darkening areas with a piece of foil to slow down browning.

So the pastry will hold its shape when baked empty, take care not to stretch the rolled dough when fitting it into the baking pan; the heat makes stretched dough shrink down from the rim of the pan.

Pastry dough for a double-crust 9-inch pie. In a bowl, combine 2¼ cups **all-purpose flour** and ½ teaspoon **salt**. With a pastry blender or your fingers, cut or rub in ¾ cup **solid vegetable shortening,** butter, or margarine until fine crumbs form. Sprinkle 5 to 7 tablespoons **cold water** over crumbs. Stir with a fork until dough holds together. Divide dough in half and pat each portion into a flat, smooth round. Use as specified in recipes; if made ahead, seal in plastic wrap and chill up to 3 days.

Unbaked or baked pastry for a single-crust 9-inch pie. Follow preceding recipe, using 1 cup plus 2 tablespoons **all-purpose flour;** ¼ teaspoon **salt;** 6 tablespoons **solid vegetable shortening,** butter, or margarine; and 2 to 3 tablespoons **cold water.** On a lightly floured board, roll pastry into a 12-inch-diameter round; ease pastry into a 9-inch pie pan. Fold edges under; flute rim decoratively. Prick pastry all over with a fork to prevent puffing. Bake crust in a 425° oven until golden, 12 to 15 minutes. Cool.

ORANGE BLOSSOM–STRAWBERRY PIE

- 6 to 7 cups strawberries
- ¾ cup sugar
- 3 tablespoons cornstarch
- 1 teaspoon grated orange peel
- 6 tablespoons water
- 2 to 3 tablespoons orange-flavor liqueur or 2 tablespoons thawed frozen orange juice concentrate
  Baked pastry for a single-crust 9-inch pie (see box, facing page)

Rinse strawberries and drain dry on absorbent towels; hull fruit.

In a 1- to 1½-quart pan, combine sugar, cornstarch, and orange peel. In a blender or food processor, whirl 2 cups of the least perfect strawberries with water until smoothly puréed; pour purée into pan, mixing well. Cook, stirring often, over medium-high heat until mixture comes to a full boil, about 5 minutes. Stir in orange liqueur to taste.

Arrange remaining strawberries, tips up, in pastry shell; evenly spoon the hot cooked berry glaze mixture over whole fruit, covering completely. Chill until glaze is cool and set, at least 1 hour or, covered, up until next day. Cut into wedges. Serves 8 or 9. — *Amy Swanson, Thousand Oaks, Calif.*

PER SERVING: 253 calories, 2.4 g protein, 40 g carbohydrates, 9.1 g fat, 0 mg cholesterol, 62 mg sodium

HUCKLEBERRY OR BLUEBERRY PIE

- 5 cups huckleberries or blueberries
- ¾ cup sugar
- 3 tablespoons cornstarch
- ½ teaspoon grated lemon peel
- 1 tablespoon lemon juice
- ½ cup water
  Baked pastry for a single-crust 9-inch pie (see box, facing page)
  Sweetened whipped cream (optional)

Rinse berries and drain dry on absorbent towels. In a 1- to 1½-quart pan, stir together the sugar and cornstarch; add 2 cups berries, lemon peel, lemon juice, and water. Cook, stirring often, over medium-high heat until mixture comes to a full boil, 5 to 7 minutes.

Amy Swanson shows off her favorite strawberry pie; perfect sun-ripened strawberries, tip up in flaky crust, are cloaked by glistening orange-flavored berry glaze.

Gently stir remaining berries into cooked berry mixture; spoon evenly into pastry shell. Chill at least 1 hour or, covered, up until next day. Spoon dollops of whipped cream onto pie. Cut into wedges. Makes 8 or 9 servings. — *Joe Besso, Billings, Mont.*

PER SERVING: 250 calories, 2.2 g protein, 41 g carbohydrates, 9 g fat, 0 mg cholesterol, 65 mg sodium

(Continued on next page)

Blackberries in a double-crust pie were gathered by Mary Jane Campbell of Geyserville, California. The pie's a summer winner served with ice cream.

BOYSENBERRY OR DOUBLE BLACKBERRY PIE

If berries are firm-ripe, use minimum tapioca; if soft-ripe, use the maximum.

    6 cups boysenberries or blackberries
    1 cup sugar
    3 to 4 tablespoons quick-cooking
       tapioca
    ½ teaspoon ground cinnamon
    ¼ teaspoon ground nutmeg
    1 tablespoon lemon juice
    3 tablespoons blackberry-flavor
       liqueur (cordial or brandy),
       optional
       Pastry for a double-crust 9-inch
       pie (see box, page 132)

Rinse berries and drain dry on absorbent towels. In a large bowl, stir together sugar, tapioca, cinnamon, and nutmeg. Add berries, lemon juice, and liqueur; mix gently. Let stand at least 15 minutes or up to 1 hour to soften tapioca, stirring gently now and then.

On a lightly floured board, roll half the pastry into a 12-inch-diameter round; ease into a 9-inch pie pan. Fill with berry mixture. On floured board, roll out remaining pastry into an 11-inch-diameter round; if desired, cut center in several places with a decorative 1-inch-wide cooky cutter; remove cutouts, brush bottoms of cutouts with water, and place on pastry in a decorative way. Lay pastry over fruit. Trim pastry to within 1 inch of pan rim; fold edges under, flush to rim, and flute to seal. If top is not cut, slash in several places so steam can escape.

Set pie in a foil-lined 10- by 15-inch pan (pie bubbles as it cooks). Bake in a 400° oven on the lowest rack until pastry is golden brown and filling is bubbly, 55 to 60 minutes. If rim begins to darken excessively, drape with strips of foil.

Serve warm or at room temperature. If made ahead, let cool, then cover loosely and store at room temperature up until next day. Cut into wedges. Serves 8 or 9.—*Mary Jane Campbell, Campbell Ranch Inn, Geyserville, Calif.*

PER SERVING: 406 calories, 4.2 g protein, 60 g carbohydrates, 18 g fat, 0 mg cholesterol, 124 mg sodium

LATTICE-TOPPED APRICOT PIE

About 2 pounds firm-ripe
apricots, pitted and quartered;
you need 6 cups fruit
1½ tablespoons lemon juice
½ cup *each* granulated sugar and
firmly packed brown sugar
3 to 4 tablespoons quick-cooking
tapioca
Pastry for a double-crust 9-inch
pie (see box, page 132)

In a large bowl, combine apricots and
lemon juice. Stir together granulated
sugar, brown sugar, and tapioca, then
mix gently with fruit. Let stand at least
15 minutes or up to 1 hour to soften tapioca; mix gently now and then.

On a lightly floured board, roll half
the pastry into a 12-inch-diameter
round; ease into a 9-inch pie pan. Fill
with apricot mixture. On floured board,
roll remaining pastry into a 10-inch
square. With a pastry wheel or knife, cut
into 8 equal strips. Arrange pastry strips
on top of pie in lattice pattern; trim off
strips as they lap over pan rim. Fold the
bottom crust over lattice, flush with pan
rim; flute pastry to seal.

Set pie in a foil-lined 10- by 15-inch pan
(pie bubbles as it cooks). Bake in a 400°
oven on the lowest rack until pastry is
golden brown and filling is bubbly, 55 to
65 minutes. If rim begins to darken
excessively, drape with strips of foil.

Serve warm or at room temperature. If
made ahead, let cool, then cover loosely
and store at room temperature up until
next day. Cut into wedges. Serves 8 or
9. — *Susan Johnson, Ridgecrest, Calif.*

PER SERVING: 413 calories, 4.6 g protein, 61 g carbohydrates, 18 g fat,
0 mg cholesterol, 127 mg sodium

SPICED PLUM CUSTARD PIE

About 1½ pounds firm-ripe plums
such as Friar, Laroda, Elephant
Heart, or prune plums, pitted
and cut into about ½-inch-wide
slices; you need 4 to 5 cups fruit
Unbaked pastry for a single-crust
9-inch pie (see box, page 132)
10 tablespoons sugar
⅛ teaspoon *each* ground allspice and
ground cardamom
2 large eggs
¾ cup half-and-half (light cream) or
whipping cream

Put plums in pastry, arranging top layer
of fruit in overlapping circles. Combine 2
tablespoons sugar with the allspice and
cardamom; sprinkle over fruit. Bake in a
375° oven on lowest rack for 20 minutes.
Meanwhile, in a small bowl, beat eggs to
blend with cream and remaining sugar.
Pour mixture over plums. Continue baking pie until custard appears set in center when gently shaken and pastry is
golden brown, 30 to 40 minutes longer.
If rim begins to darken excessively, drape
with strips of foil.

Serve warm or at room temperature. If
made ahead, cool, cover, and chill up
until next day. Cut into wedges. Serves 8
or 9. — *Wanda Knarr, Las Vegas.*

PER SERVING: 332 calories, 4.5 g protein, 43 g carbohydrates, 17 g fat,
69 mg cholesterol, 81 mg sodium

MIXED BERRIES & CREAM PIE

¾ cup currant jelly
1 tablespoon black raspberry-
or strawberry-flavor liqueur
(optional)
About 1 cup *each* (4 cups *total*)
blueberries, blackberries,
raspberries, and strawberries
½ cup whipping cream
1 tablespoon powdered sugar
Baked pastry for a single-crust
9-inch pie (see box, page 132)

In a 1- to 2-cup pan on medium heat, stir
jelly until melted; mix in liqueur. Let
glaze cool to room temperature, about
10 minutes.

Rinse berries and drain dry on absorbent towels; hull strawberries, then cut
in half.

In a small bowl, whip cream at high
speed with an electric mixer until it
holds soft peaks. Stir in the sugar, then
spread cream evenly in pastry shell. Pile
berries onto whipped cream. Spoon
glaze evenly over fruit. Cut into wedges
and serve at once. Serves 8 or 9. — *Frances
Winick, Tucson.*

PER SERVING: 283 calories, 2.5 g protein, 40 g carbohydrates, 13 g fat,
15 mg cholesterol, 70 mg sodium

*Utah's sweet dark cherries inspired Marcella
Borrowman's lattice-topped pie.*

SWEET CHERRY PIE

6½ cups pitted Bing or other dark
sweet cherries
1 tablespoon lemon juice
¼ teaspoon almond extract
½ cup sugar
3 tablespoons cornstarch
Pastry for a double-crust 9-inch
pie (see box, page 132)

In a large bowl, combine cherries, lemon
juice, and almond extract. Mix sugar and
cornstarch, then stir into fruit.

On a lightly floured board, roll half
the pastry into a 12-inch-diameter
round; ease into a 9-inch pie pan. Fill
with cherry mixture. On a floured
board, roll out remaining pastry into a
10-inch square. With a pastry wheel or
knife, cut into 8 equal strips. Arrange
pastry strips on top of pie in lattice pattern; trim off strips as they lap over rim.
Fold bottom crust over lattice, flush with
pan rim; flute to seal.

Set pie in a foil-lined 10- by 15-inch pan
(pie bubbles as it cooks). Bake in a 400°
oven on the lowest rack until pastry is
golden brown and filling is bubbly, 55 to
65 minutes. If rim begins to darken
excessively, drape with strips of foil.

Serve warm or at room temperature. If
made ahead, let cool, then cover loosely
and store at room temperature up until
next day. Cut into wedges. Serves 8 or
9. — *Marcella Borrowman, Sandy, Utah.*

PER SERVING: 394 calories, 4.5 g protein, 55 g carbohydrates, 18 g fat,
0 mg cholesterol, 123 mg sodium

(Continued on next page)

COLORADO PEACH CREAM PIE

¾ cup sugar
3½ tablespoons quick-cooking tapioca
½ teaspoon vanilla
¼ teaspoon ground nutmeg
½ cup whipping cream
6 cups peeled and sliced firm-ripe peaches
  Unbaked pastry for a single-crust 9-inch pie (see box, page 132)
¼ cup sliced almonds

In a small bowl, stir together sugar and tapioca; mix in vanilla, nutmeg, and cream. Let stand 15 minutes for tapioca to soften.

Pour peaches into pastry, then pour cream mixture evenly over fruit. Set pie in a foil-lined 10- by 15-inch pan. Bake in 375° oven on lowest rack until filling is bubbly and lightly browned and pastry is golden brown, 45 to 50 minutes. If rim begins to darken excessively, drape with strips of foil. About 5 minutes before pie is done, sprinkle almonds on it.

Serve warm or at room temperature. If made ahead, cool, cover, and chill up until next day. Cut into wedges. Serves 8 or 9. — *Pam Butler, Longmont, Colo.*

PER SERVING: 325 calories, 3.6 g protein, 47 g carbohydrates, 15 g fat, 15 mg cholesterol, 66 mg sodium

MANGO CREAM PIE IN MACADAMIA NUT CRUST

Mangoes are of fine quality and reasonable price in June.

1 package (3 oz.) cream cheese
6 tablespoons powdered sugar
½ teaspoon vanilla
½ cup whipping cream
  Macadamia nut crust (recipe follows)
2 large (about 1 lb. each) firm-ripe mangoes, peeled
  Fresh orange glaze (recipe follows)

In a small bowl, whip cream cheese, sugar, vanilla, and 2 tablespoons of the cream with an electric mixer until smoothly blended. In another bowl, whip remaining cream until it holds soft peaks, then fold, gently but thoroughly, into cream cheese mixture. Spoon filling into baked crust.

Slice mangoes thinly and in small pieces (no longer or wider than 1 in.) and lay evenly in overlapping circles on filling. Spoon glaze evenly over fruit. Chill until glaze is set, at least 1 hour or, cov-

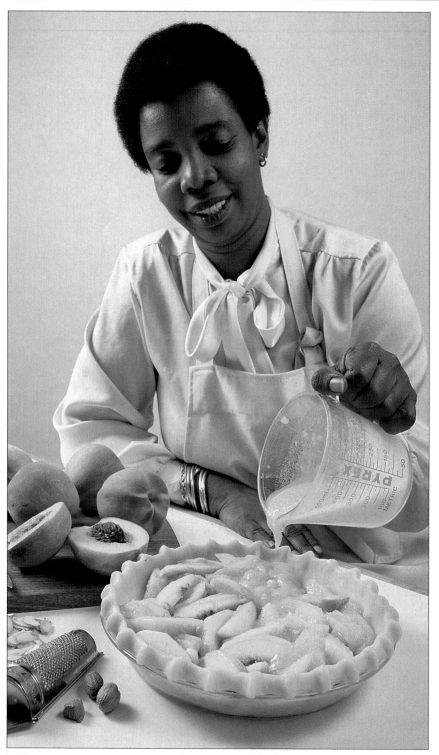

Peaches rate highest as Western cooks' favorite pie fruit. Sunset's Louise Jones tests Pam Butler's Colorado peach cream pie.

ered, up to 10 hours. Cut into wedges. Serves 8 or 9. —*Rosemarie Ferge, Kaneohe, Hawaii.*

PER SERVING: 325 calories, 3.6 g protein, 47 g carbohydrates, 15 g fat, 15 mg cholesterol, 66 mg sodium

Macadamia nut crust. In a food processor or with your fingers, whirl or rub together 1 cup **all-purpose flour;** 6 tablespoons **butter** or margarine, cut up; and ½ cup finely chopped **salted macadamia nuts.** Add 1 **large egg;** process or stir with a fork until dough holds together. Press dough evenly over bottom and up sides of a 9-inch pie pan. Bake crust in a 325° oven until golden, 25 to 30 minutes; let cool.

Fresh orange glaze. In a 1- to 1½-quart pan, combine ⅓ cup **granulated sugar,** 2 tablespoons **cornstarch,** and 1 teaspoon grated **orange peel;** stir in 1 cup **orange juice** and 1 tablespoon **lemon juice.** Cook, stirring frequently, over medium-high heat until mixture comes to a full boil, about 5 minutes. Let cool to room temperature and stir before using.

PER SERVING: 362 calories, 4.1 g protein, 41 g carbohydrates, 21 g fat, 72 mg cholesterol, 153 mg sodium

NECTARINE-MULBERRY PIE

If you can't buy mulberries and don't grow them, substitute other berries.

- 2 cups mulberries, ollalieberries, or blackberries
- ¾ cup sugar
- 3 tablespoons cornstarch
- 1 cup water
- 2½ cups sliced ripe nectarines
  Baked pastry for a single-crust 9-inch pie (see box, page 132)

Rinse berries and drain dry on absorbent towels. In a 1- to 1½-quart pan, combine sugar and cornstarch. Add 1 cup of the berries and the water. Cook, stirring often, over medium-high heat until mixture comes to a full boil, 5 to 7 minutes.

Distribute nectarines and remaining berries in an even layer in pastry; spoon hot berry mixture over fruit. Chill until glaze is set, at least 1 hour or, covered, up until next day. Cut into wedges. Makes 8 or 9 servings. —*Rose Marie Davis, Talent, Ore.*

PER SERVING: 245 calories, 2.3 g protein, 40 g carbohydrates, 9 g fat, 0 mg cholesterol, 61 mg sodium

Nectarines turn crimson under a mulberry glaze (or use blackberries or ollalieberries if you can't get mulberries). Pie, from Rose Marie Davis, travels well on Oregon outing.

Steak & Sauce Together on the Barbecue

IT'S DOUBLY TANTALIZING: *a show-stopping steak sizzling on the barbecue and an aromatic sauce or fresh relish simmering alongside as its complement.*

You start with a 2-inch-thick steak, either a bone-in cut or an easy-to-slice boneless piece, big enough to serve 4 to 6 people. You might order the thick cut in advance to ensure your choice.

As the meat cooks, grill vegetables alongside, then use them to make a simple sauce or relish. Choose a grilled tomato-and-basil relish, soy- and onion-seasoned sake, or a red wine-and-shallot sauce.

GRILLED STEAK WITH GRILLED TOMATO RELISH

- 1 **bone-in beefsteak (2½ to 3 lb.) such as T-bone or porterhouse, or a boneless beefsteak (1½ to 2 lb.) such as top round or sirloin, about 2 inches thick**
- 8 **medium-size (about 1¾ lb. total) Roma-type tomatoes, cored and cut in half lengthwise**
- 2 **tablespoons olive oil**
- 1 **large onion, chopped**
- 1 **clove garlic, pressed or minced**
- ½ **cup chopped fresh or ¼ cup dry basil leaves**
  Salt and pepper

Trim excess fat off meat. Set steak on a grill 4 to 6 inches above a solid bed of medium coals (you can hold your hand at grill level only 4 to 5 seconds). Turn steak, as needed, to brown evenly and cook until a thermometer inserted in thickest part registers 135° to 140° for rare, 20 to 25 minutes total.

Meanwhile, place the tomatoes, cut side up, on grill and brush tops lightly with olive oil. When tomatoes are browned on bottom, 2 to 3 minutes, turn them over and continue cooking until soft when pressed, 4 to 6 minutes longer.

As tomatoes cook, combine remaining oil, onion, and garlic in a metal-handled 8- to 10-inch frying pan and set on grill over coals; stir often until onions are limp and tinged with gold, 8 to 10 minutes. Stir in basil. When tomatoes are soft, add them to onion mixture and set pan on cooler part of grill or remove from barbecue and keep warm.

When meat is done, place on a board with a well or on a platter.

Cut meat away from bone, if present, then cut across grain in thin slices. If desired, spoon accumulated meat juices into warm tomato relish. Offer tomato mixture to spoon over meat slices. Season portions to taste with salt and pepper. Serves 4 to 6.

PER SERVING: 266 calories, 26 g protein, 9.2 g carbohydrates, 14 g fat, 70 mg cholesterol, 69 mg sodium

GRILLED BEEF WITH SOY-SEASONED SAKE

- 1 **bone-in beefsteak (2½ to 3 lb.) such as T-bone or porterhouse, or a boneless beefsteak (1½ to 2 lb.) such as top round or sirloin, about 2 inches thick**
- 1 **tablespoon Oriental sesame oil or salad oil**
- 2 **cloves garlic, pressed or minced**
- 2 **tablespoons minced fresh ginger**
- ½ **cup thinly sliced green onion**
- ⅔ **cup sake (rice wine) or dry sherry**
- 3 **tablespoons soy sauce**
- 12 **green onions, ends trimmed**
  Salt and pepper

Trim excess fat from meat. Set steak on a grill 4 to 6 inches above a solid bed of medium coals (you can hold your hand at grill level only 4 to 5 seconds).

Turn steak, as needed, to brown evenly and cook until a thermometer inserted in thickest part registers 135° to 140° for rare, 20 to 25 minutes total.

Meanwhile, place a metal-handled 6- to 8-inch frying pan with the oil, garlic, ginger, and sliced green onion on grill over the coals. Stir often until onions are limp, 5 to 8 minutes; then add sake and soy sauce and cook until mixture boils. Move to cooler part of grill or remove from barbecue, if done before steak.

Also lay whole green onions on grill and cook until lightly browned on both sides, 2 to 4 minutes total.

Place meat and grilled onions on a board with a well or on a platter. Reheat sauce on grill, if cool. Cut meat away from bone, if present, then cut meat in thin slices across grain. If desired, pour accumulated meat juices into warm sauce. Spoon warm sauce mixture over meat. Season portions to taste with salt and pepper. Makes 4 to 6 servings.

PER SERVING: 236 calories, 26 g protein, 6.7 g carbohydrates, 11 g fat, 70 mg cholesterol, 576 mg sodium

GRILLED BEEF WITH WINE-SHALLOT SAUCE

- 1 **bone-in beefsteak (2½ to 3 lb.) such as T-bone or porterhouse, or a boneless beefsteak (1½ to 2 lb.) such as top round or sirloin, about 2 inches thick**
- 2 **or 3 small (about 5 oz. each) unpeeled red onions, cut in half lengthwise**
- 2 **tablespoons butter or margarine**
- ½ **cup chopped shallots**
- ¾ **cup dry red wine**
- 1 **tablespoon Dijon mustard**
- 1 **teaspoon Worcestershire**
- ½ **teaspoon coarsely ground pepper**
- ½ **teaspoon dry tarragon leaves**
  Salt

Trim excess fat off meat. Set steak on a grill 4 to 6 inches above a solid bed of medium coals (you can hold your hand at grill level only 4 to 5 seconds). Place onions, cut side down, on grill. Turn steak, as needed, to brown evenly and cook until a thermometer inserted in thickest part registers 135° to 140° for rare, 20 to 25 minutes total. When onions are browned on cut side, about 10 minutes, turn over and cook until they are soft when pressed, about 10 minutes more.

Meanwhile, place a metal-handled 6- to 8-inch frying pan containing the butter and shallots on grill over the coals; stir shallots occasionally. When shallots are tinged with brown, after 6 to 8 minutes, stir in wine, mustard, Worcestershire, pepper, and tarragon. Cook until sauce is reduced to about ¾ cup, about 10 minutes; set on cooler part of grill or remove from barbecue.

Place meat and onions on a board with a well or on a platter. Reheat sauce on grill, if cool. Cut meat away from bone, if present, then cut across grain in thin slices. If desired, pour accumulated meat juices into sauce. Spoon sauce over slices. Season portions to taste with salt. Makes 4 to 6 servings.

PER SERVING: 253 calories, 26 g protein, 6.9 g carbohydrates, 13 g fat, 80 mg cholesterol, 185 mg sodium

While steak sizzles, grill Roma-type tomatoes until soft; then add tomatoes to onion-basil mixture to make relish. To serve, cut meat away from bone, then slice crosswise into thin pieces. Offer relish to eat with juicy beef. This 2-inch-thick steak serves 4 to 6.

The Japanese Breakfast with a Western Twist

A S MORE JAPANESE TRAVEL TO THE WEST, *the Japanese breakfast is joining American and Continental breakfasts on menus. Here we present two ways to enjoy this cultural merger: a typical Japanese morning meal, and a Western adaptation of it.*

Some of the Japanese foods may seem unfamiliar, but many correspond to familiar American breakfast items. For example, Japanese preserved fish as a way to start the day often causes Westerners to hesitate. But when you offer smoked salmon as an alternative, the relationship in choices is more apparent. We list parallel choices: you can be traditional or innovative, Eastern or Western, as you select something from each category. Shop in an Asian market or well-stocked supermarket for the authentic ingredients, or choose readily available Western alternatives.

Much of the charm of a Japanese meal is in the presentation. Serving each food in a separate container, with an eye to the over-all arrangement, lends such a breakfast the quality of a still life.

RICE

For either cuisine, offer hot cooked short- or medium-grain rice, about 1 cup per serving. Plain rice accompanies the Japanese breakfast. Westerners can eat rice or another hot or cold cereal, topped with sugar, cream, and fruit.

SOUP

Serve any hot broth, or make one of these combinations; the miso soup is traditional.

Miso soup. In a 1- to 1½-quart pan, combine 2 tablespoons **light miso,** 1 bag (¾ oz.) **dashi-no-moto** (seasoning for soup stock), and about 3 cups **water** (check package directions). Simmer, uncovered, for 15 minutes. Discard bag. Add three or four 1- by 1½- by 1½-inch pieces (1 oz. each) rinsed and drained **soft tofu** (optional); when hot, ladle into bowls. Serves 3 or 4.

NUTRITIONAL INFORMATION NOT AVAILABLE.

Gingered broth. In a 1- to 1½-quart pan, bring to boiling 2½ cups **regular-strength beef broth** and 2 teaspoons minced **fresh ginger.** Ladle into bowls. Serves 3 or 4.

PER SERVING: 12 calories, 0.3 g protein, 1.9 g carbohydrates, 0.4 g fat, 0 mg cholesterol, 3.1 mg sodium

TOFU

Typically, tofu is served separately or in miso soup. Allow about 1 ounce (see size above) per serving. Serve cool or warm (immerse in hot water for 1 to 2 minutes, then drain). Season with soy, mirin (sweet rice wine), or toasted sesame seed (optional).

For the Western breakfast, offer 1 ounce of cheese (such as cream cheese) with smoked fish for a serving.

Typical Japanese morning meal features (clockwise from preserved fish) soy, sweet omelet, green tea, miso soup, rice, and nori. In center are pickles and strawberry. Artistic presentation of food, each kind in its separate container, adds charm to Asian meal.

FISH

For each portion, allow 1 to 2 ounces of preserved fish, 2 to 3 ounces of fresh fish. Japanese markets sell the fish favored for breakfast: salted salmon, or partially dried mackerel or pike (both often seasoned with teriyaki sauce). Whatever your choice of fish, broil and eat warm.

Western choices might include cold smoked salmon (lox), smoked trout, tiny sardines, warmed Alaskan (black) cod, sautéed trout, or sand dabs.

EGGS

Both cuisines feature eggs cooked in the shell, hard or soft. Japanese also favor the sweet rolled omelet; Westerners may prefer scrambled or poached eggs.

Sweet rolled omelet. Whisk to blend 2 **large eggs,** 1 teaspoon **mirin** (sweet rice wine), and ¼ teaspoon **soy sauce.** Over high heat, place a nonstick frying pan with sloping sides and a bottom that measures 7 to 9 inches across. When pan is hot enough to make a drop of water dance, remove from heat and at once add 1 teaspoon **salad oil,** then pour in egg mixture. Mixture starts to set at once. Quickly, with a wide spatula, push cooked portions to center from opposite sides, and let uncooked egg flow onto bare pan underneath. You want a pale, not browned, omelet.

When mixture no longer flows, lift opposite edges over center, making a straight-sided shape. Flip omelet, bottom up, onto a plate; let cool. If made ahead, cover and chill up until the next day. Cut crosswise into 1-inch slices. Serves 2.

PER SERVING: 102 calories, 6.3 g protein, 1.6 g carbohydrates, 7.3 g fat, 213 mg cholesterol, 105 mg sodium

PICKLES

Pickled vegetables (onions, mushrooms, gobo—burdock root), seaweed, and ginger (often sold in little plastic bags) are Japanese choices to go with rice.

Westerners relish capers, salsa, prepared horseradish, or chopped onion as condiments for the fish.

NORI

As a crisp element, Japanese offer nori (seaweed). A Western substitute is thinly sliced toasted bagels, or any toast.

FRUIT

Japanese choose perfect pieces, such as 1 long-stemmed strawberry or a small cluster of grapes. Westerners serve larger portions and place less emphasis on perfection.

TEA

In the East, green tea comes hot and plain. Westerners often like black tea, to which they add milk or cream.

Western counterpart (clockwise from scrambled eggs): lox with capers and diced onions; cream cheese with sliced, toasted bagels; rice with sliced bananas; cream; gingered broth; and tea. Attention to colors, textures, and composition sets an Oriental mood.

Gallos: Central American Tacos

FOR LUNCH OR A SNACK *in Central America, it's common to see sandwiches made with fresh corn tortillas instead of bread. The soft tortillas are wrapped around savory tidbits. In Costa Rica, they're called* gallos; *in Mexico,* tacos.

For this meal, you offer several fillings with soft tortillas. Guests mix foods as they wish. Eat slaw as a relish in tortillas or as a salad. The tortillas and most of the fillings can be made ahead.

Tortillas start with dehydrated masa flour (corn tortilla flour); look for it in your supermarket's flour section or in Mexican and Central American food stores. Or buy warm, freshly made corn tortillas.

CENTRAL AMERICAN TORTILLA SANDWICHES

Fresh corn tortillas (recipe follows)
Black bean filling (recipe follows)
Picadillo filling (recipe follows)
Browned chorizos (recipe follows)
Cabbage slaw relish (recipe follows)
Salsa (homemade or purchased)
About 1½ cups guacamole (homemade or purchased)

Set warm tortillas, wrapped in a napkin, in a basket. Offer bean and picadillo fillings, chorizos, slaw, salsa, and guacamole in separate containers. Add your choice of fillings to a tortilla, then roll up to eat. Makes 16 to 18 sandwiches; serves 6 to 8.

Fresh corn tortillas. In a bowl, stir 2¾ to 3 cups warm **water** into 5 cups **dehydrated masa flour** (corn tortilla flour), adding just enough water so dough holds together well but is not sticky. Shape into a ball. Cover dough with plastic wrap.

For each tortilla, place a ¼-cup ball of dough on a piece of plastic wrap; cover with another piece of the wrap. Pat with your hands to form an even, 6-inch-diameter round slightly less than ⅛ inch thick. Peel off plastic wrap.

As tortillas are formed, cook over medium-high heat on a hot ungreased griddle or in a 10- to 12-inch frying pan, turning them often. After first turning, press occasionally with a wide spatula. Cook until tortillas look dry and are lightly flecked with brown, 1½ to 3 minutes.

Stack tortillas as cooked. Wrap them in a towel, then in foil; keep warm. (If made ahead, cool, wrap airtight in foil, and chill up to overnight. To reheat, place foil-wrapped tortillas in a 350° oven until hot, about 15 minutes.) Makes about 18.

PER TORTILLA: 119 calories, 2.5 g protein, 25 g carbohydrates, 0.8 g fat, 0 mg cholesterol, 0.3 mg sodium

Black bean filling. Sort debris from 1½ cups (10 oz.) **dry black beans.** Rinse and drain beans. In a 3- to 4-quart pan, combine 2 tablespoons **salad oil;** 1 large **onion,** chopped; and 3 cloves **garlic,** pressed or minced. Cook, stirring, over medium heat until onion is limp.

Add beans and 1 quart **regular-strength chicken broth.** Bring to boiling, then simmer, covered, until tender to bite, 1 to 1½ hours. With a potato masher, coarsely mash beans. Add **salt** to taste. Beans should have texture of thin mashed potatoes; if thinner, stir and simmer, uncovered, until thicker. (If made ahead, cool, cover, and chill up to overnight. To reheat, stir over low heat; add a little water if beans stick.) Pour into a bowl and sprinkle with 2 tablespoons shredded **jack cheese.**

PER TABLESPOON: 73 calories, 3.8 g protein, 10 g carbohydrates, 2.2 g fat, 0.6 mg cholesterol, 15 mg sodium

Picadillo filling. In a 10- to 12-inch frying pan, crumble ¾ pound **ground lean beef.** Stir over medium-high heat until browned and crumbly. Add 1 medium-size **onion,** chopped, and 2 cloves **garlic,** pressed or minced; stir until onion is limp. Add 1 tablespoon **canned tomato paste;** ⅓ cup lightly packed chopped **cilantro** (coriander); 1 large **thin-skinned potato** (½ lb.), peeled and cut into ½-inch cubes; and 1½ cups **water.** Cover and cook over low heat for 10 minutes.

Trim ends and dice ¾ pound **patty pan squash;** add to pan. Cover and cook over low heat until vegetables are tender when pierced, 10 to 15 minutes longer. (If made ahead, cool, cover, and chill up to overnight; reheat, covered, over low heat.) If soupy, simmer uncovered, stirring often, until most of the liquid evaporates. Add **salt** and **pepper** to taste. Garnish with **cilantro sprigs.**

PER TABLESPOON: 37 calories, 2.2 g protein, 2 g carbohydrates, 2.2 g fat, 8 mg cholesterol, 12 mg sodium

Browned chorizos. Pierce 6 to 8 **chorizo sausages** (about 1½ lb. total) in several places with a fork (if casings are inedible, remove meat and crumble). Place meat in a 10- to 12-inch frying pan and cook on low heat, turning often (or stirring crumbled sausage), until browned, 10 to 15 minutes; spoon off and discard fat as it accumulates. Cut whole sausages in half lengthwise. Drain on paper towels.

PER ½ SAUSAGE: 126 calories, 4.5 g protein, 0.3 g carbohydrates, 12 g fat, 23 mg cholesterol, 273 mg sodium

Cabbage slaw relish. In a large bowl, mix ⅓ cup **salad oil** and 3 tablespoons **white wine vinegar.** Add 6 cups lightly packed shredded **cabbage,** ½ cup shredded peeled **carrot,** and ¼ cup thinly sliced **green onion;** mix. Add **salt** and **pepper** to taste. Pour into serving bowl. Dice 1 large firm-ripe **tomato** and place on top of salad.

PER ¾-CUP SERVING: 100 calories, 0.9 g protein, 4.7 g carbohydrates, 9.1 g fat, 0 mg cholesterol, 14 mg sodium

In sandwiches Central American–style, soft corn tortillas are the bread; fillings include picadillo (ground beef and vegetable mixture), black beans, chorizo sausages, guacamole, and salsa. Spoon your favorite fillings into a warm tortilla, wrap to enclose, and eat like a taco or sandwich.

Exotic Eggs

SCRAMBLED, POACHED, OR FRIED—*any question what we're talking about? But how about if we say salted and coated with ash, packed in mud, or tiny and speckled? For each, the answer is the same: eggs.*

Here we offer inviting ways to use unusual eggs—from duck eggs preserved in two ancient Oriental ways to fresh, speckled quail eggs.

Preserved duck eggs (about $1.75 for 4) come in two forms: thousand-year-old (sometimes chicken instead of duck) and salted; check Asian markets. Both look quite strange, but even our timid tasters were intrigued by the distinctive flavors. In these recipes, they are used as seasonings for chicken eggs and sushi. Neither type of preserved egg needs refrigeration, but use within 2 weeks of purchase.

Thousand-year-old eggs are considerably younger than their name, though they do look as if they've been around for quite a while. Raw eggs in the shell are coated with clay, dry lime (calcium oxide), and rice husks, then buried in earth-filled clay pots for 90 days. The coating preserves the egg as the yolk firms and the white gels. Yolks turn green-black; whites become dark amber. The flavor grows earthy and slightly fermented, similar to fermented black beans.

Salted duck eggs start with raw eggs in the shell; they're submerged in brine, then coated with ash. Yolks harden and turn bright orange; the white stays clear and liquid. Flavor resembles rich, intensely flavored, salty chicken eggs.

Look for quail eggs in supermarkets and Asian food markets (about $1.50 for 10). They taste much like chicken eggs, but their charming look and size attract attention. Here, three recipes take advantage of these attributes.

STEAMED THREE EGGS

- 1 **thousand-year-old duck or chicken egg**
- 1 **salted duck egg**
- 2 **large chicken eggs**
- ¼ **cup regular-strength chicken broth**
- 2 **tablespoons dry sherry or dry white wine**
- 1 **tablespoon rice vinegar**
- ¼ **cup chopped green onion**
  Sliced pickled ginger

Rinse clean the thousand-year-old egg, then peel and rinse again; pat dry. Cut into 8 wedges and arrange in an oiled shallow (about 2-inch-deep) 2-cup bowl.

Rinse clean the salted egg. Crack shell and pour the white into a small bowl. Chop yolk; sprinkle over thousand-year-old egg. To salted white, add chicken eggs, broth, sherry, and vinegar; beat to blend.

Set bowl with salted yolk on a rack over at least 1 inch water in a 5- to 6-quart pan or wok. Slowly pour beaten egg mixture over egg wedges, taking care to keep pattern.

Bring water to a boil over high heat; cover and steam until eggs are just firm to touch, about 10 minutes. Remove from heat; let stand until room temperature or up to 2 hours. Run a knife around edge and along bottom of dish; invert eggs onto a flat plate. Sprinkle with onion. Cut into wedges; accompany with ginger. Serves 6.—*Su Yung Li, San Francisco.*

PER SERVING: 73 calories, 5.2 g protein, 1.5 g carbohydrates, 4.9 g fat, 277 mg cholesterol, sodium data unavailable

TINY EGGS-IN-A-NEST WITH CAESAR SALAD

- 12 **baguette slices, each about 3 inches wide and ½ inch thick**
- 3 **tablespoons butter or margarine**
- 12 **quail eggs**
  Caesar salad (recipe follows)
- 2 **tablespoons grated parmesan cheese**

Tear a hole about 1½ inches wide from the center of each baguette slice. Melt 1 tablespoon butter in an 8- to 10-inch frying pan over medium-high heat. Add 4 baguette slices and cook until bottoms are golden brown, about 3 minutes. Turn slices and carefully break a quail egg (see directions on facing page) into each hole.

Cover pan and cook until eggs are done to your liking, about 2½ minutes for soft yolks. With a wide spatula, carefully transfer eggs to paper towels to drain; keep warm. Repeat to cook remaining eggs.

Divide salad evenly among 4 salad plates; sprinkle with cheese. Set 3 baguette slices on each plate. Makes 4 servings.

PER SERVING: 428 calories, 11 g protein, 33 g carbohydrates, 28 g fat, 255 mg cholesterol, 524 mg sodium

Caesar salad. Discard coarse leaves from 1 large head (about 1 lb.) **romaine lettuce;** rinse and drain remaining leaves. Wrap lettuce in paper towels, put in a plastic bag, and chill until crisp, 30 minutes to 1 day.

In a salad bowl, mix ¼ cup **extra-virgin olive oil** or salad oil, 2 tablespoons **lemon juice,** 1½ teaspoons **Worcestershire,** 1 teaspoon **anchovy paste,** and ¼ teaspoon **pepper.** Shred lettuce, add to bowl, and mix.

Thousand-year-old egg

Salted duck egg

Chicken eggs (large size)

Fresh, speckled quail eggs

Chicken eggs (left) give scale for exotic eggs (right). Thousand-year-old egg is coated with lime and rice husks for 3 months; salted duck egg has black ash coating. Wash off coatings, then shell to use. Fresh quail eggs resemble chicken eggs but are about ⅓ the size.

SUSHI WITH THOUSAND-YEAR-OLD EGG

- 4 sheets toasted nori (seaweed), each about 8 inches square
  Sushi rice (recipe follows)
- 2 thousand-year-old duck or chicken eggs, rinsed well, shelled, rinsed again
- ½ cup drained pickled scallions
- 3 large green onions, ends trimmed

Cut nori into quarters. Fan out beside (but not touching) rice on a platter. Cut each duck egg into 8 equal pieces, chop the scallions, and cut onions lengthwise into fine 2-inch-long slivers; place separately in small bowls.

Invite each person to assemble sushi, 1 piece at a time, by spooning rice into the center of a piece of nori and adding a piece of egg, scallion, and slivers of onion. Roll nori around filling; hold to eat. Makes 16 pieces, 2 or 3 servings.

PER PIECE: 44 calories, 1.7 g protein, 6.3 g carbohydrates, 1.2 g fat, 77 mg cholesterol, 21 mg sodium

Sushi rice. In a 1½- to 2-quart pan, combine ¾ cup **water** with ½ cup **short-grain white rice**. Bring to a boil on high heat, cover, and simmer until water is absorbed, about 10 minutes. Uncover; let stand until cool. Stir in 2 tablespoons **seasoned rice vinegar** (or 2 tablespoons rice vinegar and 2 teaspoons sugar). Serve within 4 hours.

MINIATURE SCOTCH EGGS

- 1 pound ground turkey
- 2 tablespoons water
- 1 teaspoon dry basil leaves
- ½ teaspoon dry crumbled tarragon
- ½ teaspoon salt
- 12 hard-cooked quail eggs, shelled (directions follow)
- ½ cup mayonnaise mixed with 2 tablespoons Dijon mustard

In a food processor, whirl turkey, water, basil, tarragon, and salt to a smooth paste. Divide into 12 equal portions. Between your palms, flatten each portion into a 3½-inch-wide round; set 1 egg in center. Fold meat around egg to cover; pat to smooth. Place in a 10- by 15-inch pan.

Bake in a 350° oven until turkey is browned, about 35 minutes, turning to brown evenly. Let cool to room temperature. If made ahead, cover and chill up until next day. Cut each egg in half; serve cool or at room temperature. Offer mayonnaise in a bowl for dipping. Makes 24 pieces, 4 to 6 servings.

PER PIECE: 72 calories, 4 g protein, 0.3 g carbohydrates, 6.1 g fat, 54 mg cholesterol, 126 mg sodium

Hard-cooked quail eggs. Place 12 **quail eggs** in a 1½- to 2-quart pan; add 2 inches water. Bring just to a boil on high heat; hold just below an active simmer for 5 minutes. Immerse eggs in cold water. Tap shells to crack, then pull off.

POLENTA WITH BAKED QUAIL EGGS

- 3 tablespoons butter or margarine
- 3 ounces thinly sliced prosciutto, minced
- 1 clove garlic, minced or pressed
- 2 cups regular-strength chicken broth
- ½ cup nonfat or low-fat milk
- 1½ cups polenta or yellow cornmeal
- 16 quail eggs

In a 2- to 3-quart pan, melt 2 tablespoons butter over medium-high heat. Add prosciutto and garlic; stir often until meat is browned, about 5 minutes. Stirring, add broth, milk, and polenta; bring to a boil over high heat. Reduce heat to low; stir often until polenta is thick enough to hold its shape when mounded, about 5 minutes.

Spread polenta evenly in a greased 8- by 12-inch baking pan. With a knife, lightly score polenta into quarters. Score each quarter to make 4 triangles, drawing lines diagonally from each corner. In the center of each triangle, use a round 1-teaspoon measure or your thumb to make an indentation about ¾ inch deep and 1¼ inches wide. Cover polenta and chill until firm, at least 1 hour or up to 2 days.

Melt remaining butter and brush over polenta. Bake in a 350° oven until hot, 10 to 15 minutes. Gently break an egg (see directions below) into each indentation. Bake until yolks are set to your liking, about 7 minutes for soft yolks. Cut polenta, following scored lines. With a spatula, transfer to a platter. Makes 16 pieces, 8 servings.

PER PIECE: 970 calories, 3.8 g protein, 10 g carbohydrates, 4.2 g fat, 84 mg cholesterol, 103 mg sodium

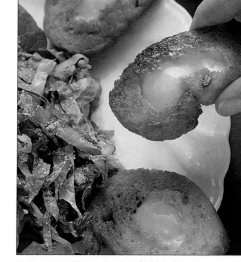

Butter-toasted baguette slices, with holes cut in the middle, cradle quail eggs as they cook. Serve in nest of Caesar salad.

Tiny bull's-eyes in baked polenta-and-prosciutto triangles are quail eggs; offer with soup. Eat with fork or fingers.

How to break a quail egg. Gently tap the side of a **quail egg** on a hard surface to make a small crack. With the tip of a small sharp knife or scissors, make a slit through the tough inner membrane, then pull the shell apart.

Finnish Squeaky Cheese

WHEN YOU BITE INTO IT, *this home-made Finnish cheese is mild and creamy—and slightly squeaky. But it's not ready to eat until it's been toasted beneath the broiler; this gives the cheese its distinctive look and taste. Once it's toasted, you can eat it warm or cold, plain or with savory or sweet accompaniments.*

Squeaky cheese is good with lox, herring, or salad for lunch. Or, in the Finnish manner, try it for breakfast or dessert, baked with a brown-sugar glaze.

Making the cheese is an enjoyable day's project. Hands-on time isn't long, but the cheese has to rest for a number of hours during the process; drawings on the facing page show steps involved. To coagulate milk and cream for the first step, you'll need cheese rennet—sold in some feed and fuel stores; or you can mail-order it from New England Cheesemaking Supply Company, Box 85, Ashfield, Mass. 01330; (413) 628-3808. A package of 10 tablets costs $6, including shipping.

After cutting the coagulated mixture, you slowly heat it to separate curds from whey. Then drain, shape, and compact the curds. Broiling the cheese is the last step.

Maintaining a constant temperature is critical. You can heat the milk and cream in a microwave oven, if it has a temperature probe that works in the 90° to 100° range.

Or, warm the mixture in a sink of hot water; use a medical, photography, or other thermometer to check heat.

FINNISH SQUEAKY CHEESE
(Kainuun leipäjuusto)

> Water
> ¼ rennet tablet
> 7½ cups whole milk
> ½ cup whipping cream
> About ½ teaspoon salt (optional)

In a 1- to 1½-quart pan, bring about ⅓ cup water to a boil over high heat. Remove from heat. Discard all but 2 tablespoons. Let cool to 90° or slightly lower; add rennet and crush completely with the back of a spoon. It takes at least 5 minutes for the rennet to dissolve, but it can stand until milk mixture is heated.

Place milk and cream in a nonmetal 2½- to 3-quart bowl; in a microwave oven, using the temperature probe, heat on full power (100 percent) to 90°.

(Or place liquids in metal or nonmetal bowl, and set in a sink full of hot water; water level should equal level of liquid in bowl. Stir until milk mixture is 90°; add hot water to sink as required.)

Thoroughly stir rennet mixture into milk mixture. Insert probe, and program

microwave oven to hold liquid at 90° until a soft-firm curd is set, about 3 hours. The mixture will feel like soft yogurt when you push a finger into it (step 1).

(Or cover bowl and let stand undisturbed in water until curd is set, 3 to 3½ hours; add hot water to sink as needed to maintain mixture at 90°.)

With a long knife, cut through curd to bottom of bowl to form columns with ½-inch-square tops on surface (step 2). Next, tilt the knife blade at a 45° angle and make diagonal cuts at ½-inch intervals to cut through the columns. Repeat from opposite side of bowl. Gently stir with a slotted spoon to check curd size; cut up chunks bigger than ½ inch.

Using probe, return curds to 90° in microwave oven. Then raise temperature of curds by 2° and hold it there for 5 minutes. Repeat until curds reach 100°.

(Or return bowl to sink of hot water and heat curds to 90°, stirring gently. Add hot water to slowly raise temperature of curds to 100°, stirring gently to avoid breaking up curds. Temperature should not rise more than 2° every 5 minutes; to slow, lift bowl out of water.)

Hold temperature at 100° for 5 minutes. The mixture separates to form white curds and clear whey.

Wedges of broiled mild cheese go on dark rye bread with dill, herring, radishes, and lettuce for Finnish-style lunch. You can make cheese as a summer-day project using a microwave oven to heat milk and cream.

1 *After standing for about 3 hours at 90°, rennet-curdled milk-and-cream mixture has consistency of yogurt.*

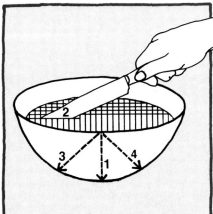

2 *Cut curd vertically (1 and 2), then diagonally (3 and 4) at ½-inch intervals. Heat to separate whey from curds.*

3 *Briefly drain whey from curds in cheesecloth-lined colander, then tie cloth and let drain longer over a sink.*

4 *In cloth-lined cheesecake pan with removable bottom, compress curds beneath pan weighted with cans.*

5 *Broil flat, drained cheese until it has brown speckles. It's ready to eat hot or cool, now or later.*

Line a colander with 2 layers of damp cheesecloth (each about 20 in. square); let ends hang over rim. Set colander in sink with drain open.

Pour curds and whey into colander. Let drain for 10 minutes, then gather edges of cloth and tie with string just above curds. Tie cloth ends together, hook bag onto long faucet over sink, and let drain for 1 hour (step 3).

Meanwhile, prepare the mold: separate rim from an 8- to 9-inch-diameter cake pan with a removable bottom. Snap and discard heads from 4 wooden matches. Evenly space matchsticks horizontally around the inside of rim's bottom lip; tape in place. Set pan bottom on matches in rim (the matches elevate the bottom so that liquid from cheese can drain). Set pan in a larger rimmed pan.

Set cloth-wrapped curds in prepared cake pan mold. Open up cloth, scrape curds to center, and thoroughly mix in salt to taste. Smooth cloth neatly against pan side and bottom, draping edges over rim. Pat curds in an even layer to pan edge. Neatly fold cloth over cheese to cover.

Set a matching-size cake pan on top of cheese; fill top pan with 1-pound cans (step 4). Chill until whey stops dripping. Check occasionally and pour off whey; let drain at least 4 hours or up to overnight.

Remove cans and top pan. Lift cheese mold from larger pan. Drain and rinse larger pan.

Holding edges of cloth, gently lift cheese from mold and lay flat; fold cloth back to expose cheese. Lay removable bottom of cake pan on top of cheese. Supporting cheese with cloth, flip cheese over onto pan bottom; pull cloth free. Set cheese, on pan bottom, back in pan rim, then set in the larger rimmed pan.

Broil cheese 2 to 3 inches below heat until speckled brown, 5 to 10 minutes (step 5). Remove pan rim. Slide a long, thin spatula under cheese to loosen, then ease cheese onto a plate. Serve wedges warm or cool. Or let whole cheese cool completely, cover, and chill up to 1 week. Makes about 12 ounces.

PER OUNCE: 89 calories, 4.2 g protein, 1.5 g carbohydrates, 7.6 g fat, 32 mg cholesterol, 95 mg sodium

SUGAR-GLAZED FINNISH SQUEAKY CHEESE

Prepare **Finnish squeaky cheese** (recipe precedes). Place warm or chilled cheese in an 8- to 9-inch-diameter baking dish. Drizzle 1 tablespoon **whipping cream** over cheese and sprinkle evenly with 3 tablespoons firmly packed **brown sugar**. Bake in a 400° oven until sugar melts, 10 to 12 minutes. Serve wedges of cheese with ½ cup *each* **raspberries** and **blueberries** (or use all one kind of berry). Serves 6.

PER SERVING: 224 calories, 8.8 g protein, 13 g carbohydrates, 16 g fat, 68 mg cholesterol, 193 mg sodium

Fresh-Fruit Salad Dressings

MADE FROM FRESH FRUIT, *these brightly colored dressings complement the flavors of mild or bitter salad greens, fruits, and cold meats such as chicken, duck, or pork.*

Slightly thickened with cornstarch, the dressings of puréed fruit or fruit juice cling nicely as they flow over salad ingredients. Two pluses: the dressings contain virtually no fat, and they will keep in the refrigerator for several days.

STRAWBERRY-TARRAGON DRESSING

1½ cups strawberries, rinsed, drained, and hulled
About ¼ cup lemon juice
About 1 tablespoon sugar

1 tablespoon minced shallots
1 teaspoon chopped fresh or ½ teaspoon dry tarragon leaves
½ teaspoon cornstarch
2 tablespoons orange juice

Purée berries in a blender or food processor, then rub through a fine strainer into a 2-cup glass measure. Add ¼ cup lemon juice and enough water to make 1 cup. Pour into a 1- to 1½-quart pan and add sugar to taste, shallots, and tarragon. Mix cornstarch with orange juice; stir into pan. On high heat, stir until boiling. Let cool; add a little lemon juice for tarter dressing (depending on sweetness of berries). Use, or cover and chill up to 3 days. Makes about 1 cup; allow 2 or 3 tablespoons per serving.

PER TABLESPOON: 9.8 calories, 0.1 g protein, 2.4 g carbohydrates, 0.1 g fat, 0 mg cholesterol, 1 mg sodium

PLUM & PORT DRESSING

About ¾ pound (3 or 4 medium-size) firm-ripe red-skin plums
2 tablespoons port
About 2 tablespoons orange juice (or omit port and use ¼ cup orange juice)
About 1 tablespoon lemon juice
2 teaspoons honey
½ teaspoon cornstarch

Rinse plums, cut from pits, and drop into a 1- to 1½-quart pan. Add port, 2 tablespoons orange juice, 1 tablespoon lemon juice, and honey. Bring to a boil, cover, and simmer until fruit is very soft, about 10 minutes.

Purée mixture in a blender or food processor; rub through a fine strainer into a 2-cup glass measure. Add enough water to make 1 cup. Return mixture to pan. Blend about 2 teaspoons water with cornstarch and stir into purée. Bring to a boil, stirring. Taste, and add a little lemon juice for tarter dressing, or add a little orange juice for thinner dressing (varies with sweetness and texture of fruit). Use, or cover and chill the dressing up to 3 days. Makes about 1 cup; allow 2 or 3 tablespoons per serving.

PER TABLESPOON: 16 calories, 0.2 g protein, 3.9 g carbohydrates, 0.1 g fat, 0 mg cholesterol, 0.4 mg sodium

ORANGE DRESSING

2 medium-size (about ¾ lb.) juice oranges
¼ cup white wine vinegar
1 tablespoon sugar
1 teaspoon cornstarch

With a vegetable peeler, pare the orange-colored skin of oranges; cut peel into very thin shreds. Ream oranges; pour juice into 2-cup glass measure. Add vinegar and enough water to make about 1 cup.

Put peel in a 1- to 1½-quart pan. Add 1 cup water and bring to a boil on high heat; drain; repeat. To drained peel, add ½ cup water and the sugar. Boil, uncovered, until almost no liquid is left; stir to prevent scorching. At once, add juice mixture.

Blend cornstarch smoothly with 2 teaspoons water and stir into pan; stir until boiling. Let cool; use, or cover and chill up to 3 days. Makes about 1 cup; allow 2 or 3 tablespoons per serving.

PER TABLESPOON: 9.5 calories, 0.1 g protein, 2.3 g carbohydrates, 0 g fat, 0 mg cholesterol, 0.1 mg sodium

Strawberry dressing, seasoned with tarragon and citrus juices, adds color and tang to chicken-lettuce salad. Virtually free of fat, salad dressing starts with fresh fruit.

Knife & Fork Appetizer Tarts

BAKED IN A CRUST, *cheese is the foundation of these two savory appetizer tarts. In the first, ricotta laced with nutty emmenthal and a dash of parmesan bakes in a butter pastry. In the second, you slather a sheet of purchased puff pastry with sautéed mushrooms and jarlsberg cheese.*

Both tarts taste best warm from the oven; make-ahead steps offer quick assembly. If you serve larger portions, the tarts and salad or soup make a light meal.

Suitable beverages include chilled apple juice, hard cider, dry Sauvignon Blanc, or a mellow Chianti.

THREE-CHEESE TART

> Butter pastry (recipe follows)
> 1 large egg
> 1 carton (8 oz., about 1 cup) part-skim ricotta cheese
> 1½ cups (6 oz.) shredded emmenthal cheese
> 1 tablespoon grated parmesan cheese

Press butter pastry evenly over bottom and up sides of a 9-inch tart pan with removable rim.

Bake in a 325° oven until pale gold, about 20 minutes. If made ahead, cool, cover, and store at room temperature until the next day.

Meanwhile, in a food processor or blender, whirl together the egg and ricotta cheese until mixture is smooth. Stir in emmenthal cheese. Spread mixture evenly into crust. Sprinkle parmesan cheese evenly over filling.

Bake in a 350° oven until golden all over, about 15 minutes. Cool on rack. Serve warm; cut into wedges. Makes 8 to 10 servings.

PER SERVING: 219 calories, 10 g protein, 11 g carbohydrates, 15 g fat, 84 mg cholesterol, 167 mg sodium

Butter pastry. In a food processor or bowl, combine 1 cup **all-purpose flour** and 6 tablespoons **butter** or margarine, cut in small chunks. Whirl or rub the mixture with your fingers until fine crumbs form. Whirl or stir in 1 **large egg** until dough forms a ball.

Enclosed in a flaky pastry crust, three-cheese tart goes with a green salad for first course or lunch. It's best served warm from the oven.

MUSHROOM-CHEESE TART

> 1 sheet frozen puff pastry (½ of a 17¼-oz. package)
> 1 tablespoon butter or margarine
> ¾ pound mushrooms, thinly sliced
> 1 teaspoon dry thyme leaves
>   Salt and white pepper
>   About 1 tablespoon beaten egg
> 1 cup (4 oz.) shredded jarlsberg or Swiss cheese

Let puff pastry stand at room temperature just until pliable, 20 to 30 minutes.

Meanwhile, in a 10- to 12-inch frying pan, melt butter over high heat. Add mushrooms and thyme. Stir often until all liquid evaporates and mushrooms brown, about 8 to 10 minutes. Add salt and pepper to taste; let cool. If made ahead, cover and chill up until the next day.

Unfold puff pastry in a lightly greased 10- by 15-inch baking pan. Brush pastry with the egg and prick surface all over with a fork. Scatter mushrooms and cheese evenly over pastry.

Bake in a 425° oven until richly browned, about 20 minutes. Cut pastry in wedges or squares. Serve hot or warm. Makes 10 to 12 servings.

PER SERVING: 138 calories, 4.1 g protein, 9.1 g carbohydrates, 9.2 g fat, 16 mg cholesterol, 154 mg sodium

Main-Dish Salads

MEAT AND VEGETABLES *team up in distinctive ways in these two main-dish salads. The first pairs tongue with a mixture of herb-seasoned white kidney beans and tomatoes. You have a choice of meats: because veal tongues (which are usually much smaller than beef tongues) are sometimes difficult to find, we offer an easy alternative of using sliced cooked beef tongue from the delicatessen.*

The second salad combines eggplant, zucchini, and onion with slices of beef tenderloin. Although the recipe looks long, it breaks down into easy steps. Up to a day ahead, roast vegetables and the beef (in sequence if you have only one oven). These ingredients go onto peppery arugula and are topped with parmesan cheese; accompanying them is a dried tomato mayonnaise.

TONGUE & WHITE BEAN SALAD

For a quick version of this salad, skip cooking the tongue and buy 1 pound thinly sliced beef tongue (shaped in a loaf) at the delicatessen. Since you won't have broth from cooked veal tongue, moisten the beans with 1 tablespoon olive oil.

- 2 **pounds veal tongues**
- 3 **cups water**
- 2 **cans (15 oz. each) cannellini (white kidney beans), drained and rinsed**

- ½ **pound firm-ripe Roma-type tomatoes, cored and coarsely chopped**
- ¼ **cup firmly packed fresh basil leaves, finely chopped; or 2 teaspoons dry basil leaves**
- 1 **tablespoon chopped fresh or 1 teaspoon dry oregano leaves**
- 2 **tablespoons cider vinegar**
- 1 **tablespoon butter or margarine**
- 6 **large lettuce leaves, rinsed and crisped**
  Salt and freshly ground pepper
  Dijon mustard

Rinse tongues well and put in a 3- to 4-quart pan; add water. Cover and bring to a boil over high heat; reduce heat and simmer until tongues are very tender when pierced, about 2 hours. Lift out tongues and set aside. Boil broth, uncovered, on high heat until reduced to ½ cup, about 10 minutes; set aside.

When tongues are cool enough to handle, pull off and discard skin, and trim off any bones, gristle, or fat. If made ahead, cover tongues and broth; chill up until next day. To use broth, reheat until it liquefies.

In a bowl, mix beans with tomatoes, basil, oregano, vinegar, and ¼ cup of the broth.

Cut tongues crosswise and on the diagonal to make ¼-inch-thick slices. Melt butter in a 10- to 12-inch frying pan over medium-high heat. Fill pan, without crowding, with tongue slices; cook until browned on both sides, about 2 minutes total, turning slices over once. Drain on paper towels. Repeat to brown remaining tongue.

Lay 1 lettuce leaf on each of 6 dinner plates. Spoon ⅙ of the bean mixture onto each leaf. Arrange equal portions of tongue beside beans; moisten meat with remaining broth. Add salt, pepper, and mustard to taste. Serves 6.

PER SERVING: 288 calories, 25 g protein, 24 g carbohydrates, 9.7 g fat, cholesterol data not available, 446 mg sodium

ROASTED BEEF & VEGETABLE SALAD

- About ¼ **cup extra-virgin olive oil or salad oil**
- 4 **Asian eggplants (about ½ lb. total), stems trimmed, cut in half lengthwise**
- 3 **tablespoons balsamic vinegar or red wine vinegar**

- 4 **small (about ¾ lb. total) zucchini, ends trimmed, cut in half lengthwise**
- 4 **small (about 1½ lb. total) red onions, peeled and cut in half crosswise**
- 1½ **pounds beef tenderloin, external fat trimmed**
- 4 **cups (about 4 oz.) arugula, rinsed and crisped**
- 2 **ounces thinly shaved or finely shredded parmesan cheese**
  Dried tomato mayonnaise (recipe follows)
  Salt and freshly ground pepper

Line a 10- by 15-inch pan with foil and coat lightly with oil. Lay eggplant, cut side up, in a single layer in pan. Mix 2 tablespoons oil with vinegar and brush ⅓ of the mixture over eggplant. Bake in a 475° oven until eggplant is browned and very soft when pressed, 25 to 30 minutes. Slide foil with eggplant off pan.

Line same pan and another 10- by 15-inch pan with foil. Oil both lightly. Arrange zucchini, cut side up, in a single layer in 1 pan. Put onion, cut side down, in the other pan. Brush vegetables with remaining oil-vinegar mixture. Bake in a 500° oven until vegetables are well browned, 30 to 40 minutes; switch pan positions halfway through baking. Slide foil with vegetables off pans and set aside to cool. If made ahead, put separately into containers, cover, and chill up until the next day. Bring to room temperature to use.

Set beef in center of 1 of the pans; bake in a 450° oven until a thermometer inserted in thickest part registers 125° for rare (cut to test), about 25 minutes. Let cool to room temperature. If made ahead, wrap airtight and chill up until the next day.

Slice meat ¼ inch thick across grain. Mix arugula with 1 tablespoon oil and divide among 4 dinner plates; top with cheese. Alongside, arrange equal portions of eggplant, zucchini, onion, and beef. Offer tomato mayonnaise, salt, and pepper to add to taste. Makes 4 servings.

PER SERVING WITHOUT TOMATO MAYONNAISE: 508 calories, 44 g protein, 17 g carbohydrates, 29 g fat, 115 mg cholesterol, 339 mg sodium

Dried tomato mayonnaise. Mince ¼ cup drained **oil-packed dried tomatoes;** mix with ¾ cup **mayonnaise.** If made ahead, cover and chill the mixture up to 2 days. Makes 1 cup.

PER TABLESPOON: 86 calories, 0.2 g protein, 0.7 g carbohydrates, 9.3 g fat, 6.1 mg cholesterol, 139 mg sodium

Pan-browned slices of simmered tongue fan out beside salad of canned white beans.

Cooking with Mint

ADDING A COOL DIMENSION *to sweet-sour seasonings, mint flavors these three dishes. In the first, salmon broiled with a honey–balsamic vinegar glaze is strewn with the fragrant herb. In the second, a sauce of mint, sweet onion, and tart sorrel tops poached salmon. In the last dish, tabbouleh features the natural sweetness of wheat, with refreshing mint and lemon.*

BALSAMIC-BROILED SALMON WITH MINT

¼ cup balsamic or raspberry vinegar
2 tablespoons honey
2 teaspoons salad oil
4 skinned salmon fillets (6 to 7 oz. each), about 1 inch thick
¾ cup firmly packed fresh mint leaves, minced
   Fresh mint sprigs (optional)
   Salt and lemon halves or wedges

In a small bowl, mix together vinegar, honey, and oil. Rinse fish and pat dry; lay fillets slightly apart in a lightly oiled 10- by 15-inch baking pan and brush tops with half the vinegar mixture.

Broil fish 6 inches from heat until no longer translucent but still moist-looking in thickest part (cut to test), 8 to 10 minutes. Brush several times during broiling with remainder of vinegar mixture.

With a wide spatula, carefully transfer salmon to a platter and sprinkle with mint; garnish with mint sprigs. Add salt and lemon to taste. Makes 4 servings.

PER SERVING: 297 calories, 33 g protein, 9.5 g carbohydrates, 13 g fat, 93 mg cholesterol, 75 mg sodium

POACHED SALMON WITH SORREL & MINT

1 quart water
½ cup dry white wine
10 black peppercorns
2 tablespoons lemon juice
1 dry bay leaf
4 salmon steaks (6 to 8 oz. each), about 1 inch thick
   Mint sorrel sauce (recipe follows)
   Fresh mint sprigs (optional)

In a 5- to 6-quart pan, bring water, wine, peppercorns, lemon juice, and bay leaf to a boil over high heat; cover and simmer for 15 minutes. Return water to boiling, add salmon, cover, and remove

Chopped mint, warmed by the heat of broiled salmon fillets, creates an aromatic complement to cooking glaze of balsamic vinegar and honey.

from heat. Let stand until fish is no longer translucent but still moist-looking in center of thickest part (cut to test), about 8 minutes. If fish is not cooked, cover and let stand, testing every 1 minute until done.

Lift salmon from liquid; drain briefly and pat dry with paper towels. Place each steak onto a dinner plate. At once, spoon mint sorrel sauce onto fish; garnish with mint sprigs. Serves 4.

PER SERVING: 352 calories, 34 g protein, 2.2 g carbohydrates, 2 g fat, 124 mg cholesterol, 193 mg sodium

Mint sorrel sauce. In a 7- to 8-inch frying pan, melt ¼ cup (⅛ lb.) **butter** or margarine over medium-high heat. Add ¼ cup minced **onion** and stir often until lightly browned, about 5 minutes; keep warm. When fish is cooked, add to onions in pan ½ cup minced **fresh mint leaves** and 2 tablespoons minced **sorrel;** stir sauce, then use at once (heat turns sorrel dark).

COOL MINT TABBOULEH

2 cups bulgur (cracked wheat)
2 cups cold water
4 cups firmly packed fresh mint leaves
½ cup lemon juice
2 tablespoons extra-virgin olive oil or salad oil
   Salt and freshly ground pepper
6 to 8 large butter lettuce leaves, rinsed and crisped
2 large (about 1 lb. total) firm-ripe tomatoes, cored and thinly sliced

In a deep bowl, mix bulgur and water; let stand until grains are tender to bite and water is absorbed, about 1 hour; stir several times. Mince mint in a food processor or with a knife. Add to bulgur with lemon juice, oil, and salt and pepper to taste; mix well. If made ahead, cover and chill up until next day.

Line a platter with lettuce leaves. Arrange tomatoes in an overlapping ring on lettuce near platter edge; mound tabbouleh in center. Makes 6 to 8 servings.

PER SERVING: 172 calories, 5.4 g protein, 31 g carbohydrates, 4.3 g fat, 0 mg cholesterol, 14.8 mg sodium

Make-Ahead Thai Casserole

*C*OCONUT AND SPICES *are used freely with potatoes and eggplant by Thai cooks. The humble basic ingredients get an exotic twist from such additions as turmeric, coriander, crushed dried hot red chilies, garlic, and ginger. This make-ahead vegetable casserole combines some typical Thai seasonings.*

THAI EGGPLANT & POTATO CASSEROLE

About ¼ cup salad oil
3 medium-size (about 3½ lb. total) eggplants, stems trimmed
3 medium-size (about 1 lb. total) onions, sliced
3 large (about 2 lb. total) russet potatoes, scrubbed and pierced
Coconut sauce (recipe follows)
Salt and pepper

Oil 2 rimmed baking pans, each 10 by 15 inches. Cut eggplants crosswise into ¾-inch-thick slices and arrange in pans in a single layer; brush tops of slices lightly with oil. Separate onion slices into rings and scatter over eggplant. Put in a 450° oven; put potatoes on rack alongside pans. After 25 minutes, turn eggplant slices over with a spatula (let onions scatter) and alternate pan positions in the oven. Bake potatoes and eggplant until eggplant is browned and both vegetables are very soft when pressed, about 45 minutes total.

Cut potatoes into ¼-inch slices. Arrange ½ the eggplant and onion in an even layer in a shallow 3½- to 4-quart baking dish. Place potatoes in an even layer on eggplant mixture, then cover evenly with remaining eggplant and onion. Pour coconut sauce evenly over the vegetables; cover tightly with foil. (If made ahead, chill up until next day.)

Bake in a 400° oven until liquid is bubbling, about 30 minutes (about 45 minutes if chilled). Uncover and bake until top is tinged with brown, about 30 minutes longer. Let casserole stand at least

Eggplant, onions, and potatoes form a sturdy foundation for layered vegetable casserole made bold with coconut and ginger. Serve with barbecued meat or poultry.

10 minutes before serving. Add salt and pepper to taste. Makes 8 to 10 servings.

PER SERVING: 301 calories, 5.1 g protein, 32 g carbohydrates, 19 g fat, 0 mg cholesterol, 29 mg sodium

Coconut sauce. In a 10- to 12-inch frying pan over medium-high heat, combine 3 tablespoons **salad oil;** 1 cup minced **shallots** or red onion; 4 cloves **garlic,** minced or pressed; 3 tablespoons minced **fresh ginger;** 1 teaspoon **ground turmeric;** ½ to 1 teaspoon **crushed dried**

hot red chilies (to taste); and ½ teaspoon **ground coriander.** Stir often until shallots are limp, about 5 minutes. Add 1 can (14 oz.) **coconut milk** and 1½ cups **regular-strength chicken broth** (or 1 cup whipping cream and 2 cups broth with 1½ teaspoons coconut flavoring); stir until hot. Add ¼ cup **lemon juice.** Use hot or cool.

A Hot Cooking Tool: The Propane Torch

LITERALLY ONE OF THE HOTTEST *professional kitchen tools is the hand-held propane torch. Chefs often use the torch to melt sugar for shiny caramel glazes on tarts and custards; its flame is also effective for melting cheese.*

Home cooks, too, will find the torch an efficient way to evenly brown or heat many foods, and not as heavy-handed as it might seem. You can precisely control both the intensity and location of the heat, whereas ovens tend to broil unevenly. With a little practice, a torch is surprisingly easy to handle, whether you're making crème brûlée or raclette.

Propane torches are sold in hardware stores for about $14; propane cartridges (about 14-oz. size) cost about $3 each. One cartridge provides roughly 8 hours of heat on a medium setting.

HOW TO BROIL WITH A PROPANE TORCH

Before using a torch, read all directions and safety instructions carefully. You can use it indoors, as long as the room is well ventilated.

Turn on valve to low and ignite fuel with a match or spark igniter. Practice first with flame on lowest setting, then try it on medium (at full blast, the flame is too hot for use on foods). Hold flame 4 to 6 inches from surface of food and move it in an even, sweeping motion, slowing as needed for browning. Take care not to scorch.

CRÈME BRÛLÉE

1 quart half-and-half (light cream)
1 cup sugar
1 tablespoon vanilla
6 large egg yolks

Set 8 ramekins (½-cup size) or an oval or round 8- by 11-inch dish in a baking pan (9 by 13 in. and about 2 in. deep).

In a 2- to 3-quart pan, combine cream and ½ cup sugar. Stir frequently over medium-high heat until scalding; add vanilla and remove from heat.

In a bowl, beat yolks to blend; whisk in hot cream. Divide custard mixture evenly among ramekins (or pour all into larger dish). Carefully set pan on center rack in a 325° oven. Pour boiling water into pan to level of custard.

Bake until custard jiggles only slightly when gently shaken, about 30 minutes for individual custards, 45 to 55 minutes

for large custard. At once, lift from hot water and let cool slightly, then cover and chill at least 4 hours or up to 2 days.

About 1 hour before serving, sprinkle custard tops evenly with remaining sugar. (For large custard, use only ⅓ cup sugar.) Light propane torch; adjust flame to low. Hold torch about 5 inches away from sugar on 1 custard at a time, sweeping heat over surface until sugar is melted and evenly browned, 30 to 45 seconds. (On large custard, apply heat using a wide circular motion, moving the flame constantly to avoid scorching.) Chill up to 1 hour for sugar to harden (after it's chilled about 2 hours, sugar begins to melt). Serves 8.

PER SERVING: 380 calories, 5.3 g protein, 30 g carbohydrates, 27 g fat, 239 mg cholesterol, 53 mg sodium

CARAMEL-GLAZED FRUIT TART

¾ pound frozen puff pastry sheets (part of a 17¼-oz. box), thawed
1 tablespoon milk
4 medium-size (about 2 lb. total) firm-ripe bananas, peeled; or 1½ pounds apples or pears, peeled and cored
2 tablespoons lemon juice
2 tablespoons butter or margarine
About ½ cup sugar
1 teaspoon ground cinnamon
¼ teaspoon ground nutmeg

On a lightly floured board, roll out pastry to form a 10- by 12-inch rectangle. Place on a greased 12- by 15-inch baking sheet. Prick pastry all over with a fork and brush with milk. Bake in a 350° oven until well browned, about 30 minutes.

Meanwhile, cut fruit into ¼-inch slices. Sprinkle with lemon juice. In a 10- to 12-inch frying pan, melt butter over medium-high heat. Stir in 2 tablespoons of the sugar, cinnamon, and nutmeg; cook until bubbling, about 1 minute. Add fruit and turn occasionally with a wide spatula until fruit is warm and glazed, about 3 minutes for bananas or 5 to 6 minutes for apples or pears. Cool slightly.

Arrange fruit decoratively in a single layer over pastry, covering it completely. Sprinkle ⅓ cup sugar over fruit. Ignite propane torch and adjust flame to low. Holding torch about 5 inches from fruit, sweep it over tart until sugar is evenly browned and bubbling, about 4 minutes. Serve hot or warm. Serves 6 to 8.

PER SERVING: 325 calories, 2.9 g protein, 45 g carbohydrates, 15 g fat, 8 mg cholesterol, 233 mg sodium

PORTABLE RACLETTE

1¾ pounds (about 2-in.-diameter) thin-skinned red potatoes, scrubbed
About ¾ pound red radishes, rinsed and drained, with all but prettiest leaves removed
About ½ pound green onions, ends trimmed
½ cup drained tiny gherkin pickles
1 wedge (1 lb.) raclette or fontina cheese, wax trimmed off

In a 4- to 5-quart pan, cover the potatoes with water. Bring to boiling, then cover and simmer gently until the potatoes are very tender when pierced, 35 to 40 minutes; drain.

In individual baskets or platters, mound the potatoes, radishes, and onions. Put pickles in a small bowl.

Lay cheese on a heatproof plate. Ignite propane torch and turn heat to medium. Holding flame 5 to 6 inches from cheese, move it in a sweeping motion over cheese until surface melts, about 30 seconds; cheese can brown some, but do not scorch. Scrape melted cheese onto potatoes; eat with vegetables. Repeat each time you want another portion. Turn off torch between uses. Makes 6 servings.

PER SERVING: 448 calories, 23 g protein, 36 g carbohydrates, 24 g fat, 87 mg cholesterol, 775 mg sodium

As raclette cheese melts, scrape it onto potatoes; eat with onions, radishes, and tiny gherkins.

SMOKED SALMON & CHEESE SALAD

Mix salmon, greens, gorgonzola, and croutons for salad.

2 **tablespoons pine nuts**
6 **tablespoons olive oil**
1 **cup (about 1¼ oz.) ½-inch cubes French bread**
2 **ounces sliced smoked salmon**
3 **ounces gorgonzola cheese**
8 **cups (about 10 oz.) bite-size pieces romaine lettuce, rinsed and crisped**
2 **cups (about 3 oz.) bite-size pieces Belgian endive, rinsed and crisped**
½ **cup thinly sliced green onion**
3 **tablespoons white wine vinegar**
1 **teaspoon Dijon mustard**
 Salt and pepper

In an 8- to 10-inch frying pan over medium heat, toast nuts, shaking often, until golden, 3 to 4 minutes. Pour out of pan. Add 1 tablespoon olive oil and bread cubes to pan. Stir often over medium heat until bread is golden, about 5 minutes; set aside.

Cut salmon into ½-inch-wide strips. Crumble cheese. In a large bowl, combine salmon, cheese, nuts, bread cubes, romaine, endive, and onion. Combine remaining oil, vinegar, and mustard; pour over salad and mix. Add salt and pepper to taste. Makes 6 servings.—*Susie Cabell, Boulder, Colo.*

PER SERVING: 227 calories, 7 g protein, 6.4 g carbohydrates, 20 g fat, 13 mg cholesterol, 336 mg sodium

BAKED QUESADILLAS

4 **flour tortillas (7 in. wide), at room temperature**
 Chili sauce (recipe follows)
1½ **cups (about 6 oz.) shredded jack or cheddar cheese**
2 **small (about ¼ lb. total) Roma-type tomatoes, cored and thinly sliced crosswise**
½ **cup chopped red onion**
⅓ **cup lightly packed fresh cilantro (coriander) leaves, optional**
 About ½ cup prepared green taco sauce

Fill tortillas with cheese, vegetables, sauce; bake until crisp.

Lightly brush both sides of tortillas with water. On half of each tortilla spread ¼ of the chili sauce. Evenly distribute ¼ of the cheese, tomato, onion, and cilantro over sauce. Fold plain half of tortilla over to cover filling. Set quesadillas slightly apart on a 12- by 15-inch baking sheet.

Bake in a 500° oven until crisp and golden, 7 to 10 minutes. With a spatula, transfer to plates. Offer taco sauce to add to taste. Makes 4 servings.—*Ann Angulo, Provo, Utah.*

PER SERVING: 332 calories, 15 g protein, 29 g carbohydrates, 17 g fat, 42 mg cholesterol, 631 mg sodium

Chili sauce. Mix ¼ cup reduced-calorie or regular **mayonnaise**, 2 teaspoons **wine vinegar**, 1 teaspoon **chili powder**, and **salt** and **pepper** to taste.

POUNDED PORK TENDERLOIN WITH ORANGE-PEPPER SAUCE

Pork tenderloin, sliced and pounded, gets zest from an orange-pepper sauce.

¾ **pound pork tenderloin**
 About ¼ cup all-purpose flour
2 **to 3 tablespoons butter or margarine**
¼ **cup chopped shallots**
¾ **teaspoon black peppercorns, coarsely crushed**
⅓ **cup dry white wine**
1 **tablespoon finely shredded orange peel**
⅔ **cup orange juice**

Cut pork crosswise into slices about ½ inch thick. Place slices between pieces of plastic wrap and pound evenly and gently until ¼ inch thick. Coat pork lightly with flour.

Melt 2 tablespoons butter in a 10- to 12-inch frying pan over medium-high heat. Cook pork in a single layer until lightly browned on both sides, about 1 minute total. Transfer to a warm serving dish. Keep meat warm in a 200° oven. Cook remaining pork, adding more butter if meat sticks.

Add shallots and pepper to pan; stir until shallots are limp, about 2 minutes. Add wine, orange peel, and juice. Boil over high heat until reduced to ½ cup, 4 to 5 minutes. Pour sauce over pork. Serves 3 or 4.—*L. K. Ross, Elk Grove, Calif.*

PER SERVING: 190 calories, 19 g protein, 9.9 g carbohydrates, 7.9 g fat, 71 mg cholesterol, 103 mg sodium

Jessie's Golden Griddlecakes

- 2 cups all-purpose flour
- 4 teaspoons baking powder
- ½ teaspoon salt (optional)
- 2 large eggs, separated
- 2 tablespoons sugar
- 2¼ cups milk
- ⅓ cup butter or margarine, melted

In a bowl, stir together flour, baking powder, and salt.

In a small bowl, beat egg whites with an electric mixer until foamy. Gradually beat in sugar until stiff moist peaks form; set aside. In a large bowl, beat egg yolks to blend with milk and butter. Stir in flour mixture and beat until smooth; fold in whipped egg whites.

Heat a lightly greased griddle or 10- to 12-inch frying pan over medium to medium-high heat; ladle about ¼ cup batter for each cake onto hot griddle. Cook until tops are bubbly and appear dry, then turn over and brown other sides, about 2 minutes total. Serve hot. Makes about 24 pancakes, each 4 inches wide; allow 4 per serving. —*Jessie Cook, Mesa, Ariz.*

Per Serving: 340 calories, 9.5 g protein, 41 g carbohydrates, 15 g fat, 111 mg cholesterol, 454 mg sodium

Serve pancakes with sour cream, powdered sugar, and fruit.

Stir-Fried Turkey Salad

- 12 cups (about 10 oz.) bite-size pieces butter lettuce, rinsed and crisped
- 1 large firm-ripe tomato, cored and cut in wedges
- 1 large firm-ripe avocado, peeled, pitted, and sliced
- ¼ cup thinly sliced green onion
- 4 slices bacon, cut in thin slivers
- 1 pound turkey thigh, skinned, boned, and cut in thin strips
  Dressing (recipe follows)
- ¼ cup grated parmesan cheese

In a large salad bowl, arrange lettuce, tomato, avocado, and onion.

In a wok or 12-inch frying pan, stir bacon over medium-high heat until crisp, about 4 minutes. With a slotted spoon, lift out bacon and reserve. Discard all but 1 tablespoon fat.

Turn heat to high. Add the turkey to pan and stir-fry until lightly browned, 3 to 4 minutes; pour turkey and juices over greens. Pour dressing over the salad; add the cheese and bacon, then mix. Makes 4 to 6 servings. —*Mary Benham, Spokane.*

Per Serving: 318 calories, 13 g protein, 7 g carbohydrates, 27 g fat, 43 mg cholesterol, 285 mg sodium

Dressing. Blend ¼ cup **olive oil**, 3 tablespoons **mayonnaise**, 3 tablespoons **wine vinegar**, 1 tablespoon **Dijon mustard**, and 1 teaspoon **dry thyme leaves.**

Mix creamy dressing with stir-fried turkey on a bed of lettuce.

Gingersnap Ice Cream Sandwiches

- ¾ cup (⅜ lb.) butter or margarine
- 1 cup plus 3 tablespoons sugar
- ¼ cup molasses
- 1 large egg
- 2 cups all-purpose flour
- 2 teaspoons baking soda
- ¼ teaspoon salt
- 1 teaspoon *each* ground ginger, ground cinnamon, and ground cloves
  About 1¼ quarts vanilla ice cream

In a large bowl, beat butter and 1 cup sugar until blended. Beat in molasses and egg. In a small bowl, mix the flour, baking soda, salt, ginger, cinnamon, and cloves. Gradually add to butter mixture, beating until blended.

Roll dough into 1½-inch balls; coat in remaining sugar. Place 3 inches apart on greased 12- by 15-inch baking sheets. Bake in a 350° oven until light gold, about 12 minutes. Cool on pans 2 minutes, then transfer to racks.

For each sandwich, place a ¼-cup scoop of ice cream on bottom of 1 cooky; gently press another cooky, bottom down, over ice cream. Serve, or wrap in foil and freeze up to 2 weeks. Makes 18 to 24 servings. —*Julie Hack, Yes Bay, Alaska.*

Per Serving: 195 calories, 2.4 g protein, 27 g carbohydrates, 9 g fat, 37 mg cholesterol, 177 mg sodium

Sandwich ice cream between chewy ginger cookies; wrap in foil.

Chefs of the West®

The Art of Cooking . . . by men . . . for men

A BURNING MARSHMALLOW *on the end of a stick—this is typically the budding Western chef's first barbecue experience. He will go on to frankfurters, and eventually to chicken, steak, perhaps even turkey. Whatever the subject, the experience is a primal one—nothing between the cook and the fire except the meat, as it was in the beginning, before stoves and boutique cookware were invented.*

John Prince's Marinated Beef on a Stick requires a higher degree of skill than toasting a marshmallow, but it's still easy. Nevertheless, the taste is rich and complex. The marinade really penetrates the thin slices of meat, becoming a part of it and not just a cosmetic.

MARINATED BEEF ON A STICK

1½ **pounds boneless top sirloin steak, trimmed of all fat**

½ **cup soy sauce**

2 **tablespoons** *each* **salad oil, honey, and red wine vinegar**

1 **clove garlic, minced or pressed**

¼ **teaspoon pepper**

½ **teaspoon ground ginger**

Cut steak across the grain into ¼-inch-thick slices, each about 4 inches long. (For easier slicing, you can place the steak in the freezer until partially firm, 30 to 45 minutes, before cutting it.)

Put meat in a bowl and add soy, oil, honey, vinegar, garlic, pepper, and ginger. Mix well; cover and chill 1 to 2 hours.

Lift meat from marinade, drain briefly, then weave thin skewers in and out of slices so meat lies flat.

Place skewers on a lightly greased barbecue grill 4 to 6 inches above a solid bed of hot coals (you should be able to hold your hand at grill level for only 2 to 3 seconds). Cook, turning to brown evenly, and baste frequently with reserved marinade until done to your liking (cut to test), 4 to 5 minutes total for medium-rare. Makes 6 servings.

PER SERVING: 257 calories, 24 g protein, 8.3 g carbohydrates, 14 g fat, 68 mg cholesterol, 1,435 mg sodium

John E. Prince

Santa Cruz, Calif.

"Barbecuing is a primal experience—nothing between the cook and the fire except the meat."

WHATEVER EMBELLISHMENT *Chuck Forsyth gives his barbecue sandwich, it isn't in the forthright name: Pig Sandwich. But the name fits. Not only is this a sandwich, and not only does the meat come from a pig, but the end result is a down-home dish that stands on its own merits, without any ballyhoo.*

Just take a taste and you'll see. The meat is so thoroughly cooked that it can be shredded by forks or fingers; in the vernacular of its native mid-South, it is pulled, as opposed to sliced, barbecue.

The sauce also takes its origin from the mid-South, but Forsyth has given it a Southwestern spin with green chilies and added some Northwestern sweetness with apple cider. If you or your guests are fire-eaters, you can add crushed dried hot red chilies or a sprinkle of cayenne.

PIG SANDWICH

1 **bone-in pork butt or shoulder (5 to 6 lb.)**

½ **to 1 teaspoon liquid smoke**

½ **cup cider vinegar**

1 **cup apple cider or juice**

1 **cup prepared barbecue sauce**

1 **can (4 oz.) diced green chilies**

10 **to 12 hamburger buns or English muffins, halved and toasted**

1 **or 2 medium-size red or white onions, thinly sliced**

Salt and pepper

Trim and discard excess fat from meat. Brush meat evenly with liquid smoke, then wrap in foil, sealing edges. Set packet in a 9- by 13-inch baking pan. Bake in a 300° oven until meat is tender enough to fall apart when prodded with a fork, 3½ to 4 hours. Remove from oven, unwrap, and let cool.

Meanwhile, combine vinegar, apple cider, barbecue sauce, and chilies in a 4- to 5-quart pan. Bring to a boil over high heat, stirring often. Cover; remove pan from heat.

When meat is cool enough to touch, shred it with your fingers or 2 forks, discarding bone, fat, and connective tissue. Measure green chili mixture and return to pan. Skim fat from drippings and discard; add drippings to green chili mixture and boil, uncovered, until reduced to original amount. Stir in the pork and heat to simmering. If made ahead, cover and chill up to 2 days.

"Whatever embellishment Chuck Forsyth gives his barbecue sandwich, it isn't in the forthright name."

Reheat meat and sauce until simmering, then spoon onto toasted buns; add onions, and salt and pepper to taste. Serve as open-faced or covered sandwiches. Makes 10 to 12 sandwiches.

PER SANDWICH: 363 calories, 31 g protein, 28 g carbohydrates, 14 g fat, 95 mg cholesterol, 536 mg sodium

Seattle

S TUFFED PASTA *must be a good idea, because many cuisines employ it. The Chinese may have been the first (with won ton), but kreplach go back a long way in Jewish cooking, as do pelmeni in Russian.*

But for exuberance in invention the Italians are far ahead of the field with their ravioli and its many descendants — agnolotti, cappelletti, mezzelune, pansotti, tortellini, tortelloni, to name only the best known. And these are only the shapes; the fillings, and especially the sauces, display even wider variety.

Charles Doody serves his tortellini in a Mornay sauce enlivened by gorgonzola cheese and walnuts. The sauce can be thinned (with broth) or thickened (with more cornstarch diluted with a little of the broth) to a texture you like. To lessen the burden of preparation, he uses packaged fresh tortellini. (Only the most dedicated or masochistic will trouble to make tortellini when good fresh ones can be purchased.)

TORTELLINI WITH WALNUT & GORGONZOLA SAUCE

- ½ cup chopped walnuts
- 3 tablespoons butter or margarine
- ¼ cup finely chopped onion
- 2 cloves garlic, minced or pressed
- 2 teaspoons cornstarch
- 1½ cups half-and-half (light cream)
- ½ cup regular-strength chicken broth
- 3 ounces (about ⅔ cup, packed) gorgonzola or blue cheese, crumbled
- 1½ teaspoons lemon juice
- 1 tablespoon dry sherry
- ¼ teaspoon *each* dry thyme leaves, dry rubbed sage, and dry marjoram leaves
- ⅛ teaspoon ground nutmeg
  Freshly ground pepper
- 2 packages (9 oz. each) fresh tortellini with meat filling

In a 10- to 12-inch frying pan, stir or shake walnuts often over medium-high heat until toasted, about 5 minutes. Pour from pan and set aside.

Melt butter in the frying pan over medium heat; add onion and garlic and stir often until onion is limp, 8 to 10 minutes. Smoothly blend cornstarch with 1 to 2 tablespoons cream; add cornstarch mixture, remaining cream, and broth to pan. Bring to a boil on high heat, stirring. Turn heat to low and add cheese, lemon juice, sherry, thyme, sage, marjoram, nutmeg, and pepper; stir until the cheese melts. Keep warm.

When you start the sauce, also bring about 3 quarts water to boiling on high heat in a 5- to 6-quart pan. Add tortellini; cook on high heat until tender to bite, about 8 minutes. Drain well. Add sauce to pan and mix with pasta; pour into a bowl and top with nuts. Makes 4 to 6 servings.

PER SERVING: 508 calories, 21 g protein, 47 g carbohydrates, 27 g fat, 98 mg cholesterol, 674 mg sodium

Portland

T HIS BANANA BRAN BREAD *tastes so good that you won't even think about how healthy it is. Try a slice at night when the temptation to have a candy bar is strong.*

To be even more wholesomely practical, toast slices of banana bread for breakfast, or cut it very thin and spread with softened cream cheese for a light lunch.

BANANA BRAN BREAD

- 1 cup all-purpose flour
- ¾ cup oat bran
- 1¼ teaspoons baking powder
- ½ teaspoon baking soda
- ¼ teaspoon salt
- 1 teaspoon grated lemon peel
- ⅓ cup (⅙ lb.) butter or margarine
- ⅔ cup sugar
- 2 large eggs
- 1 cup mashed ripe bananas (about 2 medium-size)
- ½ cup chopped walnuts

In a bowl, stir together flour, bran, baking powder, baking soda, and salt; set aside. In a mixer bowl, beat lemon peel, butter, and sugar until well blended; then add eggs, 1 at a time, beating well after each addition. Add flour mixture, banana, and nuts; stir until evenly moistened.

Spoon batter into a buttered 4½- by 8½-inch loaf pan. Bake in a 350° oven until bread begins to pull away from sides of pan and a toothpick inserted in the center comes out clean, about 55 minutes. Let cool in pan for 10 minutes, then turn out onto a rack to cool completely. Serve or, if made ahead, wrap airtight and chill up to 2 days; freeze to store longer. Makes 1 loaf, about 1¾ pounds.

PER 1 OUNCE: 87 calories, 1.7 g protein, 12 g carbohydrates, 4.1 g fat, 21 mg cholesterol, 80 mg sodium

Long Beach, Calif.

"Try a slice at night when the temptation to have a candy bar is strong."

June Menus

SUMMER BRINGS *an even more urgent need for quick, easy meals that get you out of the kitchen as fast as possible. Here we offer three fitting menus: a sandwich supper to enjoy outdoors, a festive Father's Day dinner, and a bountiful brunch starring some of the season's best fruits.*

SUMMER'S EVE PICNIC

**Chicken Sandwiches
with Mustard Vinaigrette
Cooked Green Beans & Potatoes
Niçoise Olives
Minted Raspberries with
White Chocolate
Mint Spritzers   Iced Tea**

Make-ahead steps and portability create an ideal meal for outdoor dining.

The day before the picnic, cook a chicken; a 3-pound bird should yield enough for 4 servings, or buy a cooked chicken at the deli. Also make the mint syrup and vinaigrette. In the morning, boil or steam green beans (about 1 lb.), then plunge into ice water until cold to preserve color; cook small, scrubbed thin-skinned potatoes (about 1¼ lb.) and let cool. Use vinaigrette to season the sandwiches and vegetables.

For spritzers, stir mint syrup to taste into sparkling water.

CHICKEN SANDWICHES
WITH MUSTARD VINAIGRETTE

- 4 **crusty rolls,** each 4 inches long
- 8 **small butter lettuce leaves,** rinsed and crisped
- 2 **medium-size** (about ¾ lb. total) **ripe tomatoes,** sliced ¼ inch thick
- 2 **cups** (9 to 10 oz.) **boned, skinned, and thinly sliced cooked chicken**
  Mustard vinaigrette (recipe follows)

Split rolls in half horizontally. On bottom half of each roll, lay 2 lettuce leaves, ¼ of the tomato slices, and ¼ of the chicken. Top with remaining roll halves. Offer vinaigrette to add to taste. Serves 4.

PER SERVING WITHOUT VINAIGRETTE: 307 calories, 26 g protein, 33 g carbohydrates, 6.9 g fat, 63 mg cholesterol, 380 mg sodium

Mustard vinaigrette. Mix together ½ cup **extra-virgin olive oil** or salad oil, ⅓ cup **balsamic vinegar,** and 1 tablespoon **Dijon mustard.** Makes about ¾ cup.

PER TABLESPOON: 82 calories, 0 g protein, 0.4 g carbohydrates, 9.4 g fat, 0 mg cholesterol, 37 mg sodium

Ideal menu for an evening picnic: chicken sandwiches, cool green beans, and small potatoes share mustard vinaigrette. Finale is fresh raspberries.

MINTED RASPBERRIES WITH WHITE CHOCOLATE

6 cups raspberries, rinsed and drained
Mint syrup (recipe follows)
1 ounce white chocolate, grated

Spoon raspberries into 4 dessert dishes; drizzle each with about 4 teaspoons of the syrup. Sprinkle with chocolate. Serves 4.

PER SERVING: 199 calories, 2 g protein, 44 g carbohydrates, 3.1 g fat, 1.2 mg cholesterol, 5.9 mg sodium

Mint syrup. In a 2- to 3-quart pan, bring to boiling on high heat 1 cup **water,** 1½ cups **sugar,** and 1 cup firmly packed chopped **fresh mint leaves;** stir, then boil until reduced to 1⅓ cups, 8 to 10 minutes. Let stand 30 minutes. Pour syrup through a strainer into a jar; discard leaves. Cover and chill syrup at least 4 hours or up to 4 weeks. Makes 1⅓ cups.

PER TABLESPOON: 53 calories, 0 g protein, 13 g carbohydrates, 0 g fat, 0 mg cholesterol, 0.1 mg sodium

---

FATHER'S DAY DINNER

Grilled London Broil
Blue Cheese–Onion Relish
Black Bean, Corn & Pepper Salad
Jicama & Celery Sticks
Warm Flour Tortillas
Coffee Macaroon Sundaes

This meal, with its steak-and-relish entrée and colorful make-ahead salad, should please the guest of honor.

Prepare relish for steak and salad in the morning or the day before. Barbecue a London broil (first cut of the top round; allow 4 to 5 oz. of meat per person) or a flank steak (also called London broil when grilled). For dessert, crumble almond macaroons over individual bowls of coffee ice cream.

BLUE CHEESE–ONION RELISH

In a 10- to 12-inch frying pan, combine 1 tablespoon **salad oil** and 2 large **onions,** sliced. Stir over medium-high heat until onions are limp, about 15 minutes. Pour onions into a bowl and add ¼ cup **balsamic** or red wine **vinegar** and 1 teaspoon **sugar;** mix well. Cool completely, then stir in 4 ounces (1 cup packed) crumbled **cambozola** or gorgonzola **cheese.**

Serve at room temperature with sliced hot **beef steak.** If made ahead, cover relish and let stand up to 4 hours at room temperature, or chill up until next day. Makes 3 cups, 6 servings.

PER ½ CUP: 108 calories, 4.6 g protein, 5.4 g carbohydrates, 7.8 g fat, 14 mg cholesterol, 264 mg sodium

BLACK BEAN, CORN & PEPPER SALAD

2 cans (15 oz. each) black beans or cannelli (white kidney beans), drained and rinsed
1½ cups cooked fresh corn kernels or 1 package (10 oz.) frozen corn kernels, thawed
1 large red bell pepper, stemmed, seeded, and diced
2 small fresh jalapeño chilies, stemmed, seeded, and minced
½ cup firmly packed chopped fresh cilantro (coriander)
¼ cup lime juice
2 tablespoons salad oil
Salt and pepper
Rinsed and crisped lettuce leaves

In a bowl, mix beans with corn, bell pepper, jalapeño, cilantro, lime juice, oil, and salt and pepper to taste. Cover and chill 1 hour or up until next day. Pour into a bowl lined with lettuce leaves. Serves 6.

PER SERVING: 210 calories, 10 g protein, 32 g carbohydrates, 5.5 g fat, 0 mg cholesterol, 553 mg sodium

(Continued on next page)

For Dad, colorful salad accompanies grilled steak with blue cheese–onion relish. Crunchy vegetables, warm tortillas, and coffee macaroon sundaes complete meal.

FESTIVE SUMMER BRUNCH

Apricot-Blackberry Cornmeal Kuchen
Sliced Nectarines
Thick-cut Bacon
Mushroom & Green Onion Omelets
Cinnamon Coffee   Orange Juice

Take advantage of a lazy morning and the season's abundant fruits with this brunch.

Cook omelets and bacon as kuchen cools. Add cinnamon sticks as swizzles to flavor cups of hot coffee.

APRICOT-BLACKBERRY CORNMEAL KUCHEN

½ cup yellow cornmeal
½ cup all-purpose flour
1½ teaspoons baking powder
1 large egg
¼ cup firmly packed brown sugar
½ cup buttermilk
2 tablespoons melted butter or margarine
5 medium-size (about ¾ lb. total) ripe apricots, halved and pitted
10 blackberries, rinsed and drained
2 tablespoons granulated sugar

In a bowl, mix cornmeal, flour, and baking powder. In another bowl, beat to blend egg, brown sugar, buttermilk, and butter; stir into dry ingredients until evenly moistened.

Pour batter into a greased 8-inch-diameter cake or quiche pan. Gently press apricot halves, pitted side up, decoratively into dough; put 1 berry in the hollow of each apricot.

Bake in a 350° oven until kuchen feels firm to touch in center, 30 to 35 minutes; sprinkle with granulated sugar. Cool slightly, then cut into wedges. Makes 6 to 8 servings.

PER SERVING: 160 calories, 3.4 g protein, 28 g carbohydrates, 3.9 g fat, 34 mg cholesterol, 135 mg sodium

Pickled Ginger Shrimp Salad (page 167) with Pineapple Sangria (page 178)

Celebrate the joys of summer with good foods that reflect the season's riches: warm days, flourishing gardens, sun-ripe produce, impromptu outings. Picnic at breakfast to watch the sky, carry lunch to the garden, keep the barbecue aglow, cool off with ices and punches. For leisurely July meals, mix and match our easy-going salads and sandwiches with homemade pickled vegetables, chilled soups, and simple desserts. Invite special friends to share a Northwest summer classic: fresh Puget Sound salmon grilled with young Walla Walla onions.

EARLY MORNING LIGHT *is an invitation to get up and go while the hour is young and the day is still quiet. If the sunrise promises to be spectacular, if the fish bite better as dawn cracks, or if you'd just enjoy a peaceful moment as the day begins, pack a quick breakfast for one or more and take off. The following menus make brief, although differing, time demands.*

Warm burritos with eggs and sausage fortify early morning fishermen.

BURRITOS TO GO

Apricots or Seedless Grapes
Breakfast Burritos
Hot Coffee or
Chocolate-flavored Milk

A flat omelet topped with browned bits of Italian sausage is the heart of this morning burrito; chunks of avocado get tucked into it just before you eat.

Allow about 15 minutes to get this meal together; you can heat the tortillas in the oven or the microwave. For the traveler, put the hot coffee or cold or heated milk in a thermos, and the fruit in a crushproof container.

BREAKFAST BURRITOS

1 hot Italian sausage (about 3 oz.)
2 flour tortillas (8- to 10-in. diameter)
3 large eggs
1 tablespoon water
2 tablespoons canned diced green chilies
1 tablespoon butter or margarine
1 small firm-ripe avocado
  Salt and pepper

Remove and discard casing from sausage. Crumble meat into an 8- to 10-inch frying pan. Cook, stirring often, over medium heat until browned, about 10 minutes; set aside and keep warm.

Meanwhile, moisten tortillas, stack, and seal in foil. Heat in a 325° oven for 10 to 12 minutes. Or stack moistened tortillas on a paper towel and put in a plastic bag; loosely close. Cook in a microwave oven on full power (100 percent) until steaming hot, about 30 seconds.

In a small bowl, beat eggs to blend with the 1 tablespoon water and the chilies. Melt butter in a 7- to 8-inch omelet pan over medium-high heat; when butter is faintly browned, pour in egg mixture. As eggs begin to set, lift with a wide spatula to allow uncooked eggs to flow beneath; cook until eggs are softly set but still moist-looking on top (or to doneness you prefer). With a slotted spoon, scatter sausage over eggs.

Remove from heat and cut eggs in half crosswise. Transfer each half onto 1 side of each tortilla, fold end over rounded side of eggs, then fold sides over to enclose eggs.

To transport, lay each burrito, folded side down, on a piece of foil; fold foil to seal in burrito. Wrap burritos in a warm towel and place in a small insulated container; burritos will stay warm for about 1 hour.

To serve, cut avocado in half (bring along a small knife and spoon), discard pit, then scoop out avocado and tuck pieces into burritos, adding salt and pepper to taste. Makes 2 servings.

PER SERVING: 500 calories, 21 g protein, 31 g carbohydrates, 33 g fat, 359 mg cholesterol, 708 mg sodium

---

AL FRESCO, ITALIAN-STYLE

Fresh Figs or Nectarines
Venetian Fishermen's Cookies
Caffe Latte

Sturdy cookies, made with whole-wheat flour and not too sweet, stand ready to go at a moment's notice as nourishment for an impromptu outing.

Translated, the name for these Italian cookies is "bread of the fishermen"; like hearty biscotti, they make excellent dunkers for caffe latte (an equal blend of strong coffee and hot milk).

VENETIAN FISHERMEN'S COOKIES
(Pan del Pescatore)

1 cup all-purpose flour
1 cup whole-wheat flour
1 teaspoon baking powder
½ teaspoon ground cinnamon
¼ teaspoon *each* ground nutmeg and ground cloves
½ cup (¼ lb.) butter or margarine, at room temperature
¾ cup firmly packed brown sugar
1 tablespoon grated orange peel
1 large egg
1 large egg yolk
3 tablespoons orange juice
1 cup chopped walnuts or almonds
½ cup raisins

Carry warm muffins, made from ready-bake batter, to the garden for breakfast. Serve with pats of cream cheese and juicy whole strawberries.

READY-BAKE WHOLE-GRAIN MUFFINS

- 1 cup *each* whole-bran cereal, untoasted wheat germ, and quick-cooking rolled oats
- 1 cup boiling water
- 2 large eggs
- 2 cups buttermilk
- ½ cup salad oil
- 1 cup chopped dried apricots, raisins, or chopped pitted dates
- ½ teaspoon salt
- 2 teaspoons pumpkin pie spice
- 2½ teaspoons baking soda
- 1 cup sugar
- 2½ cups all-purpose flour

In a large bowl, stir together whole-bran cereal, wheat germ, and rolled oats. Add boiling water and stir to moisten evenly; let cool. Add eggs, buttermilk, oil, and apricots; beat to blend well. Stir together salt, pumpkin pie spice, baking soda, sugar, and flour, then stir into cereal mixture. Bake muffins—all or several at a time in the oven, or 1 at a time in the microwave. Keep extra batter tightly covered and store up to 2 weeks in the refrigerator; stir before using.

To bake in the oven: spoon batter into paper-lined 2½-inch muffin cups, filling ⅔ to ¾ full. Bake in a 425° oven until muffins are slightly darker color and tops spring back when lightly touched, about 20 minutes.

To cook in the microwave: for each muffin, set 1 paper baking cup in a 6-ounce glass custard cup; or nest 2 paper baking cups, 1 inside the other, then invert and wrap a strip of tape around middle of outside cup to support shape. Fill each cup, as ready to cook, with a scant ¼ cup batter. Cook 1 muffin at a time on full power (100 percent) until muffin looks dry on top and springs back when lightly touched (it may feel moist, but it shouldn't be sticky), 40 to 50 seconds; rotate muffin after 20 to 30 seconds if it seems to be baking unevenly. If muffin isn't done, continue cooking, testing at 10-second intervals.

If you want to transport muffins warm, wrap individually in paper towels and pack in a small insulated bag; they should stay warm up to about 1 hour. Serve muffins hot, warm, or cool. Makes 2 to 2½ dozen.

PER MUFFIN: 150 calories, 4.1 g protein, 24 g carbohydrates, 4.9 g fat, 15 mg cholesterol, 153 mg sodium

In a bowl, stir together all-purpose and whole-wheat flours, baking powder, cinnamon, nutmeg, and cloves; set aside.

In large mixer bowl, beat butter with brown sugar and orange peel until fluffy. Beat in egg and egg yolk, then add orange juice and flour mixture. Stir to mix, then beat to blend well. Stir in walnuts and raisins.

Drop dough in ¼-cup-size mounds about 3 inches apart on greased 12- by 15-inch baking sheets. Bake in a 350° oven until golden brown, 15 to 20 minutes. Cool on racks. Eat, or store airtight up to 3 days; freeze to store longer. Makes about 18.

PER COOKY: 192 calories, 3.2 g protein, 24 g carbohydrates, 10 g fat, 37 mg cholesterol, 84 mg sodium

MUFFINS IN MINUTES

Whole Strawberries
Ready-bake Whole-grain Muffins
Cream Cheese
Herb Tea

Refrigerated bran muffin batter is ready to cook in the microwave in 1-minute, 1-muffin batches or to bake by the panful.

If you plan to enjoy this breakfast as a picnic away from home, carry hot tea in a thermos and bring along a pat of cream cheese for each muffin. Rinse berries and carry in a crushproof container; a meal for one or two fits easily into a backpack.

THE GOOD FOODS OF SUMMER: Festive Ices

S TIMULATE APPETITES *with one of these cooling ices as a prelude to a meal. Or conclude a meal, particularly a rich one, with an ice for a light dessert.*

Festive combinations include port with orange juice enriched by aromatic bitters; sweet vermouth or orange juice with ruby Campari or aromatic bitters; and champagne or apple juice with ginger and peach-flavor liqueur.

Freeze the ices in the freezer or in a self-refrigerated machine, following the manufacturer's directions.

To freeze in freezer. *Pour ice mixture into a metal pan (8- or 9-in. square or 9 by 13 in.); cover and freeze until solid, at least 2 hours or up to 1 month. Break into small chunks with a heavy spoon and whirl in a food processor or beat with a mixer until a smooth slush forms; serve in chilled glasses.*

If you want slush firmer, put in freezer up to 1 hour. Slush can be stored in freezer up to 1 month; to make it soft enough to scoop, beat before serving.

PORT ICE

1½ cups water
½ cup sugar
1 cup port or cream sherry
¼ cup orange juice
1 teaspoon aromatic bitters

In a 1- to 2-quart pan, stir water and sugar over high heat until boiling. Let cool. Add port, juice, and bitters. Cover and chill until cold, about 1 hour. Freeze as directed, preceding. Serves 6 to 8.

PER SERVING: 99 calories, 0.1 g protein, 17 g carbohydrates, 0 g fat, 0 mg cholesterol, 2.9 mg sodium

ITALIAN ICE

1½ cups water
½ cup sugar
1 cup sweet vermouth or orange juice
2 tablespoons Campari or 2 teaspoons aromatic bitters
1 tablespoon lime juice
Lime slices (optional)

In a 1- to 2-quart pan, stir water and sugar over high heat until boiling. Let cool; then add vermouth, Campari, and lime juice. Chill until cold, about 1 hour,

Ready in the freezer, refreshing champagne ice with essences of peach and ginger is a tongue-tingling way to start or end a summer party.

then freeze as directed, preceding. Garnish individual portions with lime slices. Serves 6 to 8.

PER SERVING: 107 calories, 0 g protein, 17 g carbohydrates, 0.3 g fat, 0 mg cholesterol, 1.6 mg sodium

GINGER-PEACH ICE

1½ cups water
½ cup sugar
2 tablespoons minced crystallized ginger
1 cup champagne, sparkling wine, or sparkling apple juice
3 tablespoons peach-flavor liqueur
Fresh mint sprigs (optional)

In a 1- to 2-quart pan, stir water, sugar, and 1 tablespoon ginger over high heat until boiling. Let cool, then add champagne and liqueur. Cover and chill until cold, about 1 hour. Freeze as directed, preceding. Top portions with remaining ginger and mint. Serves 6 to 8.

PER SERVING: 102 calories, 0 g protein, 18 g carbohydrates, 0 g fat, 0 mg cholesterol, 4 mg sodium

THE GOOD FOODS OF SUMMER: Vine-Ripe Tomatoes

VINE-RIPENED TOMATOES *are a summer treat not yet mastered by technology. Enjoy them simply sliced and lightly seasoned to your heart's content. But also use them for a flavorful impact with other foods. Here, sweet, petite cherry tomatoes team up with fail-safe basil to make a great salad; fleshy Roma-style tomatoes are oven-roasted to intensify their taste, then become the base of a thick frittata; and any good, ripe tomato cooks down to make a delicious, pungent relish that goes extremely well with grilled fish and poultry.*

RED & GOLD TOMATO SALAD

  8 to 12 red butter lettuce or red-leaf lettuce leaves, rinsed and crisped
  2 cups *each* red and yellow cherry tomatoes, stemmed, rinsed, drained, and cut in halves
      Fresh basil dressing (recipe follows)
  8 thin slices (about 2½ oz.) prosciutto or (about 4 oz.) cooked ham
12 to 16 oil-cured olives or niçoise olives
      Salt and freshly ground pepper

Line 4 salad plates with lettuce. Top each with ¼ of the tomatoes; drizzle with dressing, using it all. Roll prosciutto slices and put 2 beside each salad; garnish with olives. Season to taste with salt and pepper. Makes 4 servings.

PER SERVING: 254 calories, 6.7 g protein, 6.6 g carbohydrates, 24 g fat, 13 mg cholesterol, 569 mg sodium

Fresh basil dressing. In a blender or food processor, whirl until smoothly puréed ¼ cup lightly packed **fresh basil leaves**, 2 tablespoons grated **parmesan cheese**, ⅓ cup **extra-virgin olive oil**, 2 tablespoons **red wine vinegar**, and 1 clove **garlic**. Makes about ½ cup.

Bite-size red and yellow tomatoes mingle compatibly with basil dressing in this salad.

ROASTED TOMATO FRITTATA

1½ pounds Roma-style tomatoes, rinsed, cored, and cut in half lengthwise
      About 2 tablespoons olive oil
  1 small onion, finely chopped
  2 cups coarsely shredded Swiss chard leaves (white stems reserved for other uses) or escarole
  6 large eggs
 ⅛ teaspoon *each* pepper and ground nutmeg
 ⅓ cup grated parmesan cheese
 ½ cup fresh basil leaves

Lay tomatoes, cut side up, in a 9- by 13-inch pan; brush tops with olive oil. Bake in a 450° oven for 40 minutes. Mix onion with 1 tablespoon olive oil, then scatter over tomatoes and continue to bake until edges of tomatoes begin to brown and juices in pan are dark but not scorched, 20 to 30 minutes longer. Use hot to room temperature.

Pour 2 teaspoons oil into a nonstick 10- to 12-inch frying pan on high heat. Add chard and stir just until wilted. Pour out of pan and set aside. Fit tomatoes, cut side down, in frying pan; strew with onion pieces, then chard. Place pan over medium-low heat.

In a bowl, beat eggs to blend, then beat in pepper, nutmeg, cheese, and basil. Pour mixture over tomatoes. Let cook, undisturbed, until eggs begin to set around pan rim (they turn opaque) but still jiggle slightly in center when pan is shaken, 8 to 10 minutes.

Transfer frittata to broiler and broil about 8 inches from heat until the top feels set when lightly touched but is still moist looking, 2 or 3 minutes. Remove from broiler and run a knife inside pan rim. Invert a platter (wider than frying pan) onto pan; holding together, turn over and lift off pan. Serve warm or at room temperature, cut into wedges. Makes 6 servings.

PER SERVING: 163 calories, 9.5 g protein, 7.1 g carbohydrates, 11 g fat, 216 mg cholesterol, 179 mg sodium

TOMATO–ORANGE RELISH

  1 medium-size orange
  4 medium-size (about 1½ lb. total) firm-ripe tomatoes, cored and cut into 1-inch chunks
  2 tablespoons *each* tomato paste and cider vinegar
  1 tablespoon salad oil
  1 small dried hot red chili
  1 teaspoon *each* mustard seed and cumin seed
 ¼ teaspoon ground allspice
 ¼ cup firmly packed brown sugar
 ½ cup raisins

Grate 1 teaspoon orange peel and set it aside. Cut away and discard remaining peel and white membrane from orange. Cut orange into chunks.

In a food processor or blender, combine orange chunks, tomatoes, tomato paste, and vinegar; whirl until coarsely puréed. Set mixture aside.

In a 2- to 3-quart pan, warm oil over medium-high heat. Add chili, mustard seed, and cumin seed; stir until seeds begin to pop, 2 to 3 minutes. Mix in allspice, tomato mixture, brown sugar, raisins, and reserved orange peel. Stir until sugar dissolves, about 3 minutes, then reduce heat so mixture boils gently. Cook, uncovered and stirring often, until consistency is jam-like, 20 to 30 minutes. Serve hot or at room temperature. If made ahead, cool, cover, and chill up to 3 days, then reheat if desired. Makes about 2 cups.

PER TABLESPOON: 24 calories, 0.3 g protein, 5 g carbohydrates, 0.5 g fat, 0 mg cholesterol, 10 mg sodium

THE GOOD FOODS OF SUMMER: Cool Company Appetizers

EXPECTING GUESTS *to drop by for an afternoon visit and a little refreshment? What could be handier than a cool appetizer waiting in the refrigerator? Here are three contrasting choices; each appetizer stands on its own, or serve them all as a colorful array.*

For the first appetizer, pink prosciutto encases an herb-seasoned cream cheese filling; the meat makes the torta easy to remove from its loaf pan mold. Cut it to eat on crisp breadsticks or toast.

The second choice is a fresh twist on cabbage rolls. Instead of cooking the leaves and tuna filling, you roll crisp raw leaves around a flavorful cabbage slaw to munch out of hand.

The last choice adds a new dimension to olives. Flavors of lemon peel, lemon juice, a little garlic, and olive oil seep into ripe olives thoroughly; they'll taste as if they'd grown this way.

The first and the last appetizers can be made as much as a day ahead. The cabbage mixture holds well for a few hours.

Crinkly savoy cabbage leaf holds slaw of albacore and tomatoes. Roll up to eat.

LEMON HERB TORTA

- ¾ cup lightly packed parsley
- 1½ teaspoons grated lemon peel
- 1 green onion (ends trimmed), coarsely chopped
- 1 large package (8 oz.) cream cheese, at room temperature
- ¼ cup (⅛ lb.) unsalted butter or margarine, at room temperature
- 2 ounces very thinly sliced prosciutto or cooked ham
  Sesame-coated breadsticks or unsalted crackers

In a food processor, combine parsley, lemon peel, and onion. Whirl until minced. Add cream cheese and butter and whirl until well blended; scrape container sides often. (Or mince vegetables, combine with cream cheese and butter, and beat with an electric mixer to blend well.)

To assemble, line bottom and sides of a 3- by 5-inch loaf pan with a single layer of prosciutto. Spoon half the cheese mixture into pan and level gently, without moving meat. Cover cheese with another layer of meat. Top with remaining cheese; make level. Cover with remaining meat. Fold any meat that overlaps the pan rim back onto the filling. Cover and chill until the torta is firm when touched, at least 2 hours or up until next day.

To serve, run a knife inside pan rim, then invert the torta onto a small platter. Use a small, sharp knife to cut portions, then press cheese and meat onto breadsticks. Makes 10 to 12 servings.

PER SERVING WITHOUT BREADSTICK: 110 calories, 2.6 g protein, 0.9 g carbohydrates, 11 g fat, 34 mg cholesterol, 129 mg sodium

CABBAGE SLAW ROLLS

- 1 head (about 1½ lb.) green, red, or Savoy cabbage
- 1 can (6 to 7 oz.) albacore, packed in oil
- ¼ to ½ teaspoon crushed dried hot red chilies
- ¼ cup lemon juice
- ¼ cup drained dried tomatoes packed in oil, cut into ¼-inch slivers
- 1 tablespoon drained capers

Carefully remove 8 large outer leaves from cabbage. Rinse, drain, wrap in paper towels, enclose in a plastic bag,

Thinly sliced prosciutto encases herb-cheese torta; it's shaped in a loaf pan.

and chill. Finely shred remaining cabbage. If made ahead, cover and chill shredded cabbage and leaves up until next day.

In a bowl, mix shredded cabbage with albacore and its oil, chilies, lemon juice, tomatoes, and capers. Present slaw in a serving bowl surrounded by cabbage leaves. Let guests spoon slaw into cabbage leaves and roll up to eat. Makes 8 servings.

PER SERVING: 81 calories, 6.3 g protein, 6 g carbohydrates, 4 g fat, 5.9 mg cholesterol, 281 mg sodium

OLIVES ARLESIENNE

- 2 tablespoons olive oil
- 1 clove garlic, minced or pressed
- ½ teaspoon grated lemon peel
- 1 teaspoon lemon juice
- 1 can (5¾ oz.) pitted jumbo ripe olives, drained well

In a bowl or pint jar, combine oil, garlic, lemon peel, and lemon juice; mix until well blended. Add olives and mix lightly to coat thoroughly. Cover and chill for at least 4 hours or up to 1 week. Makes about 1½ cups, 6 to 8 servings.

PER SERVING: 65 calories, 0.2 g protein, 0.8 g carbohydrates, 7.1 g fat, 0 mg cholesterol, 140 mg sodium

Tiny, pink, *and ready-to-eat shrimp, sold shelled and cooked, are easy to use. Conveniently, they are also one of the most widely available shellfish, and usually a good buy. Shrimp harvests tend to come in cycles; currently, they're particularly bountiful.*

Tiny shrimp are the basis for three quick-to-prepare main-dish salads. To refresh the shrimp's delicate flavor, give them a quick rinse just before using.

PICKLED GINGER SHRIMP SALAD

1 to 1¼ **pounds shelled cooked tiny shrimp**

3 **tablespoons seasoned rice vinegar (or 3 tablespoons rice vinegar or white wine vinegar with 1 teaspoon sugar)**

2 **tablespoons slivered pickled ginger**

1 **tablespoon salad oil**

½ **teaspoon Oriental sesame oil**
About 8 cups rinsed and crisped leaves of butter lettuce, red- or green-leaf lettuce, mizuna, or curly chicory (1 kind or a combination)
Wasabi cones (directions follow)

Place shrimp in a colander and rinse with cool water; drain well. In a bowl, mix shrimp with vinegar, ginger, salad oil, and sesame oil.

Arrange leaves on each of 4 dinner plates. Mound shrimp and dressing onto leaves. Place a wasabi cone on each plate, adding it to taste with bites of salad. Makes 4 servings.

PER SERVING: 163 calories, 24 g protein, 3.3 g carbohydrates, 5.3 g fat, 221 mg cholesterol, 256 mg sodium

Wasabi cones. Stir 2 tablespoons **wasabi powder** (Japanese hot horseradish powder) with 1 tablespoon **water** until smooth. Divide into 4 equal portions. Pinch each into a small cone. If made ahead, cover and chill up until next day.

CONFETTI VEGETABLES WITH SHRIMP

1 to 1¼ **pounds shelled cooked tiny shrimp**

1 **tablespoon salad oil**

¼ **cup white wine vinegar**

2 **teaspoons Worcestershire**

1 **cup ¼-inch-dice carrot**

1 **cup ¼-inch-dice red bell pepper**

1½ **cups ¼-inch-dice European cucumber**

½ **cup finely chopped green onion, including tops**

2 **cups rinsed and crisped watercress sprigs**
Salt and pepper

In a colander, rinse shrimp with cool water; drain well. Cover and chill.

To a 10- to 12-inch frying pan over medium-high heat, add oil, vinegar, Worcestershire, carrot, and bell pepper. Stir often until bell pepper is tender to bite, about 5 minutes. Remove from heat and stir in cucumber and onion.

Make a wreath of watercress around edge of each of 4 dinner plates. Mound shrimp equally in the middle of each wreath. Spoon vegetables and liquid equally around and over shrimp. Add salt and pepper to taste. Makes 4 servings.

PER SERVING: 207 calories, 25 g protein, 7.3 g carbohydrates, 8.3 g fat, 221 mg cholesterol, 305 mg sodium

SHRIMP & ASPARAGUS WITH MUSTARD YOGURT CREAM

1 **pound thick asparagus spears**

1 to 1¼ **pounds shelled cooked tiny shrimp**

2 **lemons, cut in half**
Mustard yogurt cream (recipe follows)

Snap tough ends from asparagus and discard. Peel the stalks with a vegetable peeler, if desired. In a 10- to 12-inch frying pan over high heat, bring about 1 inch water to a boil. Add asparagus and cook until bright green and just tender when pierced, about 5 minutes. Drain and immediately immerse spears in ice

Bright bits of diced carrot and red bell pepper, lightly cooked, encircle shrimp on watercress.

water until cool. Drain well; if made ahead, cover and chill up until next day.

Place shrimp in a colander and rinse with cool water; drain well.

Lay asparagus equally on each of 4 dinner plates; mound shrimp over asparagus. Set a lemon half on each plate to add juice to taste, and offer mustard yogurt cream. Makes 4 servings.

PER SERVING: 126 calories, 26 g protein, 2.2 g carbohydrates, 1.4 g fat, 221 mg cholesterol, 255 mg sodium

Mustard yogurt cream. In a 1½- to 2-quart pan, stir together to mix well 1 **large egg yolk,** ¼ cup **Dijon mustard,** 2 tablespoons **white wine vinegar,** and 1 tablespoon *each* **butter** or margarine, **sugar,** and **mustard seed.**

Stir over low heat until mixture is thick enough to coat a metal spoon in a smooth, velvety layer. Set the pan in ice water; stir often until sauce is cool. Stir in 1 carton (6 oz.) **unflavored yogurt.** If made ahead, cover and chill up until next day. Makes 1 cup.

PER TABLESPOON: 28 calories, 0.9 g protein, 2.3 g carbohydrates, 1.6 g fat, 16 mg cholesterol, 128 mg sodium

THE GOOD FOODS OF SUMMER: Watermelon Fun

NOTHING REFRESHES LIKE *the cool, succulent juiciness of chilled ripe watermelon; it revives flagging spirits even in the toughest hot weather.*

Enjoy crisp-fleshed watermelon icy cold and plain, or try these simple low-fat serving suggestions. Use big, red-fleshed melons with black seeds or try the smaller, almost seedless varieties with red or yellow flesh, and cut with a flourish to make these dishes.

When you shop, it's easier to check the quality of a cut melon: look for firm flesh and rich color. When buying a whole melon, search for one with a symmetrical shape, a dull surface, and an underside that has a creamy or yellowish tinge.

CHICKEN & WATERMELON WITH HERBS

- **2 pounds boned and skinned chicken breast, rinsed and patted dry**
- **1⅓ cups orange juice**
- **1 teaspoon ground coriander**
- **1 piece (about 2½ lb.) seedless or seed-in watermelon**
- **½ teaspoon grated orange peel**
- **1 clove garlic, pressed or minced**
- **1 tablespoon finely chopped fresh or dry mint**
- **1 tablespoon finely chopped fresh dill or 1 teaspoon dry dill weed**
- **1 tablespoon finely chopped fresh cilantro (coriander)**
- **1 tablespoon balsamic or red wine vinegar**
  Salt and pepper

Cut chicken into 1½-inch cubes. In a bowl, mix chicken with ⅓ cup orange juice and coriander. If made ahead, cover and chill up to 2 hours. Thread chicken equally onto 6 to 8 thin skewers.

Cut watermelon flesh free from rind; then cut flesh into 1-inch cubes. Impale cubes equally on 6 to 8 thin skewers.

Mix remaining orange juice, orange peel, garlic, mint, dill, cilantro, and vinegar. Pour into a small serving bowl.

Cook chicken on a grill 4 to 6 inches above a solid bed of hot coals (you can hold your hand at grill level only 2 to 3 seconds) until meat is white in thickest part (cut to test), 10 to 14 minutes; turn to brown evenly. Accompany chicken and watermelon with orange–herb sauce to pour over both. Add salt and pepper to taste. Makes 6 to 8 servings.

PER SERVING: 169 calories, 27 g protein, 10 g carbohydrates, 1.7 g fat 66 mg cholesterol, 76 mg sodium

Skewered cubes of rosy–watermelon pair well with grilled chicken. Ladle orange–herb sauce over both.

WATERMELON, JICAMA & CHILI SALT

- **4 seedless or seed-in watermelon wedges (each about 3 in. wide and 9 in. long), 4 to 5 pounds total**
- **1 small whole or 1 piece (about 1¼ lb.) jicama, peeled and rinsed**
  Chili salt (recipe follows)
- **1 lemon, cut into quarters**

Slide a short, sharp knife between rind and flesh of watermelon wedges to free flesh, but keep flesh in place. Cut through melon to the rind at 1½-inch intervals.

Cut jicama in ¼-inch-thick slices that are about 2 by 3 inches. Insert jicama

Crisp jicama slices alternate with juicy watermelon bites. Season with chili salt and squeeze lemon over melon to enhance flavors.

slices in melon slits. Sprinkle chili salt and squeeze lemon juice on melon to taste. Makes 4 servings.

PER SERVING: 135 calories, 3.6 g protein, 31 g carbohydrates, 1.4 g fat, 0 mg cholesterol, 13 mg sodium

Chili salt. Mix ½ teaspoon *each* **salt** and **cayenne.** Makes 1 teaspoon.

PER ¼ TEASPOON: 0.7 calories, 0 g protein, 0.1 g carbohydrates, 0 g fat, 0 mg cholesterol, 275 mg sodium

WATERMELON BLOSSOMS WITH BASIL VINEGAR

1 **piece (4 to 4½ lb.) seedless or seed-in watermelon**

⅓ **cup seasoned rice vinegar (or 3 tablespoons cider vinegar plus 2 tablespoons water)**

2 **tablespoons chopped fresh or 2 teaspoons dry basil**

2 **teaspoons honey**

With a melon baller, cut watermelon flesh into balls to make about 4 cups; set aside or cover and chill up to 6 hours. Cut remaining flesh from shell; reserve for another use.

Cut shell into 4 to 6 ovals (roughly 2 by 4 in.). With a small, sharp knife, cut ovals into leaf shapes. Make thin, wedged cuts in skin side to incise leaf veins (the white rind beneath the green skin makes a distinctive pattern). If made ahead, cover and chill up to 6 hours.

Arrange ¼ of the fruit and 1 or 2 shell leaves on each of 4 dinner plates. Mix vinegar, basil, and honey; spoon over fruit to taste. Makes 4 servings.

PER SERVING: 90 calories, 1.6 g protein, 21 g carbohydrates, 1 g fat, 0 mg cholesterol, 5.3 mg sodium

The Good Foods of Summer: The 30 Percent Solution

A WHOLESOME CHALLENGE *in planning good, balanced menus is to keep the number of calories from fat in your diet at 30 percent or less.*

Actually, it's easier than you might think, even when you serve cuts of meats that have a reputation for being "rich." Success depends on thoroughly trimming the meat of fat, cooking the meat with little or no added fat (barbecuing is tailor-made for the task), and balancing the meat with carbohydrates in appropriate proportions. That's why these main dishes are paired with salads of grains, legumes, or pasta.

They are tasty, handsome, satisfying, and easy to prepare. And they include lots of make-ahead steps.

Grilled Minted Lamb Chops & Mushrooms with Pilaf Salad or Lentil Salad

  4 **lamb loin chops, cut about 1 inch thick (about 1½ lb. total)**
  1 **teaspoon olive oil**
  2 **tablespoons dry vermouth**
  ½ **teaspoon pepper**
  ¼ **cup coarsely chopped fresh mint leaves**
 16 **medium-large (with caps about 1½ in. wide) mushrooms**
     Pilaf salad or lentil salad (recipes follow)
  4 **or 5 cherry tomatoes**
     Mint sprigs
     Salt

Trim and discard fat from chops. Rinse meat, pat dry, and put in a plastic bag, about 4-quart size. To bag add oil, vermouth, pepper, and chopped mint. Seal bag and rotate to mix ingredients well. Set in a bowl and chill at least 30 minutes or up until the next day.

Rinse and drain mushrooms; trim off discolored stem ends. Thread mushrooms through caps onto slender skewers.

Lift chops from marinade, and pour marinade into a small bowl. Brush mushrooms with marinade. Place chops on a lightly greased grill 4 to 6 inches above a solid bed of hot coals (you can hold your hand at grill level for only 2 to 3 seconds); place mushroom skewers around edges where heat is less intense.

Serve juicy grilled lamb chops and skewered plump mushrooms with a rice pilaf salad. Garnish with red cherry tomatoes and sprigs of fresh mint.

Cook chops until browned but still pink in center (cut to test), about 10 minutes, turning once. Cook mushrooms until lightly browned, about 10 minutes, turning several times. Serve chops, mushrooms, and salad from a large platter; garnish with cherry tomatoes and mint sprigs. Add salt to taste. Makes 4 servings.

PER SERVING WITH PILAF: 426 calories (25 percent from fat), 29 g protein, 52 g carbohydrates, 12 g fat, 63 mg cholesterol, 168 mg sodium

PER SERVING WITH LENTILS: 488 calories (28 percent from fat), 42 g protein, 49 g carbohydrates, 15 g fat, 62 mg cholesterol, 70 mg sodium

Pilaf salad. Rinse and drain ½ cup **wild rice.** Put in a 2- to 3-quart pan; add 1¾ cups (1 can, 14½ oz.) **regular-strength chicken broth** and 1 cup **water** and bring to a boil on high heat. Reduce heat and simmer 20 minutes.

Rinse and drain ¾ cup **long-grain brown rice;** add to wild rice. Continue to cook until both rices are tender to bite, 20 to 25 minutes longer. Remove from heat and, with a fork, stir in 3 tablespoons **lemon juice** and ¼ cup sliced **black ripe olives.** Cover and chill until cool, about 30 minutes, or up until next day. With a fork, stir in ⅓ cup **unflavored low-fat yogurt,** 1 cup halved **cherry tomatoes,** and **salt** and additional **lemon juice** to taste. Makes 4 cups.

Lentil salad. Sort and remove any debris from 1½ cups (10 to 11 oz.) **lentils**; rinse and drain lentils, then put in a 3- to 4-quart pan. Add to pan 1 tablespoon **mixed pickling spices** and 3 cups **water.** Bring to boiling on high heat, then cover and simmer until lentils are just tender to bite, 20 to 25 minutes. Drain lentils well, then add ¼ cup **cider vinegar**, 2 cloves **garlic** (minced or pressed), and 2 tablespoons **olive oil** or salad oil. Let stand until cool; if made ahead, cover and chill up until next day.

Core, peel, and chop 1 large **firm-ripe tomato;** also stem, seed, and finely chop 1 small **fresh hot green chili.** Mix tomato, chili, ⅓ cup sliced **green onions** (including tops), 2 tablespoons slivered **fresh mint leaves,** and **salt** to taste with lentils. Makes 5 cups.

BARBECUED BRISKET WITH KASHA SALAD

Brisket is usually simmered long and gently, but it is also excellent when treated with meat tenderizer and grilled just until rare; grilled longer, the meat gets tough.

- 1 **piece (3 to 3½ lb.) center-cut fresh beef brisket**
- 1 **medium-size onion, finely chopped**
- ½ **cup catsup**
- 2 **teaspoons prepared horseradish**
- ½ **teaspoon whole cloves**
- 1 **cinnamon stick, about 2 inches long**
- 2 **tablespoons** *each* **cider vinegar and firmly packed brown sugar**
- ⅓ **cup** *each* **water and dry white wine**
  Unsalted meat tenderizer
  Kasha salad (recipe follows)
  About ½ cup finely chopped green onions, including tops

Trim and discard surface fat from brisket. Put meat in a plastic bag, about 4-quart size; add onion, catsup, horseradish, cloves, cinnamon, vinegar, brown sugar, water, and wine. Seal bag and rotate to mix ingredients well. Set bag in a pan and chill for at least 2 hours or up to 1 day.

Lift brisket from bag and pour marinade into 1- to 1½-quart pan. Pat meat dry and apply tenderizer according to package directions. Place meat on a lightly greased grill 4 to 6 inches above a solid bed of low coals (you can hold your hand at grill level only 6 to 7 seconds). Cook, turning often, until a meat thermometer inserted in thickest part registers 135° to 140° for rare to medium-rare, 25 to 30 minutes (cooked longer, the meat gets very chewy). Transfer meat to a carving board, drape with foil, and let stand for 10 minutes for juices to settle.

Meanwhile, bring marinade to a boil and simmer, uncovered, for about 5 minutes, stirring occasionally; pour through a strainer over kasha salad, then sprinkle green onions on salad.

Thinly slice brisket across the grain, cutting at a slant to make wide pieces. Accompany with salad. Makes 8 to 10 servings.

PER SERVING: 322 calories (27 percent from fat), 23 g protein, 38 g carbohydrates, 9.6 g fat, 60 mg cholesterol, 207 mg sodium

Kasha salad. Rinse 1½ cups **buckwheat groats** (kasha) and drain well. Put in a 10- to 12-inch nonstick frying pan and stir over medium-high heat until grains are dry and smell lightly toasted. Add 2 cups **regular-strength chicken broth** and 3 tablespoons **lemon juice.**

Bring to boiling over high heat, then cover, reduce heat, and simmer 10 minutes; remove from heat and let stand until liquid is absorbed, at least 10 minutes or until cool. Pour into a salad bowl; rinse and dry frying pan. Use kasha warm or let stand at room temperature up to 2 hours. If made ahead, cover and chill up until next day; stir with a fork to separate the grains.

Stem enough **seedless green grapes** to make 4 cups; rinse and drain.

When brisket is cooked and resting to slice, place frying pan over high heat. When hot, add 3 cups of the grapes and swirl about until grapes are hot and skins begin to pop, 1 or 2 minutes. Pour into bowl with kasha and mix gently; top with remaining grapes. Makes 5 cups.

GRILLED PORK TENDERLOIN WITH COUSCOUS SALAD

- 2 **pork tenderloins (¾ to 1 lb. each)**
- ¼ **cup soy sauce**
- 2 **tablespoons sake or dry sherry**
- 1½ **tablespoons honey**
- 1 **tablespoon grated fresh ginger**
- 1 **clove garlic, minced or pressed**
- 1 **pound edible-pod peas, ends and strings removed**
  Couscous salad (recipe follows)

Rinse meat and pat dry; trim silvery membrane and any fat from tenderloins. Fold thin end of each tenderloin under to make meat evenly thick; tie to secure.

Put meat in a plastic bag, about 4-quart size; add soy, sake, honey, ginger, and garlic. Seal bag and rotate to mix ingredients well. Set bag in a bowl; chill at least 30 minutes or up until next day.

Rinse and drain peas. Bring about 3 quarts water to boil in a 5- to 6-quart pan over high heat. Add peas and cook, uncovered, just until they turn a brighter green; drain and, at once, immerse in cold water until peas are cool. Drain and use, or cover and chill up until next day.

Lift meat from marinade; pour marinade into a small bowl. Lay meat on a lightly greased grill 4 to 6 inches above a solid bed of medium coals (you can hold your hand at grill level only 4 to 5 seconds). Cook and turn to brown evenly, brushing frequently with reserved marinade, just until meat is no longer pink in thickest part (cut to test) or until a meat thermometer inserted in center of thickest part registers 150° to 155°, 20 to 25 minutes. Put meat on a large platter; mound peas and the salad alongside. Thinly slice meat and serve with peas and salad. Makes 6 to 8 servings.

PER SERVING: 335 calories (8.5 percent from fat), 27 g protein, 48 g carbohydrates, 3.2 g fat, 55 mg cholesterol, 588 mg sodium

Couscous salad. In a 3- to 4-quart pan, bring to a boil on high heat 3½ cups **regular-strength chicken broth.** Add 3 tablespoons **rice vinegar,** 1 tablespoon **honey,** 1 tablespoon minced **fresh ginger,** and ½ teaspoon **dry mustard;** stir in 2 cups **couscous.** Cover and remove from heat. Let stand 10 minutes; stir with a fork to fluff, then let stand, uncovered, until room temperature; if made ahead, cover and chill up until next day. Stir with a fork before serving. Makes 8 cups.

THE GOOD FOODS OF SUMMER: A Buy & Serve Party

THE OVERFLOWING BOUNTY *and vibrant, colorful appeal of a summer produce stand inspired this showy feast of fruit and vegetables backed up by heartier, purchased, ready-to-eat foods.*

It's a buy-and-serve, self-paced, nibble-as-you-chat party, so it's wise to provide generously; good-value in-season produce creates the abundant look. You can easily scale the party up or down.

WHAT DO YOU NEED?

For each adult, allow about:

• 3 to 4 ounces savories. Choose from cooked, boneless **meat** (pâtés, roast beef, cold ham), smoked or preserved **fish** (smoked salmon, trout, or sturgeon; pickled herring), or 2 hard-cooked in-shell **chicken eggs** (or 1 chicken egg and 2 or 3 quail eggs)

• 1 to 2 ounces **cheese** (big wedges or small whole cheeses)

• 4 ounces **bread**

• ¾ pound (ready-to-eat) to 2 pounds *total* (including rinds and stems) fresh **fruit** and **vegetables**

Nibblers of any age find wholesome choices at produce party.

• ¼ to ½ cup **dip,** purchased or homemade (for vegetables, try curry-flavor mayonnaise, guacamole, or yogurt with herbs; for fruit, offer sour cream and brown sugar)

• 2 to 4 cups of your choice of **beverage** (keep bottles in ice-filled tubs; serve coolers in pitchers)

HOW DO YOU SET UP THE PARTY?

Stage it on large or small tables, grouping savories with vegetables; present fruits separately. For a small party (18 or fewer), 1 large table for the savories and 1 small table for the fruits work well. For larger groups, small tables spaced apart reduce congestion. You can duplicate foods on tables, or create a different combination at each station.

To cover tables, use greenery such as tough and handsome kale or clean, non-toxic leaves such as aspidistra (cloths beneath if you like). Then position meat, fish, eggs, cheeses, and dips with compatible vegetables and fruits. Mound them in everyday containers: trays, boards, baskets, pots, crocks, even folded-down paper bags (see bread, below left and on facing page).

To hold dips for savories, you might cut hollows in cabbages or eggplants, or use natural hollows in bell peppers. (Leftover cabbages and eggplants can be trimmed and cooked for subsequent meals.)

Dips for fruit can be served in a cut melon, half a coconut, or citrus shells.

When the edibles are in place, add opulence by filling bare spaces with whole fruits and vegetables like eggplants, tomatoes, potatoes, onions, melons, pineapples; plan to use them in later meals. Soften the look of your arrangement or camouflage containers with more greenery, such as sprays of rosemary or washed ivy, or the kale. Remember that large pieces of foods stay fresh longest. For example, a big wedge of cheese, for guests to cut as they eat, will taste and look better longer than precut cubes of cheese that dry out.

Select produce you can eat raw and out of hand, and handle it with care. Take fragile fruits out of rigid, cutting containers at once and spread out on towel-lined trays to reduce bruising and rate of spoilage. Rinse all produce (including tops) well by immersing in water; drain on paper towels. If produce has to stand more than a few minutes (or up until next day) keep cool and moist by enclosing (within towels) in plastic.

Harvest or buy fresh fruit and vegetables to create your own produce stand for a party spread. Fill in with hearty, purchased, ready-to-eat foods.

Colorful vegetables and hard-cooked chicken and quail eggs share dips in hollowed cabbages (use for soup or slaw later). Purchase loaves of crusty bread and large cheese wedges to complement seasonal fare. For large groups, use several stations with different combinations or duplicate foods.

THE GOOD FOODS OF SUMMER: Hearty Sandwiches & Salads

THESE ATTRACTIVELY ARRANGED *sandwiches and salads contain all you need for a hearty lunch or light supper—meat or fish, bread or pasta, and vegetables. Present them on trays, as individual servings.*

ANTIPASTO FOCACCIA SANDWICHES

- 1 loaf (1 lb.) frozen white or whole-wheat bread dough, thawed
- 1 jar (6 oz.) marinated artichoke hearts
- 2 ounces dry jack cheese or parmesan cheese
- 1 can (6 to 7 oz.) albacore or salmon, drained
- 1 jar (4 oz.) pimiento strips, drained

Roll dough out on a floured board to make a 10- by 15-inch rectangle. Drain about 1 tablespoon marinade from artichokes into a 10- by 15-inch pan and rub over interior. Transfer dough to pan and pat to fit. Rub 3 more tablespoons marinade over dough. Cover with plastic wrap; let stand until puffy, about 20 minutes. Uncover and poke holes all over dough with fingertips. Bake on lowest rack in a 450° oven until focaccia is golden brown, 12 to 15 minutes.

Meanwhile, use a cheese plane (the type you pull across a piece of cheese) to slice cheese paper thin; you should have about 1 cup slices. Ease hot focaccia onto a platter. Distribute artichokes and any marinade, fish chunks, and pimiento evenly over bread, then scatter cheese on top. Cut into pieces; hold or eat with a knife and fork. Makes 4 to 6 servings.

PER SERVING: 319 calories, 17 g protein, 40 g carbohydrates, 11 g fat, 18 mg cholesterol, 767 mg sodium

DANISH BEEF SANDWICHES

- 1 tablespoon reduced-calorie or regular mayonnaise
- ½ teaspoon *each* prepared horseradish and coarse-grain mustard
- 2 slices pumpernickel or dark rye bread, regular or dense texture
- 4 large butter lettuce leaves, rinsed and crisped
  About ¼ pound thinly sliced rare roast beef
  Crisp-fried onions (recipe follows)
  Salt

Spoon half the mayonnaise, horseradish, and mustard onto each slice of bread, then spread over slice, mixing the ingredients as you go.

Top each slice with lettuce leaves, then pile beef on lettuce. Mound as many onions as you can onto the beef.

Accompany sandwiches with remaining onions; add salt to taste. Eat with a knife and fork. Makes 2 sandwiches.

PER SANDWICH: 399 calories, 22 g protein, 32 g carbohydrates, 21 g fat, 49 mg cholesterol, 276 mg sodium

Crisp-fried onions. Thinly slice 1 medium-size (about 5 oz.) **onion** and separate it into rings. Place 3 tablespoons **all-purpose flour** in a plastic or paper bag. Add onion slices and shake to coat evenly with flour.

Pour about 1½ inches **salad oil** into a deep 2½- to 3-quart pan; heat to 300°. Lift half the onions from bag, shake off excess flour, and drop into oil. Cook until golden and most of the sizzling stops, 3 to 4 minutes; adjust heat to keep oil at 300°. Transfer onions with a slotted spoon to paper towels to drain; repeat to cook remaining onions. If desired, keep warm up to 15 minutes in a paper towel–lined pan (8 to 9 in. wide) in a 250° oven. Serve warm or at room temperature.

If made ahead, let cool, wrap airtight, and chill up to 3 days. To reheat, spread onions in a 10- by 15-inch pan; place in a 300° oven until warm, about 2 minutes. Makes about 4 cups.

Crisp onion rings crown lavish beef and pumpernickel sandwich; serve open-faced on tray, with vegetable garnish and beverage, to eat with knife and fork.

COLD SMOKED SALMON PASTA PRIMAVERA

8 ounces (about 2¼ cups) dry small shell-shaped pasta
  Parmesan dressing (recipe follows)
½ cup frozen petite peas
½ cup thinly sliced green onions (including tops)
2 medium-size carrots
½ pound small, tender green beans, ends trimmed
6 ounces sliced smoked salmon or lox
10 to 12 large red-leaf lettuce or butter lettuce leaves, rinsed and crisped
1 small firm-ripe tomato, peeled, cored, and chopped
  Salt and freshly ground pepper

In a 5- to 6-quart pan over high heat, cook pasta, uncovered, in 4 quarts boiling water just until tender to bite, 8 to 10 minutes. Drain, immerse in cold water until cool, drain well, and pour pasta into a large bowl. Add dressing, peas, and green onions; set aside.

Cut carrots into 2-inch lengths, then cut each section into ⅛-inch-thick sticks. Also cut beans in half lengthwise. Bring 2 quarts water to a boil in the 5- to 6-quart pan over high heat. Add carrots; when water returns to a boil, add beans. Cook, uncovered, until beans are just tender to bite. Drain; immerse in ice water until cool, then drain well. Mix the vegetables with pasta.

Divide smoked salmon in 5 or 6 portions; shape each portion in rolls. Lay lettuce equally on 5 or 6 dinner plates. Mound pasta salad equally on lettuce, then arrange salmon beside pasta. Sprinkle the salads with chopped tomato. Season to taste with salt and pepper. Makes 5 or 6 servings.

PER SERVING: 327 calories, 13 g protein, 37 g carbohydrates, 15 g fat, 7.8 mg cholesterol, 290 mg sodium

Parmesan dressing. Mix together 3 tablespoons **white wine vinegar**, 1 large clove **garlic** (minced or pressed), ½ teaspoon **crushed dried hot red chilies**, 2 tablespoons **grated parmesan cheese**, and ⅓ cup **extra-virgin olive oil**.

Asian flavors seep through Chinese noodles and grilled five-spice chicken. Arrange atop spinach leaves and garnish with sliced green onions.

CHINESE NOODLE SALAD WITH FIVE-SPICE CHICKEN

10 ounces (3 cups, part of a 14-oz. package) fresh Chinese-style noodles
  Five-spice dressing (recipe follows)
½ cup chopped fresh cilantro (coriander)
1 tablespoon grated fresh ginger
½ teaspoon grated lemon peel
2 whole chicken breasts (about 1 lb. each), skinned, boned, and split
4 to 6 cups spinach leaves, rinsed and crisped
¼ cup thinly sliced green onions (including tops)

In a 5- to 6-quart pan, bring 3 quarts water to boiling on high heat. Add noodles and cook, uncovered, just until tender to bite, 2 or 3 minutes. Drain, immerse in cold water until cool, drain again, and put in a large bowl. Add ⅓ cup dressing, cilantro, ginger, and lemon peel; mix gently and set aside.

Rinse chicken and pat dry. Place on a lightly greased grill 4 to 6 inches above a solid bed of medium-hot coals (you can hold your hand at grill level only 3 to 4 seconds). Cook until meat is no longer pink in thickest part (cut to test), 6 to 8 minutes; turn once and baste several times with dressing. On a board, cut chicken into ½-inch-wide slices.

Line 4 dinner plates with spinach. Top equally with warm chicken and noodles, arranging separately. Moisten with remaining dressing; sprinkle with onions. Makes 4 servings.

PER SERVING: 576 calories, 46 g protein, 58 g carbohydrates, 20 g fat, 86 mg cholesterol, 961 mg sodium

Five-spice dressing. Combine 2 tablespoons **seasoned rice vinegar** (or 2 tablespoons rice vinegar and 1 teaspoon sugar), 1 tablespoon *each* **soy sauce** and **lemon juice**, 1 clove **garlic** (minced or pressed), ½ teaspoon **Chinese five spice**, 1 tablespoon **Oriental sesame oil**, and ¼ cup **salad oil**.

THE GOOD FOODS OF SUMMER: Two Versatile Barbecue Sauces

GIVE VARIETY to the season's procession of grilled meats, seafood, and poultry by basting them as they cook with one of these barbecue sauces. When foods are served, offer more of the sauce used as a baste to add to taste.

Your choices are a spirited, sweet-tart, thick red sauce and a mild, mellow, thinner red chili blend. Both barbecue sauces keep well in the refrigerator, ready to use within a couple of weeks.

Look for the crinkly pasilla chilies and shiny California (also called New Mexico) chilies in Mexican markets and some supermarkets.

UNCLE BOB'S BARBECUE SAUCE

Spicy and sweet, this red sauce makes a good glaze for beef, chicken, and pork (it's especially good on pork baby back ribs); 1 cup sauce makes enough to baste about 3 pounds meat.

To prevent charring or burning sauce as meats cook, place meats on grill over indirect heat. On a charcoal barbecue, no coals should be directly beneath the meat (push coals equally to each side of the fire grate); on a gas barbecue, there should be no flame beneath the food.

- 3 **medium-size (about 1 lb. total) onions, chopped**
- 3 **cloves garlic, minced or pressed**
- 1 **tablespoon salad oil**
- 2 **cups catsup**
- 1 **cup *each* cider vinegar and dry red wine**
- ⅓ **cup firmly packed brown sugar**
- 1 **tablespoon dry mustard**
- 1 **teaspoon ground ginger**
- ½ **teaspoon *each* cayenne and pepper**

In a 5- to 6-quart pan over medium-high heat, mix onions, garlic, and oil. Cook, stirring often, until onions are limp, about 10 minutes.

Add catsup, vinegar, wine, brown sugar, dry mustard, ground ginger, cayenne, and pepper. Stirring, bring to a boil on high heat. Reduce heat to medium-low and simmer, uncovered, stirring occasionally until sauce is reduced to 4 cups, about 1½ hours. Use sauce, or cool, cover, and chill up to 2 weeks. Makes about 1 quart. —*Bob Reynolds, Moraga, Calif.*

PER TABLESPOON: 21 calories, 0.3 g protein, 4.5 g carbohydrates, 0.3 g fat, 0 mg cholesterol, 90 mg sodium

RED CHILI SAUCE

A cup of this chili sauce makes enough baste for about 3 pounds of meat; try on beef, chicken, or pork. Because the sauce contains no sugar, you can cook meat directly over the hot coals.

Offer extra sauce, lime, and salt to season individual servings.

- 8 **dry pasilla chilies (about 5 oz. total)**
- 8 **dry California (New Mexico) chilies (about 2 oz. total)**
- 3 **cups boiling water**
- 2 **cloves garlic, chopped**
- 1 **teaspoon pepper**

Break off and discard stems from pasilla and California chilies and shake out seeds. Rinse chilies and place in a bowl; add boiling water and let stand until chilies soften, about 1 hour.

With a slotted spoon, lift chilies from liquid and place in a blender. To blender, add 2 cups of the liquid, garlic, and pepper; whirl until chilies are very smoothly puréed.

Use sauce, or cover and chill up to 2 weeks. Makes about 4 cups. —*Marie E. Torres, San Jose, Calif.*

PER TABLESPOON: 10 calories, 0.4 g protein, 1.8 g carbohydrates, 0.5 g fat, 0 mg cholesterol, 1 mg sodium

Barbecued chicken gets its terra cotta tones from mellow chili barbecue basting sauce; serve more of the sauce with chicken at table.

THE GOOD FOODS OF SUMMER: Baking on the Barbecue

WHEN YOU PLAN *to fire up the barbecue for the main dish, whether it's fish fillets or flank steak, allow some time before or after this course to do a little barbecue baking.*

You might make a bread to serve with dinner: both the olive-studded rolls and the marinara-flavored crescents use purchased doughs.

Or, after the main dish is cooked, have apples ready to bake.

Shaped into pull-apart portions, olive-studded bread ring finishes browning as sausages heat. To bake on the barbecue, use indirect heat, open vents, and cover with lid.

PULL-APART OLIVE BREAD RING

    All-purpose flour
1 loaf (1 lb.) frozen whole-wheat or white bread dough, thawed
⅔ cup coarsely chopped pimiento-stuffed Spanish-style olives
    About 1 tablespoon olive oil

On a lightly floured board, flatten dough. Sprinkle with olives, then knead until they are well distributed. Divide dough into 8 equal portions; knead each into a ball. Set balls against rim of an oiled 8- to 9-inch-diameter pan (or disposable foil pan). Brush dough with olive oil. Cover lightly with plastic wrap and let stand in a warm place until almost doubled in size, 35 to 40 minutes; discard plastic wrap.

In a barbecue with a lid, set pan in grill center over indirect heat (see directions at right). Cover barbecue, open vents, and bake bread until well browned, 45 to 50 minutes; start checking at 30 minutes. Serve warm. Makes 8 servings.

PER SERVING: 181 calories, 4.5 g protein, 29 g carbohydrates, 5.2 g fat, 2.8 mg cholesterol, 408 mg sodium

ITALIAN TOMATO CRESCENTS

    All-purpose flour
1 package (10 oz.) refrigerated pizza crust
1½ tablespoons olive oil
⅓ cup canned marinara sauce
⅓ cup grated parmesan cheese

On a lightly floured board, roll or pat crust to make a 12-inch square. Brush with 1 tablespoon of the oil, then spread evenly with marinara sauce. Sprinkle sauce with 3 tablespoons of the cheese.

Cut dough into 4 equal squares; then cut each diagonally into 2 triangles. Roll each piece from widest side toward point. Set rolls, points under, well apart on an oiled 12- by 15-inch baking sheet. Brush rolls lightly with remaining oil, then sprinkle with remaining cheese.

In a barbecue with a lid, set pan in the center of grill over indirect heat (see directions at right). Cover barbecue, open vents, and bake until rolls are golden brown, 30 to 40 minutes; start checking at 20 minutes. Makes 8.

PER ROLL: 134 calories, 4.5 g protein, 17 g carbohydrates, 4.9 g fat, 2.6 mg cholesterol, 296 mg sodium

MARZIPAN-BAKED APPLES

6 medium-size (2½- to 3-in.-diameter, about 1½ lb. total) red Gravenstein or Jonathan apples
¼ cup (about 3 oz.) marzipan (sweetened almond paste)
    Butter or margarine
⅓ cup whipping cream
    Whole nutmeg to grate

Core apples; starting at stem end, pare about ¼ of the peel from the top of each apple. Fill cavities equally with marzipan. Set apples in a buttered 8- to 9-inch square or round pan (or disposable foil pan). Pour cream over apples, then grate nutmeg lightly over fruit.

In a barbecue with a lid, set pan in the center of grill over indirect heat (see directions below). Cover barbecue, open vents, and bake until fruit is tender when pierced, 50 to 60 minutes. After 20 minutes, baste fruit occasionally with cream. Serve hot or warm. Serves 6.

PER SERVING: 157 calories, 1.2 g protein, 29 g carbohydrates, 5 g fat, 15 mg cholesterol, 6 mg sodium

Indirect-Heat Cooking

For indirect cooking on the barbecue, ignite 40 charcoal briquets on firegrate. When coals are dotted with gray ash, after 30 to 40 minutes, push coals equally to opposite sides of the grate or arrange them around the grate's perimeter. Evenly distribute 6 more briquets on the coals; if you plan to cook for more than 1 hour, add 6 more briquets every 30 minutes to maintain heat level.

To increase temperature for direct grilling, add the desired number of briquets about 20 minutes before baking is to conclude. Then the coals will be ready to use about 10 minutes after baking is done.

The Good Foods of Summer: Summer Fruit Coolers

FRESH FRUIT, backed up by fruit juices, fruit-flavored ice creams, sorbets, or other beverages, is the starting point for these smooth coolers. They taste rich enough to be dessert.

Strawberry Cherry Soda

About ½ cup strawberry ice cream
About ½ cup mashed strawberries
About 1 cup (8 oz.) cherry-flavor sparkling mineral water
Whole strawberry, rinsed and drained (optional)

Place ice cream and strawberries in a tall mug (about 14 oz.). Slowly pour in mineral water, then stir with a spoon to blend in some of the melting ice cream. Garnish rim of glass with the strawberry. Serve with a straw and a long spoon. Makes 1 serving.

PER SERVING: 163 calories, 3 g protein, 23 g carbohydrates, 7.5 g fat, 30 mg cholesterol, 59 mg sodium

Frozen Watermelon Daiquiris

4 cups peeled, seeded, and diced watermelon
1 large egg white (optional; before separating, see cracking eggs, following)
About 6 tablespoons sugar
¾ cup apple juice or light rum
3 tablespoons lime juice
Thin watermelon triangles or lime slices (optional)

Set watermelon pieces slightly apart in a single layer in a 10- by 15-inch pan. Cover and freeze until solid, at least 2 hours or overnight.

To frost glasses (about 10-oz. size), whisk egg white in a small bowl until it is slightly frothy. Dip rims of glasses in egg white, then in sugar. Chill until frosted rims are set, at least 5 minutes.

In a blender, combine half the frozen watermelon pieces with apple juice, lime juice, and ⅓ cup sugar. Whirl until watermelon is reduced in volume; add remaining watermelon and whirl until mixture is a thick slush. Pour or spoon into prepared glasses, garnishing each

A refreshing beverage: dark sweet cherries whirled creamy-smooth with orange juice, nectarines, and yogurt.

with a watermelon triangle or lime slice. Serve with straws for sipping. Makes about 3½ cups, 4 servings.

PER SERVING: 151 calories, 1.9 g protein, 36 g carbohydrates, 0.7 g fat, 0 mg cholesterol, 20 mg sodium

Cracking eggs. To sterilize egg shell before cracking, immerse the egg in boiling water to cover, then lift out, crack, and, if desired, separate white from yolk. Keep uncooked eggs covered and cold until ready to use.

Cherry Yogurt Flamingo

1 cup *each* unflavored nonfat yogurt and orange juice
½ cup crushed ice
2 cups pitted dark sweet cherries
1 medium-size ripe nectarine, pitted and coarsely chopped
1 to 2 tablespoons sugar
Orange wedges

In a blender or food processor, smoothly purée yogurt, orange juice, ice, cherries, nectarine, and 1 tablespoon sugar. Taste, then add more sugar, if desired. Pour into glasses (about 8-oz. size) and garnish with orange wedges. Makes about 5 cups, 4 servings.

PER SERVING: 113 calories, 3.9 g protein, 24 g carbohydrates, 0.8 g fat, 0.9 mg cholesterol, 35 mg sodium

Pineapple Sangria

1 lemon
1 medium-size orange
2 tablespoons sugar
2 cups refrigerated pineapple juice
2 cups dry white wine
1 small bottle (12 oz., 1½ cups) sparkling water
About 2 cups ice cubes
4 medium-size strawberries, hulled, rinsed, drained, and sliced
Mint sprigs

Cut 2 or 3 thin slices from centers of lemon and orange; put slices in a 2- to 3-quart pitcher. Squeeze juice from ends of fruit and add to pitcher along with sugar; stir to dissolve sugar. Add pineapple juice, wine, sparkling water, ice, and strawberries. Stir, then pour into stemmed glasses; garnish with mint sprigs. Makes about 8 cups, 8 servings.

PER SERVING: 97 calories, 0.6 g protein, 15 g carbohydrates, 0.1 g fat, 0 mg cholesterol, 4 mg sodium

Sparkling Peach Punch with Sorbet

2 pints peach sorbet or peach frozen yogurt
2 medium-size (about ¾ lb. total) ripe peaches
1 can (6 oz.) frozen lemonade concentrate
2 quarts chilled refrigerated pineapple-orange juice
1 bottle (750 ml.) chilled sparkling wine or 4 cups chilled sparkling water

Place a 10- by 15-inch pan in the freezer; when cold, scoop sorbet into about 2-inch balls and place on pan. Return to freezer; if held longer than 1 hour or up until next day, seal pan with foil.

Peel, pit, and slice peaches; smoothly purée with lemonade concentrate in a blender or food processor. Pour into a 5- to 6-quart punch bowl and add pineapple-orange juice, sparkling wine, and sorbet; stir. Ladle into punch cups. Makes about 17 cups, 18 to 20 servings.

PER SERVING: 143 calories, 0.9 g protein, 30 g carbohydrates, 0.1 g fat, 0 mg cholesterol, 12 mg sodium

THE GOOD FOODS OF SUMMER: Meringue Cloud

A BILLOWY PUFF of white meringue, piled high and cooked in the microwave just enough to slightly firm its tiny bubbles, makes an ideal backdrop for a spectrum of summer fruits. In this light-to-rich (as your taste dictates) dessert, the partners are berries, but also consider sweet slices of ripe plums, peaches, and nectarines—alone, or in combination with berries.

It's important to cook the meringue just enough to bring the internal temperature to 140° but not to heat it further—otherwise, the bubbles begin to collapse and the cloud shrinks and gets rubbery in the center. To check the temperature, use your microwave probe or a quick-register thermometer.

You have a series of options to add variety to this simple dessert. The lightest version is the meringue alone with the berries; or make the custard sauce, using low-fat or whole milk, and serve it hot or cold. Or omit the custard and offer whipped cream in its place. If you serve the tender foamy meringue warm with cool whipped cream, the contrast of textures and temperatures is particularly pleasing. For complete indulgence, also serve the custard sauce.

MICROWAVE MERINGUE CLOUD

- 4 large egg whites
- ¼ teaspoon cream of tartar
- ½ cup sugar
  Ground nutmeg (optional)
- 3 to 4 cups rinsed and drained berries such as hulled strawberries, raspberries, blueberries, boysenberries, and blackberries (all of 1 kind or a mixture)
  Custard sauce (recipe follows)
  Sweetened whipped cream (optional)

In a large bowl, combine egg whites and cream of tartar. Beat at high speed with an electric mixer until whites are foamy. Continue beating at high speed and add sugar, about 1 tablespoon at a time, until whites hold stiff peaks.

Onto a shallow-rimmed microwave-safe platter (at least 10 in. wide), pile spoonfuls of the meringue into a tall mound that is about 5 inches at the base. If you like, swirl meringue decoratively, using a narrow spatula. Cook, uncovered, in a microwave oven on half-power (50 percent) until meringue is softly set when touched lightly and temperature in center is 140° (watch closely, and use the microwave probe or a quick-register thermometer), 1 to 2 minutes; check after 1 minute, rotate platter 180°, then cook in 15-second intervals just until done. (If overcooked, meringue condenses in the center and gets tough.)

Serve meringue warm, or let stand up to 1 hour (on longer standing, it begins to weep—release a clear liquid). If desired, sprinkle a little nutmeg onto meringue, then surround with berries. To serve, cut meringue into wedges or scoop with spoon and place in dessert bowls. Add fruit and custard sauce or whipped cream (or both) to taste. Makes 6 servings.

PER SERVING MERINGUE WITH BERRIES: 107 calories, 2.8 g protein, 24 g carbohydrates, 24 g fat, 0 mg cholesterol, 38 mg sodium

Custard sauce. In a 1-quart glass measuring cup, whisk to blend 4 **large egg yolks,** ¼ cup **sugar,** and 1½ cups **low-fat** or regular **milk.** Cook, uncovered, in a microwave oven on half-power (50 percent), stirring well with a whisk every 2 minutes until custard is thick enough to opaquely coat a metal spoon, 6 to 10 minutes. Add ½ teaspoon **vanilla** and ⅛ teaspoon **ground nutmeg.** Serve hot, warm, or chilled; if made ahead, cover and chill until cold, about 2 hours, or up until next day. Makes about 1⅔ cups.

PER ¼ CUP SAUCE: 103 calories, 3.9 g protein, 12 g carbohydrates, 4.6 g fat, 147 mg cholesterol, 35 mg sodium

Pile meringue to make a tall cloud; cook in microwave. Carefully check temperature with probe or instant-read thermometer.

A fine summer dessert, delicate meringue is wreathed with mixed berries; garnish with mint sprigs. Scoop dessert into bowls and pour in custard sauce.

THE GOOD FOODS OF SUMMER: Pack Snacks

For a surge of renewed energy, light refreshments give a boost to active outings, whether you choose to nibble without breaking stride or stop occasionally for a short rest and a bite to eat.

Here are snacks that need no refrigeration and can be stuffed into a pocket or day pack, as well as cool foods that travel chilled in a small insulated bag or vacuum bottle to offer relief from heat within 3 hours of your start.

When the snacks are dry, like the peanut and popcorn mixtures, be sure to bring along (or know where you can get) beverages. Aseptic packages of fruit juice are especially light and convenient.

For crisp, juicy, but simple snacks on the trail, choose vegetables with a yogurt dip, celery stalks filled with cheese, or tender berries (packed to protect against bruising) to eat with a delicate cottage cheese dip.

Or bring along a vacuum bottle filled with a smooth but calorie-light yogurt-blueberry drink.

PICANTE PEANUTS & SUNFLOWER SEEDS

- 1 tablespoon olive oil or salad oil
- 3 to 5 small dried hot red chilies
- 3 cloves garlic, quartered lengthwise
- 1 jar (12 oz. or 2½ cups) dry-roasted unsalted peanuts
- ½ cup unsalted shelled sunflower seed
- ½ teaspoon chili powder
  Salt

Pour oil into a 10- to 12-inch frying pan over medium heat. When oil is hot, add chilies and garlic. Stir often until garlic is lightly browned, 2 to 3 minutes. Discard garlic. Add peanuts and sunflower seed to pan; stir until nuts are hot, about 3 minutes. Mix in chili powder and add salt to taste, then let mixture stand until cool. Serve, or store airtight up to 1 week. To transport, put desired amount in a small plastic bag and close tightly. Makes about 3 cups.

PER ¼ CUP: 217 calories, 8.5 g protein, 9.2 g carbohydrates, 19 g fat, 0 mg cholesterol, 1.5 mg sodium

POSH POPCORN

- 2 quarts warm popped corn (¼ to ⅓ cup unpopped)
- ½ cup salted shelled pistachios
- 1 cup sugar
- ½ cup light corn syrup
- ¼ cup (⅛ lb.) butter or margarine
- ¼ cup whipping cream
- 1 teaspoon ground cinnamon
- 1 teaspoon vanilla

Combine popped corn and pistachios in a buttered 10- by 15-inch baking pan; place in a 250° oven to keep warm.

In a 1½- to 2-quart pan, combine sugar, corn syrup, butter, cream, and cinnamon. Place over medium-high heat; stir often until sugar dissolves. Continue to boil gently, without stirring, until mixture reaches 280° on a thermometer.

Remove from heat and, at once, stir in vanilla; immediately pour syrup over popcorn mixture, stirring gently until evenly coated.

Let stand until mixture is cool and syrup no longer sticky. Use your hands to break up mixture slightly. Serve, or keep airtight to prevent the candy coating from absorbing moisture and softening. Store up to 3 days. To transport, put desired portion in a plastic bag and close tightly. Makes about 8 cups.

PER ½ CUP: 150 calories, 1.3 g protein, 24 g carbohydrates, 6.1 g fat, 12 mg cholesterol, 38 mg sodium

ON-THE-TRAIL VEGETABLES

- 24 tiny carrots (about ½ lb. total), with tops
  About 12 red radishes with tops
- 1 piece (about ½ lb.) jicama
- ½ cup unflavored low-fat yogurt
- ¼ cup chopped fresh mint leaves
- ¼ teaspoon seasoned pepper
  Liquid hot pepper seasoning
  Salt

Immerse carrots and radishes, with tops, in cool water to rinse well. Pinch wilted leaves from carrots, then scrub or carefully peel carrots. Pinch off all but a few pretty leaves from each radish; trim root ends. Rinse vegetables again.

Peel jicama, rinse well, and cut ½-inch-thick sticks that are about 3 inches long.

Lay vegetables on paper towels, arranging so stems won't break, then wrap towels around vegetables; slip package into a plastic bag and close. Chill vegetables at least 1 hour or up until next day.

Meanwhile, in a bowl, combine yogurt, mint, seasoned pepper, and hot pepper seasoning and salt to taste. If made ahead, cover and chill up until next day.

To transport, put a packet of frozen cooler gel (or 10 to 12 ice cubes sealed in a plastic bag) in an insulated bag; lay vegetables (in plastic bag) and sauce (in a nonbreakable container with secured lid) in insulated bag.

Or put sauce in a chilled wide-mouth 1-cup vacuum bottle and carry separately; serve within 3 hours. To eat, dip vegetables into yogurt sauce. Makes 4 to 6 snack servings.

PER SERVING: 43 calories, 1.9 g protein, 8.3 g carbohydrates, 0.5 g fat, 1.1 mg cholesterol, 30 mg sodium

CELERY CHEESE STALKS

- ¼ cup slivered almonds
- ½ cup port-flavor or hickory smoke–flavor processed cheddar cheese
- 2 tablespoons mayonnaise
- ⅛ teaspoon curry powder
- 6 celery stalks, each about 8 inches long, rinsed and crisped

Stir almonds in a 10- to 12-inch frying pan over medium-high heat until golden, about 3 minutes; let cool.

Beat together to blend well the cheese, mayonnaise, and curry powder; stir in the almonds.

Cut each celery stalk crosswise into 3 equal pieces. With a small spatula, spread equal portions of cheese into curve of each celery piece. Serve or, if made ahead, cover and chill up until next day.

To transport, put celery in a plastic bag (if cheese is soft, first enclose each piece with plastic wrap) and carry in an insulated bag with a packet of frozen cooler gel (or 10 to 12 ice cubes sealed in a plastic bag); serve within 3 hours. Makes 18 pieces, 3 or 4 servings.

PER SERVING: 199 calories, 7.1 g protein, 7.1 g carbohydrates, 17 g fat, 24 mg cholesterol, 353 mg sodium

CHERRIES, BERRIES & FRENCH CREAM

- ½ cup small-curd cottage cheese
- 1 to 2 tablespoons sour cream
- 1½ tablespoons powdered sugar
- ¼ teaspoon vanilla
- ⅛ teaspoon ground nutmeg
- 2 cups strawberries, rinsed and drained
- 2 cups sweet cherries, rinsed and drained

In a blender or food processor, whirl until smooth the cottage cheese, sour cream, powdered sugar, vanilla, and nutmeg. If made ahead, cover and chill up until next day.

To transport, use paper towels to line a 5- to 6-cup rigid container that has a tight-fitting lid. Put strawberries and cherries in container, with a layer of paper towels between each layer of fruit; put on lid. Scrape cheese mixture into a chilled wide-mouth 1-cup vacuum bottle and cover tightly. Serve within 3 hours. To eat, dip fruit into cheese mixture. Makes 5 or 6 servings.

PER SERVING: 81 calories, 3.1 g protein, 14 g carbohydrates, 1.9 g fat, 3.7 mg cholesterol, 73 mg sodium

BLUEBERRY-LEMON YOGURT REFRESHER

- 1 cup unflavored low-fat yogurt
- ½ cup *each* orange juice and crushed ice
- 1½ cups blueberries
- ½ teaspoon grated lemon peel
- 1 tablespoon lemon juice
- 2 to 3 tablespoons sugar

In a blender or food processor, whirl until smooth the yogurt, orange juice, ice, blueberries, lemon peel, and lemon juice. Season to taste with sugar, then whirl again. To transport, pour into a chilled 3- to 4-cup vacuum bottle. Shake well before drinking; serve within 3 hours. Makes about 3 cups, 3 or 4 servings.

PER SERVING: 105 calories, 3.6 g protein, 22 g carbohydrates, 1.1 g fat, 3.4 mg cholesterol, 43 mg sodium

Energy break on the biking trail: cool dip with warm berries; celery sticks with port-flavored cheese; apple juice. Carry in insulated bag and vacuum bottle.

PLAYTIME AND APPETITES *have a way of merging on active summer days. When the simple ingredients for the following treats are on hand, young cooks can engineer their own refreshments. Some require no cooking; those that need heat use the microwave oven. Once mastered, most of these dishes are easy enough to be duplicated from memory.*

The cheese crisps are merely cubes of cheese melted in the microwave oven to make crisp wafers. A sprinkling of chili powder or a few sesame seeds dress up the crisps. You need cooking parchment on which to melt the cheese; it's available in some supermarkets (next to the waxed paper) and cookware stores.

If your young cooks are familiar with tools, they can make spread for the little rice cakes and dip for the melon cubes in the food processor with the plastic blade (or metal blade, if they are very careful when cleaning up).

The cheese crisps, rice cakes, and melon bites are also quite suitable for grown-up refreshments.

Scaled down to snack size from a chili dog is the chili cheese pup: half a frankfurter heated in a small bun with chili and cheese.

And when a sweet is in order, use the microwave oven for fancy s'mores, warmed one at a time, or peanut butter and chocolate fudge—made in a big measuring cup.

CHEESE CRISPS

> About 1 teaspoon chili powder
> or sesame seed (or ½ teaspoon
> of each)
> 3 ounces jack or Swiss cheese,
> cut into ½-inch cubes

Spread chili powder or sesame seed (or a combination) on a piece of waxed paper. Turn cheese cubes in chili powder to coat on all sides.

Set a piece of cooking parchment (about 12 in. square) in a microwave oven; arrange 3 cubes, at least 2 inches apart, on paper. Cook on full power (100 percent), turning parchment several times, until cheese melts, bubbles, and gets slightly darker in color, 1 or 2 minutes. Let stand until cool and firm, about 2 minutes. Lift off paper.

To make each additional batch of crisps, wipe off parchment with a paper towel and add 3 more cheese cubes. Eat crisps or put them in a jar or plastic bag and keep airtight up to 2 days. Makes about 3 dozen pieces.

PER PIECE: 9 calories, 0.6 g protein, 0 g carbohydrates, 0.7 g fat, 2 mg cholesterol, 13 mg sodium

RICE CAKE & RADISH SNACK

> 1 hard-cooked large egg
> 1 small package (3 oz.) cream cheese
> About 2 teaspoons prepared
> mustard
> 12 small (2-in.-diameter) rice cakes
> 6 or 8 red radishes (ends trimmed),
> rinsed
> Salt and pepper

Peel shell off egg, then break egg into pieces. Put pieces into a food processor with plastic or metal blade. Add cheese and whirl until well mixed. (Or mash egg on a plate with a fork, then add cream cheese and mash until well mixed.) Add mustard to taste.

Spread egg mixture equally on each rice cake. Slice radishes over each cake to cover cheese; sprinkle with salt and pepper to taste. Makes 12 pieces.

PER PIECE: 27 calories, 1 g protein, 2.3 g carbohydrates, 1.5 g fat, 21 mg cholesterol, 31 mg sodium

CHILI CHEESE PUPS

> 2 chicken, turkey, or beef
> frankfurters (3 to 4 oz. total)
> 4 pieces (about 1 oz. total) cheddar
> cheese, each about ½ by 2 inches
> 4 small (about 3-in.-long) soft oval
> dinner rolls, split almost in half
> ¼ cup canned or homemade chili
> without beans
> Prepared mustard (optional)

Cut frankfurters in half crosswise; cut a slit about ½ inch deep in each piece. Lay a piece of cheese in the slit in each piece of frankfurter, then nest each piece in a roll. Spoon about 1 tablespoon of the chili into each roll.

Fold a square (about 12 in.) of waxed paper loosely around each sandwich. Heat sandwiches, 1 at a time, in a microwave oven on full power (100 percent) just until roll feels warm, about 30 seconds. Fold back waxed paper and add mustard to taste to sandwiches. Makes 4.

PER SANDWICH: 201 calories, 7.9 g protein, 18 g carbohydrates, 11 g fat, 30 mg cholesterol, 610 mg sodium

Roll cubes of jack or Swiss cheese in chili powder or sesame seed, place on cooking parchment in microwave oven, then ZAP to make crisp wafers.

Honey-Spice Melon Bites

1 small package (3 oz.) cream cheese
¼ teaspoon ground cinnamon
1 tablespoon honey
1 tablespoon lemon juice
½ medium-size (about 3 lb. whole) cantaloupe, honeydew, or other similar melon, seeded

In a food processor with plastic or metal blade, whirl cream cheese, cinnamon, honey, and lemon juice (or beat together with a spoon until well mixed). Scrape mixture into a small bowl. If made ahead, cover and chill up until next day.

Cut melon half in half again. Cut flesh from peel with a grapefruit knife, then cut meat in about 1-inch cubes and pile into a small bowl. Spear each melon piece on a toothpick and scoop through cream cheese mixture to eat. Makes about 30 pieces.

PER PIECE: 20 calories, 0.4 g protein, 2.6 g carbohydrates, 1 g fat, 3 mg cholesterol, 11 mg sodium

Snazzy S'mores

8 rectangular petit beurre cookies (French-style butter cookies), about 1¾ by 2¼ inches
1 bar (about 2¼ oz.) white chocolate with almonds
2 tablespoons semisweet chocolate baking chips
4 marshmallows, each about 1 inch tall

Place 1 cooky, bottom side up, on each of 4 small paper plates. Top each cooky with ¼ of the chocolate bar and ¼ of the chocolate chips.

Put 1 plate in a microwave oven; cook on full power (100 percent) until chocolate just begins to soften, about 30 seconds. Set another cooky, bottom side up, on same plate and set a marshmallow on plain cooky.

Continue to cook until marshmallow just starts to puff, about 10 seconds. Remove plate from oven and press filled sides of cookies lightly together.

Repeat to make each additional s'more; eat while warm (take a little bite first to be sure s'more isn't too hot). Makes 4 servings.

PER SERVING: 189 calories, 2.6 g protein, 23 g carbohydrates, 20 g fat, 7.7 mg cholesterol, 56 mg sodium

Honey and cinnamon cream cheese dip hangs onto square edges of cantaloupe. To eat, spear melon cube on a toothpick and scoop through spicy dip.

Microwave Peanut Butter Fudge

1 small can (5 oz.) evaporated milk
1 cup granulated sugar
⅓ cup firmly packed brown sugar
¼ cup (⅛ lb.) butter or margarine
1 cup (6 oz.) semisweet chocolate baking chips
¾ cup or ½ jar (7-oz. size) marshmallow creme
¼ cup peanut butter
1 teaspoon vanilla

In a 2-quart glass measuring cup, combine evaporated milk, granulated and brown sugars, and butter.

Cook the mixture, uncovered, in a microwave oven on full power (100 percent), stirring once or twice after mixture is hot enough to dissolve sugars, about 2 minutes; then cook until mixture boils and bubbles vigorously, 2 or 3 minutes. Continue to boil for 4 minutes.

Using a pot holder to protect hands, lift cup from oven and quickly add chocolate and stir until melted. As soon as chocolate melts, quickly add marshmallow creme, peanut butter, and vanilla and stir until well mixed; scrape into a buttered 8-inch-square pan. Let fudge stand until pan is cool enough to touch, then cover fudge with foil and put in the refrigerator until firm, 45 minutes to 1 hour. Cut into 1-inch squares. Makes about 5 dozen pieces.

PER PIECE: 52 calories, 0.6 g protein, 7.4 g carbohydrates, 2.5 g fat, 2.8 mg cholesterol, 16 mg sodium

Overnight Sensations: Appetizer Pickles

ETER PIPER HAD A PECK of pickles to pack, but we propose smaller quantities. Pack a pint in just minutes, then age them overnight or longer in the refrigerator. No canning or processing is needed. You just fit raw, cooked, or canned vegetables into a jar with a few herbs, add a hot vinegar-sugar solution, then chill to make these no-salt pickles.

Start with one or several kinds of vegetables. Each of these recipes makes about a pint. Although you can eat pickles the day after you make them, they keep well up to 2 weeks, ready for calorie-wise nibbling.

For party appetizers, guests choose from an assortment of freshly pickled vegetables to nibble with cheese, cold meats, and bread.

CRISP PICKLED CARROTS

- 1 **pound baby carrots, peeled, or regular carrots, peeled and cut lengthwise into ½-inch-thick sticks**
- 4 **fresh lavender sprigs with blossoms (each about 4 in. long), or ¼ teaspoon dry lavender**
- ¾ **cup rice or white wine vinegar**
- ⅓ **cup sugar**

Trim length of carrots, if needed, so they will fit vertically ¾ inch below rim of a 1-pint wide-mouth glass jar. In a 10- to 12-inch frying pan over high heat, bring about 1 inch water to boiling. Add carrots and cook, uncovered, until barely tender when pierced, 5 to 7 minutes. Drain.

Lay jar on its side; loosely pack carrots vertically into it. As you fill jar, tuck lavender sprigs between carrots.

In a 1- to 1½-quart pan, combine vinegar and sugar and bring to a boil; cook, stirring, until sugar dissolves. Pour hot liquid over vegetables to cover. (Reserve extra liquid.) Cover with lid and shake jar to release any trapped bubbles. Chill until next day; check and add reserved marinade, if needed, to cover vegetables (they may have shrunk and become more loosely packed). Serve, or chill up to 2 weeks; turn jar over occasionally to keep pickle tops moist. Makes 1 pint, 8 to 10 servings.

PER SERVING: 22 calories, 0.4 g protein, 5.3 g carbohydrates, 0.1 g fat, 0 mg cholesterol, 14 mg sodium

CRISP PICKLED GREEN BEANS

Follow recipe for **crisp pickled carrots** (preceding), except omit carrots and lavender. Instead, use about ¾ pound **green beans,** ends trimmed. Cook beans in boiling water until barely tender when pierced, about 3 minutes. Drain, immerse in ice water until cold, then drain again. When you pack beans in jar, add **fresh purple** or green **basil sprigs** or 1 teaspoon dry basil; also add 1 teaspoon **cumin seed.** Fill jar with hot liquid.

PER SERVING: 15 calories, 0.6 g protein, 3.6 g carbohydrates, 0.1 g fat, 0 mg cholesterol, 2.2 mg sodium

PICKLED ASPARAGUS WITH THYME

Follow recipe for **crisp pickled carrots** (preceding), except use a 1½-pint wide-mouth glass jar and omit carrots and lavender. Instead, use about 1½ pounds **asparagus,** tough ends trimmed off. Cook in boiling water until barely tender when pierced, 5 to 7 minutes. Drain, immerse in ice water until cold, then drain again. You also need 4 **fresh thyme sprigs** (about 4 in. long) or 1 teaspoon dry thyme leaves. Pack asparagus vertically, adding thyme. Fill jar with hot liquid.

PER SERVING: 13 calories, 1.1 g protein, 2.7 g carbohydrates, 0.1 g fat, 0 mg cholesterol, 0.8 mg sodium

(Continued on page 186)

Take your pick from this spectrum of vegetable pickles (clockwise from top right): asparagus, okra, jicama, eggplant, carrots, green beans, red bell peppers, and cactus with tomato. No processing is needed; just age packed jars for up to 2 weeks in the refrigerator.

To pack roasted eggplant, lay jar on its side and fill with trimmed, narrow strips; tuck in oregano, garlic, ginger. Turn upright and add pickling liquid.

PICKLED JICAMA

Follow recipe for **crisp pickled carrots** (page 184), except omit carrots and lavender. Use about ¾ pound **jicama,** peeled, rinsed, and cut into ½-inch-thick sticks.

Also use about 4 **fresh purple** or green **basil sprigs** or 1 teaspoon dry basil; pack jicama vertically in jar, adding basil. Fill jar with hot liquid.

PER SERVING: 18 calories, 0.5 g protein, 4.1 g carbohydrates, 0.1 g fat, 0 mg cholesterol, 2 mg sodium

PICKLED CACTUS WITH TOMATOES

Follow recipe for **crisp pickled carrots** (page 184), except omit carrots and lavender. Use 1 jar (14-oz. size) canned sliced **cactus** (*nopales* or *nopalitos*), rinsed and drained; ⅓ cup thinly sliced **red onion;** 4 or 5 **red cherry tomatoes;** 2 tablespoons **fresh cilantro leaves.** Do not cook vegetables. In jar, alternate cactus, onion, tomatoes, cilantro, and **cumin seed** (1 teaspoon total). Fill jar with hot liquid.

PER SERVING: 14 calories, 0.3 g protein, 3.6 g carbohydrates, 0.1 g fat, 0 mg cholesterol, 43 mg sodium

MUSTARD & OKRA PICKLES

Follow recipe for **crisp pickled carrots** (page 184), except omit carrots and lavender. Use about ¾ pound **okra** (about 3 in. long); trim surface of stem ends.

Cook okra in boiling water until barely tender when pierced, 7 to 10 minutes. Drain and immerse in ice water until cold; drain again. Pack okra vertically in jar with 2 tablespoons thinly sliced **red onion** and 1 teaspoon **mustard seed.** Fill jar with hot liquid.

PER SERVING: 18 calories, 0.7 g protein, 3.8 g carbohydrates, 0.1 g fat, 0 mg cholesterol, 2.5 mg sodium

PICKLED RED PEPPERS & ONIONS

Follow recipe for **crisp pickled carrots** (page 184), except omit carrots and lavender. Use 3 medium-size (1¼ lb. total) **red bell peppers;** do not boil. Cut peppers in half lengthwise; lay them, cut sides down, in a 10- by 15-inch pan. Broil 4 to 6 inches from heat until charred, 7 to 10 minutes. Let cool; pull off and dis-

card stems, seeds, and skin. (Or use 2 jars, 7-oz. size, roasted red peppers, drained.) Cut peppers into ½-inch-wide strips.

Also use 4 **fresh rosemary sprigs** (about 4 in. long) or 1 teaspoon dry rosemary. Fill jar with peppers, rosemary, and 2 tablespoons drained **pickled cocktail-size onions.** Fill jar with hot liquid.

PER SERVING: 16 calories, 0.4 g protein, 3.9 g carbohydrates, 0.2 g fat, 0 mg cholesterol, 38 mg sodium

PICKLED EGGPLANT

It is important to use a slender variety of eggplant (which may be called Asian, Oriental, French, or Italian at the market), so that each narrow strip of the vegetable will have an edge of skin to hold it together.

> About 2 tablespoons olive oil
> 1 **pound slender Oriental eggplants,** stems trimmed
> 4 **fresh oregano sprigs** (about 4 inches long), or 1 teaspoon dry oregano leaves
> 1 **clove garlic,** thinly sliced
> ½ **teaspoon red preserved ginger** in syrup, thinly sliced; or ½ teaspoon thinly shredded fresh ginger
> ¾ **cup white wine vinegar**
> ⅓ **cup sugar**
> ½ **teaspoon Oriental sesame oil**

Line a 10- by 15-inch pan with foil; brush with oil. Cut eggplants in quarters lengthwise; lay, skin down, in a single layer in pan. Brush cut sides with olive oil. Bake, uncovered, in a 475° oven until eggplant is browned and soft when pressed, 15 to 25 minutes. Cool.

Lay a wide-mouth 1-pint jar on its side. Fill jar with eggplant (so strips are vertical when jar is upright), trimming pieces to make them ¾ inch short of rim. Intersperse eggplant with oregano, garlic, and ginger. Set jar upright.

In a 1- to 1½-quart pan, combine vinegar, sugar, and sesame oil. Bring to a boil, stirring until sugar dissolves; pour over vegetables to cover. Reserve extra liquid. Put lid on jar and shake to release bubbles. Chill overnight; if needed, add reserved liquid to cover vegetables. Serve, or chill up to 2 weeks; turn jar over occasionally to keep tops moist. Makes 1 pint, 8 to 10 servings.

PER SERVING: 39 calories, 0.4 g protein, 3.3 g carbohydrates, 2.8 g fat, 0 mg cholesterol, 13 mg sodium

Barbecue Accessories

THIS ARRAY of barbecue accessories, some new and some updated, responds to complaints often voiced by outdoor chefs.

Handling charcoal is messy; igniting it takes time and effort. *Older systems that still work well, such as the chimney-type and electric starters, can be supplemented with nontoxic fuel cubes, to tuck among briquets (cubes catch fire readily from a flame), or replaced with paraffin-coated hardwood charcoal—enough for 1 round of cooking—that lights in its own bag. The butane lighter, also used in kitchens with gas ranges, is a good outdoor tool because it works well even in the wind.*

It's difficult to control the amount of smoke flavor. *A little smoke goes a long way, so premeasured or easy-measure chips or bits control the intensity. When smoking in a gas barbecue, the chips usually need to be contained in a pan and used according to the manufacturer's directions.*

Small bits of food fall through the grill or cook faster than you can turn them. *Simple solutions for these situations are the small-mesh grill that can sit atop a regular grill, or a hinged basket.*

Cleanup is a chore. *A metal brush does a good job if grill is hot. The bucket ash catcher (below) holds residue of several rounds of cooking, then is easy and neat to empty. Be sure ashes are completely cold (sparks linger for many hours) if you dump them into a paper container.*

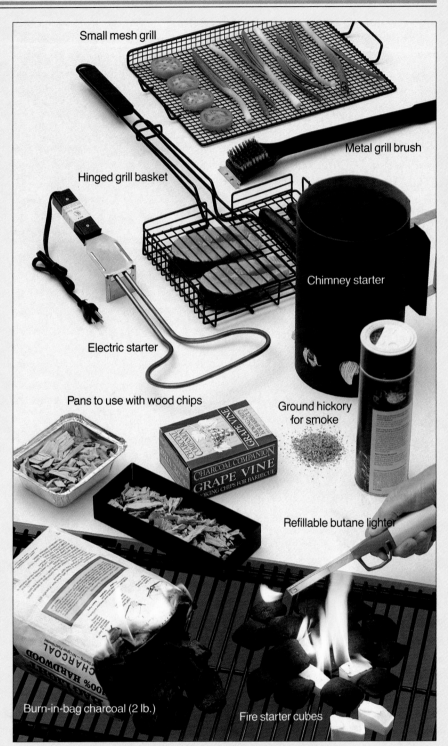

Small mesh grill

Metal grill brush

Hinged grill basket

Chimney starter

Electric starter

Pans to use with wood chips

Ground hickory for smoke

Refillable butane lighter

Burn-in-bag charcoal (2 lb.)

Fire starter cubes

CHARCOAL COMPANION
GRAPE VINE
COOKING CHIPS FOR BARBECUE

Cone-shaped ash catcher (about $14) fits under kettle-type barbecue. Base pulls out for easy dumping when ash is cold.

To make barbecuing easier, small-mesh grill and basket keep small pieces from falling through; chimney-type and electric starters, butane lighter, burn-in-bag charcoal, and fuel cubes offer neater ways to start fire; wood chips flavor food; metal brush cleans grill.

Salmon & Walla Wallas

TWO LEGENDARY NORTHWEST *treats form the heart of this barbecue dinner from Seattle. Sharing the grill with a fresh salmon fillet glazed with brown sugar are young, sweet, green-topped Walla Walla onions—but you could use any large-bulbed new onion. Since Washington is a major producer of wheat and berries, these, too, earn a place on this regional menu serving 6 to 8 people.*

NORTHWEST SUMMER FEAST

Puget Sound Barbecued Salmon with Walla Walla Onions on the Stem
Washington Cracked-wheat Salad
Green Salad   Crusty Loaves
Berries with Late-harvest Gewürztraminer

Early in the day, you can fit the salmon onto its foil cooking base, blanch the onion stems, soak the wheat, and rinse and drain an assortment of berries.

PUGET SOUND BARBECUED SALMON WITH WALLA WALLA ONIONS ON THE STEM

If you can't find onions with tops, use any onion that is 2 to 2½ inches in diameter; cooked, even the hottest onion is sweet.

12 **to 16 Walla Walla or other young bulb onions with green tops (optional); bulbs should be 2 to 2½ inches wide**
1 **salmon fillet with skin, 2½ to 3 pounds**
3 **lemons**
2 **tablespoons firmly packed brown sugar**
  Olive oil
1 **tablespoon chopped fresh or 1 teaspoon dry tarragon leaves**
  Salt and pepper
  About ½ cup honey mustard

Plump young onion bulbs get sweet, knotted stems get crispy brown as onions cook gently on grill with fillet of fresh Puget Sound salmon. Turn onions as needed to brown evenly and keep stems from burning; if stems begin to char, lean them onto fish.

Trim root ends, any coarse outer skin, and yellowed stems from onions; rinse onions well and drain. Bring about 1½ inches water to boiling in a 10- to 12-inch frying pan. A few at a time, hold onion bulbs and push green tops into hot water just until wilted, about 30 seconds. At once, immerse onions in ice water until cold; drain. Fold tips of stems down to top of white on each onion, then make a knot in stems to hold them together. If done ahead, cover and chill up to 6 hours.

Rinse fish and pat dry. Lay fillet, skin down, on 2 stacked pieces of foil. Fold or trim foil to fit fish. Ream juice from half a lemon and brush juice over fish, then rub sugar through a strainer evenly over fish.

Ignite 50 charcoal briquets on firegrate of a barbecue with a lid. When coals are well spotted with gray ash, about 30 minutes, push equally to opposite sides of grate.

Pat onions dry, rub lightly with olive oil, and lay on grill over direct heat; turn occasionally to brown evenly. After 10 minutes, set fish on foil in center of grill; sprinkle fish with tarragon. If onion stems begin to char, lean them onto fish. Cover grill, open dampers, and cook until fish is moist-looking but opaque in thickest part (cut to test), 20 to 25 minutes. As needed, turn onions to brown evenly and keep stems from burning.

Transfer onions and fish (supporting with 2 large, wide spatulas) to a large platter. Cut remaining lemons in wedges and place with salmon. Lift fish from skin to serve. Season to taste with lemon, salt, pepper, and honey mustard. Makes 6 to 8 servings.

PER SERVING: 346 calories, 33 g protein, 41 g carbohydrates, 13 g fat, 70 mg cholesterol, 247 mg sodium

WASHINGTON CRACKED-WHEAT SALAD

3 **cups cracked wheat or 2 cups bulgur**
2 **tablespoons bouillon granules**
¼ **cup mustard seed**
6 **cups boiling water**
½ **cup lemon juice**
¼ **cup extra-virgin olive oil**
  Salt and pepper
8 **to 10 rinsed and crisped large romaine or other lettuce leaves**
2 **large ripe tomatoes, peeled, cored, and chopped**

Rinse wheat well with cool water and drain. Put wheat into a large bowl with bouillon granules, mustard seed, and boiling water; let stand, stirring occasionally, until the wheat is puffed and tender to bite, about 1 hour.

Drain wheat well and add lemon juice, oil, and salt and pepper to taste. If made ahead, cover and chill up until the next day. Line a bowl with lettuce, pour salad into it, and top with tomatoes. Mix to serve. Makes 6 cups, 6 to 8 servings.

PER SERVING: 287 calories, 9.1 g protein, 46 g carbohydrates, 9.6 g fat, 0 mg cholesterol, 648 mg sodium

Salmon, grilled on foil base over indirect heat, lifts cleanly from skin for serving. Menu includes grilled onions with stems, green salad, cracked-wheat salad with chopped tomatoes, crusty bread, butter, and honey mustard.

"Seviche" Salads

LIGHT, REFRESHING, AND PIQUANT, these salads based on cooked seafood taste much like seviche, the classic Mexican seafood appetizer.

In authentic seviche, uncooked fish marinates in tart citrus juice; the acid slowly firms the flesh, giving it an opaque, cooked appearance. In these salads, the seafood cooks quickly in a tart liquid to acquire characteristic seviche flavors while bypassing any concerns one might have about eating raw fish. Once cool, mix the seafood with vegetables to make light summer entrées or first courses.

LEMON SHRIMP SEVICHE SALAD

- 1 pound raw medium-large shrimp (36 to 42 per lb.), or shelled cooked tiny shrimp
- ¾ cup *each* lemon juice and cider vinegar
- 1 tablespoon drained capers
- 1 teaspoon Dijon mustard
- 4 green onions (ends trimmed), thinly sliced
- 2 medium-size (about 5 oz. total) Roma-type tomatoes, cored and diced
- 1 small yellow bell pepper, cored, seeded, and thinly sliced
  Lemon wedges (optional)
  Salt and pepper

Peel raw shrimp (leave shell on tail tip, if desired). Devein shrimp and rinse.

In a 10- to 12-inch frying pan, mix lemon juice, vinegar, capers, and Dijon mustard. Bring to a boil on high heat. Add raw shrimp and simmer, covered, just until shrimp are opaque but still moist-looking in thickest part (cut to test), 3 to 4 minutes; with a slotted spoon, transfer shrimp to a bowl. (Do not cook tiny shrimp.) Boil liquid over high heat, uncovered, until reduced to 1 cup, about 4 minutes. Pour liquid over shrimp (either kind). Chill until cool, at least 1½ or up to 8 hours.

Mix onion, tomatoes, and bell pepper with shrimp and spoon into 4 or 6 shallow soup bowls; distribute liquid among bowls. Garnish with wedges of lemon. Offer salt and pepper to add to taste. Makes 6 first-course or 4 entrée servings.

PER FIRST-COURSE SERVING: 85 calories, 13 g protein, 6 g carbohydrates, 1.3 g fat, 93 mg cholesterol, 161 mg sodium

LIME & CHIPOTLE SCALLOPS

- 1 pound sea or bay scallops
- 1 teaspoon olive or salad oil
- ½ cup minced shallots
- ½ teaspoon minced canned chipotle chilies in sauce, or ½ teaspoon crushed dried hot red chilies
- ½ cup *each* lime juice, white distilled vinegar, and water
- ½ pound jicama
- ⅓ cup minced fresh cilantro (coriander)
  Lime halves (optional)
  Salt and pepper

Rinse scallops and drain on paper towels. If scallops are more than ½ inch thick, cut in half to make thinner rounds; set aside. In a 10- to 12-inch frying pan over medium heat, stir olive oil, shallots, and chipotle until shallots are limp, about 3 minutes. Stir in lime juice, vinegar, and water; bring to a boil on high heat. Add scallops in a single layer; reduce heat, cover, and simmer just until opaque but still moist-looking in center (cut to test), about 2 minutes. With a slotted spoon, transfer scallops to a bowl. Boil liquid on high heat, uncovered, until reduced to 1 cup; pour over scallops and chill until cool, at least 1½ or up to 8 hours.

Meanwhile, peel jicama, rinse well, and cut into ¼-inch-thick matchsticks. Gently mix jicama with scallops and spoon into 4 or 6 shallow soup bowls; distribute liquid among bowls. Garnish salads with cilantro and lime halves. Add salt and pepper to taste. Makes 6 first-course or 4 entrée servings.

PER FIRST-COURSE SERVING: 106 calories, 14 g protein, 10 g carbohydrates, 1.5 g fat, 25 mg cholesterol, 130 mg sodium

SEVICHE WITH RADISHES & PEAS

- ¾ cup *each* rice vinegar and water (or 1 cup distilled white vinegar and ½ cup water)
- 2 tablespoons minced crystallized ginger
- ½ teaspoon coriander seed
- 1 pound boned and skinned firm-texture lean fish such as halibut, mahimahi, or swordfish, cut into ½-inch chunks
- 1 cup frozen petite peas, thawed
- 1 cup sliced red radishes
  Salt and pepper

In a 10- to 12-inch frying pan over high heat, bring vinegar, water, ginger, and coriander to boiling. Add fish; reduce heat, cover, and simmer until opaque but still moist-looking in thickest part (cut to test), 3 to 4 minutes. With a slotted spoon, transfer fish to a bowl. Boil liquid over high heat, uncovered, until reduced to 1 cup; pour over fish and chill until cool, at least 1½ or up to 8 hours.

Stir in peas and radish slices. Spoon into 4 or 6 shallow soup bowls; distribute liquid among dishes. Offer salt and pepper to add to taste. Makes 6 first-course or 4 entrée servings.

PER FIRST-COURSE SERVING: 130 calories, 17 g protein, 11 g carbohydrates, 2 g fat, 24 mg cholesterol, 92 mg sodium

Shrimp, poached quickly in lemon juice, mix with sweet pepper rings, sliced green onion, and diced tomatoes in a version of the classic Mexican seafood appetizer.

Cool & Colorful Vegetable Soups

A SMOOTH ESCAPE *from summer's heat, these cold vegetable soups are chilled even further with brightly colored vegetable ices. In the first recipe, a fiery tomato-jalapeño ice is soothed by a creamy avocado soup. In the second, a golden yellow bell pepper and carrot ice complements velvety potato soup.*

If you like, you can mix and match the ices and soups to create other flavor combinations.

AVOCADO SOUP WITH SPICED TOMATO ICE

- **1 large (about ½ lb.) firm-ripe avocado**
- **6 tablespoons lime juice**
- **3 cups regular-strength chicken broth**
- **½ teaspoon ground cumin**
- **Salt and pepper**
- **1 small (about ¼ lb.) firm-ripe avocado**
- **Spiced tomato ice (recipe follows)**

Peel and pit large avocado, and cut in chunks; put into a blender or food processor. Add 5 tablespoons lime juice, broth, and cumin. Whirl until very smooth; add salt and pepper to taste. Cover and chill until cool, 1 to 6 hours.

Peel and pit small avocado, and cut in thin wedges; coat with remaining lime juice.

Ladle soup into 6 wide, shallow soup bowls. Divide ice into 6 equal scoops and add 1 to each bowl. Lay avocado slices on soup. Makes 6 servings.

PER SERVING: 129 calories, 4 g protein, 14 g carbohydrates, 7.7 g fat, 0 mg cholesterol, 361 mg sodium

Spiced tomato ice. Drain juice from 1 large can (28 oz.) and 1 small can (14½ oz.) **Italian-style tomatoes;** save juice to drink. Smoothly purée tomatoes in a blender or food processor. Pour or rub purée through a fine strainer into a metal pan (8 in. square to 9 by 13 in.); discard seeds.

With a knife, finely chop ½ cup firmly packed **fresh cilantro** (coriander) and 2 stemmed and seeded **fresh jalapeño chilies.** Stir cilantro and chilies into pan.

To freeze, cover pan tightly with foil and put in freezer until tomato mixture is solid, at least 4 hours or up to 1 week.

Let ice stand at room temperature until you can break it in chunks with a heavy spoon. Whirl chunks in a food processor or beat with a mixer until mix-

ture forms a smooth slush. Return to pan and firm slightly in freezer, 30 minutes to 1 hour. If ice gets too hard to scoop easily, let stand a few minutes at room temperature.

VICHYSSOISE WITH ROASTED PEPPER & CARROT ICE

- **2 large (¾ to 1 lb. total) russet potatoes, peeled and diced**
- **3 cups regular-strength chicken broth**
- **1 large onion, chopped**
- **3 large (about ¾ lb. total) carrots, peeled and cut into 1-inch pieces**
- **2 tablespoons olive oil**
- **1 cup milk or half-and-half (light cream)**
- **2 tablespoons lemon juice**
- **Salt and pepper**
- **Roasted pepper and carrot ice (recipe follows)**
- **½ cup chopped green onion**

In a 2- to 3-quart pan, bring potatoes and broth to a boil over high heat; cover and simmer until potatoes are very tender when pierced, about 25 minutes. Let cool.

Place chopped onion at 1 end of a 10-by 15-inch baking pan; put carrots at other end. Drizzle vegetables with oil and mix separately. Roast, uncovered, in a 400° oven until sweet and tender to bite, about 30 minutes; reserve carrots for ice.

Whirl potatoes, broth, and onions in a food processor or blender until smooth. Mix in a bowl with milk, lemon juice, and salt and pepper to taste. Cover soup and chill until cool, 4 hours or up until next day.

Ladle soup into 6 wide, shallow soup bowls. Shape ice into 6 equal scoops and add 1 to each bowl; sprinkle green onion over the ice. Serves 6.

PER SERVING: 222 calories, 6.7 g protein, 32 g carbohydrates, 8.1 g fat, 8.5 mg cholesterol. 86 mg sodium

Roasted pepper and carrot ice. Cut 4 large (about 2 lb. total) **yellow bell peppers** in half lengthwise; discard stems and seeds. Lay peppers, cut side down, in a 10- by 15-inch pan. Broil 4 inches from heat until skin is blistered and charred, about 15 minutes. Drape peppers with foil and set aside until cool enough to handle. Pull off and discard skins.

Smoothly whirl peppers, reserved **carrots,** and ½ cup **milk.** Freeze as directed for spiced tomato ice (preceding).

Spicy, frozen tomato-jalapeño ice slowly melts into cool, creamy avocado soup. Just before serving, garnish with thin wedges of avocado.

Malted Desserts

USED GENEROUSLY, *malted milk powder leaps beyond its role as a supporting flavor to lend its own sweetness to these four desserts.*

The powder, made with extracts of wheat and malted barley, is available unflavored (often called original) and with chocolate. Both are sweet, but the chocolate powder has sugar added. You can use either flavor in these recipes; add sugar as desired.

In the supermarket, look for malted milk powder near other milk-drink mixes.

MALTED CHOCOLATE DECADENCE

- ½ cup (¼ lb.) butter or margarine
- ¼ cup water
- 6 ounces semisweet chocolate, chopped
- 2 ounces unsweetened chocolate, chopped
- 4 large eggs
- ¾ cup malted milk powder
- 2 tablespoons sugar

In a 2- to 3-quart pan over low heat, stir butter, water, and semisweet and unsweetened chocolate just until smooth. In a mixer bowl, whip eggs at high speed until doubled in volume. Beat in powder, then chocolate mixture and sugar.

Butter a 9-inch cake pan with removable rim. Set pan on 2 sheets of heavy foil, each about 12 inches square; press foil firmly against sides of pan (take care not to tear foil), letting ends extend above pan rim. Set pan with foil into a larger baking pan; pour batter into cake pan.

Put pans in a 350° oven; fill outer pan with about 1 inch boiling water. Bake until center of cake feels set when gently touched, about 45 minutes. Lift foil sides to remove cake from water; cool on rack. Chill at least 2 hours or up until the next day. Remove pan rim. Serves 12 to 16.

PER SERVING: 192 calories, 3.8 g protein, 17 g carbohydrates, 14 g fat, 71 mg cholesterol, 156 mg sodium

MALTED CREAM CHEESE TORTE

- 1 large package (8 oz.) cream cheese
- ½ cup malted milk powder
- 1 cup whipping cream
- 1 to 2 tablespoons sugar
  Malted crust (recipe follows)
- 3 cups strawberries, rinsed, drained, hulled, and cut in half

Strawberry-topped cream cheese torte has malted milk flavoring in both crisp zwieback crust and smooth, creamy filling.

With an electric mixer, smoothly combine cream cheese and powder. Beating at high speed, add cream in a steady stream so mixture remains thick (if cream is added too fast, mixture thins and will not rethicken). Stir in sugar to taste. Spread mixture evenly in crust; cover and chill at least 2 hours or up until next day. Mound berries on filling. Remove pan rim. Cut in wedges. Serves 10 to 12.

PER SERVING: 361 calories, 6.3 g protein, 30 g carbohydrates, 25 g fat, 70 mg cholesterol, 319 mg sodium

Malted crust. Break 6 ounces (about 24 pieces, 1 in. wide and 3½ in. long) **zwieback cookies** into a food processor; add ¼ cup **pecans** and whirl to a fine powder. (Or crush cookies and mince nuts.)

Add ½ cup **malted milk powder** and ½ cup (¼ lb.) cold **butter** or margarine, in chunks. Whirl or rub mixture with fingers to form fine crumbs; pat into a ball. Press dough over bottom and 1 inch up sides of a 9-inch cake pan with removable rim.

Bake in a 325° oven until golden brown, 15 to 25 minutes. Cool in pan. If made ahead, wrap airtight and store up until next day.

MALTED COOKY SHORTBREAD

Follow recipe for **malted crust** (preceding) except press dough evenly over bottom of a 10-inch tart pan with removable rim. While warm, cut baked cooky into 10 to 12 wedges but leave in place. Let cool, then remove pan rim. Serve, or store airtight up to 3 days. Makes 10 to 12 pieces.

PER PIECE: 183 calories, 2.9 g protein, 18 g carbohydrates, 11 g fat, 26 mg cholesterol, 184 mg sodium

MALTED ICE CREAM PIE

- ½ gallon vanilla ice cream
- ½ cup malted milk powder
  Malted crust (recipe precedes)

Transfer ice cream to a large bowl and place in refrigerator until soft enough to stir but not melted, about 45 minutes. Add powder and beat until well blended. Quickly spread ice cream mixture evenly in crust; cover and freeze until firm, at least 4 hours. If made ahead, seal airtight and freeze up to 2 weeks. Remove pan rim; cut into wedges. Serves 10 to 12.

PER SERVING: 401 calories, 7 g protein, 46 g carbohydrates, 22 g fat, 67 mg cholesterol, 333 mg sodium

More July Recipes

OTHER JULY RECIPES *include a black bean torte layered with cilantro pesto, roasted red peppers and feta cheese; candy-coated matzo crisp snacks; and a cool-looking ice cream with a potent punch.*

BLACK BEAN TORTE

Bordered in black and flavorful throughout, this colorful salad or appetizer torte takes its shape in a loaf pan.

First you cook black beans in a cumin-seasoned broth. When cool, mash and layer them compactly in a plastic wrap–lined loaf pan with bright tiers of green cilantro pesto, red pepper, and white feta cheese. When chilled, the loaf gets firm enough to slice and the plastic liner makes it easy to get out of the pan.

- ¾ **pound (1⅔ cups) dried black beans**
- 6 **cups regular-strength chicken broth**
- 1½ **teaspoons ground cumin**
  Cilantro pesto (recipe follows)
- 1 **jar (12 oz.) whole roasted red peppers, rinsed and patted dry**
- 1 **cup (4 oz.) crumbled feta cheese**
- ½ **cup unflavored yogurt or sour cream**
  Crackers or toasted baguette slices (optional)

Sort black beans and discard debris; rinse beans. In a 4- to 5-quart pan, combine beans, broth, and cumin. Over high heat, bring to a boil. Cover and simmer, stirring occasionally, until beans are tender to bite, about 2 hours; drain. Mash 1 cup beans and mix with whole beans; let cool.

Smoothly line a 4- by 8-inch loaf pan with a sheet of plastic wrap with edges overlapping pan rim. Put ⅓ of the bean mixture in pan and gently press to make a smooth layer. Gently spread cilantro pesto over beans. Discard any seeds on peppers, then mince peppers; set aside 2 tablespoons. Make an even layer of remaining peppers on pesto. Sprinkle peppers with feta, then top cheese with remaining beans, pressing gently to make a smooth, compact loaf. Cover tightly with plastic wrap and chill until loaf feels firm when gently pressed, at least 2 hours or up to 3 days.

Uncover pan and invert a platter onto it; holding pan and platter together, invert. Lift off pan and gently pull off plastic wrap. Spoon yogurt in a band down the middle of the loaf, then sprinkle yogurt with reserved minced red peppers.

To serve as an appetizer, present loaf with crackers. Use crackers to scoop torte to eat. To serve as a salad, use a sharp serrated knife to gently cut loaf into about ¾-inch-thick slices; with a spatula, lay slices on salad plates. Makes 10 to 12 servings. —*Fred Carlo, Portland.*

PER SERVING: 186 calories, 11 g protein, 21 g carbohydrates, 7.1 g fat, 8.9 mg cholesterol, 147 mg sodium

Cilantro pesto. In a food processor or blender, purée 3 cups slightly packed **fresh cilantro** (coriander) **leaves;** 4 teaspoons **olive** or salad **oil;** 2 cloves **garlic,** minced or pressed; and ⅓ cup **pine nuts.**

BUTTER PECAN MATZO CRISPS

Thin, crisp unflavored matzos make a neutral base for these candy-coated snacks. This is a two-step operation: cook the candy, then spread it on matzos and bake (line baking pan with foil to avoid sticky bubble-overs).

- 2 **unsalted matzos, each about 6 inches square**
- ⅓ **cup (⅙ lb.) butter or margarine**
- ⅓ **cup firmly packed brown sugar**
- ⅓ **cup chopped pecans**
- ½ **teaspoon vanilla**
- ½ **cup semisweet chocolate baking chips (optional)**

Lay matzos, side-by-side, in a foil-lined 10- by 15-inch rimmed baking pan. In a 1½- to 2-quart pan, melt butter over medium heat. Add sugar and pecans and stir often until mixture comes to a rolling boil, then boil until big, shiny bubbles form, 1 to 2 minutes. Remove from heat, stir in vanilla, and at once pour hot mixture equally onto matzos. Spread sugar mixture quickly and evenly with back of spoon or spatula up to but not over edges of matzos.

Bake in a 375° oven just until matzos are crisper, 3 to 6 minutes. Remove from oven. If desired, scatter chocolate over hot matzos; when chocolate softens, spread evenly with spatula. Let cool.

Break cool candy-topped matzos into small chunks. If made ahead, cover airtight and store in a cool place up to 4 days; freeze to store longer. Serves 8.

PER SERVING: 161 calories, 1.2 g protein, 16 g carbohydrates, 11 g fat, 21 mg cholesterol, 80 mg sodium

JALAPEÑO-LEMON ICE CREAM

Deceptively cool-looking, this ice cream is more than meets the eye. It packs an intriguing, latent punch. After its cold first taste laced with a touch of lemon, it melts with prickling heat. The fire comes from steeping a fresh jalapeño chili in the ice cream base before it is frozen.

- 1½ **cups milk**
- ¾ **cup sugar**
- 8 **strips lemon peel (each about ½ by 4 in., yellow part only)**
- 1 **medium-size (about 3-in.-long) fresh jalapeño chili, stemmed and chopped**
- 2 **large eggs**
- 1½ **cups whipping cream**
- 1 **teaspoon vanilla**
  Crushed ice and salt (use 8 parts ice to 1 part salt, optional)

In a 2- to 3-quart pan over medium heat, frequently stir milk, sugar, lemon peel, and chili until milk is just boiling.

Meanwhile, in a bowl, beat eggs to blend. Stir in hot milk mixture, then add cream and vanilla. Cover and chill until mixture is cold, about 1½ hours, or until next day.

Pour liquid through a fine strainer into a 1-quart or larger ice cream freezer container (self-refrigerated or with ice and salt); discard peel and chili. Freeze according to manufacturer's directions or until dasher is hard to crank; serve ice cream softly frozen. Or, if made ahead, pack ice cream in a container, cover, and freeze up to 1 week. Makes 1 quart.

PER ½ CUP SERVING: 254 calories, 4 g protein, 23 g carbohydrates, 17 g fat, 125 mg cholesterol, 55 mg sodium

Grilled lamb and bacon-wrapped prunes are interspersed on skewers.

NORTH AFRICAN SHISH KEBAB

- 2 pounds boned, fat-trimmed lamb (leg or shoulder), cut into 1-inch pieces
- 3 tablespoons lemon juice
- 3 cloves garlic, minced or pressed
- 1½ tablespoons ground cumin
- 1 package (12 oz., about 3 dozen) pitted prunes
  About 12 slices (about ¾ lb.) bacon, cut crosswise into thirds
  About 3 dozen dry bay leaves
  Lemon wedges
  Salt and pepper

In a bowl, mix lamb, lemon juice, garlic, and cumin. Wrap prunes in bacon. Alternately thread meat, wrapped prunes, and bay leaves onto 7 or 8 skewers, leaving gaps between prunes and meat so bacon cooks evenly.

Place skewers on a grill 4 to 6 inches above a solid bed of medium coals (you should be able to hold your hand at grill level for 4 to 5 seconds). Cook, turning skewers often to prevent flare-ups, until bacon is browned and lamb is browned but still pink in center (cut to test), 10 to 15 minutes. Squeeze lemon wedges over servings, and add salt and pepper to taste. Serves 7 or 8. —*Monica Jaworski, San Diego.*

PER SERVING: 314 calories, 28 g protein, 31 g carbohydrates, 10 g fat, 79 mg cholesterol, 203 mg sodium

Bell pepper, onion, cooked potatoes brown with aromatic spices.

INDIAN POTATOES

- 1½ pounds cooked, unpeeled thin-skinned potatoes
- 1 medium-size red bell pepper
- 1 medium-size onion, chopped
- 1 tablespoon ground cumin
- 1 teaspoon ground coriander
- ⅛ teaspoon cayenne
- 2 to 3 tablespoons butter or margarine
- ⅓ cup chopped fresh cilantro (coriander)
- ½ cup sour cream (optional)
  Salt and pepper

Cut potatoes into ¼-inch-thick slices. Stem, seed, and chop bell pepper.

In a 10- to 12-inch frying pan on medium-high heat, cook bell pepper, onion, cumin, coriander, and cayenne in 2 tablespoons butter until onion is limp and begins to brown slightly, about 7 minutes; stir frequently. Add potatoes and cook, turning as needed with a wide spatula, until lightly browned, about 7 minutes longer; add more butter if potatoes stick.

Remove pan from heat. Sprinkle potatoes with cilantro, mixing gently, then spoon into a bowl and top with sour cream. Season to taste with salt and pepper. Makes 5 or 6 servings. —*June Burbick, Menlo Park, Calif.*

PER SERVING: 140 calories, 2.8 g protein, 23 g carbohydrates, 4.4 g fat, 10 mg cholesterol, 52 mg sodium

Mint, olives, olive oil embellish chilled cucumber-yogurt salad.

COOL-AS-A-CUCUMBER SALAD

- 3 medium-size (about 2 lb. total) cucumbers
  About ½ teaspoon salt
- 2 cups unflavored nonfat yogurt
- 3 cloves garlic, minced or pressed
- 2 tablespoons lemon juice
- 1 tablespoon minced fresh or 1½ teaspoons dry dill weed
- 1 tablespoon minced fresh or 1½ teaspoons dry mint leaves
  About 2 teaspoons extra-virgin olive oil
- 8 to 16 large butter lettuce leaves, rinsed and crisped

Peel cucumbers, then scrape out and discard seeds; coarsely chop cucumbers. In a colander, mix cucumbers with ½ teaspoon salt; let drain 15 minutes. In a bowl combine cucumbers, yogurt, garlic, lemon juice, and dill weed. Cover and chill 3 hours or up until next day.

Pour cucumber mixture into a serving bowl; sprinkle with ⅓ of the mint, then drizzle with 2 teaspoons olive oil. Serve salad on lettuce leaves, adding mint, olive oil, and salt to taste. Makes about 4 cups, 6 to 8 servings. —*Laurie Wilcox, Palm Desert, Calif.*

PER SERVING: 59 calories, 4 g protein, 8.4 g carbohydrates, 1.2 g fat, 1.1 mg cholesterol, 118 mg sodium

WHOLE-WHEAT SCONES

1½ cups whole-wheat flour
½ cup toasted wheat germ
⅓ cup sugar
2 teaspoons baking powder
1½ teaspoons ground cinnamon
½ teaspoon ground nutmeg
½ teaspoon salt
½ cup (¼ lb.) cold butter or margarine
1 large egg
½ cup buttermilk
½ cup raisins or currants

In a bowl, combine whole-wheat flour, wheat germ, sugar, baking powder, cinnamon, nutmeg, and salt. With 2 knives or a pastry blender, cut in butter until coarse crumbs form.

In a small bowl, beat egg with buttermilk to blend. Add egg mixture and raisins to flour mixture; stir just enough to moisten evenly. Scrape dough onto an ungreased 10- by 15-inch pan; pat into a 1-inch-thick round. With a sharp knife, cut round into 8 wedges. Bake in a 375° oven until well browned, 30 to 35 minutes. Serve warm or at room temperature. Cut or break scone into wedges to eat. Serves 8. — *Julia White, Flagstaff, Ariz.*

PER SERVING: 282 calories, 6.8 g protein, 37 g carbohydrates, 14 g fat, 58 mg cholesterol, 387 mg sodium

Raisin-studded scones are made with whole-wheat flour, wheat germ.

PORK POCKET PASTIES

1 pound ground lean pork
2 cups (7-oz. package) frozen hash brown potatoes
1 large carrot, finely diced
¼ cup chopped onion
½ teaspoon coarsely ground black pepper
1 cup (¼ lb.) shredded jack cheese
Salt
3 pocket bread rounds (6 in. across), cut in half crosswise
About 2 teaspoons melted butter or margarine

Crumble pork into a 10- to 12-inch frying pan; stir often on high heat until meat barely begins to brown, about 3 minutes. Add potatoes, carrot, onion, and pepper. Stir often until carrots are tender to bite, about 4 minutes. Remove from heat and stir in cheese. Add salt to taste.

Equally fill bread pockets with pork mixture. Lay in a 10- by 15-inch pan; brush bread with butter. Bake in a 500° oven until bread is slightly browner, about 4 minutes. Offer hot or at room temperature. Serves 6. — *Lois Dowling, Tacoma.*

PER SERVING: 417 calories, 20 g protein, 27 g carbohydrates, 25 g fat, 75 mg cholesterol, 354 mg sodium

Pocket bread halves bake with meat filling; carry to a picnic.

COLD RASPBERRY SOUFFLÉ

2 envelopes (2 teaspoons each) unflavored gelatin
⅓ cup each orange juice and lemon juice
4 cups raspberries, rinsed and drained
6 large egg whites
1 cup sugar
1½ cups whipping cream, whipped to hold soft peaks

In a 1- to 2-cup pan, mix gelatin with orange and lemon juices; let stand until liquid is absorbed. Stir on medium heat until melted. Purée raspberries in a blender or food processor; add gelatin mixture. Rub purée through a fine strainer into a bowl; discard seeds. Chill, stirring often, just until mixture barely thickens, 10 to 15 minutes.

With a mixer on high speed, whip egg whites until foamy. Slowly add sugar, beating until soft peaks form. Fold whites and whipping cream into purée. Form a 3-inch-wide foil collar on the rim of a 5- to 6-cup soufflé dish; pour in mixture. Cover and chill until firm, 3 hours or until next day. Discard foil. Serves 10. — *Carmela Meely, Walnut Creek, Calif.*

PER SERVING: 223 calories, 4.6 g protein, 28 g carbohydrates, 11 g fat, 40 mg cholesterol, 48 mg sodium

Extra berries, mint decorate chilled raspberry soufflé.

W HAT'S IN A NAME? *A great deal, at least in the case of boiled cornmeal. If you call it mush, people giggle; if, on the other hand, you call it polenta, people will genuflect. Such is the current popularity of Italian cuisine.*

It was not always so. A San Francisco–bred friend of Italian extraction remembers how her family survived on polenta during the Great Depression, pasta being prohibitively expensive. They supplemented their diet with crab (from a fisherman father) and artichokes and an occasional rabbit (from farm relatives in nearby Half Moon Bay).

She has no deep, abiding love for polenta. But if she tried it lavished with Fred Herzer's sausage sauce, richly flavored with fresh and dried tomatoes, basil, and parmesan cheese, her memories of polenta might glow more brightly.

SPEEDY POLENTA WITH SAUSAGE SAUCE

   3 **ounces (about 2 cups) dried tomatoes**
      About 1¼ pounds (5 large) Roma-type tomatoes, cored and coarsely chopped
   1 **pound mild Italian sausages**
   1 **large onion, chopped**
   5 **cloves garlic, minced or pressed**
  ½ **pound mushrooms, sliced**
   1 **cup *each* dry red wine and regular-strength chicken broth**
  ¼ **teaspoon ground cinnamon**
      Freshly ground pepper
  ¼ **cup chopped fresh basil leaves**
      Microwave polenta (recipe follows)
      Freshly grated parmesan cheese

Place dried tomatoes in a small bowl. Add boiling water to cover and let soak for 2 to 3 minutes, then lift out tomatoes. Whirl dried and fresh tomatoes in a food processor or blender until puréed.

Remove sausage casings and discard. Crumble meat into a 5- to 6-quart pan over medium heat; stir often until sausage is well browned, about 20 minutes. Discard all but 2 tablespoons of the drippings. Add onion and garlic to pan; stir often until onion is limp, about 10 minutes. Stir in puréed tomato mixture, mushrooms, wine, broth, cinnamon, pepper, and basil.

"If you call boiled cornmeal polenta, people will genuflect."

Bring the mixture to a boil over high heat; stir often until sauce is thick enough to leave a path when a spoon is scraped across pan bottom, 30 to 40 minutes. To avoid scorching, stir more frequently as the sauce thickens.

Spoon hot cooked polenta onto a rimmed platter; spread so mixture is 1 to 1½ inches thick, then ladle sauce onto polenta. Spoon portions onto plates and add cheese to taste. Makes 6 to 8 servings.

PER SERVING: 360 calories, 15 g protein, 36 g carbohydrates, 18 g fat, 42 mg cholesterol, 482 mg sodium

Microwave polenta. In a 4- to 5-quart microwave-safe bowl, combine 1½ cups **polenta,** 2 tablespoons **butter** or margarine, 3½ cups (2 cans, each 14½-oz. size) boiling regular-strength **chicken broth,** and 1⅔ cups boiling **water;** stir until well blended.

Cover polenta and cook in a microwave oven at full power (100 percent) until mixture boils and thickens, 18 to 20 minutes, stirring every 5 minutes. Mixture stays soft enough to spoon for only 3 or 4 minutes.

San Lorenzo, Calif.

T HE ARGUMENT *over the cholesterol-cutting capabilities of oat bran may still be raging, but there's no dispute over its claim to virtue as a source of fiber. Moreover, as bulk, it lessens the amount of space available in a recipe for ingredients of higher calorie count.*

There are many people who believe that oat bran enhances the texture (and possibly even the flavor) of breadstuffs. Certainly chef Tom Anderson's waffles are delicious, as well as being low in cholesterol. (Of course, if you insist on a big pat of butter, all bets are off.)

Apple Bran Waffles

1 cup buttermilk baking mix (biscuit mix)
1 cup oat bran
1 teaspoon baking powder
1 teaspoon ground cinnamon
About 2 tablespoons salad oil
2 large egg whites
1¼ cups nonfat milk
1 small (about 2½-in.-diameter) apple, peeled, cored, and finely chopped
Maple syrup

In a large bowl, whisk together the baking mix, bran, baking powder, cinnamon, 2 tablespoons oil, egg whites, and milk until smooth. Stir in the apple.

Set a waffle iron on medium-high heat (or at 375°). When hot, brush grids with salad oil. Ladle batter over hot grids (about 1 cup for 8-in.-square grid). Close pan and bake until waffle is well browned, 7 to 8 minutes. Serve, or place directly on racks in a 200° oven to keep warm for up to 30 minutes. Serve with maple syrup. Makes 3 waffles, each 8 inches wide.

PER SERVING: 379 calories, 14 g protein, 56 g carbohydrates, 16 g fat, 2 mg cholesterol, 700 mg sodium

Tom Anderson

Sandy, Utah

WHILE IN NEW ORLEANS, *Martin Yonke sampled a "barbecued" shrimp preparation he deemed worth stealing. Borrowing the steps, he added a Sichuan touch with Chinese chili paste: use with caution; too much will make you glow in the dark.*

Hot & Spicy Shrimp

2 tablespoons butter or margarine
1 medium-size onion, chopped
2 cloves garlic, minced or pressed
1 large (about 9 oz.) firm-ripe tomato, peeled, cored, seeded, and chopped

"Too much chili paste will make you glow in the dark."

½ to 1 teaspoon (or to taste) hot Chinese chili paste with garlic, or other hot chili paste
¼ pound mushrooms, thinly sliced
½ cup dry white wine
½ pound large shrimp (30 to 32 per lb.), shelled, halved lengthwise, and deveined
½ cup regular-strength chicken broth
1 tablespoon chopped parsley
1 green onion (including top), ends trimmed and thinly sliced
Crusty bread

In a 10- to 12-inch frying pan, melt butter over medium heat. Add onion and garlic and stir often until onion is limp, 10 to 15 minutes. Stir in tomato, chili paste, mushrooms, and wine. Bring to a boil over high heat; boil, uncovered, until most of the wine has evaporated, about 8 minutes.

Reduce heat to medium; add shrimp and stir often just until shrimp begin to curl, 1 to 2 minutes. Stir in broth, parsley, and green onion. When hot, ladle into soup bowls and eat with bread. Makes 2 servings.

PER SERVING: 260 calories, 22 g protein, 12 g carbohydrates, 14 g fat, 173 mg cholesterol, 292 mg sodium

Palo Alto, Calif.

CHEESECAKE *is one of the great triumvirate of restaurant desserts, along with caramel custard and chocolate mousse. It is often served with a topping of fruit or a touch of flavor, but the purist sticks to unadorned vanilla or lemon.*

When Bob Jones left home to go to college, his mother, Betty, sent two recipes with him: he threw away the meat loaf recipe at once, but worked on the cheesecake until he considered it perfect. He has been generous in sharing it with us.

Collaboration Cheesecake

1½ cups graham cracker crumbs
About ¼ cup (⅛ lb.) butter or margarine, melted
1 cup sugar
2 large packages (8 oz. each) cream cheese, at room temperature
3 large eggs
1¾ teaspoons vanilla
1 pint sour cream

In a bowl, mix graham cracker crumbs with ¼ cup butter and ¼ cup of the sugar. Pat crumbs evenly over bottom and about 1½ inches up the sides of a lightly buttered 9-inch cheesecake pan with removable rim. Chill 15 to 20 minutes.

In a large mixer bowl, beat ½ cup of the sugar with cream cheese, eggs, and ¾ teaspoon of the vanilla until very smooth. Pour mixture into chilled crust. Bake in a 375° oven until center jiggles only slightly when gently shaken, about 20 minutes. Remove cheesecake from the oven and let cool for 15 minutes. Meanwhile, turn oven up to 425°.

In a small bowl (or the carton), stir sour cream to blend with remaining ¼ cup sugar and remaining 1 teaspoon vanilla. Gently spoon mixture over cheesecake, then spread evenly. Return cheesecake to oven and bake until sour cream appears set when gently shaken, 12 to 14 minutes. Let cool to room temperature, then cover and chill until cold, at least 3 hours or up to 2 days. Cut into wedges. Makes 14 to 16 servings.

PER SERVING: 296 calories, 4.9 g protein, 23 g carbohydrates, 21 g fat, 92 mg cholesterol, 209 mg sodium

Los Gatos, Calif.

July Menus

MINIMIZE TIME *in the kitchen this month with quick-to-assemble meals. Start with an updated version of the traditional picnic to celebrate our nation's birthday. For a speedier meal, delegate preparation of the simple recipes to others.*

Summer's bounty of produce headlines the next menu. Star attraction features quickly sautéed red and yellow cherry tomatoes to go over pasta.

It takes only minutes to get the hot-cold salad supper on the table. Stir-fry strips of fresh tuna, then tumble onto greens.

FIREWORKS PICNIC

Cucumber Sticks   Pink Onion Dip
Potato Salad with Seed Vinaigrette
Grilled Hamburgers on Toasted Buns
Red, White & Blue Sundaes
Roman Candle Cookies
Lemonade   Beer

Two traditional basics of the holiday picnic, potato salad and a creamy dip, take on a leaner, fresher profile.

Make the salad and cookies ahead. Offer cucumber sticks to dip in the refreshing pink onion dip as the hamburgers cook on the grill. Show off the nation's colors with vanilla ice cream topped with sweetened sliced strawberries and whole blueberries. Garnish with Roman candle cookies.

PINK ONION DIP

1 medium-size red onion, finely chopped
2 tablespoons sugar
2 tablespoons red wine vinegar
1 cup unflavored yogurt
   Salt and pepper

Mix the onion, sugar, and vinegar. Let stand until onion is limp, about 30 minutes. Drain onion, pressing out excess liquid. Just before serving, mix onion and yogurt. Add salt and pepper to taste. Makes about 1⅓ cups, 6 to 8 servings.

PER SERVING: 36 calories, 1.7 g protein, 6.5 g carbohydrates, 0.5 g fat, 1.7 mg cholesterol, 20 mg sodium

Grilled hamburgers go with potato salad, fragrant with herb seeds. Pickled red onions lace cool yogurt dip for cucumbers. Salad and dip add lighter flavors to old-fashioned picnic.

POTATO SALAD WITH SEED VINAIGRETTE

2 pounds (about 5 large) red thin-skinned potatoes
1½ cups thinly sliced celery
½ cup thinly sliced green onion
   Seed vinaigrette (recipe follows)
   Salt and pepper

Scrub potatoes. In a 5- to 6-quart pan, combine potatoes and about 2 quarts water. Bring to a boil over high heat. Reduce heat, cover, and simmer until potatoes are tender when pierced, 20 to 25 minutes. Drain, then immerse in cold water until cool; drain again. Cut into ¾-inch cubes.

In a large bowl, gently mix potatoes, celery, onion, and vinaigrette. Add salt and pepper to taste. Serve, or cover and chill up until the next day. Serves 6 to 8.

PER SERVING: 183 calories, 2.6 g protein, 23 g carbohydrates, 9.4 g fat, 0 mg cholesterol, 30 mg sodium

Seed vinaigrette. In a 10- to 12-inch frying pan, combine 1 teaspoon *each* **mustard seed, cumin seed,** and **fennel seed.** Cook over medium heat, shaking pan often, until fragrant, 5 to 7 minutes. Coarsely crush seeds with the back of a heavy spoon. Remove from heat and add ⅓ cup **salad oil,** ⅓ cup **cider vinegar,** ½ teaspoon **coarsely ground pepper,** and 1 clove **garlic,** pressed or minced.

ROMAN CANDLE COOKIES

  1 **package (20 oz.) refrigerated sugar cooky dough**
     About 1 tablespoon red-colored coarse sugar

Unwrap the dough and cut in half crosswise, then cut each half lengthwise into 8 equal pieces, making 16 pieces total. On a floured board, roll each piece into a stick 13 to 14 inches long and about ⅜ inch thick. Lay sticks about 1½ inches apart on lightly greased 12- by 15-inch baking sheets. Sprinkle with sugar.

Bake in a 350° oven (if using 1 oven, change pan positions halfway through) until golden brown, 14 to 16 minutes. Cool on pans about 3 minutes, then transfer, with a wide spatula, to racks to cool further. If made ahead, store airtight up to 2 days. Makes 16 cookies.

PER COOKY: 153 calories, 1.5 g protein, 23 g carbohydrates, 6 g fat, cholesterol not available, 143 mg sodium

---

SUPPER FROM THE GARDEN

Avocado & Zucchini Salad
Linguine with Red & Yellow Tomatoes
Crusty Bread   Extra-virgin Olive Oil
Peach Gingerbread Shortcake
Dry Sauvignon Blanc or Chianti

Pick the bounty from your garden or the market for this summer supper.

Use a homemade or purchased gingerbread to make the base for the peach

Lift up linguine to mix with halved red and yellow cherry tomatoes spiced by chili and basil. Shredded zucchini with avocado, dressed with oil and lemon juice, completes all-vegetable menu.

shortcake. Assemble salad, then cook the pasta. Instead of butter for the bread, offer extra-virgin olive oil in a little bowl and dunk the bread in it.

AVOCADO & ZUCCHINI SALAD

  4 **cups (about 1 lb.) shredded zucchini**
  1 **large firm-ripe avocado**
1½ **cups (about 2 oz.) tender arugula or watercress sprigs, rinsed and crisped**
  ⅓ **cup extra-virgin olive oil**
  3 **tablespoons lemon juice**
  8 **to 12 Greek olives or oil-cured olives (optional)**
     Salt and pepper

Place zucchini in a wide, shallow bowl. Peel, pit, and slice the avocado. Lay avocado and arugula on zucchini.

Mix oil with lemon juice and pour over salad. Garnish with olives. Mix ingredients and, individually, add salt and pepper to taste. Makes 4 to 6 servings.

PER SERVING: 164 calories, 1.7 g protein, 4.9 g carbohydrates, 17 g fat, 0 mg cholesterol, 11 mg sodium

LINGUINE WITH RED & YELLOW TOMATOES

  1 **pound dry linguine**
  2 **tablespoons olive oil**
  1 **clove garlic, pressed or minced**
  ¼ **teaspoon crushed dried hot red chilies**
  1 **large onion, chopped**
  6 **cups (about 2 lb.) red or yellow cherry or other tiny tomatoes (use half of both colors or all of 1), stemmed and halved**
  2 **cups (about 3 oz.) tightly packed fresh basil leaves or ¼ cup dry basil**
     Grated parmesan cheese
     Salt and pepper

In a 5- to 6-quart pan, bring about 3 quarts water to a boil. Add linguine and cook, uncovered, until noodles are just tender to bite, 7 to 9 minutes. Drain well; pour into a warm shallow bowl.

Meanwhile, in a 12-inch frying pan or 6-quart pan, stir oil, garlic, chilies, and onion over high heat until onions are lightly browned, about 5 minutes. Add tomatoes and basil; stir gently until tomatoes are hot, about 2 minutes. Pour over noodles. Add cheese, salt, and pepper to taste. Serves 4 to 6.

PER SERVING: 367 calories, 12 g protein, 67 g carbohydrates, 6.2 g fat, 0 mg cholesterol, 19 mg sodium

(Continued on next page)

STIR-FRIED SALAD SUPPER

Stir-fried Tuna on Iceberg
Rice or Sesame Crackers
Canary Melon or Honeydew Wedges
Iced Sake or Iced Tea

Try this salad for a quick weekday supper.

Rinse and crisp the lettuce, then prepare the dressing for the salad. Quickly stir-fry fresh tuna and spoon over the cool greens.

STIR-FRIED TUNA ON ICEBERG

10 cups (about 1 lb.) bite-size pieces rinsed and crisped iceberg lettuce
2 tablespoons sesame seed
2 tablespoons salad oil
2 tablespoons finely shredded fresh ginger
¾ pound fresh tuna or halibut, cut into strips about ½ by 3 inches
Soy dressing (recipe follows)
½ cup thinly sliced green onion
1 cup thinly sliced red radishes
4 green onions, ends trimmed

Mound lettuce equally on 4 dinner plates.

In a wok or 12-inch frying pan, stir sesame seed over medium heat until golden, 3 to 6 minutes. Pour seed out of pan.

Add oil to pan and place on high heat. When pan is hot, add ginger and stir-fry until lightly browned, about 30 seconds.

Add tuna and stir-fry just until fish turns opaque, 2 to 3 minutes. Add soy dressing and remove from heat. Spoon ¼ of the fish and dressing over lettuce on each plate. Sprinkle with sliced green onion, radishes, and sesame seed. Garnish with whole green onions. Makes 4 servings.

PER SERVING: 281 calories, 23 g protein, 14 g carbohydrates, 14 g fat, 32 mg cholesterol, 568 mg sodium

Soy dressing. In a small bowl, stir together 3 tablespoons **mirin** (sweet sake) or cream sherry, 6 tablespoons **rice vinegar** or cider vinegar, 2 tablespoons **soy sauce**, and 1 teaspoon **prepared horseradish**.

AUGUST

Fruit-based Drinks (page 204)

Savor the warm, lazy days of midsummer, and plan your menus and entertaining using ideas that are easy on the cook. For a casual gathering, invite guests to concoct their own beverages using fresh fruit, juices, and other ingredients ready on a fruit-punch bar. Plan a Thailand-style picnic featuring spicy chicken or seafood cooked on the barbecue. The bounty of summer fruits and vegetables offers opportunities for easy experimentation— with colorful new tomato varieties, with sweet young corn, and with fruit shortcakes for breakfast.

Tomato Dazzlers

Tomatoes multiply this month— *and not only in traditional red, but also in a spectrum of orange, yellow, white, green, and a multicolored mosaic.*

You'll find many of the varieties pictured here at markets and produce stands. Home gardens remain the best source for hollow stuffer and white varieties.

We offer ways to use tomatoes fresh in salad, filled with couscous, and in gazpacho. Slight differences in flavor and texture show up—tomatoes range from tart to sweet, watery to meaty—but varieties are interchangeable in these recipes (except for stuffers; they're the best for filling).

You can also capture the essence of fresh tomatoes in a basic sauce, made while tomato season is at its peak. Use it now, or freeze small portions to use throughout the year. For sauce, choose any of the tomatoes except the stuffers. Flavor, color, and yield of this sauce vary with the kind of tomato you use. Meaty varieties result in thicker sauce; juicy tomatoes render thinner sauce. One pound of tomatoes yields about ¾ cup sauce. Cooking can improve some tomatoes, intensifying their flavor and color.

Pour the sauce over hot pasta; add fresh basil and grated parmesan cheese to taste. Or try it in a creamy sauce for fish and poultry, or in spicy salsa.

Hollow stuffer tomato looks like bell pepper but tastes like tomato. Fill with mint-spiked couscous and bake. Serve with poultry or meat.

Tomatoes with Shallot Vinaigrette

- 4 large butter lettuce leaves, rinsed and crisped (optional)
- 2 large (about 1¼ lb. total) tomatoes, cored and sliced
  Shallot vinaigrette (recipe follows)
  Salt and pepper

Place lettuce and tomatoes on a serving platter or 4 salad plates. Spoon vinaigrette evenly over tomatoes. Add salt and pepper to taste. Makes 4 servings.

PER SERVING: 151 calories, 13 g protein, 7 g carbohydrates, 14 g fat, 0 mg cholesterol, 50 mg sodium

Shallot vinaigrette. Mix ¼ cup **olive oil,** 2 tablespoons **wine vinegar,** 2 tablespoons minced **shallots,** 1 teaspoon **Dijon mustard,** and 1 teaspoon **fresh thyme** or ½ teaspoon dry thyme leaves. Makes ½ cup.

Tomatoes with Minted Couscous

- 2 tablespoons olive oil
- 1 small red bell pepper, stemmed, seeded, and chopped
- 1 small onion, chopped
- 1 clove garlic, pressed or minced
- ¾ cup regular-strength chicken broth
- ½ teaspoon ground cumin
- ⅛ teaspoon cayenne
- ½ cup couscous
- 1 tablespoon chopped fresh or dry mint leaves
  Salt and pepper
- 6 large (4 to 5 oz. each) stuffer tomatoes, or large (about 8 oz. each) regular tomatoes
  Fresh mint sprigs

In a 2- to 3-quart pan, combine oil, bell pepper, onion, and garlic. Stir often over medium-high heat until onion is faintly browned, about 10 minutes. Add broth, cumin, and cayenne; bring to a boil. Stir in couscous, cover, and remove from heat. Let stand until liquid is absorbed, about 5 minutes. Stir in chopped mint and salt and pepper to taste.

Meanwhile, cut around top of each tomato to make a lid. Scoop out seeds and any pulp, leaving shell. Reserve pulp for another use or discard. Fill tomatoes with couscous. Place in a shallow 1- to 1½-quart baking dish. Bake, uncovered, in a 400° oven until hot in

Multicolored tomatoes, sliced and drizzled with shallot vinaigrette, create yellow and red mosaic. Tart dressing accents tomatoes' flavor.

center, about 20 minutes. Set lids on tomatoes or alongside. Garnish with mint sprigs. Serves 6.

PER SERVING: 124 calories, 3.2 g protein, 17 g carbohydrates, 5 g fat, 0 mg cholesterol, 16 mg sodium

Tomato Gazpacho

This cool soup embodies the essence of fresh tomato. Simply purée the tomatoes, season with vinegar and oil, then offer condiments to add texture and flavor.

- 2½ pounds ripe tomatoes
- ¼ cup wine vinegar
- 2 tablespoons olive oil
  Salt
- 4 ripe tomato slices
- 1 small firm-ripe avocado
- 1 tablespoon lime juice
- ⅔ cup thinly sliced cucumber
- ⅓ to ½ cup sour cream
- ⅓ cup chopped red or white onion
- ⅓ cup chopped fresh cilantro (coriander)
- 1 to 2 tablespoons minced fresh hot chili such as jalapeño
  Lime wedges

Dip 2 or 3 tomatoes at a time in boiling water to cover for 20 to 30 seconds, lift out, then peel and core. If tomatoes are juicy, cut in half crosswise and squeeze gently to push out and discard seed pockets. Cut tomatoes into 1-inch chunks.

Purée tomatoes, a portion at a time, in a blender or food processor. In a large bowl, mix puréed tomatoes, vinegar, olive oil, and salt to taste. Cover and chill until cold, at least 1 hour or up to overnight.

In each of 4 shallow bowls, pour equal portions of tomato mixture. Lay 1 tomato slice on top. Peel, pit, and thinly slice avocado. Brush lime juice over avocado slices. Offer avocado, cucumber, sour cream, onion, cilantro, chili, and lime wedges to add to each bowl to taste. Serve cold. Makes 4 servings.

PER SERVING WITH CONDIMENTS: 223 calories, 4 g protein, 18 g carbohydrates, 17 g fat, 8.3 mg cholesterol, 40 mg sodium

CHEESE CRISPS WITH TOMATO SALSA

1 cup basic tomato sauce (recipe follows)

1 can (7 oz.) diced green chilies

¼ cup chopped fresh cilantro (coriander)

¼ cup thinly sliced green onion

2 to 4 tablespoons lime juice
Salt

8 flour tortillas (7 in. wide)

2 cups (8 oz.) shredded jack cheese or jalapeño jack cheese

Pour tomato sauce into a fine strainer and let drain about 10 minutes; discard liquid. Mix drained tomato sauce, chilies, cilantro, onion, and lime juice and salt to taste.

Tart green tomatoes, made into sauce, combine with green chilies and cilantro. Scoop up chunky salsa with oven-crisped cheese-filled tortillas.

Spoon creamy sauce, made from white tomatoes, over grilled salmon steaks. To vary flavor and hue of sauce, use different colored tomatoes.

Brush 1 side of tortillas lightly with water. Place 2 tortillas, wet side down and slightly apart, on a lightly greased 12- by 15-inch baking sheet. Sprinkle each evenly with ½ cup cheese. Cover each with another tortilla, wet side up. Repeat with remaining tortillas and cheese on a second baking sheet.

Bake in a 500° oven until tortillas are crisp and golden, about 10 minutes. (If using 1 oven, switch pan positions halfway.) Remove from oven and cut each round into 10 to 12 wedges. Offer warm tortilla wedges to scoop up tomato salsa. Makes about 16 appetizer servings.

PER SERVING: 98 calories, 4.9 g protein, 8.4 g carbohydrates, 5.4 g fat, 12 mg cholesterol, 225 mg sodium

BASIC TOMATO SAUCE

5 pounds ripe tomatoes
Salt and pepper

In a 3- to 4-quart pan, bring about 2 quarts water to a boil. Dip 2 or 3 tomatoes at a time in the water for 20 to 30 seconds, then peel off skins and core. If tomatoes are juicy, cut in half crosswise and squeeze gently to push out and discard contents of seed pockets. Cut into about 1-inch chunks.

Purée tomatoes, a portion at a time, in a blender or food processor.

Pour purée into a 5- to 6-quart pan. Bring to a boil, then reduce heat and boil gently, uncovered, until most of the liquid has evaporated and sauce is reduced by about half, 45 minutes to 1½ hours. Add salt and pepper to taste. If made ahead, cover and chill up to 2 days, or freeze airtight up to 6 months. Makes 3½ to 4 cups.

PER ½ CUP: 49 calories, 2.3 g protein, 11 g carbohydrates, 0.5 g fat, 0 mg cholesterol, 21 mg sodium

Creamy tomato sauce. In a 2- to 3-quart pan, stir 3 tablespoons minced **shallots** in 1 tablespoon **salad oil** over medium heat until faintly browned, about 5 minutes. Add 2 cups **basic tomato sauce** (recipe precedes), ½ teaspoon **fresh tarragon leaves** or ¼ teaspoon dry tarragon leaves, and 3 tablespoons **whipping cream.** Bring to a boil. Add **salt** and **white pepper** to taste. Serve with hot cooked fish or chicken. Makes about 2 cups. —*Suzanne Ashworth, Sacramento.*

PER ½ CUP: 118 calories, 2.7 g protein, 13 g carbohydrates, 74 g fat, 12 mg cholesterol, 25 mg sodium

Mix Your Own Fresh Fruit Creations

COOL FRUIT-BASED DRINKS *suit sweltering summer days. Set up a bar with the makings for refreshing thirst quenchers, then invite guests to sip away the afternoon.*

This attractive beverage service pleases all palates and ages because drinks are made to individual taste. As the host, you can mix drinks to order or let your guests design and make their own. We offer some basic ideas for combinations and recommend proportions; to help guests decide,

you could write these out on a simple menu card.

All these drinks start with fruit—in pieces, as juice, or as flavored beverages or syrups. In some, you purée fruit with sparkling water, sparkling wine, or milk. In others, you blend juice or syrup with water or wine in the glass. Beverages can be clear and light or thick and filling. Add pieces of fruit or fresh mint as garnishes, or thread fruit on thin wooden skewers to create edible swizzle sticks.

STOCKING YOUR FRUIT-PUNCH BAR

You can adjust ingredients to a group of any size. Select the drinks you want to offer, including at least 1 nonalcoholic choice. If you plan to use a blender, set up the bar near an electrical outlet. Keep beverages cold in an ice bucket.

Here are some suggestions:

Fresh fruit. Choose whole raspberries, blueberries, whole or sliced strawber-

At mix-your-own-beverage party, guests prepare fruit concoctions—some in blender, some in glass. Mixers include milk, sparkling water, juice, wine (still and sparkling), sugar, and syrups. Garnish with citrus wedges, berries, mint sprigs, skewered fruit.

Create concoctions such as guava spritzer (guava juice, sparkling water, lemon squeeze); white sangría (white wine, orange juice, tamarind syrup, lime); cassis splash (cassis syrup, sparkling water, raspberries); melon slush (purée of honeydew, white grape juice, ice, and sugar with strawberry garnish); peach sparkler (purée of peach and sparkling wine, mint garnish); berry frullato (raspberries puréed with milk, ice, dash of cassis syrup).

ries, bite-size pieces of peeled and seeded cantaloupe or honeydew melon, sliced peeled peaches (coated with lemon juice), sliced firm-ripe plums, peeled and cored pineapple chunks. Place in separate bowls. Allow ⅓ to ½ cup trimmed fruit per serving.

Wine. Choose 1 or several wines—a sparkling dry wine like Asti Spumante or champagne; a fruity white such as a Johannisberg Riesling, Gewürztraminer, or Chenin Blanc; or a young fruity red such as Beaujolais or Merlot. Allow about 6 ounces per serving.

Sparkling water. Allow about 8 ounces per serving.

Milk. Allow about 4 ounces per serving.

Fruit juices and beverages. Choices might include orange, apple, white grape, cranberry, pineapple, or guava.

Syrups. Choose among flavored syrups such as mint, tamarind, grenadine, and cassis. (Look for them in delicatessens, supermarkets, liquor stores, and Italian, Asian, and Mexican markets.) Or use fruit-flavored pancake syrup. You'll need 3 to 4 tablespoons per serving.

Other essentials. Include a bowl of sugar, lemon or lime wedges, lots of coarsely crushed ice (or small cubes), a blender, swizzle sticks or long slender wooden skewers for stirrers, a pitcher of water to rinse the blender, and a dump bucket to collect the rinse water. If you like, offer a bouquet of fresh mint sprigs for garnish.

HOW TO MAKE THE DRINKS

Use a serving glass as a measuring cup; fill with desired ingredients, eyeballing ratios. Mix drink with a stirrer or, if you want a purée, pour the contents of the glass into a blender and whirl.

Juice spritzer. In a glass, mix 2 parts **fruit juice** and 1 part **sparkling water** or wine. Add **ice** and **lemon** or lime. If desired, float a few **fruit** pieces or add a skewer with fruit.

Sangría. In a glass, mix 2 parts **red** or white **wine** with 1 part **orange juice.** Add **tamarind syrup** or sugar, **lime,** and **ice** to taste. Float a few **fruit** pieces, if desired.

Syrup splash. In a glass, mix 3 parts **sparkling water** with about 1 part **flavored syrup** (or to taste). Add **ice** and **lemon** or lime. If desired, float a few **fruit** pieces or add a skewer with fruit.

Fruit slush. In a blender, smoothly purée equal portions of **fruit, juice,** and **ice.** Add **flavored syrup** or sugar to taste. Add a skewer with **fruit,** if desired.

Fruit sparklers. In a blender, smoothly purée 1 part **fruit** with 2 parts **sparkling wine** or water. Garnish with **fresh mint,** if desired.

Frullato. In a blender, smoothly purée equal portions of **fruit, milk,** and **ice.** Add **flavored syrup** or sugar to taste.

Barbecue Picnic Ideas from Thailand

AMONG THE SIMPLER PLEASURES *of Thailand's complex cuisine are grilled foods served with explosive seasoning sauces. These two barbecue picnics are good examples.*

The grilled chicken originates in the northern part of the country, near the 3,300-foot-high city of Chiang Mai. The seafood beach barbecue is from Phuket, an island resort in the south. Each barbecue features a dipping sauce made from chilies to season the main course.

You can serve these grill menus in your own garden or cook them at home and transport them to a favorite picnic spot. The few special ingredients, offered primarily in Asian markets, have readily available supermarket alternatives.

CHIANG MAI CHICKEN BARBECUE

Grilled Chicken Chiang Mai–style with Red Chili Sauce
Green Papaya & Bean Salad
Sticky Rice (optional)
Fresh Litchis or Strawberries
Juice from Young Coconut or Iced Tea

In the Mae Sa Valley, northwest of Chiang Mai, locals often bring a lunch to enjoy while relaxing on big boulders at a cascading waterfall. Before hiking up to the falls, some people purchase carry-out foods from vendors at the base. A popular choice is grilled split chicken, skewered spread-eagle fashion, with a salad made from shredded green papayas. Dessert is fresh seasonal fruit.

Make the seasoning paste for the chicken and skewer the chicken up to 1 day ahead. If you don't have glutinous rice to make sticky rice, season 3 cups cooked short- or medium-grain rice to taste with about ¼ cup seasoned rice vinegar. Pinch into small bites to eat out of hand.

The salad can be made 2 hours ahead. Look for firm green papayas in stores that specialize in Southeast Asian foods; green cabbage is a surprisingly good substitute. Mexican groceries and many supermarkets carry the mild dried chilies.

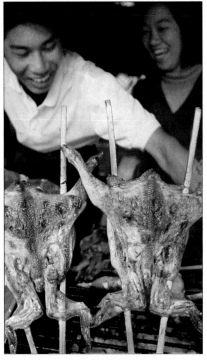

In Thailand, you can buy garlic-seasoned barbecued chicken, displayed upright on bamboo skewers; they hold chicken flat as it cooks on grill.

At Mae Sa Falls, picnickers feast on grilled chicken with sweet-tart red chili sauce and a green papaya salad. Sip cool juice from young coconut. Peel red-skinned litchis for dessert.

GRILLED CHICKEN CHIANG MAI–STYLE WITH RED CHILI SAUCE

> 1 broiler-fryer chicken (3 to 3½ lb.)
> 6 large cloves garlic, chopped
> ¼ cup thinly sliced green onion
> 1 tablespoon chopped fresh ginger
> ½ teaspoon ground coriander
> ½ teaspoon coarsely ground pepper
> 2 tablespoons fish sauce (*nam pla* or *nuoc mam*) or soy sauce
> Red chili sauce (recipe follows)

Reserve chicken giblets and necks for another use. Rinse chicken and pat dry. With poultry shears or a knife, split chicken lengthwise through breastbone. Pull bird open and place, skin side up, on a flat surface; press firmly, cracking bones slightly, until bird lies flat.

Thread chicken on sturdy 15- to 20-inch metal skewers, forcing 1 skewer through thigh—perpendicular to bone and just above drumstick—into the breast, and out through the middle joint of wing in extended position (see left photo above). Repeat on the other side of the chicken.

With a mortar and pestle or in a blender, grind garlic, onion, ginger, coriander, pepper, and fish sauce into a coarse paste. Rub all over chicken. If made ahead, cover and chill up until the next day.

Place chicken on a grill 4 to 6 inches above a solid bed of medium-hot coals (you can hold your hand at grill level only 3 to 4 seconds). Cook, turning as needed to brown evenly, until meat at thigh bone is no longer pink (cut to test), 25 to 30 minutes total. Remove chicken from skewers; cut up chicken and serve with chili sauce. Makes 4 servings.

PER SERVING: 385 calories, 43 g protein, 3.2 g carbohydrates, 21 g fat, 132 mg cholesterol, 124 mg sodium

Red chili sauce. Remove stems and seeds from 3 large (about 1 oz. total) **dried California** or New Mexico **chilies** and 2 or 3 small **dried hot red chilies.** Rinse chilies, coarsely chop, and place in a bowl. Add ¾ cup hot **water.** Soak until soft, about 10 minutes. In a blender, combine chili-water mixture and 3 cloves **garlic,** chopped; whirl until coarsely puréed.

In a 1- to 1½-quart pan, combine chili mixture, ½ cup **distilled white vinegar,** and ⅓ cup **sugar.** Cook over high heat, stirring, until reduced to about ¾ cup,

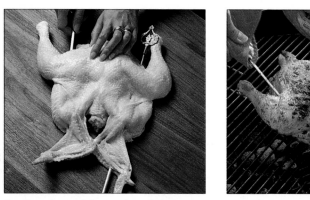

Insert sturdy metal skewers through chicken thigh, into breast, and through extended wing, holding garlic-seasoned split birds flat. (In Thailand, bamboo skewers are more typical.) Grill the chicken over medium-hot coals, turning as needed to brown evenly.

5 to 10 minutes. Stir in **salt** to taste. Serve the sauce warm or cool. If made ahead, cover and chill up to 1 week. Makes ¾ cup.

PER TABLESPOON: 27 calories, 0.2 g protein, 6.9 g carbohydrates, 0.2 g fat, 0 mg cholesterol, 0.6 mg sodium

GREEN PAPAYA & BEAN SALAD

> 1 small (about 1 lb.) green papaya or 4 cups (about ¾ lb.) finely shredded cabbage
> 2 cloves garlic, coarsely chopped
> 2 tablespoons dry shrimp (optional)
> 3 or 4 (about 1½ oz. each) fresh jalapeño chilies, stemmed, seeded, and chopped
> ¼ cup lime juice
> 1 tablespoon firmly packed brown sugar
> ¼ pound Chinese long beans or green beans, ends trimmed
> 1 medium-size ripe tomato, cored and cut into thin wedges
> 1 to 2 tablespoons fish sauce (*nam pla* or *nuoc mam*) or soy sauce
> Leaf lettuce leaves, rinsed and crisped

Peel papaya, cut in half, and discard seeds; finely shred enough fruit to make about 4 cups. In a blender, finely grind garlic, shrimp, and chilies.

In a large bowl, combine garlic mixture, lime juice, and brown sugar; stir until sugar dissolves. Thinly slice half of the beans crosswise; cut remaining beans into 3-inch lengths and set aside. Add to the bowl sliced beans, papaya, tomato, and fish sauce to taste; mix

together. Spoon onto a lettuce-lined plate; garnish with reserved beans. If made ahead, cover and chill up to 2 hours. Makes 4 servings.

PER SERVING: 75 calories, 2.1 g protein, 17 g carbohydrates, 0.7 g fat, 0 mg cholesterol, 11 mg sodium

STICKY RICE

Rinse 2 cups **sticky rice** (also called glutinous or sweet rice) until water runs clear. Cover rice with water and soak at least 2 hours or up until the next day. Drain and place rice in a cloth-lined steamer rack or tie it loosely in a towel and set on rack. Steam on rack, covered, over at least 1 inch boiling water until tender to bite, about 20 minutes. Serve warm or cool. Makes 4 servings.

PER SERVING: 342 calories, 6.3 g protein, 76 g carbohydrates, 0.5 g fat, 0 mg cholesterol, 6.5 mg sodium

---

NAGA NOI SEAFOOD GRILL

Phuket Grilled Shellfish
with Green Chili Sauce
Leaf-wrapped Grilled Fish (optional)
Marinated Cucumbers
Sticky Rice (optional)
Fresh Pineapple, Mangoes, or Papayas
Beer or Lemonade

In southern Thailand, near Phuket, lies Naga Noi, an island noted for its South Sea pearl farm and quiet white sand beaches. En route to the island, friends gather just-caught seafood from the Andaman Sea to grill for lunch.

(Continued on next page)

Grill large shrimp in the shell, then peel and dip into green chili sauce. Serve with thinly sliced red onion and cucumber seasoned with vinegar, sugar, salt, and hot chilies to taste.

The seafood selection varies with the day's catch. When we were there, small live crab were the choice; since their availability in the West is limited, our menu substitutes large prawns in the shell. If you like, steam a banana leaf–wrapped fish alongside on the grill.

Cook rice (recipe on page 207) ahead, or serve plain hot cooked rice. Make chili sauce up to 4 hours before serving. For a simple salad, season sliced cucumbers and red onion with vinegar, sugar, salt, and crushed dried hot red chilies to taste.

While the coals ignite, 30 to 45 minutes, devein the shrimp and wrap the fish in banana leaf or foil. Look for banana leaves in the freezer at Asian markets.

PHUKET GRILLED SHELLFISH WITH GREEN CHILI SAUCE

1½ **pounds extra-colossal (fewer than 10 per lb.) or colossal (10 to 15 per lb.) shrimp**
    Green chili sauce (recipe follows)

Devein unshelled shrimp by inserting a toothpick through joints in back of shell beneath vein in several places and gently pulling to remove vein. (Or, if desired, shell and devein shrimp.)

Place shrimp on a grill 4 to 6 inches above a solid bed of medium-hot coals (you can hold your hand at grill level only 3 to 4 seconds) and cook until flesh is opaque in thickest part (cut to test), 3 to 5 minutes a side. Transfer seafood to a large platter.

To eat, peel off shell and dip shrimp into green chili sauce. Serves 4 to 6.

PER SERVING (NO SAUCE): 98 calories, 19 g protein, 0.8 g carbohydrates, 1.6 g fat, 140 mg cholesterol, 137 mg sodium

Green chili sauce. In a blender, coarsely purée 4 to 6 (about 1½ oz. each) **fresh green jalapeño chilies,** stemmed, seeded, and chopped; 3 large cloves **garlic,** chopped; ½ cup **lime juice;** and 1 to 2 tablespoons firmly packed **brown sugar.**

PER TABLESPOON: 17 calories, 0.2 g protein, 4.4 g carbohydrates, 0 g fat, 0 mg cholesterol, 3.4 mg sodium

LEAF-WRAPPED GRILLED FISH

1 **whole (2⅓ to 3⅓ lb.) fish such as rockfish, cleaned and scaled; or 2 pounds white-flesh fish fillets or steaks (1½ in. thick) such as lingcod or grouper**
   Salt and ground white pepper
1 **stalk lemon grass or 3 strips (½ by 3 in. each, yellow part only) lemon peel**
6 **thin slices (each about the size of a quarter) fresh ginger**
1 **large (about 15- by 20-in.) banana leaf or piece of heavy foil**
   Green chili sauce (recipe precedes)

If desired, remove and discard head from fish. Rinse fish and pat dry. Sprinkle fish cavity or pieces lightly with salt and white pepper. Remove coarse outer leaves from lemon grass and trim off top leaves. Rinse stalk well, then pound with mallet to crush slightly. Lay lemon grass and ginger inside fish cavity or on top of pieces. Lay fish about 6 inches from 1 end of banana leaf and roll up to enclose fish (or wrap and seal in foil).

Place fish on a grill 4 to 6 inches above a solid layer of medium-hot coals (you can hold your hand at grill level only 3 to 4 seconds). Cook, turning once, until a thermometer inserted in thickest part reaches 140°, or until flesh in thickest part is opaque but still moist-looking (cut through leaf to test), 10 to 12 minutes a side for whole fish, 6 to 8 minutes a side for pieces. Unwrap fish and place on a platter. Eat chunks of fish with chili sauce added to taste. Makes 4 servings.

PER SERVING (NO SAUCE): 215 calories, 43 g protein, 0.3 g carbohydrates, 3.6 g fat, 80 mg cholesterol, 136 mg sodium

A Lesson in Salad Making: Preparing the Greens

THE FIRST STEP *in making a great salad is to prepare the greens. This process is easy for youngsters to manage, and it provides a good lesson for aspiring cooks.*

The basic routine is pretty much the same for all greens—they need to be rinsed, dried, and crisped. But there are also specific ways of handling different types of greens. Here, we focus on leafy greens that most cooks use frequently: lettuces (such as iceberg, butter, red-leaf, romaine), spinach, chicories (including Belgian endive, curly endive, escarole, frisée, and radicchio), and parsley. The procedures can also be applied to any other similarly shaped greens and fresh herbs.

Start by plucking out and discarding any bruised, old, yellowed, or tough leaves. If you aren't going to use stems or roots (as in salads with spinach or watercress), cut them off before washing leaves.

Spin-dry salad leaves and herbs that will be used right away. The salad spinner bruises leaves slightly, so use before they begin to discolor.

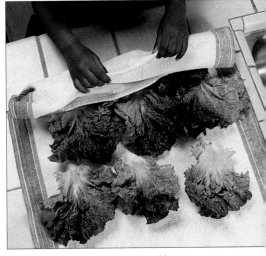

Gentle way to dry greens: wrap rinsed leaves in towel, put in plastic bag, chill about 30 minutes.

RINSING: A COOL BATH

Just running water over loose-leaf greens doesn't do an adequate job of removing unwelcome salad ingredients like dust, dirt, sand, and insects that collect on greens as they grow.

Leaves need to be immersed in cool water in a sink or a bowl and swished about. Then lift the leaves from the water to drain rather than just pulling the plug or pouring the water from the bowl. Otherwise, debris you washed off will get stuck on the leaves again.

A cool bath also gives tender leaves the moisture they need to be crisp and flavorful. Even if they're a bit limp, they'll perk up after being rinsed and chilled.

To rinse loose-leaf lettuces like butter, romaine, or red-leaf, or greens like escarole, break leaves from core into cool water; wash other loose leaves such as spinach or watercress the same way.

To rinse loose heads of greens like curly endive or frisée, hold by the stem end and swish up and down in cool water.

To rinse bunched parsley or other bunched herbs such as fresh dill, hold by the stems and swish the leafy ends in water.

To rinse tight heads of greens like iceberg lettuce, Belgian endive, or cabbage, you proceed differently. Core lettuce, run cool water into the cut and over the leaves, then invert to drain (the water also makes leaves easier to separate). Just rinse heads of Belgian endive and cabbage under cool running water, or give them a good dip.

DRYING & CRISPING

Because water left on leaves will dilute salad seasonings, you need to remove most of the moisture. To do this, you can shake the greens, whirl them in a salad spinner, or wrap them in towels (cloth or paper). Then, to crisp the greens, they must be chilled.

Shaking leaves individually works but is time-consuming. It's efficient with greens that have stems, such as heads of curly endive or parsley; just hold, shake vigorously—and watch out for the spray.

A salad spinner is fast, but it bruises the leaves slightly, so you'll need to use them fairly soon. After a day in the refrigerator, fine bruise lines will begin to discolor leaves that have been dried in a spinner. A gentler alternative is to gather the leaves in a towel, hold towel ends together, and swing the greens around.

Drying with towels is the gentlest way to remove moisture. Place leaves (in 1 or 2 layers) or heads of greens on towels and wrap them up gently.

To crisp the greens (dried by any of these three methods), wrap in towels, put in a plastic bag, and chill for at least 30 minutes. The bag must be loosely closed to allow greens to "breathe." Greens get crisper because the leaves actually "drink" the water, pulling it into their cells, which swell and firm.

The towels keep excess moisture away from the leaves (too much water makes them get slimy faster), and the plastic keeps the moisture from evaporating. Uncovered leaves, even in the refrigerator, wilt quickly.

HOW LONG WILL GREENS STAY FRESH?

Even in the best environment, greens won't keep forever. But as long as the leaves look and smell good, they're good to eat. And if portions discolor or decay, just break off and discard.

Tender greens such as spinach and lettuces may keep 4 days. Romaine lettuce lasts up to a week. Iceberg lettuce and parsley may keep 2 to 3 weeks.

Breakfast Shortcakes

DESSERT FOR BREAKFAST? *The answer is yes, with these breakfast shortcakes. You just dress up a traditional breakfast favorite—biscuits—to create the shortcakes. Then you fill each shortcake with generous amounts of fresh fruit, and yogurt or spiced cottage cheese instead of the usual whipped cream or custard.*

Bran Shortcake with Berries & Yogurt

    1   cup bran-flake cereal
    3   tablespoons milk
    ½   cup all-purpose flour
    ½   cup whole-wheat flour
        About ½ cup sugar
    1   tablespoon grated orange peel
    2   teaspoons baking powder
    1   teaspoon ground cinnamon
    3   tablespoons butter or margarine
    2   large eggs, beaten to blend
    3   cups mixed berries (2 or more
        kinds, including sliced
        strawberries, raspberries,
        blueberries, or blackberries)
    2   cups unflavored or fruit-flavor
        nonfat or low-fat yogurt

In a small bowl, stir bran flakes with milk; set aside to soften. In another bowl, mix together all-purpose flour, whole-wheat flour, 3 tablespoons sugar, orange peel, baking powder, and cinnamon. With a pastry blender or your fingers, cut or rub in butter until mixture is texture of coarse meal. Add bran mixture and eggs; stir just to moisten evenly.

On a greased 10- by 15-inch baking sheet, pat dough into an even 6-inch-diameter round. With a floured knife, lightly score top of round into 6 wedges, making cuts no more than ¼ inch deep.

Bake in a 400° oven until shortcake is lightly browned, 15 to 20 minutes. Transfer to a rack to cool until warm. If made ahead, cool completely, wrap airtight, and store at room temperature up until next day. To reheat, wrap in foil and bake in a 350° oven until warm, about 10 minutes.

With a long, serrated knife, carefully split shortcake in half horizontally. Place bottom half on a serving platter. In a bowl, mix together 2 cups berries, yogurt, and sugar to taste (omit sugar if yogurt is flavored). Spoon mixture onto

Make breakfast a special occasion with healthy bran shortcake, generously filled with mixed berries and yogurt. Another version uses thinly sliced peaches.

shortcake base; set top on fruit. Cut shortcake into wedges, following the scored lines. Serve with remaining berries and sugar, if desired. Makes 6 servings.

PER SERVING: 309 calories, 10 g protein, 50 g carbohydrates, 8.5 g fat, 89 mg cholesterol, 344 mg sodium

Peaches & Cream Breakfast Shortcake

        About 1 cup all-purpose flour
    2   teaspoons baking powder
    ¼   teaspoon baking soda
    3   tablespoons butter or margarine
    ⅓   cup buttermilk
    1   cup low-fat cottage cheese
        At least 3 tablespoons honey
    ⅛   teaspoon ground nutmeg
    2   large (about 1 lb. total) firm-ripe
        peaches, peeled, pitted, and
        thinly sliced

In a bowl, stir together 1 cup flour, baking powder, and baking soda. With a pastry blender or your fingers, cut or rub in butter until mixture is texture of coarse meal. Add buttermilk and stir only enough to moisten evenly.

Knead the dough on a lightly floured board until it is smooth, about 1 minute. Divide the dough into fourths. On an ungreased 10- by 15-inch baking sheet, pat each portion into a round about 3 inches in diameter.

Bake rounds in a 450° oven until lightly browned, about 15 minutes. Transfer to a rack and let stand until warm. If made ahead, cool completely, wrap airtight, and store at room temperature up until next day. To reheat, wrap in foil and bake in a 350° oven until warm, 5 to 10 minutes.

Whirl cottage cheese, 3 tablespoons honey, and nutmeg in a blender or food processor until smooth.

Using your fingers or a knife, split each shortcake in half horizontally. Set the bottom halves on 4 plates. Spoon ¼ of the cottage cheese mixture and ¼ of the peaches onto each base; set tops on shortcakes. Offer additional honey to add to taste. Makes 4 servings.

PER SERVING: 326 calories, 12 g protein, 49 g carbohydrates, 9.8 g fat, 26 mg cholesterol, 604 mg sodium

Cooking with Fresh Corn

THE SWEETNESS OF CORN *adds a flavorful dimension to these hearty dishes. The first is a whole-meal salad with shrimp, the second is a fresh relish to eat with chips or with meats, and the last is a toasted corn pudding to serve as a vegetable.*

CORN & SHRIMP SALAD

½ cup sweetened shredded dry coconut

3 ears (each about 8 in. long) corn, husks and silk removed

1 large head (about 1½ lb.) red-leaf lettuce, rinsed and crisped

1 pound shelled cooked tiny shrimp

1 large (about ½ lb.) red bell pepper, stemmed, seeded, and finely chopped

¼ cup thinly sliced red onion

4 ounces feta cheese, crumbled
Dressing (recipe follows)

In an 8- to 10-inch frying pan, stir coconut over medium-high heat until golden, about 6 minutes. Pour from pan. If made ahead, cover and let stand up to 2 days.

In a 5- to 6-quart pan, bring about 3 quarts water to boiling on high heat. Add corn and cook, covered, until hot, 4 to 6 minutes. Drain and let cool. Cut kernels from cob with a sharp knife.

Line a wide salad bowl with large lettuce leaves, then break remaining leaves into bite-size pieces into bowl. Mound separately on lettuce the coconut, corn, shrimp, pepper, onion, and cheese. Add dressing and mix gently. Makes 6 main-dish servings.

PER SERVING: 327 calories, 22 g protein, 19 g carbohydrates, 19 g fat, 167 mg cholesterol, 530 mg sodium

Dressing. Blend ¼ cup **olive oil** with 3 tablespoons **reduced-calorie** or regular **mayonnaise,** 2 tablespoons **balsamic vinegar,** 1 tablespoon **Dijon mustard,** and 1 teaspoon **dry dill weed.**

CORN RELISH

3 ears (each about 8 in. long) corn, husks and silk removed

½ cup finely chopped European cucumber

⅓ cup lime juice

¼ cup finely chopped green onion, including tops

A substantial meal in itself, Corn & Shrimp Salad also contains bell pepper, shredded coconut, crumbled feta cheese, and sliced red onion. Ladle dill dressing over salad.

1 tablespoon grated orange peel

3 tablespoons orange juice

2 tablespoons chopped fresh or 1 teaspoon dry mint leaves

1 teaspoon cumin seed

1 to 2 fresh jalapeño chilies, stemmed, seeded, and minced
Salt

In a 5- to 6-quart pan, bring about 3 quarts water to boiling on high heat. Add corn, cover, and cook until hot, 4 to 6 minutes. Drain and let cool. With a sharp knife, cut kernels from cob.

In a bowl, mix corn with cucumber, lime juice, onion, orange peel, orange juice, mint, cumin, and chilies; salt to taste. If made ahead, cover and chill up until next day. Makes 3 cups, about 12 servings.

PER ¼ CUP: 25 calories, 0.8 g protein, 5.7 g carbohydrates, 0.3 g fat, 0 mg cholesterol, 5 mg sodium

ROASTED CORN PUDDING

7 ears (each about 8 in. long) corn, husks and silk removed

3 tablespoons butter or margarine

5 to 6 ounces soft goat cheese or cream cheese

¼ cup all-purpose flour

2¼ cups low-fat milk

1 can (4 oz.) diced green chilies

¼ teaspoon cayenne
Salt

4 large eggs

In a 10- to 12-inch nonstick frying pan on medium heat, toast corn ears, a few at a time, until ⅓ of the kernels are tinged with brown, about 15 minutes; let cool.

With a sharp knife, cut kernels from cobs into pan. With dull side of knife, scrape cobs lengthwise, adding pulp to pan. Add butter and cheese. Stir over medium heat until butter and cheese melt. Sprinkle corn mixture with flour and stir until blended. Remove from heat and stir in milk, chilies, cayenne, and salt to taste. Beat eggs with corn mixture to blend.

Pour mixture into a buttered 2-inch-deep 7- by 12-inch casserole. Bake, uncovered, in a 350° oven until center is firm when pressed and edges are browned, 55 to 65 minutes. Serves 12.

PER SERVING: 173 calories, 7.8 g protein, 16 g carbohydrates, 9.5 g fat, 93 mg cholesterol, 212 mg sodium

Fragrant Refreshments from Lemon Grass

A STAPLE HERB *in many Southeast Asian cuisines, lemon grass has the fragrance of lemon peel but with more complex and tantalizing floral overtones. It often adds interest to spicy curries or stir-fries, and to pungently seasoned soups and salads.*

Western cooks have welcomed lemon grass, using it in both Asian and nontraditional ways. These three simple refreshments each incorporate a syrup infused with lemon grass. The first is an exotic lemonade, the second a fruit salad, and the third a cool, frosty ice.

Fresh lemon grass is widely available in Asian markets and well-stocked produce stores and supermarkets; a handful (about 8 stalks) costs as little as $1. The herb keeps up to 1 month in the refrigerator.

LEMON GRASS LEMONADE

5 cups water
1 cup lemon grass syrup (recipe follows)
6 tablespoons lemon juice

In a 7- to 8-cup pitcher, mix water, lemon grass syrup, and lemon juice. Cover and chill up to next day. Pour into ice-filled glasses. Makes 1½ quarts, 6 to 8 servings.

PER SERVING: 132 calories, 0 g protein, 32 g carbohydrates, 0 g fat, 0 mg cholesterol, 3.5 mg sodium

Lemon grass syrup. Cut off leafy top and peel tough outer layer from 3 stalks of fresh **lemon grass.** Trim off and discard discolored or dry part of root ends. Cut trimmed, woody sections into 2-inch lengths and crush lightly with a mallet, or thinly slice crosswise.

In a 1- to 1½-quart pan, combine lemon grass and 1 cup *each* **sugar** and **water.** Bring to a boil over high heat; simmer, uncovered, until reduced to 1 cup, about 30 minutes. Cool; if made ahead, cover and chill up to 2 weeks. Discard grass before using syrup. Makes 1 cup.

PER TABLESPOON: 48 calories, 0 g protein, 12 g carbohydrates, 0 g fat, 0 mg cholesterol, 0.1 mg sodium

LEMON GRASS SYRUP WITH FRUIT

2 cups mixed berries (blueberries, raspberries, hulled strawberries), rinsed and drained
½ cup lemon grass syrup (preceding)
1 small (about 2 lb.) honeydew melon or cantaloupe, peeled and seeded
   Pieces of lemon grass leaves, 4 to 5 inches long (optional)

If using strawberries, slice them. Mix berries in a bowl with lemon grass syrup. Cut melon into 18 wedges; fan 3 on each of 6 dessert plates. Spoon berries onto melon slices. Garnish with leaves. Serves 6.

PER SERVING: 122 calories, 0.8 g protein, 31 g carbohydrates, 0.3 g fat, 0 mg cholesterol, 12 mg sodium

Long stalks of fresh lemon grass look and feel coarse. Peel off toughest outer layer; use light-colored woody interior.

LEMON GRASS ICE

Pour 1 cup cold **lemon grass syrup** (preceding), 1 cup cold **water,** and 2 tablespoons **lemon** or lime **juice** into container of an ice cream maker (self-refrigerated, or use 1 part salt and 12 parts ice). Freeze until dasher no longer turns. Serve, or cover and store in freezer up to 1 month. Makes about 1½ quarts, 5 to 6 servings.

PER SERVING: 129 calories, 0 g protein, 33 g carbohydrates, 0 g fat, 0 mg cholesterol, 1.4 mg sodium

Syrup made from lemon grass flavors lemonade, fresh fruit, and refreshing ice. Herb has fragrance of lemon peel but more complex overtones.

More August Recipes

OTHER AUGUST RECIPES *include a party salad combining sweet pears and arugula with hazelnuts, and colorful turkey and tomato kebabs served with a clam sauce.*

HAZELNUT, PEAR & ARUGULA SALAD

Contrasting flavors and textures complement one another in this simple party salad. Sweet, buttery Bartlett pears and the delicate fruitiness of raspberry vinegar tame the peppery taste of arugula leaves. A hazelnut flavor—from both chopped nuts and hazelnut oil—further enhances the combination.

Look for arugula with salad greens or fresh herbs in the market, and for hazelnut oil with the oils or fancy foods.

- ⅓ cup **hazelnuts,** coarsely chopped
- 2 tablespoons **hazelnut** or **salad oil**
- ¼ cup **raspberry vinegar** or **rice vinegar**
- 2 medium-size (about ¾ lb. total) firm-ripe **Bartlett** or other **pears**
- 8 cups (about 6 oz., or 10 oz. with stems) lightly packed **arugula leaves** or **watercress leaves,** rinsed and crisped
- **Salt** and freshly ground **pepper**

Place hazelnuts in a 6- to 8-inch frying pan over medium-high heat. Stir or shake until nuts are toasted, 3 to 4 minutes. Pour from pan and let cool.

In a salad bowl, whisk together the hazelnut oil and raspberry vinegar. Halve, core, and thinly slice pears into bowl; add arugula. Gently mix with dressing to coat. Divide among 6 to 8 salad plates; sprinkle evenly with nuts. Season to taste with salt and pepper. Serves 6 to 8.—*Amey Shaw, Maltese Grill, San Francisco.*

PER SERVING: 95 calories, 1.5 g protein, 9.5 g carbohydrates, 6.8 g fat, 0 mg cholesterol, 9 mg sodium

TURKEY KEBABS WITH CLAM SAUCE

Shellfish with fowl make a lightened-up version of the old lobster-and-beef (surf-and-turf) combination. In this case, a piquant clam sauce, made with canned clams, complements the mild flavor of grilled cubes of turkey breast.

- 1 can (6½ oz.) **minced clams**
- 2 tablespoons **salad oil**
- 1 teaspoon **ground sage**
- ½ teaspoon **dry thyme leaves**
- 2 pounds **boneless turkey breast,** cut into 1½-inch cubes
- 24 **cherry tomatoes**
- **Clam sauce** (recipe follows)

Drain clam juice into a bowl; reserve clams. To juice add oil, sage, thyme, and turkey; mix well. Cover and chill at least 1 hour or up to 6 hours.

Thread turkey and tomatoes alternately on 6 to 8 skewers. Place on a grill 4 to 6 inches above a solid bed of hot coals (you can hold your hand at grill level only 2 to 3 seconds) until meat is white in center (cut to test), 9 to 12 minutes; turn to brown evenly. Place on a platter; offer sauce to add to taste. Serves 6 to 8.—*Roxanne Chan, Albany, Calif.*

PER SERVING: 166 calories, 26 g protein, 1.4 g carbohydrates, 5.2 g fat, 70 mg cholesterol, 106 mg sodium

Clam sauce. Mix ¾ cup **sour cream;** reserved **clams** (see above); 1 can (4¼ oz.) **chopped black ripe olives,** drained; ¼ cup chopped **green onions;** and 2 crisp-cooked **bacon strips,** crumbled.

PER TABLESPOON: 33 calories, 1.4 g protein, 0.9 g carbohydrates, 2.6 g fat, 6.8 mg cholesterol, 62 mg sodium

Threaded on skewers, cubes of turkey breast and bright cherry tomatoes grill in just a few minutes. Serve kebabs with a piquant sour cream–clam sauce.

Yogurt-dressed fruit and cottage cheese make a handsome salad.

PINEAPPLE, STRAWBERRY & APPLE SALAD

- 1 medium-size (about 3 lb.) pineapple
- 1 small Gravenstein or other apple, rinsed
- 1 cup coarsely chopped strawberries
- ⅓ cup unflavored or lemon-flavor yogurt
- 8 to 16 medium-size lettuce leaves, rinsed and drained
- 8 whole strawberries, rinsed and drained
- 1 cup small-curd cottage cheese

Cut peel and eyes from pineapple. Cut off ⅓ of the pineapple at narrow end; trim out and discard core, then chop fruit. Put chopped fruit into a bowl. Cut remaining pineapple lengthwise into 8 wedges, trimming off core.

Core apple and cut into ½-inch pieces. Add apple, chopped strawberries, and yogurt to chopped pineapple; mix gently. If made ahead, cover fruits and chill up to 4 hours.

Arrange lettuce, pineapple wedges, whole strawberries, cottage cheese, and chopped fruit mixture equally on 8 salad plates. Makes 8 servings. —*Valerie Kleinman, Monument, Colo.*

PER SERVING: 92 calories, 4.4 g protein, 16 g carbohydrates, 1.8 g fat, 4.5 mg cholesterol, 15 mg sodium

Chinese-style egg pancake gets Italian flavors.

ITALIAN-STYLE EGG FOO YUNG

- ½ pound mild Italian sausage, casings removed
- ½ cup shredded carrot
- ½ cup *each* thinly sliced green onion, celery, and green bell pepper
- 4 large eggs
  About 4 teaspoons salad oil
- 1 cup homemade or purchased spaghetti sauce, heated

In a 10- to 12-inch nonstick frying pan over medium-high heat, crumble sausage. Stir often until browned, about 12 minutes; discard fat. Add carrot, onion, celery, and bell pepper; stir just until limp, about 2 minutes. Pour into a bowl; let cool. Beat in eggs to blend.

Rinse and dry pan; return to medium-high heat. Add about 1 teaspoon oil; when pan is hot, ladle batter into it in ¼-cup portions. Spread each portion into a 3½-inch round with back of spoon; do not crowd. Cook until rounds are lightly browned on bottom, then turn with a wide spatula and brown other side. Remove rounds from pan. Repeat until all mixture is cooked, adding oil to prevent sticking. Serve with spaghetti sauce to add to taste. Makes 4 servings, 2 or 3 rounds each. —*Lyn McNeel, Tularosa, N.M.*

PER SERVING: 331 calories, 16 g protein, 14 g carbohydrates, 23 g fat, 245 mg cholesterol, 773 mg sodium

Pink shrimp, green pea pods make colorful stir-fry.

SHRIMP & PEA POD STIR-FRY

- 1 pound medium-size (43 to 50 per lb.) shrimp
- ¼ pound edible-pod peas
- 2 tablespoons soy sauce
- 1 tablespoon minced fresh ginger
- ¼ cup *each* dry sherry or water, and rice vinegar
- 1½ teaspoons cornstarch
- 2 tablespoons salad oil
- 1 cup sliced mushrooms
- 1 clove garlic, minced or pressed
  About 3 cups hot cooked rice
- ¼ cup thinly sliced green onion

Peel and devein shrimp. Remove ends and strings from peas. In a small bowl, mix together soy sauce, ginger, sherry, vinegar, and cornstarch.

Place a wok or 12-inch frying pan on high heat; add 1 tablespoon oil. When oil is hot, add mushrooms and garlic; stir-fry until mushrooms are lightly browned, about 4 minutes. Pour into a bowl. Add 1 more tablespoon oil to pan; when hot, add shrimp and stir-fry until pink and opaque in center when cut, about 3 minutes. Return mushroom mixture to pan with peas and soy mixture. Stir until sauce boils; pour over a bed of rice. Garnish with green onions. Serves 4. —*Mike Humason, Thousand Oaks, Calif.*

PER SERVING: 393 calories, 25 g protein, 51 g carbohydrates, 9 g fat, 140 mg cholesterol, 660 mg sodium

BARBECUED PORK TENDERLOIN WITH PEANUT SAUCE

2 (about 1½ lb. total) pork
  tenderloins, fat trimmed, rinsed
  and patted dry
Peanut sauce (recipe follows)
Lemon halves (optional)

Ignite 60 charcoal briquets on firegrate of
a barbecue with a lid. When coals are
ignited, push half to each side of grate.
Burn until coals are medium-hot (you
can hold your hand at grill level only 3 to
4 seconds). Or heat a gas barbecue for
indirect medium-hot cooking. Brush
meat with sauce and lay on grill (not
over coals or flame); cover barbecue and
open drafts. After 10 minutes, turn meat
and brush with sauce. Cook until a thermometer registers 155° in center of thickest part and meat is no longer pink in
center (cut to test), 10 to 15 minutes. Slice
and offer with remaining sauce and
lemon to add to taste. Serves 5 or 6. —
Maureen W. Valentine, Seattle.

PER SERVING: 291 calories, 32 g protein, 6.9 g carbohydrates, 15 g fat,
84 mg cholesterol, 506 mg sodium

Peanut sauce. In a 1- to 1½-quart pan over
medium heat, stir until bubbling ¾ cup
water; ½ cup **creamy-style peanut butter;** 2 cloves **garlic,** minced or pressed; ½
teaspoon **curry powder;** 1 tablespoon
firmly packed **brown sugar;** and 2 tablespoons *each* **lemon juice** and **soy sauce.**
Use hot or cool.

*Grilled pork
tenderloins are served
with peanut sauce.*

VEGETABLE MOUSSAKA

2 or 3 medium-size (about 1 lb.
  total) thin-skinned potatoes
1 medium-size (about 1 lb.)
  eggplant
3 medium-size (about 1 lb. total)
  zucchini, ends trimmed, thinly
  sliced
½ cup minced fresh or ¼ cup dry
  basil leaves
2 jars (6 oz. each) marinated
  artichoke hearts
½ pound shredded münster cheese

Scrub potatoes and thinly slice. Trim off
and discard eggplant stem; thinly slice
eggplant.

In an oiled 9- by 13-inch baking dish,
layer potatoes, eggplant, zucchini, and
basil; drizzle with artichoke marinade.
Cover tightly with foil. Bake in a 400°
oven until the vegetables are very tender
when pierced, about 1 hour.

Uncover and tuck artichokes among
the vegetables. Return to oven and bake,
uncovered, until the liquid evaporates,
about 30 minutes longer. Sprinkle
cheese over vegetables and bake just
until top is golden brown, about 10 minutes longer. Let stand about 10 minutes.
Makes 8 servings. — *Alice Schindall,
Poway, Calif.*

PER SERVING: 219 calories, 10 g protein, 20 g carbohydrates, 12 g fat,
27 mg cholesterol, 406 mg sodium

*Marinated and raw
vegetables bake to
make moussaka.*

PEACH & RASPBERRY CRISP

8 medium-size (about 2 lb. total)
  firm-ripe peaches, peeled and
  sliced (about 4 cups fruit)
¾ cup sugar
2 tablespoons lemon juice
½ teaspoon ground cinnamon
2 cups raspberries, rinsed and
  drained
1 cup all-purpose flour
½ cup (¼ lb.) butter or margarine
¼ teaspoon ground nutmeg
  Vanilla ice cream (optional)

In a shallow 1½- to 2-quart baking dish,
mix together peaches, ¼ cup sugar,
lemon juice, and cinnamon. Sprinkle
raspberries over peaches.

In a food processor or a bowl, whirl or
rub with your fingers the remaining
sugar, flour, butter, and nutmeg until
the mixture has the texture of coarse
cornmeal. Squeeze topping to compact,
then crumble over fruit to cover.

Bake in a 375° oven until bubbling in
center and golden brown on top, about
45 minutes. Cool at least 10 minutes;
spoon dessert, hot or cool, into bowls. If
desired, top with ice cream. Makes 8
servings. — *Rachelle Thornburgh,
Bainbridge Island, Wash.*

PER SERVING: 284 calories, 2.6 g protein, 44 g carbohydrates, 12 g fat,
31 mg cholesterol, 118 mg sodium

*Crumbled
topping
bakes golden
on fruit.*

Chefs of 🄬 the West

The Art of Cooking ... by men ... for men

THE POOR PEANUT has some awfully undignified connotations—ball games, elephants, insubstantial emoluments. But this humble legume is serious food, with high protein and fat contents (30 and 47 percent, respectively). In Earle Presten's Satay Sauce, it is taken as seriously as it deserves to be—and its flavor triumphs, despite a host of additional ingredients including such heavy hitters as garlic, ginger, jalapeño chilies, oyster sauce, soy sauce, and taco sauce.

Mr. Presten concocted his sauce for satay (or saté), a dish Indonesian in origin but sometimes found on Chinese and Indian menus, too. Simply put, satay consists of bite-size morsels of meat soaked in a spicy sauce, then grilled (or broiled) on a skewer and served with more sauce. Or you can grill the meat by itself, then add the sauce. A similar sauce also dresses cooked vegetables in an Indonesian dish known as gado gado—and you can certainly use Mr. Presten's that way, too.

SATAY SAUCE

- 1 tablespoon salad oil
- ½ cup raw peanuts
- 1 small onion, chopped
- 2 small fresh jalapeño chilies, stemmed and seeded
- 1 piece fresh ginger (about a 1-in. cube), thinly sliced
- 4 cloves garlic, quartered
- ¼ cup peanut butter
- ½ cup canned coconut cream (or ¼ teaspoon coconut extract, ¼ cup sugar, and ½ cup whipping cream)
- 1 tablespoon soy sauce
- 1 tablespoon oyster sauce (optional)
- 1 tablespoon lime juice
- ¼ cup *each* dry sherry and orange juice
- 3 tablespoons prepared taco sauce
  Grilled beef, chicken, or pork

Pour oil into an 8- to 10-inch frying pan over medium heat. When the oil is hot, add peanuts and onion and stir often until golden. Pour peanuts, onion, and oil into a blender; whirl to form a coarse

"The poor peanut has some undignified connotations, but this humble legume is serious food."

paste. Add the chilies, ginger, garlic, peanut butter, coconut cream, soy sauce, oyster sauce, lime juice, sherry, orange juice, and taco sauce; whirl until mixture is smoothly blended. If made ahead, cover and chill up to 1 week.

Pour sauce into a 1- to 1½-quart pan. Stir over medium heat until hot, about 10 minutes. Spoon onto (or serve as a dip for) grilled beef, chicken, or pork. Makes about 2⅓ cups.

PER TABLESPOON: 42 calories, 1.3 g protein, 2 g carbohydrates, 3.4 g fat, 0 mg cholesterol, 55 mg sodium

St. Helena, Calif.

CHEFS OF THE WEST ARE, *on the whole, a boastful lot who give their recipes such names as "Harold's Best-Ever Hush Puppies" or "Irving's Incomparable Garlic Fudge." Also generally not notably permissive, they insist that their directions be followed to the letter. Henry Caldwell, in contrast, is modest (within the bounds of good sense) and casual. He sends a recipe for Henry's Real Good Ribs and allows us to finish the ribs with a prepared sauce of our own choosing.*

These differ from conventional ribs in that they are first boiled in water and vinegar, then marinated in Worcestershire sauce, garlic and pepper before being finished over the coals.

HENRY'S REAL GOOD RIBS

- 4 **pounds country-style spareribs**
- ½ **cup cider vinegar**
- 2 **tablespoons Worcestershire**
- ¼ **teaspoon pepper**
- 2 **cloves garlic, minced or pressed**
  About ⅔ cup prepared barbecue sauce

Trim and discard excess fat from ribs. Put meat in a 6- to 8-quart pan, add water to barely cover, then add vinegar. Cover and bring to a boil over high heat; reduce heat, and boil gently for 20 minutes. Drain ribs and arrange in an 11- by 13-inch pan.

In a small bowl, combine Worcestershire, pepper, and garlic. Evenly brush over ribs. Cover and chill 30 minutes to 4 hours; turn ribs over several times.

In a barbecue with a lid, ignite 50 to 60 charcoal briquets on the firegrate. When coals are dotted with gray ash, push an equal amount to each side of grate. Place a metal drip pan on grate in the center. Place grill 4 to 6 inches above coals. Lay ribs on grill over drip pan. Cover barbecue, open drafts, and cook 20 minutes. Turn ribs over, brush with barbecue sauce, and continue to cook until ribs are richly glazed and thickest section of meat is no longer pink at the bone (cut to test), 15 to 20 minutes more. Baste several times with sauce. Makes 4 to 6 servings.

PER SERVING: 445 calories, 27 g protein, 5.2 g carbohydrates, 36 g fat, 104 mg cholesterol, 354 mg sodium

HENRY F. CALDWELL

Seattle

WHEN YOU HAD NO CHOICE *but to buy turkey massively whole, its use was mostly restricted to holidays. Leftovers went through a series of costume changes, but no matter how artfully they were refashioned the bits and scraps remained leftovers. As Andrea del Sarto said, a common grayness silvered all.*

Now, however, you can buy turkey in pieces and cook only as much as you want for a single meal—such as Stevie B.'s Enchiladas de Pavo.

By using tortillas and green chili salsa, Stephen Patterson is reestablishing links between the turkey and its point of origin. Native to much of North, Central, and South America, the turkey was first raised in Mexico and was, besides the dog, the only creature domesticated there.

Easy to assemble, these enchiladas are just the supper dish to prepare when you get home late in the afternoon.

"The turkey was first raised in Mexico."

STEVIE B.'S ENCHILADAS DE PAVO

- 2 **cups (¾ to 1 lb.) shredded, cooked turkey**
- 2 **cups prepared mild to hot (to taste) green chili salsa**
- 2 **cups (8 oz.) shredded sharp cheddar cheese**
- 8 **ounces lemon-flavored yogurt**
- 2 **tablespoons chopped fresh cilantro (coriander)**
- ½ **teaspoon ground cumin**
- ¼ **to ½ teaspoon crushed dried hot red chilies**
- 6 **flour tortillas (each about 8 in. in diameter)**
- 6 **large pitted ripe olives, halved lengthwise**

In a large bowl, combine turkey, 1 cup salsa, 1 cup cheese, yogurt, cilantro, cumin, and dried chilies to taste. Place tortillas on a flat surface; top evenly with turkey mixture. Roll up and place, seam down, in a greased 8- by 12-inch baking pan. Evenly top with the remaining salsa and cheese.

Bake, uncovered, in a 400° oven until cheese is bubbly and enchiladas are hot in center, 20 to 25 minutes. Top each enchilada with 2 olive halves. Makes 6 servings.

PER SERVING: 428 calories, 31 g protein, 37 g carbohydrates, 16 g fat, 85 mg cholesterol, 1,026 mg sodium

Denver

August Menus

FOR A LAZY AUGUST, *try meals that diners assemble to their own liking. For the soup supper, pick and choose the ready-to-eat ingredients from a colorful selection, then warm with steaming broth. Try the same tack on a picnic, packing sandwich makings instead of sandwiches. And let the season dictate vegetable and fruit choices for a mixed grill dinner.*

NOODLE BOWL DINNER

Self-styled Noodle Bowl
Litchis & Strawberries in Syrup
Iced Mandarin Orange Tea

Noodles in a flavorful broth with tidbits of meat, fish, and vegetables are a popular Asian choice for fast dining; here's an attractive supermarket version.

As much as a day ahead, you can cook, cut, and arrange all the condiments, including the noodles, that become part of the soup. You might also season the broth ahead, then just reheat it at serving time.

For a simple dessert for 4 to 6, chill 1 can (14 oz.) litchis, then mix fruit and syrup with 1 to 2 cups whole, hulled, rinsed strawberries; eat from small bowls.

Brew a flavored tea and pour over ice.

SELF-STYLED NOODLE BOWL

- ½ **pound dry vermicelli or capellini**
  Condiments (choices follow)
- 6 **cups regular-strength chicken broth**
- ⅓ **cup soy sauce**
- 3 **tablespoons *each* peanut butter and firmly packed brown sugar**
- 2 **tablespoons distilled white vinegar**
- 1 **teaspoon hot chili oil or ½ teaspoon crushed dried hot red chilies**
- 2 **tablespoons Oriental sesame oil**

In a 4- to 5-quart pan, bring 3 quarts water to boiling on high heat. Add vermicelli and cook, uncovered, until tender to bite, 2 to 8 minutes. Drain and cover pasta with cold water. When cool, drain pasta and divide into 4 to 6 portions; twist each portion with fingers to

Tailor soup to taste by ladling hot broth into bowls over your choice of hard-cooked eggs, cooked pasta, peas, shrimp, shredded carrots and onions, sliced cucumbers, and ham.

shape into a mound. Arrange on a platter. On platter or in separate bowls, arrange the remaining condiments. If made ahead, cover and chill up until next day.

In the same pan, combine broth, soy sauce, peanut butter, sugar, vinegar, and chili oil. Stirring occasionally with a whisk, bring to a boil on high heat. Add sesame oil and pour broth into a large bowl. While broth is very hot (you can keep it warm over a candle or on an electric warming tray), invite each person to add a portion of pasta and desired condiments to a soup bowl. Ladle hot broth into the bowl. Makes 4 to 6 servings. — *Janice McCormick, Berkeley.*

PER SERVING WITH EQUAL PORTIONS OF ALL CONDIMENTS: 483 calories, 37 g protein, 45 g carbohydrates, 19 g fat, 334 mg cholesterol, 1,482 mg sodium

Condiments: 6 hard-cooked **large eggs,** halved; 4 ounces **cooked ham,** cut into thin strips; ¾ pound **tiny cooked shrimp;** 1 large **carrot,** shredded; 1 medium-size **cucumber,** thinly sliced; ¼ pound **edible-pod peas,** ends and strings removed; 3 **green onions** (ends trimmed), including tops, slivered.

SANDWICH PICNIC

Fresh Herb Cream Cheese
Sliced Tomatoes
Sliced Red Onions
Extra-virgin Olive Oil
Crisp Lettuce
Whole-wheat Bread to Slice
Delicatessen Salads
Fruit Juice   Nectarines

At the picnic (perhaps no farther from home than the sandbox), present elements and let each person make his or her own sandwich—open-faced or closed.

Bring whole tomatoes, onions, and bread; also bring a sharp knife and a cutting board. For salads, either buy or make 1 or 2 easy travelers like a shredded carrot salad or coleslaw, allowing about ½ cup total for each serving.

To carry, pack beverages and perishables in a chilled insulated chest.

Offer bottled olive oil to drizzle over sandwiches.

Build your own picnic sandwiches, either open-faced or closed, starting with hearty whole-wheat bread and fresh herb cheese spread.

FRESH HERB CREAM CHEESE

1 large (8 oz.) package cream cheese or neufchâtel cheese
3 tablespoons *each* minced parsley and chives or green onions
1 tablespoon *each* minced fresh basil leaves and fresh tarragon leaves, or 1 teaspoon *each* of the dry herbs
1 small clove garlic, minced or pressed
Salt and pepper

In a food processor or with an electric mixer, blend cheese with parsley, chives, basil, tarragon, and garlic; add salt and pepper to taste. Mound cheese into a bowl and serve or, if made ahead, cover and chill up until next day. To transport, keep cold. Makes 1 cup, 6 servings.

PER TABLESPOON: 51 calories, 1.4 g protein, 0.6 g carbohydrates, 5 g fat, 16 mg cholesterol, 42 mg sodium

(Continued on next page)

MIXED GRILL DINNER

Cumin Vinaigrette
Stuffed Chicken Legs with
Roasted Bells
Portuguese or Polish Sausages
Sliced Yellow Tomatoes
French Bread
Watermelon Wedges

Vegetables, chicken, and sausages share space on the barbecue.

First, bell peppers go onto the grill when coals are hot. Then, when coals are cooler, you cook the chicken. About 15 minutes before chicken is done, add sausages (a total of 1 lb. for 6 servings) to heat. Splash the cumin vinaigrette to taste over chicken, peppers, sausage, and tomatoes.

CUMIN VINAIGRETTE

Combine ¼ cup *each* **white wine vinegar, extra-virgin olive oil,** and minced **shallots;** 2 tablespoons drained **capers;** and ½ teaspoon **ground cumin.** Use, or cover and chill up to 1 week. Makes about ¾ cup.

PER TABLESPOON: 43 calories, 0.1 g protein, 0.7 g carbohydrates, 4.7 g fat, 0 mg cholesterol, 37 mg sodium

STUFFED CHICKEN LEGS WITH ROASTED BELLS

½ cup *each* packed fresh cilantro (coriander), fresh basil leaves, and grated parmesan cheese
3 chicken legs (thigh and drumstick attached), about 1½ pounds total
3 large red bell peppers
Salt and pepper

In a food processor or blender, mince cilantro, basil, and cheese.

Cut a slit just through skin at joint on outside of each chicken leg. Slide your fingers between skin and meat to separate it from thigh and drumstick, but leave skin in place. Tuck cilantro mixture under skin, pushing to distribute equally.

Place peppers on a grill over a solid bed of hot coals (you can hold your hand at grill level for only 2 to 3 seconds); turn peppers as skin chars and blackens, about 15 minutes. Set peppers aside to cool.

When coals have cooked down to medium heat—about when peppers are charred (you can hold your hand at grill level for only 4 to 5 seconds)—lay chicken on grill and cook, turning as needed to brown evenly, until meat is no longer pink at thigh bone (cut to test), about 40 minutes.

Meanwhile, pull skin, stems, and seeds from bell peppers. Place peppers and chicken on a platter; cut thighs and drumsticks apart. Season to taste with salt and pepper. Makes 6 servings.

PER SERVING: 180 calories, 19 g protein, 3.2 g carbohydrates, 10 g fat, 58 mg cholesterol, 202 mg sodium

Sautéed Chicken with Sage (page 222)

Poultry takes the spotlight
this month in a comprehensive review of new ways we now
purchase and cook chicken and turkey. Learn about new cuts
available in the supermarket and easy, quick-cooking ways
to prepare them. Enjoy the last days of summer outdoors
with a grilled meat salad or rustic flat breads cooked on the
barbecue. For a change of pace, plan an afternoon tea party
featuring Southwestern flavors. Other September articles
suggest fresh ways with eggplant, beef soups, and take-along
breakfasts for commuters.

The Poultry Revolution

THE MODERN SUPERMARKET BIRD has come a long way since the 1940s, when large-scale commercial production of chickens and turkeys began in this country. Before World War II, chicken was a Sunday dinner treat, turkey graced the table only on holidays, and most poultry in the markets was sold whole.

Today, less than a quarter of chickens and turkeys make it to the counters whole; the rest are cut into selected parts or further processed into delicatessen items. The trend in fresh poultry now is toward skinned and boned pieces. This has created a new category of packaged meat cuts.

It's not surprising, then, that Americans are eating more chicken and turkey—about 85 pounds per capita last year compared to 34 pounds in 1960. Aside from the convenience of ready-to-use cuts, poultry's healthful image has certainly boosted sales in recent years. With less than 130 calories and 2 grams of fat in a 4-ounce serving, the light meats of chicken and turkey—without skin—are considerably lower in calories and fat than most red meats. Although poultry seems to have a lot of fat, there's a difference between it and other meats. Poultry's fat is almost all in the skin or just underneath, where it's easily removed; very little fat is marbled through the meat.

Economy is another reason for poultry's popularity. Production today is highly automated, with a few large firms involved in all phases, from breeding and hatching to packaging retail products. As a result, poultry prices have dropped relative to other meats.

The birds, the result of several decades of selective breeding, are raised in climate-controlled houses on scientifically formulated feed. Modern chickens reach maturity in less than 7 weeks, turkeys in 14 to 22 weeks. They are more docile, larger and younger at harvest, and more tender; they also have proportionately more breast meat than birds of the past.

The system is so efficient that it now takes less than 2 pounds of feed to produce a pound of chicken, about 2.6 pounds of feed to produce a pound of turkey (cattle and sheep, on the other hand, require about 8 pounds of feed to produce the same weight). The yield of cooked meat for turkey—55 to 60 percent of the live weight—tops the yield of all other meats.

Poultry's nearly boundless culinary possibilities have long appealed to good cooks. And now the new boned and skinned cuts—made to order for quick, low-fat meals—are even better suited to the needs of today's busy cooks.

HOW TO COOK THE NEW CUTS

The new poultry cuts call for updated techniques to make the most of their quick-cooking convenience and to maximize the value of their low fat content.

Here we present flexible and easy ways to cook boned and skinned cuts of chicken and turkey. Each recipe is based on 1 pound of meat from any of the boneless or boned and skinned cuts shown and described on the facing page. You'll also find two recipes featuring ground poultry. All recipes use minimal amounts of added fat.

Nutritional data with each recipe are based on chicken breast. Figures here compare the nutritional composition of ¼ pound of light and dark chicken and turkey meats. You can use them to calculate the nutritional content of the poultry you cook.

CHICKEN BREAST MEAT: 125 calories, 26 g protein, 1.4 g fat, 66 mg cholesterol

CHICKEN THIGH MEAT: 135 calories, 22 g protein, 4.4 g fat, 94 mg cholesterol

TURKEY, LIGHT MEAT: 129 calories, 27 g protein, 1.8 g fat, 70 mg cholesterol

TURKEY, DARK MEAT: 139 calories, 23 g protein, 4.7 g fat, 85 mg cholesterol

1 PAN-FRYING

Poultry sliced or pounded to ¼-inch thickness cooks in 2 to 3 minutes.

SAUTÉED CHICKEN OR TURKEY WITH SAGE

- 1 **pound boned, skinned chicken or turkey**
- 2 **teaspoons minced fresh or dry sage leaves**
- 12 **fresh whole sage leaves (optional)**
  About 2 teaspoons olive oil or salad oil
  Pepper and salt
- 2 **limes or lemons, halved**

Prepare poultry of your choice (directions follow). Sprinkle prepared poultry equally with minced sage on a cut side of each piece, pressing into meat. If using fresh whole sage leaves, turn pieces over and press leaves onto surfaces.

Place a 10- to 12-inch frying pan over medium-high heat. When hot, add 2 teaspoons oil and tilt pan to coat bottom. Fill pan with meat (whole leaf side or dry sage side down) without crowding. Cook until golden on bottom, about 1½ minutes. Turn pieces and cook until no longer pink in center (cut to test), 30 to 60 seconds longer. Repeat until all pieces are cooked, adding more oil if needed to prevent sticking. Keep warm on a platter as cooked. Grind pepper over meat. Add salt and lime to taste. Makes 4 servings.

PER SERVING WITH CHICKEN BREAST: 156 calories, 26 g protein, 3.7 g carbohydrates, 3.8 g fat, 66 mg cholesterol, 74 mg sodium

To prepare poultry, rinse, pat dry, and place all pieces to be pounded between sheets of plastic wrap. Pound chicken breast halves or thighs until ¼ inch thick. Use thinly sliced turkey breast as is, or pound thicker slices until ¼ inch thick. Split turkey tenderloins lengthwise, cutting away tendon in center, then pound until ¼ inch thick. Pound turkey thigh to ¼ inch, letting it separate at natural seam lines; divide into serving-size pieces.

(Continued on page 224)

Today's Chicken & Turkey Cuts

MOST SELF-SERVICE MARKETS featuring packaged poultry now carry a variety of boned products, but these vary somewhat from store to store. Poultry counters where you can place an order often sell turkey tenderloins, boned turkey and chicken breasts, and occasionally boned turkey thighs.

Some markets may be willing to bone a turkey breast or thigh for you. If not, bone-in poultry breasts and thighs are readily available and easy to bone yourself; we provide illustrated instructions for boning your own turkey and chicken cuts on pages 228–229.

Boned, skinned chicken breast halves (or fillets) are usually sold with three or four half-breasts (about 4 oz. each) to a package. Bone-in breast halves weighing 6 to 6½ ounces each will yield about 4 ounces meat.

Boned, skinned chicken thighs (or fillets) and **thigh-drumstick combinations** are typically sold in 1-pound packages. Use smaller drumstick pieces interchangeably with thighs. It takes 1¾ to 2 pounds bone-in thighs for 1 pound meat.

Turkey tenderloins (or fillets). Each is a boneless whole muscle from the inside center of a breast half. Large tenderloins (about 8 oz. each) are usually sold 2 to a package, smaller ones 3 or 4 to a package. When split lengthwise, these pieces may be called **tenderloin steaks.**

Turkey breast slices (or cutlets) are thin crosswise slices cut from boned, skinned breast; they're typically ⅛ to ⅜ inch thick. **Breast steaks** are about ½ inch thick.

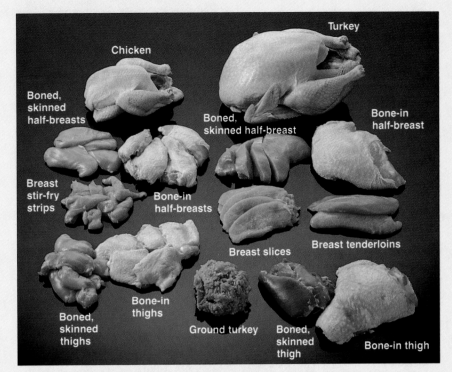

Quick-to-cook boned and bone-in pieces of chicken and turkey, as well as ground meat from breasts and thighs, greatly increase choices when buying poultry.

Boned turkey breast half (or roast) is sold with or without the skin. One half usually provides meat for several recipes. It takes 1¼ to 1⅓ pounds of bone-in breast to yield about 1 pound of meat.

Boned turkey thigh. It takes a medium-size (about 1½-lb.) bone-in thigh to yield 1 pound meat.

Chicken or turkey breast strips (sometimes called stir-fry strips, tenders, or chicken tenderloins) are boneless pieces ready to use for stir-frying.

Ground turkey and chicken. Most is primarily dark meat and has less than 15 percent fat (ground beef can be as high as 30 percent). Ground chicken has a milder taste than turkey and is usually slightly moister in texture; both products resemble ground beef. Use either meat in our recipes.

2 MICROWAVE

Use these directions any time you want cooked boneless poultry for salads, sandwiches, or other dishes. Here we offer one way to present the cooked meat in a cool main dish.

MICROWAVE POULTRY PLATTER WITH BULGUR

- 1 **pound boned, skinned chicken or turkey**
- 1 **cup bulgur (cracked wheat)**
- 2 **cups boiling water**
- ¾ **cup lime juice**
- ½ **cup minced red-skinned apple**
- 2 **tablespoons sugar**
- 2 **tablespoons minced tomato**
- 2 **teaspoons anchovy paste or 1 anchovy fillet, minced**
- 1 **teaspoon crushed dried hot red chilies**
- 2 **cloves garlic, minced**
- ½ **cup minced fresh mint or parsley**
- ¼ **cup olive oil or salad oil Salt**
- 1 **large head (about 1½ lb.) romaine lettuce, rinsed and crisped Lime wedges and fresh mint leaves (optional)**

Cook poultry in a microwave oven (directions follow). Cover cooked meat and chill until cold or up to 2 days. Drain meat.

Rinse bulgur, then pour into a bowl and add boiling water. Let bulgur stand, covered, until grains are tender to bite and most of the liquid is absorbed, about 1 hour.

Meanwhile, combine lime juice, apple, sugar, tomato, anchovy, chilies, and garlic. Thinly slice the cold poultry and arrange equally on 4 dinner plates; spoon about half the dressing over meat. Add mint and olive oil to remaining dressing.

Drain bulgur, mix with remaining dressing, add salt to taste, then spoon equally onto plates beside the meat. Reserve large romaine leaves for other

Crisp romaine makes edible holder for microwave-cooked turkey, bulgur salad.

uses; arrange smaller leaves on plates. Garnish with lime and mint leaves. To eat, scoop bulgur and poultry onto romaine leaves. Serves 4.

PER SERVING WITH CHICKEN BREAST: 432 calories, 33 g protein, 42 g carbohydrates, 16 g fat, 66 mg cholesterol, 134 mg sodium

Poultry cooked in the microwave oven. Rinse and pat dry 1 pound boned and skinned poultry. Arrange cut of your choice (see list below) in a single layer in a 9-inch square or round microwave-safe dish. Cover with microwave-safe plastic wrap and cook on full power (100 percent) until meat is no longer pink in center of thickest part (cut to test); see suggested cooking times with each choice below. If meat is not done, continue to cook on full power; check at 1-minute intervals.

Chicken breast halves. Fold thin ends under and press pieces to make evenly thick in dish. Cook on full power for 5 minutes; after 2½ minutes, turn pieces over. Let stand, covered, for 5 minutes.

Chicken thigh. Roll pieces into compact shapes and arrange in dish. Cook on full power for 7 minutes; after 3½ minutes, reverse pieces so center parts face outward. Let stand, covered, for 5 minutes.

Turkey breast. Press the meat (in 1 piece) to make evenly thick in dish. Cook on full power for 9 minutes; after 4½ minutes, turn piece over. Let stand, covered, for 5 minutes.

Turkey tenderloins. Cut each in half lengthwise, trimming away tendon in center. Place pieces in dish, fold thin ends under, and press to make as evenly thick as possible. Cook on full power for 8 minutes; after 4 minutes, reverse pieces so center parts face outside. Let stand, covered, for 5 minutes.

Turkey thigh. Lay flat in dish. Fold thin parts under; press thicker parts to make evenly thick. Cook on full power for 9 minutes; after 4½ minutes, rotate pan a half-turn. Let stand, covered, for 5 minutes.

3 NUGGETS

Here's a way to brown skinned poultry without adding many calories.

ROASTED THAI POULTRY NUGGETS

- 1 **pound boned, skinned chicken or turkey**
- 3 **tablespoons minced fresh cilantro (coriander)**
- 2 **teaspoons coarsely ground pepper**
- 8 **cloves garlic, minced**
- ⅓ **cup (part of an 8-oz. can) tomato sauce**
- 1 **tablespoon *each* firmly packed brown sugar and distilled white or cider vinegar**
- ½ **cup raisins**

Prepare poultry of your choice (directions follow). Rub poultry with a mixture of cilantro, pepper, and 6 cloves garlic. Place pieces well apart in an ungreased 10- by 15-inch baking pan.

Bake in a 500° oven until meat is lightly browned and no longer pink in center (cut to test). Allow 12 to 15 minutes for chicken breast, 18 to 20 minutes for chicken thigh, 10 to 12 minutes for turkey breast or tenderloin, and 15 to 18 minutes for turkey thigh.

Meanwhile, in a food processor or blender, whirl remaining garlic, tomato sauce, brown sugar, vinegar, and raisins

Spicy-sweet Thai flavors mingle in crisp coating and sauce for roasted nuggets.

until raisins are chopped. Serve with nuggets. Makes 4 servings.

PER SERVING WITH CHICKEN BREAST: 210 calories, 28 g protein, 22 g carbohydrates, 1.6 g fat, 66 mg cholesterol, 200 mg sodium

To prepare poultry, rinse pieces and pat dry. Cut each chicken breast half diagonally across grain into 2 equal pieces; tuck thin ends under. Roll each chicken thigh into a compact shape. Cut turkey breast or thigh into 8 equal-size pieces no more than 1½ inches thick. Cut turkey tenderloins in half lengthwise, trimming off the tendon; divide into 8 equal-size pieces.

4 STEEPING

This gentle, low-temperature poaching method results in succulent poultry. Lively seasonings distinguish the salad or sandwiches; serve meat either warm or cold.

STEEPED POULTRY WITH CHILI & ANISE

- 1 **pound boned, skinned chicken or turkey**
- 4 **cups water**
- 2 **cups regular-strength chicken broth**

- ¼ **cup New Mexico or regular chili powder**
- ¼ **cup firmly packed brown sugar**
- 2 **teaspoons dry oregano leaves**
- 1 **star anise or 1 teaspoon anise seed**
- 3 **tablespoons** *each* **olive oil and red wine vinegar**
- 2 **tablespoons** *each* **chopped fresh cilantro (coriander) and minced green onion**

Prepare poultry cut of your choice (directions follow). In a 4- to 5-quart pan with tight-fitting lid, combine water, broth, chili powder, brown sugar, oregano, and anise; bring to boiling. Remove pan from heat and immediately add poultry pieces, opened out flat. Cover pan and let stand (do not lift cover until ready to test) until meat is no longer pink in center (to test, lift out of water and cut), 15 to 20 minutes. If not done, return meat to hot water, cover, and let steep slightly longer, testing after 2 to 3 minutes. Drain meat, reserving 2 cups liquid. Boil liquid in pan on high heat, uncovered, until reduced to ⅓ cup—watch carefully to prevent scorching as liquid becomes concentrated.

Serve warm; or to serve cold, cover meat and liquid and chill up to 2 days. Mix liquid with olive oil, vinegar, cilantro, and green onion. Cut poultry pieces across the grain into thin, slanting slices and serve with the dressing in salad or sandwiches (directions follow). Makes 4 servings.

To prepare poultry, rinse, pat dry, and place all pieces to be pounded between sheets of plastic wrap. Use chicken breast halves or thighs as is. Cut 1-pound turkey breast across grain into 1-inch-thick pieces. Or pound whole turkey tenderloins or turkey thigh until ½ to ¾ inch thick.

For salad, arrange meat on washed and crisped large **butter lettuce leaves** (8 to 12) on each of 4 plates; spoon dressing over salad. Garnish with **pickled red chilies,** Spanish-style olives, or cilantro sprigs.

PER SERVING WITH CHICKEN BREAST: 263 calories, 27 g protein, 10 g carbohydrates, 13 g fat, 66 mg cholesterol, 124 mg sodium

Baguette sandwiches feature moist, tender slices of steeped turkey and savory dressing.

For sandwiches, split 1 long, slender **baguette** (about 8 oz.) lengthwise, and then cut in quarters crosswise (or split 4 French bread rolls, 6-in. size); moisten cut surfaces evenly with dressing. Fill the bread with meat and 8 to 12 washed and crisped large **butter lettuce leaves.**

PER SERVING WITH CHICKEN BREAST: 428 calories, 33 g protein, 42 g carbohydrates, 14 g fat, 68 mg cholesterol, 453 mg sodium

5 BARBECUING

Our first presentation features spicy, glazed meat and green onions threaded on skewers. In the second, prosciutto and romaine leaves enclose poultry, trapping juices to keep meat moist during grilling.

POULTRY KEBABS WITH ONION BANNERS

- 1 **pound boned, skinned chicken or turkey**
- ⅓ **cup orange marmalade**
- 2 **tablespoons Dijon mustard**
  About 12 green onions
  Salt and lemon wedges

Prepare poultry of your choice (directions follow). Mix poultry in a bowl with marmalade and mustard. Trim onion ends to make 6 inches long. Alternately thread meat and onions (through white part only, so green ends hang free) onto 4 skewers, beginning and ending with meat.

Place skewers on a lightly greased grill 4 to 6 inches above a bed of medium coals (you can hold your hand at grill level only 4 to 5 seconds). Let onion ends extend on grill beyond coals to prevent burning. For gas grills, follow manufacturer's directions for direct cooking at medium.

Cook until meat is no longer pink in center (cut to test); turn to brown evenly, and baste with remaining marmalade mixture. Allow 15 to 18 minutes for chicken or turkey breast, 20 to 25 minutes for chicken or turkey thigh or turkey tenderloin. Add salt and lemon to taste. Serves 4.

PER SERVING WITH CHICKEN BREAST: 224 calories, 28 g protein, 25 g carbohydrates, 2 g fat, 66 mg cholesterol, 306 mg sodium

To prepare poultry, rinse meat and pat dry. Cut chicken or turkey breast or turkey thigh into 1½-inch cubes. Roll each chicken thigh into a compact shape. Cut turkey tenderloins in half lengthwise, trimming away tendon; cut meat into 1½-inch cubes.

GRILLED POULTRY IN ROMAINE WRAPS

> **1 pound boned, skinned chicken or turkey**
> **Green dressing (recipe follows)**
> **Salt and pepper**

Prepare wrapped poultry (directions follow), then place on a grill 4 to 6 inches above a bed of medium coals (you can hold your hand at grill level only 4 to 5 seconds). For gas grills, follow manufacturer's directions for direct cooking at medium.

Turn meat occasionally until it is no longer pink in center (cut to test). Or use an instant-read thermometer and cook until breast meat at center of thickest part is 160° and thigh meat at center of

Romaine-wrapped turkey tenderloin is grilled; serve with green herb dressing.

thickest part is 180° to 185°. Allow about 20 minutes for chicken breast, 20 to 25 minutes for turkey breast or tenderloin, 25 to 30 minutes for chicken or turkey thighs.

Cut meat across grain into 1-inch-thick slices. Arrange slices, cut side up, equally on 4 dinner plates. Add dressing and salt and pepper to taste. Makes 4 servings.

PER SERVING WITH CHICKEN BREAST: 159 calories, 30 g protein, 0.4 g carbohydrates, 3 g fat, 76 mg cholesterol, 341 mg sodium

To wrap poultry, select cut desired (following); rinse and pat dry. You will need a total of 4 thin slices (about 2½ oz.) **prosciutto** and 2 large, 4 medium-size, or 8 small **romaine lettuce leaves** (size depends on poultry used). In a 10- to 12-inch frying pan, bring about 1 inch **water** to boiling. Plunge romaine into water for 1 minute. Lift out and immerse in cold water until cool. Drain and pat dry.

Wrap each of 4 chicken breast halves in 1 slice prosciutto and 1 medium-size romaine leaf. Roll each chicken thigh (roughly 8) into a compact shape and wrap in a half-slice of prosciutto and 1 small romaine leaf. Cut a turkey breast piece or thigh into 4 equal-size logs, 1 to 1½ inches thick; wrap each in 1 slice prosciutto and 1 medium-size romaine leaf. Wrap each of 2 large (about 8 oz. each) turkey tenderloins in 2 slices prosciutto and 1 large romaine leaf.

Green dressing. In a blender or food processor, purée ⅓ cup **olive oil** or salad oil, ¼ cup **white wine vinegar,** 2 tablespoons minced **onion,** 1 tablespoon minced **parsley,** and 2 teaspoons *each* minced **fresh sage** and **thyme leaves** (or ¾ teaspoon *each* of the dry herbs). Makes ½ cup.

PER TABLESPOON: 81 calories, 0 g protein, 0.6 g carbohydrates, 8.9 g fat, 0 mg cholesterol, 0.3 mg sodium

6 STIR-FRYING

Choose from two different sauces to season stir-fried poultry strips and onions.

STIR-FRIED POULTRY ON BITTER GREENS

> **1 pound boned, skinned chicken or turkey**
> **2 to 3 tablespoons olive oil or salad oil**
> **1 small onion, cut into 1-inch squares**
> **Caper sauce or sherry-oyster sauce (recipes follow)**
> **About 4 cups rinsed and crisped arugula, watercress, Belgian endive, or a combination of greens**

Prepare poultry of your choice (directions follow). Cut larger poultry pieces into 1-inch squares. Place a 12-inch frying pan or wok over high heat. When hot, add 1 tablespoon olive oil and onion; stir-fry until onion edges are brown, about 2 minutes. Pour onion into a bowl.

Add 1 tablespoon oil to pan, then half the poultry in a single layer; cook on high heat until it begins to brown, about 1 minute. Turn pieces over and cook until no longer pink in center (cut to test), about 30 seconds; add to onion. Repeat with remaining poultry; add oil if needed to prevent sticking.

Add sauce to pan; stir to free browned bits. If using caper sauce, boil until reduced to ¼ cup. Just heat sherry-oyster

Bitter greens are foil for stir-fried chicken and onions served with caper sauce.

sauce. Remove from heat and stir in poultry mixture. Distribute greens equally on 4 dinner plates; spoon meat over greens. Makes 4 servings.

PER SERVING WITH CHICKEN BREAST, CAPER SAUCE: 198 calories, 28 g protein, 1.7 g carbohydrates, 8.5 g fat, 66 mg cholesterol, 209 mg sodium

PER SERVING WITH CHICKEN BREAST, SHERRY-OYSTER SAUCE: 225 calories, 28 g protein, 5 g carbohydrates, 8.2 g fat, 66 mg cholesterol, 625 mg sodium

To prepare poultry, rinse pieces, pat dry, and place all meat to be pounded between sheets of plastic wrap. Use chicken or turkey stir-fry strips or chicken tenderloins as is. Pound chicken breast halves or thighs until ¼ inch thick. Pound turkey breast slices until ¼ inch thick, if needed. Cut turkey tenderloins lengthwise, cutting away tendon in center; cut ¼-inch slices across grain. Cut turkey thigh across the grain into ¼-inch slices.

Caper sauce. Mix ¾ cup **regular-strength chicken broth**, 1 tablespoon **lemon juice**, and 2 tablespoons drained **capers**.

Sherry-oyster sauce. Combine 3 tablespoons *each* **dry sherry** and **Oriental oyster sauce**, 1 clove **garlic** (minced), and ¾ teaspoon minced **fresh ginger** or ⅓ teaspoon ground ginger.

7 GROUND MEAT

You can serve either the patties or meatballs in meal-size sandwiches. Or try meatballs in curry soup.

POULTRY PATTIES OR MEATBALLS

  1 **pound ground turkey or chicken**
  ⅓ **cup catsup or tomato-based chili sauce**
  ⅓ **cup fine dry bread crumbs**
  1 **large egg**
  1 **tablespoon olive oil or salad oil (optional)**
  4 **English muffins or hamburger buns, split and toasted; or 4 pocket bread rounds, cut in half crosswise**
    Condiments of your choice
    Salt

In a bowl, mix ground turkey, catsup, crumbs, and egg. Form mixture into 4 patties (about ¾ in. thick) or into 24 meatballs (about 1-in. diameter).

To cook patties, place a 10- to 12-inch frying pan over medium-low heat. When hot, add oil and tilt pan to coat bottom. Add the patties and cook until browned on bottom. Turn with a wide spatula and continue to cook until bottom is browned and patties are no longer pink in center (cut to test), about 20 minutes total. Serve in muffins with condiments; add salt to taste. Makes 4 servings.

To cook meatballs, place meat in a well-greased 10- by 15-inch baking pan. Bake in a 500° oven until lightly browned, about 10 minutes. Fill pocket bread halves equally with the meatballs and condiments; add salt to taste. Makes 4 servings, 2 sandwiches each.

PER SERVING, GROUND TURKEY PATTIES AND NO CONDIMENTS: 385 calories, 26 g protein, 33 g carbohydrates, 16 g fat, 139 mg cholesterol, 620 mg sodium

PER SERVING, GROUND TURKEY MEATBALLS AND NO CONDIMENTS: 410 calories, 28 g protein, 49 g carbohydrates, 11 g fat, 136 mg cholesterol, 781 mg sodium

Ground turkey balls and vegetables mingle in meal-size bowl of curry soup.

MILD CURRY SOUP

  1 **tablespoon salad oil**
  2 **tablespoons raisins**
  1¾ **teaspoons curry powder**
  ½ **teaspoon dry thyme leaves**
  5 **cups regular-strength chicken broth**
  12 **baby carrots, peeled (or ¾ cup thinly sliced carrots)**
  ½ **cup fresh or frozen shelled peas**
  24 **cooked poultry meatballs (see preceding recipe); or 1 pound boned, skinned chicken or turkey, rinsed and patted dry, then cut into ¼-inch-wide strips**
    Parsley sprigs (optional)

Pour oil into a 3- to 4-quart pan over medium heat. When hot, add raisins, curry powder, and thyme; stir until spices begin to sizzle, about 30 seconds. Add broth, carrots, peas, and meat.

Bring to a boil, then simmer until vegetables are tender and meatballs are warm in center (or strips are no longer pink in center; cut to test), 10 to 15 minutes. Garnish with parsley. Serves 4 to 6.

PER SERVING WITH GROUND TURKEY: 231 calories, 18 g protein, 15 g carbohydrates, 11 g fat, 91 mg cholesterol, 329 mg sodium

How to Bone Poultry Parts

OW-FAT POULTRY DISHES *like the quick* *entrées on pages 222 to 227 call for boned, skinned pieces of turkey or chicken. Most supermarkets carry a selection of ready-to-use cuts such as turkey breast slices and boned chicken breasts and thighs. But if you're willing to do some simple boning yourself, you can take advantage of the less-expensive bone-in cuts. As a bonus, you can save the left-over bones and skin and use them to flavor homemade soups.*

Turkey half-breasts and thighs and chicken thighs are widely available and especially easy to bone, as we show on the facing page. All you need are a sharp boning or short, narrow-bladed knife and a cutting board. You can also follow these directions to bone a whole turkey breast or chicken breast. In addition, we suggest you review the information at right on safe handling of poultry.

To bone a whole turkey breast. Follow directions on facing page for boning a half-breast, but remove skin first. Place breast on work surface, skinned side up, and cut along one side of breastbone ridge; repeat on other side.

To bone a whole chicken breast. Holding breast with skin side down, firmly grasp each end. Bend ends backward until soft, dark-colored breastbone snaps. Run your fingers underneath and pull out breastbone and cartilage. Cut breast in half lengthwise with a sharp, sturdy knife, slicing through wishbone. Working with one breast side at a time, insert knife over long first rib; then cut meat from ribs as directed for half-breast on facing page.

HOW TO HANDLE POULTRY SAFELY

In poultry-processing plants—even those with the highest standards of sanitation—bacterial contamination cannot be completely eliminated. Bacteria exist in all living things, in air, in water, and on all surfaces.

Two types of bacteria can cause trouble in raw poultry. One type causes meat to rot or spoil; these bacteria also affect taste and usually create "off" odors as warning signals that the meat shouldn't be eaten. The second type of bacteria causes food poisoning; these usually can't be seen, smelled, or tasted. When present in sufficient numbers, they cause illnesses that are sometimes severe.

Most bacteria thrive at room or warmer temperatures, but grow very slowly in a refrigerator. Small populations can survive almost everything except cooking. A few simple precautions prevent contamination and keep the bacteria from multiplying enough to cause harm.

Keep poultry cold. Pick up meat last when shopping; store it in coldest part of the refrigerator as soon as possible. Don't hold at room temperature more than 3 hours. Thaw frozen poultry in the refrigerator. To thaw faster, immerse in cold water; change water often. Or thaw in a microwave oven, following manufacturer's directions.

Avoid cross-contamination. After handling raw meat, wash hands, work surface, and utensils with hot soapy water before exposing them to other foods—especially foods eaten without cooking. Periodically wipe meat-cutting boards with household bleach, then rinse well.

Cook poultry adequately. For small cuts, cook until meat in the thickest part is no longer pink. For large cuts and whole birds, a thermometer should register 160° at breastbone or in center of thickest part of boneless white meat and 180° to 185° in dark meat. (Harmful bacteria in poultry are killed at 140°, but the meat isn't palatable for most tastes unless cooked further.) Don't interrupt cooking; if meat does not reach at least 140° internally, any bacteria present can resume growing as the meat cools.

Keep hot foods hot. If you need to delay serving cooked foods, keep them between 140° and 165° (about the temperature of a chafing dish); don't hold them at room temperature for more than 2 hours. Put cooked made-ahead dishes or leftovers in refrigerator as soon as they stop steaming; don't cool them first at room temperature.

How long can you store fresh poultry? Many packaged products include a date on the label that indicates how long the product will remain at optimum freshness. With the right handling and temperature, most fresh chicken or turkey can be refrigerated safely for up to 2 days after that date. If poultry is to be kept longer, freeze it immediately. You can cover and refrigerate cooked poultry up to 4 days; if in broth or sauce, keep no longer than 2.

Turkey Half-Breast

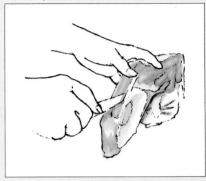

Place breast on work surface with the ridge of the breastbone facing up and ribs down. Insert knife along top edge of the breastbone and work it over the long first rib.

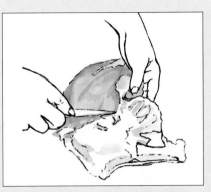

Follow contour of breastbone and rib cage as you cut and peel meat away from the bones. Cut and scrape meat from wishbone to free boned breast in one piece.

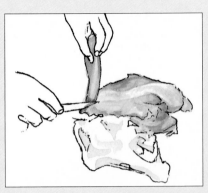

Lift out tenderloin, a long lengthwise strip of meat (usually darker-colored) in center on boned side of breast. Pull off skin; cut membrane if needed. Trim and discard fat.

Turkey or Chicken Thigh

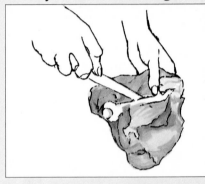

Lay thigh skin side down. Cut down to thighbone along its length, then cut on each side of bone from joint to joint.

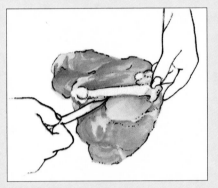

Slip knife under the bone and work it down and around the joint on one end, cutting it free.

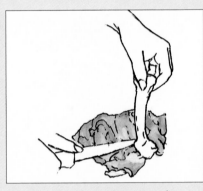

Grasp free end of bone and cut it away from meat up to and around second joint. Slice off cartilage at one end of thigh meat. Remove skin and fat.

Flat Breads Baked on the Barbecue

BAKING BREAD *over a fire was a routine chore among early-day cooks. Using the barbecue, you can still capture the rustic character of breads baked this way—and have fun watching them cook. Two that work very well are Italian pizza and Indian nan—both flat, round loaves that cook in just a few minutes.*

Here we use frozen white or whole-wheat bread dough, but you can also start with 1 pound homemade basic bread dough. For pizzas, top grilled rounds with vegetables, herbs, fruits, meat, or cheese. Make one kind or let guests fashion their own combinations.

To create a simplified version of the Indian sandwich, grill yogurt-marinated chicken breasts over medium-hot coals; then bake the bread when the coals have cooled some. Wrap the chewy bread around the chicken, and add yogurt-mint sauce and cucumber to taste.

Cooking over medium heat is the secret to baking on the grill. The time you can keep your hand at grill level is a fairly accurate gauge—4 to 5 seconds indicates medium temperature. If coals are too hot, the bread scorches before cooking.

To start barbecue fire. About 45 minutes before cooking, spread a solid single layer of charcoal briquets over the firegrate of a barbecue with a lid. Mound briquets, ignite, and let burn until coals are just covered with gray ash, about 45 minutes. Spread into an even layer; put grill in place 4 to 6 inches above coals.

GRILLED INDIVIDUAL PIZZAS

1 loaf (1 lb.) frozen whole-wheat or
  white bread dough, thawed
About 2 tablespoons olive oil
Toppings (choices follow)
Salt and pepper

Start barbecue fire (directions precede).

On a floured board, divide dough into 4 equal pieces; shape each into a ball. Roll out each to make a 5- to 6-inch-wide round. Brush top with olive oil and place, oil down, onto a piece of foil (about 10 by 12 in.). Lightly brush top with oil. With hands, flatten round to ⅛ inch thick and 7 to 8 inches wide. Let stand, uncovered, at room temperature until slightly puffy, 15 to 25 minutes.

Flavorful choices top grilled bread rounds to make individual pizzas. Clockwise from right: tomato and pesto, nectarine and basil, pepperoni and pepper, blue and white cheeses. Cooking over medium heat is the secret to baking on the grill; if coals are too hot, bread scorches.

Transport rounds (with foil) in a single layer on 12- by 15-inch baking sheets.

When coals are medium (you can hold your hand at grill level only 4 to 5 seconds), lift foil supporting a bread round; flip over to put dough on the grill. Peel off and discard foil. Repeat, placing rounds slightly apart. Cook until golden brown on bottom, 2 to 3 minutes.

With a wide spatula, transfer bread rounds to baking sheets, browned side up. Cover with topping choices; return to grill. Cover barbecue with lid, open vents, and cook until toppings are hot and bottom of bread is crisp and flecked with brown, 3 to 4 minutes. Remove from grill; add salt and pepper to taste. Serves 4.

Tomato & pesto topping. For each pizza, cut 1 large **Roma-type tomato** lengthwise into ½-inch slices. Place on a grill 4 to 6 inches above a solid bed of hot coals (you can hold your hand at grill level only 2 to 3 seconds) until browned on both sides, about 5 minutes. Set aside.

Spread 1 bread round with 2 tablespoons **pesto sauce** (homemade or prepared). Top with grilled tomato slices and ½ cup shredded **mozzarella cheese.**

PER SERVING: 691 calories, 23 g protein, 62 g carbohydrates, 40 g fat, 54 mg cholesterol, 946 mg sodium

Nectarine & basil topping. For each pizza, thinly slice 1 small pitted firm-ripe **nectarine** and mix with ½ teaspoon **balsamic** or seasoned rice **vinegar** and 1 teaspoon **extra-virgin olive oil.**

Top 1 bread round with ⅓ cup shredded **jack cheese** and 2 tablespoons finely shredded **parmesan cheese.** With a slotted spoon, scatter nectarines over cheese. Sprinkle with 2 tablespoons finely shredded **fresh** or ½ teaspoon dry **basil leaves** and 1 tablespoon **pine nuts.**

PER SERVING: 713 calories, 26 g protein, 74 g carbohydrates, 37 g fat, 46 mg cholesterol, 934 mg sodium

Pepperoni & pepper topping. For each pizza, top 1 bread round with ½ cup shredded **kuminost cheese;** ¼ cup well-drained canned **roasted red peppers,** cut into ½-inch-wide strips; and 8 thin slices (about ¾ oz.) **pepperoni sausage.**

PER SERVING: 695 calories, 27 g protein, 58 g carbohydrates, 39 g fat, 72 mg cholesterol, 1,297 mg sodium

Blue & white cheese topping. For each pizza, top 1 bread round with ½ cup shredded **münster cheese,** 3 table-

To form bread, roll dough into ¼-inch-thick round. Brush with oil, set on foil, and flatten to ⅛ inch; let rise. Flip dough onto grill and peel off foil. Cook until golden on bottom.

spoons crumbled **blue cheese,** and 1 tablespoon thinly sliced **chives** or green onions.

PER SERVING: 663 calories, 27 g protein, 55 g carbohydrates, 37 g fat, 79 mg cholesterol, 1,257 mg sodium

INDIAN-STYLE CHICKEN SANDWICHES

    1 cup unflavored nonfat yogurt
    1 teaspoon curry powder
    ¼ teaspoon cayenne
    1 clove garlic, pressed or minced
    4 skinned and boned chicken breast
       halves (about 4 oz. each), rinsed
       and patted dry
    2 tablespoons chopped fresh or dry
       mint leaves
    ½ teaspoon cumin seed
    1 loaf (1 lb.) frozen whole-wheat or
       white bread dough, thawed
    2 tablespoons salad oil
    1 small cucumber, peeled and
       thinly sliced
       Fresh mint sprigs (optional)
       Salt and pepper

In a bowl, mix ⅓ cup yogurt, curry powder, cayenne, and garlic with chicken to coat. Mix ⅔ cup yogurt, chopped mint, and cumin. If made ahead, cover both and chill up to 24 hours.

Start the barbecue fire (directions precede).

On a floured board, divide dough into 4 equal pieces and shape each into a ball. Roll out each ball into a 5- to 6-inch-wide round. Brush top with oil and place, oil side down, onto a piece of foil (about 10 by 12 in.). Lightly brush top with oil.

With your hands, flatten round to ⅛ inch thick and 7 to 8 inches wide. Let stand, uncovered, at room temperature until slightly puffy, 15 to 25 minutes.

Transport rounds (with foil) in a single layer on 12- by 15-inch baking sheets.

When coals are medium-hot (you can hold your hand at grill level only 3 to 4 seconds), lift chicken from marinade and place on grill. Cook, turning once, until chicken is white in thickest part (cut to test), about 10 to 12 minutes total. Remove from grill; keep warm.

When coals have cooled to medium (you can hold your hand at grill level for 4 to 5 seconds), lift foil supporting a bread round; flip over to put dough onto grill. Peel off and discard foil. Repeat with remaining rounds.

When dough is golden on bottom, 2 to 3 minutes, turn over with a wide spatula; cook until bottom is golden but still pliable, 2 to 3 minutes longer.

Transfer chicken, bread, cucumber, and yogurt sauce to a platter. To eat, place chicken in a warm bread round; add yogurt sauce, cucumber, mint sprigs, and salt and pepper to taste; fold bread over to enclose. Makes 4 servings.

PER SERVING: 531 calories, 38 g protein, 60 g carbohydrates, 14 g fat, 73 mg cholesterol, 667 mg sodium

Add yogurt-mint sauce to barbecued chicken breast and cucumber in grilled bread round; fold to eat as sandwich.

Salad Bowl Meal for Four

A STUDY IN COMPLEMENTS, *each of these artful arrangements combines a grilled meat with vegetables, fruit, or grain; a distinctive dressing adds the finishing touch. Serve as a main-dish salad for four on a hot September day.*

For convenience, you can grill meats and prepare many parts of the salads ahead.

A wide, shallow bowl or rimmed platter shows off ingredients best. You can add seasonings and mix the salad, or let guests design their own salads and add dressing to taste.

FRUIT & BARLEY BEEF SALAD

1 pound boneless lean beefsteak, such as eye of the round, cut 1 inch thick; or 1 pork tenderloin, ¾ to 1 pound, trimmed of fat

½ cup slivered almonds

¾ cup pearl barley, rinsed and drained

3 cups regular-strength chicken broth

2 heads (about 1½ lb. total) butter lettuce, rinsed and crisped
  Orange dressing (recipe follows)

2 cups seedless grapes, halved

1 cup pitted dried prunes, cut into ½-inch pieces

1 cup thin, diagonally cut celery slices

2 cups (3 oz.) loosely packed watercress, rinsed and crisped
  Salt

Place meat on a grill, 4 to 6 inches above a solid bed of hot coals (you can hold your hand at grill level only 2 to 3 seconds). Cook, turning to brown evenly, until beef is browned on both sides but still pink in center of thickest part (cut to

Three main-dish salads focus on cold, thin-sliced barbecued meats. From left, beef (or pork), grapes, prunes, and barley with orange dressing; turkey, cantaloupe, and cucumbers with honey marinade; steak, potatoes, carrots, and bell peppers with garlic sauce.

test), 15 to 20 minutes total. Or cook pork until no longer pink in thickest part (cut to test), about 25 minutes. Let cool. If made ahead, cover and chill up until next day.

In a 2- to 3-quart pan, stir almonds over medium-low heat until toasted, about 8 minutes. Pour out nuts.

Add barley and broth to pan. Bring to a boil; cover and simmer until tender to bite, about 25 minutes. Drain and let cool. If made ahead, cover nuts and barley; chill barley up until next day.

Line a wide, shallow serving bowl with lettuce. Thinly slice meat and arrange in about ⅓ of the bowl. Moisten meat with about 1 tablespoon of the orange dressing. Mix barley with half the remaining dressing and mound in bowl beside meat. Mix grapes, prunes, celery, watercress, and remaining dressing; mound mixture in bowl.

Mix, or let guests take some of each element. Offer toasted almonds and salt to add to taste. Serves 4. —*Mrs. L.K. Ross, Elk Grove, Calif.*

PER SERVING: 754 calories, 39 g protein, 88 g carbohydrates, 30 g fat, 61 mg cholesterol, 167 mg sodium

Orange dressing. Mix together ⅓ cup thawed **frozen orange juice concentrate,** ¼ cup **salad oil,** and ½ teaspoon **pepper.**

TURKEY, CANTALOUPE & CUCUMBER SALAD

1¼ pounds turkey breast tenderloins (fillets)
    Honey marinade (recipe follows)
1 medium-size (2½ to 3 lb.) cantaloupe

(Continued on next page)

Lettuce leaves, rinsed and crisped (optional)
1 medium-size (about 1¼ lb.) European cucumber, thinly sliced
Lime wedges (optional)
Fresh basil sprigs (optional)
½ cup minced fresh basil leaves
⅓ cup thinly sliced green onion
Salt and pepper

Rinse turkey and pat dry. Pour ½ cup marinade into a plastic food bag; add turkey, seal bag, and rotate to coat with marinade. Set bag in a pan and chill 30 minutes or up until next day; turn it over occasionally.

Reserve remaining marinade; cover and chill up until next day.

Lift turkey from marinade and discard liquid. Place turkey on a grill 4 to 6 inches above a solid bed of medium coals (you can hold your hand at grill level only 4 to 5 seconds).

Basting with about 2 tablespoons reserved marinade and turning often, cook until turkey is white in thickest part (cut to test), about 20 minutes. Let cool. If made ahead, cover and chill up until next day.

Meanwhile, seed and peel cantaloupe; cut into ½-inch-thick wedges. Line about ⅓ of a wide, shallow serving bowl with lettuce leaves; pile cantaloupe wedges onto lettuce. Thinly slice turkey and arrange beside melon. Arrange cucumber slices between meat and melon. Garnish with lime wedges and basil sprigs.

Add minced basil and green onion to remaining marinade. Mix with salad or let guests select salad elements, adding marinade to taste. Season with salt and pepper. Serves 4.

PER SERVING: 279 calories, 36 g protein, 20 g carbohydrates, 6.6 g fat, 88 mg cholesterol, 114 mg sodium

Honey marinade. Mix together ½ cup *each* **seasoned rice vinegar** (or ⅓ cup cider vinegar and 2 tablespoons water) and **lime juice,** ¼ cup **extra-virgin olive oil,** and 1 tablespoon *each* **honey** and **hot chili oil** (or ½ teaspoon cayenne).

PER TABLESPOON: 36 calories, 0 g protein, 12 g carbohydrates, 3.7 g fat, 0 mg cholesterol, 1.7 mg sodium

STEAK & POTATO SALAD

6 medium-size (about 1½ lb. total) thin-skinned potatoes
2 medium-size (about ½ lb. total) carrots
Marinated beef (recipe follows)
Garlic sauce (recipe follows)
1 *each* small green and red bell pepper
1 head (about ½ lb.) romaine lettuce, coarse leaves discarded, rinsed and crisped
¼ cup finely diced red onion
Salt
Coarsely ground pepper

Scrub potatoes well, then put them in a 5- to 6-quart pan. Add water to cover potatoes. Cover pan and bring water to boiling over high heat. Reduce heat and simmer until potatoes are very tender when pierced, 35 to 40 minutes. Lift potatoes from water with a slotted spoon and let cool; if made ahead, cover and chill up until next day.

Meanwhile, peel and thinly slice carrots on the diagonal.

Bring water in pan back to a boil and add carrots. Cook just until tender to bite, about 5 minutes. Drain and let cool; if made ahead, cover and chill up until next day.

Lift steak from marinade and discard liquid. Place steak on a grill over a solid bed of hot coals (you can hold your hand at grill level only 2 to 3 seconds). Cook, turning to brown evenly, just until meat is still red in center for rare (cut to test), 15 to 20 minutes. Let cool; if made ahead, cover and chill up until next day.

Peel potatoes and cut into ½-inch cubes. In a small bowl, mix half the garlic sauce with potatoes. Thinly slice the meat.

Stem, seed, and thinly slice the green and red bell peppers.

Line about ⅓ of a wide, shallow serving bowl with 4 or 5 large lettuce leaves; tear remaining leaves into bite-size pieces and put in bowl beside leaves. Mound carrots and bell peppers on leaves; neatly arrange meat beside vegetables, then mound potatoes next to meat. Sprinkle onion on potatoes. Either pour remaining garlic sauce over salad and mix, or let guests select elements

of the salad and add dressing and salt and pepper to taste. Serves 4. —*Rose R. Ramsay, Ashland, Ore.*

PER SERVING WITHOUT ADDITIONAL GARLIC SAUCE: 605 calories, 31 g protein, 46 g carbohydrates, 33 g fat, 80 mg cholesterol, 761 mg sodium

Marinated beef. Put 1 piece (about 1 lb.) **fat-trimmed tender beefsteak,** such as sirloin or rib eye, cut 1 inch thick, in a plastic food bag and add ½ cup **red wine vinegar** and ¼ cup *each* **olive oil** and **soy sauce.** Seal bag and rotate several times to mix ingredients. Chill meat at least 30 minutes or up until next day; turn steak over occasionally.

Garlic sauce. Smoothly stir together ¼ cup **red wine vinegar,** 1 tablespoon **sugar,** 2 teaspoons minced or pressed **garlic,** and ¾ cup **mayonnaise.** If made ahead, cover and chill up until next day. Makes 1 cup.

PER TABLESPOON: 78 calories, 0.1 g protein, 1.3 g carbohydrates, 8.2 g fat, 6.1 mg cholesterol, 59 mg sodium

BREADSTICKS TO MATCH SALADS

Complement each salad, preceding, with bread seasoned one of three ways.

2 slender baguettes (½ lb. each), cut lengthwise into quarters
About ⅓ cup olive oil
Seasonings (choices follow)

Lay wedges crust side down and slightly apart on 12- by 15-inch baking sheets. Mix oil with seasonings and brush lightly on cut edges of bread. Bake in a 400° oven until golden brown, about 8 minutes. Alternate pan positions after 5 minutes. Serves 4 to 6.

PER SERVING: 324 calories, 6.9 g protein, 42 g carbohydrates, 14 g fat, 0 mg cholesterol, 439 mg sodium

Seasonings. To go with **fruit and barley beef salad,** mix oil with 1 tablespoon **coarsely ground pepper** and lightly sprinkle bread wedges with **coarse** or kosher **salt.** To go with **turkey, cantaloupe, and cucumber salad,** add to oil 2 tablespoons *each* **minced fresh dill** and **fresh cilantro** (coriander). To go with **steak and potato salad,** add to oil 2 tablespoons *each* minced **fresh oregano leaves** and **fresh rosemary leaves.**

Eggplant Appetizer & Sandwich

*S*MOOTH AND CREAMY *oven-roasted eggplant slices form a mellow base for bold cheeses and seasonings.*

Try slices crowned with tangy chèvre cheese, dried tomatoes, and rosemary as a knife-and-fork appetizer or first course.

Replace bread with roasted eggplant rounds for open-faced cheese-and-onion sandwiches lavished with a chunky, chili-spiked avocado salsa. Once the eggplant is cooked, both dishes go together in a few minutes.

EGGPLANT APPETIZER WITH CHÈVRE

- 1 medium-size (about 1 lb.) eggplant
- 3 tablespoons oil from dried tomatoes packed in oil, or olive oil
- ½ pound chèvre cheese, thinly sliced
- ¼ cup drained dried tomatoes packed in oil, cut in strips
- 1 tablespoon chopped fresh or dry rosemary leaves
  Freshly ground pepper
  Fresh rosemary sprigs (optional)

Trim off eggplant stem. Cut eggplant crosswise into ½-inch-thick slices. Lay slices in a single layer in a lightly oiled 10- by 15-inch baking pan. Brush tops lightly with the oil. Bake in a 450° oven until browned and very soft when pressed, 20 to 25 minutes.

Divide cheese among eggplant slices, breaking it to fit on top of each round. Return to oven and continue baking until cheese is warm to touch, about 2 minutes. With a wide spatula, carefully transfer to a platter. Distribute tomatoes and chopped rosemary evenly over slices; sprinkle with pepper to taste. Drizzle any remaining oil over cheese. Garnish with rosemary sprigs. Serve warm or at room temperature. Makes 4 or 5 servings.

PER SERVING: 300 calories, 9.7 g protein, 11 g carbohydrates, 25 g fat, 42 mg cholesterol, 543 mg sodium

Dried tomatoes, rosemary, and chèvre are placed on sliced rounds of oven-roasted eggplant to create robust-tasting appetizers.

EGGPLANT SANDWICH WITH AVOCADO SALSA

- 1 medium-size (about 1 lb.) eggplant
- 2 to 3 tablespoons olive oil
- ¼ pound sliced münster cheese
- 4 thin slices red onion, separated into rings
  Avocado salsa (recipe follows)
  Fresh cilantro (coriander) sprigs

Trim off eggplant stem. Cut eggplant crosswise into ½-inch-thick slices. Lay slices in a single layer on a lightly oiled 10- by 15-inch baking pan. Brush tops lightly with olive oil. Bake in a 450° oven until browned and very soft when pressed, 20 to 25 minutes.

Top each eggplant slice with cheese, trimming slices to fit. Return to oven until cheese melts, about 3 minutes. With a wide spatula, carefully transfer rounds equally onto 4 dinner plates. Place ¼ of the onion and ¼ of the avocado salsa over each portion. Garnish with cilantro sprigs. Makes 4 servings.

PER SERVING: 275 calories, 9.4 g protein, 14 g carbohydrates, 22 g fat, 22 mg cholesterol, 191 mg sodium

Avocado salsa. Peel, pit, and dice 1 large (about ½ lb.) firm-ripe **avocado.** Add 2 tablespoons **lime juice;** 1 medium-size firm-ripe **tomato,** cored and coarsely chopped; 2 tablespoons chopped **fresh cilantro** (coriander); and 1 to 2 tablespoons chopped **fresh hot chili** to taste.

Beef Soups

SLOWLY SIMMERED *or quickly cooked, beef soups fit the bill for satisfying main dishes that suit different cooking schedules.*

When you expect to be home for a few hours, let beef shank soup bubble away untended. Then chill up to several days before adding the finishing touches. Because there is so much natural gelatin in shanks, the chilled broth softly thickens. It can be served cold or steaming hot.

For a fast meal, stir-fry tender beef chunks and serve in a hot seasoned broth.

BEEF SHANK SOUP, HOT OR COLD, WITH PICKLED BEETS & SOUR CREAM

- 5 pounds beef shanks, in 1½-inch-thick slices
  About 9 cups regular-strength beef broth
- 1 large (about ¾ lb.) onion, chopped
- 1 medium-size (about ½ lb.) turnip, peeled and chopped
- 1 large (about 6 oz.) carrot, sliced
- ½ cup chopped parsley
- 4 cloves garlic, peeled and sliced
- 2 dry bay leaves
- 8 black peppercorns
- ¾ cup pearl barley, rinsed
- 1 can (15 oz.) pickled beets—diced, julienne, or sliced
- 1 cup sour cream or unflavored nonfat yogurt
  Lemon wedges
  Salt and pepper

In an 8- to 10-quart pan, combine shanks, broth, onion, turnip, carrot, parsley, garlic, bay, and peppercorns; bring mixture to a boil over high heat. Reduce heat and simmer, covered, until meat is very tender when pierced, about 2½ hours.

With a slotted spoon, put shanks in a bowl; set aside. Line a colander with muslin or a double layer of cheesecloth; set in a large bowl. Pour broth into colander and drain, then lift cloth ends and gather to close; twist cloth to remove as much liquid as possible. Discard residue. Skim fat from broth; measure broth and add more broth as needed to make 5 cups. Rinse pan; add broth and barley. Bring to a boil on high heat, then cover and simmer until tender to bite, about 40 minutes.

Meanwhile, when shanks are cool enough to touch, discard bones and gristle. Break meat into ½-inch chunks.

Cover and chill meat. Separately cover and chill broth until fat on broth hardens, about 8 hours or up to 2 days. To speed process, set pan of broth in ice (in the sink or a large bowl) and stir occasionally; add more ice to replace what melts. Lift or spoon off solid fat and discard.

If soup is to be served cold, the broth should be gelled softly. If it is firm, stir over medium heat just until it barely begins to liquefy at edges, then remove from heat and stir until pan feels cold. Add meat.

To serve soup hot, add meat to broth and place over high heat until simmering.

Drain beets; if using slices, dice. Put beets and sour cream into small bowls. Ladle cold or hot soup into wide bowls; to each, add beets, sour cream, lemon, and salt and pepper to taste. Makes 6 to 8 servings.

PER SERVING: 543 calories, 43 g protein, 34 g carbohydrates, 26 g fat, 95 mg cholesterol, 292 mg sodium

BISTRO BEEF SOUP

- 1 medium-size (about 6 oz.) white onion, quartered
- ¼ cup olive or salad oil
- ½ pound thin-skinned potatoes, peeled and cut into ½-inch cubes
- ½ pound carrots, thinly sliced
- ½ teaspoon coarsely ground pepper
- 4 cups regular-strength beef broth
- 1 pound boneless, fat-trimmed tender beef steak, such as rib eye, about 1 inch thick
- 2 tablespoons red wine vinegar
- ⅓ cup minced parsley, chives, or basil leaves, or a combination
  Basil sprigs (optional)

Thinly slice 2 onion quarters; chop remaining onion.

In a 4- to 5-quart pan over medium heat, combine 2 tablespoons oil, chopped onion, potato, carrots, and pepper; cover. Stir occasionally until onions are golden, about 15 minutes. Add broth to vegetables; cover and simmer until potatoes are tender to bite, about 12 minutes more.

Meanwhile, cut meat into ½- by 1-inch cubes. Place a 10- to 12-inch nonstick frying pan over high heat. Add remaining oil; when hot, add beef and sliced onion, about ¼ at a time. Stir-fry until meat is lightly browned but still pink in center (cut to test), about 4 minutes. With a slotted spoon, transfer mixture as cooked to soup bowls. Stir vinegar in frying pan to release browned bits; pour into broth along with herbs. Ladle broth into bowls. Garnish with basil sprigs. Makes 4 servings. —*Atwater's Restaurant, Portland.*

PER SERVING: 407 calories, 26 g protein, 22 g carbohydrates, 24 g fat, 67 mg cholesterol, 106 mg sodium

Spoon pickled beets and sour cream onto softly gelled beef shank and barley soup. Soup can be made up to several days in advance; serve it either hot or cold.

A Southwestern Tea Party

CONTEMPORARY FLAVORS *of the South-west inspired this tea party menu. Serve for the traditional Mexican meri-enda—a late-afternoon refreshment—or as a light meal at any hour.*

TAOS TEA-TIME

Chili-Corn Scones
Jack Cheese
Lime Marmalade   Tomatillo Jam
Black Bean Salsa
Cucumber & Jicama Slices
Skewered Watermelon Chunks
Brown Sugar Masa Shortbreads
Iced or Hot Hibiscus-flavor Tea

Chilies give the corn scones a gentle bite; serve them with slices of jack cheese and a choice of the more exotic preserves available in supermarkets, such as lime marmalade and tomatillo jam or cactus and jalapeño jellies.

Spoon the mellow bean salsa onto slices of cucumber and jicama, adding lime juice to taste. Munch seeded chunks of water-melon with corn tortilla–flavor short-breads. For the tea, use any herbal mixture with hibiscus (noted on the label); the flower gives tea a bright pink color.

You can make the cookies several days ahead, the meal several hours ahead.

CHILI-CORN SCONES

2½ cups all-purpose flour
2 teaspoons baking powder
1½ teaspoons crushed dried hot red chilies
¼ teaspoon ground nutmeg
½ cup (¼ lb.) butter or margarine, cut into chunks
2 large eggs
1 small can (8¾ oz.) creamed corn
¼ cup sugar

In a food processor or large bowl, whirl or mix flour, baking powder, chilies, and nutmeg. Add butter; whirl or rub with your fingers until coarse crumbs form.

Beat eggs, creamed corn, and sugar to blend. Add to flour mixture and stir just until evenly moistened.

Scrape dough onto a floured board, dust lightly with flour, and knead 6 to 8 turns. Flour board well and roll dough ½ inch thick. With a floured 2½-inch-diameter cutter, cut rounds from dough

and place slightly apart on an ungreased 12- by 15-inch baking sheet.

Or, divide dough in half and shape each into a ball. Pat each ball into a ½-inch-thick round. Set rounds 2 inches apart on an ungreased 12- by 15-inch baking sheet. With a floured knife, cut each round not quite through to form 6 equal wedges.

Bake in a 400° oven until golden, 20 to 25 minutes. Serve hot or cool; if made ahead, package airtight and hold up until the next day. Makes about 14 rounds, or 12 wedges.

PER ROUND: 178 calories, 3.6 g protein, 24 g carbohydrates, 7.6 g fat, 48 mg cholesterol, 188 mg sodium

BLACK BEAN SALSA

1 can (about 15 oz.) black beans
2 tablespoons lime juice
⅓ cup minced fresh cilantro (coriander)
½ cup diced white onion
    About ¼ pound (about 3 small) Roma-type tomatoes, cored
    Salt and pepper
    Cilantro sprigs
    About 2 tablespoons crumbled feta cheese (optional)

Drain beans, reserving 1 tablespoon liquid. Place reserved liquid and half the beans in a bowl. Add lime juice and mash the beans until smooth. Stir in remaining beans, minced cilantro, and onion.

Cut tomatoes in half crosswise and squeeze gently to push out seeds. Chop tomato and add to bean mixture. Season with salt and pepper to taste. If made ahead, cover and chill up to 4 hours.

To serve, spoon into a small bowl, gar-nish with cilantro sprigs, and sprinkle with cheese. Makes 2 cups.

PER TABLESPOON: 14 calories, 0.8 g protein, 2.7 g carbohydrates, 0.1 g fat, 0 mg cholesterol, 52 mg sodium

BROWN SUGAR MASA SHORTBREADS

½ cup sweetened shredded dry coconut
1 cup *each* dehydrated masa flour (corn tortilla flour) and all-purpose flour
1 cup firmly packed dark brown sugar

Southwestern tea includes hibiscus-flavored tea, chili-corn scones, skewered watermelon, cheese, masa shortbreads, cucumber and jicama slices, black bean salsa, and preserves.

1 cup (½ lb.) butter or margarine, cut into chunks
1 teaspoon vanilla
¼ cup granulated sugar mixed with ¼ teaspoon ground cinnamon

In a blender or food processor, whirl coconut until finely ground. In pro-cessor or a large bowl, combine coconut, masa flour, all-purpose flour, and brown sugar; whirl or stir to mix. Add butter and vanilla; whirl or rub with fingers until dough holds together. With floured hands, pat dough into a ball. If made ahead, cover and chill up to 3 days; use at room temperature.

Divide dough into 24 equal pieces. With floured hands, roll each piece between palms into a 2½-inch-long log. Place about 1 inch apart on ungreased 12- by 15-inch baking sheets. With fore-finger and thumb, pinch ends of each cooky to form points. Then, with fore-fingers or thumbs close together, impress centers.

Bake in a 300° oven until golden brown and firm (press lightly to test), about 50 minutes (if using more than 1 pan, alternate pan positions halfway through baking). Immediately sprinkle hot cookies evenly with cinnamon-sugar mixture; cool on pans. Serve, or store air-tight in the refrigerator up to 5 days. Makes 2 dozen.

PER COOKY: 157 calories, 1.1 g protein, 20 g carbohydrates, 8.4 g fat, 21 mg cholesterol, 85 mg sodium

Malfatti: Italian-Style Dumplings

RICOTTA CHEESE *is the basis for these Italian-style dumplings, which make a wholesome main dish. The mixture resembles ravioli filling—giving credibility to the story of how the dish was born.*

It is speculated that, long ago in Italy, some ravioli lost their jackets while cooking; the result was decried as malfatti ("badly made"). But a wise cook found virtue in the results and skipped the dough deliberately next time around.

MALFATTI

1 package (10 oz.) thawed frozen chopped spinach

1 cup low-fat, part-skim, or regular ricotta cheese

About ½ cup freshly grated parmesan cheese

1 cup fine dry bread crumbs

¼ cup minced green onions (with tops)

3 tablespoons chopped fresh or 2½ teaspoons dry basil leaves

2 large eggs

1 clove garlic, minced or pressed

¼ teaspoon ground nutmeg
About ½ cup all-purpose flour
About 1⅔ cups homemade or purchased (1 jar, 14-oz. size) pasta sauce with meat

Put spinach in a colander; press with back of a spoon to remove excess liquid. In a large bowl, beat to blend the spinach, ricotta cheese, ¼ cup parmesan cheese, crumbs, onions, basil, eggs, garlic, and nutmeg. Divide mixture into 16 equal portions. With your hands, form spinach mixture, a portion at a time, into smooth 3-inch-long logs. Roll each log lightly in flour and place, so logs sit slightly apart, on a baking sheet (about 12- by 15-in. size). If made ahead, cover spinach logs airtight and chill up until next day.

In a 1- to 2-quart pan over medium heat, stir pasta sauce occasionally until steaming; keep warm.

Meanwhile, in a 5- to 6-quart pan, bring about 3 inches water to boiling over high heat. Reduce heat and add malfatti; simmer uncovered until malfatti look dry in centers (cut to test), about 8 minutes. With a slotted spoon, transfer malfatti to dinner plates or a platter; spoon pasta sauce over and around the dumplings. Offer with additional parmesan cheese to add to taste. Makes 4 servings, 4 malfatti each.—*Ida Duren, Watsonville, Calif.*

PER SERVING: 478 calories, 24 g protein, 56 g carbohydrates, 18 g fat, 136 mg cholesterol, 1,153 mg sodium

Plump malfatti—ricotta cheese laced with spinach, onions, and herbs, then poached—are tender morsels served in red pasta sauce. Top with grated parmesan cheese.

Carry-Along Breakfasts

WHOLESOME SPREADS *and hearty breads are the makings of a carry-along breakfast for the commuter or anyone else on a tight schedule. These nutritious spreads keep for several days in the refrigerator.*

APPLE-NUT SPREAD

Try this on toasted cinnamon-raisin or oat bran bread.

- ½ cup chopped almonds
- 1 cup unsweetened applesauce
- ¾ cup small-curd cottage cheese
- 1 tablespoon grated orange peel
- 1 teaspoon ground cinnamon
- ¼ teaspoon ground nutmeg
  About 2 tablespoons sugar

In a 6- to 8-inch frying pan, stir almonds over medium-high heat until golden, about 4 minutes. Pour from pan.

In a food processor or blender, whirl to a smooth purée the applesauce, cottage cheese, orange peel, cinnamon, and nutmeg; scrape container sides often. Stir in almonds and sugar to taste. Cover and chill at least 2 hours or up to 3 days. Makes 2 cups.

PER TABLESPOON: 32 calories, 1.4 g protein, 3 g carbohydrates, 1.7 g fat, 1 mg cholesterol, 27 mg sodium

Commuter takes advantage of wait-for-the-train pause to eat a pack-along breakfast.

Pack-along breakfast contains juice, fruit, and peanut butter–cream cheese mixture spread on bran muffin halves.

PEANUT BUTTER SPREAD

Swirl this on whole-wheat toast or a split bran muffin to make a breakfast sandwich; top with small chunks of banana.

- ½ cup peanut butter
- 1 small package (3 oz.) cream cheese, at room temperature
- 2 teaspoons honey (optional)

With a mixer or spoon, smoothly blend peanut butter, cream cheese, and honey to taste. Use, or cover and chill up to 3 days. Makes ¾ cup.

PER TABLESPOON: 88 calories, 3.6 g protein, 1.9 g carbohydrates, 7.9 g fat, 7.8 mg cholesterol, 71 mg sodium

YOGURT-GRANOLA SPREAD

Choose any fruit-flavored yogurt and any kind of granola you like. Spoon the mixture into half-rounds of pocket bread to eat neatly out of hand; bring along an apple to complete the meal.

- 1 cup fruit-flavored yogurt
- 1 cup granola

Mix together the yogurt and granola. Cover and chill at least 2 hours or up to 2 days. Makes about 1½ cups.

PER TABLESPOON: 32 calories, 1 g protein, 4.7 g carbohydrates, 1 g fat, 0.4 mg cholesterol, 7.3 mg sodium

Bright kiwi fruit make colorful, flavorful dressing for salad greens; serve with slices of goat cheese.

GREEN SALAD WITH KIWI DRESSING

    Kiwi dressing (recipe follows)
6 **cups (about ½ lb. total, untrimmed) lightly packed, rinsed and crisped iceberg lettuce leaves**
6 **cups (about ½ lb. total, untrimmed) lightly packed, rinsed and crisped butter lettuce leaves**
8 **ounces soft ripe goat cheese**
    Salt

Pour kiwi dressing into a large salad bowl. Tear iceberg and butter lettuce leaves into bite-size pieces and place in bowl. Gently but thoroughly mix dressing with greens. Accompany individual servings with slices of cheese; add salt to taste. Makes 8 to 10 servings. —*A. Grupp, Salem, Ore.*

Kiwi dressing. Rinse, drain, peel, and cut into chunks 2 medium-size (about ½ lb. total) **kiwi fruit.** In a blender, smoothly purée kiwi with 2 tablespoons *each* **salad oil** and **white grape juice,** 2 teaspoons **lime juice,** and **sugar** to taste.

Use or, if made ahead, cover and chill up to 6 hours. Makes about 1 cup.

PER SERVING: 107 calories, 3.9 g protein, 6 g carbohydrates, 7.8 g fat, 16 mg cholesterol, 109 mg sodium

SWEET POTATO SOUP

3 **pounds (about 4 medium-size) sweet potatoes or yams, peeled and diced**
    About 6 cups regular-strength chicken broth
1½ **tablespoons curry powder**
¼ **cup tomato paste**
2 **tablespoons lemon juice**
¼ **cup dry sherry (optional)**
    Fresh cilantro (coriander) leaves (optional)
    Salt and pepper

In a 4- to 5-quart pan, combine potatoes and 6 cups broth. Bring to a boil; cover and simmer gently until potatoes are soft enough to mash readily, about 20 minutes. With a slotted spoon, transfer potatoes to a food processor or blender; add curry powder and whirl with enough broth to smoothly purée.

Pour mixture back into pan; add tomato paste, lemon juice, and sherry. If made ahead, cover and chill up until next day. Stir over medium heat until hot. Soup is thick; thin with more broth if you like. Ladle into bowls and top with cilantro. Add salt and pepper to taste. Makes 8 to 10 servings. —*Dian Burke, Boulder Creek, Calif.*

PER SERVING: 130 calories, 3.3 g protein, 27 g carbohydrates, 1.4 g fat, 0 mg cholesterol, 98 mg sodium

Curry and sherry enrich flavor of thick, smooth sweet potato soup garnished with cilantro.

Browned bacon and onions season fritter batter.

BACON & ONION FRITTERS

4 **slices bacon, finely chopped**
1 **large (about 8 oz.) onion, finely chopped**
¾ **cup all-purpose flour**
½ **cup nonfat dry milk**
1 **tablespoon toasted wheat germ**
1 **teaspoon baking powder**
1 **teaspoon dry tarragon leaves**
¼ **cup cider vinegar**
¼ **cup water**
    Salad oil

In a 10- to 12-inch frying pan over medium heat, stir bacon often until crisp, 5 to 8 minutes. With a slotted spoon, transfer bacon to paper towels; let drain. Discard all but 1 tablespoon of drippings. Add onion to pan; stir often over medium heat until golden, about 20 minutes.

In a bowl, mix flour, milk, wheat germ, baking powder, and tarragon. Add bacon, onion, vinegar, and water; stir until evenly moistened.

In a deep 3- to 4-quart pan, heat 2 inches oil to 325°. Drop batter, 1 tablespoon at a time, into oil. Cook without crowding, turning until golden, 2 to 3 minutes; drain on paper towels. Serve hot. Makes 6 to 8 servings. —*Barbara Keenan, Fort Morgan, Colo.*

PER SERVING: 163 calories, 4.3 g protein, 14 g carbohydrates, 10 g fat, 4.6 mg cholesterol, 136 mg sodium

OLD-FASHIONED BROWN BREAD

2 cups graham or whole-wheat flour
1 cup all-purpose flour
1 teaspoon baking soda
½ teaspoon salt
1 cup dark molasses
1 cup buttermilk
½ cup low-fat milk
  Cream cheese, butter, or margarine

In a small bowl, mix graham flour, all-purpose flour, baking soda, and salt; set aside. In a large bowl, combine molasses, buttermilk, and milk. Add flour mixture to molasses mixture, and stir until well blended.

Pour batter into an oiled 5- by 9-inch loaf pan. Bake in a 325° oven until bread begins to pull from pan sides and a toothpick inserted in center comes out clean, 60 to 75 minutes.

Turn loaf out onto a rack and let cool. If made ahead, cover and store up to 2 days. Cut bread into thin slices; spread with cream cheese or butter. Makes 1 loaf, about 2¼ pounds. —*Helen Littrell, Stockton, Calif.*

PER OUNCE: 59 calories, 16 g protein, 13 g carbohydrates, 0.3 g fat, 0.5 mg cholesterol, 71 mg sodium

Dense-textured brown bread gets its color from dark molasses.

SHRIMP WITH SAUCE VERDE

¼ cup almonds
2 cups lightly packed, rinsed, and drained parsley sprigs
⅓ cup olive oil
3 tablespoons white wine vinegar
1 clove garlic
1 tablespoon drained capers
1 fresh jalapeño chili, stemmed and seeded
  Salt
1 pound large (31 to 35 per lb.) shrimp, shelled, deveined, and rinsed

In an 8- to 10-inch frying pan, stir almonds over medium heat until golden under the skin, about 8 minutes. Pour almonds into a food processor; let cool.

Add parsley, oil, vinegar, garlic, capers, and chili. Whirl until smoothly puréed. Add salt to taste.

In a 4- to 5-quart pan, bring 2 quarts water to boiling on high heat. Add shrimp to pan, cover, and remove at once from heat. Let stand until shrimp are opaque in center (cut to test), 2 to 3 minutes.

Drain shrimp and mound on a platter. Spoon sauce onto the warm shrimp. Makes 4 servings. —*L.K. Ross, Elk Grove, Calif.*

PER SERVING: 317 calories, 21 g protein, 5.5 g carbohydrates, 24 g fat, 140 mg cholesterol, 204 mg sodium

Sauce for shrimp combines parsley, almonds, chili.

PRALINE CHEESECAKE

1½ cups graham cracker crumbs
½ cup pecans
¼ cup (⅛ lb.) butter or margarine, cut into chunks
2 large packages (8 oz. each) cream cheese
⅔ cup firmly packed brown sugar
2 large eggs
⅓ cup sour cream
2 tablespoons maple syrup or rum
2 tablespoons all-purpose flour
1 teaspoon vanilla
½ cup coarsely chopped (about 2½ oz.) chocolate-coated toffee

Whirl crumbs, pecans, and butter in a food processor until mixture holds together. Press evenly over bottom and 1 inch up sides of a 9-inch-diameter pan with removable rim. Bake in a 350° oven until slightly firm when pressed, about 10 minutes.

With a mixer or food processor, blend cheese, sugar, eggs, sour cream, syrup, flour, and vanilla. Pour into crust.

Bake in a 350° oven until filling jiggles only slightly in center when pan is gently shaken, 35 to 40 minutes.

Let the cheesecake cool, then chill 2 hours or up until next day (cover when cold). Mound toffee candy in center of cake. Makes 12 to 16 servings. —*Paulette Dunlap, Gillette, Wyo.*

PER SERVING: 282 calories, 4.5 g protein, 24 g carbohydrates, 19 g fat, 68 mg cholesterol, 207 mg sodium

Toffee tops cheesecake baked in pecan crust.

CONVENTIONAL CHILI *usually has, along with a robust flavor and mystery ingredients, a floating layer of liquid fat. This undoubtedly contributes to the flavor, but it also contributes to calorie and cholesterol counts. Robert House makes a chili that is loaded with flavor but carries only a small charge of fat. Low-fat ground turkey and a lone slice of bacon are the secret ingredients. You are, of course, free to raise the temperature by adding extra chili powder.*

TURKEY CHILI

- 1 slice bacon, diced
- 1 pound ground turkey
- 1 large onion, chopped
- 1 large red bell pepper, stemmed, seeded, and diced
- 3 cloves garlic, minced or pressed
- 2 tablespoons chili powder
- 1 can (7 oz.) diced green chilies
- 1¾ cups or 1 can (14½ oz.) regular-strength chicken broth
- 1 can (14½ oz.) diced tomatoes
- ¼ cup catsup
- 1 teaspoon *each* ground cumin, dry oregano leaves, and ground coriander
- 1 can (about 15 oz.) kidney beans, drained
  Shredded cheddar cheese
  Salt and pepper

"Low-fat ground turkey is a secret ingredient."

In a 4- to 5-quart pan over medium-high heat, stir bacon and turkey until crumbled and lightly browned, about 10 minutes. Add onion, bell pepper, and garlic and stir frequently until onion is limp, about 10 minutes. Add chili powder, stir well, then add chilies, broth, tomatoes and their liquid, catsup, cumin, oregano, coriander, and beans. Bring to a boil over high heat, stirring to free browned bits. Reduce heat, cover, and simmer until flavors are well blended, about 45 minutes; stir often. Ladle into wide bowls. Add cheese, salt, and pepper to taste. Makes 4 to 6 servings.

PER SERVING: 244 calories, 18 g protein, 23 g carbohydrates, 9.5 g fat, 58 mg cholesterol, 731 mg sodium

Robert B House

Mount Vernon, Wash.

FLOWERS ARE POPULAR *as salad ingredients and garnishes, but one flower— the artichoke—stands out as real food. (Technically what we eat is not the flower, but the receptacle and the bases of the bracts of the flower head.) We in the West know how to eat them, but it wasn't always so.*

Anyone old enough to remember the Mack Sennett comedies will recall that Harry Langdon, Ben Turpin, or one of the other Sennett comedians, when confronted with an artichoke on a platter, would tear off the outer leaves and discard them in a crescendo of concern, looking for the supposed treasure within. With a final gesture of frustration, the comedian would throw away the denuded heart.

Tom Eckstein offers an easier way to get the delectable artichoke flavor; just use frozen artichoke hearts.

"The artichoke stands out as real food."

CHILLED ARTICHOKE SOUP

- 2½ cups regular-strength chicken broth
- 1 package (9 oz.) frozen artichoke hearts
- 2 tablespoons whipping cream
- 1 to 2 teaspoons lemon juice
  Diced red bell pepper
  Thinly sliced green onions, including tops
  Salt and white pepper

In a 3- to 4-quart covered pan over high heat, bring broth to a boil with artichokes; reduce heat and simmer until artichokes are very tender when pierced, about 8 minutes.

Smoothly purée artichokes and liquid in a blender; pour into a fine strainer and rub through into a bowl. Add cream and lemon juice to taste. Cover and chill until cold, about 2 hours, or up until next day.

Stir soup well, then ladle into small bowls or mugs; garnish each with bell pepper and green onions, and add salt and pepper to taste. Makes about 3 cups, 3 or 4 servings.

PER SERVING: 90 calories, 4.9 g protein, 11 g carbohydrates, 3.8 g fat, 8.3 mg cholesterol, 96 mg sodium

Tom

Seal Beach, Calif.

A MEDIEVAL THEORY *of medicine held that health consists of a balance among the elements; these could be expressed as fire, earth, water, and air, or hot, cold, wet, and dry. Dean Silvers' recipe is, by the balance theory, a thoroughly healthy salad. Ginger, curry, and onion are considered hot (or at least warm). The cucumber is proverbially cool, as are the apple and yogurt. The yogurt, again, is moist; mushrooms and raisins are dry (the latter by definition).*

CURRIED CUCUMBER SALAD

- 1 **cup unflavored nonfat or low-fat yogurt**
- 3 **tablespoons lemon juice**
- 1½ **teaspoons curry powder**
- ¼ **teaspoon ground ginger**
- 1 **European cucumber (about ¾ lb.), thinly sliced**
  About ¼ pound mushrooms, rinsed and thinly sliced
- 2 **green onions (ends trimmed) with tops, thinly sliced**
- ½ **cup raisins**
- 1 **medium-size Red Delicious apple**
  About 3 cups tender spinach or romaine leaves, rinsed and crisped
  Salt and pepper

In a small bowl, stir yogurt to mix with lemon juice, curry powder, and ginger; cover and keep cold.

In a large bowl, combine cucumber, mushrooms, onions, and raisins. Quarter and core apple; cut each wedge in half crosswise, then thinly slice lengthwise. Add to cucumber mixture along with yogurt sauce. Mix gently; cover and chill at least 1 hour or up to 6 hours.

Line 5 or 6 salad plates with spinach leaves. Stir cucumber mixture, then mound equally onto leaves. Add salt and pepper to taste. Makes 5 or 6 servings.

PER SERVING: 95 calories, 4.1 g protein, 21 g carbohydrates, 0.5 g fat, 0.8 mg cholesterol, 55 mg sodium

Dean A. Silvers

Santa Cruz, Calif.

"A healthy salad balances ingredients."

September Menus

THE LAST HOT BREATHS *of summer mingle with clues of cooler days ahead to mark September's temperament. Menus this month anticipate these swings and feature some of the season's produce. Lunch for a warm day is cold, soup for a cool evening is hot, and a hearty brunch takes the chill out of a fall morning.*

BIG NOODLE SALAD LUNCH

Lasagna Ribbon Salad
Salad Greens
Balsamic Vinegar   Olive Oil
Crusty Bread
Hot Fudge Sundaes with Strawberries
Chianti   Ice Water with Lemon

Wide ribbons of lasagna step out of their usual place in layered casseroles and team up with tender-crisp stir-fried vegetables to make a robust salad. The noodles are boiled, then cooled before they are mixed with the colorful seasonings.

You can start the pasta salad ahead. Serve it with rinsed, crisped salad greens and offer balsamic vinegar, extra-virgin olive oil, salt, and pepper to add to taste.

For sundaes, use the microwave to warm prepared fudge sauce right in the jar.

LASAGNA RIBBON SALAD

At least 3 tablespoons extra-virgin olive oil
½ cup pine nuts
¼ cup minced shallots or red onions
1 large (about ½ lb.) red bell pepper, stemmed, seeded, and finely slivered
8 ounces dry wide lasagna noodles
2 chicken or beef bouillon cubes
About ¼ pound edible-pod peas, ends and strings removed
About 1 cup shredded parmesan cheese
Salt and fresh ground pepper
Balsamic vinegar

Outdoor lunch features wide lasagna noodles with bright vegetables; serve with salad greens and add balsamic vinegar and olive oil to taste.

In a 10- to 12-inch frying pan over medium-high heat, stir 3 tablespoons olive oil, pine nuts, and shallots until nuts and shallots are just golden, about 2 minutes. Add bell pepper and stir often until limp, about 2 minutes; remove from heat.

Meanwhile, in a 5- to 6-quart pan, bring 2 quarts water to a boil over high heat. Add lasagna noodles and bouillon cubes; stir to separate noodles. Cook, uncovered, until just tender to bite, about 12 minutes (when boil resumes, turn heat down to maintain a gentle simmer). Drain pasta; add cold water to pan. When pasta is cool, drain but leave pasta in pan.

If made ahead, cover peppers and pasta and let stand up to 3 hours.

Return pan with peppers to medium-high heat and add peas; stir until peas turn bright green, about 2 minutes. Pour over pasta and lift with 2 forks to mix. Season salads with cheese, salt, pepper, olive oil, and balsamic vinegar to taste. Makes 4 or 5 servings.

PER SERVING: 413 calories, 17 g protein, 42 g carbohydrates, 21 g fat, 13 mg cholesterol, 747 mg sodium

---

SUPER CHICKEN SOUP SUPPER

Lemon Chicken Soup
Warm Croissants
Cucumber, Banana &
Pineapple Salad
Shortbread Cookies
Orange-Spice Tea

This chicken soup from scratch goes together in simple steps.

While the chicken simmers, make the salad by thinly slicing a tender European (thin-skinned) cucumber, about a 2-pound piece of peeled and cored pineapple, and 2 ripe bananas. Arrange slices on a platter and drizzle with 1 tablespoon honey and 1 or 2 tablespoons lime juice, then sprinkle with about 2 tablespoons chopped fresh mint. Add salt to taste.

LEMON CHICKEN SOUP

1 **cut-up broiler-fryer chicken (3 to 3½ lb.)**
6 **cups regular-strength chicken broth**
1 **medium-size onion, chopped**
2 **large (about 1 lb. total) ripe tomatoes, peeled, cored, and diced; or 1 can (14½ oz.) tomatoes**
1 **tablespoon fresh or 1 teaspoon dry tarragon leaves**
1 **teaspoon grated lemon peel**
¼ **teaspoon pepper**
About ½ pound (about 2 medium-size) thin-skinned potatoes, scrubbed and cut into ½-inch cubes
2 **medium-size mild red or green Anaheim (California or New Mexico) chilies, stemmed, seeded, and chopped**
1 **medium-size husked ear of corn, kernels cut from cob**
1 **large firm-ripe avocado, pitted, peeled, and diced**
2 **tablespoons lime juice**

Rinse and drain chicken; reserve giblets for other uses. In a 5- to 6-quart pan, combine all chicken but breast pieces with broth, onion, tomatoes and liquid, tarragon, lemon peel, and pepper; bring to boiling over high heat. Cover and simmer for 20 minutes. Add breast; cover and simmer until breast is no longer pink in center of thickest part and thighs are no longer pink at bone (cut to test), 15 to 20 minutes longer. Lift out chicken and let stand until cool enough to touch.

Add potatoes to broth; cover and simmer gently until potatoes are tender to bite, 25 to 30 minutes.

Meanwhile, skin and bone chicken; tear meat into bite-size pieces.

When the potatoes are done, skim and discard the fat from the broth. Add chicken, chilies, and corn. Let the soup cook just until ingredients are hot. Mix avocado with lime juice. Ladle soup into bowls and offer avocado to add to taste. Makes 6 to 8 servings. —*Kathy VerValn, Valley Center, Calif.*

PER SERVING: 233 calories, 22 g protein, 18 g carbohydrates, 8.6 g fat, 57 mg cholesterol, 115 mg sodium

Baked egg nestles in hearty beans flavored with spicy linguisa and cheese. Eat for brunch with salsa, tortillas, and Asian pears.

BAKED EGGS FOR BRUNCH

Fiesta Brunch Casseroles
Asian Pears
Coffee   Steamed Milk

The spicy flavor of linguisa, a Portuguese-style sausage, is the only seasoning you need for the main dish.

These individual casseroles get a fast start with canned beans. Mix with cooked potatoes and linguisa and heat in the oven. Then add eggs and cheese and bake until eggs are set. The result is a hearty peasant-style dish that will appeal to both family and guests.

To froth milk, use a steam jet or whirl hot milk in a blender.

(Continued on next page)

FIESTA BRUNCH CASSEROLES

- 2 **cans (14½ oz. each) pinto beans**
- ½ **pound linguisa sausage, chopped**
- 2 **medium-size (about ¾ lb. total) cooked thin-skinned potatoes, peeled and diced**
- 4 **large eggs**
- 1¼ **cups (5 oz.) shredded cheddar cheese**
- 4 **flour tortillas (7-in. size)**
- 4 **green onions, ends trimmed About 1 cup prepared salsa**

Drain beans, reserving ½ cup liquid. Pour half the beans into a bowl; add reserved liquid. Mash until fairly smooth. Stir in remaining beans, linguisa, and potatoes.

Into 4 shallow casseroles, each about 2-cup size, spoon equal amounts of bean mixture. Set casseroles in 1 or 2 shallow pans (10 by 15 in.). Bake in a 400° oven about 10 minutes; stir. Bake 5 minutes more, then remove from oven. With back of a spoon, impress an egg-size cavity in center of each casserole; break an egg into it. Sprinkle cheese equally over beans. Return casseroles in pans to oven.

Stack tortillas and seal in foil; put in oven. Bake casseroles until egg yolks are set the way you like; allow about 15 minutes for firm but moist yolks. Garnish each dish with an onion; serve with warm tortillas and salsa. Makes 4 servings. — *Barbara J. Jones, Albuquerque.*

PER SERVING: 809 calories, 36 g protein, 74 g carbohydrates, 41 g fat, 288 mg cholesterol, 2,091 mg sodium

OCTOBER

Autumn's apple bounty (page 254)

Apples arrive in a big way
in October. With the harvest in full swing, we sample the
new apple varieties and compare their characteristics with old
favorites; you'll also find updated versions of classic apple
recipes. Savor the flavors of Italy in three dinner parties, each
featuring uncomplicated and make-ahead dishes. For more
casual entertaining, celebrate Halloween with your
neighborhood witches and goblins at a pumpkin party. Other
ideas from our autumn cornucopia include lean ways to cook
fish, no-fat salad dressings, and stuffed baked potatoes.

Italian-Style Dinner Parties

DINING IN ITALY *proceeds at a leisurely pace, with ample time to savor several courses, each deserving of its own place in the meal.*

Duplicate the experience in your home with these dinners we sampled in Italy. Two come from southern Italy, near Rome, and one comes from the north, near Milan. The dishes are uncomplicated and easy to achieve in a Western kitchen; many can be made ahead.

Each Italian dinner menu concludes with a dessert featuring the delicate flavor and creaminess of Italian cheeses.

Widely available ricotta—a soft, mild fresh cheese—fills the Roman-style tart. Mascarpone, the Italian version of cream cheese, imparts a velvety mantle to the other two desserts. Look for this premium-priced cheese at some supermarkets, cheese stores, and delicatessens; use firmer domestic cream cheese as a substitute.

Traditionally, the last two desserts use raw eggs. For people who are concerned about the possibility of salmonella in uncooked eggs, especially those vulnerable to disease—young children, pregnant women, the elderly, those with an illness or who take medication that affects their immune system—we give alternative cooked recipes. With these egg-safe variations, use cream cheese for more consistent results.

To serve the meals in traditional Italian style, present each course separately on its own dish, starting with antipasto. Follow with the first plate, which often includes pasta or rice; then offer the second plate, which usually consists of a small piece of meat, fish, or poultry. Salad can precede or follow the main dish.

Or you can present the meal more casually, offering the first and second courses together. To lighten and further simplify the meal, eliminate one of the courses and substitute a selection of fruit and cheeses for any of the rich desserts suggested here. Whichever presentation you choose, these menus will earn you accolades.

In her kitchen, Paola di Mauro crushes fresh rosemary for lamb.

COLLE PICCHIONE WINERY DINNER

Bucatini all' Amatriciana
Hunter's-style Lamb
Green Beans
Mixed Baby Greens with Olive Oil & Vinegar
Ricotta Cheese Tart
Colle Picchione Rosso or Zinfandel
Coffee

Paola di Mauro, winemaker from Marino—south of Rome—incorporates food from her garden into this menu for 8.

She serves bucatini (pasta shaped like drinking straws) with tomatoes and chilies that she grows. Fresh rosemary, garlic, and vinegar give the lamb stew a refreshing piquant edge. Serve the salad before the pasta or after the lamb.

You can get a head start on preparing this meal by completing a number of steps in advance. Make pasta sauce, lamb stew, and ricotta cheese tart up to a day ahead. You can also rinse and crisp salad greens (you'll need about 1 lb.) any time from a day ahead to 30 minutes before serving.

As the stew cooks or reheats, serve the pasta. Cook beans (1½ to 2 lb.) shortly before stew is ready.

BUCATINI ALL' AMATRICIANA

- 2 **tablespoons olive oil**
- 3 **ounces (½ cup) pancetta or prosciutto, finely chopped**
- 1 **large onion, thinly sliced**
- 1 **clove garlic, pressed or minced**
- 2 **to 4 fresh jalapeño chilies, stemmed, seeded, and minced**
- ⅔ **cup dry white wine**
- 3 **pounds Roma-type tomatoes, peeled, cored, and chopped (about 6 cups)**
- 1 **pound dry bucatini, perciatelli, or spaghetti**
   Salt and pepper
   Grated parmesan cheese

In a 10- to 12-inch frying pan, combine oil and pancetta. Stir over medium-high heat until pancetta begins to brown, about 3 minutes. Add onion, garlic, and jalapeños. Stir until onion begins to brown, 6 to 8 minutes. Add wine and tomatoes. Boil gently, uncovered, until sauce is reduced to about 1 quart, 20 to 30 minutes. If made ahead, cool, cover, and chill up until next day; reheat until hot.

Meanwhile, in a 5- to 6-quart pan, bring about 3 quarts water to a boil on high heat. Add bucatini; when boil resumes, reduce heat to maintain a gentle boil and cook, uncovered, until pasta is just tender to bite, 8 to 14 minutes. Drain pasta well; pour into warm serving bowl. Pour sauce over pasta; mix well. Add salt, pepper, and parmesan cheese to taste. Makes 8 servings.

PER SERVING: 297 calories, 11 g protein, 52 g carbohydrates, 5.5 g fat, 6.1 mg cholesterol, 155 mg sodium

(Continued on page 250)

Gathered round the dining table for a Sunday supper, Mauro family and guests enjoy garden's bounty: fresh rosemary for lamb, simmered tomatoes and chilies mixed with pasta, lightly cooked fresh green beans, dressed salad greens. Sugar-dusted ricotta cheese tart ends the feast.

HUNTER'S-STYLE LAMB

About ¼ cup olive oil

3½ pounds round-bone lamb shoulder chops, cut into about 1½-inch chunks

1 cup dry white wine

3 cloves garlic

3 tablespoons fresh or dry rosemary leaves

2 tablespoons red wine vinegar

Salt and pepper

Fresh rosemary sprigs (optional)

Pour 2 tablespoons oil into a deep 12-inch frying pan or 5- to 6-quart pan; set over high heat. Add about half the lamb to the pan. Brown well, stirring often, about 10 minutes. Lift lamb from pan; set aside. Brown remaining lamb, adding more oil if needed. Return browned lamb (and any juices) to pan. Add wine and cover; reduce heat and simmer until meat is very tender when pierced, about 1½ hours. Skim and discard fat. If made ahead, cool, cover, and chill up until the next day. Reheat, covered, until hot; stir often.

Meanwhile, with a mortar and pestle crush garlic and rosemary (or coarsely chop). Mix with vinegar and 2 tablespoons oil. Stir into pan with lamb and bring to a boil. Add salt and pepper to taste. Pour into a dish. Garnish with rosemary sprigs. Makes 8 servings.

PER SERVING: 273 calories, 28 g protein, 1.5 g carbohydrates, 17 g fat, 94 mg cholesterol, 102 mg sodium

RICOTTA CHEESE TART

Pastry dough (recipe follows)

4 large eggs

4 tablespoons granulated sugar

2 tablespoons armagnac or rum

1 carton (15 oz.) part-skim ricotta cheese

⅓ cup *each* golden raisins and diced candied orange peel

Powdered sugar

Press pastry dough in an even layer over bottom and sides of a 9-inch-diameter cake pan with removable rim. Bake in a 350° oven until golden, about 30 minutes.

Separate 2 eggs. In a small bowl, beat 2 whites until foamy. Gradually beat in 2 tablespoons granulated sugar until whites hold moist, stiff peaks; set aside.

In a food processor or blender, smoothly blend the 2 egg yolks, 2 whole eggs, 2 tablespoons granulated sugar, armagnac, and cheese. Add cheese mixture, raisins, and orange peel to whites; fold to blend. Pour ricotta mixture into baked pastry.

Bake in a 350° oven until center of filling barely jiggles when gently shaken, 35 to 40 minutes. Let cool on a rack. If made ahead, cover and chill up until the next day. Sprinkle cheese tart with powdered sugar and serve cool. Cut into wedges. Makes 8 servings.

PER SERVING: 329 calories, 12 g protein, 35 g carbohydrates, 16 g fat, 173 mg cholesterol, 188 mg sodium

Pastry dough. Mix 1 cup **all-purpose flour,** ⅓ cup **sugar,** and 6 tablespoons **butter** or margarine, cut into chunks. Rub with fingers until fine crumbs form. Stir in 1 **large egg yolk** until well distributed; press into a ball. (In a food processor, whirl flour, sugar, and butter into coarse crumbs. Add yolk and whirl until dough begins to lump; press into a ball.)

MILAN COUNTRY INN SUPPER FOR 8 GUESTS

Shrimp & White Beans
Lasagna with Radicchio
Milan-style Veal Chops
Sautéed Mushrooms   Mashed Turnip
Mashed Pumpkin or Winter Squash
Pinot Grigio or Dry Sauvignon Blanc
Pound Cake with Cognac Cream
Malvasia Dolce   Coffee

Franco and Silvana Colombani own Albergo del Sole, a lovingly maintained country inn in Maleo, south of Milan. The inn's restaurant draws food connoisseurs from all over the country to sample Mr. Colombani's cuisine. He transforms the region's food resources into dishes that are elegant in their simplicity.

As a simple antipasto to begin this dinner for 8, Mr. Colombani presents white beans with shrimp, seasoned only with fresh basil and a fruity extra-virgin olive oil. The lasagna has layers of bitter-tinged radicchio with a béchamel sauce, emmen-

thal cheese, and thin wide noodles. Braised veal chops with sage are accompanied by sautéed mushrooms, mashed turnip, and pumpkin.

An unassuming pound cake, made with potato starch flour, is lavished with creamy cognac sauce. For a special treat, pour Malvasia Dolce—a slightly sweet, muscat-flavor sparkling wine—into flutes to sip with the dessert.

The shrimp, lasagna, and dessert can be made up to one day ahead. You can also prepare the vegetables (about 1½ lb. of each) a day in advance. Place the lasagna in the oven, then brown the veal. Put veal and vegetables (covered, in separate dishes) in oven. While they bake, complete the shrimp antipasto and serve. The second course of meat and vegetables should be ready by the time you have eaten the pasta. If you like, present a green salad before or after the second course.

SHRIMP & WHITE BEANS

16 large (31 to 35 per lb.) shrimp, shelled and deveined

2 cans (15 oz. each) Italian white kidney beans (cannellini), drained

1 small ripe tomato, cored and cut into ¼-inch cubes

¼ cup coarsely chopped fresh or 2 tablespoons dry basil leaves

About 6 tablespoons extra-virgin olive oil

Fresh basil sprigs (optional)

Salt and pepper

In a 3- to 4-quart pan, bring about 1½ quarts water to a boil on high heat. Add shrimp, cover, and return to a boil. Remove from heat and let stand until shrimp are opaque in thickest part (cut to test), about 3 minutes. Drain and immerse shrimp in ice water until cool; drain. If done ahead, cover and chill up to 1 day.

Very gently mix the shrimp, beans, tomato, chopped basil, and ¼ cup olive oil. Place equal portions on 8 plates. Garnish with basil sprigs. Add additional olive oil and salt and pepper to taste. Makes 8 appetizer servings.

PER SERVING: 160 calories, 7.3 g protein, 16 g carbohydrates, 8 g fat, 35 mg cholesterol, 274 mg sodium

Antipasto *Shrimp, white beans, and tomato dressed with basil and olive oil launch this northern Italian dinner.*

Primo *Next comes lasagna layered with radicchio and emmenthal cheese in a béchamel sauce.*

LASAGNA WITH RADICCHIO

- 8 ounces dry lasagna noodles
- 2 tablespoons butter or margarine
- 1 tablespoon salad oil
- 1 ounce pancetta or prosciutto, finely chopped
- 1 small onion, finely chopped
- 2 cloves garlic, pressed or minced
- 1½ pounds (about 3 qt.) radicchio, cut into ¼-inch strips
   Béchamel sauce (recipe follows)
- 4 cups (1 lb.) shredded emmenthal or Swiss cheese
   Salt

Bring about 3 quarts water to boiling in a 5- to 6-quart pan over high heat. Add noodles and cook, uncovered, until just tender to bite, about 8 minutes. Drain and immerse in cold water.

In a 10- to 12-inch frying pan over medium-high heat, combine butter and oil. Add pancetta, onion, and garlic; stir often until onion is faintly browned, about 5 minutes. Add radicchio, a portion at a time if it doesn't all fit; stir just until wilted, 2 to 4 minutes.

Drain noodles well. In a buttered shallow 3-quart baking dish, layer ¼ of the noodles, radicchio mixture, béchamel sauce, and cheese. Repeat layers. (If made ahead, cover and chill until the next day.)

Bake, uncovered, in a 375° oven until hot and bubbly, 35 to 55 minutes. Let stand 10 minutes. Cut into rectangles with a knife and serve with a wide spatula. Add salt to taste. Makes 8 servings.

PER SERVING: 530 calories, 26 g protein, 37 g carbohydrates, 31 g fat, 95 mg cholesterol, 352 mg sodium

Béchamel sauce. In a 2- to 3-quart pan, melt ¼ cup (⅛ lb.) **butter** or margarine over medium heat. Stir in 6 tablespoons **all-purpose flour.** Gradually whisk in 1 quart **milk.** Stir until boiling vigorously. Use hot or warm.

MILAN-STYLE VEAL CHOPS

- 8 veal loin chops (about 2 lb. total), or chicken thighs (2½ lb. total), skinned
   About 2 tablespoons all-purpose flour
- 2 tablespoons butter or margarine
- 2 ounces pancetta or prosciutto, finely chopped
- 8 fresh or 1 teaspoon dry sage leaves
- ¾ cup dry white wine
   Salt and pepper

Trim any fat from chops. Coat chops lightly with flour. In an ovenproof 10- to 12-inch frying pan, melt butter over medium-high heat. Add pancetta and sage; stir until lightly browned, about 5 minutes, then lift out with a slotted spoon. Add chops without overlapping; brown on both sides, about 6 minutes total. Set chops aside as browned. When all are cooked, return meat, pancetta, and sage to pan; add wine.

Cover pan tightly. Bake in a 375° oven until chops are tender when pierced, 40 to 45 minutes. Place chops on dinner plates; keep warm. Measure pan juices; if less than ¾ cup, add water and bring to a boil; if more than ¾ cup, boil juices, uncovered, until reduced to ¾ cup. Spoon pan juices over each chop. Add salt and pepper to taste. Makes 4 servings as part of a smaller meal, 8 servings if served as part of this whole menu.

PER SERVING: 123 calories, 15 g protein, 1.9 g carbohydrates, 5.8 g fat, 65 mg cholesterol, 184 mg sodium

(Continued on next page)

Secundo *Sage-scented oven-braised veal chop accompanies mashed pumpkin, turnip, and sautéed mushrooms.*

Dolce *Cognac-spiked mascarpone cream cloaks fine-textured cake for dessert; garnish with whole strawberries.*

POUND CAKE WITH COGNAC CREAM

- ¾ cup (⅜ lb.) butter or margarine
- 1 cup granulated sugar
- 2 large eggs
- ⅔ cup cake flour
- ⅔ cup potato flour or cornstarch
- ¼ cup cognac or brandy
  About 2 tablespoons fine dry bread crumbs
  Powdered sugar
  Cognac cream (recipe follows)
  Whole strawberries, rinsed

In a large bowl, beat butter and granulated sugar until creamy. Add eggs, 1 at a time, beating well after each. Beat in cake flour and potato flour. Beat in cognac.

Butter the bottom and sides of a 9-inch-diameter cake pan with removable rim. Sprinkle pan bottom and sides with bread crumbs. Pour batter into pan and bake in a 350° oven until a toothpick inserted in center comes out clean, about 45 minutes. Cool in pan on a rack. If made ahead, cover and store up until the next day. Remove rim; sprinkle with powdered sugar and cut into wedges.

Offer cognac cream to spoon over pieces. Garnish with berries. Makes 8 to 10 servings.

PER SERVING OF PLAIN CAKE: 279 calories, 2 g protein, 35 g carbohydrates, 15 g fat, 80 mg cholesterol, 163 mg sodium

Uncooked cognac cream. In a small bowl, beat 2 **large egg whites** until foamy. Gradually beat in 2 tablespoons **sugar** until stiff, moist peaks form; set aside. Beat 2 **large egg yolks** with 2 tablespoons **sugar** until well blended. Add ½ pound **mascarpone** or cream **cheese**; beat to mix well. Add ⅓ cup **cognac** or brandy; mix well. Fold in beaten egg whites. Serve, or cover and chill up until the next day. Makes about 2½ cups.

PER TABLESPOON: 33 calories, 0.7 g protein, 1.4 g carbohydrates, 2.2 g fat, 17 mg cholesterol, 20 mg sodium

Egg-safe cognac cream. In the top of a double boiler or zabaglione pan, whisk together 4 **large egg yolks**, ¼ cup **sugar**, and ¼ cup **water**. Set top of double boiler over, not in, simmering water or set zabaglione pan directly over medium heat. Beat constantly with a whisk just

until mixture reaches 160° on a thermometer and is thick and frothy, 3 to 5 minutes. Remove from heat (and water) and let cool, about 5 minutes.

In a small bowl, beat ½ pound **cream cheese** until smooth. Gradually add ⅓ cup **cognac** or brandy, beating until smooth. Fold in egg mixture with a whisk. Serve, or cover and chill up until the next day. Makes about 2 cups.

PER TABLESPOON: 44 calories, 0.9 g protein, 1.8 g carbohydrates, 3.1 g fat, 34 mg cholesterol, 22 mg sodium

---

ELEGANT ROMAN DINNER

**Roman-style Chicken
Spinach & Pine Nuts
Polenta
Tiramisu
Velletri Rosso or Zinfandel
Espresso**

Mary Lou and Marco Antonini enjoy entertaining in their gracious home south of Rome. The meal on the facing page features classic dishes of the area.

While the chicken simmers, cook polenta: in a 4- to 5-quart pan, mix 1½ cups polenta with 6 cups water or regular-

strength chicken broth; stirring, bring to a boil on high heat, then stir often over low heat until it attains a very thick consistency, like a pudding, about 15 minutes. Add salt and butter to taste.

Just before you're ready to serve meal, cook about 2½ pounds rinsed and drained spinach leaves until wilted. Drain and garnish with toasted pine nuts, lightly browned golden raisins, and grated parmesan cheese to taste.

The chicken, polenta, and spinach go well together and can be served at the same time. Or, if you like to break the meal into more courses, precede the chicken with the spinach or a green salad, dressed with extra-virgin olive oil and vinegar.

Tiramisu, the espresso-flavored dessert, can be made a day in advance.

ROMAN-STYLE CHICKEN

2 tablespoons olive oil
6 chicken legs with thighs attached (about 3½ lb. total)
1 large onion, thinly sliced
2 large (about 1 lb. total) red or yellow bell peppers, stemmed, seeded, and thinly sliced
½ cup dry white wine
¼ cup water
1 can (28 oz.) tomato purée
1 tablespoon fresh or dry rosemary leaves
1 can (6 oz.) pitted black ripe olives, drained
1 tablespoon drained capers
Salt and pepper

Pour oil into a 12-inch frying pan or 5- to 6-quart pan over medium-high heat. Add chicken pieces without crowding; cook until browned on all sides, 10 to 15 minutes for each batch. Set aside as browned.

Add onion to pan; stir occasionally until limp, about 5 minutes. Add bell peppers and stir occasionally until onion is lightly browned, about 5 minutes longer. Add wine, water, tomato purée, rosemary, olives, and chicken (with any juices). Simmer, covered, until meat is no longer pink at thigh bone (cut to test), 30 to 40 minutes. Skim and discard fat.

Stir in capers, and salt and pepper to taste. Pour onto a platter. Makes 6 servings.

PER SERVING: 489 calories, 37 g protein, 18 g carbohydrates, 30 g fat, 122 mg cholesterol, 894 mg sodium

TIRAMISU

12 double ladyfingers (3 oz. total)
Espresso (recipe follows)
Rum cream (recipe follows)
1 ounce bittersweet or semisweet chocolate, finely chopped or grated

Arrange the ladyfingers, side by side, in the bottom of a 9-inch quiche dish or shallow 1- to 1½-quart dish. Drizzle evenly with hot espresso. Let cool.

Spoon rum cream over ladyfingers. Sprinkle with chocolate. Cover and chill at least 1 hour or up until the next day. Scoop out portions with a spoon. Makes 6 to 8 servings.

PER SERVING WITH UNCOOKED RUM CREAM: 209 calories, 5.6 g protein, 14 g carbohydrates, 14 g fat, 149 mg cholesterol, 116 mg sodium

PER SERVING WITH EGG-SAFE RUM CREAM: 221 calories, 4.7 g protein, 16 g carbohydrates, 15 g fat, 175 mg cholesterol, 96 mg sodium

Espresso. Place ½ cup freshly ground espresso beans in a filter-lined cone over a 1-cup glass measure. Pour 1⅓ cups boiling water over beans and let drip until all water passes through beans. Use hot. Makes about 1 cup.

Uncooked rum cream. In a small bowl, beat 3 large egg whites until foamy. Gradually beat in 2 tablespoons sugar until whites hold stiff moist peaks. In another bowl, beat 3 large egg yolks with 1 tablespoon sugar until thick and foamy. Add ½ pound mascarpone or cream cheese and 2 to 3 tablespoons rum to taste; beat to blend. Fold in beaten whites.

Egg-safe rum cream. In the top of a double boiler or in a zabaglione pan, whisk together 4 large egg yolks, ¼ cup sugar, and ¼ cup water. Set double boiler over, not in, simmering water. Set zabaglione pan directly over medium heat. Constantly beat with a whisk just until mixture reaches 160° on a thermometer and is thick and frothy, 2 to 3 minutes. Remove from heat and water and let mixture cool.

In a small bowl, beat ½ pound cream cheese with 3 tablespoons rum until smooth. Add egg mixture and fold in with a whisk to blend.

The Antoninis and guests enjoy Roman dinner of chicken and olives in tomato sauce, polenta, and spinach with nuts. For dessert, they have espresso-flavored tiramisu.

The New Apple Abundance

Apples arrive *in a big way in autumn. This month, with the apple harvest in full swing, market bins tumble forth their greatest bounty of the year. The number of choices may astound you. In response to demand for apples with more flavor and character, newer varieties—with names like Braeburn, Elstar, and Fuji—will be competing for your attention.*

This is the best time of year to try less familiar varieties: the selection is widest, and some apples that are grown in limited quantities won't be in the market for long. But with so many to choose from, how can you find the one with just the flavor, crispness, and juiciness you like? And how can you tell which will bake most evenly or make the best pie or applesauce?

To help supply some answers, a panel of Sunset *tasters evaluated 22 different varieties, both newly available ones and classic market standbys. The chart on pages 256–258 summarizes their findings. It* gives each apple's distinctive characteristics when raw and suggests its cooking potential.

But even fruits of the same variety can taste very different from one another, depending on the particular strain, the soil and climate where they've been grown, their ripeness when harvested, and how they've been handled and stored. To help you improve your chances of choosing the best apples, we offer some background on cultivation, as well as hints on what apples to look for season by season and how to choose them in the market.

HOW—AND WHY—DID THE NEW APPLES GET DEVELOPED?

In recent years, Red Delicious has set the standard for market apples—big, red, and unblemished. Color and appearance have been prime industry criteria for grading. Emphasis has been on finding "improved" strains of Red and Golden Delicious. Unfortunately, however, the old adage that beauty is only skin deep was often borne out by pretty-looking apples that were thick-skinned and bland.

Now there's a trend to put less emphasis on color and appearance and more on taste and wholesomeness. Concerns about food safety, fueled by the controversy over Alar (trade name for a no-longer-used growth regulator that gives some apples better firmness, color, and keeping quality), have stimulated interest in apples grown with fewer chemicals—even if they are undersize or imperfect.

During the 1960s and '70s, many Westerners satisfied their taste for tart apples with Granny Smiths imported in summer from New Zealand. In the '80s, Granny Smith trees were widely planted

EMPIRE
All-purpose apple
rivaling Winesap

ELSTAR
Big favorite
in Europe

NEWTOWN PIPPIN
Four-star winner
fresh and in pies

here, especially in the interior valleys of California and Washington, where the long, hot growing season suits them well. But fewer are being planted now, as the search for greater diversity continues.

Many of today's familiar apples developed, over time, from chance seedlings. Newtown Pippin appeared on Long Island in the 1750s. Granny Smith introduced itself in New South Wales, Australia, in the 1850s. McIntosh was discovered in Ontario, Canada, in the early 1800s. Red Delicious turned up in Iowa in the 1870s.

Apple trees grown from seed don't bear fruit identical to that of the parent, and—despite the well-known examples just mentioned—the chances of a seedling's fruit being better than the parent's are very remote.

Mutations, called sports, sometimes occur. Growers watch for limbs bearing fruit that's different from the other fruit on the tree. Wood from limbs bearing fruit with desirable properties can be budded or grafted onto a selected root-stock to perpetuate the strain (there are more than 150 strains of Red Delicious). The process of selection and rejection over many generations has given us the varieties grown today.

Experimentation with newer apples is going on in many parts of the West. Each kind has its own specific requirements for climate and growing conditions. Jonagold, for example, which doesn't do well in hot climates, is proving successful in western Washington and Oregon, and it is helping to revive these older apple-growing areas. Washington is now our largest apple-producing state, supplying more than 60 percent of the fresh apples sold in this country last year. California is fourth, behind Michigan and New York.

Oregon, Idaho, Colorado, and Arizona are also important producers—and experimenters.

Starting new orchards is expensive: it takes five or six years for standard trees to bear enough fruit to be harvested profitably—three years if the orchardist uses dwarf or semi-dwarf rootstock in denser plantings. This country's orchards are still mainly planted with Red Delicious (about a third of the U.S. crop), Golden Delicious, McIntosh, and Granny Smith apples. Most growers are experimenting with new kinds a few at a time. Varieties in which there is lively commercial interest now include Braeburn, Elstar, Empire, Fuji, Gala, and Jonagold.

There's also a revival of interest in certain older apples, including Winesap, Newtown Pippin, Jonathan, and Gravenstein. At farmers' markets and roadside stands, you may even discover

FUJI
Coming on strong,
snappy-crisp

CRITERION
Honey-sweet fresh,
bland when cooked

ROYAL GALA
Grand for munching,
poor for pies

...The New Apple Abundance

Fall apple bounty fills supermarket bins; produce manager points out newer choices.

"antique" apples like Northern Spy, Spitzenberg, and Winter Banana.

A YEAR-ROUND CALENDAR OF APPLES

Once seasonal, apples are now marketed year-round—because of imports from the Southern Hemisphere, and also because some varieties keep extremely well. Some last for several months in ordinary cold storage. Others can stay crisp and juicy for up to a year if held in sealed refrigerated rooms with controlled atmosphere (called CA); to slow ripening, CA reduces oxygen—something like putting the fruit to sleep.

In a typical year, most cold-storage apples are sold by the end of December or January. Then the CA rooms begin to be opened. When you shop at that time of year, ask for apples from boxes marked "CA"; they will usually be superior to the last cold-storage apples.

From midwinter until late summer, when early varieties start to ripen and the fresh-fruit season resumes, markets sell both CA-storage apples and imports.

Granny Smiths grown in Chile begin to arrive as early as February. From New Zealand, Galas usually start appearing in March or April—followed in May and June by Braeburns, Fujis, and more Granny Smiths.

In winter and early spring, apples produced mainly in the Eastern states and Canada also appear in our markets. These are primarily Cortland, Empire, Idared, McIntosh, Spartan, and Stayman Winesap.

TIPS TO HELP YOU SHOP FOR APPLES

The largest or most colorful apple may not be the best. Larger apples on a tree tend to mature more rapidly than smaller ones; they can be softer and are more likely to become mealy.

Choose apples that have a fresh appearance and feel firm to touch. They should be free of insect damage, bruises, and withered flesh. But not all blemishes are significant. The skin on apples from damp climates may be mottled with russet or brown marks, but these don't affect the quality of the fruit.

The amount of red blush on an apple has little to do with its quality or ripeness, either. But background color can be a good indicator of maturity. On red varieties with green ground color, the green should be bright; if too dark, the apple is immature, and if too yellowish, it's overripe. Solid green varieties should be light green, not too dark or too yellowish. Yellow apples should be light yellow, not greenish yellow or deep yellow.

Apples must be kept cold, especially ones brought out of storage (both cold storage and CA) after the first of the year. They lose crispness and flavor 10 times faster at room temperature than they do at 32°.

If possible, buy apples from markets that have refrigerated display counters. At home, store them in the refrigerator in a plastic bag to retain moisture and prevent the absorption of flavors from other foods.

A WORD ABOUT OUR APPLE TASTING

One's pleasure in eating an apple is influenced by the balance of sugar and acid and other subtle elements of taste as well as aroma, crispness, and texture. Some of our tasters consistently chose sweeter, milder apples; others preferred tangier ones.

When possible, we tested each variety several times, at different seasons and from different growing areas. Quality and flavor sometimes varied widely. Ranging from unacceptable (zero) to excellent (four), our ratings reflect the best samples we tested and are based on average scores of our testers.

Rating the Apple Varieties

Apple Variety	Characteristics	Fresh	Sauce	Microwave	Sauté	Pie
Akane (also called Prime Red). A Jonathan cross with bright red skin, this is most available in the Northwest. It grows best in cool climates. Watch for these apples from late August into September. They don't keep or store well.	*Fresh:* Tender-crisp flesh is fine-textured, juicy, with refreshing tart-sweet flavor. Skin is thin, tender. *Cooked:* Retains shape and lively flavor; makes creamy, pink sauce when cooked with peels, then strained.	● ● ●	● ● ●	● ● ●	● ●	● ● ●
Braeburn. Recently planted in warm inland valleys of California and the Northwest; not many are ready for harvest yet. Look for apples from New Zealand from late spring into summer. They look similar to Fujis and keep exceptionally well.	*Fresh:* Flavor is complex, moderately tart, with sweet, perfumy aftertaste. Apples are crisp, juicy; skin is tender. *Cooked:* Flavor complexity is lost, but apples retain good, tart taste. They keep shape, bake evenly.	● ● ●	● ●	● ●	● ●	● ●

Apple Variety	Characteristics	Fresh	Sauce	Microwave	Sauté	Pie
Cortland. An important variety in East and Midwest. Watch for CA-stored fruit here in winter and spring. They're quite fragile, so select them carefully.	*Fresh:* Snow white flesh is tender-crisp, fine-textured; it resists browning. Apples are juicy, with thin skin and rich, mildly tart-sweet flavor. *Cooked:* Apples retain lively flavor. They cook quickly, keep shape when baked.	• • •	• • •	• • • •	• • •	• • •
Criterion. Discovered in Washington in 1968, these handsome yellow apples (often packed in gift boxes) are difficult to handle without bruising. They keep well in CA storage, but become mealy if poorly handled.	*Fresh:* Flavor is sweet, mild, with little acid. Juicy, crisp flesh resembles Asian pear, resists browning. Skin is thin, tender. *Cooked:* Apples retain shape, taste bland. They need little sugar; lemon juice picks up flavor.	• • •	•		• •	• •
Elstar. In Europe, this Dutch apple is one of the most sought-after varieties. Plantings here are mostly in cooler areas of Northwest. Apples keep well, their tart flavor mellowing a little in storage.	*Fresh:* Intensely tart-sweet, aromatic flavor is unique. Apples are firm, juicy, with tender skin. *Cooked:* Apples retain lively flavor, cook up to creamy sauce, and bake evenly without falling apart; slices fall apart in pie.	• • •	• • •	• • •		• • •
Empire. Develop reddest color when grown in cool areas, but less colorful apples have as much flavor. Western harvest starts in October, then Eastern apples are sold here in winter. They get mealy if overripe or stored too long.	*Fresh:* Mildly tart flavor has winelike aftertaste. White flesh is tender-crisp, juicy, and resists browning. Skin is thick. *Cooked:* Apples retain rich flavor, cook quickly. Avoid overcooking when baking or sautéing.	• • •	• • •	•	• • •	• • •
Fuji. Good supply from California expected this year, with doubling of harvest in each of next few years; now being widely planted in Northwest. They keep very well. Sweetest apples are ones left on trees until late October, November.	*Fresh:* Tangy-sweet flavor is rich, complex. Juicy, snappy-crisp texture resembles Asian pears. *Cooked:* Flavor less interesting, though still enjoyable. Apples tend to retain shape, and take longer than average to cook tender.	• • • •	• •	•	• •	• •
Gala, Royal Gala. Several strains are now widely planted in West; picking starts here in late July, imported fruit in March and April. To avoid over-ripe fruit, choose apples with pale yellow background color and pink-red stripe or blush.	*Fresh:* Distinctive flavor is sweet, with tart accent. Apples are crisp, juicy, fine-grained; tender skin. *Cooked:* Flavor weaker, but still pleasantly sweet; apples need little sugar. They tend to hold shape, develop creamy texture.	• • • •	• •	• •		
Golden Delicious. They keep up to a year in CA storage but deteriorate quickly at room temperature and bruise easily. For best flavor, apples should be light (not greenish) yellow; deep yellow fruit may be overmature.	*Fresh:* In prime condition, flesh is tender-crisp and juicy, and skin is tender. Flavor is rich, sweet, aromatic. Cut pieces resist browning. *Cooked:* Apples retain shape; they have rich flavor, melting texture, need little sugar.	• • •	• • •	• • •	• • •	• • •
Granny Smith. Dependably firm and tart, they hold up well in markets. For sweetest fruit, watch for late-harvest apples after mid-October. Avoid intensely green apples; they should be light green, with even a slight yellowish blush.	*Fresh:* If well ripened, tart and sweet flavors are balanced. Flesh is firm, crisp, juicy; resists browning. *Cooked:* Apples cook into thick, coarse sauce with tangy flavor. They tend to fall apart when baked or sautéed.	• • •	• • •	• •		
Gravenstein (green and red strains). Not grown on large scale, but red strains gaining in popularity. Harvest begins in late July, but best eating apples appear in August. After September, they tend to be mealy.	*Fresh:* Renowned for old-fashioned, tart-sweet flavor. Perfectly ripe apples are crisp, juicy, aromatic. *Cooked:* Flesh cooks apart quickly into juicy sauce with rich flavor. Avoid overcooking when baking, sautéing.	• • •	• • •	• • •	• •	• • •
Idared. Though it originated in Idaho, most orchards are now in East and Midwest. Watch for CA-stored apples after the first of the year. They keep exceptionally well, becoming sweeter during storage.	*Fresh:* Lively tart-sweet flavor resembles Jonathan. Moderately firm flesh is juicy, fine textured; skin is tender. *Cooked:* Apples retain full flavor, keep shape. Cook with peels and strain for smooth, colorful sauce.	• • •	• • •	• • •	• • •	• • •

(Continued on next page)

...Rating the Apple Varieties

Apple Variety	Characteristics	Fresh	Sauce	Microwave	Sauté	Pie
Jonagold. They grow well with good color and flavor in cool, damp coastal areas of Northwest and at higher elevations. Apples store well; supplies of this newer variety should last through December this year.	*Fresh:* Complex flavor has good sweet-tart balance. Flesh is crisp, very juicy; skin is tender. *Cooked:* Milder, but with good apple flavor. They tend to retain shape, cook evenly; for best sauce, cook with peels, then strain.	• • • •	• •	• • •	• • •	• • •
Jonathan. Grown on small scale around West. Harvest starts in mid-August in California. Apples are in their prime early in season. Expect sound fruit until November, but shop carefully; they become soft and mealy quickly.	*Fresh:* Best fruit has tart, rich, distinctive flavor. Flesh is tender-crisp and juicy; skin is thin. *Cooked:* Apples retain full flavor. They cook tender quickly; make smooth, juicy sauce, retain shape when baked.	• • •	• • •	• • •	• •	• • •
McIntosh. British Columbia supplies most apples sold here in fall, winter. Not all apples get CA storage; select carefully, especially in late winter, as they tend to get soft and mealy easily.	*Fresh:* Flavor is mildly tart, aromatic. Firm, fresh apples are tender-crisp, juicy. Skin is tough and separates from flesh. *Cooked:* Apples retain rich flavor. They dissolve in sauce, tend to fall apart when baked, in pie.	• •	• • •			• •
Melrose. A Red Delicious–Jonathan cross, they grow well in western Washington and Oregon but aren't well known outside the Northwest. They are excellent keepers: their flavor improves after one to two months in cold storage.	*Fresh:* Its sweet and tart flavors have good balance. Texture is crisp, juicy; skin moderately tender. *Cooked:* Flesh cooks tender and velvety; retains shape and full flavor when baked, in pie. Needs little sugar.	• •	• •	• • •	• •	• • •
Mutsu (Crispin). Resembles Golden Delicious, one of its parents, but it's usually greener and more irregular in shape. Apples keep well. They grow well in cool areas of Northwest. Eastern-grown apples sold here in winter.	*Fresh:* Flavor is sweet-tart, with spicy accent. Flesh is dense, crisp, and juicy. *Cooked:* Apples retain shape, have fairly coarse texture. Some flavor lost, but taste is still good. For best sauce, cook with peels, then strain.	• • •	• •	•	• •	•
Newtown Pippin. These plain-looking apples are often underrated. Some are picked too green; for sweetest flavor, wait until they turn light greenish yellow. Even these fruits keep well into spring. Russeting around stem end is normal.	*Fresh:* Good, ripe apples have lively sweet-tart flavor. Flesh is dense, crisp, moderately juicy. *Cooked:* Fruit retains rich flavor. Apples tend to keep shape when baked, in pie; they cook up into thick sauce.	• • • •	• • •	• • •	• •	• • •
Red Delicious. Many strains, ranging in color from deep all-red to red striped. Apples keep for 12 months in CA storage but are very perishable at room temperature. Avoid any that look withered or bruised.	*Fresh:* Best-tasting strains are sweet, mellow, and aromatic, with hint of tartness. In prime condition, apples are tender-crisp, juicy. *Cooked:* Apples hold shape but have odd texture and weak flavor.	• • •		•	•	•
Rome Beauty (Red Rome). Large, handsome apples are market standbys until about May. Choose them carefully; apples get bland and mealy if left on display too long or if poorly handled.	*Fresh:* At best, apples are very mild, with little acid. They're firm, crisp, not very juicy. Skin is thick but fairly tender. *Cooked:* Renowned for baking, apples hold shape well. Cooking with sugar enhances flavor.	•	• •	• •	•	• •
Spartan. Developed in British Columbia, which supplies most of this variety sold here. Like McIntosh, which they resemble, apples get soft and mealy if stored too long or not handled carefully.	*Fresh:* Apples have clean, sweet flavor; they're moderately tart and quite aromatic. Flesh is tender-crisp, juicy. *Cooked:* Fine textured, keeps shape. A little sugar, lemon juice perk weak flavor.	• • •	• •		• •	• •
Stayman Winesap. Most apples sold here as Winesap or Stayman are actually a Stayman-Winesap cross. Grown in Northwest, Midwest, East, these apples keep well if stored and handled carefully.	*Fresh:* Flavor is spicy-tart, winelike. Firm, crisp flesh. Thick skin tends to separate from it. *Cooked:* Apples retain their lively flavor. They make thick, juicy sauce but retain some texture when baked or used in pies.	• •	• •	• •	• •	• •

Sunset's Apple Classics

W HEN YOU COOK APPLES, *you discover different facets of each variety's unique personality. Some kinds tend to retain their shape, and others melt into sauce. Some give up lots of juice, others very little. Cooking times vary widely. And the flavor may become more or less intense.*

Our chart on pages 256–258 points out distinctive qualities of 22 varieties and shows how testers rated each one when prepared in traditional ways. Here are our updated recipes for four apple classics. The pie recipe has been adjusted to suit each kind of apple (see chart on page 260).

APPLE ARITHMETIC

1 pound of apples consists of about:
2 large apples
3 medium-size apples
4 small apples
3 cups peeled and sliced apples

MICRO-BAKED APPLES

The microwave is more than a time-saver for "baking" apples; it also helps preserve the fruits' natural color and shape. If you use apple juice for liquid, many varieties may be sweet enough with the least amount of sugar suggested.

> **4** medium-size to large apples
> **½** cup apple juice or water
> **2** to 5 tablespoons granulated or firmly packed brown sugar
> **½** teaspoon ground cinnamon (optional)
> **2** tablespoons lemon juice (omit for tart apples)

Remove apple cores from stem end to within ½ inch of base; peel top third of stem ends. Arrange apples, peeled end up, in an 8- to 9-inch-wide microwave-safe dish. In a small bowl, mix together apple juice, sugar, cinnamon, and lemon juice; pour over apples.

Cover dish with microwave-safe plastic wrap and cook at full power (100 percent) until apples are tender throughout when pierced, 6 to 20 minutes, depending on variety. After 5 minutes, rotate apples in dish a half-turn and baste with juices in dish. Continue cooking, checking doneness and basting about every 2 minutes.

Remove apples to a serving dish and spoon cooking liquid over them. Makes 4 servings.

PER SERVING: 121 calories, 0.3 g protein, 31 g carbohydrates, 0.5 g fat, 0 mg cholesterol, 2.6 mg sodium

Apples with raisin-rum sauce. Prepare apples and juice mixture as for **micro-baked apples,** preceding. Arrange apples in dish and fill cores with ½ cup **raisins** (pour excess into the dish); pour juice mixture over fruit. Cook as directed, then remove apples to serving dish. Add juice or water to pan liquid to make 1 cup; pour into a 1- to 1½-quart pan. Mix in 2 teaspoons **cornstarch** blended with 3 tablespoons **light rum.** Stir on high heat until boiling. Spoon over apples. Makes about 4 servings.

PER SERVING: 204 calories, 0.9 g protein, 47 g carbohydrates, 0.6 g fat, 0 mg cholesterol, 5 mg sodium

TWO-WAY APPLESAUCE

For chunky sauce, peel apples, using juicy ones that cook quickly. For smooth sauce, use peeled or unpeeled apples, and rub through a strainer (discard peel residue; red-skinned varieties will tint sauce pink). Apple juice sweetens the sauce.

Combine 1 quart peeled, cored, sliced **apples** (or 5 cups unpeeled, cored, sliced apples) with ½ cup **apple juice** or water in a 2½- to 3-quart pan. Bring to a boil; reduce heat and simmer, covered, until fruit is soft and begins to dissolve, 4 to 20 minutes, depending on variety. Add juice to thin or if liquid cooks away.

If desired, mix in 1 to 4 tablespoons **granulated sugar** or firmly packed brown sugar and **ground cinnamon** to

taste. Rub unpeeled apple mixture through a food mill or coarse strainer; discard peels. Makes about 2 cups, 4 servings.

PER SERVING: 77 calories, 0.2 g protein, 20 g carbohydrates, 0.4 g fat, 0 mg cholesterol, 0.9 mg sodium

SAUTÉED APPLE SLICES

These apple wedges glazed in butter and sugar make a sparkling companion for pork, lamb, chicken, or sausage.

Quarter 2 medium-size to large unpeeled **apples;** remove cores and cut fruit into slices about ¾ inch thick. In a 10- to 12-inch pan, melt 1 tablespoon **butter** or margarine over medium heat; when bubbly, add apples and turn to coat with butter. Cover and cook until apples are tender when pierced, 2½ to 10 minutes. Sprinkle with 1 teaspoon **sugar** and cook, uncovered, turning gently as needed, until liquid evaporates and apples brown lightly, 3 to 16 minutes. Makes about 4 servings.

PER SERVING: 71 calories, 0.2 g protein, 12 g carbohydrates, 3 g fat, 7.8 mg cholesterol, 29 mg sodium

Tasters evaluated each apple variety fresh, as well as cooked in four different ways.

CLASSIC APPLE PIE

We baked pies with 22 different apple varieties, fine-tuning the ingredients for each one. Although typical recipes call for as much as a cup of sugar for a 9-inch pie, we found that a quarter of that amount was ample for sweet apples and let more of the apple flavor come through. Use the greater amount of sugar if apples are underripe and extra firm, or if you prefer sweeter desserts.

For pastry, use refrigerated crust, pie crust mix, or your own recipe. The bran cereal in this recipe virtually disappears in the baking, but it helps keep the bottom crust crisp and flaky.

> 8 cups thinly sliced, peeled, cored apples
> Sugar (see chart at right)
> Quick-cooking tapioca or cornstarch (see chart)
> ½ to 1 teaspoon ground cinnamon
> ¼ to ½ teaspoon ground ginger or ground nutmeg
> Lemon juice (see chart)
> Pastry for a double-crust 9-inch pie
> 1 cup bran flake or raisin-bran flake cereal (optional)

In a large bowl, mix apples with sugar, tapioca, cinnamon, ginger, and lemon juice; set aside. Roll out half the pastry on a floured board to fit a 9-inch pie pan. Line pan with pastry. Sprinkle cereal over pastry, then pile in apple mixture, heaping it in the center. On a floured board, roll out remaining pastry to cover pie. Lay pastry over fruit; flute edges and cut vent holes in the top.

Bake on the lowest shelf of a 425° oven until top is browned and filling is bubbly, 45 to 55 minutes. If browned after 30 minutes, cover loosely with foil. Serve warm or at room temperature. Makes 6 to 8 servings.

PER SERVING: 204 calories, 1.5 g protein, 34 g carbohydrates, 7.9 g fat, 0 mg cholesterol, 138 mg sodium

Apple Variety	Sugar (cup)	Tapioca (tablespoon)	Lemon juice (tablespoon)
Akane	¼ to ⅓	0	0
Braeburn	⅓ to ½	2	0
Cortland	¼ to ⅓	1	2
Criterion	¼ to ⅓	0	2
Elstar	⅓ to ½	0	0
Empire	⅓ to ½	0	0
Fuji	⅓ to ½	1	0
Gala	¼ to ⅓	1	2
Golden Delicious	¼ to ⅓	2	2
Granny Smith	½ to ¾	0	0
Gravenstein	⅓ to ⅔	0	0
Idared	¼ to ⅓	0	1
Jonagold	¼ to ⅓	1	2
Jonathan	¼ to ⅓	0	0
McIntosh	⅓ to ½	0	0
Melrose	¼ to ⅓	1	0
Mutsu	⅓ to ½	0	0
Newtown Pippin	½ to ⅔	0	0
Red Delicious	¼ to ⅓	2	2
Rome Beauty	¼ to ⅓	0	3
Spartan	¼ to ⅓	0	2
Stayman Winesap	¼ to ⅓	0	0

Smooth Soups

THE HUMBLE ELEMENTS *of these soups, puréed together, form smooth, flavorful collaborations. Vegetables thicken and color them, while garnishes add textural contrast and seasoning. Such smooth soups are sometimes called bisques.*

Potatoes lend silkiness to the sweet golden pepper bisque. Creamy pinto beans, sweet tomatoes, and carrots make another winning combination.

GOLDEN PEPPER BISQUE

- 2 large (about 1 lb. total) yellow bell peppers
- 1 tablespoon salad oil or olive oil
- 1 large onion, chopped
- 2 large (about 1 lb. total) thin-skinned potatoes, peeled and cut into ½-inch chunks
- 2 large (about ½ lb. total) carrots, peeled and sliced ½ inch thick
- 1 large stalk celery, ends trimmed, thinly sliced
- 6 cups regular-strength chicken broth
  Extra-virgin olive oil
  Salt and pepper
  Finely shredded parmesan cheese
  Croutons (recipe follows)

Rinse bell peppers. Place in a 9-inch pie or cake pan and broil about 4 inches from heat, turning as needed, until all sides are charred, 12 to 17 minutes. Let cool. Remove and discard stems, seeds, and skin; rinse peppers and cut into chunks.

In a 5- to 6-quart pan, combine salad oil and onion. Stir occasionally over medium-high heat until onion is faintly browned, about 10 minutes. Add bell peppers, potatoes, carrots, celery, and chicken broth. Bring to a boil, then cover and simmer until carrots are very soft to bite, 20 to 25 minutes.

In a blender or food processor, smoothly purée vegetable mixture, a portion at a time. (If made ahead, cool, cover, and chill up until the next day.) Return to pan. Warm soup, covered, over medium heat; stir often. Ladle into wide soup bowls. Add extra-virgin olive oil, salt, pepper, cheese, and croutons to taste. Makes 6 to 8 servings.

PER PLAIN SERVING: 109 calories, 3.7 g protein, 17 g carbohydrates, 3.2 g fat, 0 mg cholesterol, 59 mg sodium

Croutons. Cut 4 ounces **French bread** into ¾-inch cubes. In a 10- by 15-inch baking pan, mix bread with 2 table-spoons **olive oil.** Bake in a 350° oven until croutons are golden and crisp, 10 to 12 minutes. If made ahead, cool and store airtight up to 2 days. Makes 4 cups.

PER ½-CUP SERVING: 71 calories, 1.3 g protein, 7.9 g carbohydrates, 3.8 g fat, 0.4 mg cholesterol, 82 mg sodium

BEAN & TOMATO BISQUE

- 3 medium-size (about 1¼ lb. total) firm-ripe tomatoes
  Extra-virgin olive oil
- 1 large onion, chopped
- 2 cloves garlic, pressed or minced
- 2 large (about ½ lb. total) carrots, peeled and thinly sliced
- 1 can (15 oz.) pinto beans, drained
- 1 quart regular-strength chicken broth
- ⅓ cup chopped fresh basil leaves or fresh cilantro (coriander)
  Salt and pepper

In a 4- to 5-quart pan, bring about 2 quarts water to a boil. Drop 2 of the tomatoes into the water for about 30 seconds; lift out and drain. Pull off skin and cut out core; discard. Coarsely chop peeled tomatoes.

Dry pan and add to it 1 tablespoon olive oil, onion, and garlic. Stir often over high heat until onion is faintly brown, 6 to 8 minutes. Add chopped tomato, carrots, pinto beans, and chicken broth. Bring to a boil; then simmer, covered, until carrot is very soft to bite, about 10 minutes.

In a blender or food processor, smoothly purée soup a portion at a time. (If made ahead, cool, cover, and chill up until the next day.) Return to pan. Warm soup, covered, over medium heat; stir often.

Core and dice remaining tomato. Ladle soup into wide bowls and garnish each with equal portions of tomato and basil. Add olive oil and salt and pepper to taste. Makes 4 to 6 servings.

PER SERVING: 140 calories, 6.4 g protein, 21 g carbohydrates, 3.9 g fat, 0 mg cholesterol, 350 mg sodium

Yellow peppers and carrots give this soup its golden hue and mild sweetness. A drizzle of olive oil, shredded parmesan, and croutons complete it.

Halloween Pumpkin Party

Invite witches, *pirates, and other ghoulish guests to this Halloween celebration. The feasting focuses on a giant pumpkin filled with a witches' brew of chicken and barley soup. Use smaller pumpkins as soup bowls. When you're done, rinse the shells and carve jack-o'-lanterns.*

HALLOWEEN PUMPKIN PARTY FOR 10 TO 12

Roasted Pumpkin Teeth
(Pumpkin Seeds)
Spider Eggs in a Cocoon (*Peas in a Pod*)
Celery Broomsticks or Jicama Bones
Bloodshot Eyeballs (*Cherry Tomatoes*)
Witches' Brew in Pumpkin Shell
(Chicken and Barley Soup)
Black Widow Rolls (*Poppy Seed Rolls*)
Butter
Milk or Apple Cider
**Caramel Cheese Apples or
Plain Apples**

Roast pumpkin seeds to make appetizers. Also offer raw vegetables for hungry guests to nibble. Gjetost cheese adds extra protein to the caramel apples.

Allow 1½ to 2 pounds vegetables for appetizers; choose several kinds. Fringe the broad ends of celery sticks to make broomsticks; immerse in ice water. Cut peeled jicama to resemble bones. Rinse pea pods and cherry tomatoes.

The soup can be made up to 1 day ahead. You can clean the pumpkin shells at the same time, but keep them cool if they're ready more than 4 hours ahead. Save the seeds for roasting. Make caramel apples up to 2 days in advance.

ROASTED PUMPKIN TEETH

Pull and discard fibers from **seeds** (see pumpkin shells, far right); rinse seeds and drain well. In each 10- by 15-inch baking pan, place 2 to 3 cups seeds. Sprinkle lightly with **salt**. Bake in a 300° oven until golden and crisp, about 45 minutes; stir occasionally. If made ahead, cool and store airtight up to 3 days. A 14-pound pumpkin yields about 1½ cups seeds.

PER ¼-CUP SERVING: 71 calories, 3 g protein, 8.6 g carbohydrates, 3.1 g fat, 0 mg cholesterol, 2.9 mg sodium

WITCHES' BREW IN PUMPKIN SHELL

- 2 **tablespoons salad oil**
- 1 **large onion, chopped**
- 1 **large red bell pepper, stemmed, seeded, and chopped**
- 1 **clove garlic, minced or pressed**
- 1 **teaspoon ground cumin**
- 3½ **quarts regular-strength chicken broth**
- 1 **broiler-fryer chicken (about 3½ lb.), cut up**
- ¾ **cup pearl barley, rinsed**
- 2 **to 2½ pounds fresh pumpkin, or banana or hubbard squash, peeled and cut into ½-inch cubes (about 6 cups)**
  Pumpkin shells (directions follow)
- 1 **package (10 oz.) frozen corn**
- ¾ **pound Swiss chard, tough stems trimmed, cut crosswise into thin shreds**
  Condiments (choices follow)
  Salt and pepper

In an 8- to 10-quart pan, combine oil, onion, bell pepper, and garlic. Stir often over medium-high heat until onion is slightly browned, about 7 minutes. Stir in cumin and broth. Bring to a boil over high heat. Add chicken (except breast) and barley. Cover and simmer 20 minutes. Add breast; cover and simmer until breast is white in center of thickest part, about 15 minutes. Lift out chicken; let cool. Skim and discard fat from soup. Add pumpkin to soup; cover and simmer until tender when pierced, about 15 minutes.

When chicken is cool enough to touch (about 10 minutes), remove and discard skin and bones; tear meat into bite-size pieces and return to soup. If soup is made ahead, cool, cover, and chill up until the next day. Remove fat from top.

About 10 minutes before serving, pour boiling water into large and small pumpkin shells; cover and let stand to warm.

Bring soup to a boil. Add corn and chard; cook until chard wilts, about 2 minutes.

Drain water from pumpkin shells. Pour hot soup into big pumpkin shell. To serve, ladle soup into smaller pumpkin shells. Offer condiments and salt and pepper to add to taste. Makes about 6 quarts, 10 to 12 servings.

PER PLAIN SERVING: 222 calories, 19 g protein, 22 g carbohydrates, 6.5 g fat, 45 mg cholesterol, 170 mg sodium

Pumpkin shells. Cut tops out to make lids from 1 large (14 to 18 lb.) **pumpkin** and 10 to 12 small (1 to 3 lb. each) **pumpkins.** Scrape out fibers and seeds; reserve seeds for roasted teeth, preceding.

Condiments. Select 3 or 4: 1 large firm-ripe **avocado**, peeled, pitted, diced, and coated with 1 tablespoon **lemon juice**; 1½ cups (6 oz.) shredded **jack cheese**; 1 cup **fresh cilantro** (coriander) **sprigs**; and ½ cup thinly sliced **green onion.**

CARAMEL CHEESE APPLES

- 10 **to 12 small (4 to 5 oz. each) apples**
- 10 **to 12 wooden ice cream sticks**
- 1 **package (14 oz.) vanilla caramels, unwrapped**
- 1 **package (8.8 oz.) gjetost cheese, cut into ½-inch cubes**
- 3 **tablespoons water**

Wash and dry apples. Twist off stems. Insert sticks into 1 end of each apple. Butter a 10- by 15-inch baking pan.

To cook on direct heat. In a deep 1½- to 2-quart pan, stir caramels, cheese, and water over medium-low heat, just until melted and smooth, 10 to 12 minutes.

To cook in a microwave oven. Place caramels, cheese, and water in a small, deep microwave-safe bowl or 1-quart glass measuring cup. Cook at full power (100 percent) in a microwave oven, stirring once or twice, until smoothly melted, about 4 minutes.

Holding sticks, dip apples, 1 at a time, into caramel mixture; swirl apples in caramel or spoon caramel over apples to coat sides of fruit. Lift out of caramel and drain briefly; set on buttered pan. Repeat with remaining apples, placing them slightly apart. If caramel gets too thick, stir over low heat or reheat in microwave oven until fluid. Chill until caramel is set, at least 4 hours. If made ahead, cover and chill up to 2 days. Makes 10 to 12 apples.

PER SERVING: 290 calories, 3.5 g protein, 50 g carbohydrates, 9.9 g fat, 0.7 mg cholesterol, 200 mg sodium

From a giant pumpkin cauldron, ladle chicken and barley soup into smaller pumpkin bowls. Guests add condiments to soup and munch on appetizers of roasted pumpkin seeds and raw vegetables. For dessert, bite into an apple cloaked in caramel and cheese.

Baking with Soy Flour

To boost the protein of breads, pastries, and similar baked products, soy flour can be an effective—and flavorful—ingredient. Because soy flour behaves quite differently from wheat flour, one cannot be substituted for the other in recipes. But together, they're a starting point for good-tasting baked foods. We suggest several uses.

Found for years in health-food stores, soy flour is increasingly available in supermarkets, generally in 1- to 2-pound bags. At a glance, the flour, made from toasted soy beans, resembles fine cornmeal, but it has a damper feel.

When moistened, soy flour has a strong vegetable smell, and the dough can be somewhat sticky to work with. As it bakes, however, the flour develops a sweet, nut-like fragrance and taste. Breads and pastries made with soy flour brown more rapidly, so watch closely as food cooks. The yeast bread is noticeably springier. Soy flour also adds a distinctive crispness, evident in thin shortbread, flatbread, and pizza crust.

While soy flour has four times the protein of all-purpose flour, it lacks the gluten necessary to support leavened breads.

To slow any changes in flavor, refrigerate any unused portions of soy flour in an airtight container. Note, too, that it declines in quality after 4 months.

Fine, springy texture and golden color in loaf come from soy flour. Bread browns rapidly, so watch closely as food cooks.

Soy Bread

> 1 package active dry yeast
> 1½ cups warm water (110°)
> ½ teaspoon salt
> ½ cup soy flour
> About 3½ cups all-purpose flour

In a large bowl, combine yeast and water; let stand to soften, about 5 minutes. Add salt and soy flour; mix well. Add 3 cups all-purpose flour; stir to moisten well.

To knead by hand, scrape dough onto a board generously coated with all-purpose flour. Knead until smooth and elastic, 8 to 10 minutes; add flour as required to prevent sticking. Rinse, dry, and oil bowl. Turn dough over in bowl to oil top.

To knead with a dough hook, mix until dough no longer feels sticky to touch and pulls from side of bowl; if necessary, add all-purpose flour, 1 tablespoon at a time.

Cover dough, kneaded by either method, with plastic wrap; let stand in a warm place until doubled in size, 1 to 1½ hours.

Punch dough down, then scrape onto a board lightly coated with all-purpose flour. Kneading gently, shape dough into a smooth ball. Place on an oiled 12- by 15-inch baking sheet. Pat ball to flatten into a 6-inch round. Cover lightly with plastic wrap and let stand until puffy-looking, about 40 minutes.

Bake, uncovered, in a 350° oven until crust is richly brown, about 40 minutes. Transfer to a rack to cool slightly. Serve warm or cool.

If made ahead, wrap airtight when cool and hold at room temperature up to 1 day; freeze to store longer. Makes 1 loaf, about 1¾ pounds.

PER SERVING: 60 calories, 2.6 g protein, 12 g carbohydrates, 0.1 g fat, 0 mg cholesterol, 46 mg sodium

Soft Soy Shortbread Cookies

> 1 cup (½ lb.) butter or margarine
> ½ cup sugar
> 1½ cups all-purpose flour
> ½ cup soy flour

In a food processor, whirl butter, sugar, all-purpose flour, and soy flour until dough forms a ball. (To prepare by hand, rub mixture with your fingers until mixture forms fine crumbs, then press dough firmly to form a ball.)

Pat the dough evenly into an ungreased 9-inch-square pan. Pierce dough all over with a fork at ½-inch intervals.

Bake in a 325° oven until golden, about 35 minutes. While warm, cut the pastry into 1½-inch squares and, with a spatula, transfer cookies to a rack to cool. Serve, or package airtight and chill up to 3 days; freeze to store longer. Makes 36.

PER COOKY: 79 calories, 1.2 g protein, 7.2 g carbohydrates, 5 g fat, 14 mg cholesterol, 52 mg sodium

Crisp soy shortbread cookies. To make thinner, crisper cookies, prepare dough as directed, preceding. Instead of using a 9-inch-square pan, pat dough out on a 12- by 15-inch baking sheet to make a neat 9- by 13-inch rectangle.

Pierce dough all over with a fork at ½-inch intervals. Bake in a 275° oven until a rich, golden brown, about 45 minutes.

While warm, cut into 1½-inch squares and transfer with a wide spatula to racks to cool. Makes 48.

PER COOKY: 60 calories, 0.9 g protein, 5.4 g carbohydrates, 3.9 g fat, 10 mg cholesterol, 39 mg sodium

SOY FLATBREAD

- 1 package active dry yeast
- ¾ cup warm water (110°)
- 2 tablespoons olive or salad oil
  About ½ teaspoon salt
  About 1½ cups all-purpose flour
- ¾ cup soy flour

In a bowl, combine yeast and water; let stand until softened, about 5 minutes. Add 1 tablespoon oil, ½ teaspoon salt, 1 cup all-purpose flour, and soy flour; beat to mix well. Scrape dough onto a board coated lightly with all-purpose flour. Knead until dough is smooth and elastic, about 5 minutes; add all-purpose flour as required to prevent sticking.

Rinse, dry, and oil bowl. Turn dough over in bowl to oil top. Cover with plastic wrap and let rise in a warm place until almost doubled in volume, about 45 minutes. Punch dough down and knead on a lightly floured board to expel air. Divide dough into 16 equal pieces. Shape each piece into a ball, flatten slightly, then cover with plastic wrap.

Roll out 1 piece of dough to make a 6- to 7-inch round; add flour and turn frequently to prevent sticking. Gently lift round onto an oiled 12- by 15-inch baking sheet. Roll out 1 more round and put on pan; don't overlap. Brush rounds lightly with oil and, if desired, sprinkle with salt.

Bake in a 325° oven until golden brown on edges (watch closely; they darken quickly), about 15 minutes. Repeat to shape and bake remaining dough (if using 2 baking sheets in 1 oven, alternate positions halfway through baking). Transfer rounds to racks; they crisp as they cool. Serve, or, when cool, package airtight at once to preserve crispness, then freeze. Thaw unwrapped. Makes 16.

PER PIECE: 52 calories, 2.9 g protein, 6.3 g carbohydrates, 1.8 g fat, 0 mg cholesterol, 69 mg sodium

Herbed soy flatbread. Make **soy flatbread,** preceding, adding 1½ teaspoons **dry basil leaves** and/or **dry oregano leaves** along with all-purpose and soy flours. Brush unbaked rounds with **water** and sprinkle each with about ½ teaspoon grated **parmesan cheese** (3 tablespoons total).

PER PIECE: 56 calories, 3.3 g protein, 6.4 g carbohydrates, 2.1 g fat, 0.7 mg cholesterol, 18 mg sodium

PIZZA WITH CRISP SOY CRUST

Make **soy flatbread** dough, preceding. Divide dough in half. On a board lightly coated with all-purpose flour, roll each half into an 8-inch round. Place rounds on an oiled 12- by 15-inch baking sheet and pierce all over with a fork. Bake in a 400° oven for 5 minutes.

Divide ¾ cup homemade or purchased **pizza sauce** between the rounds; spread evenly. Sprinkle equally with 2 cups (8 oz.) shredded **mozzarella cheese,** and 1 teaspoon *each* crumbled **dry oregano leaves** and **dry thyme leaves. Optional toppings** include 1 cup crumbled browned Italian sausage, 1 cup thinly sliced mushrooms, ½ cup black ripe olives.

Bake pizzas on lowest rack of a 400° oven until crust is brown on bottom (lift with a spatula to check), about 25 minutes. Cut into wedges. Makes 4 to 6 servings.

PER SERVING: 338 calories, 20 g protein, 23 g carbohydrates, 19 g fat, 44 mg cholesterol, 678 mg sodium

Crisp golden soy flatbread goes well with herb butter or other spreads. For a variation, add dried herbs along with flours and sprinkle rounds with grated parmesan.

No-Fat Salad Dressings Made with Chilies

CHILIES LEND COLOR, *heat, and body to these oil-free salad dressings.*

Dried red chilies give the first dressing a vivid hue and spicy flavor. Puréed mild green chilies and hot jalapeños make the second one tart.

Use either with orange onion salad (recipe follows) or with another of your choosing.

RED CHILI DRESSING

- 3 large (¾ oz. total) dry California or New Mexico chilies
- ¾ cup water
- 6 tablespoons cider vinegar
- 2 tablespoons sugar
- 1 tablespoon chopped fresh ginger
  Salt

Remove and discard stems and most of the seeds from chilies. Rinse chilies and cut with scissors into ½-inch strips. In a 1- to 1½-quart pan, combine chilies and water. Bring to a boil. Remove pan from heat; let chilies soak until soft, about 5 minutes.

In a blender or food processor, combine chili mixture, vinegar, sugar, and ginger; whirl until smoothly puréed. Add salt to taste. Serve; or cool, cover, and chill up to 1 week. Makes about 1 cup.

PER TABLESPOON: 11 calories, 0.2 g protein, 2.7 g carbohydrates, 0.2 g fat, 0 mg cholesterol, 0.5 mg sodium

GREEN CHILI DRESSING

- 1 can (4 oz.) green chilies
- ⅓ cup lime juice
- ¼ cup chopped fresh cilantro (coriander)
- ¼ cup water
- 1 clove garlic
- 1 or 2 fresh jalapeño chilies, stemmed, seeded, and chopped
- 1½ teaspoons sugar
  Salt

In a blender or food processor, combine green chilies, lime juice, cilantro, water, garlic, jalapeño chilies, and sugar; whirl until smoothly puréed. Add salt to taste. Serve or, if made ahead, cover and chill up to 1 day. Makes about 1 cup.

PER TABLESPOON: 5 calories, 0 g protein, 1.3 g carbohydrates, 0 g fat, 0 mg cholesterol, 44 mg sodium

Pour spicy red chili dressing over colorful salad of crisp leaf lettuce, tiny shrimp, orange, cucumber, onion, and avocado.

ORANGE ONION SALAD WITH CHILI DRESSING

- 4 quarts (about 1 lb.) rinsed and crisped leaf lettuce, in bite-size pieces
- ½ pound (1 cup) tiny cooked shelled shrimp or 2 cups bite-size pieces cooked chicken or beef steak
- ½ cup thinly sliced red onion
- 1 small cucumber, ends trimmed, thinly sliced
- 3 small (about 1 lb. total) oranges
- 1 medium-size firm-ripe avocado
- 1 cup green or red chili dressing (recipes precede)

Place lettuce in a large, shallow salad bowl. Arrange shrimp, onion, and cucumber on lettuce.

With a short, sharp knife, cut peel and white membrane from oranges. Cut oranges crosswise into ¼-inch-thick slices; arrange on salad. Peel and pit avocado, thinly slice lengthwise, and place slices on salad. Pour dressing over salad and gently mix. Makes 6 to 8 servings.

PER SERVING WITH GREEN DRESSING: 114 calories, 7.8 g protein, 13 g carbohydrates, 4.4 g fat, 55 mg cholesterol, 160 mg sodium

Leaner Ways with Fish

F ROM EVERY QUARTER, *the interest in creating dishes that are equally well balanced in nutrition and flavor is producing delightful dining choices. When Casa Madrona chef Kirke Byer, of Sausalito, California, took on this task, he came up with these handsome, lean fish preparations.*

First, a foursome of citrus fruits becomes the sauce for broiled fish and fragrant basmati rice. In the second dish, grilled scallops are flanked by a ginger-pear purée; serve with black beans, sliced oranges, and a green salad.

CITRUS LINGCOD WITH ORANGE ALMOND RICE

- 4 or 5 small (about 2 lb. total) oranges
- 1 large (about ¾ lb.) pink grapefruit
- 1 medium-size lemon
- 1 medium-size lime
- ¼ cup slivered almonds
- ¼ cup olive oil
- ¼ cup chopped onion
- ½ teaspoon almond extract
- 1½ cups white basmati or long-grain rice
- 2 pounds boned and skinned mild, white-flesh fish fillets (such as lingcod, striped bass, or grouper), about 1 inch thick
- ¼ cup rice vinegar
- 2 tablespoons minced shallots
  Salt and pepper

Finely shred enough peel (colored part only) from oranges and grapefruit to make 1½ tablespoons *each*. Finely shred colored peel from lemon and lime to make 1 teaspoon *each*. Mix citrus peels together; set aside.

With a short, sharp knife, cut peel and white membrane from 2 oranges, the grapefruit, lemon, and lime. Over a bowl, cut between white membranes to release citrus segments into bowl. Ream remaining oranges to make 1¼ cups juice.

In a 2- to 3-quart pan, stir almonds over medium heat until golden, 5 to 9 minutes. Pour out of pan; reserve. To pan add 1 tablespoon oil and onion; stir over medium-high heat until limp, 3 to 5 minutes. Add ¾ cup orange juice, 1¼ cups water, and almond extract. Bring to a boil and stir in rice. Cover and simmer on low heat until rice is tender to bite, 20 to 30 minutes. Just before serving, stir in the almonds.

Orange, grapefruit, lemon, and lime segments, citrus juices, and zests add lively flavor to broiled fish and basmati rice with almonds.

Rinse fish and pat dry. Cut into 4 to 6 equal pieces. Brush fish all over with about 2 tablespoons oil. Place on rack in a 12- by 14-inch broiler pan. Broil about 4 inches from heat, turning once, until fish is opaque but still moist-looking in thickest part (cut to test), 10 to 12 minutes.

In a 10- to 12-inch frying pan, combine vinegar, shallots, remaining ½ cup orange juice, citrus segments and accumulated juices, and 1 tablespoon olive oil. Cook over medium heat, shaking pan often, just until sauce is warm, about 2 minutes.

On 4 to 6 dinner plates, place equal portions of the rice, fish, and warm sauce. Garnish with citrus peel. Add salt and pepper to taste. Makes 4 to 6 servings.

PER SERVING: 503 calories, 34 g protein, 51 g carbohydrates, 18 g fat, 103 mg cholesterol, 112 mg sodium

GRILLED SCALLOPS WITH PEAR & GINGER COULIS

- 1 pound sea scallops
- 2 tablespoons olive oil
- 1 small onion, diced
- 2 tablespoons chopped fresh ginger

- 3 medium-size (about 1½ lb. total) firm-ripe pears, peeled, cored, and diced
- ¼ cup rice vinegar
  Salt and pepper

Rinse scallops and pat dry. If needed, cut in half crosswise to make rounds about ½ inch thick. Mix with 1 tablespoon oil. Divide into 4 equal portions; thread scallops through sides on 4 thin skewers.

In a 2- to 3-quart pan over medium-high heat, stir onion often in 1 tablespoon oil until limp, about 8 minutes. Add ginger, pears, and vinegar. Simmer, uncovered, until pears are tender when pierced, 15 to 20 minutes. Smoothly purée in a blender or food processor. Keep warm, or cover and chill up to 3 days; reheat to use.

Place scallops on a grill 4 to 6 inches above a solid bed of hot coals (you can hold your hand at grill level for only 2 to 3 seconds). Cook, turning once, until scallops are opaque but still moist-looking in thickest part (cut to test), 8 to 10 minutes.

On 4 warm dinner plates, mound equal portions of warm pear mixture. Lay a scallop skewer on each. Add salt and pepper to taste. Makes 4 servings.

PER SERVING: 260 calories, 20 g protein, 28 g carbohydrates, 8.3 g fat, 38 mg cholesterol, 186 mg sodium

Main Dishes from the Microwave

FAST, NUTRITIOUS, EVEN *elegant dishes can be prepared in the microwave. It saves cooking time, helps food retain nutrients and color, and minimizes cleanup.*

In the first of these two entrées, seabass fillets are slashed to lie flat, then cook quickly, seasoned with orange juice and soy sauce. In the second recipe, a preheated microwave browning dish is used to give tenderized beef steaks a quick browning before meat is cooked briefly in the microwave oven.

SEABASS WITH GINGER

For a light, lean, and flavorful entrée, enhance seabass with orange and fresh ginger. Chinese pea pods or buttered baby carrots make colorful companions.

- ¾ **to 1 pound white seabass fillets (each 1 to 1½ in. thick)**
- 2 **tablespoons orange juice**
- 4 **teaspoons soy sauce**
- 2 **teaspoons finely shredded fresh ginger**
- 1 **teaspoon finely shredded orange peel**
  Fresh cilantro (coriander) sprigs
  Orange wedges

Rinse fish and pat dry. To butterfly fish, cut each fillet in half horizontally almost all the way through; open fillets out flat. On both sides of each opened-out fillet, make crosswise cuts at 1-inch intervals; cut toward center of fillet, leaving about a 1½-inch-wide strip uncut at center.

Set fish pieces in a 9- by 13-inch microwave-safe baking dish and drizzle evenly with orange juice and soy. Sprinkle ginger and orange peel evenly over fish. Cover and cook in a microwave oven on full power (100 percent) for 2 minutes. Let stand, covered, for 3 minutes. Fish should be opaque but still moist-looking in center of thickest part (cut to test). If necessary, cover and cook on full power for 1 to 2 minutes longer, testing for doneness every 30 seconds.

Arrange fish on plates; garnish with cilantro and orange wedges. Makes 2 servings.

PER SERVING: 210 calories, 38 g protein, 3 g carbohydrates, 4 g fat, 82 mg cholesterol, 823 mg sodium

STEAK WITH MUSTARD-CAPER SAUCE

The lean, boneless steaks labeled "cube steaks" or "minute steaks" in the meat market are actually beef round steak—first cut into individual portions, then run through a mechanical tenderizer. The meat sizzles on a microwave browning dish; the dish is heated in the microwave before the meat goes onto it.

- 2 **cube beef steaks (about 6 oz. each)**
- 4 **teaspoons prepared steak sauce**
- 2 **tablespoons dry sherry**
- 2 **teaspoons Dijon mustard**
- ¼ **teaspoon Worcestershire**
- 1 **tablespoon drained capers**
- 2 **tablespoons butter or margarine**
  Watercress sprigs

Brush each steak on each side with 1 teaspoon steak sauce. Set steaks aside.

Preheat a 2- to 2½-quart or 10-inch-square microwave browning dish in a microwave oven on full power (100 percent) for 4½ minutes. Meanwhile, stir together sherry, mustard, Worcestershire, and capers; set aside.

Using oven mitts, carefully transfer browning dish to a heatproof surface. Add steaks and wait until sizzling stops. Then turn steaks over and cook in microwave oven, uncovered, on full power for 45 seconds. Transfer steaks to a plate, cover loosely, and let stand for 2 minutes.

Meanwhile, add butter to browning dish and heat, uncovered, on full power until butter melts, 25 to 30 seconds. Stir in sherry mixture and heat, uncovered, on full power until hot, about 45 seconds. Pour sauce over steaks and garnish with watercress. Makes 2 servings.

PER SERVING: 534 calories, 33 g protein, 5 g carbohydrates, 42 g fat, 143 mg cholesterol, 656 mg sodium

Orange and ginger season seabass fillets, butterflied for even cooking.

Baked Potatoes Stuffed with Good Things

S TURDY AND SATISFYING, *economical and handy appropriately describe these supper dishes based on steaming baked (russet or sweet) potatoes. Each is filled with mixtures quickly composed from ingredients found in most pantries and refrigerators.*

POTATOES FAJITAS

4 large (about 2¾ lb. total) russet potatoes
About ¼ pound fat-trimmed cold cooked beef, such as steak or roast
⅓ cup lime juice
1 clove garlic, minced or pressed
1 tablespoon salad oil
1 medium-size onion, coarsely chopped
About 1½ cups purchased salsa
Lime wedges
Fresh cilantro (coriander) sprigs
Sour cream (optional)

Scrub potatoes and pierce several times with a fork. Bake on the rack in a 350° oven until very tender when pierced, about 1 hour.

Meanwhile, thinly slice beef across the grain. Mix in a small bowl with lime juice and garlic. Pour oil into a 10- to 12-inch frying pan over high heat. Add onion and stir just until limp, about 5 minutes. Transfer meat to pan with a slotted spoon; stir just until hot, about 1 minute. Add meat marinade and ½ cup salsa; stir until hot, about 1 minute. Remove from heat.

Using potholders to protect your hands, cut a deep slit lengthwise down the center and an equally deep one across the middle of each potato. Grasping potato between the slits, press firmly to split top open wide. Set potatoes on plates and top with meat mixture. Accompany with more salsa, lime wedges, cilantro, and sour cream to add to taste. Makes 4 servings.

PER SERVING: 372 calories, 14 g protein, 65 g carbohydrates, 6.1 g fat, 22 mg cholesterol, 586 mg sodium

CURRIED HUMMUS WITH BAKED POTATOES

4 large (about 2¾ lb. total) russet potatoes
1 can (15½ oz.) garbanzos, drained
About ¾ cup regular-strength chicken broth

Golden curry and hummus make russet potato (left) an all-vegetable main dish; melted cheese tops yam (right), which cradles mellow onions, bacon, and chutney.

3 tablespoons lemon juice
2 cloves garlic
2 teaspoons curry powder
½ teaspoon cumin seed
Finely slivered green onions
Salt and pepper

Scrub potatoes and pierce in several places with a fork. Bake on a rack in a 350° oven until very tender when pierced, about 1 hour.

Meanwhile, in a blender or food processor, make hummus by whirling garbanzos, ¾ cup broth, lemon juice, garlic, curry, and cumin until very smooth. Pour into a 2- to 3-quart pan; stir over medium-high heat until mixture is reduced to 1½ cups. Keep warm. If made ahead, let stand up to 2 hours; reheat (thin, if desired, with a little more broth).

Using potholders to protect your hands, cut a deep slit lengthwise down the center and an equally deep one across the middle of each potato. Grasping potato between the slits, press firmly to split top open wide. Put potatoes on plates; generously spoon hummus into splits. Garnish with onions; offer remaining hummus, salt, and pepper to add to taste. Makes 4 servings.

PER SERVING: 402 calories, 12 g protein, 84 g carbohydrates, 2.4 g fat, 0 mg cholesterol, 377 mg sodium

ONION, BACON & CHUTNEY WITH YAMS

4 large (about 2¾ lb. total) yams or sweet potatoes
4 large (about 2½ lb. total) onions, thinly sliced
4 slices bacon, chopped
About ½ cup chutney (any kind), coarsely chopped
½ cup shredded gouda, fontina, or jack cheese

Scrub yams and pierce several times with a fork. Set in a 10- by 15-inch pan. Bake in a 350° oven until very tender when pierced, about 1 hour and 10 minutes.

Meanwhile, in a 10- to 12-inch frying pan over medium-high heat, stir onions and bacon often until onions are golden and sweet tasting, about 20 minutes. (If made ahead, set aside up to 2 hours; reheat.) Off heat, add ¼ cup chutney.

Using potholders to protect your hands, cut a deep slit lengthwise down the center and an equally deep one across the middle of each potato. Grasping potato between the slits, press firmly to split top open wide. Pile onion mixture equally into splits, then sprinkle with cheese. Return to pan and broil about 4 inches from heat until cheese is melted, 1 to 2 minutes. Put potatoes on plates and accompany with remaining chutney. Makes 4 servings.

PER SERVING: 572 calories, 12 g protein, 92 g carbohydrates, 18 g fat, 31 mg cholesterol, 373 mg sodium

Stay-Fresh Rolled Sandwiches

BROWN-BAG LUNCHERS *will find merit in these two rolled sandwiches. Both are easy to eat out of hand and can safely wait at room temperature until lunch time without loss of freshness. One has a bright green wilted-lettuce wrapper; the other is rolled up in a thin flour tortilla.*

You can make either of the sandwiches the night before and chill them overnight to keep them as fresh as possible. Slip the sandwich into your lunch bag with a few cookies and some fruit, then hit the road.

ROMAINE DOLMAS

   ½ **cup short- or medium-grain rice**
   3 **ounces dry salami, diced**
   2 **tablespoons drained capers**
   2 **tablespoons seasoned rice vinegar or 2 tablespoons rice vinegar and 2 teaspoons sugar**
   2 **teaspoons grated lemon peel**
   8 **large romaine lettuce leaves**

In a 2- to 3-quart pan, combine rice and 1¼ cups water. Bring to boiling over high heat. Cover and simmer until liquid is absorbed, about 20 minutes. Uncover, stir with a fork, and let cool. With fork, mix in salami, capers, vinegar, and lemon peel.

In a 10- to 12-inch pan, bring about 1 inch water to a boil. Immerse leaves 1 at a time, just until limp, about 5 seconds. Immediately immerse leaves in ice water until cold. Lift out and lay flat on paper towels; blot dry.

At stem end of each leaf, mound ⅛ of rice. Fold sides over filling, then roll from stem end, tucking in edges as you go to form a neat package. Serve, or seal in plastic wrap to store or carry. If made ahead, put in refrigerator up until next day. Dolmas hold well up to 5 hours at room temperature. Makes 8; allow 2 for a serving.

PER DOLMA: 93 calories, 3.6 g protein, 10 g carbohydrates, 3.8 g fat, 8.4 mg cholesterol, 255 mg sodium

ROLLED TORTILLA SANDWICH WITH RED PEPPER SPREAD & CHEESE

You will have enough red pepper spread for 4 sandwiches.

   1 **flour tortilla, 10- or 12-inch diameter**
   2 **tablespoons red pepper spread (recipe follows)**
   1½ **ounces thinly sliced havarti or jack cheese**

Lay tortilla flat. Spread the red pepper filling over the tortilla, leaving bare a quarter-moon section (1 in. wide at midpoint) along 1 edge. Lay the cheese slices in a single layer across center of tortilla, parallel to the plain edge; brush plain edge lightly with water.

Starting opposite plain edge, tightly roll tortilla around filling, tucking in cheese. Press firmly against moist edge to seal. If made ahead, wrap airtight and chill up until next day. Cut tortilla diagonally into 2-inch-wide slices; seal in a plastic bag to transport. Sandwich stays fresh at room temperature up to 5 hours. Makes 1 serving.

PER SERVING: 308 calories, 14 g protein, 31 g carbohydrates, 14 g fat, 43 mg cholesterol, 554 mg sodium

Red pepper spread. Put 1 cup drained **canned roasted red bell peppers** or drained canned pimientos in a food processor or blender with ¼ cup **firmly packed basil leaves,** 1 tablespoon **balsamic vinegar,** and 2 teaspoons **olive oil;** whirl until smooth. Pour into a 1½- to 2-quart pan; boil and stir over medium-high heat until reduced to ½ cup, about 2 minutes. Cool. Use, or cover and chill up to 4 days. Makes ½ cup.

PER TABLESPOON: 25 calories, 0.5 g protein, 3.3 g carbohydrates, 1.4 g fat, 0 mg cholesterol, 12 mg sodium

Neat bundles—blanched lettuce leaves, rolled over filling of cooked rice and salami—travel unchilled to the office for a nutritious desk lunch.

Salsa Cousins

THE POPULARITY OF SALSA *has given us cause to take a new look at relishes. No longer are they predictable concoctions that keep forever; any flavor-dense mixture complementary to meats, poultry, or fish qualifies—and ingredients may be short-lived.*

HOT PINEAPPLE & DAIKON RELISH

1 **can (8 oz.) unsweetened crushed pineapple, drained, or ½ cup chopped fresh pineapple**

2 **tablespoons lime juice**

1 **tablespoon minced fresh ginger**

1 **tablespoon dry mustard mixed with 1 tablespoon water**

2 **teaspoons prepared horseradish**
  About ⅓ pound daikon, peeled and finely shredded
  Salt

Mix pineapple, lime juice, ginger, mustard, horseradish, daikon; add salt to taste. Serve, or cover and chill up until next day. Makes 1⅓ cups.—*Paulette Rossi, Portland.*

PER TABLESPOON: 9.4 calories, 0.2 g protein, 2.2 g carbohydrates, 0.2 g fat, 0 mg cholesterol, 2 mg sodium

PICKLED TOMATO RELISH

6 **medium-size (about 1¼ lb.) Roma-type tomatoes**

½ **cup seasoned rice vinegar, or ½ cup rice or distilled white vinegar with 1 teaspoon sugar**

2 **tablespoons firmly packed brown sugar**

½ **teaspoon *each* coriander seed, cumin seed, and mustard seed**

⅛ **teaspoon cayenne**

Drop tomatoes into about 2 quarts boiling water in a 3- to 4-quart pan over high heat; after 5 seconds, lift out, let cool, then pull off peel. Cut tomatoes into bite-size pieces; place in a deep bowl.

Empty pan and add vinegar, sugar, coriander, cumin, mustard, and cayenne. Bring to boiling over high heat; pour at once over tomatoes.

Let tomatoes stand 20 minutes, stirring gently about every 5 minutes. Serve warm or at room temperature. If made ahead, cover and chill up to next day. Makes about 2 cups.

PER ¼-CUP SERVING: 32 calories, 0.7 g protein, 7.9 g carbohydrates, 0.3 g fat, 0 mg cholesterol, 7.1 mg sodium

Fresh relishes of highly seasoned fruits and vegetables go well with beef and other meats. All four shown here can be made a few hours ahead and refrigerated.

CONFETTI CRACKED-WHEAT RELISH

2 **medium-size (about ½ lb. total) carrots, shredded**

2 **medium-size (about ¾ lb. total) zucchini, shredded**

1 **medium-size (about 4 oz.) red or green bell pepper, stemmed, seeded, and slivered**

3 **cloves garlic, minced or pressed**

2 **teaspoons olive or salad oil**

⅓ **cup bulgur (cracked wheat)**

1 **cup regular-strength chicken broth**

2 **tablespoons soy sauce**

In a 10- to 12-inch nonstick frying pan over medium-high heat, stir-fry carrots, zucchini, bell pepper, and garlic in oil until limp, about 5 minutes. Stir in bulgur, broth, and soy. Bring to a boil, cover, remove from heat, and let stand until liquid is absorbed and bulgur is tender to bite, about 20 minutes. Serve warm or at room temperature. If made ahead, cover and chill up to 2 days. Makes 5 cups.—*Sydni Rozenfeld, San Francisco.*

PER ¼-CUP SERVING: 47 calories, 1.7 g protein, 8.1 g carbohydrates, 1.3 g fat, 0 mg cholesterol, 221 mg sodium

CUCUMBERS & JICAMA SALSA WITH BASIL

1 **large (about ½ lb.) cucumber, peeled, seeded, and diced**

1 **piece (about 1 lb.) jicama, peeled, rinsed, and diced**

⅓ **cup *each* chopped fresh basil leaves and green onion with tops**

¼ **cup *each* lemon juice and unflavored nonfat yogurt**

1 **small fresh jalapeño chili, stemmed, seeded, and minced**
  Salt

Mix cucumber, jicama, basil, green onion, lemon juice, yogurt, jalapeño, and salt to taste. Serve, or cover and chill up to 6 hours. Makes 6 cups.

PER ½-CUP SERVING: 23 calories, 1 g protein, 4.9 g carbohydrates, 0.1 g fat, 0.1 mg cholesterol, 8.1 mg sodium

For burrito, roll apple slices in buttered flour tortilla, then heat in microwave oven.

FRUIT-FILLED BREAKFAST BURRITO

1 flour tortilla (9- to 10-in. diameter)
Filling (choices follow)

Spread tortilla with filling. Fold opposite sides over filling, then roll from 1 end to enclose. Set seam side down on a microwave-safe plate; rub tortilla lightly all over with water. Cook, uncovered, in a microwave oven on full power (100 percent) until tortilla is hot to touch, 1 to 2 minutes; check after 1 minute. Let cool slightly to eat. Makes 1 serving. —Gail Aagaard, Angwin, Calif.

Banana–Peanut Butter. Spread tortilla with 1 tablespoon **peanut butter** and top with 1 ripe small **banana**, sliced. If desired, drizzle with **honey** to taste.

Berry-Ricotta. Spread tortilla with 2 tablespoons **part-skim ricotta** or cream **cheese**; top with ½ cup **berries** (sliced strawberries or whole raspberries) and sprinkle with **sugar** to taste.

Apple-Spice. Spread tortilla with 1 teaspoon melted **butter** or margarine. Top with 1 small **apple**, cored, thinly sliced. Sprinkle with ½ teaspoon **sugar** and ¼ teaspoon **ground cinnamon.**

PER SERVING WITH BANANA: 293 calories, 8.8 g protein, 48 g carbohydrates, 8.9 g fat, 0 mg cholesterol, 285 mg sodium

PER SERVING WITH BERRIES: 179 calories, 7.2 g protein, 30 g carbohydrates, 3 g fat, 9.5 mg cholesterol, 248 mg sodium

PER SERVING WITH APPLE: 219 calories, 3.5 g protein, 42 g carbohydrates, 4.5 g fat, 10 mg cholesterol, 248 mg sodium

Lemon is final flavor accent for grilled chops; baste with spicy sauce as they cook.

RED-GLAZED PORK CHOPS

½ cup hot-seasoned catsup
1 tablespoon honey
1 tablespoon lemon juice
¼ teaspoon cayenne
6 center-cut pork chops, about 1 inch thick (about 2½ lb. total), excess fat trimmed off
2 large lemons, cut into wedges

In a small bowl, mix catsup, honey, lemon juice, and cayenne. Brush top of chops thickly with sauce. Lay chops sauce side down on a grill over a solid bed of hot coals (you can hold hand at grill level for only 2 to 3 seconds). Brush tops of chops thickly with sauce.

Cook meat, turning as needed for even browning, just until no longer pink at bone (cut to test), 10 to 14 minutes. Baste frequently with remaining sauce.

(Or put chops on a rack in a 9- by 13-inch baking pan and broil 6 inches from heat until meat at bone is no longer pink, 12 to 15 minutes. Turn chops 1 or 2 times, basting often with remaining sauce.)

Transfer pork chops to a platter and garnish with lemon wedges. Squeeze lemon juice onto meat to taste. Makes 3 to 6 servings. —Rachel Walter, Lewistown, Mont.

PER SERVING: 243 calories, 28 g protein, 8.4 g carbohydrates, 9.4 g fat, 88 mg cholesterol, 310 mg sodium

Season vegetables with mustard and caraway seed.

HOMESTYLE SWISS CHARD

About 1 pound Swiss chard
1 tablespoon butter or margarine
1 small red onion, chopped
1 cup thinly sliced celery (about 4 stalks)
1 large (about ½ lb.) red bell pepper, stemmed, seeded, and cut into thin strips
½ teaspoon caraway seed
1½ tablespoons Dijon mustard
Salt and freshly ground pepper

Rinse chard well and drain. Trim off and discard discolored ends of stems. Trim leafy part from stems; coarsely chop leaves and mince stems.

In a 10- to 12-inch frying pan over medium-high heat, melt butter. Add chard stems, onion, celery, red bell pepper, and caraway seed. Stir often until vegetables are tender to bite, about 7 minutes.

To pan, add chard leaves and mustard; mix well. Stir often until leaves wilt, then stir over high heat until all liquid evaporates, about 1 minute. Pour vegetables into a bowl. Add salt and pepper to taste. Makes 4 to 6 servings. —Sylvia Bryant, San Francisco.

PER SERVING: 48 calories, 1.7 g protein, 6 g carbohydrates, 2.5 g fat, 5.2 mg cholesterol, 298 mg sodium

HARVEST SOUP

½ pound ground turkey
½ pound mild Italian sausages, casings discarded
½ cup chopped onion
6 cups regular-strength beef broth
1 cup tomato juice
1 cup dry red wine
3 large (about 1¼ lb. total) firm-ripe tomatoes, cored and chopped
3 large carrots, peeled and sliced
2 cups coarsely chopped zucchini
1 tablespoon Worcestershire
2 teaspoons dry oregano leaves
About 1 teaspoon liquid hot pepper seasoning

In a 3- to 4-quart pan over medium-high heat, combine turkey, sausage, and onion. Stir often until meat is lightly browned, about 15 minutes. Transfer meat mixture with a slotted spoon to drain on paper towels. Discard fat in pan; wipe pan clean.

Return meat mixture to pan; add broth, tomato juice, wine, tomatoes, carrots, zucchini, Worcestershire, and oregano. Cover and simmer over medium heat until the carrots are tender to bite, 20 to 30 minutes. Add liquid hot pepper seasoning to taste. Makes about 13 cups, 6 to 8 servings. —*Barbara Keenan, Fort Morgan, Colo.*

PER SERVING: 178 calories, 11 g protein, 13 g carbohydrates, 9 g fat, 30 mg cholesterol, 381 mg sodium

Vegetable-laced soup is made hearty with ground turkey, Italian sausage.

BROWN RICE GRATIN

2 cups broccoli flowerets
3 cups cooked brown rice
1 cup (8 oz.) shredded Swiss or jarlsberg cheese
¾ cup regular-strength chicken broth
½ cup sour cream
½ cup chopped green onion
¼ cup minced fresh cilantro (coriander)
2 tablespoons Dijon mustard
¼ teaspoon pepper
¼ cup fine dry bread crumbs mixed with 2 teaspoons melted butter or margarine

In a wok or 4- to 5-quart pan, place broccoli on a rack above 1 inch of boiling water. Cover and steam until flowerets are just tender when pierced, about 9 minutes.

In a large bowl, mix broccoli, rice, cheese, broth, sour cream, onion, cilantro, mustard, and pepper. Spread evenly in a 9- by 13-inch oval or rectangular casserole. Sprinkle with bread crumbs.

Bake in a 350° oven until casserole is hot in center and crumbs are browned, 15 to 20 minutes. Makes 6 servings. —*Sally Vog, Springfield, Ore.*

PER SERVING: 344 calories, 16 g protein, 31 g carbohydrates, 17 g fat, 46 mg cholesterol, 324 mg sodium

Broccoli bakes with savory brown-rice mixture; add cooked meat for a main dish.

CRUMBLE-TOP PUMPKIN GINGERBREAD

2 cups all-purpose flour
1 cup whole-wheat flour
1 cup sugar
1 teaspoon ground cinnamon
1 teaspoon ground ginger
½ teaspoon ground nutmeg
¾ cup (⅜ lb.) butter or margarine
2 large eggs
1 can (1 lb.) pumpkin
½ cup light molasses
¼ cup milk
1½ teaspoons baking soda
Whipped cream (optional)

In a large bowl, stir together all-purpose flour, whole-wheat flour, sugar, cinnamon, ginger, and nutmeg. With your fingers, rub in butter until texture of coarse meal; set aside ⅔ cup.

In a small bowl, beat eggs, pumpkin, molasses, milk, and soda to blend. Stir into dry ingredients to moisten evenly. Pour into a greased 8- by 12-inch or 9- by 13-inch pan. Sprinkle with reserved flour mixture.

Bake in a 350° oven until top is firm to touch, about 50 minutes. Serve warm with whipped cream. Serves 8 to 10. —*J. Hill, Sacramento.*

PER SERVING: 407 calories, 6.3 g protein, 63 g carbohydrates, 16 g fat, 80 mg cholesterol, 285 mg sodium

For a Halloween treat, offer warm pumpkin gingerbread with whipped cream.

J ERKY, *once just a hiker's food, has become a favorite at-home snack. It was probably created long ago when some hunter discovered that smoke from his campfire not only kept away flies but also flavored and preserved meat. Later refinements included cutting the meat into strips for quick drying and adding seasonings to enhance the flavor.*

Dean Terrell gave his co-workers a sample of his jerky. One of them, who had grown up in Hawaii, was reminded of the paniolo's food (a paniolo is a Hawaiian cowboy; the name is derived from the word español *because early cowboys in the Islands were Mexican). He suggested that the jerky could be improved by adding some ginger. What was the result? You can find out for yourself. Aloha.*

"One tester said this jerky reminded him of the Hawaiian cowboys' food."

PANIOLO BEEF JERKY

- 1 **flank steak, 1½ to 2 pounds**
- 2 **tablespoons reduced-sodium soy sauce**
- 2 **tablespoons Worcestershire**
- ¼ **cup lime juice**
- ¼ **teaspoon coarsely ground black pepper**
- ⅛ **teaspoon liquid smoke**
- 1 **teaspoon crushed dried hot red chilies**
- 1 **tablespoon grated fresh ginger**

Trim and discard fat from flank steak. With a sharp knife, cut steak across the grain into ¼-inch-thick slanting slices.

In a large bowl, stir together soy sauce, Worcestershire, lime juice, pepper, liquid smoke, crushed chilies, and ginger. Add meat and mix well. Cover and chill until next day, stirring occasionally.

Lay meat slices side by side on foil-covered 12- by 15-inch baking sheets. Place in a 115° to 120° oven until meat feels dry and firm and looks dry in center when a piece is broken, 10 to 11 hours. Makes about ¾ pound.

PER OUNCE: 95 calories, 12 g protein, 1.3 g carbohydrates, 4.5 g fat, 28 mg cholesterol, 170 mg sodium

D. Dean Terrell

Burbank, Calif.

O NCE UPON A TIME, *neither the first crocus nor the return of swallows to Capistrano was as sure a sign of spring (to the gourmet, at least) as the appearance of asparagus in the market.*

When the feasting paled and asparagus lovers could think beyond the basic spear, other indulgences were explored . . . such as sipping instead of chewing. Gerry Cutler has engineered a fitting liquid version: a soup that is the essence of asparagus. Other ingredients serve mainly to enhance the asparagus flavor.

Nowadays you can enjoy this fine soup almost anytime, because as asparagus season fades away here, it blossoms south of the equator and flies north (with some mechanical assistance) a bit before the swallows leave Capistrano.

GERRY'S ASPARAGUS SOUP

- 1½ **to 2 pounds asparagus**
- 1 **tablespoon butter or margarine**
- 3 **green onions (ends trimmed), including tops, thinly sliced**
- ¼ **pound mushrooms, sliced**
- 1¾ **cups (or 1 can, 14½ oz.) regular-strength chicken broth**
- ¼ **cup purchased salsa**
- 1 **cup milk**
- ½ **cup shredded jack cheese**
  Salt and pepper

Break off and discard tough ends of asparagus. Rinse asparagus well and drain.

In a 4- to 5-quart pan over medium heat, melt butter with onions and mushrooms. Stir often until onions are limp, about 3 minutes. Add broth and asparagus. Bring to a boil, then reduce heat and simmer until asparagus is just tender when pierced, about 5 minutes. Snip off tips of 8 spears and set aside.

"As asparagus fades here, it blossoms south of the equator and flies north."

Continue to simmer remaining asparagus until very tender when pierced, about 5 minutes.

In a blender, smoothly whirl asparagus spears with broth mixture and salsa, a portion at a time. Pour and rub mixture through a fine strainer back into pan; add milk and stir over medium heat until steaming hot. Ladle into soup bowls, sprinkle with cheese, then float asparagus tips in soup. Season to taste with salt and pepper. Makes 4 servings.

PER SERVING: 161 calories, 9.9 g protein, 9.5 g carbohydrates, 10 g fat, 29 mg cholesterol, 252 mg sodium

Gerry Cutler

Redmond, Wash.

IN WINE WRITERS' LANGUAGE, *one might describe Carl Lange's Chili Verde as being assertive and full-bodied, with green pepper overtones and a long (but not interminable) finish, suitable for immediate consumption but improved if chilled for a day or two and reheated. Some may say that wine writers' language is not appropriate for describing a stew. But is it appropriate applied to wine? The jury is still out.*

If you prefer to serve your chili verde with a warm tortilla, try Lange's trick of rolling up the tortilla in a paper towel and heating it in a microwave oven for 10 to 20 seconds before serving.

CHILI VERDE

1½ pounds lean boned pork shoulder
2 cans (1 lb. each) tomatoes
1 large onion, chopped
1 cup finely sliced celery
1 teaspoon dry oregano leaves
½ teaspoon rubbed dry sage
2 large cans (7 oz. each) diced green chilies
2 dry bay leaves
Hot cooked rice
Fresh cilantro (coriander) sprigs

Trim and discard excess fat from pork. Cut meat into ¾-inch cubes and put them in a 10- to 12-inch frying pan. Drain about ½ cup juice from tomatoes into pan. Cover and cook on high heat until boiling; reduce heat and simmer 30 minutes.

Uncover pan; add onion, celery, oregano, and sage. Stir often until liquid evaporates and drippings in pan are richly browned.

Add tomatoes and their remaining juice. Stir to free browned bits, then add chilies and bay leaves. Cover and simmer until meat is very tender when pierced, about 1 hour; stir occasionally. If mixture is too thin, uncover and let simmer until chili is reduced to the consistency you like; stir frequently.

Spoon chili mixture over rice; garnish with cilantro. Makes 4 to 6 servings.

PER SERVING: 234 calories, 24 g protein, 13 g carbohydrates, 9.4 g fat, 76 mg cholesterol, 732 mg sodium

Scottsdale, Ariz.

"Carl Lange's Chili Verde is assertive and full-bodied."

WHEN YOU ANNOUNCE *to family or friends that Indian pudding is the main course for dinner, warn them not to get their hopes up for an early dessert. Terrance McCarthy's Island Indian Pudding is not, repeat not, conventional Indian pudding made with molasses and served with ice cream. It is, rather, a version of tamale pie, a hearty Cal-Mex casserole that contains your basic tamale ingredients.*

European influence is present, but the basics are all New World, so the name is justifiable. As for the island part—well, Alameda is an island.

ISLAND INDIAN PUDDING

3 large eggs
1½ cups buttermilk
1 can (17 oz.) cream-style corn
1 cup peeled, seeded, and chopped firm-ripe tomatoes
1 medium-size onion, finely chopped
1 medium-size green bell pepper, stemmed, seeded, and chopped
1 can (4 oz.) sliced or chopped pimientos
1 can (6 oz.) pitted medium-size black ripe olives, drained
About ½ teaspoon salt
1 teaspoon chili powder
¼ teaspoon *each* pepper and liquid hot pepper seasoning
1 cup yellow cornmeal
¼ cup (⅛ lb.) butter or margarine, melted

In a large bowl, beat eggs to blend with buttermilk, corn, tomatoes, onion, bell pepper, pimientos, olives, ½ teaspoon salt, chili powder, pepper, hot pepper seasoning, cornmeal, and butter. Pour into a buttered 9- by 13-inch baking dish or pan.

Bake in a 350° oven until firm when lightly touched in center, about 1 hour. Let stand 10 minutes, then serve. Add salt to taste. Makes 8 to 10 servings.

PER SERVING: 194 calories, 5.7 g protein, 25 g carbohydrates, 8.8 g fat, 78 mg cholesterol, 401 mg sodium

Terrance J. McCarthy

Alameda, Calif.

October Menus

CHILLY MORNINGS *and cool evenings are to be expected this month; so are glorious warm afternoons. To take advantage of one of these golden Indian summer days, put together an easy-to-tote picnic and enjoy it after a brisk bike ride. For supper, try the warming casserole. And for a simple breakfast, highlight the flavors of autumn's bounty.*

BICYCLE PICNIC FOR 3 OR 4

Cucumber-Mint Soup
Cherry Tomatoes
Chicken Chutney Pockets
White & Dark Chocolate
Chip Cookies
Apples   Fruit-flavor Mineral Water

If the weather looks great, pop this refreshing lunch in a pack and whiz away.

Steep the chicken (or use 2 cups cooked chicken) and make the sandwich filling up to 4 hours ahead. Assemble sandwiches just before departing. Put them in a thermal bag, the soup in a thermos. Sip soup from cups. Make or buy cookies.

CUCUMBER-MINT SOUP

  1 European cucumber (about 1 lb.)
  ½ cup regular-strength chicken broth
  ½ cup unflavored nonfat or low-fat yogurt
  ¼ cup lightly packed fresh mint leaves
  2 tablespoons lime juice
     Salt

Peel cucumber and cut into chunks. Whirl in a blender or food processor with broth, yogurt, mint, and lime juice until very smoothly puréed. (If ingredients are not cold enough to make soup cold, add about ½ cup ice cubes and whirl until crushed.) Season to taste with salt.

Serve or, to transport, pour soup into a chilled thermos and serve within 2 hours (shake before pouring into cups). Makes 3 or 4 servings.

PER SERVING: 37 calories, 2.6 g protein, 6.3 g carbohydrates, 0.4 g fat, 0.6 mg cholesterol, 32 mg sodium

After a vigorous bike ride, satisfy hearty appetites with chicken chutney pocket sandwiches, cool cucumber-mint soup, and tomatoes; offer cookies and apples for dessert.

CHICKEN CHUTNEY POCKETS

  3 chicken breast halves (about 1½ lb. total)
  ½ cup *each* thinly sliced celery and green onion
  ¼ cup Major Grey chutney, chopped
  ¼ cup mayonnaise
  ½ teaspoon curry powder
  3 or 4 pocket bread rounds (about 6-in. diameter), cut in half

  ¼ cup coarsely chopped salted cashews
  6 or 8 large red-leaf lettuce leaves, rinsed and crisped

Put chicken in a 4- to 5-quart pan; add water to cover by 2 inches. Bring water to boiling over high heat; cover pan and remove from heat. Let stand until meat is white in center of thickest part (cut to test), 18 to 20 minutes. Drain, then cover chicken with ice water; when meat is cold, drain. Pull off and discard skin and bones. Tear chicken into bite-size pieces.

In a bowl, stir together celery, onion, chutney, mayonnaise, and curry powder; add chicken and mix well. If made ahead, cover chicken mixture and chill up to 4 hours.

Gently open pockets in bread halves. Mix cashews with chicken salad. Tuck a lettuce leaf into each pocket and fill with equal portions of salad. Pack in a rigid container (or individually in sandwich bags) and transport in a thermal bag. Makes 3 or 4 servings. —*Bonnie Frederick, Pullman, Wash.*

PER SERVING: 509 calories, 34 g protein, 43 g carbohydrates, 23 g fat, 86 mg cholesterol, 517 mg sodium

---

CASSEROLE SUPPER

Potato, Prosciutto & Spinach Lasagna
Mesclun Greens Salad   Breadsticks
Baked Amaretti Pears
Zinfandel   Sparkling Water

Instead of pasta, layers of tender potatoes separate the creamy sauce and filling in this simple, hearty make-ahead variation of lasagna.

As the lasagna and pears bake in the same oven, set the table, then toss ready-to-use mesclun greens (mixed salad leaves) or other lettuce with an olive oil and wine vinegar dressing.

POTATO, PROSCIUTTO & SPINACH LASAGNA

  1 **package (10 oz.) frozen chopped spinach, thawed**
  5 **large (about 2½ lb. total) russet potatoes**
  1 **large red onion, thinly sliced**
 ¼ **pound thinly sliced prosciutto or cooked ham, cut into slivers**
     Three-cheese sauce (recipe follows)
 ½ **cup freshly grated parmesan cheese**

Squeeze moisture from spinach; set aside. Peel potatoes; cut into ⅛-inch-thick slices.

Butter a 9- by 13-inch baking dish. Arrange ⅓ of the potato slices, overlapping slightly, to cover bottom of dish in an even layer. Cover evenly with ½ the onion, ½ the prosciutto, and ½ the spinach; then spoon ⅓ of the cheese sauce over these ingredients. Repeat; finish with potatoes, then cheese sauce. If made ahead, cover and chill up until next day; let stand at room temperature 1 hour before baking.

Bake, covered, in a 375° oven for 30 minutes; remove cover and continue baking until top is richly browned and potatoes are tender when pierced, about 1 hour longer. Sprinkle parmesan over lasagna and bake 5 minutes longer. Let stand 10 minutes before serving. Makes 6 servings. —*Paula Bennett, Seattle.*

PER SERVING: 679 calories, 32 g protein, 52 g carbohydrates, 38 g fat, 120 mg cholesterol, 1,055 mg sodium

Three-cheese sauce. In a 2- to 3-quart pan over medium-high heat, stir ½ cup (¼ lb.) **butter** or margarine with ½ cup **all-purpose flour** until mixture is bubbling. Off heat, whisk in 2 cups *each* **milk** and **regular-strength chicken**

broth, and ¼ teaspoon **ground nutmeg.** Stir on medium-high heat until boiling. Off heat, add 1 cup (4 oz.) *each* shredded **havarti, provolone,** and **Swiss cheeses** (or all 1 kind); stir until smooth. Add **pepper** to taste.

BAKED AMARETTI PEARS

  6 **medium-size (about 2¾ lb. total) firm-ripe pears**
 ¼ **cup almond-flavor liqueur (optional)**
 ⅓ **cup sugar**
     About ½ cup coarsely crushed amaretti (Italian-style almond macaroons)

Peel pears and set upright in an 8- to 9-inch-diameter shallow baking dish. Sprinkle evenly with liqueur, then sugar. Bake, uncovered, in a 375° oven until fruit is delicately browned and tender when pierced, about 1 hour; baste occasionally with pan juices.

Spoon pears into individual bowls, adding pan juices. Serve hot or at room temperature, sprinkled with cooky crumbs. Makes 6 servings.

PER SERVING: 196 calories, 1.2 g protein, 46 g carbohydrates, 2.2 g fat, 3.4 mg cholesterol, 22 mg sodium

(Continued on next page)

Potato lasagna? Beneath the golden brown surface are layers of prosciutto, spinach, onion, and mellow cheese sauce; thinly sliced potatoes stand in for pasta.

AUTUMN BREAKFAST

Pomegranate-Citrus Compote
Pumpkin Oat Bran Muffins
Crisp Bacon   Mocha Java Coffee

In the fresh fruit compote, brilliant pomegranate seeds give fall flavor to juicy grapefruit segments. Pumpkin in moist muffins carries the seasonal spirit one step further. For the coffee, pick your favorite blend of beans.

Make compote while muffins bake. Put ½ cup pink grapefruit segments in each bowl; scatter ½ cup pomegranate seeds over portions. Per 4 servings, mix 1 teaspoon each grated orange and lime peels, ¼ cup each orange juice and lime juice, and sugar to taste; spoon over fruit.

PUMPKIN OAT BRAN MUFFINS

    1 cup oat bran
    ½ cup *each* all-purpose flour and
       whole-wheat flour
    ½ cup firmly packed brown sugar
    2 teaspoons baking powder
    ½ teaspoon *each* baking soda,
       ground cinnamon, and ground
       ginger
    2 large egg whites
    ⅓ cup nonfat or low-fat milk
    ⅓ cup salad oil
    1 cup canned pumpkin

In a bowl, mix bran, all-purpose flour, whole-wheat flour, sugar, baking powder, baking soda, cinnamon, and ginger. In another bowl, beat whites to blend with milk, oil, and pumpkin. Add to dry ingredients; stir just until evenly moistened.

Spoon batter equally into 12 paper-lined 2½-inch muffin cups. Bake in a 375° oven until tops are well browned, 30 to 35 minutes. Serve warm. Makes 1 dozen. — *Nancy Tabor, Bend, Ore.*

PER MUFFIN: 155 calories, 3.6 g protein, 24 g carbohydrates, 6.7 g fat, 1.3 mg cholesterol, 87 mg sodium

NOVEMBER

Petite Pumpkins with Herb Cheese (page 286)

Join us this month in celebrating the bounty of the autumn harvest. Our festive Thanksgiving menu comes in two versions: an elegant, dressed-up dinner for guests and a simpler, more informal family-style bill of fare. In November we also highlight some treasures of the Western harvest: persimmons, quince, pomegranates, chestnuts, and miniature pumpkins. Ideas for winter entertaining feature Northwest-style gumbo, made with Pacific shellfish, and hearty dishes inspired by the traditional cuisines of Czechoslovakia and Hungary.

A Dress-Up/Dress-Down Thanksgiving Dinner

THIS FESTIVE, BOUNTIFUL MEAL *accommodates every taste, whether your Thanksgiving gathering is for the family— with mixed ages and somewhat cautious palates—or for dinner guests with more adventurous outlooks.*

Put the meal together following the left-hand column of the menu below and it has a wholesome, friendly, and rather economical character. Follow the options on the right-hand side, and you dress up the basics of each dish with more extravagant ingredients.

As a third possibility, mix and match dishes from both sides of the menu.

Each dish has make-ahead steps to help you bring this meal together smoothly. The salads share some elements, but one can be served family-style from a large bowl, while the other is designed for presentation on individual plates. The turkey is roasted unstuffed; to have lots of gravy for the family, you simmer the giblets.

For a more intensely flavored, concentrated gravy to serve in smaller quantities—like a sauce—the giblets get roasted before simmering. The cranberry relish, the dressing, the three vegetable dishes (carrots and onions, green beans, and potato casserole), and the pumpkin dessert each offer variations with distinctive seasoning alternatives.

THE SALAD

WATERCRESS & SHRIMP SALAD WITH BUTTER LETTUCE

 3 tablespoons mustard seed
 6 tablespoons olive oil or salad oil
 3 cups ½-inch cubes French bread
 ½ cup balsamic or red wine vinegar
 1½ tablespoons Dijon mustard
 12 cups butter lettuce leaves, rinsed and crisped
 6 cups watercress sprigs, rinsed and crisped
 1 pound shelled cooked tiny shrimp

Put mustard seed in a small bowl and add about ½ cup boiling water. Let stand 10 minutes to 8 hours; drain.

In a 10- to 12-inch nonstick frying pan over medium-high heat, combine ¼ cup of the oil with the bread cubes; stir until cubes are lightly browned, about 15 minutes. Drain on paper towels. If croutons are made ahead, store airtight up until next day.

In a large bowl, mix vinegar, 2 tablespoons oil, mustard seed, and mustard. Tear lettuce into bowl in bite-size pieces. Add watercress and shrimp. Mix well; top with croutons. Makes 12 servings.

PER SERVING: 144 calories, 10 g protein, 7.1 g carbohydrates, 8.4 g fat, 74 mg cholesterol, 193 mg sodium

BELGIAN ENDIVE SALAD WITH FOIE GRAS

 12 pieces thin-sliced firm-texture white bread, crusts trimmed (if desired)
 3 tablespoons mustard seed
 3 large heads (about ¾ lb. total) Belgian endive, leaves separated, rinsed, and crisped
 6 ounces (about 6 cups) watercress sprigs, rinsed and crisped
 ½ pound fresh (or 1 can, 7¼ oz.) duck foie gras
 ¾ cup raspberry vinegar
 ¼ cup extra-virgin olive oil (optional)

Cut bread slices in half diagonally. Arrange in a single layer on 2 baking sheets, 12- by 15-inch size. Bake in a 350° oven until toasted, 10 to 15 minutes. Let cool. If made more than 1 hour ahead, package airtight and hold at room temperature up until next day.

Put mustard seed in a small bowl and add about ½ cup boiling water. Let stand 10 minutes to 8 hours; drain.

On each of 12 salad plates, fan an equal amount of the endive leaves. Put an equal amount of watercress at the base of each fan and 2 pieces of toast beside greens on each plate.

Cut foie gras into 12 equal slices. Place a 10- to 12-inch nonstick pan over medium-high heat. When pan is hot, add foie gras without crowding. Cook just enough to warm and tinge with brown, about 40 seconds. Turn slices over and repeat, 30 to 40 seconds. Transfer slices to a plate as browned and keep warm; add remaining foie gras to pan until all is heated.

THANKSGIVING DINNER FOR A DOZEN

Frankly family	*Gussied up for guests*
SALAD	
Watercress & Shrimp with Butter Lettuce	Belgian Endive with Foie Gras
ROAST TURKEY GRAVY	
Simmered Giblet	Roasted Giblet
CRANBERRY RELISH	
With Ginger	With Port
ROASTED CARROTS & ONIONS	
Sliced Vegetables with Orange	Petite Vegetables with Orange Liqueur
GREEN BEANS	
With Mushroom Duxelles	With Shiitake Duxelles
MASHED POTATO CASSEROLE	
With Green Olives & Cream Cheese	With Tapenade & Mascarpone
BARLEY-CORN DRESSING	
With Sausage	With Prosciutto
PUMPKIN TART	
& Whipped Cream	& Warm Ginger Cream

Stir vinegar, mustard seed, and—if using canned foie gras—oil into pan with foie gras drippings. At once spoon dressing equally over salads. Set a slice of foie gras on a piece of toast on each plate. Makes 12 servings.

PER SERVING: 198 calories, 5.1 g protein, 15 g carbohydrates, 14 g fat, 26 mg cholesterol, 116 mg sodium

THE GRAVY

SIMMERED GIBLET GRAVY

> Neck and giblets from a 22- to 24-pound turkey, rinsed
> About 2 quarts regular-strength chicken broth
> 2 cups dry white wine
> 2 large onions, quartered
> 4 large carrots, peeled and sliced
> 3 stalks celery
> ½ teaspoon dry thyme leaves
> 1 dry bay leaf
> At least 2 tablespoons fat-skimmed roasted turkey drippings, or as much as you have (optional)
> ⅓ cup cornstarch dissolved in ½ cup water

Place neck and giblets, except liver, in a 5- to 6- quart pan. Add 2 quarts broth, wine, onions, carrots, celery, thyme, and bay leaf. Bring to a boil over high heat, then cover and simmer until gizzard and neck meat are very tender when pierced, about 1½ hours. Add liver (if desired) and simmer 5 minutes longer.

Pour broth through a strainer into a large bowl; skim and discard any fat. Discard vegetables; finely chop neck meat and giblets (and liver, if desired).

Measure broth. If more than 6 cups, return to pan; boil, uncovered, until reduced to that amount. If you have less than 6 cups, add more broth to make up the difference. If made ahead, cool, cover, and chill broth and giblets up until next day.

Return broth and giblets to pan; add turkey drippings. Reheat to boiling; stir in enough cornstarch mixture to thicken to your preference. Pour into a bowl. Makes about 8 cups, or 12 servings of about ⅔ cup each.

PER ⅔ CUP: 97 calories, 8.9 g protein, 8.2 g carbohydrates, 2.9 g fat, 40 mg cholesterol, 8.3 mg sodium

(Continued on next page)

Family turkey trimmings include mashed potatoes with chopped green olives, roasted carrots and onions, green beans and mushrooms, barley-corn dressing with sausage.

Lavish salad alternative includes Belgian endive, watercress, warm foie gras on toast. Greens are dressed with warm raspberry vinegar and foie gras drippings.

ROASTED GIBLET GRAVY

Follow directions for **simmered giblet gravy** (preceding), but first place giblets (except liver) and neck into an 8- to 9-inch baking pan; reserve liver for another use. Bake, uncovered, in a 400° oven until well browned, about 1 hour; stir occasionally.

Put giblets in a 5- to 6-quart pan. To roasting pan add about ½ cup **regular-strength chicken broth** and stir to free browned bits; pour into pan with giblets. Add only 3½ cups more broth. Instead of white wine, use 1 cup **dry red wine** and ½ cup **brandy.** Bring to a boil with vegetables and herbs; simmer as directed, until giblets are tender. Lift out giblets; reserve for another use.

Boil liquid down to about 3 cups. Pour broth through a strainer into a 1-quart measure; discard residue. Skim and discard any fat. You should have 3 cups liquid. If more, return broth to pan and boil to reduce. If less, add more broth to equal 3 cups. If made ahead, cool, cover, and chill up until next day.

Return broth to pan; add turkey drippings. Bring to boiling over high heat. Dilute only 2 tablespoons **cornstarch** in

¼ cup **water;** stir enough into broth to thicken to your preference.

Pour into a bowl. Makes 3 to 4 cups, or 12 servings of about ¼ cup each.

PER ¼ CUP: 87 calories, 8.2 g protein, 7.7 g carbohydrates, 2.4 g fat, 40 mg cholesterol, 64 mg sodium

THE RELISH

CRANBERRY RELISH WITH GINGER

    2 large (about 6 oz. total) tangerines
       or 1 medium-size orange
    1 bag (12 oz.) fresh or frozen
       cranberries
    ¼ cup crystallized ginger
    ⅓ to ½ cup sugar

Cut tangerines in half, remove and discard seeds, and cut fruit into 1-inch chunks. Coarsely chop or grind tangerines in a food processor or a food chopper fitted with a medium blade.

Add cranberries and ginger; coarsely chop or grind. Stir in sugar to taste. Serve, or cover and chill up until the next day. Makes 3 cups.

PER TABLESPOON: 14 calories, 0 g protein, 3.7 g carbohydrates, 0 g fat, 0 mg cholesterol, 0.9 mg sodium

CRANBERRY RELISH WITH PORT

Follow recipe for **cranberry relish with ginger** (preceding), omitting ginger and adding ⅓ to ½ cup **apricot jam** (to taste) and ¼ cup **port.** Makes 3 cups.

PER TABLESPOON: 18 calories, 0 g protein, 4.2 g carbohydrates, 0 g fat, 0 mg cholesterol, 0.5 mg sodium

THE VEGETABLES

SLICED ROASTED CARROTS & ONIONS WITH ORANGE

    4 pounds carrots
    2 tablespoons *each* butter or
       margarine and salad oil
    1 large (about ½ lb.) onion,
       chopped
    1 teaspoon grated orange peel
    ⅓ cup orange juice
    1 tablespoon lemon juice
       Parsley sprigs (optional)
       Thin orange slices
       Salt and pepper

Peel carrots and cut into long diagonal slices about ¼ inch thick. Melt butter with oil in a 12- by 14-inch roasting pan; add carrots and stir to mix.

Bake, uncovered, in a 475° oven until carrots begin to brown, about 25 minutes. Add onion; turn vegetables often with a wide spatula until darkly browned on edges, 1¼ to 1½ hours.

Mix in orange peel, orange juice, and lemon juice. If made ahead, let stand at room temperature (cover when cool) up to 3 hours; cover and chill up to 8 hours. Reheat, uncovered, in a 350° oven until warm, 15 to 20 minutes. Spoon into a bowl; garnish with parsley and orange. Add salt and pepper to taste. Serves 12.

PER SERVING: 105 calories, 1.6 g protein, 16 g carbohydrates, 4.5 g fat, 5.2 mg cholesterol, 67 mg sodium

ROASTED PETITE CARROTS & ONIONS WITH ORANGE LIQUEUR

Follow directions for **sliced roasted carrots and onions with orange,** but instead of sliced carrots, chopped onion, and orange juice, use 4 pounds peeled **baby carrots,** 2 packages (10 oz. each) **frozen pearl onions,** and ¼ cup **orange-flavor liqueur.** Makes 12 servings.

PER SERVING: 120 calories, 1.8 g protein, 20 g carbohydrates, 4.5 g fat, 5.2 mg cholesterol, 71 mg sodium

Green Beans with Mushroom Duxelles

1 pound mushrooms, rinsed and drained

2 tablespoons butter or margarine

1 small onion, minced

½ cup dry sherry

¾ cup water

1 tablespoon soy sauce

2 tablespoons balsamic vinegar or red wine vinegar

1 teaspoon Oriental sesame oil (optional)

1 teaspoon cornstarch

3 pounds green beans, ends and strings removed

Trim and discard discolored stem ends of mushrooms. Mince mushrooms.

Melt butter in a 10- to 12-inch frying pan over medium-high heat. Add onion and stir often until limp. Add mushrooms and ¼ cup *each* sherry and water; stir often until liquid evaporates and mushrooms are slightly browned, about 15 minutes.

Stir together remaining sherry and water, soy sauce, balsamic vinegar, sesame oil, and cornstarch; add to mushrooms. Stir until sauce boils. (If made ahead, cool, cover, and chill up until next day; stir to reheat and continue.)

In a 5- to 6-quart pan, bring 3 quarts water to boiling on high heat. Add beans; cook, uncovered, until just tender to bite, 4 to 6 minutes; drain. (If made ahead, immerse in cold water until cool; drain, cover, and chill up until next day. To reheat, immerse in hot water for 3 to 4 minutes; drain.)

Arrange beans on a platter and spoon mushroom mixture onto beans. Serve hot to room temperature. Makes 12 servings.

PER SERVING: 55 calories, 2.1 g protein, 8.3 g carbohydrates, 2.1 g fat, 5.2 mg cholesterol, 112 mg sodium

Green Beans with Shiitake Duxelles

Follow directions for **green beans with mushroom duxelles,** but instead of fresh mushrooms use about 16 **dried shiitake mushrooms** (about 1-in.-diameter caps; 1¼ oz.).

Soak mushrooms in hot water to cover until soft and pliable, about 20 minutes.

Fancier menu features shiitake mushrooms on the beans, baby carrots and pearl onions, tapenade on the potatoes, dressing with prosciutto.

Rub gently to release any grit, then lift mushrooms from water. Discard water.

Squeeze mushrooms gently to remove most of the moisture; trim off and discard tough stems. Mince caps.

Instead of regular green beans, use **haricots verts** or other tiny slender green beans. Makes 12 servings.

PER SERVING: 54 calories, 1.6 g protein, 8.8 g carbohydrates, 2 g fat, 5.2 mg cholesterol, 111 mg sodium

(Continued on next page)

Mashed Potato Casserole with Green Olives & Cream Cheese

- 6 large (about 4¼ lb. total) russet potatoes
- 1 large package (8 oz.) cream cheese, cut into chunks
  Salt and pepper
- 2 large eggs
- 2 cups pitted green ripe olives, minced

Peel and dice potatoes. Put in a 5- to 6-quart pan with about 1 inch water. Cover and bring to a boil on high heat; reduce heat and simmer until potatoes mash easily when pressed, 30 to 35 minutes. Drain well. Either leave potatoes in pan or put them in a large bowl; add cheese.

With a masher or an electric beater, mash potatoes (or squeeze mixture through a potato ricer) until smooth. Add salt and pepper to taste, then beat in eggs. Spread potatoes evenly in a 3- to 3½-quart shallow casserole. If casserole is made ahead, cool, cover, and chill up to next day.

With the tip of a small spoon, make 4 evenly spaced shallow, diagonal trenches across the top of the potatoes. Spoon olives into the trenches. Cover casserole snugly with foil. Bake in a 375° oven until hot in center, about 35 minutes (45 minutes if chilled). Serves 12.

PER SERVING: 229 calories, 5.7 g protein, 28 g carbohydrates, 11 g fat, 56 mg cholesterol, 622 mg sodium

Mashed Potato Casserole with Tapenade & Mascarpone Cheese

Follow directions for **mashed potato casserole with green olives and cream cheese** (preceding), but instead of cream cheese use 1¼ cups (10½ oz.) **mascarpone** or herb-flavor soft **cheese**. Instead of topping potatoes with ripe green olives, fill trenches with **tapenade** (directions follow). Makes 12 servings.

PER SERVING: 300 calories, 7.6 g protein, 32 g carbohydrates, 17 g fat, 60 mg cholesterol, 1,086 mg sodium

Tapenade. Pit 2 cups **niçoise olives** (or other black olives). Place pitted olives in a food processor or blender with ¼ cup drained **capers**, 1 tablespoon **Dijon mustard**, 6 drained **canned anchovy fillets**, ½ teaspoon *each* crumbled **dry bay leaves** and **dry thyme leaves**, 1 large **garlic** clove, and 3 tablespoons **regular-strength chicken broth** or water. Whirl until smoothly puréed. If made ahead, cover and chill up to 2 days. Or use about 1 cup purchased **tapenade**.

The Dressing

Barley-Corn Dressing with Sausage

- 1¾ cups (or a 12-oz. package) pearl barley, rinsed
- 6 cups regular-strength chicken broth
- ¾ pound bulk pork sausage
- 1 tablespoon *each* olive or salad oil and butter or margarine
- 2 to 3 large (about 2 lb. total) onions, chopped
- 1 tablespoon minced fresh or 1½ teaspoons dry rubbed sage
- ½ teaspoon pepper
- 4 cups fresh corn kernels (cut from about 5 medium-size ears), or 2 packages (10 oz. each) frozen corn kernels
  Fresh sage leaves (optional)
  Salt

Bring barley and broth to a boil in a 4- to 5-quart pan on high heat; cover and simmer until barley is tender to bite, about 10 minutes. Drain; save broth. Set broth and barley aside. Rinse and dry pan; add sausage and crumble over medium-high heat; stir often until richly browned, about 10 minutes. Spoon meat onto paper towels.

Add oil, butter, onion, rubbed sage, and pepper to pan. Stir often until onion is tinged with brown and sweet-tasting, about 40 minutes. Add corn and stir often for 5 minutes; add barley and sausage. Pour dressing into a shallow 9- by 13-inch casserole and add 1 cup reserved broth (save extra broth for other uses). Cover dish snugly with foil. If made ahead, chill up until next day. Bake in a 350° oven until hot in center, about 40 minutes (1 hour if cold). Uncover and garnish with sage leaves. Add salt to taste. Serves 12.

PER SERVING: 325 calories, 9.9 g protein, 39 g carbohydrates, 15 g fat, 22 mg cholesterol, 238 mg sodium

Barley-Corn Dressing with Prosciutto

Follow directions for **barley-corn dressing with sausage** (preceding), but omit sausage. Use ¼ pound thinly sliced **prosciutto**, slivered. Stir often in pan over medium-high heat with an added 2 teaspoons **olive oil** until meat is browned and crisp, 12 to 15 minutes. Set aside. Mix ½ the prosciutto with dressing. Sprinkle reserved prosciutto over baked dressing. Serves 12.

PER SERVING: 224 calories, 8.7 g protein, 39 g carbohydrates, 4.8 g fat, 8.2 mg cholesterol, 190 mg sodium

The Dessert

Pumpkin Tart & Whipped Cream

- 1 can (16 oz.) pumpkin
- 1 can (12 oz.) evaporated milk
- 2 large eggs
- ¾ cup firmly packed brown sugar
- ½ cup sour cream
- 1 teaspoon ground cinnamon
- ½ teaspoon ground ginger
- ¼ teaspoon ground nutmeg
  Tart shell (directions follow)
  Sweetened whipped cream

In a large bowl, whisk to blend pumpkin, milk, eggs, sugar, sour cream, cinnamon, ginger, and nutmeg. Pour into warm or cool tart shell. Bake in a 325° oven until center jiggles only slightly when gently shaken, about 40 minutes. Let cool. If made ahead, cover and chill up until next day. Remove rim; place tart on a platter. Top with a puff of whipped cream; offer remaining cream to add to individual taste. Serves 12.

PER PLAIN SERVING: 347 calories, 6.7 g protein, 42 g carbohydrates, 18 g fat, 98 mg cholesterol, 180 mg sodium

Tart shell. In a food processor or bowl, combine 2 cups **all-purpose flour**, ⅓ cup **sugar,** and ¾ cup (⅜ lb.) **butter** or margarine, in chunks. Whirl or rub with fingers until fine crumbs form. Add 1 **large egg;** whirl or mix with a fork until dough holds together. Press over bottom and sides of a 12-inch tart pan with removable rim. Bake on bottom rack in a 300° oven until pale gold, 35 to 40 minutes.

Traditional ending for a traditional dinner: whipped cream cloud dusted with nutmeg perches on golden pumpkin tart; for a sophisti-cated variation, serve wedges with warm ginger cream. To minimize last-minute tasks, make the tart the day before your festive meal.

PUMPKIN TART & WARM GINGER CREAM

Follow directions for **pumpkin tart and whipped cream** (preceding), but omit whipped cream. Instead combine ½ cup **half-and-half** (light cream) and ¼ cup slivered **crystallized ginger** in a 1- to 1½-quart pan. Stir over low heat until hot (do not boil), about 7 minutes. Serve warm. Makes about 1¾ cups, 12 servings.

PER TABLESPOON SAUCE: 25 calories, 0.4 g protein, 2.5 g carbohydrates, 1.5 g fat, 4.8 mg cholesterol, 6.6 mg sodium

Western Harvest Treasures

TREASURES OF FALL HARVEST are presented here as celebrations of the season: pointed, soft-ripening Hachiya-type persimmon; flat-bottomed, crisp Fuyu-type persimmon; knobby quince; ruby pomegranate; glossy chestnuts; and miniature pumpkins. We feature each in dishes that complement a festive holiday meal—and are simple enough to make more than once while the seasonal ingredients are available.

The steamed pumpkins and Fuyu persimmon salad are quick and easy to make. Peeling boiled fresh chestnuts for the handsome casserole is time-consuming, but this step can be done ahead. And if you are so inclined, the quince chutney, pomegranate sorbet, and Hachiya persimmon puddings can also be made ahead.

PETITE PUMPKINS WITH HERB CHEESE

- 4 miniature pumpkins (7 to 8 oz. each), such as Jack Be Little or Munchkin
- 1 package (4 oz.) herb- and garlic-flavor soft cheese
- 1 small package (3 oz.) cream cheese
- 1 large egg
- 4 to 8 fresh sage leaves (optional)

First-course mini-pumpkin cradles soft herb cheese; steam squash, fill, steam again.

Rinse pumpkins and set on a rack over 1 inch boiling water in a 5- to 6-quart pan or wok. Cover and steam over medium-high heat until pumpkins are tender when pierced, about 20 minutes.

Lift pumpkins from rack and let stand until cool. Slice off top quarter of each pumpkin. With a small spoon, gently scoop out seeds, taking care not to break shell. If done ahead, cover and chill up until next day.

In a food processor or with a mixer, beat herb cheese, cream cheese, and egg until smooth. Spoon mixture equally into each squash. Lay 1 or 2 sage leaves on filling. Set pumpkins on rack over boiling water in the 5- to 6-quart pan. Cover and steam until filling puffs slightly and looks set, about 10 minutes. After 5 minutes, fit squash lids on rack (not on squash) to heat. To serve, return lid to each pumpkin and put on a plate. Makes 4 servings.

PER SERVING: 219 calories, 7.5 g protein, 12 g carbohydrates, 17 g fat, 105 mg cholesterol, 187 mg sodium

FUYU PERSIMMON SALAD

- ¾ cup tangerine or orange juice
- ½ teaspoon grated tangerine or orange peel
- 2 teaspoons cornstarch
- ¼ cup orange-flavor liqueur (or tangerine or orange juice)
- 1 tablespoon lemon juice
- 4 to 6 firm-ripe Fuyu-type persimmons (5 to 6 oz. each)
- 3 to 4 tablespoons pomegranate seeds

In a 1- to 1½-quart pan, blend tangerine juice and peel with cornstarch. Bring to a boil, stirring, on high heat. Remove from heat and add orange liqueur and lemon juice. Use warm or cool; if made ahead, cover and chill up until next day. Stir before serving.

Rinse persimmons. The peel is tender to eat, but you can peel persimmons into "petals" if fruit is at just the right stage of ripeness for the skin to pull free rather easily. To test, cut a small slash under stem end and pull gently. If skin tears, immerse fruit in boiling water for 15 seconds and let stand until cool. Then test fruit again.

Set fruit, stem end down, on individual salad plates. Cut almost but not quite through each persimmon, dividing it into 6 to 8 wedges. Then, if you want to create a petal effect, slip the tip of a short sharp knife under the skin at the apex of 1 of the wedge cuts. Gently pull or cut peel free from top of fruit, then let it fall backward around fruit. Repeat for remaining wedges to complete the petal pattern. Spoon the tangerine sauce equally onto persimmons and sprinkle with the pomegranate seeds. Makes 4 to 6 servings.

PER SERVING: 144 calories, 0.8 g protein, 34 g carbohydrates, 0.4 g fat, 0 mg cholesterol, 1.8 mg sodium

CHESTNUTS WITH SAUSAGE & GRAPES

- 1½ pounds (about 1 qt.) chestnuts in the shell
- ¼ pound mild Italian sausage
- 1 cup minced onions
- ¾ cup regular-strength chicken broth
- ½ cup port
- ½ cup whipping cream
- 1 tablespoon butter or margarine
- 2 cups seedless green grapes
Salt

Cut an X into flat side of chestnuts. Put in a 3- to 4-quart pan and cover with water. Bring to boiling; simmer 10 minutes. With a short-bladed sharp knife, pull shell and membrane from wet nuts. If made ahead, cover and chill up until next day.

Remove sausage casings; break meat into pieces in a 10- to 12-inch frying pan. Add onions; stir often over medium-high heat until meat is lightly browned and onion is tinged with brown, about 20 minutes.

Put sausage, onion, chestnuts, broth, and port in a shallow 8- by 12-inch oval or rectangular casserole. Cover tightly with foil and bake in a 400° oven 1 hour. Uncover, add cream, and mix gently; bake, stirring occasionally, until most of the liquid is absorbed, 10 to 12 minutes.

In the frying pan on high heat, melt butter until sizzling. Add grapes and swirl about in pan just until heated, about 2 minutes. Pour grapes over chestnuts. Add salt to taste. Makes 8 to 10 servings.

PER SERVING: 322 calories, 5.2 g protein, 52 g carbohydrates, 11 g fat, 25 mg cholesterol, 125 mg sodium

(Continued on page 288)

To create salad of crisp Fuyu persimmon, cut ripe fruit into wedges and carefully peel back skin to create petal pattern. Light dressing contains pomegranate seeds, tangerine and lemon juices, and orange-flavor liqueur.

Chestnuts baked with sausage and port, then topped with heated grapes, accompany a festive crown roast of pork.

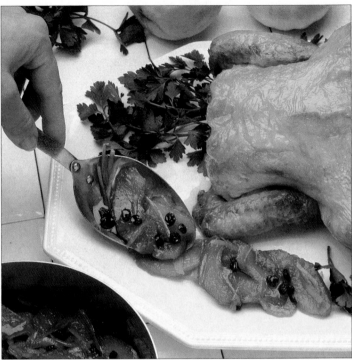

Quince chutney complements roast chicken. Quince is very hard when raw, softens like an apple when cooked. Chutney keeps well in the refrigerator.

QUINCE CHUTNEY

- 3 medium-size (1¾ to 2 lb. total) quince
- ⅔ cup finely slivered peeled fresh ginger
- 1 cup raspberry vinegar
- 1½ cups sugar
- ½ cup currants

Rinse quince; peel. Cut into quarters (quince can be very hard in the center), cut out core, then slice fruit in about ¼-inch-thick pieces.

Put ginger in a 3- to 4-quart pan and add 4 to 5 cups water. Bring to boiling, uncovered, on high heat. Drain off water and add quince, vinegar, sugar, and currants to pan. Bring to a boil, then boil gently, uncovered, until only about ½ cup syrup remains. Stir occasionally. Serve warm or cool. If made ahead, cover and chill up to 2 weeks, or freeze. Makes 3⅔ cups.

PER TABLESPOON: 29 calories, 0.1 g protein, 7.7 g carbohydrates, 0 g fat, 0 mg cholesterol, 0.7 mg sodium

POMEGRANATE SORBET

- 3 medium-size (about 1½ lb. total) pomegranates
  About ⅔ cup tangerine or orange juice
- 2 tablespoons lime juice
- 2 tablespoons melted currant or raspberry jelly
- 2 to 4 tablespoons sugar
  About 1 pint vanilla ice cream (optional)
- 3 to 4 tablespoons pomegranate seeds (optional)

Cut pomegranates in half and ream juice and pulp from shells, taking care not to break shells. With a spoon, scrape shells to remove any remaining bits of fruit and add to juice. If you want to serve the sorbet from the pomegranate shells, wrap the shells airtight and freeze.

Put pomegranate juice, fruit, and pulp in a fine strainer set over a bowl; press to extract as much juice as possible (do not rub); discard residue. Measure juice and add enough tangerine juice to make 2 cups total. Add lime juice, jelly, and sugar to taste.

Pour liquid into a metal pan (such as an 8- to 10-in.-square pan) and freeze until hard, at least 2 hours, or cover airtight and store in freezer up to 1 month.

Break pomegranate ice into chunks and whirl in a food processor or beat with a mixer just until it forms a smooth slush. Scoop into a container, cover airtight, and put in freezer to firm, at least 1 hour.

(Or freeze fruit mixture—according to manufacturer's directions—in a self-refrigerated ice cream maker or in an ice cream maker with salt and ice, using 1 part salt to 8 parts ice. Use, or store as directed.)

For best flavor and texture, do not store sorbet for more than 1 month; let stand at room temperature about 10 minutes to soften enough to scoop.

Serve scooped into small dishes. Or fill about half of each pomegranate shell (cold from freezer) with sorbet, then fill remaining half with vanilla ice cream (you can do this ahead and freeze, covered, for up to 2 days). Nest shells in close-fitting bowls or wine goblets.

Brilliant pomegranate sorbet shares pomegranate half-shell, nested in glass, with vanilla ice cream. Bright pomegranate seeds decorate dessert.

Soft-ripe Hachiya persimmons pressed through strainer make smooth sauce to go with individual servings of steamed Hachiya puddings.

Sprinkle pomegranate seeds onto each portion. Makes about 2⅓ cups sorbet, or 6 servings of about ⅓ cup each (with or without ice cream).

PER SERVING SORBET: 77 calories, 0.6 g protein, 19 g carbohydrates, 0.2 g fat, 0 mg cholesterol, 3.5 mg sodium

HACHIYA PERSIMMON PUDDINGS WITH HACHIYA SAUCE

- 1 **cup sugar**
- 1 **cup all-purpose flour**
- 1 **teaspoon ground cinnamon**
- ¼ **teaspoon ground nutmeg**
- 2 **teaspoons baking soda**
- 2 **tablespoons hot water**
- 1 **cup soft-ripe Hachiya-type persimmon pulp**
- 2 **large eggs**
- ¾ **cup golden raisins**
- ½ **cup dark rum**
- 1 **teaspoon vanilla**
- 2 **teaspoons lemon juice**
- ½ **cup (¼ lb.) butter or margarine, melted and cooled to lukewarm**
  Hachiya sauce (recipe follows)

Mix sugar, flour, cinnamon, and nutmeg. In a bowl, stir together baking soda and water, then mix in persimmon pulp and eggs; beat until blended. Add sugar mixture, raisins, ¼ cup rum, vanilla, lemon juice, and butter. Stir to mix well.

Butter 10 (6-oz.-size) or 12 (4-oz.-size) plain pudding molds such as custard cups or individual metal pudding molds. Equally fill molds with batter. Cover each mold snugly with a piece of foil. Set the molds on a rack over at least 1 inch of boiling water in a 5- to 6-quart pan; you will need 2 pans, or you can cook the puddings in sequence.

Cover and steam over medium-high heat until puddings feel firm when lightly pressed in center (through foil), about 1 hour and 10 minutes. Pour additional boiling water into pan as required to keep level at about 1 inch.

Remove puddings from pan, uncover, and let cool about 10 minutes. Invert onto a dish or platter and lift off molds.

If made ahead, let cool, wrap airtight, and chill up to 4 days. Freeze to store longer (thaw before reheating). To reheat, set puddings (as many as desired) close together on a plate that will fit on rack in the same pan or pans you used before; cover plate tightly with foil. Add boiling water to just below rack. Cover and steam on medium-high heat until puddings are warm, 15 to 20 minutes.

Unwrap puddings and set each on a dessert plate. Surround each pudding with a pool of hachiya sauce, or offer sauce to add to taste. Warm remaining ¼ cup rum in a 6- to 8-inch frying pan. Ignite with a match (not beneath a fan or flammables) and pour evenly over each pudding. Makes 10 to 12 servings.

PER SERVING WITHOUT SAUCE: 229 calories, 2.6 g protein, 37 g carbohydrates, 8.7 g fat, 56 mg cholesterol, 227 mg sodium

Hachiya sauce. Rub enough soft- to squishy-ripe **Hachiya-type persimmons** through a fine strainer (or whirl smooth in a blender or food processor) to make ½ cup. Beat ½ cup **whipping cream** until it holds soft peaks. Fold pulp with cream and ½ cup **purchased** or thick home-made **eggnog.** Serve, or cover and chill up until next day; stir to use. Makes 2 cups.

PER TABLESPOON: 20 calories, 0.3 g protein, 1.5 g carbohydrates, 1.5 g fat, 6.5 mg cholesterol, 3.4 mg sodium

Seattle Gumbo

THE LOUISIANA HERITAGE *of Seattle resident Reggie Kendall emerges in this Northwest gumbo made with Pacific shellfish. The dish is a lighter, simpler version of his Southern grandmother's recipe, without the traditional okra. Its rich color comes from a browned flour roux; long cooking takes away the flour's thickening ability and leaves a subtle, toasty flavor.*

Mr. Kendall accompanies his gumbo with a green salad and hot cornbread. Dessert is lemon tart or chocolate mousse.

Because ingredients are showy, part of the party is watching the gumbo come together. Make the broth ahead of time to ease preparation.

Dungeness crab, shucked oysters, shrimp in the shell, spicy sausage, and onion and green bell pepper fill up Northwest variation on gumbo.

VERINA'S NORTHWEST GUMBO

- 1 cup salad oil
- 1 cup all-purpose flour
  About 1 pound onions, minced
  About 1 pound green bell peppers, stemmed, seeded, and minced
- 3 quarts fish broth (directions follow)
- 2 pounds extra-large (26 to 30 per lb.) shrimp
- 2 large (about 3 lb. each) cooked Dungeness crabs, cleaned and cracked
- ½ pound shelled cooked Dungeness crab
- 1 to 1½ pounds kielbasa (Polish sausage), cut into 1-inch chunks
- 2 jars (10 oz. each) fresh shucked small Olympic or Pacific oysters
  Liquid hot pepper seasoning
  About ¼ cup chopped parsley
- 12 to 14 cups hot cooked long-grain white rice
  Salt

Pour oil into a heavy 10- to 12-inch frying pan on medium-high heat; when oil is hot (about 325°), add flour all at once. Stir often until roux is a rich, deep caramel color, 7 to 8 minutes. Off the heat, dump in the onions and bell peppers all at once. Stir until foaming stops and vegetables are soft, about 1 minute.

Meanwhile, in a 12- to 16-quart pan, bring broth to boiling; stir in the hot roux. If made ahead, cover and chill up until next day. Cover and reheat to simmering.

Devein shrimp in shell by sliding a thin wooden skewer into back and under vein, then gently pulling vein out; repeat in several places along back. Rinse shrimp; add all at once to broth with crab in shell, crab meat, sausage, and oysters (with liquid). Cover and simmer very gently so flavors mingle, 15 to 30 minutes. Add 2 tablespoons hot pepper seasoning.

Transfer gumbo to a large serving bowl and sprinkle with parsley. Ladle portions over rice in wide soup bowls. Add liquid hot pepper seasoning and salt to taste. Makes 12 to 14 servings.

PER SERVING: 670 calories, 37 g protein, 64 g carbohydrates, 28 g fat, 169 mg cholesterol, 719 mg sodium

Rich brown roux with chopped vegetables goes into fish broth. Next comes shellfish.

Fish broth. Rinse well 1 pound **cod** or rockfish and about 4 pounds **heads, bones,** and **trimmings from white-flesh fish** such as cod, rockfish, lingcod, sole, or halibut; put into a 10- to 12-quart pan. Add 4 quarts **water,** 2 large (about 1 lb. total) chopped **onions,** 4 **dry bay leaves,** 2 teaspoons **black peppercorns,** 2 bottles (8-oz. size) **clam juice,** and 2 stalks **celery** (chopped). Bring to a boil, cover, and simmer 5 to 6 hours.

Pour broth through a fine strainer into a large bowl; discard residue. Boil on high heat, uncovered, until reduced to 3 quarts. If made ahead, cover and chill up until next day, or freeze for longer storage. Makes 3 quarts.

Based on a classic Southern recipe, Northwest-style gumbo uses Pacific shellfish and omits the traditional okra. To serve at the table, ladle pieces of shellfish, sausage slices, and rich fish and vegetable broth over rice in wide bowls.

A Hearty Czech Meal

IN THE WINTER DISHES of traditional Czechoslovakian cuisine, long-lasting roots and fruits from the cellar were often used in a variety of ways within the same menu—with surprisingly distinctive results.

Here, celery root and carrots have dual roles: they're raw and crisp in an appetizer salad, and also cooked to make a sauce for the roast and the dumplings. Apples are sautéed and served with the roast, too.

This Czech meal for 6 starts with a cottage cheese spread and a root slaw, both to eat on crusty bread. You can munch walnuts, too, or eat them with the cheese. Then settle down to bowls of broth and liver balls, followed by a roast, vegetable sauce, stuffed dumplings, warm apples, and asparagus.

For dessert, a token taste of chocolate to go with coffee and cordial is ample.

Cottage Cheese Spread   Walnuts
Celery Root & Carrot Slaw
Sliced Baguette
Liver Balls in Broth
Beef Rib Roast with Apples
& Roasted Vegetable Sauce
Crouton Dumplings   Hot Asparagus
Dry German, Alsatian, or Domestic
Gewürztraminer
Chocolate Bon Bons
Blackberry Cordial   Strong Coffee

A day ahead, you can make the appetizers, the soup, and the crouton dumplings. You can also pare and cut the vegetables for the sauce.

If you prefer to cook the asparagus a few hours ahead, immerse it, when done, in ice water to stop the cooking and preserve the color. Before serving, place it in hot water for a few minutes to warm. While the roast cooks, you can peel and slice the apples and start heating them.

A dry but fruity white wine such as Gewürztraminer is refreshing. If you prefer, choose a dry, smooth red wine such as a mature Barbera or Cabernet Sauvignon.

COTTAGE CHEESE SPREAD

Spread cheese mixture onto thin slices of baguette or crisp rolls. Sprinkle walnut halves or pieces onto cheese.

Liver balls are cooked until firm in boiling broth; spoon broth with balls into bowls.

1½ cups small-curd cottage cheese
½ teaspoon paprika
Salt

In a blender or food processor, whirl cottage cheese and paprika until smooth; add salt to taste. Spoon cheese into a small bowl; if made ahead, cover and chill up until next day. Makes 1½ cups, 6 servings.

PER TABLESPOON: 14 calories, 1.6 g protein, 0.4 g carbohydrates, 0.6 g fat, 1.9 mg cholesterol, 53 mg sodium

CELERY ROOT & CARROT SLAW

To eat, mound onto thin slices of baguette or crisp rolls.

1 medium-size carrot, peeled and finely shredded
1 celery root (about ½ lb., or 1 piece), scrubbed, peeled, and finely shredded
¼ cup sour cream or unflavored yogurt
Salt and pepper
2 to 3 teaspoons lemon juice
Thin lemon slice (optional)

Mix together carrot, celery root, and sour cream, and add salt, pepper, and lemon juice to taste. If made ahead, cover and chill up until the next day. Serve in a small bowl, garnished with lemon slice. Makes 3 cups, 6 servings.

PER SERVING: 38 calories, 0.9 g protein, 4.6 g carbohydrates, 2.1 g fat, 4.2 mg cholesterol, 42 mg sodium

LIVER BALLS IN BROTH

¼ pound beef liver, rinsed and patted dry
½ cup dry bread crumbs
1 large egg
1 tablespoon milk or water
1 tablespoon melted butter or margarine
1 clove garlic, minced or pressed
2 tablespoons minced parsley
½ teaspoon dry marjoram leaves
¼ teaspoon *each* salt and pepper
6 cups regular-strength beef broth

Trim membrane and tubes from liver and discard. Cut liver into chunks and put in a food processor or blender with bread crumbs, egg, milk, butter, garlic, 1 tablespoon parsley, marjoram, salt, and pepper; whirl until smoothly puréed, then set aside (or cover and chill until next day).

In a 4- to 5-quart pan, bring broth to a boil over high heat. Quickly spoon liver mixture, 1 tablespoon at a time, into boiling broth. Cover pan, reduce heat to simmering, and cook until balls are firm in the center (make a small cut to test), about 5 minutes. Serve, or keep warm over lowest heat up to 2 hours. If made ahead, let cool, cover, and chill; reheat until simmering.

Ladle broth and liver balls into 6 soup bowls; sprinkle the remaining parsley on top. Makes 6 servings.

PER SERVING: 111 calories, 6.4 g protein, 10 g carbohydrates, 4.7 g fat, 119 mg cholesterol, 203 mg sodium

BEEF RIB ROAST WITH APPLES & ROASTED VEGETABLE SAUCE

1 boned and tied beef rib roast, 3½ to 4 pounds
1 medium-size carrot, peeled and cut into ½-inch dice
1 celery root (¾ lb., or 1 piece), scrubbed, peeled, and cut into ½-inch dice
1 medium-size parsnip, peeled and cut into ½-inch dice
1 medium-size onion, peeled and chopped
3 *each* black peppercorns and whole allspice
2 bay leaves
2 tablespoons melted butter or margarine

1½ cups regular-strength beef broth
1 cup whipping cream
   Warm apple slices (recipe follows)
   Parsley sprigs
   Salt and pepper

Wipe meat with a damp paper towel. In a 12- by 15-inch shallow pan, set roast with fat side up. Insert a meat thermometer in thickest part of roast. Put carrot, celery root, parsnip, onion, peppercorns, allspice, and bay leaves in pan around meat. Drizzle butter over vegetables.

Bake in a 350° oven until thermometer reads 130° for rare, 140° for medium, 1¾ to 2¼ hours. As meat cooks, stir vegetables several times with a wide spatula. Set meat on a platter; keep warm.

With a slotted spoon, quickly transfer vegetables to a blender or food processer, discarding bay leaves. Spoon off and discard fat from pan drippings, then pour drippings in with vegetables. Whirl until smoothly puréed, adding broth. Scrape back into pan, add cream, and stir over medium-high heat until steaming. Pour into a serving bowl; keep warm.

Spoon apples into a serving dish, or present with meat and garnish with parsley.

Slice roast and accompany with vegetable sauce and apples. Add salt and pepper to taste. Makes 6 to 8 servings.
—*Kristina Klee, Sacramento.*

PER SERVING: 663 calories, 34 g protein, 9 g carbohydrates, 54 g fat, 163 mg cholesterol, 173 mg sodium

Warm apple slices. Peel, core, and slice 5 medium-size (about 2 lb. total) **tart apples** such as Newtown Pippin. In a 12-inch frying pan or 4- to 5-quart pan over medium heat, melt 2 tablespoons **butter** or margarine. Add apples, 1 tablespoon firmly packed **brown sugar,** and ½ teaspoon **ground cinnamon.** Cook apples until tender when pierced, about 10 minutes. Turn heat to high; frequently turn fruit with a spatula until tinged golden brown, about 3 minutes. If made ahead, keep warm up to 30 minutes.

PER SERVING: 116 calories, 0.2 g protein, 21 g carbohydrates, 4.3 g fat, 10 mg cholesterol, 40 mg sodium

CROUTON DUMPLINGS

In a 6- to 7-inch frying pan over medium-high heat, melt 2 tablespoons **butter** or margarine. Add ¾ cup **seasoned croutons.** Stir often until croutons

begin to brown, about 5 minutes; let cool. If made ahead, cover and store up until next day.

In a large bowl, mix together 1¾ cups **all-purpose-flour** and 2 teaspoons **baking powder.** With your fingers, rub in ¼ cup (⅛ lb.) **butter** or margarine until mealy. Using a fork, stir in ½ cup **water** and 1 **large egg** until evenly moistened.

In bowl, cut through dough to divide into 6 equal pieces. Spoon a portion of dough into your lightly floured hand; spoon ⅙ of the croutons onto center of dough. With floured fingers, pull dough up and over croutons to cover completely; set stuffed dumpling on a floured surface. Repeat to shape remaining dumplings.

In a 5- to 6-quart pan, bring 3 to 3½ quarts water to boiling over high heat. Add 3 dumplings to water at a time.

Cook, uncovered, at a gentle boil until dumplings feel firm when lightly touched and look dry around croutons (make a tiny cut to test), about 8 minutes; turn after 4 minutes. Lift dumplings from water with a slotted spoon and set on a rack to drain; keep warm. Repeat to cook remaining dumplings (to speed process, you can cook in 2 pans at once). If made ahead, let dumplings cool, then cover and chill up until next day. To reheat in a microwave oven, arrange in a single layer on a nonmetal plate, cover loosely with plastic wrap, and cook on full power (100 percent) until hot in center, about 3 minutes. Or set on a rack in a deep pan over about 1 inch boiling water; cover and steam until hot in center, about 6 minutes. Makes 6 servings.

PER SERVING: 274 calories, 5.5 g protein, 31 g carbohydrates, 14 g fat, 77 mg cholesterol, 358 mg sodium

Hearty Czechoslovakian menu features roast beef with crouton-stuffed dumplings, stalks of asparagus, warm sautéed apple slices, and vegetable sauce.

Hungarian-Style Dishes with Paprika

IF YOU OVERLOOK PAPRIKA *because you consider it a bland seasoning, think again. Used with a bold hand, it's more than a dusting of color to dress up plain foods.*

Hungarian cuisine is rich with the color, flavor, and aroma of this distinctive seasoning. Hungarians have also made a specialty of producing paprika; they've been exporting this powder of dried ripe red peppers of the capsicum family for at least four centuries.

Native to the Americas, the peppers came to western Europe with the Spanish and Portuguese, who later took them to India. From there, Ottoman Turks took the peppers through Persia to eastern Europe, including present-day Hungary.

Today, you'll find Old World and New World versions of the spice on supermarket shelves. Taste varies with the type of pepper used. All paprika peppers are fully ripened to develop intense flavors and color before they are dried and ground.

The peppers that are used to make Hungarian paprika look much like small red bell peppers. From them are derived sweet (also called mild) and mildly hot varieties of the spice. Westerners will find hot paprika gentle compared with many of the chilies we use regularly.

Domestic producers—mostly in California and New Mexico—make paprika from long, slender hybrids of the Anaheim chili. These peppers lack the heat of the regular Anaheim and yield paprika comparable to Hungarian sweet.

These Hungarian-style cool-weather dishes make good use of paprika. Try the sweet cooked onions, made orange-red by paprika, atop open-faced sandwiches. But also consider them as a warm relish for any cooked meat, poultry, or fish. Goulash soup is based on brisket; mushrooms and barley form the foundation of the other soup. Pork baby back ribs bake moist and tender on a bed of sauerkraut and fresh cabbage; paprika seasons the vegetables and the light, crisp crust of crumbs on the meat.

SWEET PAPRIKA ONIONS

For delicious open-faced sandwiches, top slices of toasted bread (buttered or spread with sour cream) with cooked pork tenderloin, chicken breast, or cheese such as cream cheese, feta, gruyère, or jack. Then mound warm onion on top.

- **2 tablespoons *each* salad oil and butter or margarine**
- **2 pounds onions, thinly sliced**
- **2 tablespoons hot or sweet Hungarian paprika, or regular (domestic) paprika**

In a 10- to 12-inch frying pan over medium heat, add oil, butter, and onions. Stir occasionally until onions turn a deep gold, well tinged with brown, about 1½ hours. Remove from

Imported paprika (left) can be gently warm or sweet; mellow domestic paprika (center) comes from ripe red Anaheim chili hybrids (right).

heat and stir in paprika. Use hot, or cover and chill up to 3 days; stir over medium heat to warm before using. Makes about 1 cup.

PER TABLESPOON: 50 calories, 0.8 g protein, 4.6 g carbohydrates, 3.4 g fat, 3.9 mg cholesterol, 16 mg sodium

GOULASH SOUP

- **2 pounds fresh beef brisket, cut into 1-inch pieces**
- **2 tablespoons *each* salad oil and butter or margarine**
- **3 large (about 2½ lb. total) onions, thinly sliced**
- **1 cup *each* dry white wine and water**
- **¼ cup sweet Hungarian paprika, or regular (domestic) paprika**
- **2 medium-size green bell peppers, stemmed, seeded, and diced**
- **4 cups (2 cans, 14½-oz. size) regular-strength beef broth**
- **1 medium-size russet potato, peeled and cut into ½-inch cubes**
  Unflavored nonfat yogurt

In a 5- to 6-quart pan over medium-high heat, brown meat, about ½ at a time, in 1 tablespoon *each* salad oil and butter. Set meat aside.

To pan, add remaining oil, butter, and onions. Stir often until onions are dark gold in color and very soft, about 40 minutes. Stir in meat, wine, water, paprika, bell pepper, and broth. Bring to a boil, reduce heat, and cover and simmer until meat is tender to bite, about 2 hours.

Add potato and continue to simmer until the potato is tender to bite, about 30 minutes longer. Ladle into bowls; add yogurt to taste. Makes 6 servings.

PER SERVING: 428 calories, 35 g protein, 25 g carbohydrates, 21 g fat, 104 mg cholesterol, 172 mg sodium

Red with paprika, slow-cooked onions make delectable topping for sandwich of jack cheese. Munch with crisp radishes.

BABY BACK RIBS BAKED WITH SAUERKRAUT

1 large can (27 oz.) sauerkraut, drained
4 cups shredded red cabbage
About 3 tablespoons hot or sweet Hungarian paprika, or regular (domestic) paprika
4 cloves garlic, minced or pressed
1 can (14½ oz.) stewed tomatoes
3 pounds pork baby back ribs
½ teaspoon pepper
⅓ cup fine dry bread crumbs

Pour sauerkraut into a colander and rinse with cool running water; let drain. In a roasting pan about 10 by 14 inches, mix together sauerkraut, cabbage, 1 tablespoon paprika, garlic, and tomatoes; spread in an even layer. Lay ribs on sauerkraut mixture, curved side up; sprinkle meat evenly with pepper and about 2 teaspoons paprika. Tightly cover pan with foil. Bake in 375° oven for 1½ hours.

Mix together 2 teaspoons paprika and bread crumbs. Remove foil, turn ribs over, and sprinkle with paprika mixture. Bake, uncovered, until meat is very tender when pierced and crumbs are brown, about 20 minutes longer.

Transfer baby back ribs to a platter and spoon sauerkraut mixture into a bowl. Cut ribs apart and serve with sauerkraut. Makes 4 servings.

PER SERVING: 720 calories, 41 g protein, 25 g carbohydrates, 51 g fat, 165 mg cholesterol, 922 mg sodium

MUSHROOM, BARLEY & PARSLEY CHOWDER

2 pounds mushrooms
About ⅓ cup olive or salad oil
1 large (about 10 oz.) onion, chopped
¼ cup sweet Hungarian paprika or regular (domestic) paprika
1 can (14½ oz.) pear-shaped tomatoes
2 quarts regular-strength chicken or beef broth
2 cups water
1 cup pearl barley, rinsed
2 tablespoons red wine vinegar
2 cups minced parsley
Salt and pepper

Rinse mushrooms; trim off and discard discolored stem ends. Thinly slice mushrooms.

Pork baby back ribs, finely crusted with paprika and dry bread crumbs, are cut apart between bones. Serve with sauerkraut baked with red cabbage and more paprika.

In a 6- to 8-quart pan over high heat, combine mushrooms and ¼ cup olive oil. Stir often until mushroom juices evaporate, about 15 minutes. Add onion and stir often until onion is limp, about 5 minutes. Stir in paprika, tomatoes and juices, beef broth, water, barley, and red wine vinegar.

Over high heat, bring mixture to a boil. Reduce heat, cover, and simmer until barley is very tender to bite, about 30 minutes. (If made ahead, cool, cover, and chill up until next day. Reheat to continue.)

Meanwhile, in a 10- to 12-inch frying pan over high heat, stir 1 tablespoon olive oil with parsley until parsley turns brighter green and crisp, about 2 minutes. Spoon onto paper towels to drain; if made ahead, cool, cover, and chill up until next day.

When barley is tender, add ¾ of the sautéed parsley to soup. Ladle soup into bowls; sprinkle with remaining parsley. Add salt and pepper to taste. Makes 8 to 10 servings.

PER SERVING: 211 calories, 7.1 g protein, 27 g carbohydrates, 9.5 g fat, 0 mg cholesterol, 121 mg sodium

Starting with Squash

SMOOTH AND SWEET *baked winter squash forms the base for three attractive first courses. Chinese cuisine inspired the first dish, while India influenced the second. In the last, creamed spinach and prosciutto broil atop more squash.*

SICHUAN PORK WITH WINTER SQUASH

> 2 **tablespoons soy sauce**
> 2 **tablespoons minced fresh ginger**
> **Winter squash (directions follow)**
> ½ **pound ground lean pork**
> 2 **tablespoons salted fermented black beans, rinsed and drained**
> 1 **teaspoon cornstarch**
> ½ **cup regular-strength chicken broth**
> 2 **tablespoons slivered green onions**

Rub 1 tablespoon soy sauce and 1 tablespoon ginger on squash before baking.

In an 8- to 10-inch frying pan over medium heat, stir pork often until crumbly and well browned, about 5 minutes. To pan, add the remaining ginger and beans, mashing beans.

Mix cornstarch, remaining soy, and broth; add to pan. Stir on high heat until boiling. If made ahead, cover and chill up until the next day; reheat.

With a sharp knife, cut cooked squash into 6 equal portions. Set, skin down, on plates. Top squash equally with pork mixture and sprinkle with onions. Makes 6 servings.

PER SERVING: 169 calories, 9.7 g protein, 11 g carbohydrates, 10.2 g fat, 28 mg cholesterol, 540 mg sodium

Winter squash. Rinse 2 pounds **winter squash**—Hubbard, banana, butternut, Kabocha—or 3 acorn squash (each about ¾ lb.). Cut squash in half; scoop out and discard seeds. Put squash, skin side up, in a 9- by 13-inch pan. Add 1½ cups **regular-strength chicken broth**. Bake, uncovered, in 350° oven until tender when pierced, about 1 hour. Use hot or warm.

KHYBER LAMB & SQUASH APPETIZER

> **Winter squash (recipe precedes)**
> 1 **tablespoon curry powder**
> ½ **pound ground lean lamb**
> 1 **tablespoon tomato paste**
> ½ **teaspoon ground cardamom**
> ½ **teaspoon cumin seed**
> ¼ **teaspoon ground allspice**
> 1 **teaspoon cornstarch**
> ½ **cup regular-strength chicken broth**
> **About ½ cup sour cream**
> 2 **tablespoons slivered green onions**
> **Lemon wedges**

When preparing squash to bake, rub with 1 teaspoon of the curry powder.

In an 8- to 10-inch frying pan over medium heat, stir lamb often with remaining curry, tomato paste, cardamom, cumin, and allspice until meat is crumbly and well browned, about 10 minutes. Mix cornstarch with broth; add to pan. Stir over high heat until boiling. If made ahead, cover and chill up until next day; reheat.

With a sharp knife, cut cooked squash into 6 equal portions and set on plates, skin down. Spoon lamb mixture equally onto each serving. Put a spoonful of sour cream on meat; sprinkle with onions. Accompany with more sour cream and lemon. Makes 6 servings.

PER SERVING: 257 calories, 2.7 g protein, 21 g carbohydrates, 15 g fat, 36 mg cholesterol, 109 mg sodium

GOLDEN SQUASH FLORENTINE

> 1 **pound fresh spinach or 1 package (10 oz.) frozen chopped spinach, thawed**
> 1 **tablespoon butter or margarine**
> 1 **large shallot, minced**
> 1 **tablespoon all-purpose flour**
> ½ **cup half-and-half (light cream)**
> ½ **teaspoon Worcestershire**
> ¼ **teaspoon *each* dry mustard and pepper**
> ½ **to 1 teaspoon ground nutmeg**
> **Winter squash (recipe precedes)**
> 3 **ounces thinly sliced prosciutto**

Rinse and drain fresh spinach, discarding roots and wilted or yellowed leaves. Put leaves in a 4- to 5-quart pan on high heat. Stir often until leaves wilt, 2 to 4 minutes. Let drain in a colander. When cool, press to remove moisture.

Over medium heat, combine butter and shallot in same pan used for spinach. Stir often until shallot is lightly browned, about 5 minutes. Add flour and stir until mixture is golden. Remove from heat and whisk in half-and-half. Place on medium-high heat and stir until boiling. Mix in Worcestershire, mustard, pepper, spinach, and nutmeg to taste. If made ahead, cover and chill up until next day; reheat.

With a sharp knife, cut cooked squash into 6 equal portions. Place, skin down, in baking pan. Top squash equally with spinach mixture; drape with prosciutto. Broil 8 inches from heat until prosciutto is sizzling and tinged with brown, about 4 minutes. Set pieces on individual plates. Makes 6 servings.

PER SERVING: 137 calories, 8.3 g protein, 13 g carbohydrates, 6.8 g fat, 21 mg cholesterol, 313 mg sodium

Creamed spinach and thinly sliced prosciutto top this golden Hubbard squash appetizer. Assemble individual portions, then broil briefly just before serving.

Enjoying Pummeloes

LONG APPRECIATED BY ASIANS, *pummeloes now appear in many supermarkets during the winter. This round to pear-shaped citrus fruit looks like a large grapefruit but is sweeter, without bitterness; it's often firmer fleshed and less juicy than its more common relative.*

Inside the smooth, golden yellow skin, the fruit is buried beneath a very thick layer of spongy white pith. Remove this layer, then peel away the thick membranes encasing each segment. The flesh may be pink or white, and its texture varies in different fruit. Sometimes a pummelo is so firm that the segments readily fall apart into separate juice sacs, or it may be almost as cohesive and juicy as a grapefruit.

Enjoy pummelo segments plain, on a fruit plate for breakfast or dessert, or in salads such as these.

PUMMELO & AVOCADO SALAD

  1 large (about 10 oz.) firm-ripe avocado, peeled, pitted, and cut into lengthwise slices
  1 small (about 1½ lb.) pummelo, peeled and segmented (see pictures below)
  1 lime, cut into wedges
    Chili salt (recipe follows)

On 4 salad or dinner plates, arrange equal portions of the avocado and pummelo sections. Garnish each serving with lime wedges. To eat, squeeze lime over fruit and sprinkle to taste with chili salt. Makes 4 servings.

PER SERVING WITHOUT CHILI SALT: 131 calories, 2 g protein, 16 g carbohydrates, 8.1 g fat, 0 mg cholesterol, 6.7 mg sodium

Chili salt. Mix 2 teaspoons **salt** and ¼ teaspoon **cayenne.**

PER ⅛ TEASPOON: 0.1 calories, 0 g protein, 0 g carbohydrates, 0 g fat, 0 mg cholesterol, 245 mg sodium

THAI PUMMELO & SHRIMP SALAD

  3 tablespoons dry sweetened shredded or flaked coconut
  1 tablespoon salad oil
  2 large cloves garlic, thinly sliced
  1 large (about 2½ lb.) pummelo, peeled and segmented (see pictures below)
  ⅓ pound shelled cooked tiny shrimp
  ¼ cup thinly sliced shallots
    Tart-hot dressing (recipe follows)
    Butter or green-leaf lettuce leaves, rinsed and crisped
  ¼ cup roasted salted peanuts, chopped
    Fresh cilantro (coriander) sprigs

In a 6- to 8-inch frying pan, stir coconut over low heat until golden, 5 to 8 minutes. Pour out of pan and set aside. Add oil and garlic, and stir over medium heat just until garlic is golden brown and crisp, 2 to 3 minutes. Set aside.

Meanwhile, with your hands, gently pull pummelo segments apart to separate the tiny juice sacs (firm, dry-textured fruit segments separate easily; if fruit does not do this readily, leave segments whole). Gently mix shredded pummelo (do not mix in whole segments; set aside), shrimp, shallots, and dressing.

Line 4 salad or dinner plates with let-tuce. Spoon equal portions of shredded pummelo salad onto lettuce. (If using whole segments, lay equal portions of pummelo on lettuce; spoon shrimp mixture on fruit.) Garnish each salad equally with toasted coconut, garlic, peanuts, and cilantro. Makes 4 servings.

PER SERVING: 241 calories, 13 g protein, 27 g carbohydrates, 10 g fat, 73 mg cholesterol, 137 mg sodium

Tart-hot dressing. In a small bowl, combine 2 tablespoons **lime juice,** 2 tablespoons **fish sauce** (*nam pla* or *nuoc mam*) or soy sauce, 1 tablespoon minced **fresh ginger,** 1 teaspoon **sugar,** and ½ to ¾ teaspoon **crushed dried hot red chilies;** stir until sugar dissolves.

Dust segments of pummelo and avocado with chili-spiked salt, and drench with lime juice.

Cut thick skin and most of white pith from ends and sides with a sharp knife.

Trim away pith to expose fruit. Pull fruit open to center of sections.

Cut thick, pithy ridge of membrane away from the center of fruit sections.

Carefully pull fruit segments away from thick membrane; start from inside edge.

Light & Healthy Recipes

LIGHTEN UP YOUR COOKING *to achieve your goals of eating well and staying fit. However, a shift to better-balanced eating doesn't mean you must put aside your favorite foods. Here we present examples of pot roast and cheesecake to show how recipes can be streamlined to reduce both calories and the percentage of calories from fat. Even tortilla chips can be lean.*

NEW POT ROAST

⅓ ounce (about ¼ cup) dried porcini mushrooms (optional)

1 boneless beef bottom round or rump roast (3½ lb.), fat trimmed

2 tablespoons Worcestershire

1 large onion, chopped

2 cloves garlic, minced or pressed

2 cups low-sodium beef broth

1 cup dry red wine

1 can (6 oz.) tomato paste

1½ pounds small red thin-skinned potatoes

1½ pounds carrots, cut into ½-inch-thick sticks

In a small bowl, pour ⅓ cup boiling water over mushrooms; let soak until softened, about 20 minutes. Pour mushrooms and liquid into a cheesecloth-lined strainer, reserving liquid. Squeeze mushrooms to extract liquid. Finely chop mushrooms. Set mushrooms and liquid aside.

Meanwhile, combine meat, Worcestershire, and ½ cup water in a 5- to 6-quart pan. Cover and bring to a boil over high heat; reduce heat to medium and cook for 30 minutes. Uncover, increase heat to high, and cook, turning meat to brown evenly, until liquid has almost evaporated (if drippings begin to burn, stir 2 to 3 tablespoons water into pan). Skim off and discard fat.

Add onion, garlic, and 2 tablespoons water to pan. Reduce heat to medium-high, and stir until vegetables are glazed with drippings, about 5 minutes.

Add beef broth, wine, tomato paste, and mushrooms and their liquid. Reduce heat, cover, and simmer for 2 hours, turning meat once or twice. Tuck potatoes around meat and continue cooking for 20 minutes. Add carrots; continue cooking until meat and vegetables are tender when pierced, about 20 minutes longer.

With a slotted spoon, remove vegetables and meat. Skim and discard fat from pan juices. Slice meat and arrange on

Pot roast, lightened in calories by substantial reduction of fat, can be part of menu for wholesome dining. Add potatoes and carrots to cook during final minutes.

individual plates with vegetables. Moisten with pan juices. Makes 10 servings.

PER SERVING: 351 calories, 38 g protein, 25 g carbohydrates, 11 g total fat (4 g saturated fat), 94 mg cholesterol, 290 mg sodium

LOW-FAT CHEESECAKE

1½ cups graham cracker crumbs

3 tablespoons margarine, melted

1 cup low-fat cottage cheese

2 cups unflavored nonfat yogurt

½ cup sugar

1 tablespoon all-purpose flour

1 large egg

2 large egg whites

2 teaspoons vanilla

2 cups raspberries, other berries, or sliced fresh fruit

Stir together graham cracker crumbs and margarine until well combined. Press firmly over bottom and partway up sides of an 8-inch cheesecake pan with removable rim. Bake in a 350° oven for 7 minutes. Let cool on a rack. Reduce oven temperature to 300°.

In a blender, whirl cottage cheese and yogurt until smooth and glossy, at least 1 minute. Add sugar, flour, egg, egg whites, and vanilla; whirl until smooth.

Pour filling into crust and bake until top feels dry when lightly touched and center jiggles only slightly when pan is gently shaken, about 55 minutes. Let cool on a rack. Wrap airtight and refrigerate for at least 8 hours or until next day. Top portions with berries. Makes 10 servings.

PER SERVING: 211 calories, 8 g protein, 31 g carbohydrates, 6 g total fat (0.9 g saturated fat), 23 mg cholesterol, 292 mg sodium

WATER-CRISPED TORTILLA CHIPS

12 corn or flour tortillas (6- to 7-in. diameter)
Salt

Dip tortillas, 1 at a time, in water; let drain briefly. Season to taste with salt. Stack and cut into 6 or 8 wedges.

Arrange wedges in a single layer on 12- by 15-inch baking sheets (you'll need about 3 sheets, or reuse 1). Bake in a 500° oven for 4 minutes. Turn chips over and bake until browned and crisped, about 2 minutes longer. If made ahead, let cool; store airtight at room temperature for up to 1 week. Makes 2 quarts.

PER CUP CORN TORTILLA CHIPS: 100 calories, 3 g protein, 19 g carbohydrates, 2 g fat (0 g saturated fat), 0 mg cholesterol, 80 mg sodium

Haute Cuisine Chinoise

Combine Chinese seasonings *with French-style presentation and ingredients for an intriguing cuisine that San Francisco restaurateur Tommy Toy calls haute cuisine chinoise.*

These two examples—fried won ton filled with crab and cheese, and sautéed chicken breast marinated with Southeast Asian flavors—can easily be duplicated.

Won Ton with Crab & Cheese

- 1 large package (8 oz.) cream cheese, at room temperature
- ½ teaspoon Oriental sesame oil (optional)
- ¼ teaspoon steak sauce or soy sauce
- ¼ teaspoon pepper
- 1¼ cups (about 4 oz.) thinly sliced garlic chives, or regular chives plus 2 cloves garlic, pressed or minced
- ½ pound shelled cooked crab
- 1 package (14 oz.) won ton skins
  About 1 tablespoon beaten egg
  Salad oil
  Plum sauce, or ⅓ cup red wine vinegar mixed with 2 tablespoons water and 1 tablespoon finely shredded pickled ginger

In a small bowl, beat cream cheese, sesame oil, steak sauce, and pepper until smooth. Mix in chives and crab.

Place a won ton skin on a flat surface (cover remaining skins with plastic wrap to keep pliable). Mound 1 teaspoon filling in 1 corner. Fold that corner over filling, and roll to tuck point under. Moisten the 2 side corners with egg and bring together, overlapping slightly. Press firmly to seal; put on a flour-dusted baking sheet (or sheets) and cover while you fill the remaining skins; place slightly apart. If made ahead, cover and chill up to 8 hours.

In a wok or 3- to 4-quart pan, pour oil to a depth of 1 to 1½ inches; heat to 350°, checking with a thermometer. Fry 4 to 6 won ton at a time, turning occasionally, until golden, about 1 minute. Remove with a slotted spoon and drain on paper towels. Keep warm in a 200° oven until all are cooked, then serve with plum sauce or vinegar mixture for dipping. (If made ahead, cool, then wrap airtight and freeze. To reheat, arrange frozen won ton in one layer on baking sheet or sheets and bake in a 350° oven until hot, about 15 minutes.) Makes about 6 dozen.

Per won ton: 31 calories, 1.6 g protein, 3.3 g carbohydrates, 1.2 g fat, 7.5 mg cholesterol, 21 mg sodium

Fold corner of won ton skin over crab filling; roll to enclose. Moisten opposite side corners with egg and bring together, overlapping slightly; press to seal. Fry in oil until crisp. To eat, dip in red vinegar with pickled ginger or in plum sauce.

Chicken with Lemon Grass & Chili

- 4 boned, skinned chicken breast halves (4 to 5 oz. each)
  Lemon grass marinade (recipe follows)
- 1 pound asparagus, tough ends removed
- 2 to 3 tablespoons salad oil
  Lime wedges

Place chicken breasts between sheets of plastic wrap. With a flat mallet, gently and evenly pound chicken until about ¼ inch thick. Coat breasts with marinade; cover and chill 20 to 30 minutes.

In a 5- to 6-quart pan, bring about 2 quarts water to a boil. Add asparagus and cook, uncovered, until barely tender to bite, 3 to 5 minutes. Drain; keep warm.

Meanwhile, place a 10- to 12-inch frying pan over medium-high heat. Add 2 tablespoons oil; tilt pan to coat bottom.

Lift chicken from marinade, draining excess. Cook as many pieces as will fit without overlapping, turning once, until white in center, 4 to 5 minutes total. Remove from pan and keep warm. Repeat with remaining chicken, adding oil as needed.

Place equal portions chicken and asparagus on plates. Garnish with lime. Makes 4 servings.

Per serving: 205 calories, 28 g protein, 3 g carbohydrates, 8.6 g fat, 66 mg cholesterol, 140 mg sodium

Lemon grass marinade. Combine 2 tablespoons **dry white wine;** 1 tablespoon **soy sauce;** 1 teaspoon **sugar;** 1 teaspoon **Oriental sesame oil** (optional); 3 cloves **garlic,** pressed or minced; 1 **fresh jalapeño chili,** stemmed, seeded, and finely chopped; and ⅛ teaspoon **pepper.** Trim tough tops off 1 stalk **fresh lemon grass** and peel off dry layers. Rinse grass well and mince; add to wine mixture. (Or omit lemon grass and use ½ teaspoon grated lemon peel.)

Smoked Fish Torte

SHOWY BUT SIMPLE, *this layer cake look-alike is really a smoked fish torte that makes a cool luncheon entrée or a handsome starter for a party dinner.*

First you bake tender, unsweetened soufflé layers. Between them go dill-flavored cream cheese, smoked trout, peppery arugula, and cucumber slices. Frost torte's top with more cheese. After torte chills, it cuts neatly to reveal green and white layers inside.

It takes time to put the torte together, but you can complete it in steps up to the day before serving.

SMOKED TROUT & ARUGULA TORTE

- ¼ cup (⅛ lb.) **butter** or **margarine**
- ½ cup **all-purpose flour**
- 2 cups **milk**
- 4 large **eggs,** separated
- ⅛ teaspoon **cream of tartar**
  Cream cheese filling (recipe follows)
- 1 **smoked trout fillet** (⅓ to ½ lb.), skinned and boned
- 3 ounces (about 4 cups, loosely packed) **arugula leaves,** rinsed and crisped
- 1 small (about 8 oz.) **cucumber,** peeled and cut into ⅛-inch-thick rounds

Lightly butter 2 cake pans, each 9 inches in diameter. Line bottoms with waxed paper, then butter paper and dust pans with flour; set pans aside.

In a 2- to 3-quart pan, melt butter over medium heat. Stir in the flour. Remove from heat and smoothly whisk in the milk. Bring to a boil on medium-high heat, stirring. Whisk about ½ cup of the hot mixture into the egg yolks; stir yolk mixture back into pan and stir until mixture thickens slightly, about 5 minutes. Let stand to cool slightly.

In a large bowl, whip egg whites with cream of tartar on high speed until they hold stiff, moist peaks. Gently fold yolk mixture into white mixture, just until blended. Divide batter equally between floured pans.

Bake in a 350° oven until richly browned and firm to touch, 50 to 55 minutes; alternate pan positions halfway through baking. Cool in pan 10 minutes, then run a knife around the edge. Gently invert torte layers onto racks and carefully peel paper from them. Let cool completely.

Place 1 torte layer on a flat plate; spread layer evenly with ¼ of the cream cheese filling. Flake ½ the trout over the cheese. Set aside 8 nicely shaped arugula leaves of similar size. Lay remaining arugula flat over trout.

Gently spread another ¼ of the filling over the arugula, pushing leaves back into place as you go. Sprinkle cheese with remaining trout, then cover with an even, single layer of cucumber slices flush to the torte rim.

Spread about 1 tablespoon of the filling on the inverted (bottom) side of the other torte layer. Invert layer onto the first, aligning neatly.

Spread remaining filling on the top layer, and place reserved arugula leaves on cheese in spoke fashion, with cut edges toward center.

Cover gently but airtight with plastic wrap and chill at least 2 hours or up until next day; unwrap.

Cut torte into wedges; use a pie server to move wedges onto plates. Makes 12 first-course servings, 6 main-dish servings.

PER FIRST-COURSE SERVING: 214 calories, 10 g protein, 7.7 g carbohydrates, 16 g fat, 126 mg cholesterol, 290 mg sodium

Cream cheese filling. With a mixer, smoothly blend 1 large package (8 oz.) **cream cheese,** at room temperature; ½ cup **sour cream;** 1 tablespoon **prepared horseradish;** and 2 tablespoons chopped **fresh dill.** If made ahead, cover and chill up until next day. Bring to room temperature before using.

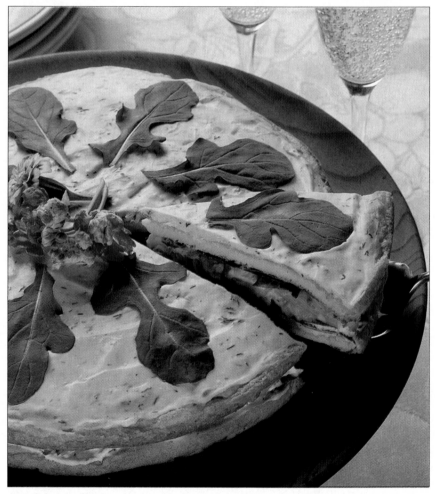

Arugula leaves, edible flowers (optional) embellish smoked fish torte; layered fillings include arugula, cucumber slices, and cream cheese filling with horseradish.

Hash Variations

A DISH OF HUMBLE ORIGINS, *well-made hash is nevertheless widely appreciated. The secret of its goodness has much to do with your patience as a cook. Whether you prepare it scrambled or in patties, you can't rush the flavorful step of browning.*

Here are three variations. While corned beef and potatoes may be the best-known hash ingredients, any leftover meat and potatoes—or even rice—will do. The first recipe is a seasoned mixture of pork and rice. The second stars roast beef and potato. The last is a lightened-up combination of chicken and rice with spinach.

PIQUANT PORK HASH WITH PAPAYA

1½ cups diced trimmed cooked pork
2 cups cooked short- or medium-grain rice
1 large carrot, peeled and shredded
½ cup chopped green onion
2 fresh small jalapeño chilies, stemmed, seeded, and minced
2 tablespoons minced fresh cilantro (coriander)
1 tablespoon butter or margarine
2 tablespoons seasoned rice vinegar (or 2 tablespoons rice vinegar mixed with 2 teaspoons sugar)
2 large (about 2¼ lb. total) firm-ripe papayas, seeded, peeled, and each cut lengthwise into 6 wedges
3 or 4 green onions, ends trimmed (optional)
Salt and pepper

Whirl pork in a food processor until coarsely ground; or mince with a knife. In a bowl, mix pork, rice, carrot, onion, chilies, and cilantro.

Melt butter in a 10- to 12-inch nonstick frying pan over medium-high heat. Add pork mixture. With a wide spatula, flatten mixture to an even thickness in pan. Cook until browned on bottom, about 5 minutes. With the spatula, turn over hash in large sections. Cook until browned on bottom, then occasionally stir hash until browned bits are well scattered through it, 7 to 10 minutes longer. Stir in vinegar.

Mound hash equally onto 3 or 4 dinner plates. Arrange papaya wedges equally on plates. Garnish with whole onions. Add salt and pepper to taste. Makes 3 or 4 servings.

PER SERVING: 356 calories, 16 g protein, 44 g carbohydrates, 12 g fat, 59 mg cholesterol, 84 mg sodium

Speckled with browned, flavorful bits of carrot, green onion, chilies, and cilantro, pork and rice hash goes well with papaya.

BEEF HASH WITH HORSERADISH CREAM

2 tablespoons butter or margarine
1 large onion, chopped
2 large (about 1½ lb. total) russet potatoes, scrubbed, peeled, and shredded
1 large (about ½ lb.) red bell pepper, stemmed, seeded, and diced
2 cups (about ¾ lb.) chopped fat-trimmed cooked beef, such as a roast or steak, coarsely chopped
Horseradish cream (recipe follows)
Salt and pepper

In a 10- to 12-inch nonstick frying pan, melt butter over medium-high heat. Add onion and stir often until limp, about 5 minutes. Add potatoes and pepper; stir often until browned, about 20 minutes. Stir meat into pan. With a spatula, press mixture into an even thickness. Cook until bottom is browned, about 5 minutes.

With spatula, turn over hash in large sections. Brown on bottom, about 7 minutes longer. Transfer to plates and accompany with horseradish cream; add salt and pepper to taste. Serves 4.

PER SERVING WITHOUT HORSERADISH CREAM: 338 calories, 28 g protein, 28 g carbohydrates, 12 g fat, 81 mg cholesterol, 124 mg sodium

Horseradish cream. Stir together ½ cup **sour cream** and 2 tablespoons **prepared horseradish.** Makes about ⅔ cup.

PER TABLESPOON: 25 calories, 0 g protein, 0 g carbohydrates, 2.4 g fat, 5 mg cholesterol, 8.9 mg sodium

CHICKEN HASH PATTIES WITH SPINACH

2 slices bacon, chopped
2 cloves garlic, minced or pressed
1 large onion, chopped
1 cup cold cooked chunks of boned and skinned chicken or turkey
2 cups cooked short- or medium-grain rice
1 cup firmly packed, rinsed and drained spinach leaves, chopped
Salt and pepper
2 large eggs
3 tablespoons butter or margarine

In a 10- to 12-inch nonstick frying pan over medium-high heat, stir bacon, garlic, and onion frequently until mixture is lightly browned, about 8 minutes.

In a food processor or with a knife, coarsely chop chicken and ½ cup rice. Put in a bowl and add bacon mixture, remaining rice, spinach, and salt and pepper to taste. Beat eggs to blend; stir into meat mixture. Shape into 8 patties, each ¾ inch thick.

Wipe frying pan clean. Melt butter in pan over medium-high heat. Add 3 or 4 patties and cook until bottoms are browned, about 4 minutes. With a wide spatula, gently turn patties and cook until brown on other side, about 4 minutes longer. Transfer to dinner plates and keep warm. Repeat to cook remaining patties. Makes 4 servings.

PER SERVING: 395 calories, 18 g protein, 33 g carbohydrates, 20 g fat, 168 mg cholesterol, 244 mg sodium

An Ancient Chinese Cooking Technique

AN ANCIENT CHINESE WAY *of cooking is tailor-made for current tastes. The process is simple: meat is stewed in a mixture of water, soy sauce, ginger, onion, and garlic. The soy tinges the meat brownish-red, giving rise to the name "red-cooking." The meat juices enrich the liquid, making a flavorful broth. And as the meat simmers, the fat melts and floats to the surface, where it can be skimmed away.*

In this updated approach, the meat choices are slow-cooking, succulent, and surprisingly lean shanks of lamb and beef which are oven-braised, untended. You can cook shanks ahead, then reheat the next day. Use broth as a sauce for the meat and for a companion such as pasta.

RED-COOKED LAMB SHANKS

6 lamb shanks (about 5½ lb. total), bones cracked, rinsed
2 cups water
⅓ cup dry sherry
¼ cup soy sauce
¼ cup minced ginger
3 tablespoons sugar
3 green onions (ends trimmed), chopped
2 cloves garlic, minced or pressed
About 1 tablespoon cornstarch
About 6 cups hot cooked pasta, rice, or mashed potatoes
Chopped parsley

Lay shanks in a single layer in a 9- by 13-inch pan. Bake, uncovered, in a 400° oven until browned, about 35 minutes.

Turn shanks over; add water, sherry, soy, ginger, sugar, onions, and garlic. Cover pan tightly with foil. Bake until meat is so tender it pulls apart easily, 2 to 2½ hours.

With a slotted spoon, transfer shanks gently to a platter; keep warm. If made ahead, cover and chill meat (on platter) and broth (in pan) up until next day.

Skim and discard fat (or lift chilled fat) from cooking broth. (If made ahead, return shanks and any broth to baking pan, cover with foil, and bake in a 400° oven until hot, 35 to 40 minutes; then put shanks on platter and keep warm.)

Measure broth; if needed, add water to make about 1½ cups. Set baking pan with broth over high heat and bring to boiling. If more than 1½ cups, boil to reduce.

In a small bowl, mix cornstarch with 2 tablespoons water; stir enough of the cornstarch mixture into boiling broth to thicken broth to consistency you like. Pour into a small bowl. Add pasta to platter with meat; sprinkle with parsley. Moisten meat and pasta to taste with broth. Makes 6 servings.

PER SERVING: 600 calories, 67 g protein, 50 g carbohydrates, 13 g fat, 184 mg cholesterol, 865 mg sodium

RED-COOKED BEEF SHANKS

Follow directions for **red-cooked lamb shanks** (preceding), omitting lamb shanks and using 6 **beef shanks** (each piece about 2 in. thick, about 6 lb. total). Bake until meat is very tender and pulls easily from the bones, about 2 hours.

PER SERVING: 598 calories, 68 g protein, 50 g carbohydrates, 12 g fat, 109 mg cholesterol, 865 mg sodium

Oven-braised lamb shanks owe succulent flavor to adaptation of Chinese method for stewing meat and poultry. Broth—enriched with meat juices, soy sauce, ginger, onion, and garlic—makes a well-seasoned sauce.

Indian-Style Barbecued Chicken or Fish

HOME COOKING, INDIAN-STYLE, *makes frequent use of the barbecue—much like family-style cooking in the West. But it's the subtle seasonings Indian cooks use that add an unusual dimension to every-day foods. For a simple Indian-style meal, try barbecued chicken breasts with fresh carrot chutney or barbecued fish fillets.*

INDIAN-STYLE BARBECUED CHICKEN

- 8 **boned and skinned chicken breast halves (about 2½ lb. total)**
- 1 **cup nonfat unflavored yogurt**
- 4 **cloves garlic, minced or pressed**
- 2 **tablespoons minced fresh ginger**
- 1 **fresh jalapeño chili, stemmed, seeded, and minced**
- 2 **teaspoons ground coriander**
- 1 **teaspoon ground cumin**
- ½ **teaspoon ground cinnamon**
- 2 **whole cloves**
- ½ **to 1 teaspoon cayenne**
  Salt

Rinse chicken and pat dry. In a bowl, mix yogurt, garlic, ginger, chili, coriander, cumin, cinnamon, cloves, and cayenne to taste. Add chicken and mix well; cover and chill for 6 hours or up until next day. Mix occasionally.

Lift meat from marinade and place on a grill 4 to 6 inches above a solid bed of hot coals (you can hold your hand at grill level for only 2 to 3 seconds). Cook, basting with remaining marinade, until meat is white in thickest part (cut to test), 12 to 15 minutes. Add salt to taste. Makes 6 to 8 servings. —*Aban Lal, Antioch, Calif.*

PER SERVING: 178 calories, 35 g protein, 3.4 g carbohydrates, 1.9 g fat, 83 mg cholesterol, 115 mg sodium

FRUIT & CARROT CHUTNEY

- ½ **cup slivered almonds**
- 1 **cup cider vinegar**
- 2 **cups firmly packed finely shredded carrots**
- ½ **cup raisins**
- ⅓ **cup coarsely chopped pitted dates**
- ⅓ **cup coarsely chopped dried figs**
- ⅓ **cup coarsely chopped dried apricots**
- 1 **cup firmly packed brown sugar**
- 3 **cloves garlic, minced or pressed**
- 1 **tablespoon minced fresh ginger**
- 1 **teaspoon dry mustard**
- ½ **teaspoon ground cinnamon**
- ½ **teaspoon cayenne**
  Salt

Aromatic spices flavor grilled chicken breast. Offer with pilaf, sliced tomatoes, and a cucumber salad. Add easy carrot chutney and unflavored yogurt to taste.

In a 2- to 3-quart pan over medium heat, stir almonds until golden brown, about 6 minutes. Add vinegar, carrots, raisins, dates, figs, apricots, sugar, garlic, ginger, mustard, cinnamon, and cayenne. Bring to a boil on high heat, then simmer, uncovered, stirring often, until liquid evaporates and mixture is reduced to about 4 cups, about 25 minutes; as mixture thickens, watch carefully and stir often to avoid scorching. Serve warm or at room temperature. Add salt to taste. If made ahead, cover and chill up to 1 week. Makes about 4 cups.

PER TABLESPOON: 32 calories, 0.4 g protein, 6.8 g carbohydrates, 0.6 g fat, 0 mg cholesterol, 2.8 mg sodium

GRILLED LINGCOD WITH MINT RELISH

- ½ **cup fresh mint leaves**
- ½ **cup fresh cilantro (coriander) leaves**
- 3 **tablespoons lemon juice**
- 1 **fresh jalapeño chili, stemmed and seeded**
- 1 **clove garlic**

- ½ **teaspoon ground cumin**
- ½ **cup sweetened shredded dry coconut**
- 2 **pounds boned and skinned lingcod or rockfish fillets, each about 1 inch at thickest part**
  Salt

In a blender or food processor, whirl mint, cilantro, lemon juice, 1 tablespoon water, chili, garlic, and cumin until smoothly puréed. Stir in coconut.

Rinse fish, pat dry, and cut into 4 equal pieces. On a grill 4 to 6 inches above a solid bed of hot coals (you can hold your hand at grill level only 2 to 3 seconds), position fish so grain is at right angles to grill bars. Cook until edges of fish begin to turn opaque; then, sliding a wide spatula along the grill bars and under the fillets, turn the fish over. Cook until fish is opaque but still moist-looking in thickest part (cut to test), 8 to 12 minutes total.

With spatula, transfer fish to a platter and top each portion equally with the mint-cilantro mixture. Add salt to taste. Makes 6 servings.

PER SERVING: 163 calories, 27 g protein, 4.1 g carbohydrates, 3.7 g fat, 79 mg cholesterol, 108 mg sodium

Chinese Artichokes

THE ODD-LOOKING MORSELS *at right are an intriguing addition to an adventurous gardener-cook's repertoire. Known as Chinese artichokes, chorogi, crosnes, knot-root, or kon loh, they can be eaten raw and crisp or cooked until tender. Their flavor is mild and delicate, sometimes sweet, sometimes faintly bitter, depending on age and growing conditions. Cooking mellows them still more. Two ways to prepare them follow.*

BUTTER-STEAMED CHINESE ARTICHOKES

2 cups (about ½ lb.) Chinese artichokes
½ cup water
1½ teaspoons butter or margarine
¼ cup minced parsley
Salt and pepper

With a stiff brush, scrub artichokes thoroughly; rinse well and drain. Trim off any dark tips. Place artichokes in a 10- to 12-inch frying pan with water and butter. Cover and cook over medium heat until liquid evaporates, about 15 minutes. Remove lid, turn heat to high, and stir often until artichokes are tinged with golden brown, about 3 minutes longer. Pour into a bowl, sprinkle with parsley, and add salt and pepper to taste. Makes 4 servings.

PER SERVING: 55 calories, 12 g protein, 9.6 g carbohydrates, 1.4 g fat, 3.9 mg cholesterol, 16 mg sodium

Curiously shaped Chinese artichokes, butter-steamed and tinged with brown, complement cooked pork chops.

PICKLED CHINESE ARTICHOKES

Red onion turns pink when pickled.

1 cup (about ¼ lb.) Chinese artichokes
1 medium-size (about 6 oz.) red or white onion, thinly sliced
1 cup distilled white vinegar
⅓ cup sugar

With a stiff brush, scrub artichokes; rinse well and drain. Trim off any dark tips.

In a 2-cup wide-mouthed jar, alternate layers of artichokes and onion. In a 1- to 1½-quart pan, combine vinegar and sugar. Bring to boil on high heat and cook, stirring, until sugar dissolves. At once, pour over vegetables in jar. Let cool, then cover and chill at least overnight, or up to 2 months. Makes about 2 cups.

PER ¼ CUP: 49 calories, 0.4 g protein, 13 g carbohydrates, 0 g fat, 0 mg cholesterol, 0.6 mg sodium

GROWING CHINESE ARTICHOKES

Here's how to grow Chinese artichokes. Plant them in the spring after danger of frost is past.

The tubers you plant are expensive and perishable. But once you get them going, you need never buy any again. They multiply like mad. Any you miss harvesting are likely to grow and flourish the following season. We planted tubers in a damp, shady spot (where most other vegetables do poorly) both in the ground and in a half-barrel. Both produced well.

As you do when planting other vegetables, loosen and amend soil about a foot deep. Work organic or controlled-release fertilizer into soil before planting (or apply low-nitrogen fertilizer every few weeks). Set tubers 3 inches deep and 6 to 10 inches apart in rows a foot apart. Plants can survive with little water, but to produce tubers of good size and texture, they need some shade and ample moisture.

When growth slows (November or later in mild-winter areas), stop watering, let plants die back, and lift tubers with a garden fork. Plants stay dormant as long as weather is cold. If it warms, lift tubers, shake or rinse off loose dirt, and store in an airtight container in the refrigerator, layered between paper towels. Tubers keep at least three weeks. Scrub them no more than a day before preparing.

Order tubers in fall or winter and plant as soon as soil is workable in spring. One well-stocked supplier is Seeds Blüm, Idaho City Stage, Boise, ID 83706 (catalog $3; 20 tubers cost $5.50).

Spoonbread or Cornbread Sticks from Blue Cornmeal

A SOUTHWEST STAPLE, *blue cornmeal is no longer a rare sight in the rest of the West. The blue-gray meal is found in specialty and health-food stores, and also in well-stocked supermarkets.*

It can be used interchangeably with white or yellow cornmeal but has its own parched-corn flavor. Depending on the recipe, its natural blue-gray color changes dramatically. If the mixture is high in acid, the color change is toward purple-pink; if low in acid or slightly alkaline, the color shifts toward blue-green. These cornbread sticks have a pinkish cast; the spoonbread is bluer.

SOUTHWEST BLUE CORNBREAD STICKS

- 2 tablespoons butter or margarine
- 1 medium-size onion, chopped
- 1 small fresh jalapeño chili, stemmed, seeded, and minced
- 1 cup all-purpose flour
  About 1 cup blue cornmeal
- 1 tablespoon baking powder
- 2 teaspoons sugar
- 1 large egg
- 1¼ cups milk
- 1 cup (about 4 oz.) shredded jack cheese

Melt butter in a 10- to 12-inch frying pan on medium-high heat. Add onion and chili, stirring often until onion is lightly browned, 8 to 10 minutes; set aside.

Mix together flour, 1 cup cornmeal, baking powder, and sugar in a large bowl. In another bowl, whisk egg and milk until blended. Stir onion, milk mixture, and cheese into the cornmeal mixture.

Butter cornstick pans (each about 5½ in. long) or tiny muffin pans (about 1½-in. diameter). Dust pans with cornmeal; shake out excess. Spoon batter into pans, filling to rims. Bake in a 375° oven until firm to touch and browned, 20 to 25 minutes. Cool about 5 minutes, then invert pans to remove cornbread; use a small knife to loosen if necessary. (If you have only 1 pan, wash, dry, butter, and dust with cornmeal again, then bake the next batch.)

Serve bread hot or at room temperature. If made ahead, let cool, then wrap airtight and chill up to 24 hours, or freeze to store longer. To reheat, lay bread (thawed, if frozen) in a single layer on a 12- by 15-inch baking sheet; place in a 350° oven until warm in centers, about 10 minutes. Makes about 18 cornbread sticks.

PER PIECE: 107 calories, 3.9 g protein, 13 g carbohydrates, 4.2 g fat, 23 mg cholesterol, 130 mg sodium

BLUE CORN SPOONBREAD WITH ROASTED GARLIC

- 1 head garlic
- 1 tablespoon olive oil
- ⅔ cup blue cornmeal
- 2 teaspoons sugar
- ¼ teaspoon cayenne
- 2 cups milk
- 2 tablespoons butter or margarine
- 4 large eggs, separated
  Salt and pepper

Cut garlic in half through cloves. Pour oil into an 8- to 9-inch-wide baking pan. Place garlic, cut side down, in pan. Bake in a 375° oven until cloves are golden brown on bottom, about 30 minutes. Let cool, then squeeze garlic from peel into a bowl; mash with a fork and set aside.

In a 3- to 4-quart pan, combine cornmeal, sugar, and cayenne. Slowly and smoothly stir or whisk in milk, then butter. Place over high heat and stir until boiling and thick. Let cool 5 minutes.

In a small bowl, beat egg yolks with garlic; stir a little of the hot mixture into bowl, then return mixture to pan.

In a large bowl, beat egg whites at high speed with an electric mixer until they hold moist but distinct peaks. Gently but thoroughly fold whites into cornmeal mixture. Pour into a buttered 1½-quart soufflé dish or deep baking dish. Bake in a 375° oven until well browned and mixture is firm when dish is shaken, 35 to 40 minutes. Scoop out portions with a spoon and serve at once. Add salt and pepper to taste. Makes 4 to 6 servings.

PER SERVING: 233 calories, 8.9 g protein, 22 g carbohydrates, 12 g fat, 163 mg cholesterol, 123 mg sodium

Blue cornbread sticks take their fanciful shape from pans; you can also bake batter in muffin tins. Serve warm with a mug of hot soup.

Puffy from oven, blue cornmeal spoonbread, flavored with caramelized garlic and cayenne, settles as it cools.

Breakfast Casseroles

EXPECTING COMPANY FOR BREAKFAST? *Dress up the occasion with a casserole based on cereal grains. In the first dish, steel-cut oats (found with fancy foods at the supermarket) bake tender and sweet in a soft custard; a separately broiled sugar topping mimics crème brûlée. In the second casserole, an apple streusel mixture bakes on bulgur (cracked wheat).*

OATS & CRÈME BRÛLÉE

    4   cups water
    1   cup steel-cut oats
    2   cups half-and-half (light cream)
    ⅓   to ½ cup sugar
    4   large egg yolks
    1   teaspoon vanilla
        Brown-sugar brûlée crust (recipe follows)

In a 1½- to 2-quart pan, combine water and oats. Bring to a boil over high heat.

Simmer, uncovered, until oats are tender to bite and liquid is absorbed, about 30 minutes; stir occasionally. Pour oats into an 8- by 12-inch oval casserole at least 2½ inches deep; set in a larger baking pan.

In the pan used to cook oats, combine cream and sugar to taste. Stir frequently over medium-high heat until scalding.

Beat yolks and vanilla in a bowl with a little of the hot cream. Stir mixture into pan, then pour over oats. Set pans on center rack in a 325° oven. Pour boiling water into outer pan to level of custard. Bake until custard jiggles only slightly in center when gently shaken, about 45 minutes. At once, lift from water.

With 2 wide spatulas or your fingers, gently transfer brown-sugar crust onto custard; if crust breaks, fit together on top. Makes 6 servings.

PER SERVING: 325 calories, 6.4 g protein, 42 g carbohydrates, 15 g fat, 176 mg cholesterol, 63 mg sodium

Brown-sugar brûlée crust. On a sheet of foil, set dish that will hold baked oats. Gently trace around the base with a pencil, taking care not to tear foil.

Coat area within outline with about 2 tablespoons soft **butter** or margarine. Set foil on a 12- by 15-inch baking sheet (without sides). Rub ½ cup **dark brown sugar** through a fine strainer to evenly coat buttered area.

Bake in a 500° oven until sugar begins to melt and bubble (some sugar doesn't melt), 2 to 5 minutes, rotating pan to melt sugar evenly. Let crust cool, then slide a slender spatula under it to release from foil. If made ahead, leave on pan, seal airtight, and hold up until next day.

BAKED BULGUR & APPLES

    3   cups milk
    ½   cup sugar
    1½   cups bulgur (cracked wheat)
    ½   cup regular rolled oats
    ⅓   cup all-purpose flour
    ½   teaspoon *each* ground cinnamon and ground ginger
    ½   cup (¼ lb.) butter or margarine
         About 1 pound Golden Delicious apples, peeled, cored, and thinly sliced
    ⅓   cup golden raisins
         Half-and-half (light cream) or milk

In a 1½- to 2-quart pan, bring 3 cups milk and ¼ cup sugar to boil over high heat, stirring often. Stir in bulgur; cover and set aside at least 20 minutes.

In a food processor or bowl, whirl or rub together with fingers remaining sugar, oats, flour, cinnamon, ginger, and butter to form fine crumbs. Then squeeze mixture to make lumps about ½ inch thick.

Pour bulgur mixture into an 8- by 12-inch oval casserole at least 2½ inches deep; spread level. Lay apples and raisins over it. Cover with foil and bake in a 375° oven until apples are tender when pierced, about 20 minutes. Uncover; scatter oatmeal lumps over fruit. Bake until topping is golden brown, 15 to 20 minutes. Spoon into bowls. Add cream to taste. Makes 8 servings.

PER SERVING: 380 calories, 8 g protein, 56 g carbohydrates, 15 g fat, 44 mg cholesterol, 168 mg sodium

Break through crisp brown-sugar crust to scoop out custard and oats. This breakfast treat goes well with fresh strawberries.

Cooky Jar Favorites from *Sunset* Readers

COOKIES YOU CAN COUNT ON—*that's what these simple-looking (and easy-to-make) favorites prove to be. Each of these four recipes, all suggested by readers, earned excellent marks at Sunset taste panels. Letters sent with some recipes said the cookies were often kept on hand, ready for snacking.*

Rolled oats give wholesome character to the first two cookies. Mashed bananas make the next cookies stay moist. And the last cooky is actually a tiny brownie baked in a paper cup.

Remember—if you have only one oven and bake two pans of cookies at a time, alternate pan positions about halfway through baking for even browning. Wipe pans clean between batches.

All the cookies keep well at room temperature for a few days if packed airtight. But they stay fresh-tasting and keep their texture best when stored in the freezer.

PECAN COOKIES

- ¾ cup (⅜ lb.) butter or margarine, at room temperature
- ¾ cup sugar
- ¼ cup molasses
- ¼ cup water
- 1 large egg
- 1 teaspoon vanilla
- 3 cups regular rolled oats
- 1⅓ cups all-purpose flour
- ½ teaspoon baking soda
- ¼ teaspoon baking powder
- 1 cup coarsely chopped pecans
- About 36 pecan halves

In a large bowl, beat together butter, sugar, and molasses. Beat in water, egg, and vanilla.

Mix oats, flour, soda, and baking powder; add to butter mixture. Stir to mix, then beat to blend thoroughly. Stir in chopped pecans.

Drop dough in rounded 2-tablespoon mounds about 2 inches apart onto ungreased 12- by 15-inch baking sheets. With the back of a floured spoon, spread each mound into a ½-inch-thick round; press a pecan half into center of each. Bake in a 350° oven until edges are golden brown, 12 to 15 minutes. Transfer with a spatula to racks; serve warm or cool. To store, let cool, then package airtight; hold at room temperature up to 2 days. Makes about 3 dozen.—*Sandra Jewett, Granada Hills, Calif.*

PER COOKY: 126 calories, 2.1 g protein, 14 g carbohydrates, 7 g fat, 16 mg cholesterol, 56 mg sodium

OAT & NUTMEG COOKIES

- 1 cup (½ lb.) butter or margarine, at room temperature
- 1 cup granulated sugar
- 1 cup firmly packed brown sugar
- 2 large eggs
- ½ cup unflavored low-fat yogurt
- 3½ cups regular rolled oats
- 2 cups all-purpose flour
- 2 teaspoons baking powder
- 1½ teaspoons ground nutmeg
- ½ teaspoon baking soda

In a large bowl, beat together until fluffy the butter, granulated sugar, and brown sugar. Add eggs and yogurt; mix well.

Mix together oats, flour, baking powder, nutmeg, and soda. Add dry ingredients to butter mixture; stir to mix, then beat to blend thoroughly.

Drop dough in rounded tablespoonfuls about 2 inches apart onto ungreased 12- by 15-inch baking sheets. Bake in a 350° oven until edges are golden brown, about 20 minutes. Transfer to racks with a spatula; serve warm or cool. To store, let cool, then package airtight; hold at room temperature up to 2 days. Makes about 4 dozen.—*Susie Brubaker, Ashland, Ore.*

PER COOKY: 114 calories, 1.9 g protein, 17 g carbohydrates, 4.5 g fat, 19 mg cholesterol, 71 mg sodium

BANANA–SUNFLOWER SEED DROPS

- ½ cup salad oil
- 2 medium-size soft-ripe bananas, peeled and mashed
- 1 cup sugar
- 1½ cups all-purpose flour
- 1 cup roasted salted sunflower seeds
- 1 teaspoon baking soda

In a large bowl, beat oil, bananas, and sugar. Mix flour with sunflower seeds and soda; add dry ingredients to banana mixture and stir until thoroughly mixed.

Drop dough by rounded tablespoonfuls about 2 inches apart onto ungreased 12- by 15-inch baking sheets. Bake in a 350° oven until edges are golden brown, about 15 minutes. Transfer to racks with a spatula. Serve warm or cool. To store, let cool, package airtight; hold at room temperature up to 4 days. Makes about 3 dozen.—*Laurie Wilcox, Palm Desert, Calif.*

PER COOKY: 96 calories, 1.2 g protein, 12 g carbohydrates, 5.2 g fat, 0 mg cholesterol, 46 mg sodium

Easy-to-enjoy cookies cool on racks. Clockwise from top: brownie bites, pecan cookies, banana–sunflower seed drops.

BROWNIE BITES

- ½ cup (¼ lb.) butter or margarine
- 4 ounces unsweetened chocolate
- 1½ cups sugar
- 1 teaspoon vanilla
- 3 large eggs
- 1 cup all-purpose flour
- About 40 walnut halves

In a 2- to 3-quart pan, stir butter and chocolate over lowest heat until melted. Remove pan from heat and stir in sugar and vanilla. Add eggs, 1 at a time, beating well after each addition. Stir in flour.

Spoon batter into paper-lined tiny (1½-in.-diameter) muffin cups, filling cups almost to the top. Place a walnut half on top of batter in each cup.

Bake in a 325° oven until tops look dry and feel firm when lightly touched, about 20 minutes.

Let brownies cool in pan 10 minutes, then transfer to racks to cool. Serve warm or cool. To store, let cool, then package airtight and hold at room temperature up to 4 days. Makes about 40.—*Jan Macauley, Spring Valley, Calif.*

PER COOKY: 95 calories, 1.4 g protein, 11 g carbohydrates, 5.6 g fat, 22 mg cholesterol, 29 mg sodium

More November Recipes

OTHER NOVEMBER ARTICLES *featured a pair of fruit-vegetable soups, a stir-fry pairing liver with colorful vegetables, an unusual dip for raw vegetables, and crisp, whole-wheat bran crackers.*

SWEET POTATO & PEAR SOUP

A hint of sweetness from pear, balanced by a savory body of vegetables, infuses this soup with an intriguing flavor complexity.

- 1 **large onion, chopped**
- ½ **teaspoon dry thyme leaves**
- 1 **tablespoon butter or margarine**
- 2 **large (about 2 lb. total) sweet potatoes or yams**
- 2 **medium-size (about 1 lb. total) ripe Bartlett pears**
- 1½ **quarts regular-strength chicken broth**
- ⅛ **teaspoon pepper**
- 2 **to 3 tablespoons lime juice**
  Thin strips lime peel

In a 5- to 6-quart pan, stir onion and thyme in butter over medium-high heat until limp, about 5 minutes.

Meanwhile, peel sweet potatoes and cut into 1-inch pieces (submerge in water once peeled). Peel and core 1 pear. Add drained potatoes, peeled pear, broth, and pepper to onion. Bring to a boil; simmer, covered, until potato is very tender when pierced, 20 to 25 minutes.

Pour soup through a fine strainer set over a bowl. Return broth to pan and boil, uncovered, until reduced to 4½ cups, about 5 minutes. Meanwhile, in a blender or food processor, smoothly purée potato mixture. Return purée to reduced broth. Add lime juice to taste. If made ahead, cool, cover, and chill up until the next day. To reheat, stir over high heat until hot.

Peel and core remaining pear; cut into 24 thin wedges. Pour soup into bowls and garnish with pear wedges and lime peel. Makes 8 first-course servings.

PER SERVING: 159 calories, 3.5 g protein, 30 g carbohydrates, 3.1 g fat, 3.9 mg cholesterol, 66 mg sodium

FENNEL-APPLE SOUP

This soup has a subtle fruitiness that works well as a prelude to roast pork, ham, or poultry.

- 1 **large onion, chopped**
- 1 **tablespoon salad oil**
- 3½ **cups regular-strength chicken broth**

Ginger-accented vegetables—onion, mushrooms, bell pepper, and zucchini—accompany calf's liver and hot cooked rice in this stir-fry.

- 1 **cup dry white wine**
- 2 **large heads (about 1 lb. total, stems trimmed) fennel, sliced; feathery leaves reserved**
- 2 **medium-size (about 1 lb. total) Golden Delicious apples, peeled, quartered, and cored**
- ¼ **teaspoon pepper**
  Salt
- ¼ **cup whipping cream**

In a 5- to 6-quart pan, stir onion in oil over medium-high heat until limp, about 5 minutes. Add broth, wine, fennel, apples, and pepper. Bring to a boil; simmer, covered, until fennel and apples are very tender when pierced, about 20 minutes.

Spoon mixture, about half at a time, into a blender or food processor. Whirl until smoothly puréed. Return to pan. Add salt to taste. If made ahead, cool, cover, and chill up until the next day. To reheat, stir over high heat until hot.

Ladle soup into 6 soup bowls. To garnish, pour ⅙ of the cream into each bowl and stir slightly to swirl. Top each with a fennel leaf. Makes 6 first-course servings.

PER SERVING: 124 calories, 2.7 g protein, 15 g carbohydrates, 6.5 g fat, 11 mg cholesterol, 98 mg sodium

LIVER STIR-FRY

Indulge liver lovers with this quick recipe, which also includes colorful vegetables.

- 2 **tablespoons salad oil**
- 1 **tablespoon Oriental sesame oil**
- 1 **medium-size onion, chopped**
- ¼ **pound mushrooms, sliced**
- 1 **small red or green bell pepper, stemmed, seeded, and cut into thin strips**
- 2 **tablespoons minced fresh ginger**
- 2 **small (about ½ lb. total) zucchini, ends trimmed, cut into matchstick-size pieces**

½ pound calf's liver or chicken livers, rinsed and cut into thin strips

1½ cups hot cooked rice

2 tablespoons rice vinegar mixed with 1 tablespoon soy sauce

In a 10- to 12-inch frying pan, combine 1 tablespoon *each* salad oil and sesame oil over high heat. Add onion, mushrooms, pepper, and ginger. Stir-fry until liquid evaporates and vegetables are lightly browned, 5 to 6 minutes. Divide vegetables among 2 or 3 dinner plates; keep warm. Add zucchini to pan; stir-fry over high heat just until hot, about 1 minute, then place equal portions on plates.

Pour remaining salad oil into pan over high heat; add liver and stir-fry just until browned, 1 to 2 minutes. Divide the rice and liver among plates. Sprinkle with vinegar mixture. Makes 2 or 3 servings. —*Betty Hamilton, Hazelton, Idaho.*

PER SERVING: 388 calories, 18 g protein, 39 g carbohydrates, 17 g fat, 332 mg cholesterol, 411 mg sodium

GREEN DILL TAHINI

A Middle Eastern sauce made from ground sesame seed, tahini gets a refreshing new look and flavor in this dip for raw vegetables.

Fresh dill, used generously, is puréed with tahini and gives it a pale green tint and a delicate, cool taste. Unflavored yogurt smooths and lightens the dip.

In the market, look for tahini in cans or jars alongside nut butters or with fancy foods. Or you can toast your own sesame seed and grind it to a fine paste.

Fresh dill colors, flavors, and garnishes smooth tahini dip; serve with raw vegetables.

3 tablespoons tahini (sesame sauce), purchased or homemade (recipe follows)

2 to 3 tablespoons water

¼ to ½ cup chopped fresh dill

3 tablespoons unflavored nonfat yogurt

2 to 3 tablespoons lemon juice

Salt and pepper

About 4 cups raw vegetables such as jicama slices, cucumber slices, sugar snap peas, carrot sticks

In a blender or food processor, smoothly purée tahini, 2 tablespoons water, and dill (larger amount for more color and flavor). Mix in yogurt, lemon juice, and salt and pepper to taste; add water to thin, if desired. Serve, or cover and chill up to 3 days. Scoop onto vegetables to eat. Makes about 1 cup sauce.

PER TABLESPOON SAUCE: 30 calories, 1.1 g protein, 3.3 g carbohydrates, 1.6 g fat, 0.1 mg cholesterol, 9.8 mg sodium

Homemade tahini. Stir ¼ cup **sesame seed** in an 8- to 10-inch frying pan over medium heat until golden. Pour into a blender or food processor; smoothly purée with 4 teaspoons **olive oil.**

WHOLE-WHEAT BRAN CRACKERS

These whole-wheat crackers are easier to make than you might think. You pour a very thin liquid batter into pans, tilt to cover pan bottoms evenly, then bake. (Pans that warp with heat won't do the job well.) Cut crackers in pans when partially baked, then continue baking until brown. Watch carefully; browning tends to be uneven and you must remove crackers as they are ready.

1 cup all-purpose flour

½ cup whole-wheat flour

½ cup oat bran

1 tablespoon sugar

2 teaspoons baking powder

½ teaspoon baking soda

About 5 tablespoons butter or margarine, melted

2 large eggs

1 cup low-fat milk

1 cup water

5 tablespoons grated parmesan cheese

In a bowl, stir together all-purpose flour, whole-wheat flour, oat bran, sugar, baking powder, and baking soda. In another bowl, beat to blend 3 tablespoons butter, eggs, milk, and water. Add to dry ingredients; whisk briskly until smooth. Or, in a food processor,

Crackers owe their surprisingly thin and crisp texture to a liquid-batter base; they keep well.

whirl dry ingredients, add liquids, and whirl until smooth.

Generously butter 2 rimmed baking pans, each 10 by 15 inches. At the end of 1 pan, pour ⅔ cup batter. Tilt and swirl pan to cover bottom evenly with batter; it will be a very thin coating. Repeat to coat other pan. Set remaining batter aside.

Put pans in a 350° oven; bake until crackers are just firm to touch, about 5 minutes. Brush tops lightly with some remaining melted butter, then sprinkle crackers in each pan with 1 tablespoon parmesan.

While hot, cut each cracker sheet with a sharp knife (or sharp pizza cutter) lengthwise into 3 equal strips, crosswise into 6 equal strips. Take care not to tear the still-soft crackers as you cut. Continue baking until crackers begin to become brown and crisp, 10 to 20 minutes more. If oven heat is uneven, crackers in some areas of pan will brown faster; gently lift from pan as browned and put on racks to cool. Wash pans, dry, butter, and repeat process to bake remaining batter.

Serve, or store airtight up to 5 days. Freeze to store longer. Makes 7½ dozen.

PER CRACKER: 22 calories, 0 g protein, 2.7 g carbohydrates, 1 g fat, 8.1 mg cholesterol, 32 mg sodium

Crushed saffron threads, fresh ginger, and chili season wilted cabbage, carrots, and bell pepper.

SAFFRON GINGER VEGETABLES

½ pound (about 3 small) carrots, peeled and finely shredded

1 small (1¼ lb.) head cabbage, cut into fine shreds

1 medium-size red bell pepper, stemmed, seeded, and cut into thin slivers (about 3 in. long)

¼ teaspoon saffron threads, crushed, or 1 teaspoon curry powder

¼ cup salad oil

¼ cup white wine vinegar

3 tablespoons minced fresh ginger

1 fresh jalapeño chili, stemmed, seeded, and minced

Salt and pepper

In a 5- to 6-quart pan, bring about 3 quarts water to a boil. Add carrots, cabbage, and bell pepper; cook, uncovered, stirring several times, just until barely wilted, about 1 minute. Drain and rinse with cold water until cool; drain well.

Mix the saffron with 1 tablespoon hot water until water turns orange. Add oil, vinegar, ginger, and chili. Pour saffron mixture over vegetables; mix well. Add salt and pepper to taste. Serve or, if made ahead, cover and chill up to the next day. Makes 6 servings. — *Anne Duffield, Los Altos Hills, Calif.*

PER SERVING: 126 calories, 1.6 g protein, 10 g carbohydrates, 9.3 g fat, 0 mg cholesterol, 30 mg sodium

Serve homemade sesame-speckled wheat crackers for appetizers, with cheese and grapes.

WHEAT & OAT CRACKERS

1¼ cups whole-wheat flour

1 cup regular rolled oats

2 tablespoons oat or rice bran

1 tablespoon sugar

⅔ cup buttermilk

2 tablespoons salad oil

¼ cup sesame seed

Seasoned salt or dry herb seasoning mix

In a small bowl, mix the flour, oats, bran, and sugar. Add buttermilk and oil. Mix until dough forms a ball. Add a little water, if needed, to make dough hold together.

Divide dough in half. On a floured board, roll each half into a 7- by 9-inch rectangle. Generously grease and flour 2 rimless baking sheets, each 12 by 15 inches. Center a dough rectangle on each. With a floured rolling pin, roll dough to evenly cover pan (edges may be irregular). Evenly sprinkle with sesame seed and salt. Roll lightly into surface. Cut into 2-inch squares.

Bake in a 325° oven until golden all over, 30 to 35 minutes (switch pan positions midway through cooking if using 1 oven). Cool about 3 minutes, then transfer to racks and cool. Serve, or store airtight up to 1 week. Makes about 6 dozen. — *Edith Harmer, Arcata, Calif.*

PER CRACKER: 20 calories, 0.6 g protein, 2.7 g carbohydrates, 0.7 g fat, 0.1 mg cholesterol, 2.6 mg sodium

Sweet and hot mustard makes a good gift for the holidays.

CARLA'S HOT & SWEET MUSTARD

1⅓ cups champagne vinegar or white wine vinegar

1⅓ cups (4 oz.) dry mustard

2 cups sugar

6 large eggs

In a small bowl, mix vinegar and dry mustard; let stand for 1 hour.

Add sugar and eggs to mustard mixture; beat with whisk until smooth. Pour into a heavy 1½- to 2-quart pan. Stir with a whisk often over medium heat until mixture thickens and begins to bubble, 10 to 12 minutes. Remove from heat.

Pour into jars. If made ahead, cool, cover, and chill up to 3 months.

To seal, pour hot mustard into hot, clean sterilized jars to within ⅛ inch of top. Clean jar rim. Top with hot, clean canning lids. Let cool 24 hours. Press down on lid. If it stays down, jar is sealed; if it pops up, refrigerate as above. Store sealed jars in a cool, dry place up to 1 year. Makes 4 cups. — *Carla Van Dyke, Ketchum, Idaho.*

PER TABLESPOON: 42 calories, 1.1 g protein, 6.7 g carbohydrates, 1.2 g fat, 20 mg cholesterol, 6.1 mg sodium

HAM & CHEESE MEAT LOAF

    About 3 ounces French bread
 1 small onion, minced
 2 pounds ground lean beef
 ½ cup tomato juice
 2 large eggs
 1 teaspoon dry oregano leaves
 ½ teaspoon pepper
 ¼ teaspoon salt (optional)
 3 ounces thinly sliced cooked ham
 1¼ cups (5 oz.) shredded Swiss
    cheese

Cut bread into 1-inch chunks. Whirl in a blender or food processor to make 1½ cups coarse crumbs.

In a large bowl, mix bread crumbs, onion, beef, juice, eggs, oregano, pepper, and salt. On a 12- by 15-inch piece of foil, pat meat mixture into a 10- by 12-inch rectangle. Overlap ham slices on meat mixture to within 1 inch of edges. Sprinkle ham evenly with 1 cup cheese. Starting at a 10-inch end, roll up meat, lifting foil to guide. Pinch meat ends to seal. Place roll, seam down, in a 10- by 15-inch baking pan.

Bake in a 350° oven until well browned, about 1 hour and 15 minutes. Top with ¼ cup cheese. Let stand 5 to 10 minutes. Transfer to a platter; cut in thick slices. Makes 8 servings. —*Jane Cross, Albuquerque.*

PER SERVING: 365 calories, 30 g protein, 7.8 g carbohydrates, 23 g fat, 142 mg cholesterol, 385 mg sodium

Pinwheel of Swiss cheese and thinly sliced ham swirls through heart of this meat loaf.

NEWPORT VEGETABLE CHOWDER

 2 stalks (about ¼ lb. total) celery
 3 medium-size (about 1½ lb. total)
    thin-skinned potatoes
 1 medium-size firm-ripe tomato
 1 tablespoon salad oil
 1 medium-size onion, chopped
 1 quart regular-strength chicken
    broth
 1 can (11½ oz.) tomato-vegetable
    juice cocktail
 1 can (7 oz.) diced green chilies
 1 package (10 oz.) frozen corn
    kernels
 2 cans (6½ oz. each) albacore tuna
    packed in water, drained
 1 can (6½ oz.) chopped clams

Trim ends of celery; thinly slice stalks. Cut potatoes into ½-inch cubes. Core and dice tomato.

In a 5- to 6-quart pan over medium-high heat, combine oil, onion, and celery; stir often until onion is faintly brown, about 8 minutes. Add broth, tomato-vegetable juice cocktail, chilies, and potatoes. Bring to a boil; cover and simmer until potatoes are tender when pierced, about 20 minutes. Add corn, tomato, tuna, and clams and their liquid. Simmer, covered, until hot, about 3 minutes. Ladle into bowls. Makes 8 servings. —*Maxine Tinsley, Newport, Ore.*

PER SERVING: 229 calories, 19 g protein, 29 g carbohydrates, 4.3 g fat, 26 mg cholesterol, 536 mg sodium

Easy chowder holds chunks of canned tuna and clams.

PUMPKIN ALMOND TORTE

 ½ cup slivered blanched almonds
 4 large eggs, separated
 ⅔ cup sugar
 1 cup canned pumpkin
 1½ teaspoons grated lemon peel
 6 tablespoons all-purpose flour
 ¾ teaspoon baking powder
 ½ teaspoon ground nutmeg
 ¼ teaspoon ground cinnamon
    Glaze (recipe follows)

Whirl nuts in a blender until powdery.

In a small bowl with an electric mixer, beat egg whites until foamy. Gradually add 3 tablespoons of the sugar, beating until stiff, moist peaks form; set aside.

In a large bowl beat egg yolks with remaining sugar until pale. Beat in pumpkin and lemon peel, then stir in flour, baking powder, nutmeg, and cinnamon. Fold in beaten whites and nuts. Pour into a greased and floured 9-inch cheesecake pan with removable rim.

Bake in a 325° oven until a toothpick inserted in center comes out clean, 40 to 45 minutes. Cool on rack 10 minutes. Remove pan rim. Spoon glaze over cake; cool. Cut in wedges. Makes 8 servings. —*Sally Vog, Springfield, Ore.*

Glaze. Smoothly mix ¼ cup **powdered sugar,** 1 tablespoon **lemon juice,** and ¼ teaspoon **grated lemon peel.**

PER SERVING: 199 calories, 5.8 g protein, 30 g carbohydrates, 7.1 g fat, 106 mg cholesterol, 75 mg sodium

Garnish pumpkin almond torte with whipped cream and thin lemon slices.

WHY SHOULD YOU COOK A TURKEY *on the barbecue? First, a barbecue out-of-doors will make it easier to accommodate the candied sweet potatoes, mashed potatoes, and the various pies and puddings that clog the oven during the holiday season. Second, since traffic in the kitchen—especially in and around the stove—is also very likely to be congested, things will be considerably cooler if the item that cooks the longest is parked on the back porch.*

Third, but no less important, the flavor of the bird stands to benefit—in this case, from Ken Churches's marinade.

KETTLE-COOKED MARINATED TURKEY

  1 turkey, about 12 pounds
  ½ cup *each* soy sauce, dry sherry, and regular-strength chicken broth
  ¼ cup lemon juice
  1 clove garlic, minced or pressed
  ¾ teaspoon ground ginger
  ½ teaspoon pepper

Remove neck and giblets from turkey; reserve for other uses (like gravy). Rinse turkey inside and out; pat dry, then pull skin over neck cavity and secure to back with a skewer. Place turkey in a large plastic food bag.

Add to bag 1 cup water, soy, sherry, broth, lemon juice, garlic, ginger, and pepper. Seal bag and rotate several times to distribute seasonings over bird. Set bag in a pan and chill 4 hours or up until next day; turn bag over several times.

On the firegrate in a covered barbecue, ignite 50 charcoal briquets. When coals are covered with gray ash, bank coals equally on opposite sides of grate; put a drip pan in middle. Add 10 briquets to coals now, and every 30 minutes as you cook, to maintain heat. Place grill 4 to 6 inches above coals. Place turkey, breast side down with wings akimbo, on grill directly above drip pan; reserve marinade. Cover barbecue, open dampers, and cook for 45 minutes. Turn turkey breast up and continue to cook until meat at bone in thickest part of breast registers 160°, about 1¾ hours total. Baste bird often with reserved marinade.

"To preserve his sanity and temper, he keeps the carving chore in the kitchen."

Set turkey on a platter, drape loosely with foil, and let stand at least 20 minutes before carving. Makes 10 to 12 servings.

PER SERVING: 383 calories, 66 g protein, 59 g carbohydrates, 11 g fat, 172 mg cholesterol, 511 mg sodium

Ken R. Church

Yuba City, Calif.

RESOLVING *a persistent controversy—to carve the turkey at the table or in the kitchen—Arnie Kamrin graces Chefs not with a recipe, but with a technique. His stand is well reasoned: to preserve his sanity and temper, he advocates keeping the chore in the kitchen. But because he also values presentation, he devised a way to divide, slice, and reorganize the bird, with light and dark meats neatly arranged on a platter.*

You can use this method with any size turkey. (Mr. Kamrin recommends using an electric knife for tidy slices; a really sharp long-bladed knife also works well.) If you don't have a recipe for turkey on hand, try Kettle-cooked Marinated Turkey, preceding, which uses the barbecue instead of the oven for roasting.

KAMRIN'S CARVED TURKEY

1. Let roast turkey stand at least 20 minutes so juices can settle back into meat. On a carving board with rim (to catch juices), cut wings and thighs free at joints. Cut into breast meat as little as possible, and be sure to include with the thighs the "oysters" from the hollows in the backbone. Cut wings apart at joints; cut drumsticks from thighs at joints.

2. Hold the turkey upright (for a more secure grip and to protect hands from heat, wear rubber gloves). Cut closely down along keel bone (center of breast) to separate half the breast from the carcass. Repeat to cut breast free on other side. Take care to keep breast sections whole, and avoid tearing skin; use your fingers to pull and ease meat free.

Lay breast sections skin up. With an electric knife or sharp long-bladed knife, cut each breast half lengthwise into ¼- to ½-inch-thick slices, keeping slices in place. Using a wide spatula, place the cut breast halves on a large platter.

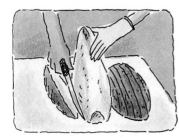

3. Turn thighs skin side down. With a sharp short-bladed knife, cut lengthwise along bone in 1 thigh to expose it, then slide knife around bone to release it, keeping thigh intact; turn thigh skin side up. Repeat to bone remaining thigh. With an electric knife or very sharp knife, cut thighs lengthwise into about ½-inch-thick slices, keeping slices in place. With a wide spatula, transfer thighs to platter.

4. Fit drumsticks and wing pieces between sliced meats. Garnish with parsley or watercress. Serve warm or cold.

ARNIE KAMRIN

Los Altos Hills, Calif.

THE PEOPLE OF CALABRIA—*a region at the toe of boot-shaped Italy—have learned to dine well on what the land affords in vegetables. Robert Gigliotti's interpretation of Vegetables alla Calabrese reveals this Mediterranean ingenuity.*

Gigliotti's grandparents came here from Calabria in the early 1900s. From them he acquired a taste for the richly prepared vegetables of their Italian homeland.

VEGETABLES ALLA CALABRESE

- 1 ounce (about ⅓ cup) dried tomatoes
- 2 tablespoons olive oil
- 1 medium-size onion, chopped
- 3 cloves garlic, minced or pressed
- 1 medium-size carrot, diced
- 1 medium-size red or yellow bell pepper, stemmed, seeded, and diced
- ½ pound mushrooms, thinly sliced
- 1 cup finely diced eggplant
- 2 to 4 drained canned pepperoncini peppers, seeded and minced
  About 1 pound Roma-type tomatoes, cut into eighths
- 2 small (about 5-in.-long) zucchini, ends trimmed, thinly sliced
- 6 large pitted black ripe olives, thinly sliced
  Hot cooked spaghetti (optional)
  Freshly grated parmesan cheese
  Salt and pepper

Put dried tomatoes and ½ cup hot water in a bowl; let stand to soften.

Meanwhile, pour oil into a 5- to 6-quart pan over medium heat; add onion, garlic, carrot, bell pepper, mushrooms, and eggplant. Stir often until all liquid evaporates and vegetables are soft and sweet-tasting, about 20 minutes.

Drain soaked tomatoes and chop. Add to pan with pepperoncini (using maximum amount for most piquant flavor), fresh tomato, zucchini, and olives. Stir often over high heat until most of the liquid evaporates and zucchini is no longer opaque, 8 to 10 minutes.

Serve vegetables alone or spooned over hot pasta. Sprinkle with parmesan cheese and salt and pepper to taste. Makes about 5 cups, 5 to 7 servings.

PER SERVING OF VEGETABLES: 95 calories, 2.9 g protein, 13 g carbohydrates, 4.8 g fat, 0 mg cholesterol, 179 mg sodium

Robert E. Gigliotti

Edmonds, Wash.

YOU'VE BEEN WRONG *all these years if you rhyme scone with* stone. *Never mind what your dictionary may say—if you are a Scot (or in touch with Scottish traditions) you will rhyme it with* gone.

Scottish scones have a consistency something like that of a biscuit or a shortcake. They usually also contain currants and a hint of sweetness. Jerry Schroeder's Breakfast Scones are richer and more complex—with rolled oats, nuts, currants, figs, and brown sugar. With juice, coffee, and the Sunday paper, they make a satisfying breakfast.

BREAKFAST SCONES

- 1¾ cups all-purpose flour
- ¾ cup regular rolled oats
- ½ cup firmly packed dark brown sugar
- 2 teaspoons baking powder
- ¼ teaspoon baking soda
- ½ cup (¼ lb.) cold butter or margarine, cut into small pieces
- ¼ cup chopped walnuts
- ⅓ cup dried currants
- ¼ cup chopped dried figs
- 2 large eggs
- ¼ cup buttermilk
- 1 teaspoon vanilla
- 1 teaspoon melted butter or margarine

In a large bowl, mix flour, oats, brown sugar, baking powder, and soda. With a pastry blender or 2 knives, cut butter into flour mixture until it resembles coarse cornmeal. Add nuts, currants, and figs.

In another bowl, beat eggs to blend with buttermilk and vanilla. With a fork, stir liquids into flour mixture until evenly moistened.

Scrape dough onto a well-floured board. Dust lightly with flour (dough is very soft) and knead 4 or 5 turns. Place dough on an oiled 12- by 15-inch baking sheet and pat into a 9-inch-diameter round. With a floured sharp knife, cut into 8 wedge-shaped pieces, leaving wedges in place. Brush with melted butter. Bake in a 400° oven until tops are golden brown, about 20 minutes. Serve scones hot or warm. Makes 8.

PER PIECE: 375 calories, 6.9 g protein, 49 g carbohydrates, 17 g fat, 88 mg cholesterol, 294 mg sodium

Fair Oaks, Calif.

No-fuss everyday meals *give you more time to concentrate on holiday shopping and entertaining this month.*

GIANT DOUGHNUT BREAKFAST

**Sliced Oranges with Vanilla Yogurt
Buttermilk Doughnut Coffee Cake
Hot Tea or Cider with Cinnamon Swizzle**

A whimsical coffee cake that looks like a big doughnut stars at breakfast. It's formed from cake doughnut batter baked in a ring mold. The fine-textured cake soaks up a tangy orange syrup and is served with sliced oranges.

The coffee cake is best eaten fresh and warm, but it goes together quickly and cooks in less than 30 minutes. Get a head start the night before by measuring the ingredients, so they'll be ready to pour into the bowl and mix. If you don't have a ring mold, use a tube pan.

Accompany with thick orange slices topped with vanilla-flavor yogurt and grated orange peel. Peel oranges before slicing, or present plates of sliced unpeeled fruit with knives and forks and let each person cut off the peel.

For an aromatic beverage, put a cinnamon stick in a cup, then add steaming tea or apple cider.

Buttermilk Doughnut Coffee Cake

- 2 cups all-purpose flour
- 2 teaspoons baking powder
- ½ teaspoon baking soda
- 1 teaspoon ground cinnamon
- ½ teaspoon ground nutmeg
- 1 large egg
- ⅓ cup granulated sugar
- ½ cup buttermilk
- 3 tablespoons butter or margarine, melted
  Orange syrup (recipe follows)
- ⅓ cup powdered sugar

In a large bowl, stir together flour, baking powder, baking soda, cinnamon, and nutmeg. In another bowl, beat to blend egg, granulated sugar, buttermilk, and butter. Add to dry ingredients; stir just until evenly moistened (batter is stiff).

Powdered sugar emphasizes doughnut shape of mildly sweet coffee cake, moistened with fresh orange syrup. Serve with yogurt-topped orange slices and hot cider.

Spread batter evenly in a buttered 4-cup (8-in.-wide) metal ring mold or 8- to 9-inch tube pan. Bake in a 375° oven until richly browned, about 20 minutes. Remove from oven and, with a long, slender skewer, pierce through cake to pan about every ½ inch. At once, spoon orange syrup onto cake, letting it absorb liquid between additions. Let stand 5 to 10 minutes, then invert cake onto a platter. Ladle any free-flowing syrup back onto cake.

Rub powdered sugar through a fine strainer onto cake. Cut into wedges. Makes 6 to 8 servings.

PER SERVING: 313 calories, 5 g protein, 62 g carbohydrates, 5.4 g fat, 39 mg cholesterol, 227 mg sodium

Orange syrup. In a 1- to 1½-quart pan over medium-high heat, combine 2 cups **orange juice** and ⅔ cup **sugar**. Bring to a boil; boil, uncovered, until reduced to 1½ cups. Use hot; if made ahead, cover and chill up until next day, then reheat.

THANKSGIVING, ACT II

Turkey & Spinach Micro-gratin
Thanksgiving Vegetables
Pineapple-Mint Relish
Cranberry-Applesauce Sundaes
Dry Johannisberg Riesling   Milk

Bring new life to Thanksgiving leftovers with this menu. The main dish uses turkey scraps, stuffing, and gravy. Part of its appeal is that you make it up in individual servings, which you can heat and serve a portion at a time or collectively for a family meal.

With a little fresh spinach and grated cheese, you can turn bits of left-over turkey, any kind of stuffing, and gravy into these microwave casseroles. The microwave is also an ideal tool for warming left-over vegetables—briefly heated, they will taste almost fresh-cooked.

The flavor of fresh pineapple relish offers a change of pace to this encore meal; enjoy in salad-size portions. Save surplus fresh pineapple for breakfast or a dessert the next day. If you prefer, you can start with canned diced or crushed pineapple.

For the sundaes, heat together equal parts cranberry sauce (any kind) and applesauce (purchased or homemade), then spoon over scoops of vanilla low-fat frozen yogurt or ice cream.

TURKEY & SPINACH MICRO-GRATIN

2 **cups left-over stuffing**
¼ **cup left-over turkey gravy or regular-strength chicken broth**
2 **cups firmly packed rinsed and drained spinach leaves, coarsely chopped**
   About 2 cups torn bite-size pieces cooked turkey
¼ **pound Jarlsberg or Swiss cheese, shredded**
   Paprika (optional)
   Salt and pepper

Melted Jarlsberg wilts fresh spinach on turkey leftovers in individual microwaved main dish, served with cucumber-pineapple relish. Reheated vegetables join meal.

Divide stuffing and gravy evenly among 4 individual (about 1-cup) microwave-safe dishes. Pat mixture to make level. Layer in each dish ¼ of the spinach and ¼ of the turkey, then sprinkle equally with cheese. If assembled ahead, cover and chill up until next day.

Place 1 or more uncovered dishes in a microwave oven. Heat at full power (100 percent) until cheese melts and mixture is hot in center, about 1½ minutes for 1 dish, up to 5 minutes for 4 dishes; after every 1½ minutes, rotate each dish 180° and check center temperature. Continue to heat until food reaches the internal temperature you want. Remove dishes from microwave oven; dust cheese lightly with paprika. Add salt and pepper to taste. Makes 4 servings.

PER SERVING: 482 calories, 33 g protein, 92 g carbohydrates, 28 g fat, 118 mg cholesterol, 836 mg sodium

PINEAPPLE-MINT RELISH

1 **cup diced fresh or drained canned pineapple**
1 **cup diced cucumber**
2 **tablespoons minced fresh or 2 teaspoons dry mint**
2 **tablespoons cider vinegar**
1 **tablespoon honey**
   Salt

In a small bowl, stir together pineapple, cucumber, mint, vinegar, honey, and salt to taste. Serve or, if made ahead, cover and chill up to 4 hours. Makes 4 servings.

PER SERVING: 40 calories, 0.3 g protein, 10 g carbohydrates, 0.2 g fat, 0 mg cholesterol, 1.2 mg sodium

(Continued on next page)

HEARTY SOUP SUPPER

Split Pea Soup with Orange Roughy
Butter Lettuce Vinaigrette
Bread Sticks
Persimmons   Gingersnaps
Chardonnay   Mineral Water

A bowl of thick and satisfying hot soup will take the chill out of a cold November evening. This hearty version of split pea soup is rich with vegetables and bite-size chunks of fish. Simple accompaniments include a green salad, bread sticks, and fruit and cookies.

You can cook the soup base up to two days ahead. To serve, reheat base to simmering and add the cooked rice and fish at the last minute.

Split Pea Soup with Orange Roughy

2 tablespoons olive or salad oil
1 large (about ½ lb.) onion, chopped
2 cups (about ½ lb.) sliced mushrooms
¾ cup minced celery
⅓ cup dry white wine
   About 3 cups regular-strength chicken broth
3 cups water
1½ cups split peas, sorted for debris and rinsed
¼ cup minced parsley
½ teaspoon pepper
3 cups cooked brown rice
1 pound boned and skinned orange roughy or rockfish, cut into bite-size chunks
   Lemon wedges and salt

In a 5- to 6-quart pan over medium-high heat, combine oil, onion, mushrooms, and celery; stir often until onions are browned at edges, about 15 minutes.

Add wine, 3 cups broth, water, and peas. Bring to a boil over high heat, then cover and simmer until peas are soft to bite, about 1¼ hours. If made ahead, let cool, then cover and chill up to 2 days; reheat to simmering to continue (thin with broth if desired).

Stir parsley, pepper, and rice into soup. Heat to simmering. Add fish and let simmer just until fish is opaque in center but still moist-looking, about 5 minutes. Ladle into individual bowls. Add lemon and salt to taste. Makes about 2½ quarts, 6 to 8 servings. —*Judy Roy, Honolulu.*

PER SERVING: 336 calories, 21 g protein, 43 g carbohydrates, 9.1 g fat, 11 mg cholesterol, 77 mg sodium

All-Day Open House (page 320)

Welcome the festive season
with our selection of holiday parties. Readers share ideas for
gatherings that are easy on the hosts: a make-ahead buffet
lunch, an all-day open house, and a bring-your-own-chili
potluck for multiple families. Other entertaining ideas include
a walk-about party featuring bite-size appetizers, a crab feast,
and a menu featuring traditional Hanukkah foods. Holiday
projects include a cooky tree constructed from home-baked
biscotti cookies, flavored fruit vinegars in vibrant colors,
and fish-shaped planks for cooking salmon and other fish.

Holiday Parties That Are Easy on the Hosts

LUNCH THAT WAITS

Pecan Cheese Ring with Apples
Chicken with Apricots & Olives
Vegetables with Green Mayonnaise
Tabbouleh Salad
Bread Wreath   Butter
**Dry Chenin Blanc or
Johannisberg Riesling**
Bite-size Tarts
Christmas Cookies
Coffee   Tea

At her annual holiday party, Betsy Stafford of Sausalito, California, offers wreath making followed by a buffet.

She provides the wreath bases, and guests contribute the decorations. Her mother, an experienced wreath maker, helps amateurs turn the raw materials into masterpieces that they take home with them.

Guests spend about 2 hours making wreaths, then have lunch. The buffet meal, made ahead and served tepid, frees the hostess to be with her friends. It is an easy meal to eat from your lap.

The cheese ring and green dip can be made several days in advance. Serve the dip with red bell pepper strips and blanched broccoli flowerets; you'll need a total of about 3 pounds untrimmed vegetables. Prepare your favorite tabbouleh salad (except for green herbs) and cook the chicken the night before. Up to 4 hours before serving, add herbs to salad and let chicken warm to room temperature. Arrange apple slices around the cheese ring shortly before serving.

GREEN MAYONNAISE

- 1½ cups mayonnaise
- ⅓ cup chopped parsley
- ⅓ cup chopped fresh cilantro (coriander)
- ⅓ cup chopped fresh dill or 1½ tablespoons dry dill weed
- 1½ tablespoons lemon juice

At wreath-making party, guest samples pecan cheese ring on crisp apple slices.

In a food processor or blender, combine mayonnaise, parsley, cilantro, dill, and lemon juice; whirl until smooth. If made ahead, cover and chill up to 2 days. Makes about 2 cups, 14 to 16 servings.

PER SERVING: 150 calories, 0.3 g protein, 0.9 g carbohydrates, 16 g fat, 12 mg cholesterol, 119 mg sodium

PECAN CHEESE RING WITH APPLES

- ¾ cup pecan halves
- 3 packages (8 oz. each) cream cheese, cut up
- 4 ounces ripe camembert or brie cheese, cut into small pieces
- 4 ounces (about ½ cup) crumbled blue cheese
- 1 cup (4 oz.) shredded Swiss cheese
- ¼ cup milk
- 3 or 4 large (about 1¾ lb. total) Red Delicious apples, cored, thinly sliced, and coated with about ¼ cup lemon juice

Place nuts in a 9-inch-wide pan; bake in a 350° oven until golden under skin, 10 to 12 minutes. Let cool. Reserve 9 or 10 nuts for garnish; chop remainder.

With an electric mixer, beat cream cheese, camembert cheese, blue cheese, Swiss cheese, and milk until smoothly blended.

Line an 8½- to 9-inch ring mold smoothly with plastic wrap. Spoon ½ of the cheese mixture into mold; cover with chopped nuts. Spread remaining cheese over nuts. Cover with plastic wrap and press down on cheese to fill mold evenly.

Chill until firm, at least 2 hours or up to 1 week.

Uncover mold. Place a platter on mold; invert together. Remove pan and plastic wrap; garnish with pecan halves. To serve, arrange apple slices around cheese. Makes 4 cups, 14 to 16 servings.

PER TABLESPOON CHEESE: 95 calories, 2.9 g protein, 2.9 g carbohydrates, 8.2 g fat, 22 mg cholesterol, 97 mg sodium

CHICKEN WITH APRICOTS & OLIVES

- 4½ to 5 pounds boned and skinned chicken thighs
- 1 cup calamata or niçoise olives, drained
- 1 cup (6 oz.) dried apricots
- 1 cup dry vermouth
- ½ cup drained capers
- 1 teaspoon grated orange peel
- ½ cup orange juice
- ¼ cup white wine vinegar
- 3 tablespoons dry basil leaves
- 2 tablespoons olive oil
- 6 cloves garlic, pressed or minced
- 1 cup firmly packed brown sugar
   Parsley sprigs
   Thin orange slices
   Salt and pepper

Rinse chicken and pat dry. In a large bowl, combine chicken, olives, apricots, vermouth, capers, orange peel, orange juice, vinegar, basil, oil, and garlic. Cover and chill, stirring once, until the next day.

In each of 2 baking pans (10 by 15 in.), arrange half the chicken in a single layer. Pour marinade over chicken. Evenly sprinkle sugar over chicken.

Bake, uncovered, in a 400° oven until chicken is no longer pink in thickest part (cut to test), 30 to 35 minutes (if using one oven, switch pan positions halfway). Transfer chicken to a platter. Pour pan juices into a small bowl. Serve hot or cool. If made ahead, cover and chill up until the next day. To serve, let stand at room temperature up to 4 hours (acid and sugar inhibit bacteria growth). Or, to serve warm, cover loosely and place in a 300° oven just until tepid, 20 to 30 minutes. Reheat sauce in a microwave oven or over low heat. Garnish chicken with parsley sprigs and orange slices. Add sauce, salt, and pepper to taste. Makes 14 to 16 servings.

PER SERVING: 268 calories, 26 g protein, 24 g carbohydrates, 7.6 g fat, 106 mg cholesterol, 300 mg sodium

(Continued on page 320)

Make-ahead buffet lunch follows wreath making. Clockwise, from lower right: Chicken with Apricots & Olives with sauce, vegetables with Green Mayonnaise, tabbouleh salad, and a bread wreath. For dessert, offer a selection of bite-size tarts and Christmas cookies.

Santa and hostess Mary Schwarz greet guest at her holiday open house.

Hot spiced cider awaits guests at day-long holiday open house.

ALL-DAY OPEN HOUSE

Grape Wreath
Gingerbread Fence Cooky Platter
Cracker Wreath
Assorted Cheeses
Honeydew Melon Wedges &
Orange Slices with Cranberries
Holiday Breads   Muffins
Croissants   Butter Cut-outs
Preserves in Orange Cup
Cold Sliced Cooked or Cured Meats
Hot Spiced Cider

Mary Schwarz of Portola Valley, California, is a prolific craftswoman, wood carver, designer, decorator, collector, and cook. During the year, she produces an unbelievable quantity of handmade projects to share with guests at an all-day open house she hosts in December.

Every inch of her house overflows with holiday cheer—a dozen decorated trees accent the rooms, more than a hundred expressive teddy bears greet guests, and wreaths grace every door.

The dining room is decked out in holiday finery. The star attraction is the buffet table (see photo, page 317), filled from morning to late afternoon with brunch to appetizer offerings. The food isn't complicated—in fact most of it is purchased ready to eat—but the creative way the food is displayed gives it a sense of style. You'll find her simple but festive ideas easy to duplicate.

Throughout the day, Mrs. Schwarz offers fruit, cheese, cookies, and bread. In the afternoon, she brings out a selection of cold meats. Allow about 2 ounces cheese or meat, ⅓ pound untrimmed fruit, 2 to 3 ounces bread or crackers, and 1 to 2 ounces sweets for each serving.

Grape wreath. Arrange small bunches of red or green **grapes** on a platter in the shape of a wreath. Trim with a big bow.

Gingerbread fence cooky platter. On the back of small **gingerbread boy cookies** (purchased or homemade), place a dot of **frosting**. Stand cookies around inside edge of an attractive rimmed pan or dish (Mrs. Schwarz uses a heart-shaped copper pan), pressing the frosting side to the pan so the cookies form a chain around it. Fill center of pan with more cookies.

Cracker wreath. On a fir or cedar wreath, nestle **crackers** on the greenery. Place a **cheese ball** in the center.

Butter cut-outs. Slice cold **butter** (use 1-pound blocks for cooky cutters larger than 1 in.) into slabs about ½ inch thick. Using an open-top cutter, cut shapes from slab, then gently push out butter cut-out.

Or, if you have chocolate molds, firmly pack room-temperature butter into molds to fill. Close mold if hinged, or cover and freeze until firm. With the tip of a sharp knife, pry out molded butter. If needed, dip mold to rim briefly in hot water.

Use, or cover and chill until serving.

EXPANDABLE CHILI POTLUCK

Melted Nacho Cheese
Tortilla Chips
Potluck Salads
High's Expandable Chili
with Condiments
A Dozen Desserts
Beer

Geoff High explains the origins of this annual get-together with family and friends: "While growing up in Denver, I developed a tight-knit group of about 15 friends. After high-school graduation, we went in different directions but kept in close contact through letters, phone calls, and road trips. At Christmas, it became apparent that my parents felt cheated because their son, who had come home for the holidays, would immediately run off to spend time with his friends who had also returned home."

Six years ago, the parents found a solution that suits everyone. On about December 22, one house hosts a chili party. Each family brings chili in a big pot, salad, appetizers, or dessert. Larger families tend to bring bigger portions.

Each family brings a pot of chili (or a salad, an appetizer, or a dessert) to potluck dinner.

All the family members rekindle the friendships that developed while the gang was together. By now, with the addition of spouses, children, and friends, this party numbers more than 60 guests.

Because the number of guests changes from year to year, Geoff High's mother, Carol, invented this quick, expandable chili that combines fresh ingredients with canned chili. She can easily multiply the recipe as needed. Options in the basic ingredients vary the flavor. Guests choose condiments to suit their tastes.

HIGH'S EXPANDABLE CHILI WITH CONDIMENTS

1 pound ground lean beef or pork
1 large onion, chopped
2 cloves garlic, pressed or minced
3 tablespoons chili powder or ground New Mexico or California chilies
1 teaspoon ground cumin
1 can (28 oz.) cut tomatoes or whole pear-shaped tomatoes, cut up
1 large can (7 oz.) diced green chilies (optional)
2 cans (15 oz. each) chili with beans (or pinto beans, drained)
  Condiments (choices follow)

In a 3- to 4-quart pan (use a 5- to 6-qt. pan for a double recipe, 6- to 8-qt. pan for a triple recipe), stir beef occasionally over high heat until browned and crumbly, 10 to 20 minutes. Add onion and garlic; stir until limp, 5 to 8 minutes. Stir in chili powder and cumin.

Add tomatoes and juices, green chilies, and chili with beans. Bring to a boil; then simmer, uncovered, stirring occasionally, until flavors are blended, about 15 minutes. Remove and discard fat. (If made ahead, cool, cover, and chill until the next day. Reheat to serve.) Ladle into bowls; offer condiments to add to taste. Makes 2 quarts, or 8 servings of 1 cup each.

PER PLAIN SERVING: 299 calories, 17 g protein, 19 g carbohydrates, 18 g fat, 59 mg cholesterol, 748 mg sodium

Condiments. For each serving, allow ¼ cup condiments. Choose from shredded **cheddar cheese,** chopped **onion, fresh cilantro leaves** (coriander), **sour cream,** pitted and diced firm-ripe **avocado** coated with **lemon juice,** and 2 to 3 teaspoons minced **fresh** or canned **jalapeño chilies.**

Home for the holidays, young people gather with their families for sociable potluck supper featuring chili and condiments, salad, and dessert.

Bite-Size Appetizers

U NLESS YOU JUGGLE, *two hands aren't enough at a stand-up party to keep fork, glass, and plate under control. That's why Elaine Bell—caterer and culinary director at Sterling Vineyards—creates buffets with foods you simply pick up to* eat. *The menu here features seven of her utensil-free appetizers—enough for a light meal for 12 to 16. Each recipe includes convenient make-ahead steps, as helpful as an extra pair of hands during this busy entertaining season.*

To make this light meal—and cleanup afterward—run smoothly, have plenty of small paper napkins, and wastebaskets for collecting the napkins and skewers.

HERBED EGGPLANT ROLLS

- 3 tablespoons olive oil or salad oil
- 2 garlic cloves, minced or pressed
- 1 large (about 1½ lb.) eggplant, stem trimmed
- ½ pound fontina cheese, cut into 32 equal pieces, each about 2 inches long
- 3 tablespoons chopped fresh basil leaves
- 2 teaspoons *each* chopped fresh rosemary leaves and chopped fresh oregano leaves
  Salt and pepper (optional)

Mix 2 tablespoons of the oil with the garlic and set aside.

Cut eggplant lengthwise into quarters; cut quarters lengthwise into 8 slices to make a total of 32 pieces (slices will be about ⅛ in. thick).

Oil 3 baking pans (10- by 15-in. size) with some of the garlic-oil. Lay eggplant slices, side by side, in pans; brush with remaining mixture. Bake eggplant in a 375° oven until soft and lightly browned, 10 to 15 minutes. Watch closely for scorching. Slide a spatula under slices; let cool on pan. If made ahead, cover and chill up until next day. Use at room temperature.

No utensils needed for these bite-size appetizers: (clockwise from bottom) lemon-basil shrimp, apricots with blue cheese and pecans, tomato cheesecake, baked potatoes, eggplant rolls, glazed chicken, fish with lemon relish.

In a small bowl, mix cheese with remaining 1 tablespoon oil; add basil, rosemary, and oregano, and mix gently. Place 1 piece of cheese at narrow end of an eggplant slice, then roll eggplant to enclose; put on a platter. Repeat to fill remaining eggplant slices. Sprinkle lightly with salt and pepper; if made ahead, cover and let stand up to 2 hours. Makes 32 pieces.

PER PIECE: 44 calories, 2 g protein, 1.4 g carbohydrates, 3.5 g fat, 8.2 mg cholesterol, 58 mg sodium

SWORDFISH WITH LEMON RELISH

- **32 baguette slices (each about 2 in. wide and ¼ in. thick)**
- **1 pound boned and skinned swordfish, about ½ inch thick**
- **¼ cup dry white wine**
  Salt and pepper
  Lemon peel relish (recipe follows)
- **2 small Roma-type tomatoes, cored, seeded, and thinly slivered**

Arrange baguette slices in a single layer on 2 baking sheets, 12- by 15-inch size. Bake in a 350° oven until lightly toasted, about 10 minutes. Let cool; hold for 1 hour or package airtight up to 2 days.

Cut fish into 16 equal pieces (about 1 in. square), then cut each piece in half horizontally (making each piece about ¼ in. thick). Line a 10- by 15-inch baking pan with foil. Arrange fish in single layer on foil and sprinkle with wine and salt and pepper to taste. Cover loosely with more foil. Bake in a 375° oven until fish is just opaque but still moist-looking in center (cut to test), about 6 minutes. Let cool in pan; chill, covered, up to 4 hours.

Up to 30 minutes before serving, spoon equal amounts of lemon relish onto each baguette slice; cover airtight and hold at room temperature. Just before serving, drain fish and pat dry; set a piece on each baguette. Top with tomato slivers. Makes 32 pieces.

PER PIECE: 52 calories, 3.5 g protein, 6.9 g carbohydrates, 12 g fat, 5.7 mg cholesterol, 55 mg sodium

Lemon peel relish. With a vegetable peeler, pare yellow skin with a little pith from 6 large **lemons**. Mince peel. Cut and discard remaining pith from 2 lemons (reserve remaining lemons for other uses); cut the 2 lemons in chunks, picking out and discarding seeds. Coarsely chop fruit.

In an 8- to 10-inch frying pan, combine ½ cup finely chopped **onion** and 1 tablespoon **salad oil** over medium-high heat. Stir often until onion is limp but not browned, about 7 minutes. Add lemon peel, chopped lemon, ½ cup **dry white wine,** ⅓ cup **sugar,** and 1 teaspoon **pepper.**

Stir relish often until most of the liquid has cooked away and mixture is syrupy, 15 to 18 minutes. Let cool; if made ahead, cover relish and chill up to 2 weeks. Makes about 1 cup.

DRIED APRICOTS WITH BLUE CHEESE

- **32 pecan or walnut halves**
- **5 ounces (⅔ cup) cambozola or gorgonzola cheese**
- **1 small package (3 oz.) cream cheese**
- **1½ teaspoons pepper**
- **32 dried apricot halves**
- **3 tablespoons minced fresh mint**

In a 7- to 8-inch frying pan, stir nuts over medium heat until toasted, about 4 minutes. Pour from pan and let cool.

In a small bowl or food processor, beat or whirl together cambozola cheese, cream cheese, and pepper. Spread equal amounts of cheese onto each apricot half. Press a nut into the cheese on each piece.

Place mint in a small, shallow bowl. Dip apricots, cheese side down, into mint, pressing so herb clings. Put fruit, cheese side up, on a platter. If made ahead, cover and chill up to 4 hours. Makes 32.

PER PIECE: 40 calories, 1.3 g protein, 2.6 g carbohydrates, 2.9 g fat, 6.2 mg cholesterol, 70 mg sodium

SKEWERED SHRIMP WITH LEMON PESTO

- **32 large (about 1 lb.) shrimp, shelled, deveined, and rinsed**
  Lemon-basil pesto (directions follow)

Wooden skewer makes shrimp, lavished with lemon-basil sauce, easy to eat.

Thread each shrimp onto a slender wooden skewer from tail into, but not through, wide end. Pour pesto into a rimmed plate; roll shrimp in pesto. Lay shrimp, side by side, in a 10- by 15-inch baking pan. If made ahead, cover with plastic wrap and chill up to 4 hours.

Bake, uncovered, in a 400° oven until shrimp are opaque but moist-looking in center (cut to test), 5 to 6 minutes. Serve hot or warm. Makes 32 pieces.

PER PIECE: 36 calories, 2.6 g protein, 0 g carbohydrates, 2.7 g fat, 18 mg cholesterol, 23 mg sodium

Lemon-basil pesto. In a food processor or blender, purée ½ cup packed **fresh basil leaves,** ¼ cup **olive oil,** 2 tablespoons grated **lemon peel,** 2 tablespoons grated **parmesan cheese,** 1 **garlic clove,** and 1 tablespoon **pine nuts.** Use, or cover and chill up until next day.

(Continued on next page)

One-handed eating is easy, whether food arrives on a tray or you go to the buffet. Each recipe includes convenient make-ahead steps to minimize last-minute work.

ROASTED POTATOES WITH ASIAGO CHEESE

> 16 tiny (1½- to 2-in.-diameter) red thin-skinned potatoes, scrubbed
> ½ cup grated asiago or parmesan cheese
> ½ cup mayonnaise
> 2 tablespoons minced green onion
> About 1 teaspoon paprika

Pierce potatoes in several places with a fork and put in a 9-inch-wide round or square pan. Bake in a 375° oven until tender when pierced, about 1 hour. Let stand up until next day.

In a small bowl, mix together cheese, mayonnaise, and onion.

Cut each potato in half. Scoop a small cavity about ½ inch deep in each potato. Set potatoes, cut side up, in a 10- by 15-inch baking pan; you may trim a sliver off rounded side of potatoes so they sit steady. Spoon cheese mixture equally into each. Dust liberally with paprika. Bake potatoes in a 350° oven until hot throughout, about 15 minutes. Place on a platter. Makes 32 pieces.

PER PIECE: 51 calories, 1.1 g protein, 4.5 g carbohydrates, 3.2 g fat, 3.2 mg cholesterol, 49 mg sodium

APRICOT-ORANGE GLAZED CHICKEN

> 6 boned and skinned chicken breast halves (about 2 lb. total), rinsed
> 1 cup apricot jam
> 2 tablespoons firmly packed brown sugar
> 2 tablespoons prepared horseradish
> 2 tablespoons minced fresh ginger
> 2 tablespoons grated orange peel
> ¼ cup orange juice

Cover 36 slender wooden skewers with water and let soak at least 30 minutes or up to 2 hours.

Cut each breast lengthwise into 6 equal slices; weave each onto a skewer. Lay pieces on a rack in a 10- by 15-inch baking pan (or rack of a broiler pan), with chicken in center of pan. If made ahead, cover and chill up to 6 hours.

In a 1- to 1½-quart pan, combine jam, sugar, horseradish, ginger, orange peel, and orange juice. Stir over medium-high heat until jam melts. Use the sauce warm or let stand up to 6 hours, covered; reheat to continue.

Brush chicken with sauce. Broil 6 inches from heat until meat browns slightly, about 4 minutes; baste twice with sauce. Turn chicken over; baste again. Broil just until meat is no longer pink in center of thickest part (cut to test), 3 to 4 minutes longer. Baste chicken and put on a platter. Makes 36 pieces.

PER SKEWER: 49 calories, 4.4 g protein, 7.3 g carbohydrates, 0 g fat, 11 mg cholesterol, 14 mg sodium

DRIED TOMATO CHEESECAKE

> ½ cup drained oil-packed dried tomatoes plus 1 tablespoon oil
> 2 teaspoons chopped fresh or 1 teaspoon dry oregano leaves
> 6 garlic cloves
> 3 large eggs
> 2 large packages (8-oz. size) cream cheese, cut into chunks
> 1 cup sour cream
> ½ cup finely chopped green onions
> Salt and pepper
> Press-in pastry (recipe follows)

In a food processor or blender, coarsely purée tomatoes with oil, oregano, garlic, and eggs. In processor or a bowl, smoothly beat cheese and sour cream with tomato mixture. Stir in onions and salt and pepper to taste. Spread evenly onto pastry.

Bake in a 350° oven until filling is puffed and lightly browned, about 25 minutes. Let cool, then cover and chill at least 2 hours or up to 2 days. With a sharp knife, cut cheesecake into about 2-inch squares, then cut each square in half diagonally and transfer to a platter. Makes 70 pieces.

PER PIECE: 78 calories, 1.5 g protein, 4 g carbohydrates, 6.2 g fat, 29 mg cholesterol, 82 mg sodium

Press-in pastry. In a food processor or with your fingers, whirl or rub 6 tablespoons **butter** or margarine (in chunks) with 1¼ cups **all-purpose flour** until mixture resembles coarse meal. Whirl or stir in 1 **large egg** until dough holds together. Press dough evenly (it will be thin) over bottom of a 10- by 15-inch baking pan. Bake in a 350° oven until lightly browned, about 10 minutes. Use hot or cool; if made ahead, cover and chill up until next day.

Favorite Foods for Hanukkah

AMONG THE FAVORITE FOODS *cus-tomarily served during Hanukkah, the Jewish festival of lights, are the golden potato pancakes called* latkes.

Here we present latkes in a traditional meal that includes some flavorful innovations. Our menu serves 6 to 8.

Instead of serving smoked salmon or smoked whitefish, try smoked black cod (sometimes called Alaska cod or barbecued Pacific cod) for a change. The cod tastes best when warm; you can heat it in a microwave oven in a few minutes (uncovered at full power for 30-second to 1-minute intervals until the fish is warm to touch). Allow 3 to 4 ounces of this rich-tasting fish for each serving.

Accompany the fish and latkes with the following tangy relish made from pickled beets, mustard seed, chili, and horseradish. Serve it along with the usual sour cream and applesauce. You'll need at least 1 cup of sour cream; buy or make at least 2 cups applesauce.

Include a big, beautiful braided challah loaf in this meal. Make or purchase the loaf. If you buy the bread, you may need to order it ahead from your bakery.

Dessert is simple. Cut the dough for the buttery Hanukkah cookies into shapes like menorahs and dreidels (spinning tops); then decorate cookies with blue and white frosting, representing the colors of the Israeli flag.

POTATO LATKES

- 4 large eggs
- 2 large (about 1 lb. total) onions, minced
- 1½ pounds (about 3 medium-size) russet potatoes, peeled
- ½ cup matzo meal or all-purpose flour
  About ⅓ cup salad oil
  Salt and pepper

In a large bowl, mix eggs and onion; set aside. Using a food processor or hand grater, coarsely shred potatoes. At once, add potatoes and meal to bowl; stir.

Put about 1 tablespoon oil in a 10- to 12-inch nonstick frying pan over medium-high heat. Into hot pan, ladle about ¼ cup potato mixture for each latke; spread into a 3½-inch round. Cook 2 or 3 at a time until golden and crisp on both sides, 6 to 8 minutes total; add oil to prevent sticking. Drain on paper towels.

When all are cooked, lay them in a single layer on 12- by 15-inch baking sheets. If made ahead, cover and chill up until next day. To reheat and crisp, bake latkes, uncovered, in a 425° oven until sizzling hot, 10 to 15 minutes if room temperature, 15 to 20 minutes if chilled. Add salt and pepper to taste. Makes about 24, or 6 to 8 servings.

PER PIECE: 226 calories, 6.1 g protein, 25 g carbohydrates, 11 g fat, 106 mg cholesterol, 39 mg sodium

SEEDED BEET RELISH

- 1 tablespoon mustard seed
- 1 fresh jalapeño chili, stemmed and seeded
- 2 tablespoons red wine vinegar
- 1 tablespoon sugar
- 1 can (about 1 lb.) pickled beets, drained and finely chopped
- 1 to 2 teaspoons prepared horseradish

In a small bowl, pour about ½ cup hot water over mustard seed; let stand at least 5 minutes. In a blender, whirl chili, vinegar, and sugar until smooth (or mince chili and mix with vinegar and sugar). Drain liquid from mustard seed and add chili mixture, beets, and horseradish to taste. Cover and chill for 1 hour or up to 2 days. Makes about 1½ cups.

PER TABLESPOON: 17 calories, 0.3 g protein, 3.9 g carbohydrates, 0.1 g fat, 0 mg cholesterol, 50 mg sodium

HANUKKAH COOKIES

- ½ cup (¼ lb.) butter or margarine, at room temperature
- ½ cup sugar
- 1 large egg
- 1 teaspoon vanilla
  About 1½ cups all-purpose flour
- ½ teaspoon baking soda
  Purchased blue and white frosting in tubes (optional)

In a mixer bowl, beat butter and sugar until fluffy. Add egg and vanilla; beat until well mixed.

Stir together 1½ cups flour and baking soda. Add to butter mixture, stir together, then beat to blend thoroughly.

On a floured board, roll dough, a portion at a time, to ¼-inch thickness. Cut cookies with a floured cutter; transfer on a wide spatula to oiled 12- by 15-inch baking sheets, spacing cookies slightly apart. Add scraps to remaining dough.

Bake in a 350° oven until golden brown, about 12 minutes; reverse pan positions after about 5 minutes. With spatula, transfer cookies to racks to cool. Pipe frosting onto cookies to decorate. Let stand until frosting is firm to touch. Serve; or store in an airtight container, separating layers with wax paper. Chill up to 1 week; freeze to store longer. Makes about 1½ dozen cookies, 2½-inch diameter.

PER COOKY: 109 calories, 1.5 g protein, 14 g carbohydrates, 5.5 g fat, 26 mg cholesterol, 79 mg sodium

Warm smoked fish and crisp-tender potato latkes go with sour cream, pickled beet relish, and handsome braids of challah. For dessert, serve buttery cookies.

Biscotti Tree

CONSTRUCTED FROM BAKED *biscotti dough, this cooky tree is an edible centerpiece. Put it out for a party and let guests munch their way down, lifting it apart branch by branch. The firm, spiced almond cookies make good dunkers for coffee and hot chocolate.*

TIERED BISCOTTI TREE

1½ cups slivered almonds
¾ cup (⅜ lb.) butter or margarine, at room temperature
1 cup sugar
1 tablespoon grated orange peel
4 large eggs
1 teaspoon vanilla
About 4½ cups all-purpose flour
4½ teaspoons baking powder
½ teaspoon salt
½ teaspoon ground cinnamon
¼ teaspoon *each* ground cloves, ground coriander, and ground nutmeg
Marmalade icing (recipe follows)
Decorations, such as a holly sprig or small Christmas tree balls

Place almonds in an 8- to 9-inch-wide pan. Bake in a 350° oven, shaking often, until golden, about 15 minutes; cool.

In a large bowl, beat butter, sugar, and orange peel until fluffy. Add eggs, 1 at a time, beating well after each addition. Stir in vanilla. Combine 4½ cups flour, baking powder, salt, cinnamon, cloves, coriander, nutmeg, and nuts; add to butter mixture and stir to blend thoroughly.

Divide dough into 3 equal pieces. On a well-floured board, pat each piece into an evenly thick triangle (step 1) that measures 9 inches across base, 2 inches across top, and 12 inches on sides. Make edges neat by pressing with a ruler. Carefully transfer each triangle with wide spatulas to an oiled 12- by 15-inch baking sheet. Bake in a 350° oven for 15 minutes; dough can wait for oven space.

Remove from oven; cut crosswise into slices exactly ⅝ inch wide (step 2), using a long knife. Tip slices onto a cut side. Bake, turning once, until golden brown, about 20 minutes. Cool on racks. If made ahead, package airtight up until next day, or freeze.

To build the tree, pipe (use a ¼-inch tip) or spread a little frosting on 1 side of each of the longest cookies. Lay icing side down on a flat platter, tips touching, to form a triangle. Pipe or spread icing down center of each cooky on plate. Stack the 3 next-longest cookies on the first, inverting position of the triangle (see step 3). Build tree, using the next-smallest cooky trio for each level and cementing with icing. If you like, pipe icing to drip over the edge of the cookies. Decorate top with holly.

Let guests lift off cookies to eat. If made ahead, or to protect from dust, seal in plastic wrap; cookies stay fresh up to 4 days, depending on moisture in air. Kept longer, they hold their shape but get stale.

PER 2 INCHES OF COOKY: 48 calories, 0.8 g protein, 7.9 g carbohydrates, 1.6 g fat, 7.4 mg cholesterol, 29 mg sodium

Marmalade icing. Smoothly mix together ¾ cup **orange marmalade**, 1 box (1 lb.) or 4 cups sifted **powdered sugar**, and 1 tablespoon **orange-flavor liqueur** or orange juice. If icing thickens as you work, stir in a little more orange juice.

1 *Press dough edges with ruler to make a neat triangle. You bake three identical ones to get "limbs" for tiered cooky tree.*

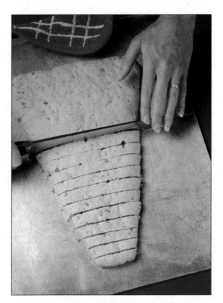

2 *With a long knife, cut half-baked cookies into ⅝-inch slices; tip slices onto a cut side, then bake until golden brown.*

3 *Make triangles of same-size cookies. Reverse position of triangle on each tier; graduate triangles from longest to shortest cookies.*

With snowy drips of icing, Grandma puts finishing touch on Betsy's cooky tree. Built using baked biscotti dough and decorated with glossy holly sprigs, the tree becomes an edible centerpiece for a holiday party. Guests munch their way down, lifting the tree apart branch by branch.

Feasting on Crab

GIVE THE SEASON'S FINEST *Dungeness crab a delicious bath in these festive yet simple preparations. Crab's good looks and flavor make it a prime candidate for splashy holiday celebrations.*

Starting with cracked cooked crab from the market, you can prepare any of these four delicious entrées in minutes. Serve the crab cloaked in an Asian stir-fry sauce with green onions or gently heated in a Riesling-infused broth. Or serve it cold, dressed in either of two refreshing marinades—one speckled with fragrant herbs, the other dotted with olives and a tricolor pepper confetti.

You need to use your hands to dig out the sweet morsels of meat. Offer each guest a shellfish or nut cracker and a small fork (or use the tip of a crab claw) for the job. Also provide plenty of napkins, finger bowls, even bibs or large napkins to tie around guests' necks.

Complete the feast with a green salad or raw vegetables and lots of crusty bread. Accompany the cold marinated crab with a dry Sauvignon Blanc or crisp Chardonnay. With the hot dishes, sip a sweeter, fruitier wine such as a medium-dry Johannisberg Riesling or Gewürztraminer.

STIR-FRIED CRACKED CRAB WITH ONION

⅓ cup *each* dry sherry and water
¼ cup oyster sauce
2 teaspoons cornstarch
1 tablespoon salad oil
3 tablespoons minced fresh ginger
14 green onions (ends trimmed), cut into 2-inch lengths
3 cooked large Dungeness crab (about 6 lb. total), cleaned and cracked

In a small bowl, blend sherry, water, oyster sauce, and cornstarch; set aside.

Pour oil into an 8- to 10-quart pan set over high heat. Add ginger and white ends of onion; stir-fry until onion just begins to brown, about 2 minutes. Add

Use a narrow fork or the tip of a crab claw to dig sweet meat out of shell.

sherry mixture and stir until boiling, about 1 minute. Add crab and green portions of onion; stir to coat crab with sauce. Cover and cook over low heat, stirring occasionally, until crab is hot, 5 to 8 minutes. Pour onto a large platter. Makes 6 servings.

PER SERVING: 154 calories, 21 g protein, 9.2 g carbohydrates, 3.4 g fat, 64 mg cholesterol, 799 mg sodium

CRAB RIESLING

¼ cup (⅛ lb.) butter or margarine
4 cups regular-strength chicken broth
2 cups fruity medium-dry Johannisberg Riesling
¼ cup thinly sliced chives or green onions
6 slices (each about the size of a quarter) fresh ginger
1 tablespoon soy sauce
1 tablespoon lemon juice
3 cooked large Dungeness crab (about 6 lb. total), cleaned and cracked

Melt butter in a 5- to 6-quart pan over medium heat. Add broth, wine, chives, ginger, soy, and lemon juice. Bring to a boil; reduce heat, cover, and simmer for 10 minutes.

Add crab to hot broth; cover and simmer until heated through, 10 to 15 minutes. Discard ginger. Ladle broth and crab into 6 large, shallow bowls. Makes 6 servings.

PER SERVING: 188 calories, 21 g protein, 3.2 g carbohydrates, 9.7 g fat, 85 mg cholesterol, 610 mg sodium

SICILIAN DRESSED CRACKED CRAB

½ cup balsamic vinegar (or 6 tablespoons red wine vinegar plus 2 tablespoons water and 1 teaspoon sugar)
¼ cup red wine vinegar
⅓ cup extra-virgin olive oil
4 cloves garlic, pressed or minced
3 fresh or dry bay leaves
¾ cup chopped fresh basil leaves (or 3 tablespoons dry basil plus ½ cup chopped parsley)
2 tablespoons chopped fresh thyme leaves or 1 teaspoon dry thyme leaves
1 tablespoon chopped fresh rosemary leaves or 1 teaspoon crumbled dry rosemary
1 tablespoon chopped fresh oregano leaves or 1 teaspoon dry oregano leaves
1 tablespoon Worcestershire
¼ teaspoon pepper
¼ to ½ teaspoon crushed dried hot red chilies
3 cooked large Dungeness crab (about 6 lb. total), cleaned and cracked
Fresh sprigs of basil, thyme, rosemary, oregano, or parsley (optional)

In a large bowl, whisk the balsamic and wine vinegars, oil, garlic, bay leaves, chopped basil, chopped thyme, chopped rosemary, chopped oregano,

Feast on cracked crab marinated in sherry vinaigrette dotted with minced bell peppers and pungent olives. Sop up the flavorful marinade with crusty bread.

Worcestershire, pepper, and chilies. Stir in crab; cover and chill, stirring occasionally, at least 10 minutes or up to 3 hours. Pour into a large serving bowl or 6 wide bowls. Garnish with herb sprigs. Makes 6 servings. —*Dan Laguna, Pacific Fresh, Sunnyvale, Calif.*

PER SERVING: 222 calories, 20 g protein, 6.1 g carbohydrates, 14 g fat, 64 mg cholesterol, 351 mg sodium

CRACKED CRAB WITH PEPPER CONFETTI

  3 **cooked large Dungeness crab (about 6 lb. total), cleaned and cracked**
      Vinaigrette (recipe follows)
¼ **cup calamata or black ripe olives**

In a large bowl, combine crab, vinaigrette, and olives. Stir to mix. Cover and chill 10 minutes or up to 4 hours, stirring occasionally. Pour crab and vinaigrette into a large serving bowl or 6 wide bowls. Makes 6 servings.

PER SERVING: 177 calories, 16 g protein, 3.3 g carbohydrates, 11 g fat, 53 mg cholesterol, 466 mg sodium

Vinaigrette. Whisk together ¼ cup **olive oil**, 1 cup **sherry vinegar** (or ¾ cup red wine vinegar plus ¼ cup water), 2 tablespoons **Dijon mustard,** and ¼ cup *each* minced **red, green,** and **yellow bell pepper** (or use ¾ cup of 1 color pepper).

Sunshine Salads

Bursting with brightness, *fresh citrus fruits enliven these three salads. Juicy navel oranges, aromatic tangerines, and sweet-tart grapefruit peak in availability this time of year, and the appealingly priced fruits are natural complements to rich holiday meats such as baked ham, roast beef, and turkey.*

The first one sets the sweetness of fresh oranges against the licorice-cool taste of fennel. Jewel-like pomegranate seeds add a scattering of rosy color, heightened by the dark green of fennel sprigs. An anise seed dressing unites the flavors.

The next salad is especially sunny-looking, and very attractive on a buffet. It combines pink or white grapefruit sections, golden orange slices, slender crescents of pale green avocado, bright green kiwi rounds, red onion rings, and shreds of crisp white jicama.

Simpler but equally pleasant in its balance of flavors is the salad of tart-sweet tangerines, delicately bitter radicchio, and mild butter lettuce—brought together by a mellow chili-flavored dressing.

ORANGE & FENNEL SALAD

- 2 large (about 1½ lb. total) partially trimmed fennel heads
- ¼ cup seasoned rice vinegar (or ¼ cup rice vinegar mixed with 4 teaspoons sugar)
- 2 tablespoons salad oil
- 1 tablespoon grated orange peel
- 1 teaspoon anise seed
- 4 large (about 2½ lb. total) oranges
  Seeds from 1 pomegranate (about 3½-in. diameter)
  Salt

Trim off and discard tough stems, ends, and any bruises from fennel. Reserve feathery green sprigs. Cut fennel head into thin slivers; place in a bowl. Finely chop 1 tablespoon feathery tops (reserve remainder); add to bowl with vinegar, oil, peel, and anise seed. Mix well. If made ahead, let stand up to 30 minutes or cover and chill up to 4 hours.

Cut off and discard peel and white membrane from oranges. Cut fruit crosswise into ¼-inch-thick slices; discard seeds.

Juicy orange slices sprinkled with shiny red pomegranate seeds team with thin slivers of fresh fennel in this holiday salad.

On 6 salad or dinner plates, spoon equal portions of fennel salad. Arrange orange slices beside the fennel and sprinkle equally with pomegranate seeds. Garnish with reserved green fennel sprigs. Add salt to taste. Makes 6 servings.

PER SERVING: 148 calories, 2 g protein, 26 g carbohydrates, 5 g fat, 0 mg cholesterol, 62 mg sodium

GRAPEFRUIT, ORANGE & KIWI SALAD

2 large (about 2 lb. total) pink or white grapefruit

2 large (about 1¼ lb. total) oranges

½ pound jicama

1 large (about ½ lb.) avocado
Celery seed vinaigrette (recipe follows)

4 to 6 large butter lettuce leaves, rinsed and crisped

5 kiwi fruit (about 1½ lb. total), peeled and cut into ¼-inch-thick slices

6 or 8 thin red onion slices, each about 3 inches in diameter
Salt

Cut off and discard peel and white membrane from grapefruit. Cut between membrane and fruit to release segments; discard seeds.

Cut off and discard peel and white membrane from oranges. Cut crosswise into ¼-inch-thick slices; discard seeds.

Peel and rinse jicama. In a food processor with a shredder blade (or using a hand grater), finely shred jicama.

Pit and peel avocado, and cut into thin wedges; moisten with a little of the dressing to prevent darkening.

Lay lettuce around edges of a platter. Group grapefruit, oranges, jicama, avocado, and kiwi fruit separately on platter, then separate onion slices into rings and scatter them over fruit. Add dressing and salt to taste to individual portions. Makes 6 servings. —*Nancy Cook, Sonoita, Ariz.*

PER SERVING WITHOUT DRESSING: 186 calories, 3.3 g protein, 36 g carbohydrates, 5 g fat, 0 mg cholesterol, 10 mg sodium

Celery seed vinaigrette. In a small bowl, mix together 1 teaspoon **Dijon mustard,** 2 teaspoons **celery seed,** 2 tablespoons **sugar,** 3 tablespoons **salad oil,** and ⅓ cup **cider vinegar.** If made ahead, cover and let stand at room temperature up until next day. Makes about ¾ cup.

PER TABLESPOON: 50 calories, 0 g protein, 4.1 g carbohydrates, 3.5 g fat, 0 mg cholesterol, 14 mg sodium

TANGERINE & RADICCHIO SALAD

6 tangerines (about 1½ lb. total)

1 large (about ¾ lb.) head butter lettuce, rinsed and crisped

1 small (about 3 oz.) head radicchio or red leaf lettuce, rinsed and crisped
Citrus-chili vinaigrette (recipe follows)
Salt

Peel tangerines. Cut between segment membrane and fruit to release fruit, or simply break segments apart. Discard seeds. Put fruit in a large salad bowl. Tear lettuce and radicchio into large pieces and add to bowl along with dressing. Mix gently; add salt to taste. Makes 6 servings.

PER SERVING: 109 calories, 1.6 g protein, 11 g carbohydrates, 7.5 g fat, 0 mg cholesterol, 14 mg sodium

Citrus-chili vinaigrette. Mix together 3 tablespoons **extra-virgin olive** or salad oil, ½ cup **lime juice,** 1 tablespoon *each* grated **lime peel** and grated **lemon peel,** 1 teaspoon **chili powder,** and 1 teaspoon **cumin seed.** Let stand at least 15 minutes. If made ahead, cover and chill up to 6 hours.

Rosy radicchio and pale green butter lettuce form a ruffled nest for bright tangerine segments. Mix gently with citrus-chili vinaigrette dressing.

Fish-on-a-Plank

THE TRADITION *of cooking on a plank has Western ties. Northwest Indians supported fish on a plank to cook in front of a fire. At the turn of the century, fish served on a plank was a specialty at one of San Francisco's grand hotels. And Sunset has a history of plank cooking—from fruit to fish. Today, the technique is enjoying a revival in some fish restaurants.*

Why cook on a plank? A plank makes cooking and serving baked fish easy and attractive. In effect, you're cooking on the serving board. When baked without sauces, fish gives up very little juice, and since you set the board in a pan in the oven (to make it easy to move), any drips will be contained. The board keeps the fish warm while you eat, and the warm wood is faintly aromatic—not enough to flavor foods, but it smells good.

You can easily make your own board or boards for large or small pieces of fish.

What woods work? Oak and maple are suitable hardwoods, but pine works, too. Buy an unfinished and untreated plank (about ¾ in. thick) without cracks.

What size, shape? Figure how big a fish you like to cook and get a plank a few inches longer and a few inches wider. You can simply sand it smooth, or cut it into another shape. To cut fish-shaped planks, enlarge a pattern on the facing page onto paper. Trace shape onto plank. Cut with a jigsaw or band saw. Sand all surfaces smooth.

To season plank so it's not inclined to crack, coat wood liberally all over with **salad oil.** Set in a large pan; place in a 200° oven for 4 hours. Frequently brush plank with oil to keep it moist in oven.

To clean, wash plank with warm water and lemon juice or vinegar. Dry; coat with salad oil. Wipe to remove excess.

Won't the plank catch fire? The cooking times and temperatures recommended here shouldn't cause a problem. However, if large areas of oiled board are not covered by fish, oil in the board gets smoky as heated. If wood begins to char, remove from oven and blot with a damp towel.

PLANKED SALMON

Large seasoned wood plank, rinsed and dried
Salad oil
1 salmon tail portion (about 2½ lb.), boned with fillets and tail attached
Cilantro butter (recipe follows)
Fresh cilantro (coriander) sprigs or parsley
Lemon slices, salt, and pepper

Rub plank liberally with oil; set on a 12-by 15-inch baking sheet and put in a 475° oven to heat for about 10 minutes.

Easy to cook and attractive to serve, salmon fillet is baked and presented at table on oak plank; individual fish steaks can also be cooked by this method. Brush cilantro butter over fish as it bakes. Hot board keeps fish warm while you eat; use pads to protect table.

Lay salmon on board, skin side down and aligned to fit the board. Dot with about 1 tablespoon cilantro butter. Put board with fish in oven; when the butter melts, brush it over surface of fish. Bake until the thickest part of the salmon is opaque but still moist-looking (cut to test), 15 to 20 minutes.

Set fish and plank on an insulated surface at the table. Garnish with cilantro and lemon. Add cilantro butter, salt, and pepper to taste. Makes 6 servings.

PER SERVING: 234 calories, 30 g protein, 0 g carbohydrates, 12 g fat, 89 mg cholesterol, 89 mg sodium

Cilantro butter. In a small bowl, stir ½ cup (¼ lb.) **butter** or margarine, at room temperature, with 1 tablespoon chopped **fresh cilantro** and 2 teaspoons **wasabi powder** or prepared horseradish to taste. Makes ½ cup.

PER TABLESPOON: 102 calories, 0.1 g protein, 0.1 g carbohydrates, 12 g fat, 31 mg cholesterol, 118 mg sodium

PLANKED FISH STEAKS

Follow directions for planked salmon (preceding), but use ¾- to 1-inch-thick **steaks of salmon,** halibut, or lingcod on individual serving–size **seasoned planks** (directions precede). Dot each portion with about 1 teaspoon cilantro butter. Bake until fish tests done, about 10 minutes. Set planks on plates.

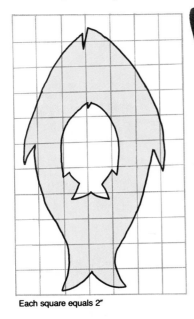

Each square equals 2″

Using the pattern above, cut a board from oak, maple, or pine to match the shape of your fish. Or create your own shapes or use rectangles or rounds. Leave at least an inch between fish and edge.

An Easy Gift Idea: Flavored Vinegars

CAPTURE VIBRANT COLOR *and fruit essence in these easy-to-make flavored vinegars. You start with purchased white wine vinegar and heat it with berries, citrus peel, or exotic passion fruit or tamarind. As the mixture cools, the vinegar absorbs flavor and color from the added ingredient.*

Poured into bottles, these vinegars make attractive gifts, simple to use and store. Here are suggestions to include with any such gift (or keep for your own reference):

Splash any of the vinegars over crisp greens. Try them without added oil for light and satisfying salads.

Try with vegetables, raw or cooked. Use tamarind or lime vinegar as an ultra-lean dip for cooked artichokes or raw jicama. Sprinkle orange or lime vinegar on cooked asparagus. Cook red cabbage with berry vinegar. Add orange vinegar to cooked onions or peas. Drizzle berry or passion fruit vinegar on baked winter squash.

Enhance fruit for salads or dessert. Try berry vinegar on berries, oranges, watermelon; passion fruit vinegar on mangoes and berries; orange or lime vinegar on oranges, kiwi fruit, berries; any citrus vinegar on melons, avocados, papaya; tamarind vinegar on bananas, pears, papaya, and oranges.

Use with meat, poultry, or fish. Splash on cooked foods, or use as a marinade. To marinate, put meat in a plastic bag and add enough vinegar to moisten; seal and chill 1 to 4 hours, turning occasionally. Then broil, barbecue, sauté, or roast.

Tissue-wrapped bottles of vinegar make festive gifts. Vinegars keep at room temperature up to 4 months.

Some striking combinations: tamarind or passion fruit vinegar with pork, lamb, or chicken; citrus vinegars with fish; berry vinegars with poultry or lamb; citrus or tamarind vinegars with beef or venison.

To find combinations you like, drop a little vinegar onto a bite of food and taste.

These vinegars keep at room temperature up to 4 months. Fruit in the bottle slowly falls apart but is not harmful. Simply pour through a strainer and discard fruit; add more fruit to bottle, if you like.

FLAVORED VINEGAR

> 3 cups white wine vinegar
> Fruit flavor (choices follow)
> 2 tablespoons honey

Combine vinegar, fruit flavor, and honey in a 2- to 3-quart pan. Cover and bring to a boil over high heat. Remove from heat and let stand, covered, until cool. If specified with fruit choice, pour liquid through fine strainer into a bowl; discard residue.

Pour vinegar through a funnel into a 1-quart bottle, plain or decorative. Close tight; let stand at least 1 day. Use, or keep at room temperature up to 4 months. If an opaque film develops on surface, you can either spoon it off or, to preserve clarity of vinegar, pour through a fine strainer into a 2- to 3-quart pan and bring to boiling. Wash bottle, then refill with vinegar. Store as before. Makes about 1 quart.

PER TABLESPOON RASPBERRY VINEGAR (OTHERS ARE SIMILAR): 8.5 calories, 0 g protein, 2.2 g carbohydrates, 0 g fat, 0 mg cholesterol, 0 mg sodium

Fruit flavor. *Berry vinegar.* Rinse and drain 4 cups fresh **raspberries, blueberries,** or **strawberries** (hull and slice); or use 1 package (12 or 16 oz.) frozen, unsweetened berries (any of the above). If desired, set aside ¼ cup berries. Add remaining fruit to vinegar and heat as directed, preceding. Pour through strainer. Add reserved fruit to filled bottle.

Citrus vinegar. Use ¼ cup finely shredded **lemon, orange,** or **lime peel.** Heat as directed, preceding. Bottle with the peel.

Passion fruit vinegar. Scrape pulp from 6 ripe (shells are crinkled) **passion fruit,** each about 2 inches in diameter. Add pulp to vinegar. Heat as directed, preceding. Bottle with fruit.

Tamarind vinegar. Pull brittle shell and strings from 1 pound **tamarind pods** (sold in Mexican and Southeast Asian markets). Add pulp and seeds to vinegar; warm slightly. With your hand, rub pulp from seeds. Heat as directed, preceding. Pour through strainer; press pulp with a spoon to extract all liquid.

Lime vinegar is a refreshing, lean seasoning for salmon steaks; it also goes well on salad greens, vegetables, and fruits.

To create berry vinegar, drain wine vinegar, colored and flavored with fruit (blueberries, above), through fine strainer; discard pulp.

Brilliant vinegars take hue and taste from (left to right) tamarind, lime, raspberry, strawberry, and orange. Blueberries, passion fruit, and lemon also work well. When presenting vinegar as a gift, include suggestions for use (see facing page).

Showpiece Roasts

N O BONES ABOUT IT, *these three roasts are easy to carve. Two come from the tender loin, a third from a more exercised muscle, which can still be tender if served rare.*

For a premium roast at an intimate dinner, coat a small, tender lamb loin with herb-garlic paste. A larger crowd can enjoy buffalo crossrib or top sirloin roast served with pan juices flavored with anise and mustard. For a gathering of 8 to 10, roast a center-cut pork loin crusted with cumin, pepper, and orange peel.

You may need to order these roasts several days in advance. Lamb loin starts at about $8 a pound, pork loin at $4 a pound. For buffalo, check suppliers under Meat or Game in the yellow pages. Since buffalo is often sold frozen, you can buy it early to store in your freezer. The crossrib starts at $3.50 per pound; more tender top sirloin costs twice as much. Some wholesalers sell directly to the consumer and may offer the best price.

Roast Lamb Loin with Herbs

- 2 tablespoons olive oil
- 2 tablespoons chopped parsley
- 1 teaspoon chopped fresh or ½ teaspoon dry thyme leaves
- 1 teaspoon chopped fresh or ½ teaspoon crumbled dry rosemary leaves
- 1 teaspoon chopped fresh or ½ teaspoon dry rubbed sage
- 4 cloves garlic, pressed or minced
- 1 teaspoon grated lemon peel
- 1 boned lamb loin (about 1½ lb.)
- 4 to 8 fresh rosemary, thyme, sage, or parsley sprigs, each 5 to 6 in. long (use 1 kind or a combination)
- Lemon wedges
- Salt and pepper

Mix oil, chopped parsley, chopped thyme, chopped rosemary, chopped sage, garlic, and lemon peel; rub all over loin. Fold meat to make a roll.

Secure a bouquet of fresh herbs on boned lamb loin as you tie it together.

Lay 3 cotton strings, each about 15 inches long, on a board, parallel to each other and about 2 inches apart. Set the lamb loin, fat side up, across center of strings. Lay 1 each of rosemary, thyme, sage, and parsley sprigs on top of lamb. Bring strings up and around the roast and tie them. If needed, tie in a few more places to secure. (If made ahead, cover and chill up until the next day.)

Place lamb, herb side up, on a rack in a 9- by 13-inch pan. Roast in a 475° oven until a thermometer inserted in center of meat registers 140° for rare, 30 to 40 minutes. Transfer to platter, keep warm, and let rest for about 5 minutes. Remove strings and garnish with additional fresh herb sprigs and lemon wedges. Season to taste with salt and pepper. Makes 6 servings.

PER SERVING: 308 calories, 19 g protein, 0.9 g carbohydrates, 25 g fat, 81 mg cholesterol, 56 mg sodium

Buffalo Roast with Honey-Seed Crust

Top sirloin is slightly more tender than the crossrib. Removing tough membrane is a crucial step to achieving tenderness.

When boned-and-tied lamb loin is sliced, vein of herb paste reveals itself where bone was removed. Squeeze lemon wedges over slices. Serve with small, whole red potatoes.

1 boned buffalo top sirloin or crossrib roast (about 8 lb.), strings removed
2½ tablespoons mustard seed
1 tablespoon anise seed
2 tablespoons honey
2 tablespoons salad oil
1 tablespoon soy sauce
1 tablespoon Dijon mustard
   Whole green onions, ends trimmed
2 cups rice wine (sake) or dry sherry
2 cups regular-strength beef broth
8 thin slices (about the size of a quarter) fresh ginger
½ cup thinly sliced green onions
   Salt and pepper

Thinly slice seed-coated buffalo crossrib roast; it's a good size for a large group. Served rare, the lean, mild meat is tender and moist; additional cooking makes it dry and tough.

Rinse roast with cool water and pat dry. Trim off any excess fat. Remove as much as possible of the heavy silver-colored membrane that covers and runs through parts of the roast. Slip a thin sharp knife under the membrane and cut meat away, holding membrane taut.

If you cut large pieces of meat off roast while trimming membrane, lay them on thinner section of roast. To keep roast compact as it cooks, tie it snugly with cotton string crosswise at 2-inch intervals and lengthwise 2 or 3 times. Set roast on a rack in a 12- by 17-inch roasting pan.

With a mortar and pestle or in a blender, coarsely crush the mustard seed and anise seed. Reserve 1½ teaspoons of the crushed seed. Mix remaining seed with honey, oil, soy sauce, and mustard; coat roast completely with the mixture.

Bake in a 450° oven for 15 minutes. Reduce temperature to 300° and continue to cook until a thermometer inserted in center of thickest part registers 130° (do not overcook), 1½ to 1¾ hours.

Transfer roast to a platter and let rest in a warm place for about 15 minutes, then snip strings free and remove them. Garnish with whole green onions.

Meanwhile, skim fat from drippings. Add rice wine, broth, reserved seed, and ginger to pan and bring to a boil, scraping browned bits free. Boil on high heat, uncovered, until reduced to 2½ cups, about 8 minutes. Discard ginger; stir in sliced onion and pour sauce into a small bowl.

With a very sharp knife, thinly slice roast. Serve with reduced pan juices. Add salt and pepper to taste. Serves 18 to 20.

PER SERVING: 219 calories, 36 g protein, 5.9 g carbohydrates, 4.9 g fat, 101 mg cholesterol, 147 mg sodium

ROAST PORK LOIN WITH CUMIN

1 tablespoon cumin seed
1 tablespoon coarse-ground pepper
¾ teaspoon grated orange peel
1 boned, rolled, and tied center-cut pork loin (3 to 3½ lb.)
½ cup minced shallots
½ cup orange juice
½ cup dry white wine
1½ cups regular-strength chicken broth
5 teaspoons cornstarch
   Fresh cilantro (coriander) sprigs
   Salt and pepper

With a mortar and pestle or in a blender, coarsely crush cumin seed; reserve ¼ teaspoon for the sauce. Combine remaining cumin seed, pepper, and ½ teaspoon orange peel. Rub mixture all over the pork loin. Place pork, fat side up, on a rack in a 12- by 15-inch roasting pan. Roast in a 375° oven until a thermometer inserted in thickest part of meat registers 155°, 55 to 60 minutes. Put roast on a platter; keep warm. Remove strings.

Tilt pan to skim off and discard fat. To pan add shallots, orange juice, wine, ¼ teaspoon orange peel, and reserved ¼ teaspoon crushed cumin seed. Stir over high heat to loosen browned bits. Boil, uncovered, until reduced to about ⅔ cup, about 4 minutes. Stir together broth, any accumulated juices from roast, and cornstarch. Mix into pan and stir until sauce boils, then pour into a small bowl.

Garnish roast with cilantro sprigs. Thinly slice meat crosswise. Offer sauce and salt and pepper to add to taste. Makes 8 to 10 servings.

PER SERVING: 319 calories, 25 g protein, 4.9 g carbohydrates, 21 g fat, 86 mg cholesterol, 72 mg sodium

Spoon sauce of shallots, orange juice, wine, broth, and pan drippings over slices of pork loin.

Black Beans, Red Beans & Lentils

THEY'RE GOOD FOR YOU, *inexpensive, and readily available. But the main reason to use beans in these dishes is that they taste good. Presoaking dry beans shortens their cooking time. Look for epazote in the spice section of Mexican markets.*

BLACK BEANS WITH VEGETABLES

- 1 pound (about 2¼ cups) dry black beans, or 5 cans (15¼ oz. each) black beans
- 2 tablespoons olive or salad oil
- 2 large (about 1½ lb. total) red onions, chopped
- 2 large (about 1¼ lb. total) green bell peppers, stemmed, seeded, and chopped
- 2 large (about 1¼ lb. total) red bell peppers, stemmed, seeded, and chopped
- 1 can (4 oz.) diced green chilies
- 1 head (about 2½ oz.) garlic, peeled and minced or pressed
- 2 tablespoons dry oregano leaves
- 3 chicken bouillon cubes or 2 cups regular-strength chicken broth
- ½ teaspoon dry epazote (optional)
- ¼ cup dry sherry (optional)
- 4 to 6 cups hot cooked brown rice

Tasty yet inexpensive, black beans and brown rice offer rich flavor and complete protein.

Sort dry beans to remove debris; rinse well and drain. To a 6- to 8-quart pan, add dry beans and 8 cups water; bring to a boil over high heat and cook 5 minutes. Remove beans from heat and let stand 1 hour. Drain; pour beans into a bowl.

In the same pan over medium-high heat, combine oil, onion, green and red bell peppers, chilies, garlic, and oregano. Stir often until vegetables are soft and tinged with brown, about 30 minutes. Add soaked beans with 6 cups water and bouillon cubes (or add undrained canned beans and broth) and epazote. Bring to a boil; reduce heat, cover, and simmer until beans are seasoned and soft to bite, about 2½ hours (45 minutes for canned beans).

Mash beans to thicken soup to consistency you like. Stir in sherry. Ladle soup into bowls; add brown rice. Makes 8 to 10 servings. — *Sydni Rozenfeld, San Francisco.*

PER SERVING: 329 calories, 14 g protein, 60 g carbohydrates, 4.8 g fat, 0.2 mg cholesterol, 413 mg sodium

OREGON CITY RED BEANS

- 1 pound (about 2⅓ cups) dry small red beans or dry kidney beans, or 6 cans (15¼ oz. each) kidney beans, drained
- 2 pounds smoked ham hocks
- 2 teaspoons olive or salad oil
- 3 large (about 1½ lb.) onions, chopped
- 4 garlic cloves, minced or pressed
- 2 dry bay leaves
- 1 teaspoon dry thyme leaves
- ½ teaspoon *each* cayenne and pepper

Sort dry beans to remove debris; rinse well and drain. In a 5- to 6-quart pan, combine dry beans and 8 cups water; bring to a boil on high heat and cook 5 minutes. Remove beans from heat and let stand 1 hour. Drain; pour beans into a bowl.

Put the pan over medium-high heat; add ham hocks and oil. Stir often until hocks begin to brown, about 7 minutes.

Add onion and garlic; stir often until onion is limp, about 20 minutes.

Add soaked beans and 5 cups water. (If using canned beans, add only 2 cups water to ham hocks; add beans later.) Stir in bay leaves, thyme, cayenne, and pepper. Bring to a boil over high heat; reduce heat, cover, and simmer, stirring often, until meat falls from bones, about 2 hours. (If using canned beans, add after meat has cooked 1½ hours.)

Lift out hocks; when cool to touch, separate meat from bones, fat, and gristle. Break meat into small chunks; return to soup.

Continue simmering soup, uncovered, until it's the consistency you like; stir occasionally. Skim off and discard fat, and discard the bay leaves. Makes 6 to 8 servings. — *Shanti Adamson, Oregon City, Ore.*

PER SERVING: 335 calories, 24 g protein, 43 g carbohydrates, 78 g fat, 32 mg cholesterol, 763 mg sodium

LENTILS & SAUSAGE

- 1 pound (about 2 cups) lentils
- 1 pound kielbasa (Polish sausage), thinly sliced on the diagonal
- 1 cup chopped celery
- 1 small (about 6 oz.) onion, diced
- 3 medium-size (about ¾ lb.) zucchini (ends trimmed), chopped
- ¼ teaspoon ground cloves
- 3 cups regular-strength chicken broth
- 4 medium-size (about ¾ lb.) Roma-type tomatoes, cored and diced

Sort lentils for debris; rinse and drain. In a 5- to 6-quart pan over high heat, stir sausage often until lightly browned; drain on paper towels. To pan add celery, onion, zucchini, and cloves. Stir often until vegetables are tinged with brown, about 20 minutes. Add lentils, broth, and 3 cups water.

Over high heat, bring mixture to a boil; reduce heat, cover, and simmer until lentils are tender to bite, about 30 minutes. Stir in sausage and tomatoes. Cook just until hot, about 10 minutes. Makes 6 to 8 servings. — *Deborah Lee-Alano, San Francisco.*

PER SERVING: 404 calories, 25 g protein, 38 g carbohydrates, 17 g fat, 40 mg cholesterol, 533 mg sodium

Light Salads Made with Grains

GRAINS ADD TEXTURE, *extra nutrients, and protein to these light-tasting salads.*

Pearl barley is flavored with rice vinegar and topped with sardines. Toasted quinoa combines with spinach and apples. Millet lends texture to a lemony shrimp salad.

Look for the grains in supermarkets or natural-food stores.

SUSHI-FLAVOR BARLEY SALAD

1 cup pearl barley
1 small carrot, peeled and cut into matchstick-size pieces
⅓ cup seasoned rice vinegar (or distilled white vinegar or rice vinegar mixed with 2 tablespoons sugar, salt to taste)
1 tablespoon Oriental sesame oil
1 cup frozen petite peas, thawed
⅓ cup thinly sliced green onion
2 tablespoons drained sliced pickled ginger, cut into thin strips
1 can (3¾ oz.) brisling sardines, drained
1 small (about ¾ lb.) European cucumber, ends trimmed, thinly sliced crosswise
Whole green onions, ends trimmed

Place barley in a fine strainer and rinse well; drain. In a 1½- to 2-quart pan, bring 2¼ cups water to a boil. Add barley, cover, and simmer 20 minutes. Sprinkle carrots over barley. Continue simmering, covered, until barley is tender to bite and most of the liquid is absorbed, about 10 minutes. Drain; let cool.

Mix the rice vinegar and sesame oil; stir into barley. Add peas, sliced onion, and ginger; mix to blend. Spoon equal portions into 4 or 5 shallow bowls or onto dinner plates. Garnish with sardines, cucumber, and whole onions. Makes 4 or 5 servings.

PER SERVING: 266 calories, 11 g protein, 44 g carbohydrates, 6 g fat, 26 mg cholesterol, 153 mg sodium

SPINACH & QUINOA SALAD

½ cup quinoa
1 cinnamon stick (about 3 in. long)
½ teaspoon cumin seed
½ cup *each* apple juice and water
2 tablespoons currants
2 quarts (about 10 oz.) bite-size pieces rinsed, crisped spinach

Healthy entrée with an Oriental flavor, whole-meal salad pairs pearl barley with rice vinegar, peas, carrot, green onion, pickled ginger, cucumber slices, and sardines.

1 small red apple, cored and thinly sliced
⅓ cup cider vinegar
2 to 2½ tablespoons honey
2 tablespoons salad oil
Salt and pepper

Rinse quinoa in a fine strainer; drain. Pour quinoa into a 1½- to 2-quart pan. Stir often over medium heat until lightly browned, 8 to 10 minutes. Add cinnamon stick, cumin seed, apple juice, and water. Bring to boil, then cover and simmer until most of the liquid is absorbed and quinoa is tender to bite, about 15 minutes. Stir in currants; use warm or cool.

In a large salad bowl, combine spinach and apple. Mound quinoa mixture onto spinach. Mix vinegar, honey to taste, and oil; pour over salad and mix. Add salt and pepper to taste. Makes 4 or 5 servings.

PER SERVING: 188 calories, 4.1 g protein, 31 g carbohydrates, 6.7 g fat, 0 mg cholesterol, 57 mg sodium

MILLET & SHRIMP SALAD

1 cup millet
1 tablespoon mustard seed
1½ cups thinly sliced celery
⅓ pound tiny cooked shelled shrimp
⅓ cup thinly sliced green onion
1 teaspoon grated lemon peel
⅓ cup lemon juice
⅓ cup salad oil
2 teaspoons Dijon mustard
Large butter lettuce leaves, rinsed and crisped

Place millet in a fine strainer and rinse well; drain. In a 2- to 3-quart pan, combine millet, mustard seed, and 1½ cups water. Bring to a boil, cover, and simmer until liquid is absorbed and millet is tender to bite, about 15 minutes. Let cool, then drain.

Add celery, shrimp, and onion. Mix lemon peel, lemon juice, oil, mustard, and 3 tablespoons water; stir into millet. Place a lettuce leaf on each of 4 or 5 dinner or salad plates. Spoon equal portions of the salad onto leaves. Makes 4 or 5 servings.

PER SERVING: 332 calories, 12 g protein, 33 g carbohydrates, 17 g fat, 58 mg cholesterol, 164 mg sodium

Flavoring Essences from Southeast Asia

REFLECTING TROPICAL ORIGINS, *flavoring essences from Southeast Asia use natural and synthetic ingredients to duplicate the flavors and aromas of the region's flowers, leaves, and fruits.*

Used much as Westerners use vanilla, these essences provide an inexpensive way to sample exotic flavors in familiar foods such as custard sauce, sponge cake, whipped cream, and butter wafers.

Green pandan essence comes from an aromatic leaf, pandanus (bai toey). It has a rich, toasted-nut taste. Use it in about the same proportions as vanilla.

Jasmine (mali) flowers produce a floral essence that is almost perfume-like. Durian is a highly esteemed and expensive fruit in Asia. Its clear extract has a pungent odor much like ripe camembert; tasters either love it or hate it. Golden banana essence tastes and smells like the common fruit it comes from; its Asian version can be milder than Western banana extract. Use these three sparingly.

You'll find these essences—and perhaps other flavors—in some Southeast Asian markets, especially Thai ones. To experiment, start with a few drops, adding to taste.

TROPICAL SOFT CUSTARD

Serve this custard sauce over berries, oranges, or poached pears. It's also delicious over sponge cake (recipe follows).

2 cups milk
⅓ cup sugar
4 large egg yolks
About 1 teaspoon pandan essence or ¼ teaspoon banana, jasmine, or durian essence

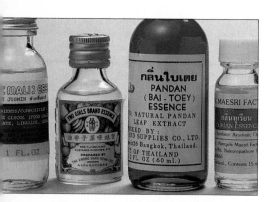

Use small amounts of Southeast Asian essences to add exotic tastes; try (left to right) jasmine, banana, pandan, and durian. They cost less than $1 an ounce.

In the top of a double boiler placed directly over medium heat, scald milk. Remove from heat. In a small bowl, mix sugar with yolks; stir in some of the hot milk, then pour mixture into pan.

Set pan in bottom of a double boiler filled with about 1 inch of simmering water (water should not touch bottom of top pan). Stir until custard thickly coats the back of a metal spoon, 15 to 20 minutes. Stir in essence to taste. Cool, cover, and chill. Makes 2¼ cups.

PER ¼-CUP SERVING: 22 calories, 0.7 g protein, 2.5 g carbohydrates, 1.1 g fat, 32 mg cholesterol, 7.8 mg sodium

SCENTED SPONGE CAKE

Serve this cake plain, embellished with fruit and the tropical soft custard (recipe precedes), or with aromatic cream (recipe follows).

For shortcake, split the layer. Fill with aromatic cream, sliced oranges, and kiwi fruit; top with more cream and fruit.

4 large eggs, separated
¾ cup sugar
1 teaspoon pandan essence or ½ teaspoon banana essence or ¼ teaspoon jasmine or durian essence
⅔ cup all-purpose flour
¾ teaspoon baking powder
¼ teaspoon salt

Butter bottom and sides of a 9-inch cake pan. Line pan bottom with waxed paper, then butter paper; set aside.

In a large bowl, beat egg whites with an electric mixer at high speed until foamy. Gradually add ¼ cup of the sugar, beating just until stiff, moist peaks form; set aside.

In a small bowl, beat egg yolks and remaining ½ cup sugar at high speed (you do not need to wash beaters), scraping bowl often, until mixture is thick and lighter in color. Stir in essence. Fold yolk mixture into white mixture just until blended. In another bowl, mix flour, baking powder, and salt. Sprinkle flour mixture over egg mixture; fold together.

Pour batter into prepared pan and spread evenly. Bake in a 375° oven until top springs back when lightly touched in center, 25 to 30 minutes. Cool on rack about 15 minutes. Cut around cake sides. Turn cake out of pan; peel off

paper. Cool cake thoroughly. Serve or, if made ahead, wrap airtight and store at room temperature until the next day; freeze for longer storage. Makes 6 to 8 servings.

PER SERVING: 151 calories, 4.1 g protein, 27 g carbohydrates, 2.9 g fat, 137 mg cholesterol, 142 mg sodium

AROMATIC CREAM

Offer over fruit or plain cake.

In a small bowl, beat 1 cup **whipping cream** until soft peaks form. Add 1½ tablespoons **sugar** and ½ teaspoon **pandan essence** or ⅛ to ¼ teaspoon jasmine, banana, or durian essence to taste. Beat flavored cream briefly just to blend. Makes about 2 cups.

PER TABLESPOON: 24 calories, 0.2 g protein, 0.8 g carbohydrates, 2.3 g fat, 8.3 mg cholesterol, 2.5 mg sodium

SCENTED BUTTER WAFERS

1 cup (½ lb.) butter or margarine, at room temperature
1⅓ cups powdered sugar
1 large egg
1½ teaspoons pandan essence or ½ teaspoon banana essence or ¼ teaspoon jasmine or durian essence
2½ cups all-purpose flour
1 teaspoon baking soda
1 teaspoon cream of tartar
About ¼ cup crystallized ginger, cut into thin slivers (optional)

In a large bowl, beat butter and sugar until creamy. Add egg and essence; beat until well blended. Mix flour, baking soda, and cream of tartar. Mix with butter mixture.

Divide mixture in half. On a piece of plastic wrap, form each portion into a roll 1½ inches in diameter; wrap airtight. Chill at least 2 hours or up to 2 days.

Unwrap and slice cookies about 3/16 inch thick; arrange slices about 1 inch apart on lightly greased 12- by 15-inch baking sheets. If desired, press a crystallized ginger sliver into center of each cooky slice.

Bake in a 375° oven (if using 2 pans, switch pans halfway through baking) until light gold around edges, 8 to 10 minutes. Cool on racks. Serve, or store airtight up to 5 days; freeze to store longer. Makes about 6 dozen.

PER COOKY: 51 calories, 0.6 g protein, 6.3 g carbohydrates, 2.7 g fat, 11 mg cholesterol, 39 mg sodium

More December Recipes

OTHER DECEMBER ARTICLES *feature a dip for vegetables made with soft tofu and a chicken entrée with tropical overtones.*

GINGER TOFU WITH VEGETABLES

The silky texture and neutral flavor of soft tofu make it an ideal medium for distinctive seasonings in this high-protein, low-fat dip for crisp vegetables.

The fresh bite of ginger stands out against the tofu, robust character comes from onion, and Oriental sesame oil contributes a mellow, nutty taste. Some liken this dip's flavor to that of hummus, *the garbanzo-bean and sesame-seed mixture so popular in Middle Eastern cuisines.*

Look for tofu in the refrigerated section of supermarkets, often with produce.

Scoop thick, creamy tofu dip onto crisp celery for a refreshing appetizer or snack.

1 carton (about 1 lb.) soft tofu
¼ cup sliced green onion
1 tablespoon minced fresh ginger
1 clove garlic, pressed or minced (optional)
1 tablespoon Oriental sesame oil
About 2 tablespoons soy sauce
⅛ teaspoon cayenne
About 6 cups raw vegetables, such as cucumber slices, carrot sticks, red or green bell pepper strips, small celery stalks, sugar snap peas, and cherry tomatoes

Rinse tofu under cool running water, let drain, then drop into a blender or food processor. Whirl smoothly with onion, ginger, garlic, oil, soy sauce, and cayenne. If made ahead, cover and chill up to 3 days. Pour into a small bowl; accompany with vegetables. Scoop onto vegetables to eat. Makes about 1¾ cups, 7 to 9 servings of 3 or 4 tablespoons each.

PER TABLESPOON (NOT INCLUDING VEGETABLES): 21 calories, 1.1 g protein, 2 g carbohydrates, 0.9 g fat, 0 mg cholesterol, 80 mg sodium

CHICKEN QUEENSLAND

Tropical overtones of coconut and spicy ginger accent this quick-to-fix chicken dish. You serve it with sliced pineapple and bananas cooked under the broiler.

6 boned and skinned (about 2¼ lb. total) chicken breast halves, rinsed and patted dry
3 tablespoons lime juice
½ cup ginger preserves
3 large (about 1¾ lb. total) ripe bananas, peeled and quartered
1 medium-size (about 3 lb.) pineapple, peeled, cored, and cut into ½-inch-thick slices
¼ cup sweetened shredded dry coconut
3 limes, cut into wedges

Arrange chicken in a single layer in a 9-by 13-inch pan. In a blender, whirl lime juice with preserves until ginger is finely

Coconut-topped chicken goes with broiled bananas and pineapple; squeeze lime over all.

minced; spoon over chicken. Bake in a 450° oven until chicken is white in thickest part (cut to test), about 12 minutes.

Meanwhile, arrange bananas, cut sides up, in a 10- by 15-inch pan with pineapple; slices can overlap slightly.

Sprinkle chicken with coconut; broil 4 inches from heat until sauce is bubbling and coconut is lightly browned, 1 to 1½ minutes. Transfer chicken to 6 dinner plates. Brush fruit with chicken pan juices and broil until warm, 1 to 2 minutes. Divide fruit evenly among plates. Offer lime wedges to add to taste. Makes 6 servings. —*Mickey Strang, Ridgecrest, Calif.*

PER SERVING: 423 calories, 41 g protein, 58 g carbohydrates, 4.1 g fat, 98 mg cholesterol, 135 mg sodium

Baked brie with roasted red and green peppers makes a colorful party appetizer.

BAKED BRIE WITH ROASTED PEPPERS

1 *each* large (about 1¼ lb. *total*) red and green bell pepper (or both 1 color)
1 clove garlic, cut in half
1 round (about 1 lb.) ripe brie cheese
Baguette slices, plain or toasted

Cut peppers in half crosswise. Cut 1 or 2 thin slices from each; wrap and chill slices. Set peppers, cut side down, in an 8- to 9-inch-wide pan. Broil 6 inches from heat, turning occasionally, until charred on all sides, about 15 minutes. Cover peppers and let stand until cool. Pull off and discard the skin, seeds, and stems; dice peppers.

Rub garlic inside an attractive 9- to 10-inch round or square rimmed baking dish. Spoon diced peppers into dish; top with brie. If made ahead, cover and chill up to 2 days.

Bake brie, uncovered, in a 350° oven until it melts at edges and the center is hot and soft, 15 to 20 minutes. Garnish cheese with raw pepper slices. If desired, set cheese on an electric warming tray to keep hot. With a knife or spoon, scoop cheese and roasted peppers onto baguette slices. Makes 12 to 16 appetizer servings. —*Beverlee Holm, Sunnyvale, Calif.*

PER SERVING (NO BREAD): 102 calories, 6.1 g protein, 1.7 g carbohydrates, 8 g fat, 28 mg cholesterol, 179 mg sodium

Fresh oysters, spinach, white wine, and nutmeg flavor this simple-to-make soup.

SPINACH OYSTER BISQUE

2 tablespoons butter or margarine
1 large onion, chopped
2 tablespoons all-purpose flour
1 teaspoon Worcestershire
¼ teaspoon white pepper
5 cups regular-strength chicken broth
½ cup dry white wine
1 package (10 oz.) frozen chopped spinach
1 jar (10 oz. or 1¼ cups) shucked fresh small Pacific or other small oysters, cut into bite-size pieces; save liquid
Whole nutmeg or ground nutmeg

Melt the butter in a 4- to 5-quart pan over medium-high heat. Add the onion; stir often until onion begins to brown, 8 to 10 minutes. Mix flour with onions, then add Worcestershire and pepper.

Remove from heat and stir in broth and wine. Add spinach and return to high heat; stir until boiling and spinach is thawed. Add oysters and their liquid; heat until steaming, stirring often. Ladle bisque into bowls. Grate a little nutmeg onto each portion. Makes 4 or 5 servings. —*Helen Kennedy, Albuquerque.*

PER SERVING: 148 calories, 8.7 g protein, 11 g carbohydrates, 7.8 g fat, 44 mg cholesterol, 219 mg sodium

Diced yams bake under layer of candied apples, cranberries, and pecans.

BAKED YAMS WITH CANDIED APPLES & CRANBERRIES

1 large (about ½ lb.) Golden Delicious apple, peeled, cored, and diced
3 cups (12-oz. bag) fresh or frozen cranberries
¾ cup firmly packed brown sugar
¾ cup coarsely chopped pecans
½ cup orange juice
¼ cup orange-flavor liqueur (or ¼ cup orange juice)
¾ teaspoon ground cinnamon
⅛ teaspoon ground nutmeg
3 medium-size (about 2 lb. total) yams or sweet potatoes

In a bowl, combine apple, cranberries, sugar, pecans, orange juice, orange liqueur, cinnamon, and nutmeg. Set aside.

Peel yams; cut into about ½-inch cubes. Spread cubes out in a buttered, shallow 2½- to 3-quart (9- by 13-in. oval or rectangular) baking dish. Spoon apple-cranberry mixture evenly over the yams.

Cover the dish tightly with foil. Bake in a 400° oven for 45 minutes. Remove cover and continue baking until yams are tender when pierced and liquid in bottom of dish has almost evaporated, 35 to 45 minutes longer. Makes 6 to 8 servings. —*Linda George, Tucson.*

PER SERVING: 311 calories, 2.6 g protein, 62 g carbohydrates, 9 g fat, 0 mg cholesterol, 16 mg sodium

Soft Crab Tacos with Citrus Salsa

2 tablespoons olive oil
1 clove garlic, minced or pressed
1 small red onion, finely chopped
1 large firm-ripe tomato, cored and chopped
1 small can (4 oz.) diced green chilies
1 pound shelled cooked crab
12 corn tortillas (6-in. size)
Salsa (recipe follows)
Salt

In a 10- to 12-inch pan over medium-high heat, stir oil, garlic, and onion often until onion begins to brown, 8 to 10 minutes. Add tomato and chilies; simmer until tomato is soft, 8 to 10 minutes. Remove from heat; add crab.

Meanwhile, stack tortillas, wrap in foil, and warm in a 350° oven, about 10 minutes. Spoon about ⅓ cup crab filling onto a tortilla; add salsa and salt to taste. Fold in half to enclose filling; repeat for remaining tacos. Makes 6 servings. — *Heather Sager, Carlsbad, Calif.*

Salsa. Mix ½ cup chopped **cucumber**; 1 fresh **jalapeño chili**, stemmed, seeded, and minced; 1 cup diced fresh or canned **pineapple**; 1 teaspoon grated **lime peel**; 3 tablespoons **lime juice**; and 2 tablespoons minced **fresh cilantro** (coriander).

PER TACO WITH SALSA: 140 calories, 10 g protein, 16 g carbohydrates, 4.1 g fat, 38 mg cholesterol, 218 mg sodium

Serve crab and salsa in tortillas with shredded lettuce, cheese, avocado.

Yorkshire Chicken with Caramelized Shallots

1 pound boned chicken thighs, skinned
1½ cups all-purpose flour
About 2 tablespoons olive oil
¾ pound small shallots, peeled
1 cup milk
2 large eggs
2 tablespoons butter or margarine
¼ teaspoon pepper
1 teaspoon dry rosemary leaves

Rinse chicken; pat dry. Cut meat into 1-inch pieces, coat with ½ cup flour, then shake off excess. Pour 2 tablespoons oil into a nonstick 10- to 12-inch frying pan over medium-high heat. When hot, add half the chicken; stir often until lightly browned, 5 to 7 minutes. Transfer with a slotted spoon to a shallow 2½- to 3-quart oval baking dish. Cook remaining meat; add oil if needed. Add shallots to pan; cover and stir often until golden brown, 10 to 15 minutes. Scatter over chicken.

In a blender or food processor, smoothly mix 1 cup flour, milk, eggs, butter, and pepper; stir in rosemary. Pour evenly over chicken. Bake in a 375° oven until top is well browned and puffy, 40 to 45 minutes. Serve at once. Makes 4 or 5 servings. — *Mrs. August Vaz, Castro Valley, Calif.*

PER SERVING: 443 calories, 28 g protein, 43 g carbohydrates, 18 g fat, 180 mg cholesterol, 183 mg sodium

Pour rosemary-scented batter, in blender, over boneless chicken; bake.

Pistachio Lace Cookies

¼ cup (⅛ lb.) butter or margarine
6 tablespoons firmly packed brown sugar
2 tablespoons light corn syrup
¼ cup all-purpose flour
1 teaspoon vanilla
1 cup shelled salted pistachios

In a 1- to 1½-quart pan over medium heat, melt butter. Off the heat, stir in sugar, syrup, flour, vanilla, and nuts.

Grease and flour 2 nonstick baking sheets, each 12 by 15 inches. Well apart on each pan, drop batter in 3 mounds, each 1-tablespoon size. Push nuts slightly apart with spoon.

Bake in a 350° oven until cookies are a rich golden brown and bubbling, about 10 minutes (if using 1 oven, alternate pan positions after 5 minutes). Remove from oven and let stand just until cookies are firm enough to ease free when a slender spatula is slipped under them, about 2 minutes (too soft, they pull apart; too hard, they break—warm in oven to soften again). Cool on racks. Bake remaining cookies.

Serve, or store airtight in a rigid container up to 2 days; freeze to store longer. Makes about 14. — *Carole Van Brocklin, Port Angeles, Wash.*

PER COOKY: 121 calories, 2.1 g protein, 12 g carbohydrates, 7.7 g fat, 8.9 mg cholesterol, 38 mg sodium

Crisp pistachio-studded cookies spread thin as they bake.

ONCE SOCIALLY OUTCAST, *meat loaf has lately risen in status—as, indeed, has its classic roadside purveyor, the diner. Meat loaf has no wasteful bones, is fork-tender (if done right), takes compatibly to all sorts of sauces and gravies, and makes a marvelous sandwich filling.*

To compare meat loaf to Cleopatra is unfair to both, but they have this in common: Age cannot wither nor custom stale their infinite variety. Take Edward Ford's meat loaf, for instance. Not only does it call for sausage as a basic ingredient, but it allows a choice of hot or mild seasoning.

MEAT LOAF PLUS

- 1½ **pounds ground lean beef**
- 1 **pound mild or hot Italian sausages, casings removed and meat crumbled**
- 2 **tablespoons butter or margarine**
- 1 **pound mushrooms, thinly sliced**
- 3 **cloves garlic, minced or pressed**
- 1 **medium-size onion, chopped**
- ¾ **cup seasoned fine dry bread crumbs**
- ½ **teaspoon** *each* **salt, pepper, dry basil leaves, and dry oregano leaves**
- 1 **can (8 oz.) tomato sauce**
- 2 **large eggs**

In a large bowl, combine beef and sausage. In a 10- to 12-inch frying pan over medium-high heat, melt butter; add mushrooms, garlic, and onion. Stir often until liquid has evaporated and onion is limp, 10 to 15 minutes. Let cool to warm.

Add to meat mixture with bread crumbs, salt, pepper, basil, oregano, tomato sauce, and eggs. Using your hands, mix well.

In a 9- by 13-inch baking pan, pat meat to make level and fill pan evenly. Bake in a 350° oven until meat is no longer pink in center (cut to test), about 1 hour and 5 minutes. Let stand for 10 minutes, then cut into thick slices; or slice after loaf is cool. To serve cold, cover and chill 3 hours or until next day. Makes 8 to 10 servings.

PER SERVING: 383 calories, 22 g protein, 11 g carbohydrates, 27 g fat, 123 mg cholesterol, 750 mg sodium

Hermosa Beach, Calif.

FOCACCIA IS A SORT *of scantily clad pizza; instead of wearing a full panoply of cheese, tomato sauce, and whatever other ingredients your kitchen can provide in the way of costume jewelry, it is simply arrayed with a touch of flavor.*

Though pizza crust and focaccia are both bread dough, focaccia is patted (not stretched) into its desired form, which is usually thicker than pizza. Before baking, it's brushed with olive oil and sprinkled with onion, some herbs, or just coarse salt (here, Greg Levin seasons his with salad dressing and herb mix). Flavorings can be worked into the dough at the final kneading.

Although Italian cook book author Marcella Hazan considers focaccia to be the most primitive form of bread—a sort of leavened tortilla cooked on the hearth (focus is Latin for hearth)—it now turns up in fancier restaurants.

SALAD HERB FOCACCIA

- ¼ **cup warm water (110°)**
- 1 **teaspoon sugar**
- 1 **package active dry yeast**
  About 2½ cups all-purpose flour
- ¼ **teaspoon salt**
- ½ **cup sour cream**
- ¼ **cup (⅛ lb.) butter or margarine, melted**
- 1 **large egg**
- 3 **tablespoons prepared Italian salad dressing or olive oil**
- 1 **tablespoon dry Italian herb seasoning mix or ¼ teaspoon** *each* **dry oregano leaves, dry rosemary leaves, dry basil leaves, and dry thyme leaves**

In a large bowl, mix water and sugar; sprinkle yeast over water and let stand for 5 minutes to soften. Stir in until evenly moistened 1 cup flour, salt, sour cream, butter, and egg. Beat with an electric mixer for 3 minutes. With a heavy spoon, stir in 1¼ cups of the remaining flour.

Scrape dough onto a well-floured board and knead until smooth and elastic, 5 to 8 minutes. Place dough in a greased bowl; turn over to grease top. Cover with plastic wrap and let rise in a warm place until doubled in size, about 1 hour.

Punch down dough, then knead on a lightly floured board to expel air. Put dough in an oiled 10- by 15-inch pan. Pat

"To compare meat loaf to Cleopatra is unfair to both."

dough out to fill pan. With your finger or the end of a wooden spoon, poke holes in dough at 1-inch intervals. Brush dough with salad dressing, then sprinkle with herb mix. Let dough rise, uncovered, until puffy, about 30 minutes.

Bake on the bottom rack in a 400° oven until well browned, 15 to 20 minutes. If made ahead, cover and let stand at room temperature until next day, or wrap airtight and freeze to store longer (thaw unwrapped). Reheat, uncovered, in pan or on foil in a 450° oven until hot, about 8 minutes. Cut bread into 12 equal pieces and serve hot, warm, or at room temperature. Makes 12 pieces.

PER SERVING: 179 calories, 3.8 g protein, 22 g carbohydrates, 8.3 g fat, 37 mg cholesterol, 133 mg sodium

Bellingham, Wash.

J AY NELSON'S REASON *for calling his stew Italian Fish Chowder remains shrouded in mystery, but the flavor is bright as the Tyrrhenian Sea and cleaner than the Gulf of Naples. Essentially a Boston clam chowder, the hearty stew has been enriched—perhaps even ennobled—by the addition of scallops, shrimp, and firm white fish. Certainly it is far above the conventional Boston or Manhattan Friday chowder du jour.*

ITALIAN FISH CHOWDER

3   cans (10 oz. each) whole baby clams
3   tablespoons butter or margarine
2   large (about 1 lb. total) onions, chopped
1   cup thinly sliced celery
4   large (about 2½ lb. total) russet potatoes, peeled, rinsed, and cut into ½-inch cubes
¾   pound boned and skinned firm white-flesh fish, such as white seabass or halibut
¾   pound scallops
½   pound large (31 to 35 per lb.) shrimp, peeled, deveined, and cut in half lengthwise
2   cups milk
½   teaspoon pepper
    Salt

Drain clam liquid into a 1-quart glass measure; add water to make 3½ cups *total*. Set the liquid and clams aside.

In a 5- to 6-quart pan, melt butter over medium-high heat; add onions and celery. Stir vegetable mixture often until onions are limp, 8 to 10 minutes. Add clam liquid and potatoes; bring to a boil, cover, reduce heat, and simmer gently until the potatoes are just tender when pierced, 10 to 15 minutes.

Meanwhile, rinse and drain fish, scallops, and shrimp. Cut fish into bite-size chunks. If scallops are 1 inch or thicker, cut in half. Add fish, scallops, and shrimp to chowder; cook until fish is just opaque but still moist-looking in center (cut to test), 3 to 4 minutes. Add clams, milk, and pepper. Heat until steaming. Ladle into bowls, and add salt to taste. Makes about 4½ quarts, 8 or 9 servings.

PER SERVING: 344 calories, 35 g protein, 31 g carbohydrates, 8.4 g fat, 110 mg cholesterol, 259 mg sodium

Salinas, Calif.

I N THE MATHEMATICS *of cookery, the whole should seem greater than the sum of its parts. What apple pie fancier would order something called Apple Flour Lard Torte? Then why does Frank Doherty call his dessert creation Raspberry Bread Cake? This is plain speech indeed for a dish that is as delicious as it is easy—and that might at least be dubbed* Gâteau de Pain aux Framboises.

Raspberry bread cake has a traceable ancestry. English cooks have long made bread and fruit concoctions known generically as summer puddings. These desserts feature what gardeners there call soft (as opposed to tree) fruits—red or black currants, gooseberries, blackberries, and raspberries. They employ layers of bread and fruit or use bread as a jacket for stewed fruit or fruit purée. Doherty's delicate use of butter makes a less rich product than many an English version.

RASPBERRY BREAD CAKE

1   loaf (1 lb.) thin-sliced firm white bread
    About 4 tablespoons (⅛ lb.) butter or margarine, at room temperature
3   packages (10 oz. each) frozen sweetened raspberries, thawed
4   to 6 tablespoons sugar
    Sweetened whipped cream

"In the mathematics of cookery, the whole should seem greater than the sum of its parts."

Trim crusts from bread slices and discard (or save for crumbs). Mash butter with a spatula to soften, then spread bread slices on 1 side equally with butter.

In a blender or food processor, smoothly purée raspberries and juices. Pour berry mixture into a fine strainer over a bowl; rub fruit through strainer and discard seeds. Stir enough sugar into the raspberries to make them taste fairly sweet.

Spread about 4 tablespoons of the berry mixture over the bottom of a 1½- to 2-quart soufflé dish or deep straight-sided bowl. Make a single layer of bread, buttered side up, in bowl; trim slices to fit and save scraps (keep pieces as large and neat as possible) to patch subsequent layers of the pudding. Evenly cover bread with about ½ cup of the raspberry mixture. Make 2 more layers of bread and fruit, turning the top layer of bread buttered side down and finishing with the raspberry purée.

Cover pudding with plastic wrap and chill at least 8 hours or up until next day. Uncover pudding and, if you like, spoon a puff of whipped cream onto it. Then scoop out pudding with a spoon and put into individual bowls, adding whipped cream to taste. Makes 10 servings.

PER SERVING: 272 calories, 4.6 g protein, 50 g carbohydrates, 6.4 g fat, 14 mg cholesterol, 280 mg sodium

Las Vegas

December Menus

THE EXPLOSION OF ACTIVITIES *this month cuts down on time for meal preparation. This month's menus give you sensible ways to handle the holiday frenzy.*

With rich and exotic foods in the limelight, a plain and comforting meal can provide welcome balance. Few choices satisfy this need better than homemade soup produced in stages to fit week-night schedules. A simple but festive breakfast works well for Christmas morning around the tree. And for evenings when time is short, try the fish supper.

> **WORK-NIGHT SOUP SUPPER**
>
> Costa Rican Beef & Vegetable Soup
> Yellow Rice
> Banana Chip Sundaes
> Coconut Cookies
> Beer or Milk

Hearty whole-meal soups made with slowly simmered meats often take more time to cook than most people have during the week. This handsome soup, with chunks of tender beef and colorful vegetables, is designed to cook in two or more stages. The meat stews during dinner on one night. Quick-cooking vegetables get added when the soup is on the menu. Spoon turmeric-tinged rice into individual bowls to complete the one-dish meal.

To get a head start on the soup, begin the rich beef base on the weekend or a night or two before you plan to eat it. Once the meat is browned, it takes about 1¾ hours of unattended cooking to become tender and succulent. To serve, cook the rice, reheat the soup, and poach the vegetables briefly in the broth.

Coarsely chop dried banana chips and sprinkle over vanilla or praline ice cream for quick sundaes.

COSTA RICAN BEEF & VEGETABLE SOUP

Add scoops of yellow rice (recipe follows) to bowls of soup.

- 2 tablespoons salad oil
- 2 pounds boneless beef stew meat, such as chuck, cut into 1½-inch chunks
- 1 large onion, thinly sliced
- 1½ cups thinly sliced celery

After work, reheat broth with tender beef chunks; add cabbage, red pepper, and wheels of corn and cook briefly. Ladle into bowls; offer golden rice to add to each serving.

- 3 cloves garlic, pressed or minced
- 1 dry bay leaf
- 8 cups regular-strength beef broth
- 1 large red bell pepper, stemmed, seeded, and cut into ¼-inch-wide strips
- ½ to ¾ pound cabbage, cut through the core into 5 to 6 1-inch-wide wedges
- 1 ear fresh corn (husks and silk removed) or 2 ears (about 1 lb. total) frozen corn, thawed
- ¼ cup chopped fresh cilantro (coriander)

  Salt and pepper

Pour oil into a 5- to 6-quart pan over high heat. Add meat and stir often until well browned, 15 to 20 minutes. Add onion, celery, and garlic; stir often until onion is lightly browned, about 8 minutes. Add bay leaf and broth; bring to a boil. Reduce heat. Simmer, covered, until meat is very tender when pierced, about 1¾ hours. (If made ahead, cover and chill up to 2 days; lift off and discard any solid fat. Heat to simmering to continue.)

Add bell pepper and cabbage. Cover and simmer until cabbage is tender when pierced, about 10 minutes. Meanwhile, cut corn through cob into 1-inch rounds (use a mallet or hammer to push knife through cob). Add corn to soup and simmer, covered, until hot, about 5 minutes. Stir in cilantro. Ladle vegetables, beef, and broth equally into 5 or 6 wide bowls. Add salt and pepper to taste. Makes 5 or 6 servings.

PER SERVING: 331 calories, 31 g protein, 13 g carbohydrates, 17 g fat, 99 mg cholesterol, 160 mg sodium

YELLOW RICE

In 2- to 3-quart pan, combine 2 tablespoons **salad oil** and 1 small **onion,** chopped; stir often over medium heat until onion is soft, 5 to 7 minutes. Add 1 cup **long-grain white rice** and ¼ teaspoon **ground turmeric;** stir until rice begins to turn opaque, about 5 minutes. Add 1¾ cups **water.** Bring to a boil; cook, uncovered, until water is below surface of rice, about 10 minutes. Cover and cook on low heat until rice is tender to bite, about 10 minutes. Makes 5 or 6 servings.

PER SERVING: 155 calories, 2.3 g protein, 25 g carbohydrates, 4 g fat, 0 mg cholesterol, 1.7 mg sodium

---

CHRISTMAS TREE BREAKFAST

Gingerbread Tree Scones
Orange Cream Cheese
Hard- or Soft-cooked Eggs in the Shell
Thinly Sliced Roast Turkey or Baked Ham
Grapes & Tangerines
Milk   English Breakfast Tea

It's difficult for breakfast to compete with Christmas morning's gift-opening rituals. This menu merges with the activities.

The scones taste best freshly baked. To get a jump on the day, measure out the dry ingredients the night before. In the morning, add liquid to dry ingredients, shape, and bake. With the scones, serve purchased orange-flavor cream cheese—or beat 1 tablespoon orange marmalade into 1 small package (3 oz.) cream cheese. Offer eggs, cooked to your liking, and thinly sliced turkey or ham (2 to 3 oz. per serving), rolled for easy eating.

GINGERBREAD TREE SCONES

    2 cups all-purpose flour
    ¼ cup firmly packed brown sugar
    1 teaspoon baking powder
    1 teaspoon ground ginger
    1 teaspoon ground cinnamon
    ½ teaspoon baking soda
    ¼ teaspoon ground allspice
    ¼ teaspoon salt
    ½ cup (¼ lb.) cold butter or
       margarine, cut into small pieces
    ⅓ cup light molasses
    ⅓ cup milk
       About 1 tablespoon beaten egg
       About 1 tablespoon coarse sugar
       or crushed sugar cubes
    4 blanched almonds

In a large bowl or a food processor, combine flour, brown sugar, baking powder, ginger, cinnamon, baking soda, allspice, and salt. Add butter and, with a pastry blender or with the food processor, cut or whirl until texture is like coarse cornmeal. Stir together molasses and milk; add to dry ingredients. Mix with a fork or whirl just until dough forms.

With floured hands, gather dough into a ball. Transfer dough to a greased 12- by 15-inch baking sheet. Pat dough into a ½-inch-thick rectangle about 5 by 10 inches. With a floured knife, cut diagonal lines through dough across the strip, forming 8 triangles with 2-inch-wide bases (see photograph below). On alternate triangles, score surface with a knife to make tree branches. Brush surface with egg. Sprinkle coarse sugar over the plain triangles. Gently press a nut into the tip of each of the 4 scored trees.

Bake in a 425° oven until tops are lightly browned, 15 to 18 minutes. Cool on racks about 5 minutes. Serve warm. Break or cut apart. Makes 8 scones.

PER PIECE: 254 calories, 3.4 g protein, 42 g carbohydrates, 13 g fat, 40 mg cholesterol, 300 mg sodium

Cut dough into triangles. Score half of them to make trees; sprinkle plain ones with coarse sugar.

SPEEDY SEAFOOD SUPPER

Poached Fish with Fennel & Tomato
Mixed Green Salad
Crusty Bread & Butter
Pears   Brie or St. André Cheese
Dry Sauvignon Blanc or Sparkling Water

Even if you're in a hurry, you can prepare this rather elegant meal in minutes. To cut time further, purchase a mesclun mix for the salad.

While the fish poaches, begin the meal with the salad (about ½ lb. rinsed, crisped bite-size salad greens), dressed with your favorite vinaigrette. Then transfer the fish and its sauce to shallow bowls to eat with crusty bread.

POACHED FISH WITH FENNEL & TOMATO

    ¾   pound (about 2 large heads)
        partially trimmed fennel
    2   tablespoons olive oil
    1   medium-size onion, thinly sliced
    ¼   teaspoon fennel seed
    1   can (28 oz.) cut-up tomatoes or
        pear-shaped tomatoes, cut up
    1   cup dry white wine
    1½ pounds lean white-fleshed fish
        fillets such as lingcod or rockfish,
        about 1 inch thick
        Salt and pepper

Trim off and discard tough stems, ends, and any bruises from fresh fennel. Reserve feathery green sprigs. Quarter fennel heads lengthwise and remove cores. Thinly slice fennel crosswise.

In a 5- to 6-quart pan, combine oil, onion, and sliced fennel; stir often over medium heat until onion is light gold, about 15 minutes. Add fennel seed, tomatoes (including juice), and wine. Boil gently, uncovered, until sauce reduces to about 4 cups, 20 to 25 minutes. Reduce to a simmer.

Rinse fish, cut into 4 or 5 equal pieces, and lay in tomato sauce. Cover pan and simmer until fish is opaque but still moist-looking in thickest part (cut to test), 10 to 12 minutes. Lift out fish and place in wide bowls. Ladle sauce evenly over each piece. Garnish with fennel sprigs. Add salt and pepper to taste. Makes 4 or 5 servings.

PER SERVING: 270 calories, 33 g protein, 14 g carbohydrates, 9.2 g fat, 89 mg cholesterol, 530 mg sodium

Articles Index

Index of Recipe Titles

General Index

Photographers

Glenn Christiansen: 52, 53, 54, 62, 77, 78, 79, 103, 104, 105, 161, 163, 165, 166 (right), 172 (bottom), 173, 178, 179, 184, 185, 191, 202, 203, 221, 223, 224, 225, 226, 227, 248, 249, 251, 252, 253, 254–255, 260, 279, 287. **Peter Christiansen:** 1, 7, 8, 9, 10, 11, 19, 20, 30, 31, 40, 43, 61, 65, 74, 75, 80, 81, 86, 87, 92, 93, 94, 95, 107, 108, 109, 115, 119, 131, 133, 134, 135, 136, 137, 139, 149, 150, 151, 152, 153, 158, 159, 162, 164, 167, 168, 169, 170, 172 (top), 174, 175, 176, 177, 181, 182, 183, 188, 189, 192, 206, 207, 208, 213, 230, 231, 237, 247, 256, 261, 264, 265, 286, 288, 289, 292, 293, 297, 299, 308, 322, 323, 324, 325, 334 (bottom right), 335, 338, 340, 341 (top right). **Stephen Cridland:** 111. **David Falconer:** 110 (bottom). **Jeff Halstead:** 110 (top). **Renee Lynn:** 328, 329. **Norman A. Plate:** 4, 100, 101, 122, 271, 294 (bottom), 295. **Kevin Sanchez:** 39, 298. **George Selland:** 166 (left). **Darrow M. Watt:** 2, 5, 6, 12, 13, 14,.15, 16, 17, 18, 21, 26, 27, 29, 34, 35, 37, 38, 41, 42, 48, 49, 51, 55, 56, 57, 58, 59, 60, 64, 66, 67, 68, 82, 83, 84, 88, 89, 90, 113, 114, 116, 117, 118, 120, 121, 123, 128, 129, 140, 141, 143, 144, 145, 146, 148, 186, 187, 190, 198, 199, 201, 204, 205, 209, 210, 211, 212, 218, 219, 232–233, 235, 236, 238, 239, 244, 245, 263, 266, 267, 269, 270, 276, 277, 281, 282, 283, 285, 294 (top), 296, 300, 301, 302, 303, 304, 305, 306, 307, 309, 314, 315, 317, 318, 319, 320, 321, 326, 327, 330, 331, 332, 333, 334 (left, top), 36, 337, 339, 341 (left), 346, 347. **Doug Wilson:** 290, 291. **Tom Wyatt:** 268.